Rave reviews for *Bed & Breakfast USA* from the press:

"The best source of nationwide information"—*Changing Times*

"The most comprehensive B&B guide"—*Sylvia Porter's Personal Finance*

"The most comprehensive B&B guide"—*Savvy*

"One of the best"—*Akron Beacon Journal*

"Your best bet"—*Philadelphia Inquirer*

"Makes enjoyable reading"—*Country Living*

"Extremely useful, well-organized guide"—*American Library Association Booklist*

"The best source for B&Bs throughout the country"—*Let's Go USA*

"Many a first-time B&B guest vows never again to stay in a motel.... Business travelers—particularly women traveling alone—have found this personal touch just the ticket."—**Karen Cure, *TWA Ambassador***

"Bed and breakfast lodging has been sweeping the United States by storm...." *Bed & Breakfast USA* is one of the "bibles of the business...." —***Chicago Tribune***

"Squeezed budgets get relief at B&Bs.... *Bed & Breakfast USA* (is) an extensive list of establishments...." —***United Press International***

"The best overall view... Betty Rundback is so enthusiastic that she even gives readers pointers on how to start their own B&Bs." —***Detroit News***

"Fills a need for travelers who are watching their wallets.... Especially helpful... especially valuable."—***New York Daily News***

"For those who have embraced the B&B way to travel, there is no going back to hotel highrises and motel monotony."—***Time***

"America's newest and hottest accommodations trend is B&B." —***Boston Globe***.

Rave reviews from hosts and guests:

Our guests write: "We were complete strangers when we arrived, and departed a few days later as good friends. Absolutely beautiful accommodations and exceptional hospitality."

"After seeing your B&B, a hotel just wouldn't do."

"All B&Bs exceeded our expectations and all hosts were very friendly. Thank you for a marvelous guide."

"The B&B was immaculate, comfortable, and inviting. Our hosts were absolutely charming. . . . It felt like a visit with friends. . . ."

"It would be difficult to come up with enough superlatives to describe your home. . . . it's the wonderful people you meet when traveling that make time away from home worthwhile."

"You know, it's not just the fact that the accommodations are comfortable, attractive, and reasonable—but it's the pleasant, gracious touch. It's being able to get directions, find out current attractions. . . ."

"At $35 a night per couple it was too good to be true. I thought I had heard the wrong price. But our bill for two nights was $70!"

"I feel I must write to you to express my complete satisfaction with your book."

"We, being English, have stayed at many B&Bs in Europe and we can truthfully say that we have never experienced such hospitality and kindness anywhere."

Our hosts report: "We've had the most interesting people in the world come up our driveway clutching *Bed & Breakfast USA* as though it were a passport to heaven."

"Your B&B book is marvelous and we bless you for doing a great job. We'd never get the people who are restored by our quiet retreat without your book. They simply wouldn't know we existed!"

"We've had a lot of fun and made many new friends who have invited us to come and visit."

"Our guests are beautiful! Nothing but good experiences."

"Thanks for all the nice people who come our way through your book!"

Bed & Breakfast USA

A GUIDE TO
Tourist Homes
AND
Guest Houses

Betty Revits Rundback
and
Nancy Kramer

Tourist House Association of America

E. P. Dutton • New York

With love to Bob Rundback
because this whole project was his idea,
and to Ann Revits,
ever the proud mother and grandma, and to Rick.

Editor: Sandra W. Soule

Designer: Stanley S. Drate/Folio Graphics Co. Inc.

Copyright © 1985 by Betty Revits Rundback and Nancy Kramer

All rights reserved. Printed in the U.S.A.

Front cover photo: Mostly Hall, Falmouth, Massachusetts, by Jim Austin

Back cover photos: bedroom, Victorian House, St. Augustine, Florida, by Daisy Morden; dining room, 1895 House, Littleton, New Hampshire, by Ronald A. Paula.

No part of this publication may be reproduced or transmitted in any form or by any means, electronic or mechanical, including photocopy, recording or any information storage and retrieval system now known or to be invented, without permission in writing from the publisher, except by a reviewer who wishes to quote brief passages in connection with a review written for inclusion in a magazine, newspaper or broadcast.

Published in the United States by E. P. Dutton,
2 Park Avenue, New York, N.Y. 10016

Library of Congress Catalog Card Number: 84-72524

ISBN: 0-525-48144-3

Published simultaneously in Canada by Fitzhenry & Whiteside Limited, Toronto and Vancouver

10 9 8 7 6 5 4

Contents

	Preface	xxvii
	Acknowledgments	xxix
1.	Introduction	1
2.	How to Start Your Own B&B	9
3.	B&B Recipes	25
4.	State-by-State Listings	35

ALABAMA
Birmingham—**Bed & Breakfast-Birmingham** 37
Mobile—Kraft's Korner 38
Montgomery—Travellers' Rest 38
Samson—Jola Bama Guest House 39
Scottsboro—The Brunton House 39
Tuscumbia—Tara 40

ALASKA
Anchorage—**Alaska Private Lodgings** 41
          Stay with a Friend 42
Juneau—**Alaska Bed and Breakfast** 42
Kodiak—**Kodiak Bed and Breakfast** 42
Valdez—The Lake House 43

ARIZONA
Bed & Breakfast in Arizona 44
Mi Casa–Su Casa Bed & Breakfast 45
Chandler—Cone's Tourist Home 45
Cochise—Cochise Stronghold Lodge 46
Flagstaff—Dierker House 46
          Rainbow Ranch 47
          Walking L Ranch 47
Phoenix—Bed 'n Breakfast in Arizona 48
Scottsdale—**Bed & Breakfast Scottsdale—Cave Creek** 48
Tucson—**Barbara's Bed and Breakfast** 49
        The Bird's Nest 49
        Myers' Blue Corn House 49

Reservation services appear here in boldface type.

v

ARKANSAS
Eureka Springs—Dairy Hollow House ... 51
                    Devon Cottage ... 52
                    Harvest House ... 52
Helena—Edwardian Inn ... 52
Hot Springs—Stillmeadow Farm ... 53
                    Williams House Bed & Breakfast Inn ... 53

CALIFORNIA
Gold Country ... 55
Hospitality Plus ... 55
Ione—The Heirloom ... 56
Mariposa—The Pelennor, B&B at Bootjack ... 56
Murphys—Dunbar House, 1880 ... 57
Sutter Creek—The Hanford House ... 57
Los Angeles Area ... 58
Bed & Breakfast of Los Angeles ... 58
California Houseguests International ... 58
CoHost, Americas Bed and Breakfast ... 59
Eye Openers Bed & Breakfast Reservations ... 59
Alhambra—Brown's Guest House ... 60
Glendale—Shroff House ... 60
Hollywood—The Traybrook ... 61
Los Angeles—Avon Bed & Breakfast ... 61
                Bev's B&B ... 62
Malibu—Casa Larronde ... 62
Northridge—Hideaway House ... 63
Rancho Palos Verdes—By-the-Sea ... 63
Seal Beach—The Seal Beach Inn & Gardens ... 64
Torrance—Hazel's Habitat ... 64
                Noone Guest House ... 65
                The Whites' House ... 65
Venice—The Venice Beach House ... 65
West Covina—Hendrick Inn ... 66
Mendocino/Wine Country ... 66
Bed & Breakfast Exchange ... 66
Angwin—Big Yellow Sunflower Bed & Breakfast ... 67
Cloverdale—The Old Crocker Inn ... 67
Elk—Elk Cove Inn ... 68
Eureka—The Carter House ... 69
              Eagle House Bed & Breakfast Inn ... 69
              Old Town Bed & Breakfast Inn ... 70

Reservation services appear here in boldface type.

CONTENTS • vii

Fort Bragg—Colonial Inn	70
The Grey Whale Inn	71
Healdsburg—Camellia Inn	71
Little River—The Victorian Farmhouse	72
Napa—The Old World Inn	73
St. Helena—Wine Country Cottage	73
Monterey Peninsula	74
Carmel—Happy Landing Inn	74
Holiday House	74
House of England	75
Sea View Inn	75
Pacific Grove—House of Seven Gables Inn	76
Pebble Beach—Ocean-Forest Hideaway	76
Santa Cruz—Chateau Victorian	77
Sacramento Area	77
Grass Valley—Murphy's Inn	77
Oroville—Jean's Riverside Bed & Breakfast	78
Sacramento—Bear Flagg Inn	78
The Briggs House	79
San Diego and Orange County Area	80
American Historic Homes Bed & Breakfast	80
Carolyn's B&B Homes	80
Digs West	80
Seaview Reservations Bed & Breakfast	81
Anaheim—Anaheim Country Inn	81
Del Mar—The Blue Door	82
Julian—Julian Gold Rush Hotel	82
La Jolla—Stay-a-Nite	83
San Clemente—Jean's Retreat	83
San Diego—Abigail	84
Britt House	84
The Cottage	85
Harbor Hill Guest House	85
The Hide-A-Way	86
Westminster—Friends-We-Haven't Met	86
San Francisco	87
American Family Inn	87
Bed & Breakfast International—San Francisco	87
Berkeley—"Creekview"	88
Point Reyes Station—Thirty-Nine Cypress	88

Reservation services appear here in boldface type.

San Francisco—Albion House	89
Bed & Breakfast Near the Park	89
Casa Arguello	90
Casita Blanca	90
Le Petit Manoir	91
Sonol—Glen Echo	91
Walnut Creek—Gasthaus zum Bären	92
San Joaquin Valley	92
Orosi Valley View Citrus Ranch	92
San Luis Obispo	93
Megan's Friends	93
San Luis Obispo—The Castles	93
Santa Barbara Area	94
Educators' Vacation Alternatives	94
Arroyo Grande—Rose Victorian Inn	94
Baywood Park—Bayview House	95
Carpinteria—D & B Schroeder Ranch	95
Santa Barbara—Blue Quail Inn	96
Glenborough Inn	96
Long's Seaview B&B	97
Ocean View House	97
Santa Paula—Laurelwood Inn	98
Solvang—Solvang Castle Inn	98
Templeton—Country House Inn	99

COLORADO
Bed and Breakfast Colorado	100
Bed & Breakfast—Rocky Mountains	101
Aspen—The Copper Horse	101
Ault—The Adams House	101
Central City—Two Ten Casey	102
Colorado Springs—Griffin's Hospitality House	102
Hearthstone Inn	103
Denver—Four Seasons	103
Dolores—Simon Draw Guest House	104
Estes Park—Wanek's Lodge at Estes	104
Green Mountain Falls—Outlook Lodge	105
Longmont—The Knox Farm	105
Manitou Springs—The Nippersink	106
Norwood—Back Narrows Inn	106
Ouray—Baker's Manor Guest House	107
The House of Yesteryear	107
Silverton—The Alma House	108

Reservation services appear here in boldface type.

CONNECTICUT
Covered Bridge Bed & Breakfast 109
Nutmeg Bed & Breakfast 110
Clinton—Harborview on Holly Place 110
East Haddam—Bishopsgate Inn 111
Groton Long Point—Shore Inne 111
Ivoryton—Ivoryton Inn 112
Mystic—Comolli's Guest House 112
    1833 House 113
    The Pentway House 113
Westbrook—Captain Stannard House 114
West Mystic—River Lodge & Boat Haven 114

DELAWARE
Bed & Breakfast of Delaware 116
Bethany Beach—The Sand Box & Sea-Vista Villas 117
Dover—Biddles Bed & Breakfast 117
New Castle—William Penn Guest House 118
Rehoboth Beach—Beach House Bedroom 118

DISTRICT OF COLUMBIA
The Bed & Breakfast League, Ltd. 119
Bed & Breakfast Ltd. of Washington, D.C. 119
Sweet Dreams & Toast, Inc. 120
Adams Inn 120
Kalorama Guest House 121
Meg's International Guest House 121
The New Manse 122
The Reeds 122

FLORIDA
A & A Bed & Breakfast of Florida, Inc. 124
Bed & Breakfast Co. 125
B & B Suncoast Accommodations 125
Bed & Breakfast of the Florida Keys & East Coast 126
Florida & England Bed & Breakfast 126
Altamonte Springs—Quail's Nest 126
Amelia Island—1735 House 127
Big Pine Key—The Barnacle 127
    Bed & Breakfast on-the-Ocean 128
Bradenton—Banyan House 129
Cedar Key—Island Hotel 130
Clearwater—Bed & Breakfast of Tampa Bay 130
Englewood—Lemon Bay B&B 131

Reservation services appear here in boldface type.

Fort Myers—Windsong Garden	131
Lake City—The Pines	132
Marathon—Hopp-Inn Guest Home	132
Miami—"The White House"	133
Naples—Feller House	133
Orlando—Avonelle's Bed & Breakfast	134
Bed & Breakfast of Orlando	134
Ormond Beach—Dancing Palms	134
Palm Harbor—Sunrise Guest House	135
Pensacola—Sunshine Inn	135
St. Augustine—Kenwood Inn	136
Victorian House B&B	136
St. Petersburg—Bayboro House	137
St. Petersburg Beach—The Walters House	137
Sarasota—The Bay-View Home	138
Tallahassee—**Tallahassee Bed & Breakfast**	138

GEORGIA
Bed & Breakfast—Atlanta	139
Quail Country Bed & Breakfast, Ltd.	140
Atlanta—Beverly Hills Inn	140
House of Friends	141
Columbus—The DeLoffre House	141
Dahlonega—Worley Homestead Inn	142
Helen—Hilltop Haus	142
Marietta—Arden Hall Inn–1880	143
Savannah—**Savannah Historic Inns and Guest Houses**	143
Bed & Breakfast Inn	143
Four Seventeen—The Haslam-Fort House	144
The Stoddard-Cooper House	145
Senoia—The Culpepper House	145

HAWAII
Bed & Breakfast—Hawaii	146
Pacific–Hawaii Bed & Breakfast	147
Alea—Alohaland Guest House	147
Hilo—Hale O' Makamaka (House of Friends)	147

IDAHO
Coeur d'Alene—Sunnie's Guest House	149
Hailey—Ellsworth Inn	150
Idaho City—Idaho City Hotel	150

ILLINOIS
Champaign—Morgan Residence	152

Reservation services appear here in boldface type.

CONTENTS • xi

Galena—Belle Aire Mansion 153
Illiopolis—Old Illiopolis Hotel 153
Wildwood—The Keplers 154

INDIANA
Michigan City—Duneland Beach Inn 155
Middlebury—Patchwork Quilt Bed and Breakfast 156
Nashville—Sunset House 156
Rockport—The Rockport Inn 157
Shipshewana—Green Meadow Ranch 157
Westfield—Camel Lot, Ltd. 158

IOWA
Bed & Breakfast in Iowa 159
Anamosa—The Inn at Stone City 160
Brooklyn—Hotel Brooklyn 160
Decorah—Fifth Avenue Guest House 161
    Montgomery Mansion 161
Homestead—Die Heimat Country Inn 162
Keosauqua/Bentonsport—Mason House Inn 162

KANSAS
Kansas City Bed & Breakfast 163
Colby—Bourquin's Bed & Breakfast on the Farm 164
Tonganoxie—Almeda's Inn 164

KENTUCKY
Kentucky Homes B & B 166
Bowling Green—Bowling Green Bed & Breakfast 167
Paducah—Ehrhardt's B&B 167

LOUISIANA
Louisiana Hospitality Services, Inc. 168
Southern Comfort Bed & Breakfast 169
Covington—Plantation Bell Guest House 169
New Iberia—Mintmere Plantation 170
New Orleans—**Bed & Breakfast, Inc.** 170
    New Orleans Bed & Breakfast 171
    The Cornstalk Fence Guest House 171
    Lafitte Guest House 172
Opelousas—The Estorge House 172
Ruston—Twin Gables 172
St. Francisville—Cottage Plantation 173

MAINE
Bed & Breakfast Down East, Ltd. 174

Reservation services appear here in boldface type.

Inland Maine — 175
Kingfield—The Country Cupboard Guesthouse — 175
West Forks—Crab Apple Acres Inn — 175
Along the Coast — 176
Bar Harbor—Birch Haven — 176
Bath—Grane's Fairhaven Inn — 176
Camden—Goodspeed's Guest House — 177
    Hawthorn Inn — 177
    Maine Stay Bed & Breakfast — 178
Cape Neddick—Wooden Goose Inn — 178
Kennebunkport—The Captain Lord Mansion — 179
    The Green Heron Inn — 179
    Old Fort Inn — 180
Litchfield—Old Tavern Inn — 180
Mt. Desert Island—Bed 'n' Breakfast at Penury Hall — 181
    The Harbor Lights — 181
    Hearthside Inn — 182
Ogunquit—Hartwell House — 182
    High Tor — 183
Pemaquid—Little River Inn — 184
Portland—The Inn at Parkspring — 184
South Bristol—The Tide's Inn — 185
South Harpswell—The Maine Stay — 185
Waterford—The Artemus Ward House — 186
Wiscasset—Roberts House Bed & Breakfast — 186
York Beach—The Jo-Mar B&B on-the-Ocean — 187

MARYLAND
Annapolis—**The Maryland Registry** — 188
Baltimore—The Unicorn House — 189
Bel Air—Heritage Hill — 189
Cabin John—The Winslow Home — 190
Easton—Hynson Tourist Home — 190
Ellicott City—Hayland Farm — 191
Girdletree—The Stockmans — 191
Harwood—Oakwood — 192
Rockville—Swift's B & B — 192
Sharpsburg—Inn At Antietam — 193
Smith Island—Frances Kitching's — 193

MASSACHUSETTS
Bed & Breakfast Associates—Bay Colony — 194
Pineapple Hospitality—B & B In All New England — 195

Reservation services appear here in boldface type.

CONTENTS • xiii

Boston Area	195
Greater Boston Hospitality	195
Host Homes of Boston	195
New England Bed & Breakfast	196
Gloucester—Williams Guest House	196
Cape Cod/Martha's Vineyard	197
Bed & Breakfast—Cape Cod	197
House Guests—Cape Cod	197
Bass River—Old Cape House	198
Brewster—Old Sea Pines Inn	198
Falmouth—Mostly Hall Bed & Breakfast Inn	199
Provincetown—Somerset House	199
Sandwich—The Summer House	200
Vineyard Haven—Captain Dexter House	201
Haven Guest House	202
West Falmouth—The Elms	202
Sjöholm Inn Bed & Breakfast	203
West Harwich—Lion's Head Inn	203
West Yarmouth—The Manor House	204
Woods Hole—The Marlborough	204
Nantucket	205
Carlisle House	205
The Carriage House	205
Cliff Lodge	206
Central/Western Massachusetts	206
Berkshire Bed & Breakfast	206
Pioneer Valley Bed & Breakfast	207
Sturbridge Bed & Breakfast	207
Buckland—Amacord	208
Great Barrington—The Turning Point Inn	208
Ware—The Wildwood Inn	209

MICHIGAN

Beulah—Windermere Inn	210
Dimondale—Bannicks B & B	211
Douglas—Rosemont Inn	211
Horton—Wellman Accommodations	212
Laingsburg—Seven Oaks Farm	212
Lakeside—The Pebble House	213
Lexington—Governor's Inn	213
Mecosta—Blue Lake Lodge	214
Port Sanilac—Raymond House Inn	215
St. Ignace—Colonial House Inn	215

Reservation services appear here in boldface type.

Saugatuck—Wickwood Inn	216
Union City—The Victorian Villa Guesthouse	216
Walled Lake—Villa Hammer	217

MINNESOTA
Bed & Breakfast Registry—North America	218
Dassel—Gabrielson's B&B	219
Hastings—Thorwood Bed & Breakfast	219
Minneapolis—Evelo's Bed & Breakfast	220
Oakdale—Oakdale Tanners Lake	220
Rochester—Canterbury Inn	221
Stacy—Kings Oakdale Park Guest House	221

MISSISSIPPI
Natchez—Monmouth Plantation	223
Pass Christian—Turn of the Century Cottage	224
Port Gibson—Oak Square	224
Woodville—Square Ten Inn	225

MISSOURI
B&B St. Louis—River Country of Missouri and Illinois, Inc.	226
Ozark Mountain Country B&B Service	227
Arrow Rock—Borgman's Bed & Breakfast	227
Camdenton—Lakeside Guest House	228
Morgan's Woodhaven	228
Carthage—Hill House	228
Hannibal—The Victorian Guest House	229
Independence—**Truman Country B&B**	229
Rogersville—Anchor Hill Lodge	230
St. Joseph—McNally House Bed & Breakfast	230
Bed & Breakfast—St. Louis	231
Washington—The Schwegmann House B&B Inn	231

MONTANA
Western Bed & Breakfast Hosts	233
Bozeman—Voss Inn	234
Whitefish—Duck Inn	234

NEBRASKA
Bed & Breakfast of Nebraska	235
Lincoln—Rogers House	236

NEVADA
Lake Tahoe—Haus Bavaria	237
Las Vegas—Las Vegas B&B	238

Reservation services appear here in boldface type.

Smith—Windybrush Ranch	238
Unionville—Old Pioneer Garden	239
Winnemucca—Shone House	239

NEW HAMPSHIRE

New Hampshire Bed & Breakfast	240
Ashland—Cheney House	241
Campton—The Campton Inn	241
Mountain-Fare Inn	242
Franconia—Sugar Hill Inn	242
Gilford—Cartway House	243
Lisbon—Bridgehouse Bed & Breakfast	243
Littleton—The Beal House Inn	244
1895 House	244
North Conway—The Scottish Lion Inn	245
Northwood—The Resort at Lake Shore Farm	245
North Woodstock—Woodstock Inn	246
Rindge—Tokfarm Inn	246
Sunapee—Times Ten Inn	247
West Plymouth—Crab Apple Inn	247

NEW JERSEY

Bay Head—Conover's Bay Head Inn	249
Cape May—The Abbey	250
Albert G. Stevens Inn	250
Barnard-Good House	251
The Brass Bed Inn	251
The Gingerbread House	252
The Mainstay Inn	252
The Open Hearth Guest House	253
The Queen Victoria	253
The Seventh Sister Guest House	254
Dennisville—The Henry Ludlum Inn	254
Denville—Lakeside Bed & Breakfast	255
Milford—Chestnut Hill on-the-Delaware	255
Ocean Grove—Cordova	256
Sea Isle City—Cape Associates	256
Spring Lake—Normanday Inn	257

NEW MEXICO

Chimayo—Casa Escondida	258
Espanola—La Puebla House	259
Lincoln—The Wortley Hotel	259
Los Alamos—Los Alamos Bed & Breakfast	260
Orange Street Bed & Breakfast	260

Reservation services appear here in boldface type.

Mesilla Park—The Elms 261
San Juan Pueblo—Chinguague Compound 261
Silver City—Bear Mountain Guest Ranch 262
Taos—American Artists Gallery-House 262
      Mountain Light Bed & Breakfast 263

NEW YORK
Catskills 264
Stamford—The Lanigan Farmhouse 264
Tannersville—The Eggery Inn 265
Central New York/Leatherstocking Area 265
Bed & Breakfast of Central New York 265
Bed & Breakfast—Leatherstocking 266
Binghamton—B & B Adagio 266
Camden—Erie Bridge Inn 266
Cooperstown—The Inn at Brook Willow Farm 267
Fly Creek—Litco Farms B & B 267
Johnson City—Libby's Lodgings 268
Finger Lakes Area 268
Bath—Wheeler Bed and Breakfast 268
Canandaigua—Bristol Bed & Breakfast 269
Canaseraga—Country House 269
Corning—Laurel Hill Guest House 270
      Rosewood Inn 270
      Victoria House 271
Elmira—"Millstones" Guest House 271
Geneva—The Cobblestones 272
Ithaca—Elmshade Guest House 272
      Rose Inn 273
      Varna Inn 273
Syracuse—Ivy Chimney 274
Hudson Valley/Albany/Kingston Area 274
Bed and Breakfast, U.S.A., Ltd. 274
Cambridge—Battenkill Bed and Breakfast Barn 275
Cold Spring—Olde Post Inn 275
      One Market Street 276
Croton-On-Hudson—Barbara's Bed & Breakfast 276
Garrison—Golden Eagle Inn 277
High Falls—House on the Hill 277
Johnson—Elaine's Guest House 278
Lebanon Springs—Brookside Manor 278
Old Chatham—Locust Tree House 279

Reservation services appear here in boldface type.

Pittstown—Maggie Towne's B & B	279
Rensselaer—Tibbitt's House Inn	280
Rhinebeck—Corner House	280
Shandaken—Two Brooks Bed & Breakfast	281
Spencertown—Spencertown Guests	281
Wappingers Falls—Best One Yet	282
Warwick—Tranquality Guest Home	282
Willow Brook Farm	283
Lake George Area	283
Bolton Landing—Hayes's B & B Guest House	283
Glens Falls—East Lake George House	284
Granville—Willow Glen Hill	284
Lake George—Corner Birches Guest House	285
Lake Placid/Adirondacks Area	285
North Country B & B Reservation Service	285
Keene—Bark Eater Inn	286
Lake Placid—Sports Palace	286
Stagecoach Inn	287
Long Lake—Adirondack Hotel	287
Long Island	288
A Reasonable Alternative	288
Hampton Bays—Hampton on-the-Water	288
Hempstead—Duvall Bed and Breakfast	289
Westhampton Beach—Seafield House	289
New York City Area	290
The B & B Group (New Yorkers at Home)	290
Urban Ventures	290
Eastchester—The Tilted Barn	290
Holliswood—I-Love-New York Bed & Breakfast	291
New York City—A Bit o' the Apple	292
Staten Island—Sixteen Firs	292
Tuckahoe—Beehive Bed & Breakfast	293
Niagara/Buffalo/Rochester Area	293
Rochester—Bed and Breakfast	293
Castile—The Eastwood House	294
Colden—Back of the Beyond	294
East Concord—Highland Springs	295
Hamburg—Bebaks Guest House	295
Medina—Craft's Place B & B	296
Newfield—The Franklin House	296
Penfield—Strawberry Castle Bed & Breakfast	297
Thousand Islands Area	297

Reservation services appear here in boldface type.

Sandy Creek—Pink House Inn 297
Three Mile Bay—Le Muguet 298

NORTH CAROLINA
Asheville—Flint Street Inn 299
　　　　The Ray House 300
Balsam—Balsam Lodge 301
Bath—Bath Guest House 301
Blowing Rock—Ragged Garden Inn 302
Brevard—The Inn at Brevard 302
Bryson City—Folkestone Lodge 303
Charlotte—Hampton Manor 303
　　　　The Library Suite 304
Edenton—The Lords Proprietors' Inn 304
　　　　Mulberry Hill Guest House 305
Franklin—The Franklin Terrace 305
Glenville—Mountain High 306
Graham—Leftwich House 306
Greensboro—Greenwood 307
Hendersonville—Havenshire Inn 307
Kill Devil Hills—Ye Olde Cherokee Inn 308
New Bern—Kings Arms Inn 308
Ocracoke—Beach House 309
Pisgah Forest—Mountain Key Lodge 309
Robbinsville—Wilson's Guest House 310
Tryon—Mill Farm Inn 310
Wilmington—Anderson Guest House 311

NORTH DAKOTA
Grassy Butte—Long X Trail Ranch 312
Medora—The Rough Riders 313

OHIO
Akron—Portage House 314
Avon Lake—Williams House 315
Cleveland—**Private Lodgings** 316
　　　　Sarah Frisch House 316
　　　　The Tudor House 316
Columbus—**Columbus Bed & Breakfast** 317
Huron—The Beach House 317
Olmsted Falls—Hamilton B. Maxon House 318
South Amherst—Birch Way Villa 319
Spring Valley—3 B's Bed 'n Breakfast 319
Warren—Shirlee's Chambers 320
Xenia—Hattle House 320

Reservation services appear here in boldface type.

OKLAHOMA

Clayton—Clayton Country Inn	321
Yukon—Tulp House	322

OREGON

Northwest Bed and Breakfast	323
Ashland—Chanticleer	324
The Coach House Inn	324
Neil Creek House	325
Royal Carter House	326
Shutes Lazy "S" Farm B&B	
Bandon—Spindrift	326
Coburg—Wheeler's Bed & Breakfast	327
Eugene—Copper Windmill Ranch	327
Griswold Bed & Breakfast	328
Gold Beach—The Cottage	328
Jacksonville—Livingston Mansion	329
Leaburg—Marjon Bed & Breakfast Inn	329
Portland—Corbett House B & B	330
Seaside—The Riverside Inn	330
Stayton—Horncroft	331

PENNSYLVANIA

Allentown Area	332
Mertztown—Longswamp Bed & Breakfast	
Bucks County	333
Holicong—Barley Sheaf Farm	333
New Hope—Pineapple Hill	333
The Wedgwood Bed & Breakfast Inn	334
Whitehall Farm	334
Central Pennsylvania	335
Rest & Repast Bed & Breakfast Service	335
Gettysburg Area	335
The Homstead	335
Gettysburg—Twin Elms	336
Hanover—Beck Mill Farm	336
Pennsylvania Dutch Area	337
Airville—Spring House	337
Bird-in-Hand—Greystone Motor Lodge	338
Ephrata—Smithton–Henry Miller 1763 House	338
Kinzer—Groff Tourist Farm Home	339
Sycamore Haven Farm Guest House	339
Lancaster—Groff Farm—"Abend-Ruhe"	340
Meadowview Guest House	340
Witmer's Tavern-Historic 1725 Inn	341

Reservation services appear here in boldface type.

Paradise—Maple Lane Guest House	341
Neffdale Farm	342
Rayba Acres Farm	342
Reading—El Shaddai	343
Smoketown—Smoketown Village Tourist Home	343
York—Fairhaven	344
Memory Lane Bed & Breakfast	344
Philadelphia Area	345
Bed & Breakfast—Center City	345
Bed & Breakfast of Chester County	345
Bed & Breakfast of Philadelphia	346
Kennett Square—Meadow Spring Farm	346
Mrs. K's	347
Pocono Mountains	347
Bed & Breakfast Pocono Northeast	347
Canadensis—Dreamy Acres	348
Nearbrook	348
Cresco—La Anna Guest House	349
Delaware Water Gap—The Mountain House	350
Greentown—Four County View B & B	350
Trails End	351
Milford—The Vines	351
Mill Rift—Bonny Bank	352
Mount Bethel—Elvern Country Lodge	352
Newfoundland—White Cloud	353
Shawnee—Eagle Rock Lodge	353
White Haven—The Redwood House	354
Scranton/North Central Pennsylvania	355
Endless Mountains Reservation Service	355
Muncy—The Bodine House	355
Tunkhannock—Anderson Acres	356
Union Dale—Powder Mill Farms	356
Western Pennsylvania	357
Pittsburgh Bed & Breakfast	357
Freeport—Hobby Horse Farm	357
Jamestown—Das Tannen-Lied (The Singing Pines)	358

RHODE ISLAND

Block Island—Old Town Inn	359
Narragansett—House of Snee	360
The Richards	360
Newport—Brinley Victorian	361
Ellery Park House	361

Reservation services appear here in boldface type.

CONTENTS • xxi

Queen Anne Inn	362
Westerly—Woody Hill Guest House	362

SOUTH CAROLINA

Beaufort—Twelve Oaks Inn	363
Camden—The Carriage House	364
The Inn	364
Charleston—**Charleston East Bed & Breakfast**	365
Historic Charleston Bed & Breakfast	365
Holland's Guest House	366
Two Meeting Street Inn	366
Dale—Coosaw Plantation	367
Georgetown—Shaw House	367
Myrtle Beach—Serendipity, An Inn	368
Salem—A Country Place	368
Yonges Island—Prospect Hill Plantation	369

SOUTH DAKOTA

Bed and Breakfast of South Dakota	370
Canova—Skoglund Farm	371
Webster—Lakeside Farm	371

TENNESSEE

Host Homes of Tennessee	372
Kingsport—Shallowford Farm	373
Knoxville—Three Chimneys of Knoxville	373
Bed & Breakfast in Memphis	374
Murfreesboro—Clardy's Guest House	374
Nashville—Miss Anne's Bed & Breakfast	375
Rogersville—Hale Springs Inn	375

TEXAS

Bed & Breakfast Texas Style	376
Big Sandy—Annie's Bed & Breakfast	377
Sand Dollar Hospitality B & B	377
The Bed & Breakfast Society of Houston	378
Houston—Hostess House B & B	378
Bed & Breakfast Hosts of San Antonio	379
San Antonio—Cardinal Cliff	379
Schertz—Seventh Haven	379
Village Mills—Big Thicket Guest House	380
Weimar—Weimar Country Inn	381

UTAH

Bed 'n Breakfast Association of Utah	382
Cedar City—Meadeau View Lodge	383

Reservation services appear here in boldface type.

Monroe—Peterson's Bed & Breakfast 383
St. George—Larkin Inn 384
    Seven Wives Inn 384
Salt Lake City—Eller Bed & Breakfast 385

VERMONT

American Bed & Breakfast—New England 386
Barre—Woodruff House 387
Bethel—Greenhurst Inn 387
    Poplar Manor 388
Bondville—The Barn Lodge 388
Brookfield—Green Trails Country Inn 389
Brownsville—The Inn at Mt. Ascutney 389
Chester—Stone Hearth Inn 390
Dorset—The Little Lodge at Dorset 391
    Maplewood Colonial House 391
East Burke—Blue Wax Farm 392
    Burke Green Lodging 392
Essex Junction—Jericho House 393
Ludlow—The Combes Family Inn 393
Manchester Center—Brook 'n' Hearth 394
Middlebury—Brookside Meadows 395
Montgomery—Fallbrook House 395
North Hero—Charlie's Northland Lodge 396
Perkinsville—Peregrine's Rest 396
Pittsfield—Pittsfield Inn 397
Proctorsville—Okemo Lantern Lodge 397
Reading—The Peeping Cow Inn 398
Rochester—Harvey Farm Country Inn 398
Rutland—Hillcrest Guest House 399
Shaftsbury—Munro-Hawkins House 399
South Strafford—Watercourse Way 400
Stowe—Ski Inn 400
    Timberhölm Inn 401
Waitsfield—Knoll Farm Country Inn 402
Waterbury—Schneider Haus 402
West Charleston—Hunt's Hideaway 403
West Dover—Snow Den 403
    Waldwinkel Inn 404
    The Weathervane 404
Weston—The Colonial House 405
Wilmington—Holly Tree 405
    Nutmeg Inn 406

Reservation services appear here in boldface type.

VIRGINIA

Alexandria—**Princely/Bed & Breakfast**	407
Blue Ridge Bed & Breakfast	408
Bridgewater—Jean's Bed & Breakfast	408
Capron—Sandy Hill Farm Bed & Breakfast	409
Charlottesville—**Guesthouses Reservation Service**	409
The English Inn Guest House	410
Chincoteague—Miss Molly's Inn	410
Churchville—Buckhorn Inn	411
Fredericksburg—The McGrath House	412
Mathews—RiverFront House	412
Bed & Breakfast of Tidewater	413
Norfolk—Cameron Residence	413
Richmond—**Bensonhouse of Richmond**	413
Griffin House	414
Sperryville—The Conyers House	414
Virginia Beach—Angie's Guest House	415
The Graters' Residence	416
Waterford—The Pink House	416
Williamsburg—**The Travel Tree**	417
Brass Lantern Lodge	417
Carter's Guest House	417
The Cedars	418
The Chateau	418
Country Cottage Guest House	419
Mi Casa	419
Thompson Guest House	420
Woods Guest Home	420

WASHINGTON

Pacific Bed & Breakfast	421
Travellers' Bed & Breakfast—Seattle	422
Anacortes—The Channel House	422
Bainbridge Island—Phoenix House	423
Deer Harbor—Palmer's Chart House	423
Edmonds—Harrison House	424
Heather House	424
Santopolo House	425
Fox Island—Lockhart's Retreat	425
Friday Harbor—San Juan Inn	426
Gig Harbor—Hillside Gardens Bed and Breakfast	426
The Olde Glencove Hotel	427
Glenwood—Flying L Guest Ranch	427

Reservation services appear here in boldface type.

xxiv • CONTENTS

Leavenworth—Brown's Farm	428
Edel Haus Bed 'n' Breakfast	428
Pateros—Lake Pateros B & B	429
Port Townsend—Lizzie's	430
Palace Hotel	430
Seattle—Chambered Nautilus Bed and Breakfast Inn	431
The College Inn Guest House	431
Tacoma—Inge's Place	432
Keenan House	432
Vashon—The Swallow's Nest	433
Whidbey Island—Guest House Bed & Breakfast	433
Sally's B & B Manor	434

WEST VIRGINIA

Horse Shoe Run—Mountain Village Inn	435
Mathias—Valley View Farm	436
Summit Point—Countryside Bed & Breakfast	436

WISCONSIN

Baraboo—The House of Seven Gables	437
Janesville—Sessler's Guest House	438
La Farge—Rainbow Retreat	438
Lake Delton—O. J.'s Victorian Village Guest House	439
Milwaukee—**Bed & Breakfast of Milwaukee**	439
Mineral Point—The Duke House	440
Prairie Du Sac—Farmhand Cottage	440
Strum—The Lake House	441
Sturgeon Bay—White Lace Inn— A Victorian Guest House	441

WYOMING

Cody—The Lockhart Inn	442
Evanston—Pine Gables Bed and Breakfast Inn	443
Jackson Hole—Captain Bob Morris	443
Wilson—Heck-of-a-Hill Homestead	444

5. CANADA

Alberta	445
Alberta Bed & Breakfast	445
British Columbia	446
North Vancouver—Grouse Mountain Bed & Breakfast	446
Nova Scotia	447
Annapolis Royal—Bread & Roses	447
Baddeck—Bute Arran	448
Parrsboro—Confederation Farm	448

Reservation services appear here in boldface type.

Ontario 449
Kingston Area Bed & Breakfast 449
Ottawa Area Bed & Breakfast 449
Stratford—**Ambassador B & B** 449
    The Maples 450
Toronto Bed & Breakfast 450
Toronto—Oppenheims 451
Wiarton—Glenbellart House 451
Prince Edward Island 453
Kensington—Sea Breeze Bed & Breakfast 453
    Woodington's Country Inn 453
O'Leary—Smallman's Bed & Breakfast 454
Summerside—Dyment Bed & Breakfast 454
Quebec 456
Montreal Bed & Breakfast 456
Montrealers at Home 456
Montreal—1550 Pine Avenue West 457

6. PUERTO RICO
    San Juan—Buena Vista Guest House 458

U.S. VIRGIN ISLANDS
    St. Thomas—The Cottage-Hart House 459

Appendix: State Tourist Offices 460

Reservation Form 465

Membership Applications 467

We Want to Hear From You! 473

Information Order Form 474

Reservation services appear here in boldface type.

Preface

If you have read earlier editions of *Bed & Breakfast USA*, you know this book has always been a labor of love. It is personally gratifying to see how it has grown from the first 16-page edition, titled *Guide to Tourist Homes and Guest Houses*, which was published in 1975 and contained 40 individual listings. Ten years later, the ninth revised edition lists 617 homes and 114 reservation agencies, giving travelers access to over 11,000 host homes. This spectacular success seems to indicate strongly that the revived concept of the guest house has recaptured the fancy of both travelers and proprietors.

All of the B&Bs described in this book are members of the Tourist House Association of America. All members are dedicated to the standards of "Cleanliness, Comfort, and Cordiality," and sincerely enjoy plumping up the pillows in anticipation of having visitors. THAA dues are $15 annually. We share ideas and experiences by way of our newsletter, and arrange regional seminars and conferences.

Our biggest problem has been the attempt to include new listings in time for publication, since we are constantly deluged with applications from additional hosts who wish to be mentioned in *Bed & Breakfast USA*. We had to stop somewhere, so we have provided a form in the back of the book that you can use to order a list of B&Bs that joined our Association after we went to press.

BETTY R. RUNDBACK
Director, Tourist House Association of America
RD 2 Box 355A Greentown, Pennsylvania 18426

January, 1985

Acknowledgments

A special thanks to Michael Frome, who saw promise in the first 16-page "Guide" and verbally applauded our growth with each subsequent edition. And many thanks to all the other travel writers and reporters who have brought us to the attention of their audience.

Many hugs to family and friends who lovingly devoted time to the "office" chores. Among them are the best stamp lickers and envelope stuffers in the world! Mike and Peggy Ackerman, John Rundback, Fred Rundback, Ricky Costanzo, Sherry and Joyce Buzlowsky, Sharon Makler, Betty Neuer, Julie Cohen, Lisa Eagleston, Chris Sakoutis, Harry Revits, Susie Scher, Elinor Scher, Robert Zucker, Harriet Frank, Joan Smith, and Karen Zane. We are most grateful to Joyce Ackerman and James McGhee for their artwork.

Our appreciation goes to our editor, Sandy Soule. She exhausted her supply of blue pencils but never her patience.

PACIFIC
(clock showing 1)

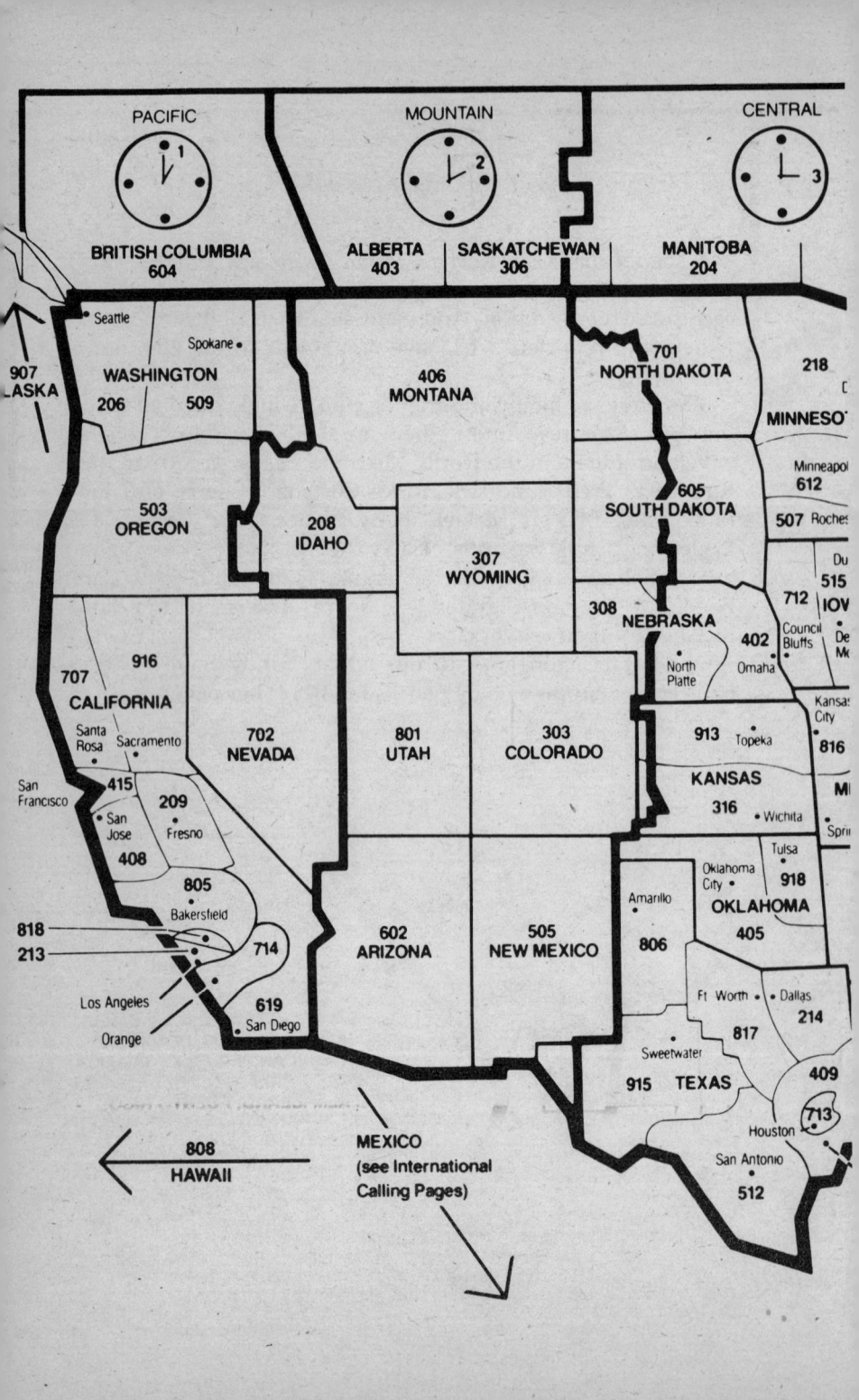

MOUNTAIN
(clock showing 2)

CENTRAL
(clock showing 3)

- BRITISH COLUMBIA 604
- ALBERTA 403
- SASKATCHEWAN 306
- MANITOBA 204
- 907 ALASKA
- WASHINGTON: Seattle 206, Spokane 509
- OREGON 503
- IDAHO 208
- MONTANA 406
- NORTH DAKOTA 701
- MINNESOTA 218, Minneapolis 612, Rochester 507, Duluth 218
- SOUTH DAKOTA 605
- WYOMING 307
- NEBRASKA 308, North Platte, Omaha 402, Council Bluffs
- IOWA 515, 712, Des Moines
- CALIFORNIA: 707, 916, Santa Rosa, Sacramento, 415, San Francisco, San Jose, 408, 209 Fresno, 805 Bakersfield, 818, 213 Los Angeles, Orange, 714, 619 San Diego
- NEVADA 702
- UTAH 801
- COLORADO 303
- KANSAS 913 Topeka, 816 Kansas City, 316 Wichita
- MISSOURI, Springfield
- OKLAHOMA 405, Oklahoma City, Tulsa 918
- ARIZONA 602
- NEW MEXICO 505
- TEXAS: Amarillo 806, Ft. Worth, Dallas 214, 817, Sweetwater 915, 409, Houston 713, San Antonio 512
- 808 HAWAII ←
- MEXICO (see International Calling Pages) ↓

Eastern / Atlantic Area Code Map

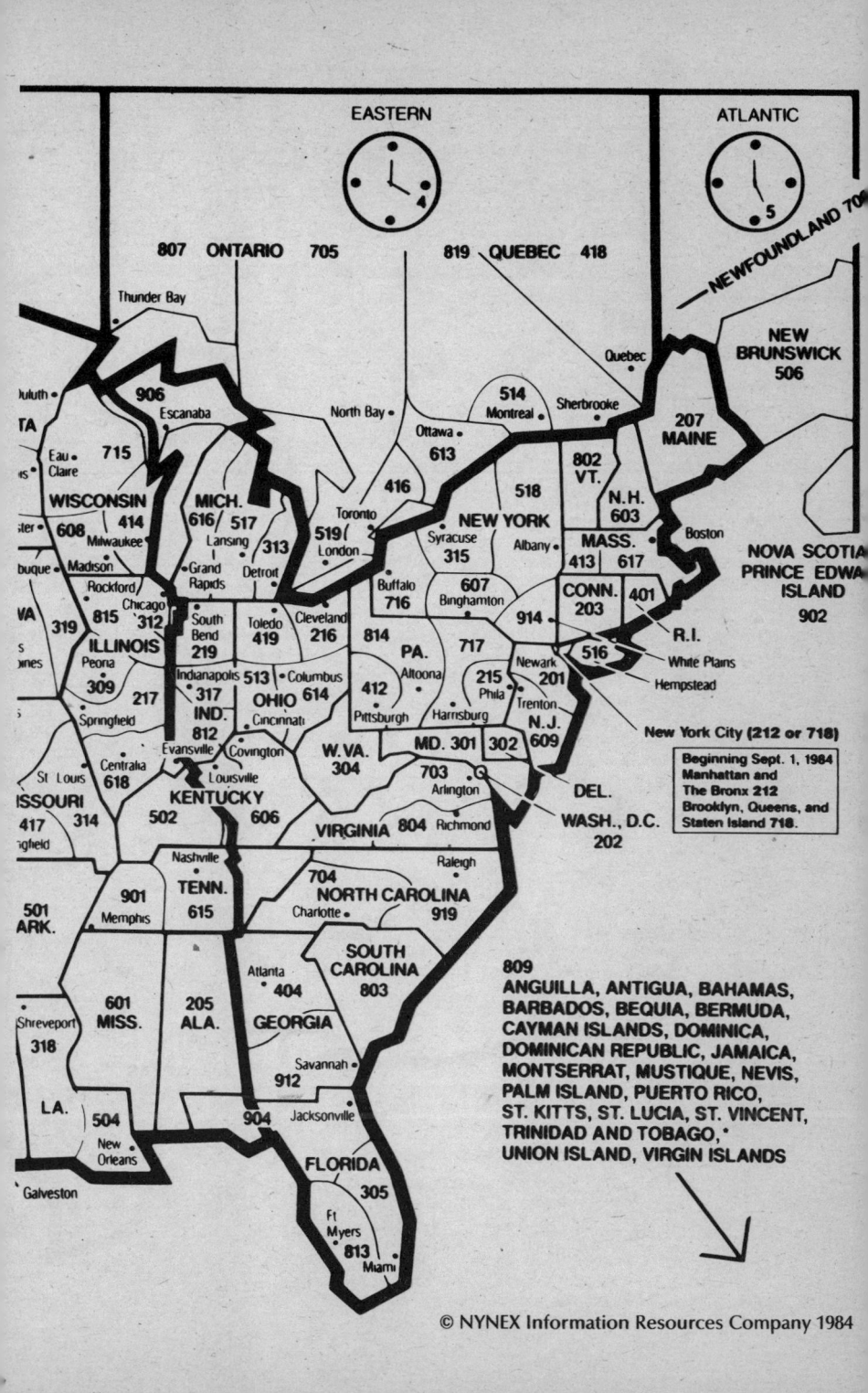

EASTERN (clock showing 4)
ATLANTIC (clock showing 5)

807 ONTARIO 705 — Thunder Bay, North Bay, Toronto, London, Ottawa
819 QUEBEC 418 — Quebec, Sherbrooke, Montreal

NEWFOUNDLAND 709
NEW BRUNSWICK 506
NOVA SCOTIA / PRINCE EDWARD ISLAND 902

MAINE 207 — Boston
N.H. 603
VT. 802
MASS. — 413 / 617
CONN. 203
R.I. 401

NEW YORK — 518 Albany, 315 Syracuse, 716 Buffalo, 607 Binghamton, 914, 516, White Plains, Hempstead
New York City (212 or 718)

Beginning Sept. 1, 1984
Manhattan and
The Bronx 212
Brooklyn, Queens, and
Staten Island 718

PA. — 814, 717 Altoona, 412 Pittsburgh, 215 Phila, Harrisburg
N.J. — 201 Newark, 609 Trenton
DEL.
MD. 301 — 302
WASH., D.C. 202
W.VA. 304
VIRGINIA 804 — 703 Arlington, Richmond

MICH. — 906 Escanaba, 616/517 Lansing, Grand Rapids, 313 Detroit
WISCONSIN — 715 Eau Claire, 414 Milwaukee, 608 Madison, Duluth
ILLINOIS — 815 Rockford, 312 Chicago, 309 Peoria, 217 Springfield, 618 Centralia
IND. — 219 South Bend, 317 Indianapolis, 812 Evansville
OHIO — 419 Toledo, 216 Cleveland, 513 Columbus, 614 Cincinnati
KENTUCKY 502 / 606 — Louisville, Covington
MISSOURI — 314 St Louis, 417 Springfield
ARK. 501
LA. 504 — New Orleans, Shreveport 318, Galveston

TENN. — 901 Memphis, 615 Nashville
NORTH CAROLINA — 704 Charlotte, 919 Raleigh
SOUTH CAROLINA 803
GEORGIA — 404 Atlanta, 912 Savannah
ALA. 205
MISS. 601
FLORIDA — 904 Jacksonville, 305 Ft Myers, 813 Miami

809
ANGUILLA, ANTIGUA, BAHAMAS,
BARBADOS, BEQUIA, BERMUDA,
CAYMAN ISLANDS, DOMINICA,
DOMINICAN REPUBLIC, JAMAICA,
MONTSERRAT, MUSTIQUE, NEVIS,
PALM ISLAND, PUERTO RICO,
ST. KITTS, ST. LUCIA, ST. VINCENT,
TRINIDAD AND TOBAGO,
UNION ISLAND, VIRGIN ISLANDS

© NYNEX Information Resources Company 1984

Bed & Breakfast USA

1
Introduction

Bed and Breakfast is the popular lodging alternative to hotel high rises and motel monotony. B&Bs are either private residences where the owners rent spare bedrooms to travelers, or small, family-operated inns offering a special kind of warm, personal hospitality. Whether large or small, B&Bs will make you feel more like a welcome guest than a paying customer.

The custom of opening one's home to travelers dates back to the earliest days of colonial America. Hotels and inns were few and far between in those days, and wayfarers relied on the kindness of strangers to provide a bed for the night. Which is why, perhaps, there is hardly a colonial-era home in the mid-Atlantic states that does not boast: "George Washington Slept Here!"

During the Depression, the tourist home provided an economic advantage to both the traveler and the host. Travelers always drove through the center of town; there were no superhighways to bypass local traffic. A house with a sign in the front yard reading "Tourists" or "Guests" indicated that a traveler could rent a room for the night and have a cup of coffee before leaving in the morning. The usual cost for this arrangement was $2. The money represented needed income for the proprietor as well as the opportunity to chat with an interesting visitor.

In the 1950s, the country guest house became a popular alternative to the costly hotels in resort areas. The host compensated for the lack of hotel amenities, such as private bathrooms, by providing comfortable bedrooms and bountiful breakfasts at a modest price. The visitors enjoyed the home-away-from-home atmosphere; the hosts were pleased to have paying houseguests.

The incredible growth in international travel that has occurred over the past 25 years has provided yet another stimulus. Millions of Americans now vacation annually in Europe and travelers have become enchanted with the bed and breakfast concept so popular in Britain, Ireland, and other parts of the continent. In fact, many well-traveled Americans are delighted to learn that we "finally" have B&Bs here. But, as you now know, they were always here . . . just a rose by another name.

Bed and breakfasts are for:

- **Parents of college kids:** Tuition is costly enough without the added expense of "Parents' Weekends." Look for a B&B near campus.

- **Parents traveling with children:** A family living room, play room, or backyard is preferable to the confines of a motel room.

- **"Parents" of pets:** Many proprietors will allow your well-behaved darling to come too. This can cut down on the expense and trauma of kenneling Fido.

- **Business travelers:** Being "on the road" can be lonely and expensive. It's so nice, after a day's work, to return to a home-away-from-home.

- **Women traveling alone:** Friendship and conversation are the natural ingredients of a guest house.

- **Skiers:** Lift prices are lofty, so it helps to save some money on lodging. Many mountain homes include home-cooked meals in your room rate.

- **Students:** A visit with a family is a pleasant alternative to camping or the local "Y."

- **Visitors from abroad:** Cultural exchanges are often enhanced by a host who can speak your language.

- **Carless travelers:** If you plan to leave the auto at home, it's nice to know that many B&Bs are convenient to public transportation. Hosts will often arrange to meet your bus, plane, or train for a nominal fee.

- **Schoolteachers and retired persons:** Exploring out-of-the-way places is fun and will save you money.

- **Antique collectors:** Many hosts have lovely personal collections, and nearby towns are filled with undiscovered antique shops.
- **House hunters:** It's a practical way of trying out a neighborhood.
- **Relocating corporate executives:** It's more comfortable to stay in a real home while you look for a permanent residence. Hosts will often give more practical advice than professional realtors.
- **Relatives of hospitalized patients:** Many B&Bs are located near major hospitals. Hosts will offer tea and sympathy when visiting hours are over.
- **Convention and seminar attendees:** Staying at a nearby B&B is less expensive than checking into a hotel.

And everyone else who has had it up to here with plastic motel monotony!

What It Is Like to Be a Guest in a B&B

The B&B descriptions provided in this book will help you choose the places that have the greatest appeal to you. A firsthand insight into local culture awaits you; imagine the advantage of arriving in New York City or San Francisco and having an insider to help you sidestep the tourist traps and direct you to that special restaurant or discount store. Or explore the countryside, where fresh air and home-cooked meals beckon. Your choice is as wide as the U.S.A.

Each bed and breakfast listed offers personal contact, a real advantage in unfamiliar environments. You may not have a phone in your room or a TV on the dresser. You may even have to pad down the hall in robe and slippers to take a shower, but you'll discover little things count:
- In Williamsburg, Virginia, a visitor from Germany opted to stay at a B&B to help improve her conversational English. When the hostess saw that she was having difficulty understanding directions, she personally escorted her on a tour of Old Williamsburg.

- In Pennsylvania, the guests mistakenly arrived a week prior to their stated reservation date and the B&B was full. The hostess made a call to a neighbor who accommodated the couple. (By the way, the neighbor has now become a B&B host!)
- In New York City, the guest was an Emmy Award nominee and arrived with his tuxedo in need of pressing. The hostess pressed it; when he claimed his award over nationwide TV, he looked well groomed!

Expect the unexpected, like a pot of coffee brewed upon your arrival or fresh flowers on the nightstand. At the very least, count on our required standard of cleanliness and comfort. Although we haven't personally visited all the places listed, they have all been highly recommended by Chambers of Commerce or former guests. We have either spoken to or corresponded with all the proprietors; they are a friendly group of people who enjoy having visitors. They will do all in their power to make your stay memorable.

Our goal is to enable the traveler to crisscross the country and stay only at B&Bs along the way. To achieve this, your help is vital. Please take a moment to write us of your experiences; we will follow up on every suggestion. Your comments will serve as the yardstick by which we can measure the quality of our accommodations. For your convenience, an evaluation form is included at the back of this book.

Cost of Accommodations

Bed and Breakfast, in the purest sense, is a private home where the owners rent their spare bedrooms to travelers. These are the backbone of this book.

However, American ingenuity has enhanced this simple idea to include more spectacular homes, mansions, small inns, and intimate hotels. With few exceptions, the proprietor is the host and lives on the premises.

Whether plain or fancy, all B&Bs are based on the concept that people are tired of the plastic monotony of motels and are disappointed that even the so-called budget motels can be quite expensive. Travelers crave the personal touch and they sincerely enjoy "visiting" rather than just "staying."

Prices vary accordingly. There are places in this book where lovely lodging may be had as low as $10 a night and others that feature a gourmet breakfast in a canopied bed for $75. Whatever the price, if you see the sign ✪, it means that the B&B has guaranteed its rates through 1985 to holders of this book, so be sure to mention it when you call or write!

Accommodations vary in price depending upon the locale and the season. Peak season usually refers to the availability of skiing in winter and water sports in summer; in the sunbelt states, the winter months are usually the peak season. Off-season rate schedules are usually reduced. Resorts and major cities are generally more expensive than out-of-the-way places. However, B&Bs are always less expensive than hotels and motels of equivalent caliber in the same area. A weekly rate is usually less expensive than a daily rate. Special reductions are sometimes given to families (occupying two rooms) or senior citizens. Whenever reduced rates are available, you will find this noted in the individual listings.

Meals

Breakfast: "Continental" refers to fruit or juice, rolls, and a hot beverage. Many hosts pride themselves on home-baked breads, homemade preserves, plus imported teas and cakes, so their continental breakfast may be quite deluxe. Several hosts have regular jobs outside the home so you may have to adjust your schedule to theirs. A "full" breakfast includes fruit, cereal and/or eggs, breakfast meats, breads, and hot beverage. The table is set family-style and is often the highlight of a B&B's hospitality. Either a continental breakfast or full breakfast is included in the room rate unless otherwise specified.

Other Meals: If listed as "available," you can be assured that the host takes pride in his or her cooking skills. The prices for lunch or dinner are usually reasonable but are not included in the quoted room rate unless clearly specified as "included."

Making Reservations

- Reservations are a MUST or you may risk missing out on the accommodations of your choice. Reserve *early* and confirm with a deposit equal to one night's stay. If your plans change and you

notify the proprietor well in advance, your deposit will be refunded. If you call to inquire about reservations, please remember the difference in time zones. When dialing outside of your area, remember to dial the digit "1" before the area code.
- Many individual B&Bs now accept charge cards. This information is indicated in the listings by the symbols "MC" for Master Card, "AMEX" for American Express, etc. A few have a surcharge for this service so inquire as to the policy.
- Cash or traveler's checks are the accepted method of paying for your stay. Be sure to inquire whether or not tax is included in the rates quoted so that you will know exactly how much your lodging will cost.
- Rates are based on single or double occupancy of a room as quoted. Expect that an extra person(s) in the room will be charged a small additional fee. Inquire when making your reservation what the charge will be.
- If a listing indicates that children or pets are welcome, it is expected that they will be well behaved. All of our hosts take pride in their homes and it would be unfair to subject them to circumstances where their possessions might be abused or the other houseguests disturbed by an unruly child or animal.
- Please note that many hosts have their own resident pets. If you are allergic or don't care to be around animals, inquire before making a reservation.
- In homes where smoking is permitted, do check to see if it is restricted in any of the rooms. Most hosts object to cigars.
- Where listings indicate that social drinking is permitted, it usually refers to your bringing your own beverages. Most hosts will provide ice; many will allow you to chill mixers in the refrigerator, and others offer complimentary wine and snacks. A few B&B inns have licenses to sell liquor. Any drinking should not be excessive.
- If "Yes" is indicated in the listings for airport pickup, it means that the host will meet your plane for a fee. If you are arriving by bus or train, ask if this service can be arranged.
- Feel free to request brochures and local maps so you can better plan for your visit.
- Do try to fit in with the host's house rules. You are on vacation; he isn't!
- A reservation form is included at the back of this book for your

convenience; just tear it out and send it in to the B&B of your choice.

B&B Reservation Services

There are many host families who prefer not to be individually listed in a book, and would rather have their houseguests referred by a coordinating agency. The organizations listed in this book are all members of the Tourist House Association. They all share our rigid standards regarding the suitability of the host home as to cordiality, cleanliness, and comfort.

The majority do a marvelous job of matching host and guest according to age, interests, language, and any special requirements. To get the best match, it is practical to give them as much time as possible to find the host home best tailored to your needs.

Many have prepared descriptive pamphlets describing the homes on their rosters, the areas in which the homes are located, and information regarding special things to see and do. *Send a self-addressed, stamped, business-sized envelope to receive a descriptive directory by return mail along with a reservation form for you to complete.* When returning the form, you will be asked to select the home or homes listed in the brochure that most appeal to you. (The homes are usually given a code number for reference.) The required deposit should accompany your reservation. Upon receipt, the coordinator will make the reservation and advise you of the name, address, telephone number, and travel instructions for your host.

A few agencies prepare a descriptive directory and *include* the host's name, address, and telephone number so that you can contact the host and make your arrangements directly. They charge anywhere from two to five dollars for the directory.

Several agencies are *membership* organizations, charging guests an annual fee ranging from $5 to $25 per person. Their descriptive directories are free to members and a few of them maintain toll-free telephone numbers for reservations.

Most reservation services have a specific geographic focus. The coordinators are experts in the areas they represent. They can often make arrangements for car rentals, theater tickets, and touring suggestions, and offer information in planning a trip best suited to your interests.

8 • INTRODUCTION

Most work on a commission basis with the host, and that fee is included in the room rates quoted in each listing. Some make a surcharge for a one-night stay; others require a two- or three-night minimum stay for holiday periods or special events. Some will accept a credit card for the reservation but the balance due must be paid to the host in cash or traveler's checks.

All of their host homes offer continental breakfast and some may include a full breakfast.

Many reservation services in the larger cities have, in addition to the traditional B&Bs, a selection of apartments, condominiums, and houses *without hosts in residence*. This may be appealing to those travelers anticipating an extended stay in a particular area.

The statewide services are listed first in the section for each state. City or regionally based organizations are listed first under the heading for that area. A few agencies are nationwide and their addresses are listed below. For a complete description of their services, look them up under the city and state where they're based.

NOTE: When calling, do so during normal business hours (for that time zone), unless otherwise stated. Collect calls are not accepted.

AMERICAN HISTORIC HOMES BED & BREAKFAST, P.O. Box 388, San Juan Capistrano, California 92693.

BED AND BREAKFAST LEAGUE, 2855 29th Street, N.W., Washington, D.C. 20008.

BED & BREAKFAST REGISTRY—NORTH AMERICA, P.O. Box 80174, St. Paul, Minnesota 55108-0174.

EVA, 317 Piedmont Road, Santa Barbara, California 93105.

HOME SUITE HOMES, 1470 Firebird Way, Sunnyvale, California 94087.

INTERNATIONAL SPAREROOM, P.O. Box 518, Solana Beach, California 92075.

2
How to Start Your Own B&B

What It's Like to Be a Host

Hosts are people who like the idea of accommodating travelers and sharing their home and the special features of their area with them. They are people who have houses too large for their personal needs and like the idea of supplementing their income by having people visit. For many, it's a marvelous way of meeting rising utility and maintenance costs. For young families, it is a way of buying and keeping that otherwise-too-large house and furnishing it, since many of the furnishings may be tax deductible. Another advantage is that many state and local governments have recognized the service that some host families perform. In browsing through this book you will note that some homes are listed in the National Historic Register. Some state governments allow owners of landmark and historical houses a special tax advantage if they are used for any business purpose. Check with the Historical Preservation Society in your state for details.

If you have bedrooms to spare . . . if you sincerely like having overnight guests . . . if your home is clean and comfortable . . . this is an opportunity to consider. It is a unique business because *you* set the time of the visit and the length of stay. (Guest houses are not boarding homes.) You invite the guests at *your* convenience, and the extras, such as meals, are entirely up to you. You can provide a cup of coffee, complete meals, or just a room and shared bath.

Although the majority of hosts are women, many couples are finding pleasure in this joint venture. The general profile of a typical host is a friendly, outgoing, flexible person who is proud of her home and hometown. The following information and suggestions represent a guideline to consider in deciding whether becoming a B&B host is really for you.

There are no set rules for the location, type, or style of a B&B. Apartments, condos, farmhouses, town houses, beach houses, vacation cottages, houseboats, mansions, as well as the traditional one-family dwelling are all appropriate. The important thing is for the host to be on the premises. The setting may be urban, rural, or suburban; near public transportation or in the hinterlands. Location is only important if you want to have guests every night. Areas where tourism is popular, such as resort areas or major cities, are often busier than out-of-the-way places. However, if a steady stream of visitors is not that important or even desirable, it doesn't matter where you are. People will contact you if your rates are reasonable and if there is something to see and do in your area, or if it is near a major transportation route.

Setting the Rates

Consider carefully four key factors in setting your rates: location, private vs. shared bath, type of breakfast, and your home itself.

Location: If you reside in a traditional resort or well-touristed area, near a major university or medical center, or in an urban hub or gateway city, your rates should be at least 40% lower than those of the area's major motels or hotels. If you live in an out-of-the-way location, your rates must be extremely reasonable. If your area has a "season"—snow sports in winter, water sports in summer—offer off-season rates when these attractions are not available. Reading through this book will help you to see what is the going rate in a situation similar to yours.

The Bath: You are entitled to charge more for a room with private bath. If the occupants of two rooms share one bath, the rate should be less. If more than five people must share one bathroom, you may have complaints, unless your rates are truly inexpensive.

The Breakfast: Figure the approximate cost of your ingredients, plus something for your time. Allow about $1 to $1.50 for a continental breakfast; $2 to $3 for a full American breakfast; then *include* it in the rate.

Your Home: Plan on charging a fair and reasonable rate for a typical B&B home, one that is warm and inviting, clean and comfortable. If your home is exceptionally luxurious, with king-size beds, Jacuzzi baths, tennis courts, or hot tubs, you will find guests who are willing to pay a premium. If your home is over 75 years old, well restored, with lots of antiques, you may also be able to charge a higher rate.

The Three B's—Bed, Breakfast, and Bath

The Bedroom: The ideal situation for a prospective host is the possession of a house too large for current needs. The children may be away at college most of the year or may have left permanently, leaving behind their bedrooms and, in some cases, the extra bath. Refurbishing these rooms does not mean refurnishing; an extraordinary investment need not be contemplated for receiving guests. Take a long hard look at the room. With a little imagination and a little monetary outlay, could it be changed into a bedroom *you'd* be pleased to spend the night in? Check it out *before* you go any further. Are the beds comfortable? Do the pillows or mattresses need replacement? Would the bed linens be appropriate if your fussy aunt slept overnight? Is the carpet

Roserox Country Inn By-The-Sea
Pacific Grove, California

clean? Are the walls attractive? Do the curtains or shades need attention? Are there sturdy hangers in the closet? Would emptying the closet and bureau be an impossible task? Is there a good light to read by? A writing table and comfortable chair? A mirror? Peek under the bed and see if there are dust balls or old magazines tucked away. While relatives and friends would "understand" if things weren't perfect, a paying guest is entitled to cleanliness and comfort.

If the idea of sprucing up the room has you overwhelmed, forget the idea and continue to be a guest rather than a host! If, however, a little "spit and polish," replacement of lumpy mattresses, sagging springs, and freshening the room in general presents no problem . . . continue! In short, your goal should be the kind of a room *you'd* be pleased to spend the night in and be willing to pay for.

The Breakfast: Breakfast time can be the most pleasant part of the guest's stay. It is at the breakfast table with you and the other guests that suggestions are made as to what to see and do, and exchanges of experiences are enjoyed. From a guest's point of view, the only expected offering is what is known as continental breakfast, which usually consists of juice, roll, and coffee or tea.

Breakfast fare is entirely up to you. If you are a morning person who whips out of bed at the crack of dawn with special recipes for muffins dancing in your head, to be drenched with your homemade preserves followed by eggs Benedict, an assortment of imported coffee or exotic tea . . . hop to it! You will play to a most appreciative audience. If, however, morning represents an awful intrusion on sleep and the idea of talking to anyone before noon is difficult, the least you should do is to prepare the breakfast table the night before with the necessary mugs, plates, and silverware. Fill the electric coffee pot and leave instructions that the first one up should plug it in; you can even hook it up to a timer, so that it will brew automatically!

Most of us fall somewhere in between these two extremes. Remember that any breakfast at "home" is preferable to getting dressed, getting into the car, and driving to some coffee shop. Whether you decide upon "continental breakfast" or a full American breakfast, consisting of juice or fruit, cereal or eggs, possibly bacon or sausage, toast, rolls, coffee, or tea, is up to you. It is most important that whatever the fare, it be included in your room rate. It is most awkward, especially after getting to know and like your guests, to present an additional charge for breakfast.

The Bath: This really is the third "B" in "B&B." If you are blessed with an extra bathroom for the exclusive use of a guest, that's super. If guests will have to share the facilities with others, that really presents no problem. If it's being shared with your family, the family must always be "last in line." Be sure that they are aware of the guest's importance; the guest, paying or otherwise, always comes first. No retainers, or used Band-Aids, or topless toothpaste tubes are to be carelessly left on the sink. The tub, shower, floor, and toilet bowl are to be squeaky clean. The mirrors and chrome should sparkle and a supply of toilet tissue, fresh soap, and unfrayed towels go a long way in reflecting a high standard of cleanliness. Make sure that the grout between tiles is free of mildew and that the shower curtain is unstained. Cracked ceilings should be repaired, the paint free of chips, and if your bath is wallpapered, make certain no loose edges mar its beauty.

Roserox Country Inn By-The-Sea

Most guests realize that in a share-the-bath situation they should leave the room ready for the next person's use. It is a thoughtful reminder for you to leave tub cleanser, a cleaning towel or sponge, and bathroom deodorant handy for this purpose. A wastepaper basket, paper towels, paper cups, should be part of your supplies. Needless to say, your hot water system should be able to accommodate the number of guests you'll have without being taxed. And a plumber should make certain that there aren't any clogged lines or dripping faucets to spoil things for you or your visitors. If more than one guest room is sharing the same bath, it makes sense to have a supply of different colored towels and to assign a color for each guest. There should be enough towel bars and hooks to accommodate the towels. You might even want to supply each guest room its own soap in its own covered soap dish. This is both popular and economical.

The B&B Business

Money Matters: Before embarking upon any business, it's a good idea to discuss it with an accountant and possibly an attorney. Since you'll be using your home for a business enterprise there are things with which they are familiar that are important for you to know. For instance, you may want to incorporate, so find out what the pros and cons are. Ask about depreciation. Deductible business expenses may include refurbishing, furnishings, supplies, printing costs, postage, etc. Although having an occasional paying guest may not necessarily subject you to the state tax applicable to hotels, your B&B income is taxable. An accountant will be able to guide you with a simple system of record keeping. Accurate records will help you analyze income and expense, and show if you are breaking even, or operating at a profit or a loss.

Insurance: It is important to call your insurance broker. Many home-owner policies have a clause covering "an occasional overnight paying guest." See if you will be protected under your existing coverage and, if not, what the additional premium would be.

Every home should be equipped with smoke detectors and fire extinguishers. All fire hazards should be eliminated; stairways and halls should be well lit and kept free of clutter. If you haven't already done so, immediately post prominently the emergency numbers for the fire department, police, and ambulance service.

Regulations: If you have read this far and are still excited about the concept of running a B&B, there are several steps to take at this point. As of this writing, there don't seem to be any specific laws governing B&Bs. Since guests are generally received on an irregular basis, B&Bs do not come under the same laws governing hotels and motels. And since B&Bs aren't inns where emphasis is on food rather than on lodging, no comparison can really be made in that regard either. As the idea grows, laws and regulations will probably be passed. Refer to the back of *Bed & Breakfast USA* and write to your state's office of tourism for information. The address and phone number are listed for your convenience. You might even call or write to a few B&Bs in your state and ask the host about her experience in this regard. Most hosts will be happy to give you the benefit of their experience, but keep in mind that they are busy people and it would be wise to limit your intrusion upon their time.

If you live in a traditional, residential area and you are the first in your neighborhood to consider operating a B&B, it would be prudent to examine closely the character of houses nearby. Do physicians, attorneys, accountants, or psychologists maintain offices in their residences? Do dressmakers, photographers, cosmeticians, or architects receive clients in their homes? These professions are legally accepted in the most prestigious communities as "Customary House Occupations." Bed and breakfast has been tested in many communities where the question was actually brought to court. In towns from La Jolla, California, to Croton-on-Hudson, New York, bed and breakfast has been approved and accepted.

Zoning boards are not always aware of the wide acceptance of the B&B concept. Possibly the best evidence that you could present to them is a copy of *Bed & Breakfast USA*, which indicates that it is an accepted practice throughout the entire country. It illustrates the caliber of the neighborhoods, the beauty of the homes, and the fact that many professionals are also hosts. Reassure the zoning board that you will accept guests only by advance reservation. You will not display any exterior signs to attract attention to your home. You will keep your home and grounds properly maintained, attractive, and in no way detract from the integrity of your neighborhood. You will direct guests to proper parking facilities and do nothing to intrude upon the privacy of your neighbors.

After all, there is little difference between the visit of a family friend and a B&B guest, because that is the spirit and essence of a

B&B. Just as a friend would make prior arrangements to be a houseguest, so will a B&B guest make a reservation in advance of arriving. Neither would just "drop-in" for an overnight stay. We are happy to share letters from hosts attesting to the high caliber, honesty and integrity of B&B guests that come as a result of reading about their accommodations in this book. There are over 12,000 B&Bs extending our kind of hospitality throughout the United States and the number is increasing geometrically every day.

You should also bring along a copy of *Bed & Breakfast USA* when you go to visit the local Chamber of Commerce. Most of them are enthusiastic, because additional visitors mean extra business for local restaurants, shops, theaters, and businesses. This is a good time to inquire what it would cost to join the Chamber of Commerce.

The Name: The naming of your B&B is most important and will take some time and consideration because this is the moment when dreams become reality. It will be used on your brochures, stationery, and bills. (If you decide to incorporate, the corporation needs a name!) It should somehow be descriptive of the atmosphere you wish to convey.

Brochure: Once you have given a name to your house, design a brochure. The best ones include a reservation form and can be mailed to your prospective guests. The brochure should contain the name of your B&B, address, phone number, best time to call, your name, a brief description of your home, its ambience, a brief history of the house if it is old, the number of guest rooms, whether or not baths are shared, the type of breakfast served, rates, required deposit, minimum stay requirement if any, dates when you'll be closed, and your cancellation policy. A deposit of one night's stay is acceptable and the promise of a full refund if cancellation is received at least two weeks prior to arrival is typical. If you have reduced rates for a specific length of stay, families, senior citizens, etc., mention it.

If you can converse in a foreign language, say so, because many visitors from abroad seek out B&Bs; it's a marvelous plus to be able to chat in their native tongue. Include your policy regarding children, pets, or smokers, and whether you offer the convenience of a guest refrigerator or barbecue. It is helpful to include directions from a major route and a simple map for finding your home. It's a good idea to include a line or two about yourself and your interests, and do mention what there is to see and do in the area as well as proximity to any major university. A line drawing of your house is a good investment since the picture can be used not only on the brochure, but on your stationery, postcards, and greeting cards as well. If you can't have this taken care of locally, write the Tourist House Association. We have a service that can handle it for you.

Take your ideas to a reliable printer for his professional guidance. Don't forget to keep the receipt for the printing bill since this is a business expense.

Confirmation Letter: Upon receipt of a paid reservation, do send out a letter confirming it. You can design a form letter and have it offset by a printer, since the cost of doing so is usually nominal. Include the dates of the stay, number of people expected, the rate including tax, as well as explicit directions by car and, if applicable, by public transportation. A simple map reflecting the exact location of your home in relation to major streets and highways is most useful. It is a good idea to ask your guests to call you if they will be traveling and unavailable by phone for the week prior to their expected arrival. You might even want to include any of the house rules regarding smoking, pets, or whatever.

Successful Hosting

The Advantage of Hosting: The nicest part of being a B&B host is that you aren't required to take guests every day of the year. Should there be times when having guests would not be convenient, you can always say you're full and try to arrange an alternate date. But most important, keep whatever date you reserve. It is an excellent idea at the time reservations are accepted to ask for the name and telephone number of an emergency contact should you have to cancel unexpectedly. However, *never* have a guest come to a locked door. If an emergency arises and you cannot reach your prospective guests in time, do make arrangements for someone to greet them and make alternate arrangements so they can be accommodated.

House Rules: While you're in the "thinking stage," give some thought to the rules you'd like your guests to adhere to. The last thing you want for you or your family is to feel uncomfortable in your own home. Make a list of House Rules concerning arrival and departure during the guests' stay and specify when breakfast is served. If you don't want guests coming home too late, say so. Most hosts like to lock up at a certain hour at night, so arrange for an extra key for night owls. If that makes you uncomfortable, have a curfew on your House Rules list. If smoking disturbs you, confine the area where it's permitted.

Some guests bring a bottle of their favorite beverage and enjoy a drink before going out to dinner. Many hosts enjoy a cocktail hour too, and often provide cheese and crackers to share with the guests. B&Bs cannot sell drinks to guests since this would require licensing. If you'd rather no drinks be consumed in your home, say so.

Many hosts don't mind accommodating a well-behaved pet. If you don't mind or have pets of your own, discuss this with your guests before they pack Fido's suitcase. Your House Rules can even be included in your brochure. That way both the host and the guest are aware of each other's likes and dislikes, and no hard feelings are made.

Entertaining: One of the most appealing features of being a guest at a B&B is the opportunity of being able to visit in the evening with the hosts. After a day of sightseeing or business, it is most relaxing and pleasant to sit around the living room and chat. For many hosts, this is the most enjoyable part of having guests. However, if you are accommodating several people on a daily basis, entertaining can be tiring. Don't feel you'll be offending anyone by excusing yourself to attend to your own family or personal needs. The situation can be easily handled by having a room where you can retreat and offering your guests the living room, den, or other area for games, books, magazines, and perhaps the use of a television or bridge table. Most guests enjoy just talking to each other since this is the main idea of staying at a B&B.

The Telephone: This is a most important link between you and your prospective guests. As soon as possible, have your telephone number included under your B&B name in the White Pages. It is a good idea to be listed in the appropriate section in your telephone directory Yellow Pages. If your home phone is used for a lot of personal calls, you should think about installing a separate line for your B&B. If you are out a lot, give some thought to using a telephone answering device to explain your absence and time of return, and record the caller's message. There is nothing more frustrating to a prospective guest than to call and get a constant busy signal or no answer at all. Request that the caller leave his name and address, "at the sound of the beep," so you can mail a reservation form. This will help eliminate the necessity of having to return long distance calls. If the caller wants further information, he will call again at the time you said you'd be home.

B&B guests don't expect a phone in the guest room. However, there are times when they might want to use your phone for a long distance call. In your House Rules list, suggest that any such calls be charged to their home telephone. Business travelers often have telephone charge cards for this purpose. In either case, you should keep a telephone record book and timer near your instrument. Ask the caller to enter the city called, telephone number, and length of call. Thus, you will have an accurate record should a charge be inadvertently added to your bill. Or, if you wish, you can add telephone charges to the guest bill. The telephone operator will quote the cost of the per-minute charge throughout the country for this purpose.

Maid Service: If you have several guest rooms and bathrooms, you may find yourself being a chambermaid as part of the business. Naturally, each guest gets fresh linens upon arrival. If a guest stays up to three days, it isn't expected that bed linen be changed every day. What is expected is the room be freshened and the bath be cleaned and towels replaced every day. If you don't employ a full-time maid you may want to investigate the possibility of hiring a high school student on a part-time basis to give you a hand with the housekeeping. Many guests, noticing the absence of help, will voluntarily lend a hand, although they have the right to expect some degree of service, particularly if they are paying a premium rate.

Keys: A great many hosts are not constantly home during the day. Some do "hosting" on a part-time basis, while involved with regular jobs. There are times when even full-time hosts have to be away during the day. If the guests are to have access to the house while you are not on the premises, it is wise to have extra keys made. It is also wise to take a key deposit of $50 simply to assure return of the key. Let me add that in the 10 years of my personal experience, as well as in the opinions of other hosts, B&B guests are the most honest people you can have. No one has ever had even a washcloth stolen, let alone the family treasures. In fact, it isn't unusual for the guest to leave a small gift after a particularly pleasant visit. On the other hand, guests are sometimes forgetful and leave belongings behind. For this reason it is important for you to have their names and addresses so you can return their possessions. They will expect to reimburse you for the postage.

Registering Guests: You should keep a regular registration ledger for the guest to complete before checking in. The information should include the full names of each guest, home address, phone number, business address and telephone, and auto license number. It's a good idea to include the name and phone number of a friend or relative in case of an emergency. This information will serve you well for other contingencies, such as the guest leaving some important article behind, or an unpaid long distance phone call, or the rare instance of an unpaid bill. You may prefer to have this information on your guest bill which should be designed as a two-part carbon form. You will then have a record and the guest has a ready receipt. (Receipts are very important to business travelers!)

Settling the Bill: The average stay in a B&B is two nights. Since a deposit equal to one night's lodging is the norm, when to collect the balance is up to you. Most guests pay upon leaving, but if they leave so early that the settling of the bill at that time is inconvenient, you can request the payment the previous night. You might want to consider the convenience of accepting a major credit card but contact the sponsoring company first to see what percentage of your gross is expected for this service. If you find yourself entertaining more business visitors than vacationers, it might be something you should offer. Most travelers are aware that cash or traveler s checks are the accepted modes of payment. Accepting a personal check is rarely risky but again, it's up to you. You might include your preference in your brochure.

Other Meals: B&B means that only breakfast is served. If you enjoy cooking and would like to offer other meals for a fee, make sure that you investigate the applicable health laws. If you have to install a commercial kitchen, the idea might be too expensive for current consideration. However, allowing guests to store fixings for a quick snack or to use your barbecue can be a very attractive feature for families traveling with children or for people watching their budget. If you can offer this convenience, be sure to mention it in your brochure. (And, be sure to add a line to your House Rules that the guest is expected to clean up.) Some hosts keep an extra guest refrigerator on hand for this purpose.

It's an excellent idea to keep menus from your local restaurants on hand. Try to have a good sampling, ranging from moderately priced to expensive dining spots, and find out if reservations are required. Your guests will always rely heavily upon your advice and suggestions. After all, when it comes to your town, you're the authority! It's also a nice idea to keep informed of local happenings that might be of interest to your visitors. A special concert at the university or a local fair or church supper can add an extra dimension to their visit. If parents are visiting with young children they might want to have dinner out without them; try to have a list of available baby-sitters. A selection of guide books covering your area is also a nice feature.

The Guest Book: These are available in most stationery and department stores, and it is important that you buy one. It should contain designated space for the date, the name of the guest, home address, and a blank area for the guest's comments. They generally sign the guest book before checking out. The guest book is first of all a permanent record of who came and went. It will give you an idea of what times during the year you were busiest and which times were slow. Secondly, it is an easy way to keep a mailing list for your Christmas cards and future promotional mailings. You will also find that thumbing through it in years to come will recall some very pleasant people who were once strangers but now are friends.

Advertising: Periodically distribute your brochures to the local university, college, and hospital, since out of town visitors always need a place to stay. Let your local caterers know of your existence since wedding guests are often from out of town. If you have a major corporation in your area, drop off a brochure at the personnel office. Even visiting or relocating executives and salesmen enjoy B&Bs. Hotels and motels are sometimes overbooked; it wouldn't hurt to leave your brochure with the manager for times when there's no room for their last-minute guests. Local residents sometimes have to put up extra guests so it's a good idea to take an ad out in your local school or church newspaper. The cost is usually minimal. Repeat this distribution process from time to time, so that you can replenish the supply of brochures.

The best advertising is being a member of the Tourist House Association since all member B&Bs are fully described in this book, which is available in bookstores, libraries, and B&Bs throughout the U.S. and Canada. In addition, it is natural for THA members to recommend each other when guests inquire about similar accommodations in other areas. The most important reason for keeping your B&B clean, comfortable, and cordial is that we are all judged by what a guest experiences in any individual Tourist House Association home. The best publicity will come from your satisfied guests who will recommend your B&B to their friends.

Additional Suggestions

Extra Earnings: You might want to consider a few ideas for earning extra money in connection with being a host. If you enjoy touring, you can plan and conduct a special outing, off the beaten tourist track, for a modest fee. In major cities, you can do such things as acquiring tickets for theater, concert, or sports events. A supply of *Bed & Breakfast USA* for sale to guests is both a source of income and gives every THA member direct exposure to the B&B market.

Several hosts tell me that a small gift shop is often a natural offshoot of a B&B. Items for sale could include handmade quilts, pillows, potholders, and knitted items. One host has turned his hobby of woodworking into extra income. He makes lovely picture frames, napkin rings, and foot stools that many guests buy as souvenirs to take home. If you plan to do this, check with the Small Business Administration to inquire about such things as a resale license and tax collection; the Chamber of Commerce can advise in this regard.

Transportation: While the majority of B&B guests arrive by car, there are many who rely on public transportation. Some hosts, for a modest fee, are willing to meet arriving guests at airports, train depots, or bus stations. Do be knowledgeable about local transportation schedules in your area and be prepared to give explicit directions for your visitors' comings and goings. Have phone numbers handy for taxi service, as well as information on car rentals.

Thoughtful Touches: Guests often write to tell us of their experiences at B&Bs as a result of learning about them through this book. These are some of the special touches that made their visit special: fresh flowers in the guest room; even a single flower in a bud vase is pretty. One hostess puts a foil-wrapped piece of candy on the pillow before the guest returns from dinner. A small decanter of wine and glasses, or a few pieces of fresh fruit in a pretty bowl on the dresser are lovely surprises. A few one-size-fits-all terry robes are great to have on hand, especially if the bathroom is shared. A small sewing kit in the bureau is handy. Writing paper and envelopes in the desk invite the guest to send a quick note to the folks at home. If your house sketch is printed on it, it is marvelous free publicity. A pre-bed cup of tea for adults or cookies and milk for children are always appreciated.

By the way, keep a supply of guest-comment cards in the desk, both to attract compliments as well as to bring your attention to the flaws in your B&B that should be corrected.

Join the Tourist House Association: If you are convinced that you want to be a host, and have thoroughly discussed the pros and cons with your family and advisers, complete and return the membership application found at the back of this book. Our dues are $15 annually. The description of your B&B will be part of the next issue of the book *Bed & Breakfast USA,* as well as in the interim supplement between printings. You will also receive the THA's newsletter; regional seminars and conferences are held occasionally and you might enjoy attending. And, as an association, we will have clout should the time come when B&B becomes a recognized industry.

Affiliating with a B&B Reservation Agency: Over 100 agencies are listed in *Bed & Breakfast USA*. If you do not care to advertise your house directly to the public, consider joining one in your area. Membership and reservation fees, as well as the degree of professionalism, vary widely from agency to agency, so do check around.

Prediction for Success: Success should not be equated with money alone. If you thoroughly enjoy people, are well organized, enjoy sharing your tidy home without exhausting yourself, then the idea of receiving compensation for the use of an otherwise dormant bedroom will be a big plus. Your visitors will seek relaxing, wholesome surroundings and unpretentious hosts who open their hearts as well as their homes. Being a B&B host or guest is an exciting, enriching experience.

For key to listings, see inside front or back cover.

○ This star means that rates are guaranteed through December 31, 1985 to any guest making a reservation as a result of reading about the B&B in *BED & BREAKFAST U.S.A.*—1985 edition.

Please enclose a self-addressed, stamped, business-sized envelope when contacting reservation services.

For more details on what you can expect in a B&B, see Chapter 1.

Always mention *Bed & Breakfast USA* when making reservations!

3
B&B Recipes

The recipes that follow are not to be found in standard cookbooks. Some are original and the measurements are sometimes from the school of "a smidgen of this," "according to taste," and "till done." But they all indicate the host's desire to pamper guests with something special. The most important ingredient is the heartful of love that is as unmeasured as the handful of flour.

We had an overwhelming response to our request for host-contributed favorite breakfast recipes. Although we could not publish them all this time, we will use most of them in future editions. The following represent, as much as possible, regional or ethnic recipes that impart the flavor and variety of B&Bs across the country.

Apple 'n' Fruit Bake

1½ c. apple cider (or apple juice) ½ c. sliced almonds
½ c. raisins   ½ c. sunflower seeds
½ c. cut-up dates   cinnamon

(Allow at least 1 large fruit, sliced thick, per person.) Apples, pears, peaches, nectarines, whole seedless grapes, and bananas.

In a large, shallow casserole, mix the apples with the liquid and sprinkle lightly with cinnamon. Bake at 350° for 10 minutes. Add remaining fruit (except bananas) and bake an additional 10 minutes. Do not overcook. Remove from oven and gently toss with sliced bananas. Serve hot or cold. (Delicious hot with French toast or pancakes!)

NOTE: The liquid portion suggested above is enough for a dozen pieces of whole fruit. The fruit should not be swimming in juice and should keep its identity and shape.

The Turning Point, Great Barrington, Massachusetts

Blueberry-Raspberry Soup

2 c. water
3 tbsp. quick-cooking tapioca
2 1½" cinnamon sticks
½ c. sugar
¼ tsp. salt

1 tsp. lemon peel (grated)
⅓ c. lemon juice
8 oz. fresh or frozen blueberries
2 packages frozen raspberries (16 oz.)

In a saucepan, combine water, tapioca, sugar, salt, cinnamon, lemon peel, lemon juice, and blueberries. Over medium-high heat, bring to a boil, stirring constantly. Reduce heat and simmer, stirring occasionally, for 5 minutes. Remove from heat and stir in raspberries. Cover and refrigerate until well chilled. Remove cinnamon sticks. Serve cold and pass bowl of sour cream. (Makes 6 large or 12 small servings.)

NOTE: Tastes great hot, too!

Barnard Good House, Cape May, New Jersey

Cheese-Baked Eggs

1 tsp. melted butter
1 tbsp. cream

1 large egg
Havarti cheese (grated)

Butter a 3½ oz. ramekin or custard dish. Add cream. Gently crack egg into dish. Season with salt and pepper. Sprinkle cheese on top. Bake in pre-heated oven at 350° for 8 to 10 minutes.

Chanticleer, Ashland, Oregon

Cheese Pudding

½ c. sharp cheese (grated)
4 eggs
¼ c. melted butter
½ tsp. salt
½ tsp. pepper
½ tsp. Dijon mustard
½ tsp. paprika
2⅔ c. milk
12 slices firm bread—remove crusts and cut in 1" cubes

Beat eggs and add butter, milk, and spices. Alternate layers of bread and cheese in a greased 9" × 13" baking pan. Pour egg mixture over the layers and refrigerate overnight. Preheat oven at 350° and bake for 1 hour. (Serves 6 to 8.) Great with sausage!

Bed & Breakfast of Delaware, Wilmington, Delaware

Bev's Chili Relleno Souffle

1 4-oz. can diced green chilis
½ lb. sharp cheddar cheese (grated)
5 eggs (separated)
2 c. milk
½ c. flour

Place chilis in 7" × 11" baking dish and cover with cheese. Beat egg yolks, add flour and milk, and pour over cheese. Beat egg whites, fold in, and bake for 45 minutes at 350° or until custard sets. (Serves 4.)

Megan's Friends, San Luis Obispo, California

Eierkuchen (German Egg Cakes)

½ c. cake flour
¼ tsp. baking soda
¾ tsp. baking powder
1 tbsp. sugar
salt (dash)
½ c. buttermilk
6 eggs (separated)
cream of tartar (pinch)
2 tbsp. sour cream
1 tsp. vanilla
1 tbsp. sweet butter

In a large bowl, mix flour, baking soda, baking powder, sugar, and salt. Add egg yolks, buttermilk, sour cream, and vanilla, then beat. In a separate bowl, add cream of tartar to egg whites and beat until stiff. Carefully fold into the yolk mixture. Preheat griddle and grease with sweet butter. Spoon onto griddle, spreading mixture slightly with side of spoon to make small round pancakes. When golden brown on one side, flip over and bake the underside. Top with fresh berries or applesauce. (Serves 4.) *Guten Appetit!*

Elk Cove Inn, Elk, California

Dutch Baby (Oven Pancake Puff)

6 eggs
1 c. flour
1 c. milk
4 tbsp. butter
½ tsp. salt

Preheat oven to 425°. Put butter into 9" × 13" pan and melt in oven. In blender, combine eggs, flour, milk, and salt. Turn oven down to 400° and pour mixture into pan. (Do not stir!) Bake 25 minutes. (Delicious served with pure maple syrup or cinnamon sugar. Serves 4 to 6.)

Lake Pateros B&B, Washington
Vermont B&B, Jericho, Vermont
Miss Anne's B&B, Nashville, Tennessee
B&B Center City, Philadelphia, Pennsylvania
Nashville Bed & Breakfast, Nashville, Tennessee

Whole-Wheat Pancakes with Orange Syrup

1 c. unbleached flour
¾ c. whole-wheat flour
1 tbsp. sugar
½ tsp. salt
1 tsp. baking powder
1 tsp. baking soda
1⅔ c. buttermilk
3 tbsp. melted butter
3 eggs (separated)

Combine flours, sugar, salt, baking powder, and baking soda. In a separate bowl, beat buttermilk, melted butter, and egg yolks with rotary beater. Add egg mixture all at once to dry ingredients. Mix well. Gently fold in stiffly beaten egg whites. Drop batter by spoonfuls (2 to 3 tbsp.) onto lightly greased hot griddle. Bake until cakes are full of bubbles on top. Turn with spatula and brown on other side. (Yields 16 to 20 4" pancakes.)

Orange Syrup

1 12-oz. can of frozen juice concentrate
1½ c. sugar

Mix together in a small saucepan. Heat to boiling, stirring occasionally.

Beach House, Ocracoke Island, North Carolina

Buttermilk Pancakes

4 c. flour
1 tsp. baking soda
1 tsp. salt
4 eggs (beaten)

½ c. melted butter
2 tsp. vanilla
4 c. buttermilk

Mix dry ingredients. Add milk, vanilla, and melted shortening to eggs. Combine mixtures and stir until smooth. Bake on hot griddle until bubbles break. Turn over and bake until golden brown. Delicious with homemade jam or pure maple syrup!

Pittsfield Inn, Pittsfield, Vermont

Maine Blueberry Scones

2 c. all-purpose flour
2 tbsp. sugar
3 tsp. baking powder
nutmeg (dash)
¾ tsp. salt

½ stick sweet butter
1 egg (beaten)
1 c. blueberries
½ c. medium cream
½–¾ c. milk

Sift dry ingredients. Cut in shortening. Add berries. Combine egg with milk. Add to dry ingredients. Stir just enough to moisten. Pat out dough quickly and gently into a circle about ¾" thick. Cut into pie-shaped wedges. Brush with cream and sprinkle with sugar. Place on cookie sheet and bake in 450° oven for 15 minutes or until golden brown. Serve warm.

Bed & Breakfast Down East, Eastbrook, Maine

Fresh Fruit Bran Muffins

1½ c. whole bran cereal
1 c. milk
1 egg
¼ c. cooking oil
1 c. all-purpose flour
¼ c. sugar (use slightly more if you want to)
2 tsp. baking powder

½ tsp. baking soda
½ tsp. salt
½ tsp. finely shredded lemon peel
½ tsp. cinnamon
1 c. fresh fruit (choice of apples, peaches, blueberries, raspberries, dark cherries)

Combine bran and milk, and let stand for 4 minutes or until liquid is absorbed. Stir in egg and oil; set aside. In a separate bowl, stir together flour, sugar, baking powder, baking soda, salt, lemon peel, and cinnamon. Add bran mixture and stir just until moist. Fold in fruit. Fill greased muffin tins ⅔ full. Bake in 400° oven for 20 to 25 minutes. (Yields 12 to 15 muffins.)

Cheney House, Ashland, New Hampshire

Jalapeño Muffins

3 c. corn bread mix
2½ c. milk
½ c. salad oil
3 eggs (beaten)
1 large onion (grated)
2 tbsp. sugar

½ c. finely chopped peppers
1½ c. sharp cheese (shredded)
¼ lb. bacon (fried and crumbled)
¼ c. chopped pimentos
½ clove garlic (crushed)

Mix first four ingredients, then add remainder. Bake in heavily greased muffin tins, or in tins with paper liners. Bake at 400° for approximately 35 minutes. (Yields 4 dozen muffins.)

NOTE: These may be frozen in packages of three. Take out the night before and heat the next morning for a delicious treat.

VARIATION: Decrease milk by ¼ c. and add 2 c. creamed-style corn.

Bed & Breakfast Texas Style, Dallas, Texas

Skyline Apple Muffins

1½ c. brown sugar
⅔ c. oil
1 egg
1 c. buttermilk
1 tsp. salt

1 tsp. baking soda
1 tsp. vanilla
2 c. all-purpose flour
1½ c. chopped apples (tart)
½ c. chopped pecans or walnuts

In a mixing bowl, mix the sugar, oil, and egg. In a measuring cup, mix the buttermilk, salt, soda, and vanilla. Stir this into the sugar mixture. Add the flour and stir thoroughly. Add the apples and nuts. Bake in greased muffin tin at 350° for 30 minutes.

The Lords Proprietors' Inn, Edenton, North Carolina

B. J.'s Apple Cake

2 c. sugar
4 c. chopped apples (pared)
2 c. flour
1½ tsp. baking soda
1 tsp. salt

2 tsp. cinnamon
2 eggs (beaten)
1 c. cooking oil
2 tsp. vanilla
1 c. nuts (optional)

Sprinkle sugar over apples in large bowl. Sift together dry ingredients twice. Add to apples. Add remaining ingredients. Stir only until mixed (by hand), not longer. Pour into greased 9" × 13" pan. Bake at 350° for 45 to 50 minutes. Serve hot or cold.

Kenwood Inn, St. Augustine, Florida

Grandma Nettie's Bread Pudding

4 kaiser rolls or half-pound challah bread
4 eggs (large)
½ c. white raisins
1 tart apple

1 qt. milk
6 c. corn flakes
½ c. sugar
1½ tsp. vanilla

Topping: 2 tsp. cinnamon and 3 tsp. sugar (mixed)

Soak bread in water and cover. Pour boiled water over raisins and cover. Squeeze water from bread and add slightly beaten eggs. Add sugar, milk, corn flakes, grated apple, and vanilla. Drain raisins and add. Mix together. Spread into 9" × 13" baking pan that has been well greased with butter or margarine. Sprinkle with topping and bake at 350° for 1 hour.

Serve warm with sweet cream. Enjoy!

A Bit o' the Apple, New York City

Cheddared Walnut Bread

2½ c. all-purpose flour
2 tbsp. sugar
2 tsp. baking powder
½ tsp. baking soda
1¼ tsp. salt
½ tsp. dry mustard

dash of cayenne
¼ c. shortening
1 c. grated sharp cheddar cheese
1 egg
1 c. buttermilk
½ tsp. Worcestershire sauce

1 c. chopped walnuts
several whole walnut pieces (for garnish)

In a bowl, sift first 7 ingredients together. Cut in the shortening. Mix in cheese with a fork. Beat egg slightly; add the buttermilk and Worcestershire sauce. Stir into dry mixture just until moistened. Add walnuts and mix through. Turn the stiff dough into a greased 8½" × 4½" loaf pan and smooth the top. Gently press large walnut pieces into top of loaf. Bake at 350° for 55 minutes or until it tests done. Let stand for 10 minutes, then turn out to cool on wire rack.

NOTE: Delicious toasted with butter!

Feller House, Naples, Florida

Lemon Yogurt Bread

3 c. flour
1 tsp. salt
1 tsp. baking soda
½ tsp. baking powder
3 eggs
1 c. oil

1¾ c. sugar
2 c. lemon yogurt
1 tbsp. lemon extract
1 c. finely chopped almonds (optional)

Sift first four ingredients; stir in nuts; set aside. Beat eggs in a large bowl; add oil and sugar; cream well. Add yogurt and extract. Spoon into 2 well-greased loaf pans, or 1 large well-greased bundt pan. Bake in preheated oven at 325° for 1 hour. (Blue Ribbon Winner at '82 Mendocino County Fair!)

The Grey Whale Inn, Fort Bragg, California

Zucchini Raisin Bread

3 eggs
1 c. sugar
1 c. vegetable oil
2 c. grated raw zucchini (peeled)
3 tsp. vanilla
3 c. flour

1 tsp. salt
1½ tsp. baking soda
1 tsp. baking powder
3 tsp. cinnamon
1 c. raisins

Beat eggs until light and foamy. Add sugar, oil, zucchini, and vanilla. Beat well. Combine flour, salt, soda, powder, and cinnamon, then add to egg mixture. Stir until well blended. Add raisins and pour into two 9" × 5" loaf pans. Bake at 350° for 1 hour. Let cool in pans for 7 minutes. Turn out on wire rack.

The Wedgwood Inn, New Hope, Pennsylvania

Easy Sausage Patties

1 lb. bulk sausage meat	1 tsp. sage (or Bell's Seasoning)
1 lb. freshly ground lean pork	2 tsp. fresh parsley (chopped)
1 tsp. garlic powder	1 tsp. fresh chives (chopped)

Mix ingredients thoroughly. Make patties ½" thick. Dust with flour. Heat skillet. (No fat required.) Brown quickly on both sides. Cover with a lid. Reduce heat and cook 8 minutes. Pour off excess fat. Turn and cook 8 minutes. Great with scrambled eggs!

Granes Fairhaven Inn, Bath, Maine

Judy's Breakfast Ideas

Prepare your favorite hot cereal with apple juice or sweet cider instead of water. Sprinkle with cinnamon.

Keep hot cereals hot in a crock pot during a leisurely breakfast. Late arrivals can help themselves.

Heat a favorite jam or jelly with an equal amount of maple syrup and a pat of butter to create a new pancake topping.

Use leftover eggnog for a quick French toast batter.

Loch Lyme Lodge, Lyme, New Hampshire

KEY TO LISTINGS

◎ This star means that rates are guaranteed through December 31, 1985 to any guest making a reservation as a result of reading about the B&B in *BED & BREAKFAST U.S.A.*—1985 edition.

Location: As indicated, unless the B&B is right in town, or its location is clear from the address as stated.

Best time to call: When indicated, the time when the host is usually home to accept calls. Some have telephone answering machines or answering services to cover other times. Remember the differences in time zones when calling.

NOTE: Reservation services are available during normal business hours (9 A.M.–5 P.M., Monday through Friday) unless otherwise indicated.

No. of rooms: Number of *guest* bedrooms.

Double: Rate for two people in one room. Double rooms may be furnished with a standard double bed, queen- or king-sized bed, or twin beds.

Single: Rate for one person in a room.

Suite: Can be either two bedrooms with an adjoining bath, or a living room and bedroom with private bath.

Guest cottage: A separate building that usually has a mini-kitchen and private bath.

pb: Private bath.

sb: Shared bath.

Max. no. sharing bath: Maximum number of people that might be sharing one bathroom. Keep in mind that some B&Bs have sinks in each bedroom.

Double/pb: Room for two with private bath.

Single/pb: Room for one with private bath.

Double/sb: Room for two with shared bath.

Single/sb: Room for one with shared bath.

NOTE: There is usually an extra charge for an additional person occupying the same room.

Open: As indicated. Keep in mind that many B&Bs are closed for Thanksgiving, Christmas, and Easter.

Breakfast: Included in the room rate unless otherwise stated. A continental breakfast consists of juice, bread, and hot beverage. Some hosts provide a gourmet breakfast with homemade cakes, breads, and preserves. A full breakfast consists of juice, cereal, eggs, breakfast meat, bread or rolls, and hot beverage. Some are so special, you may not be hungry for lunch!

Credit cards: When reservation services accept them, the deposit can be made with a credit card but the host will still require that the balance due be paid in cash or by check.

Pets: Keep in mind that the host may have resident pets. Always ask if it is convenient to bring yours, to make certain there won't be a conflict with other guests. If you are allergic to animals, inquire before making reservations.

Children: If "crib" is noted after the word "welcome," the host can accommodate children under the age of three.

Smoking: If permitted, this means it is allowed *somewhere* inside the house. Some hosts discourage smoking in the breakfast room for the comfort of other guests; some prohibit smoking in bedrooms for safety's sake. Most do not allow cigars or pipes.

Social drinking: Some hosts provide a glass of wine or sherry; others provide setups for bring-your-own.

Airport/station pickup: If "yes" is indicated, the host will meet your plane, bus, or train for a fee.

Please enclose a self-addressed, stamped, business-sized envelope when contacting reservation services.

For more details on what you can expect in a B&B, see Chapter 1.

Always mention *Bed & Breakfast USA* when making reservations!

4

State-by-State Listings

ALABAMA

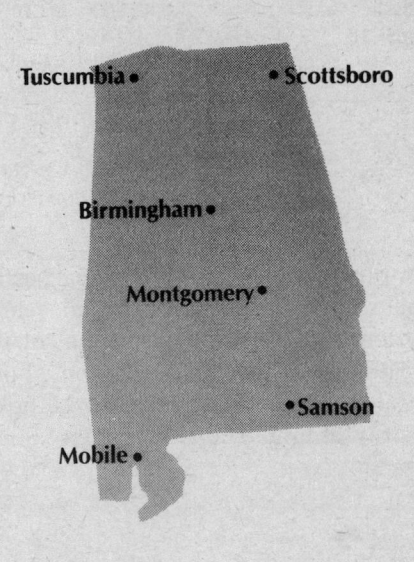

Bed & Breakfast—Birmingham ✪
P.O. BOX 31328, BIRMINGHAM, ALABAMA 35222

Tel: (205) 591-6406
Coordinator: **Ruth Taylor**
States/Regions Covered:
　**Birmingham, Franklin, Mobile,
　Montgomery, Smith Lake, Verbena**

Rates (Single/Double):
　Modest:　$28–$40
　Average:　$42–$58
　Luxury:　$60–$125
Credit Cards: **No**

See where Bear Bryant coached, Martin Luther King, Jr., led, and where the Old and New South blend in a way that never fails to surprise and please first-time visitors. Convenient to many museums and historic and cultural places, your home away from home might be a contemporary prizewinner or a country cottage. Birmingham is the site of the 1985 National Square Dance convention.

Kraft's Korner ✪
90 CARLILE DRIVE, MOBILE, ALABAMA 36619

Tel: (205) 666-6819
Best Time to Call: 6-9 AM
Host(s): Estelle and Allen Kraft
Location: 5 mi. from I-10
No. of Rooms: 2
No. of Private Baths: 1
Max. No. Sharing Bath: 2
Double/pb: $30
Single/pb: $25
Double/sb: $25
Single/sb: $20
Suites: $50 (for 4)
Open: All year
Reduced Rates: 10%, seniors
Breakfast: Full
Other Meals: Available
Pets: No
Children: Welcome
Smoking: No
Social Drinking: No
Airport/Station Pickup: Yes

This is a contemporary home in a residential section, where the temperate climate has flowers blooming all year long. Nearby Bellingrath Gardens, called the Charm Spot of the South, is a must on your itinerary. Estelle and Allen spoil guests with Southern hospitality. Estelle is a fine cook and the emphasis is on natural and healthy dining. The University of South Alabama is not far.

Travellers' Rest ✪
3664 KELLY LANE, MONTGOMERY, ALABAMA 36105

Tel: (205) 281-2772
Host(s): Joan Sullivan
Location: 2 mi. from I-65
No. of Rooms: 2
Max. No. Sharing Bath: 4
Double/sb: $27
Single/sb: $18
Open: All year
Reduced Rates: 6%, seniors
Breakfast: Full
Pets: Sometimes
Children: Welcome
Smoking: Permitted
Social Drinking: No
Airport/Station Pickup: Yes
Foreign Languages: German

This single-story brick home is located ten minutes from downtown. Furnished in colonial decor, it is warm and inviting. It is minutes away from the Governor's House and the First White House of the Confederacy. Joan offers a hearty Southern breakfast, including grits. Troy State and Alabama State Colleges are nearby.

Jola Bama Guest Home
201 EAST STREET, SAMSON, ALABAMA 36477

Tel: **(205) 898-2478**
Host(s): **Jewel M. Armstrong**
Location: **40 mi. W of Dothan**
No. of Rooms: **5**
No. of Private Baths: **2**
Max. No. Sharing Bath: **2**
Double/pb: **$26**
Single/pb: **$20**
Double/sb: **$18**
Single/sb: **$15**
Open: **All year**
Breakfast: **Continental**
Pets: **Welcome**
Children: **Welcome**
Smoking: **Permitted**
Social Drinking: **Permitted**
Foreign Languages: **Spanish**

This comfortable clapboard Victorian boasts a collection of interesting antiques. It is 85 miles directly south of Montgomery, "the Cradle of the Confederacy." The north Florida beaches, the Army Aviation Museum, and Troy State College are nearby. Jewel is a tree farmer and cattle rancher, and looks forward to welcoming you all.

The Brunton House ✪
P.O. BOX 1006, 112 COLLEGE AVENUE, SCOTTSBORO, ALABAMA 35768

Tel: **(205) 259-1298**
Host(s): **Norman and Jerry Brunton**
Location: **1 mi. from Rt. 72**
No. of Rooms: **7**
Max. No. Sharing Bath: **6**
Double/sb: **$24**
Single/sb: **$19**
Open: **All year**
Reduced Rates: **10%, seniors**
Breakfast: **Full**
Pets: **Sometimes**
Children: **Welcome**
Smoking: **Permitted**
Social Drinking: **Permitted**
Airport/Station Pickup: **Yes**

This fine old home is located on historic College Avenue. At Courthouse Square, two blocks away, an old-time drugstore operates its original soda fountain. Swimming, boating, and fishing are close by on the Tennessee River. Norman and Jerry invite you to watch TV in the living room, or use the kitchen for light snacks. The first Monday of every month (and the Sunday preceding) feature Monday Trade Day, an extravaganza of antique dealers from all over the country.

Tara
300 WEST SECOND STREET, TUSCUMBIA, ALABAMA 35674

Tel: **(205) 383-5959**
Host(s): **Reba Burke**
Location: **65 mi. W of Huntsville**
No. of Rooms: **5**
No. of Private Baths: **1**
Max. No. Sharing Bath: **5**
Single/pb: **$35**
Double/sb: **$25**
Single/sb: **$20**
Open: **Apr. 2–Nov. 14**

Reduced Rates: **Weekly, seniors, families**
Breakfast: **Full**
Other Meals: **Available**
Pets: **Sometimes**
Children: **Welcome**
Smoking: **No**
Social Drinking: **Permitted**
Airport/Station Pickup: **Yes**

Tara is a large, white frame house with front and side porches, two blocks from the historic section, where there are many handsome homes to tour. Ivy Green, the birthplace of Helen Keller, is within walking distance. Your hostess invites you to comfortable rooms with Southern accents. She serves an old-fashioned breakfast of grits, eggs, and biscuits. Local attractions include historic Natchez Trace Parkway and Courthouse Square, whose buildings are on the National Register of Historic Places.

ALASKA

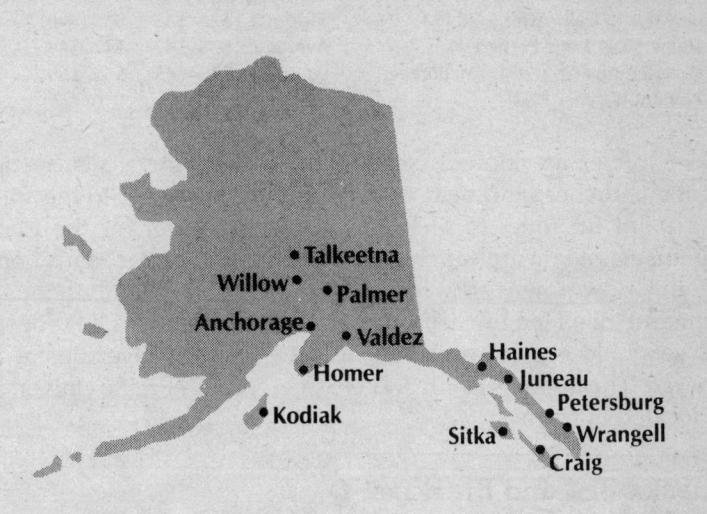

Alaska Private Lodgings ✪
P.O. BOX 110135 SOUTH STATION, ANCHORAGE, ALASKA 99511

Tel: **(907) 345-2222**
Best Time To Call: **8 AM–8:30 PM**
Coordinator: **Susan Hansen**
State/Regions Covered: **Girdwood, Homer, Kenai, Palmer, Soldotna**

Rates (Single/Double):
  Modest: **$30–$35**
  Average: **$35–$40**
  Luxury: **$40–$50**
Credit Cards: **MC, VISA**

Alaska hosts are this state's warmest resource! Susan's accommodations range from an original log house of a pioneer's homestead where the host is in the antique-doll business, to a contemporary home with guest quarters on the entire lower level, to a beautiful country guest home offering a spectacular view of the Anchorage bowl and Cook Inlet. Many are convenient to the University of Alaska and Alaska Pacific University.

Stay with a Friend
BOX 173, 3605 ARCTIC BOULEVARD, ANCHORAGE, ALASKA 99503

Tel: (907) 274-6445	Rates (Single/Double):
Best Time to Call: After 5:30 PM	Modest: $26–$35 $35–$40
Coordinator: Irene Pettigrew	Average: $35–$42 $42–$49
States/Regions Covered: Anchorage, Homer, Hatcher Pass	Luxury: $42–$45 $52–$69
	Credit Cards: No

Host homes are located convenient to shopping malls, restaurants, churches, and near enough downtown to get to the starting point for tours to McKinley, Portage Glacier, or the Kenai Peninsula. If you are watching your budget, consider that a home in the downtown area is the most expensive and the peak demand for all lodging is from June 15 to September 15. If you are 60 years old or over, you may use the People Mover Bus at no charge. The depot is at 6th and G Street. Alaska Pacific University is located in town.

Alaska Bed and Breakfast ✪
526 SEWARD STREET, JUNEAU, ALASKA 99801

Tel: (907) 586-2959	Rates (Single/Double):
Coordinator: Pat Denny	Modest: $30 $40
States/Regions Covered: Haines, Juneau, Petersburg, Sitka, Wrangell	Average: $35 $48
	Luxury: $40 $50
	Credit Cards: No

Visitors can enjoy southeast Alaskan hospitality in an historic inn, a log cabin in the woods, a modern home overlooking the water, or an old Indian village. Mendenhall Glacier, Glacier Bay, and the University of Alaska are nearby. The area is known for fine fishing and great hiking.

Kodiak Bed & Breakfast
P.O. BOX 2370, KODIAK, ALASKA 99614

Tel: (907) 486-3873	Rates (Single/Double):
Best Time To Call: 8 AM–8 PM	Average: $40–$50
Coordinator: Peter Meyburg	Credit Cards: No
State/Regions Covered: Kodiak	

Kodiak is one of the nation's top fishing ports, a hunting and sport fishing paradise, the home of the first Russian settlement in America and of the famous Kodiak bear. The people are warm and friendly and look forward to receiving you.

The Lake House ✪
MILE 6, RICHARDSON HIGHWAY, P.O. BOX 1499, VALDEZ, ALASKA 99686

Tel: **(907) 835-4752**
Best Time to Call: **Evenings**
Host(s): **Bob and Marilyn Walker**
Location: **¾ mi. from Richardson Hwy.**
No. of Rooms: **5**
Max. No. Sharing Bath: **6**
Double/sb: **$60**

Single/sb: **$55**
Open: **May 16–Sept. 30**
Breakfast: **Continental**
Pets: **Sometimes**
Children: **Welcome**
Smoking: **Permitted**
Social Drinking: **Permitted**
Foreign Languages: **French**

This two-story home has sun rooms and large decks to take advantage of its wilderness setting. The region's countless waterfalls, mountains, and lake add to its beauty. Valdez is a seaport and small-boat harbor with many interesting things to see and do. Bob and Marilyn enjoy skiing, hiking, and having guests.

For key to listings, see inside front or back cover.

✪ This star means that rates are guaranteed through December 31, 1985 to any guest making a reservation as a result of reading about the B&B in *BED & BREAKFAST U.S.A.*—1985 edition.

Please enclose a self-addressed, stamped, business-sized envelope when contacting reservation services.

For more details on what you can expect in a B&B, see Chapter 1.

Always mention *Bed & Breakfast USA* when making reservations!

ARIZONA

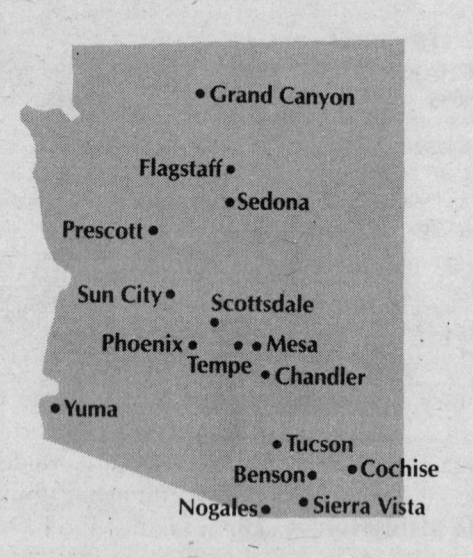

Map of Arizona showing: Grand Canyon, Flagstaff, Sedona, Prescott, Sun City, Scottsdale, Phoenix, Mesa, Tempe, Chandler, Yuma, Tucson, Benson, Cochise, Nogales, Sierra Vista

Bed & Breakfast in Arizona ✪
8433 N. BLACK CANYON, SUITE 160, PHOENIX, ARIZONA 85021

Tel: **(602) 995-2831**
Best Time to Call: **8 AM–5 PM**
Coordinator: **Bessie Lipinski**
States/Regions Covered: **Arizona (statewide)**

Rates (Single/Double):
Modest: $20 $30
Average: $25–$35 $35–$45
Luxury: $40–$90 $50–$110
Credit Cards: **MC, VISA**

Bessie offers you local color and local customs explained by friendly hosts. Arizona is a spectacular state with every kind of scenery and climate you can imagine. This is the land of the spellbinding Grand Canyon, Indian and Mexican cultures, cowboys and cattle ranches, gold mines, ghost towns, majestic mountains, and awesome deserts. Plan to spend several days to truly get the most out of your visit.

Mi Casa–Su Casa Bed & Breakfast ○
P.O. BOX 950, TEMPE, ARIZONA 85281

Tel: **(602) 990-0682**	Rates (Single/Double):
Best Time to Call: **8 AM–8 PM**	Modest: $20 $25
Coordinator: **Ruth T. Young**	Average: $25 $35
States/Regions Covered: **Benson,**	Luxury: $40 $50–$110
Flagstaff, Mesa, Nogales, Payson,	Credit Cards: **MC, VISA**
Paradise Valley, Phoenix, Prescott,	
Scottsdale, Sedona, Sierra Vista, Sun	
City, Tucson, Yuma	

Ruth's guest houses are located statewide; the above is only a partial listing. They are located in cities, suburbs, and rural settings, all of which are within easy driving range of canyons, national parks, Indian country, Colorado River gem country, the Mexican border area, historic mining towns, and water recreation areas. Send $2 for her detailed directory. Arizona State University and the University of Arizona are convenient to many B&Bs.

Cone's Tourist Home ○
2804 WEST WARNER, CHANDLER, ARIZONA 85224

Tel: **(602) 839-0369**	Double/sb: **$22**
Best Time to Call: **After 6 PM**	Single/sb: **$22**
Host(s): **Howard and Beverly Cone**	Open: **Aug. 1–May 31**
Location: **18 mi. SE of Phoenix**	Reduced Rates: **Weekly**
No. of Rooms: **2**	Breakfast: **Continental**
No. of Private Baths: **1**	Pets: **Welcome**
Max. No. Sharing Bath: **4**	Children: **Welcome**
Double/pb: **$26**	Smoking: **Permitted**
Single/pb: **$26**	Social Drinking: **Permitted**

This beautiful contemporary home is situated on two country acres. Howard and Beverly offer horseback riding for experienced riders, a large parlor for relaxing, and kitchen and barbecue facilities. It is three miles from fine restaurants and eight miles from Arizona State University; Phoenix is close too.

Cochise Stronghold Lodge ✪
RD1 BOX 51, COCHISE, ARIZONA 85606

Tel: **(602) 826-3442**
Host(s): **Rita Wilburn and Al Okemah**
Location: **65 mi. SE of Tucson**
No. of Rooms: **2**
Max. No. Sharing Bath: **3**
Double/sb: **$30**
Single/sb: **$20**
Guest Cottage: **$40; sleeps 3**

Open: **All year**
Reduced Rates: **Weekly; seniors**
Breakfast: **Continental**
Pets: **No**
Children: **Welcome, over 4**
Smoking: **Permitted**
Social Drinking: **Permitted**

Located in the foothills of the Dragoon Mountains, at an elevation of 4,400 feet, is this self-contained, solar guest cottage with lovely views through the huge picture windows. It is air-conditioned in summer and cozily heated with a wood-burning stove in winter. Nowhere is the history of the Old West more vivid than along the Cochise Trail with its spectacular Wonderland of Rocks, ghost towns, Fort Huachuca, and the Amerind Museum featuring Indian artifacts. Rita, a retired registered nurse, and Alexander, a full-blooded American Indian, look forward to sharing their home with you.

Dierker House ✪
423 WEST CHERRY, FLAGSTAFF, ARIZONA 86001

Tel: **(602) 774-3249**
Host(s): **Dorothea Dierker**
No. of Rooms: **2**
Max. No. Sharing Bath: **4**
Double/sb: **$35**
Single/sb: **$20**
Open: **All year**

Breakfast: **Continental**
Pets: **No**
Children: **Welcome, over 12**
Smoking: **Permitted**
Social Drinking: **Permitted**
Foreign Languages: **German, Spanish**

After a day of touring the Grand Canyon and Indian sites, return to Dorothea's Victorian home and enjoy a glass of wine and fresh fruit in the evening, by the fire in winter or in the pretty garden in summer. You are welcome to borrow a good book and snuggle in bed under a cozy down comforter. Activities might include a Colorado River raft trip with one of Dorothea's (grown!) children as your guide!

Rainbow Ranch ✪
2860 NORTH FREMONT, FLAGSTAFF, ARIZONA 86001

Tel: **(602) 774-3724**
Best Time to Call: **7:30–8:30 AM**
Host(s): **Miriam Pederson**
Location: **¼ mile from Hwy. 180**
No. of Rooms: **3**
Max. No. Sharing Bath: **6**
Double/sb: **$40**
Single/sb: **$20**

Open: **All year**
Breakfast: **Full**
Pets: **Sometimes**
Children: **Welcome**
Smoking: **Permitted**
Social Drinking: **Permitted**
Airport/Station Pickup: **Yes**
Foreign Languages: **French (limited)**

Miriam's 90-year-old farmhouse stands on seven acres and is comfortably furnished with lovely antiques and Miriam's good humor. After a hearty breakfast featuring home-gathered eggs and herbs, plus homemade breads and jams, you'll be ready to explore the Grand Canyon (75 miles away), Oak Creek Canyon, Sunset Crater, or the Navajo and Hopi Indian reservations. There's something doing in every season, including hiking and skiing; the tennis court is a few steps away. Children's rates are $20 each. Northern Arizona University is five miles away.

Walking L Ranch ✪
RR 4 BOX 721B, FLAGSTAFF, ARIZONA 86001

Tel: **(602) 779-2219**
Best Time to Call: **8–10 AM; 5–9 PM**
Host(s): **Jerry and Susan Ladhoff**
Location: **2 mi. from Rt. 180**
No. of Rooms: **2**
No. of Private Baths: **1**
Max. No. Sharing Bath: **4**
Double/pb: **$45**
Single/pb: **$25**
Double/sb: **$45**

Single/sb: **$25**
Open: **All year**
Breakfast: **Full**
Other Meals: **Available**
Pets: **Sometimes**
Children: **Welcome, over 12**
Smoking: **Permitted**
Social Drinking: **Permitted**
Airport/Station Pickup: **Yes**

Nestled in the pines of the Coconino National Forest, this ranch house features a lovely plant-filled spa room with hot tub, redwood deck, and patio. The homey, inviting rooms are accented with antiques, collectibles, Indian art, and Susan's handicrafts. Jerry is a professor at nearby Northern Arizona University and his hobby is woodworking. Your horse is welcome in the stable-corral for $2.50 per night. Riding, hiking, and skiing are popular pastimes after you've had your fill of the Grand Canyon.

Bed 'n' Breakfast in Arizona ○
5995 EAST ORANGE BLOSSOM LANE, PHOENIX, ARIZONA 85018

Tel: **(602) 994-3759**
Best Time to Call: **Mornings, evenings**
Host(s): **Marjorie Ann Lindmark**
No. of Rooms: **3**
No. of Private Baths: **2**
Max. No. Sharing Bath: **3**
Double/pb: **$45**
Single/pb: **$35**
Double/sb: **$40**
Single/sb: **$30**
Suites: **$75**
Open: **All year**
Reduced Rates: **Weekly**
Breakfast: **Full**
Other Meals: **Available**
Pets: **No**
Children: **No**
Smoking: **Permitted**
Social Drinking: **Permitted**
Airport/Station Pickup: **Yes**

Marjorie's charming, tri-level home is located in the exclusive Arizona Country Club area. It is furnished in an eclectic mix of contemporary and Indian artifacts. You are welcome to use the swimming pool. The delicious breakfast often features four-egg-omelettes or unusual quiche. Arizona State University is nearby.

Bed & Breakfast Scottsdale—Cave Creek
6502 N. 83 STREET, SCOTTSDALE, ARIZONA 85253

Tel: **(602) 998-7044**
Coordinator: **Lois O'Grady**
State/Regions Covered: **Scottsdale**
Rates (Single/Double):
Luxury: **$50–$110**
Credit Cards: **No**

Lois has a special group of homes where you can really enjoy sunshine every day of the year. Your hosts' Western hospitality will make you feel you've lived there for years. Many are convenient to the University of Arizona, the Center for Performing Arts, Rawhide (the Western town) and the Frank Lloyd Wright Foundation, which offers architecture tours.

Barbara's Bed and Breakfast
P.O. BOX 13603, TUCSON, ARIZONA 85732

Tel: (602) 886-5847
Coordinator: **Barbara Pollard**
State/Regions Covered: **Tucson**

Rates (Single/Double):
Modest: $20 $30
Average: $25 $35
Luxury: $30 and up $40 and up

There is a wide variety of homes in Tucson proper, close to the desert, in outlying towns, and in more remote desert locations, ranging from "nothing pretentious" to foothills elegance and charm. Most fall into the comfortable middle range. Barbara will match you with a host home where you'll feel perfectly at home. The weather is always good and you'll find many interests to keep you busy, from playing golf, to visiting Indian missions, to taking a trip south of the border to Nogales, Mexico. The University of Arizona is nearby.

The Bird's Nest ✪
6201 N. PIEDRA, SECA, TUCSON, ARIZONA 85718

Tel: (602) 299-9164
Best Time to Call: **Evenings**
Host(s): **Vic and Betty Hanson**
Location: **10 mi. from I-10**
No. of Rooms: **1**
No. of Private Baths: **1**
Double/pb: **$35**

Single/pb: **$35**
Open: **Jan. 1-May 31; Sept. 1-Nov. 30**
Breakfast: **Continental**
Pets: **No**
Children: **No**
Smoking: **No**
Social Drinking: **Permitted**

Located in the foothills of the Catalina Mountains, this one-story adobe home has a patio. It's furnished in a pleasant blend of colonial and Southwestern styles, decorated with lovely plants and original art, and it features beautiful views. Vic and Betty enjoy people and will be happy to help you with your touring plans. They'll also identify the large variety of birds that visit their backyard. The University of Arizona is nearby.

Myers' Blue Corn House ✪
4215 EAST KILMER, TUCSON, ARIZONA 85711

Tel: (602) 327-4663
Best Time to Call: **After 5 PM**

Host(s): **Barbara and Vern Myers**
Location: **5 mi. from I-10**

No. of Rooms: **2**
Max. No. Sharing Bath: **4**
Double/sb: **$35**
Single/sb: **$25**
Open: **All year**
Reduced Rates: **Families, Seniors**

Breakfast: **Full**
Pets: **Sometimes**
Children: **Welcome (crib)**
Smoking: **No**
Social Drinking: **Permitted**
Airport/Station Pickup: **Yes**

Located on a quiet residential street, it's convenient to downtown Tucson and the University of Arizona via city buses. The family room, decorated with Indian arts and crafts, and filled with history books, has bumper pool and TV. Close to seasonal recreation, it is also handy for tours of Old Tucson, Saguaro National Monument, Kitt Peak Observatory, and Nogales, Mexico. You may use the kitchen for light snacks, and the washing machine, dryer, and barbecue. The University of Arizona is nearby.

Rainbow Ranch

ARKANSAS

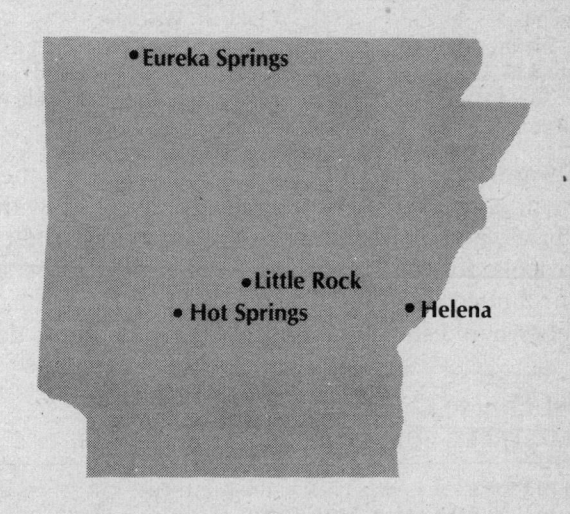

Dairy Hollow House
RTE. 2, BOX 1, EUREKA SPRINGS, ARKANSAS 72632

Tel: (501) 253-8652
Host(s): **Jan Brown, Blake Clark, Crescent Dragonwagon**
Location: **¼ mi. from Rt. 62B**
No. of Rooms: **2**
No. of Private Baths: **2**
Double/pb: **$59**
Single/pb: **$55**
Open: **All year**

Breakfast: **Full**
Other Meals: **Available**
Credit Cards: **AMEX, MC, VISA**
Pets: **No**
Children: **Welcome over 8**
Smoking: **Permitted**
Social Drinking: **Permitted**
Airport/Station Pickup: **Yes**

Built in 1881, this flower-framed hideaway has been lovingly restored, furnished with antiques and traditional Ozark folk art, and updated for creature comfort. It is a ten-minute walk to the downtown historic district. Breakfast is a leisurely affair and a gastronomic delight. The morning paper is delivered to your door, and you may enjoy your final cup of coffee while reading it in a rocker on the porch.

Devon Cottage ✪
26 EUREKA STREET, EUREKA SPRINGS, ARKANSAS 72632

Tel: (501) 253-9169
Best Time to Call: **Evenings**
Host(s): **Laura Menees**
No. of Rooms: **2**
Max. No. Sharing Bath: **4**
Double/sb: **$38–$55**
Single/sb: **$32–$45**
Open: **All year**

Reduced Rates: **Weekly; Midweek**
Breakfast: **Full**
Pets: **Sometimes**
Children: **Welcome**
Smoking: **Permitted**
Social Drinking: **Permitted**
Foreign Languages: **Spanish, French**

This Edwardian frame cottage, just a block from the historic downtown, is decorated with antiques and graced with wicker, plants, brass, and art. Laura is a psychotherapist and craftsperson and looks forward to sharing the delights of the area with you. Surrounded by the beautiful Ozarks, there are many lakes and rivers where fishing and bird-watching are fun to do.

Harvest House ✪
104 WALL STREET, EUREKA SPRINGS, ARKANSAS 72632

Tel: (501) 253-9363
Best Time to Call: **8–10 AM, 3–9 PM**
Host(s): **Margaret and Jim Conner**
No. of Rooms: **2**
No. of Private Baths: **2**
Double/pb: **$38**
Open: **All year**

Breakfast: **Full**
Other Meals: **Available**
Pets: **Sometimes**
Children: **Welcome**
Smoking: **Permitted**
Social Drinking: **Permitted**

This green-and-white Victorian house is furnished with antiques, collectibles, and family favorites. The guest rooms are downstairs, with private entrances. Located in the Ozark Mountains, the scenery is lovely. Homemade surprise snacks are always available. Margaret and Jim are wonderful hosts and will do everything possible to make your stay pleasant.

Edwardian Inn
317 BRISCOE, HELENA, ARKANSAS 72342

Tel: (501) 338-9155
Host(s): **Mac and Joan McGinty**
Location: **60 miles S of Memphis, Tenn.**

No. of Rooms: **12**
No. of Private Baths: **12**
Double/pb: **$45**
Single/pb: **$39**

Suites: **$45–$55**
Open: **All year**
Breakfast: **Continental**
Credit Cards: AMEX, MC, VISA
Pets: **Sometimes**

Children: **Welcome**
Smoking: **Permitted**
Social Drinking: **Permitted**
Airport/Station Pickup: **Yes**

Built by a wealthy merchant in 1904, this handsome mansion has been carefully restored without sacrificing the richness of a bygone era, yet it boasts every modern convenience. The original fireplace mantels, paneling, magnificent wood floors are a testament to craftsmanship. Each room is air-conditioned, has a TV, and telephone. A meeting room accommodating 30 makes this inn especially attractive for people here on business.

Stillmeadow Farm ✪
RTE. 1, BOX 434 D, HOT SPRINGS, ARKANSAS 71901

Tel: **(501) 525-9994**
Host(s): **Gene and Jody Sparling**
Location: **4 mi. S of Hot Springs**
No. of Rooms: **4**
No. of Private Baths: **2**
Max. No. Sharing Bath: **4**
Double/pb: **$55**
Single/pb: **$45**

Double/sb: **$45**
Single/sb: **$35**
Open: **All year**
Breakfast: **Continental**
Pets: **No**
Children: **Welcome, over 6**
Smoking: **Permitted**
Social Drinking: **Permitted**

Stillmeadow Farm is a reproduction of an 18th-century New England salt box, set in 75 acres of pine forest. The decor blends country antiques, baskets, and collectibles. Your hosts provide homemade snacks and fruit in the guest rooms. For breakfast, freshly baked pastries and breads are served. Hot Springs National Park, Lake Hamilton, the Mid-America Museum, and a race track are nearby.

Williams House Bed & Breakfast Inn ✪
420 QUAPAW, HOT SPRINGS, ARKANSAS 71901

Tel: **(501) 624-4275**
Host(s): **Mary and Gary Riley**
Best Time to Call: **9–11 AM; evenings**
Location: **50 mi. SW of Little Rock**
No. of Rooms: **6**

No. of Private Baths: **4**
Max. No. Sharing Bath: **4**
Double/pb: **$50–$70**
Single/pb: **$45–$60**
Double/sb: **$45–$50**

Single/sb: **$40–$45**
Suites: **$65–$80**
Guest Cottage: **$55–$135 (2-6)**
Open: **All year**
Reduced Rates: **Available**
Breakfast: **Full**

Pets: **No**
Children: **Welcome, over 6**
Smoking: **Permitted**
Social Drinking: **Permitted**
Airport/Station Pickup: **Yes**

This Victorian mansion, with its stained glass and beveled glass windows, is a nationally registered landmark. The atmosphere is friendly, and the marble fireplace and grand piano invite congeniality. Breakfast menu may include quiche, toast amandine, or exotic egg dishes. Gary and Mary will spoil you with special iced tea, snacks, and mineral spring water. World health experts recognize the benefits of the hot mineral baths in Hot Springs National Park. The inn is within walking distance of Bath House Row.

CALIFORNIA

Eureka

Westport
Little River • Fort Bragg
Elk
Cloverdale • Angwin • Oroville
Healdsburg • • Grass Valley
Pt. Reyes • St. • Sacramento
Helena • Ione Sutter Creek
San Francisco • Kensington Murphys
Santa Cruz • • San Jose
Pebble Beach • Pacific Grove
San Simeon • Carmel
San Luis Obispo • Cambria • Orosi
Arroyo Grande • • Lancaster
Santa Barbara • Montecito
Malibu Glendale
Seal Beach Los Angeles • • Torrance
Newport Beach Laguna Beach • Westminster
San Clemente • Santa Ana
San Diego • La Jolla
• Julian

GOLD COUNTRY
Hospitality Plus
P.O. BOX 388, SAN JUAN CAPISTRANO, CALIFORNIA 92693

Tel: **(714) 496-7050**
Coordinator: **Deborah Sakach**
States/Regions Covered: **California:**
  Napa, Pacific Grove, Redondo Beach, Solvang; Oklahoma: Tulsa; Montana: Billings; Texas: Dallas

Rates (Single/Double):
  Modest: $15 $25
  Average: $25 $35
  Luxury: $40 $55

Deborah's computerized service has access to over 1,000 B&Bs throughout California and in other states. Her specialty is planning complete coastal, mountain, and desert tours, staying at B&Bs all the way. Visit Yosemite where your host will lend you a bike; or stay in Honolulu, one block from the beach, with a third-generation Hawaiian family. No matter what your price range, special attention will be given to your needs.

The Heirloom
P.O. BOX 322, 214 SHAKLEY LANE, IONE, CALIFORNIA 95640

Tel: (209) 274-4468
Host(s): **Melisande Hubbs and Patricia Cross**
Location: **35 mi. E of Sacramento**
No. of Rooms: **6**
No. of Private Baths: **3**
Max. No. Sharing Bath: **6**
Double/pb: **$65**
Double/sb: **$45**
Guest Cottage: **$55–$75; sleeps 2 to 3**

Open: **All year**
Breakfast: **Full**
Pets: **No**
Children: **Welcome, over 12**
Smoking: **Permitted**
Social Drinking: **Permitted**
Airport/Station Pickup: **Yes**
Foreign Languages: **Portuguese**

Nestled in the Sierra foothills yet close to the historic gold mines, wineries, antique shops, and museums, this 1863 mansion, with its lovely balconies and fireplaces, is a classic example of antebellum architecture. It is furnished with a combination of family treasures and period pieces. Patricia and Melisande's hearty breakfast includes such delights as quiche, crepes, soufflé, and fresh fruits. Afternoon refreshments are always offered.

The Pelennor, Bed & Breakfast at Bootjack ◐
3871 HIGHWAY 49 SOUTH, MARIPOSA, CALIFORNIA 95338

Tel: (209) 966-2832
Host(s): **Dick and Gwendolyn Foster**
Location: **70 mi. N of Fresno**
No. of Rooms: **6**
Max. No. Sharing Bath: **4**
Double/sb: **$30**
Single/sb: **$25**
Open: **All year**

Breakfast: **Full**
Other Meals: **Available**
Pets: **Sometimes**
Children: **Welcome**
Smoking: **Permitted**
Social Drinking: **Permitted**
Airport/Station Pickup: **Yes**

The Pelennor is at the foothills of the Sierra Mountains, at the southern tip of the Mother Lode Gold Country. Guest accommodations are offered in the main house and in a separate B&B building. The property is also home to a friendly cat, dog, and goose. Guests are welcome to relax on the porch or use the barbecue facilities. Your hosts offer homemade croissants, muffins, strawberry jam, and omelettes for breakfast. They will gladly direct you to the oldest newspaper and courthouse in the state and Yosemite National Park, one hour away.

Dunbar House, 1880 ✪
271 JONES STREET, P.O. BOX 1375, MURPHYS, CALIFORNIA 95247

Tel: **(209) 728-2897**
Best Time to Call: **After 3 PM**
Host(s): **John and Barbara Carr**
Location: **55 mi. E of Stockton**
No. of Rooms: **5**
Max. No. Sharing Bath: **6**
Double/sb: **$50**
Single/sb: **$45**
Suites: **$55**

Open: **All year**
Reduced Rates: **Dec.-Mar. midweek**
Breakfast: **Continental**
Pets: **No**
Children: **Welcome, over 10**
Smoking: **No**
Social Drinking: **Permitted**
Foreign Languages: **Portuguese**

This 19th-century Victorian house is located in the heart of one of the best-preserved Gold Rush towns. Guests are offered rooms with lace curtains, fresh flowers, pillow shams, and bed ruffles. A generous breakfast is served in the fireplaced dining room or in the garden. Nearby attractions are Calaveras Big Trees State Park, Moaning Caves, and Stevenot Winery.

The Hanford House ✪
P.O. BOX 847, 3 HANFORD STREET, SUTTER CREEK, CALIFORNIA 95685

Tel: **(209) 267-0747**
Host(s): **Ronald Van Anda**
Location: **35 mi. E of Sacramento on Hwy. 49**
No. of Rooms: **9**
No. of Private Baths: **9**
Double/pb: **$45–$70**
Suites: **$100**
Open: **All year**

Reduced Rates: **10%; midweek**
Breakfast: **Continental**
Credit Cards: **MC, VISA**
Pets: **No**
Children: **Welcome, over 12**
Smoking: **Permitted**
Social Drinking: **Permitted**
Airport/Station Pickup: **Yes**

This charming inn is elegant yet warm and comfortable. Ron is an antiques dealer, and the furnishings reflect the graciousness of long-ago eras, but the queen-size beds are new. A rooftop redwood deck provides breathtaking views of the countryside and the scenic Gold Rush town where you can still pan for gold in the streams. A complimentary bottle of wine is part of Ron's way of welcoming guests. There is a barrier-free entrance and a special guest room for the handicapped.

LOS ANGELES AREA ✪

Bed & Breakfast of Los Angeles
32074 WATERSIDE LANE, WESTLAKE VILLAGE, CALIFORNIA 91361

Tel: **(818) 889-8870 or 889-7325**	Rates: (Single/Double):
Best Time to Call: **8–10 AM, 4–8 PM**	Modest: $24 $30
Coordinators: **Peg Marshall and Angie Kobabe**	Average: $24 $45
	Luxury: $42 $75
States/Regions Covered: **30 communities in greater Los Angeles**	Credit Cards: **No**

Peg and Angie can provide accommodations for you from Ventura in the north to Laguna Beach in the south. There's a guest house in Hollywood, a luxury suite in Beverly Hills, and a contemporary loft in Balboa, to name a few choices. After you've selected your favorite listings from their directory, Peg and Angie will make all the reservations for you. Please send a self-addressed envelope with 40 cents' postage. B&Bs are located near major colleges in Los Angeles, Orange, and Ventura counties.

California Houseguests International ✪
18533 BURBANK BOULEVARD #190, TARZANA, LOS ANGELES, CALIFORNIA 91356

Tel: **(818) 344-7878**	Rates (Single/Double):
Best Time to Call: **Early AM**	Modest: $40 $45
Coordinator: **Trudi Alexy**	Average: $50 $55
State/Regions Covered: **Greater Los Angeles Area, Agoura, the beach cities, San Diego, San Francisco**	Luxury: $60 $65
	Credit Cards: **No**
	Minimum Stay: **2 days**

Through Trudi's extensive listings, choose a private suite in a charming chalet overlooking Malibu Beach, or bask in luxury on an estate in the Hollywood Hills, or walk to Disneyland from an Anaheim condo, or steep yourself in atmosphere in a San Francisco Victorian. Membership fees are $10 per person annually.

CoHost Bed and American Breakfast
P.O. BOX 9302, WHITTIER, CALIFORNIA 90608

Tel: **(213) 699-8427**	Rates (Single/Double):
Coordinator: **Coleen Davis**	Modest: $20 $25
State/Regions Covered: **Los Angeles, Redondo Beach, Palos Verdes, San Juan Capistrano, Santa Ana, Whittier**	Average: $30–$40 $35–$45
	Luxury: $60 and up $65 and up
	Credit Cards: **No**

Outgoing and friendly, Coleen has homes for you throughout southern California. You are assured of comfortable accommodations, full American breakfast, and helpful information to find your way easily to all the sights. Located in lovely residential areas, many B&Bs offer amenities such as tours, tennis, golf, Jacuzzi, pool, or meals. CoHost is somewhat unique, in that all member hosts know each other, so that groups of friends traveling together can stay near each other.

Eye Openers Bed & Breakfast Reservations ✪
P.O. BOX 694, ALTADENA, CALIFORNIA 91001

Tel: **(818) 684-4428**	Rates (Single/Double):
Coordinator: **Ruth Judkins**	Modest: $30 $35
State/Regions Covered: **Arcadia, Hermosa Beach, Manhattan Beach, Ojai, Palm Springs**	Average: $40 $45
	Luxury: $50–$55 $60
	Credit Cards: **MC, VISA**

Ruth invites you to visit some of the friendliest people in the Los Angeles/Pasadena area. There are many beautiful homes to choose from, and one will be selected to suit you. Dodger Stadium, Disneyland, Santa Anita Racetrack, and the "usual" delights of this area will keep you busy. There is a $5 lifetime membership fee.

Brown's Guest House ○
1105 EAST NORWOOD PLACE, ALHAMBRA, CALIFORNIA 91801

Tel: **(818) 281-8853**
Best Time to Call: **Afternoon**
Host(s): **Opal Brown**
Location: **8 mi. E of Los Angeles**
No. of Rooms: **1**
No. of Baths: **1**
Double/pb: **$30**
Single/pb: **$25**
Open: **All year**
Breakfast: **Continental**
Pets: **No**
Children: **No**
Smoking: **No**
Social Drinking: **No**

Opal's modern stucco home is in a residential area just 20 minutes from Los Angeles. The Pasadena Rosebowl is five miles away, and many restaurants are within walking distance. The comfortable guest room has a private entrance. Cal. State-Los Angeles is only three miles away.

Shroff House ○
1114 PARK AVENUE, GLENDALE, CALIFORNIA 91205

Tel: **(818) 507-0774**
Best Time to Call: **8–11 AM; evenings**
Host(s): **Spencer and Gerry Shroff**
Location: **10 mi. NE of Los Angeles**
No. of Rooms: **1**
Max. No. Sharing Bath: **2**
Double/sb: **$25**
Single/sb: **$20**
Open: **All year**
Reduced Rates: **7th day free**
Breakfast: **Continental**
Pets: **No**
Children: **Welcome**
Smoking: **Permitted**
Social Drinking: **Permitted**

A Spanish-style stucco house with a red tile roof, it is furnished with 1930s motifs. It is comfortable in all seasons, being centrally heated and air-cooled. Relax on the shaded patio or in the gazebo. It is convenient to the movie studio tours, art galleries, ethnic restaurants, as well as to Forest Lawn Memorial Park. The Shroffs love to travel and will happily share tips with you on where to go. Occidental College is nearby. A minimum stay of two nights is required.

The Traybrook ✪
1772 N. ORCHID AVENUE, HOLLYWOOD, CALIFORNIA 90028

Tel: (213) 465-7680
Best Time to Call: 1–5 PM
Host(s): **Beverly Schroeder and Valerie Merrill**
No. of Rooms: 1
No. of Private Baths: 1
Double/pb: $45

Open: **All year**
Breakfast: **Continental**
Pets: **No**
Children: **Welcome**
Smoking: **No**
Social Drinking: **Permitted**

The Traybrook features an informal, comfortable, spacious room with a queen-size bed plus a kitchenette for preparing light meals or snacks. It is within walking distance of Mann's Chinese Theatre, Hollywood Bowl, movies, plays, nightclubs, and a score of restaurants.

Avon Bed & Breakfast ✪
1453 AVON TERRACE, LOS ANGELES, CALIFORNIA 90026

Tel: (213) 663-4368
Best Time to Call: 5–10 PM
Host(s): **Eileen Searson**
Location: **2 mi. from Fwy. 101**
No. of Rooms: 2
No. of Private Baths: 1
Max. No. Sharing Bath: 4
Double/pb: $35
Single/pb: $25
Double/sb: $30

Single/sb: $20
Open: **All year**
Reduced Rates: **Available**
Breakfast: **Continental**
Pets: **No**
Children: **Welcome**
Smoking: **Permitted**
Social Drinking: **Permitted**
Airport/Station Pickup: **Yes**

Eileen is a costume designer who likes nothing better than advising her houseguests on tours of "Tinsel town." Her Swiss-chalet-style home has leaded glass windows, red flocked wallpaper, and is decorated with antiques. It's 15 minutes to Universal Studios, Grauman's Chinese Theatre, and the Civic Center. You are welcome to use the kitchen, barbecue, and picnic table. The coffeepot is always on and complimentary snacks are offered.

Bev's B&B ✪
P.O. BOX 85396, LOS ANGELES, CALIFORNIA 90072

Tel: **(213) 666-1715**
Best Time to Call: **5–10 PM**
Host(s): **Beverly Foster-Yaw**
Location: **Near Hwy. 101**
No. of Rooms: **2**
Max. No. Sharing Bath: **4**
Double/sb: **$55**
Single/sb: **$45**
Open: **All year**

Reduced Rates: **10% for 2 weeks**
Breakfast: **Continental**
Other Meals: **Available**
Pets: **No**
Children: **Welcome, over 16**
Smoking: **Permitted**
Social Drinking: **Permitted**
Airport/Station Pickup: **Yes**

This 1920s Spanish stucco house is minutes away from Hollywood and Vine, the Griffith Park Observatory, Chinatown, and the Convention Center. Universal Studios and the smart shops of Beverly Hills are only 20 minutes by freeway. Bev brims with enthusiasm for people. One of the guest rooms incorporates her vast collection of hearts, and the other is attractively decorated using primary colors against a white background for a striking cabana effect.

Casa Larronde ✪
22000 PACIFIC COAST HIGHWAY, MALIBU, CALIFORNIA 90265

Tel: **(213) 456-9333**
Best Time to Call: **Mornings**
Host(s): **Jim and Charlou Larronde**
Location: **40 mi. NW of Los Angeles**
No. of Rooms: **2**
No. of Baths: **2**
Double/pb: **$60–$75**

Single/pb: **$55–$60**
Open: **All year**
Breakfast: **Full**
Pets: **Sometimes**
Children: **Welcome**
Smoking: **Permitted**
Social Drinking: **Permitted**

All the guest rooms have color TV, but if you walk down the beach you may get to see the stars live; Johnny Carson, Rich Little, Ann-Margret, and Flip Wilson are the neighborhood people here on Millionaires' Row. This house is 4,000 square feet of spectacular living space. It has floor-to-ceiling glass, ocean decks, a private beach, and a planter that's two stories high. Jim and Charlou, world travelers, enjoy entertaining, and their gourmet breakfast ranges from Scotch eggs to French toast made with Portuguese sweet bread. Champagne, cocktails, and snacks are complimentary refreshments. Pepperdine College is two miles away.

Hideaway House ✪
8441 MELVIN AVENUE, NORTHRIDGE, CALIFORNIA 91324

Tel: (818) 349-5421
Best Time to Call: 6–10 PM
Host(s): **Dean and Dorothy Dennis**
Location: **20 mi. NW of Los Angeles**
No. of Rooms: **2**
No. of Private Baths: **1**
Max. No. Sharing Bath: **2**
Double/pb: **$50**
Single/pb: **$35**
Double/sb: **$45**

Single/sb: **$30**
Open: **All year**
Breakfast: **Full**
Other Meals: **Available**
Pets: **Sometimes**
Children: **Welcome, over 10**
Smoking: **Permitted**
Social Drinking: **Permitted**
Airport/Station Pickup: **Yes**

Located in a beautiful Los Angeles suburb, this secluded country estate in the San Fernando Valley is a good base for exploring southern California. It's 30 minutes to the beach and 50 minutes to Disneyland. Dean and Dorothy welcome you to their art- and antiques-filled home and will provide local guide service by prior arrangement. Cal. State-Northridge is nearby.

By-the-Sea ✪
4273 PALOS VERDES DRIVE SOUTH, RANCHO PALOS VERDES, CALIFORNIA 90274

Tel: (213) 377-2113
Host(s): **Ruth and Earl Exley**
Location: **5 mi. SW of Los Angeles**
No. of Rooms: **2**
No. of Private Baths: **2**
Double/pb: **$50**
Single/pb: **$35**
Open: **All year**

Reduced Rates: **20%, Nov. 1–May 1;**
    10%, seniors
Breakfast: **Full**
Other Meals: **Available**
Pets: **Sometimes**
Children: **Welcome**
Smoking: **Yes**
Social Drinking: **Permitted**
Airport/Station Pickup: **Yes**

This gracious ranch-style home in suburban Los Angeles has an unobstructed ocean view. Ruth and Earl belong to a private beach club across the road, and you can use the facilities there. It is close to Marineland, Disneyland, and Hollywood. Ruth's breakfast specialties include honey-baked ham, French toast, or quiche. Your hosts offer you *hors d'oeuvres* with other pre-dinner refreshments. California State–Dominguez Hills is close by.

Seal Beach Inn & Gardens ✪
212 5TH STREET, SEAL BEACH, CALIFORNIA 90740

Tel: **(213) 493-2416**	Suites: **$90–$120**
Best Time to Call: **7 AM–11 PM**	Open: **All year**
Host(s): **Dr. and Mrs. Jack Bettenhausen**	Reduced Rates: **weekly, seniors**
	Breakfast: **Continental**
Location: **near Hwy. #1**	Credit Cards: **AMEX, MC, VISA**
No. of Rooms: **24**	Pets: **No**
No. of Private Baths: **24**	Children: **Welcome, over 12**
Double/pb: **$60–$120**	Smoking: **Permitted**
Single/pb: **$60–$120**	Social Drinking: **Permitted**

At first glance you'll think you're at a French Mediterranean *auberge*. The canopies, antique street lamps, ornate fences, and profusion of flowers have romanced travelers for over 60 years. It is beautifully appointed with antiques and comfortable furnishings. The beach is 300 yards away, and there's a pool, if you prefer. Disneyland and California State University are nearby.

Hazel's Habitat ✪
2440 CABRILLO AVENUE, TORRANCE, CALIFORNIA 90501

Tel: **(213) 328-2375**	Open: **All year**
Best Time to Call: **Evenings**	Reduced Rates: **7th night free**
Host(s): **Hazel Virginia Gilliland**	Breakfast: **Continental**
Location: **20 mi. S of Los Angeles**	Pets: **Sometimes**
No. of Rooms: **1**	Children: **Welcome**
No. of Private Baths: **1**	Smoking: **Permitted**
Double/pb: **$25–$30**	Social Drinking: **No**
Single/pb: **$20–$25**	

You can relax and enjoy the quiet of the suburbs while you are only a short distance from Marineland and Catalina Island. The beach is 10 minutes away. The local shopping center is the largest in the U.S., so don't worry if you forgot your sunglasses. Hazel welcomes married couples and women traveling alone.

Noone Guest House ✪
2755 SONOMA STREET, TORRANCE, CALIFORNIA 90503

Tel: (213) 328-1837
Best Time to Call: 6–7 PM
Host(s): Betty and Bob Noone
Location: 15 mi. SW of Los Angeles
No. of Rooms: 1 cottage
No. of Private Baths: 1
Guest Cottage: $30; sleeps 2

Open: All year
Breakfast: Continental
Pets: Welcome
Children: Welcome
Smoking: Permitted
Social Drinking: Permitted

This comfortable guest cottage has a bedroom, bath, kitchen, patio, and laundry facilities, but the special plus is the warm hospitality offered by Betty and Bob. They'll direct you to Marineland, Disneyland, Knott's Berry Farm, or the beach—all close to "home." The University of Southern California is nearby.

The Whites' House ✪
17122 FAYSMITH AVENUE, TORRANCE, CALIFORNIA 90504

Tel: (213) 324-6164
Host(s): Russell and Margaret White
Location: 15 mi. S of Los Angeles
No. of Rooms: 2
No. of Private Baths: 2
Double/pb: $30
Single/pb: $25

Open: All year
Breakfast: Continental
Pets: Sometimes
Children: Welcome
Smoking: Permitted
Social Drinking: Permitted
Airport/Station Pickup: Yes

This contemporary home with its fireplaces, deck, and patio is located on a quiet street in an unpretentious neighborhood. The airport and lovely beaches are 15 minutes away. Disneyland, Knotts Berry Farm, Marineland, and Hollywood are 30 minutes from the door. Use the laundry facilities or kitchen; Russell and Margaret want you to feel perfectly at home.

The Venice Beach House ✪
15 THIRTIETH AVENUE, VENICE, CALIFORNIA 90291

Tel: (213) 823-1966
Best Time to Call: Mornings
Host(s): Jonna Jensen and Vivian Boesch
Location: 5 mi. from I-10

No. of Rooms: 8
No. of Private Baths: 4
Max. No. Sharing Bath: 4
Double/pb: $85–$125
Double/sb: $50–$125

Suites: **$90–$125**
Open: **All year**
Reduced Rates: **15% weekly**
Breakfast: **Continental**
Credit Cards: **AMEX, MC, VISA**

Pets: **No**
Children: **Welcome, over 10**
Smoking: **No**
Social Drinking: **Permitted**
Foreign Languages: **Italian, Spanish**

This landmark house was built in 1911 and has been carefully restored to reflect the charming atmosphere of that era. Some of the rooms have fireplaces, balconies, or Jacuzzi tubs, and all are attractively furnished with antiques. It's half a block to the beach, two miles to the marina, and the house is close to restaurants, museums, shops, and U.C.L.A.

Hendrick Inn ✪
2124 E. MERCED AVENUE, WEST COVINA, CALIFORNIA 91791

Tel: **(818) 919-2125**
Host(s): **Mary and George Hendrick**
Location: **20 mi. E of Los Angeles**
No. of Rooms: **4**
No. of Private Baths: **2**
Max. No. Sharing Bath: **2**
Double/pb: **$35–$40**
Single/pb: **$25**
Double/sb: **$35–$40**

Single/sb: **$30**
Suites: **$50**
Open: **All year**
Breakfast: **Full**
Pets: **No**
Children: **Welcome, over 8**
Smoking: **Permitted**
Social Drinking: **Permitted**
Foreign Languages: **Spanish**

This lovely home is one hour from the mountains, seashore, and desert. It's less than an hour to Disneyland or busy downtown Los Angeles. The living rooms of this sprawling ranch-style house contain comfortable sitting areas and fireplaces where you may share a nightcap with your hospitable hosts. You will enjoy the backyard swimming pool and the Jacuzzi after a day of touring.

MENDOCINO AREA/WINE COUNTRY

Bed & Breakfast Exchange
P.O. BOX 88, ST. HELENA, CALIFORNIA 94574

Tel: **(707) 963-7756**
Best Time to Call: **9 AM–5 PM**
Coordinators: **Andee Beresini and Carolyn Stanley**

States/Regions Covered: **Napa and Sonoma counties, Calistoga, Boonville, Eureka, Ferndale, Healdsburg**

Rates (Single/Double): Credit Cards: **No**
  Modest: **$35**   **$35**
  Average: **$55**   **$75**
  Luxury: **$100 up**   **$100 up**

The homes on Andee's roster are all located convenient to the wineries and vineyards that have made this section of the state known as Wine Country. Wine-tasting tours are popular pastimes. The more expensive accommodations are on fabulous estates with pools, spas, and special services.

Big Yellow Sunflower Bed & Breakfast ✪
235 SKY OAKS DRIVE, ANGWIN, CALIFORNIA 94508

Tel: **(707) 965-3885**	Open: **All year**
Host(s): **Dale and Betty Clement**	Breakfast: **Full**
Location: **60 mi. N of San Francisco**	Other Meals: **Available**
No. of Rooms: **1 suite**	Pets: **Sometimes**
No. of Private Baths: **1**	Children: **Welcome, over 6**
Double/pb: **$65**	Smoking: **No**
Single/pb: **$55**	Social Drinking: **Permitted**

The guest duplex, a completely private suite with kitchenette and sundeck, is part of Betty and Dale's wood-and-brick colonial home. Charmingly decorated with some antiques, lots of plants, and flower baskets, it is only minutes away from Napa Valley. You'll be slow to leave the ample breakfast which may include fresh fruit, waffles, quiche, and other delectables. Complimentary snacks, cookies, ice cream, and beverages are offered when you return from touring.

The Old Crocker Inn
26532 RIVER ROAD, CLOVERDALE, CALIFORNIA 95425

Tel: **(707) 894-3911**	Breakfast: **Full**
Best Time to Call: **Noon–6 PM**	Credit Cards: **MC, VISA**
Host(s): **Ed and Deborah Lyons**	Pets: **No**
Location: **40 mi. N of Santa Rosa**	Children: **Welcome**
No. of Rooms: **10**	Smoking: **Permitted**
No. of Private Baths: **10**	Social Drinking: **Permitted**
Double/pb: **$50–$70**	Airport/Station Pickup: **Yes**
Single/pb: **$50–$70**	Foreign Languages: **German**
Open: **All year**	

On five landscaped acres, overlooking the Sonoma County wine region, the inn offers privacy, charm, and seclusion. This 1897 lodge consists of four redwood-and-brick buildings furnished with rural turn-of-the-century antiques. The guest rooms open onto verandas, atriums, or gardens. After visiting the more than 30 wineries, enjoy the Russian River attractions, the pool, or just relax 'round the fireplace with other guests.

Elk Cove Inn ✪
6300 SOUTH HIGHWAY ONE, P.O. BOX 367, ELK, CALIFORNIA 95432

Tel: (707) 877-3321
Best Time to Call: **10 AM–5 PM**
Host(s): **Hildrun-Uta Triebess**
Location: **On Highway 1**
No. of Rooms: 9
No. of Private Baths: 7
Max. No. Sharing Bath: 4
Double/pb: $72–$92
Single/pb: $56–$65
Double/sb: $46–$52
Single/sb: $30–$38
Open: **All year**

Reduced Rates: **10% Mon.-Thurs.**
Breakfast: **Full**
Other Meals: **Included weekends**
Credit Cards: **MC, VISA**
Pets: **No**
Children: **Welcome, over 8**
Smoking: **Permitted**
Social Drinking: **Permitted**
Airport/Station Pickup: **Yes**
Foreign Languages: **French, Italian, German, Spanish**

This 1883 Victorian inn is attractively furnished, and the beds have the freshness of sun-dried linens. Cut flowers and handmade accessories add to the loveliness. Spectacular views, a driftwood beach, and beautiful gardens make this a romantic spot. On weekends and holidays, Hildrun-Uta includes French and German gourmet dinners, which she prepares, as well as breakfast. Weekend rates increase to between $126 and $148 (private bath) and $98 to $106 (shared bath) and include meals.

The Carter House ☉
1033 THIRD STREET, EUREKA, CALIFORNIA 95501

Tel: **(707) 445-1390**
Best Time to Call: **Noon–5 PM**
Host(s): **Mark and Christi Carter**
No. of Rooms: 7
No. of Private Baths: 4
Max. No. Sharing Bath: 4
Double/pb: $75
Single/pb: $70
Double/sb: $65
Single/sb: $60
Suites: $125

Open: **All year**
Reduced Rates: **Available**
Breakfast: **Full**
Credit Cards: **AMEX, MC, VISA**
Pets: **No**
Children: **No**
Smoking: **Permitted**
Social Drinking: **Permitted**
Airport/Station Pickup: **Yes**
Foreign Languages: **Spanish**

In 1982, this Victorian mansion was precisely reproduced from architectural plans drawn in 1884. The exterior is redwood, and the interior is done in redwood and oak. All trims and moldings are handmade and the chimneys rise to 50 feet. The rooms, each with a view, are furnished with authentic antiques, down comforters, Oriental rugs, original art, and fresh flowers. Christi and Mark pamper you with breakfasts that often include eggs Benedict or unusual pastries, *hors d'oeuvres* and complimentary wine before dinner, cookies and cordials before bedtime, and (by special arrangement with Mark) limousine service in his 1958 Bentley. Wow! Humboldt State University is nearby.

Eagle House Bed and Breakfast Inn ☉
139 SECOND STREET, EUREKA, CALIFORNIA 95501

Tel: **(707) 444-9762**
Host(s): **David Lipscomb**
Location: ¼ mi. from Hwy. 101
No. of Rooms: 10
No. of Private Baths: 10
Double/pb: $60–$80
Single/pb: $50–$70

Open: **All year**
Breakfast: **Continental**
Credit Cards: **AMEX, MC, VISA**
Pets: **No**
Children: **Welcome, over 16**
Smoking: **No**
Social Drinking: **Permitted**

Eagle House provides a panoramic view of Humboldt Bay, the fishing fleet, and the old town district. Travelers have stopped here for nearly a century. The high Victorian stick-architecture, ornate woodwork, and fireplaces have made the house an area landmark, now nominated to the National Register of Historic Places. The guest rooms are filled with fine antiques, all of them for sale. Such amenities as a hot tub, wine, and *hors d'oeuvres* are always available. The lower floors of the hotel feature a bar, restaurant, and shops. Nearby sights include the Sequoia Park Zoo, Carson Mansion, and Fort Humboldt.

Old Town Bed and Breakfast Inn ✪
1521 3RD STREET, EUREKA, CALIFORNIA 95501

Tel: **(707) 445-3951**
Host(s): **Bob and Agnes Sobrito**
No. of Rooms: **5**
No. of Private Baths: **3**
Max. No. Sharing Bath: **4**
Double/pb: **$45–$55**
Single/pb: **$35–$45**
Double/sb: **$50**
Single/sb: **$40**
Open: **All year**
Reduced rates: **Off-season**
Breakfast: **Full**
Credit Cards: **MC, VISA**
Pets: **No**
Children: **Welcome**
Smoking: **No**
Social Drinking: **Permitted**
Airport/Station Pickup: **Yes**

This Greek Revival home is the last of what once was the Bay Mill. The house was built in 1871 and was later moved to its present location on a residential street. The rooms are graciously decorated with antiques. Each guest room features something different—a brass bed, or oak furnishings, or an old-fashioned armoire. Breakfast is served in the wood-stove-heated kitchen or the formal dining room. In the afternoon, unwind with wine and cheese in the parlor. Redwood parks, secluded beaches, and the Old Town are nearby. Humboldt State University and College of the Redwoods are a short distance from the inn.

Colonial Inn ✪
P.O. BOX 565, 533 EAST FIR STREET, FORT BRAGG, CALIFORNIA 95437

Tel: **(707) 964-9979**
Best Time to Call: **8–10 AM**
Host(s): **Catherine and Donald Markham**
Location: **150 mi. N of San Francisco**
No. of Rooms: **8**
No. of Private Baths: **8**
Double/pb: **$45–$70**
Single/pb: **$36–$40**
Open: **All year**
Breakfast: **No**
Pets: **Sometimes**
Children: **Welcome**
Smoking: **Permitted**
Social Drinking: **Permitted**

Located in a quiet, residential area, surrounded by a well-manicured lawn and lovely trees, the inn is convenient to antique shops, restaurants, museums, tennis, and other recreational activities. The beach is nearby and famous Mendocino is 12 miles away. Catherine and Donald look forward to helping you get the most pleasure out of your visit.

The Grey Whale Inn ✪
615 NORTH MAIN STREET, FORT BRAGG, CALIFORNIA 95437

Tel: (707) 964-0640 (toll-free in California: 1-800-FT BRAGG)
Best Time to Call: 8 AM–9 PM
Host(s): John and Colette Bailey
Location: 165 mi. NW of San Francisco
No. of Rooms: 13
No. of Private Baths: 11
Max. No. Sharing Bath: 4
Double/pb: $45–$75
Single/pb: $40–$70
Double/sb: $65–$70
Single/sb: $60–$65
Suites: $65–$75 (for 2); $100 (for 4)
Open: All year
Reduced Rates: Available
Breakfast: Continental
Credit Cards: AMEX, MC, VISA
Pets: No
Children: Welcome, over 6
Smoking: Permitted
Social Drinking: Permitted

An imposing three-story weathered redwood inn, with beautifully landscaped grounds, can be your home away from home. It is attractively furnished and boasts an extensive art collection. The warm colors, varied woods, plump comforters, and collection of books make for a cozy environment. Area attractions include the Noyo Harbor, Redwood Forest, and the Skunk Railway. John and Colette will advise where and when to watch the fascinating whales. Breakfast features Colette's prize-winning breads and coffee cakes. The College of the Redwoods is a block away.

Camellia Inn ✪
211 NORTH STREET, HEALDSBURG, CALIFORNIA 95448

Tel: (707) 433-8182
Best Time to Call: Mornings
Host(s): Ray and Del Lewand
Location: 65 mi. N of San Francisco
No. of Rooms: 6
No. of Private Baths: 4
Max. No. Sharing Bath: 4
Double/pb: $50–$65
Single/pb: $30–$65
Double/sb: $40–$50

72 • CALIFORNIA

Single/sb: **$40–$50**
Open: **All year**
Reduced Rates: **Off-season**
Breakfast: **Full**
Credit Cards: **MC, VISA**

Pets: **No**
Children: **Welcome, over 10**
Smoking: **Permitted**
Social Drinking: **Permitted**

This elegant Italianate Victorian town house (circa 1869) is an architectural delight. It is convenient to the Russian River, wineries, golf, tennis, and more. Ray and Del serve a hearty breakfast buffet in the dining room, and wine is served in the afternoon in the grand parlor or on the pool terrace.

The Victorian Farmhouse
P.O. BOX 357, LITTLE RIVER, CALIFORNIA 95456

Tel: **(707) 937-0697**
Best Time to Call: **9 AM–9 PM**
Host(s): **Tom and Jane Szilasi**
Location: **150 mi. N of San Francisco**
No. of Rooms: **6**
No. of Private Baths: **6**
Double/pb: **$63**

Open: **All year**
Breakfast: **Continental**
Pets: **No**
Children: **No**
Smoking: **Permitted**
Social Drinking: **Permitted**

Built in 1877, the farmhouse has been completely renovated and furnished in period antiques to enhance its original beauty and Victorian charm. It's close to Mendocino with its many galleries, boutiques, and restaurants. There's an apple orchard and gardens, and the ocean is a short walk away. Whale-watching in the winter months is popular. Tom and Jane will pamper you with breakfast brought to your room, and will invite you to join them for evening sherry.

The Old World Inn
1301 JEFFERSON STREET, NAPA, CALIFORNIA, 94559

Tel: **(707) 257-0112**
Host(s): **Geoffrey and Janet Villiers**
Location: **35 mi. NE of San Francisco**
No. of Rooms: **8**
No. of Private Baths: **8**
Double/pb: **$70–$90**
Open: **All year**
Reduced rates: **Off-season; weekdays**

Breakfast: **Continental**
Credit Cards: **AMEX, MC, VISA**
Pets: **No**
Children: **No**
Smoking: **No**
Social Drinking: **Permitted**
Airport/Station Pickup: **Yes**

The bright, fresh colors of Swedish artist Carl Larson dominate the rooms of this Victorian inn. Each is a unique blend of antiques, exclusive fabrics and linens, with special touches such as a skylight or canopy bed. In the afternoon, wine and cheese are served in a lovely morning room. This is also the breakfast room, or you may have goodies brought to your private quarters. Your hosts are pleased to direct you to local wineries, the Petrified Forest, glider flights, hot spring baths and many fine restaurants. An outdoor Jacuzzi is a fine way to begin or end a day of touring.

Wine Country Cottage ✪
400 MEADOWOOD LANE, ST. HELENA, CALIFORNIA 94574

Tel: **(707) 963-0852**
Host(s): **Jan Strong**
Location: **In the Napa Valley**
Guest Cottage: **$80; sleeps 2**
Open: **All year**

Breakfast: **Continental**
Pets: **Sometimes**
Children: **Sometimes**
Smoking: **Permitted**
Social Drinking: **Permitted**

A private woodland retreat for two, boasting a patio under the pines, a comfortable bed-sitting room, private bath with shower, and complete kitchen. Jan will direct you to the nearby spas, Napa Valley wineries, hot-air ballooning, tennis, golf, or swimming facilities. When you tire of your own cooking, there are many renowned restaurants for you to enjoy.

MONTEREY PENINSULA
Happy Landing Inn ✪
P.O. BOX 2619, CARMEL, CALIFORNIA 93921

Tel: **(408) 624-7917**	Suites: **$85–$105**
Best Time to Call: **11 AM–9 PM**	Open: **All year**
Host(s): **Bob Alberson, Dick Stewart, and Jewell Brown**	Breakfast: **Continental**
	Credit Cards: **AMEX, MC, VISA**
Location: **120 mi. S of San Francisco**	Pets: **Sometimes**
No. of Rooms: **7**	Children: **Welcome, over 12**
No. of Private Baths: **7**	Smoking: **No**
Double/pb: **$60–$75**	Social Drinking: **Permitted**
Single/pb: **$60–$75**	Foreign Languages: **Japanese**

Located on Monte Verde between 5th and 6th, this early Comstock-style inn is a charming and romantic place to stay. Rooms with cathedral ceilings open onto a beautiful garden with gazebo, pond, and flagstone paths. Lovely antiques and personal touches, including breakfast served in your room, make your stay special.

Holiday House
P.O. BOX 782, CARMEL, CALIFORNIA 93921

Tel: **(408) 624-6267**	Single/pb: **$60**
Best Time to Call: **8 AM–9 PM**	Double/sb: **$68**
Host(s): **Dieter and Ruth Back**	Single/sb: **$62**
Location: **1 mi. from Hwy. 1**	Open: **All year**
No. of Rooms: **6**	Breakfast: **Full**
No. of Private Baths: **4**	Pets: **No**
Max. No. Sharing Bath: **4 (shower and toilet in separate rooms)**	Children: **Welcome, over 8**
	Smoking: **No**
Double/pb: **$75**	Social Drinking: **Permitted**

Centrally located on Camino Real (near 7th Street), three blocks from the beach and town, this 73-year-old *grande dame* of guest houses is the perfect spot to relax and reflect. All the bedrooms have either a view of the Pacific Ocean or open onto the garden. Breakfast features homemade breads, coffee cakes, ham and cheese strata, or baked deviled eggs and cheese. Dieter and Ruth invite you to enjoy a glass of sherry by the fireplace.

House of England ✪
25020 VALLEY WAY, CARMEL, CALIFORNIA 93923

Tel: **(408) 624-3004**
Host(s): **Dr. Gene England**
Location: **On Rt. 1**
No. of Rooms: **4**
No. of Private Baths: **1**
Max. No. Sharing Bath: **6**
Double/pb: **$50**
Double/sb: **$40–$50**

Open: **All year**
Reduced Rates: **20% mid-week off-season**
Breakfast: **Full**
Pets: **Sometimes**
Children: **Welcome**
Smoking: **No**
Social Drinking: **Permitted**

This Mediterranean-style house has a large front yard and a deck in the backyard for your leisure. Gene, a psychologist and former Stanford professor, will pamper you with a glass of wine while you relax in the hot tub. It's a mile to the beach and charming shops, and the Monterey Institute of International Studies is close by.

Sea View Inn ✪
P.O. BOX 4138, CAMINO REAL, CARMEL, CALIFORNIA 93921

Tel: **(408) 624-8778**
Best Time to Call: **9 AM–7 PM**
Host(s): **Marshall and Diane Hydorn**
Location: **2 mi. from Hwy. 1**
No. of Rooms: **8**
No. of Private Baths: **6**
Max. No. Sharing Bath: **4**
Double/pb: **$53–$65**
Single/pb: **$53–$65**

Double/sb: **$45**
Single/sb: **$45**
Open: **All year**
Breakfast: **Continental**
Credit Cards: **MC, VISA**
Pets: **No**
Children: **Welcome, over 12**
Smoking: **No**
Social Drinking: **Permitted**

Located between 11th and 12th streets, three blocks from the ocean, this is one of Carmel's few remaining stately old homes. Marshall and Diane have furnished the guest rooms with fine antiques. Complimentary light sherry and pretzels are served in the living room by the fireplace. You're always made to feel special because of the personal attention your hosts extend.

House of Seven Gables Inn ✪
555 OCEAN VIEW BOULEVARD, PACIFIC GROVE, CALIFORNIA 93950

Tel: **(408) 372-4341**	Open: **All year**
Host(s): **The Flatley Family**	Reduced Rates: **10%, weekly**
Location: **1 mi. W of Monterey**	Breakfast: **Continental**
No. of Rooms: **14**	Pets: **No**
No. of Private Baths: **14**	Children: **Welcome, over 12**
Double/pb: **$75–$110**	Smoking: **No**
Single/pb: **$70–$105**	Social Drinking: **Permitted**
Suites: **$110**	Foreign Languages: **Arabic, French, Spanish**
Guest Cottage: **$85; sleeps 2**	

This Victorian seaside mansion overlooks Monterey Bay and the coastal mountains. The guest rooms all have beautiful views and are furnished in eclectic style, with many antiques. The house boasts many Tiffany glass windows, pier mirrors, Persian rugs, and comfortable easy chairs. Your hosts serve freshly baked breads and assorted coffees and teas in an elegant, sunny dining room. Stroll the gardens or relax on one of four porches. A secluded beach is just steps from the house. Other attractions include Carmel Mission, Cannery Row, Old Fisherman's Wharf, and 17-Mile Drive.

Ocean-Forest Hideaway ✪
P.O. BOX 1193, PEBBLE BEACH, CALIFORNIA 93953

Tel: **(408) 372-7425**	Suites: **$60**
Host(s): **Bill George**	Open: **All year**
Location: **3 mi. from Hwy. 1**	Reduced Rates: **10%, Sunday to Thursday; groups**
No. of Rooms: **3**	Breakfast: **Continental**
No. of Private Baths: **1**	Pets: **No**
Maximum No. Sharing Bath: **4**	Children: **Welcome, over 9**
Double/pb: **$60**	Smoking: **No**
Single/pb: **$60**	Social Drinking: **Permitted**
Double/sb: **$55**	Airport/Station Pickup: **Yes**
Single/sb: **$55**	

It's two minutes to scenic beaches on the famous 17-Mile Drive adjacent to golf courses in the exclusive Pebble Beach forest. On the way to Carmel, just five minutes away, you'll see historic castles overlooking the ocean. A path through the woods brings you to the private entry of the hideaway suite with private bath. The other guest rooms have king-size beds, and you will be pampered with cozy comforters, flowers, and wine. Enjoy breakfast overlooking the woods, where deer and squirrels play.

Chateau Victorian ○
118 FIRST STREET, SANTA CRUZ, CALIFORNIA 95060

Tel: **(408) 458-9458**	Breakfast: **Continental**
Host(s): **Franz Benjamin**	Credit Cards: **AMEX, MC, VISA**
Location: **1½ mi. from hwys. 1 and 17**	Pets: **No**
No. of Rooms: **7**	Children: **No**
No. of Private Baths: **7**	Smoking: **No**
Double/pb: **$55–$95**	Social Drinking: **Permitted**
Open: **All year**	Foreign Languages: **German**

This 100-year-old home has been restored to its former opulence. Five of the bedrooms have working fireplaces, and all the rooms are tastefully decorated. After a hearty breakfast, you can walk a block to the beach, the Municipal Wharf, or the world-famous casino and boardwalk. Complimentary wine and cheese are served in the late afternoon as a prelude to dining in one of the area's superb restaurants. UC-Santa Cruz is close by.

SACRAMENTO AREA

Murphy's Inn
318 NEAL STREET, GRASS VALLEY, CALIFORNIA 95945

Tel: **(916) 273-6873**	Reduced Rates: **10%, off-season**
Host(s): **Marc and Rose Murphy**	Breakfast: **Full**
Location: **25 mi. from I-80**	Credit Cards: **AMEX, MC, VISA**
No. of Rooms: **7**	Pets: **No**
No. of Private Baths: **5**	Children: **Welcome**
Max. No. Sharing Bath: **4**	Smoking: **Permitted**
Double/pb: **$48–$68**	Social Drinking: **Permitted**
Double/sb: **$48–$68**	Airport/Station Pickup: **Yes**
Open: **All year**	

This 100-year-old Victorian inn, on magnificent grounds, is framed by a majestic sequoia tree. The house's beauty is enhanced by the spacious veranda and hanging ivy baskets. Guest rooms are meticulously clean and graced with antiques, lace curtains, and brass beds. Marc and Rose invite you to join other guests in the sitting room. Centrally located in the historic district, it is minutes away from Nevada City and within walking distance of restaurants and unique shops.

Jean's Riverside Bed & Breakfast ✪
P.O. BOX 2334, OROVILLE, CALIFORNIA 95965

Tel: **(916) 533-1413**
Best Time to Call: **Before 8 AM, after 10 PM**
Host(s): **Jean Pratt**
Location: **1½ mi. from Hwy. 70**
No. of Rooms: **6**
No. of Private Baths: **3**
Max. No. Sharing Bath: **4**
Double/pb: **$40**
Single/pb: **$30**
Double/sb: **$35**

Single/sb: **$25**
Open: **All year**
Reduced Rates: **Available**
Breakfast: **Full**
Other meals: **Available**
Pets: **Sometimes**
Children: **Welcome**
Smoking: **Permitted**
Social Drinking: **Permitted**
Airport/Station Pickup: Yes
Foreign Languages: **French**

Located on the banks of the Feather River, there are views of the dam and Table Mountain. Swimming, boating, fishing, gold-panning, and canoeing are available on private waterfront. Jean will happily direct you to Feather Falls (fourth highest in the U.S.), Oroville Lake with its 160 miles of shoreline, the most authentic Chinese temple in this country, and other historical sites.

Bear Flag Inn ✪
2814 I STREET, SACRAMENTO, CALIFORNIA 95816

Tel: **(916) 448-5417**
Host(s): **Robert West and Jennifer Dowley**
Location: **80 mi. E of San Francisco**
No. of Rooms: **2**
No. of Private Baths: **2**
Double/pb: **$50**
Single/pb: **$40**
Open: **All year**

Reduced Rates: **After 4 days**
Breakfast: **Continental**
Credit Cards: **MC, VISA**
Pets: **No**
Children: **Welcome**
Smoking: **Permitted**
Social Drinking: **Permitted**
Airport/Station Pickup: **Yes**
Foreign Languages: **German**

This European-style hostelry is located in a residential neighborhood of downtown Sacramento. It is a handsomely restored California "Arts and Crafts Style" bungalow decorated with period furnishings and within walking distance of fine restaurants. Complimentary wine, a fireplace in the living room, and a hammock in the garden all add up to relaxation.

The Briggs House ✪
2209 CAPITOL AVENUE, SACRAMENTO, CALIFORNIA 95816

Tel: **(916) 441-3214**
Best Time to Call: **9 AM–Noon; 4–9 PM**
Host(s): **Sue Garmston, Barbara Stoltz, Kathy Yeates, Paula Rawles**
Location: **1 mi. from I-80**
No. of Rooms: **7**
No. of Private Baths: **5**
Max. No. Sharing Bath: **2**
Double/pb: **$55–$70**
Single/pb: **$55–$70**
Double/sb: **$50–$60**
Single/sb: **$50–$60**
Guest Cottage: **$80–$90**
Open: **All year**
Reduced Rates: **10% less, 6 days**
Breakfast: **Full**
Credit Cards: **AMEX, MC, VISA**
Pets: **No**
Children: **Cottage only**
Smoking: **Permitted**
Social Drinking: **Permitted**

Just a few blocks from the State Capitol, this is an elegantly restored Victorian house surrounded by stately trees. Antiques add to the splendor of the rich wood paneling, inlaid floor, Oriental rugs, and lace curtains. You'll be pampered with flowers in your room, and English china and fine silver for your gourmet breakfast. Relax in the spa or sauna after a busy day of sightseeing. Evening treats include wine, fruit, nuts, and unhurried conversation in the living room. California State University-Sacramento is nearby.

SAN DIEGO AND ORANGE COUNTY AREA

American Historic Homes Bed & Breakfast
P.O. BOX 388, SAN JUAN CAPISTRANO, CALIFORNIA 92693

Tel: (714) 496-7050
Coordinator: **Deborah Sakach**
State/Regions Covered: **Nationwide**

Rates (Single/Double):
Modest: $20 $25–$35
Average: $30–$35 $36–$55
Luxury: $50–$60 $56–$85
Credit Cards: **No**

All the homes on Deborah's roster are historically significant. They range from a three-story Victorian in San Francisco to a North Carolina plantation, including sea captains' houses, bayside retreats, Georgian mansions and Early American colonials. Many are designated National Landmarks and all share the common element of warmth and hospitality.

Carolyn's B&B Homes
P.O. BOX 84776, SAN DIEGO, CALIFORNIA 92138

Tel: (619) 435-5009
Coordinator: **Carolyn Waskiewicz**
States/Regions Covered: **San Diego: La Jolla, Del Mar, Catalina Island, Jamul, Coronado**

Rates (Single/Double):
Average: $20–$60 $30–$70
Cottages: $55–$125
Credit Cards: **No**

Carolyn represents a wide variety of private homes in the San Diego area. Accommodations vary from simple to luxurious, including an oceanfront home in La Jolla; an historical mansion close to Balboa Park; a farmhouse with stained glass windows and beamed ceilings; a Victorian mansion on the ocean, where presidents and kings have been entertained, and much more. Send $5 for her directory of listings, and make your reservations directly with the host of your choice.

Digs West
8191 CROWLEY CIRCLE, BUENA PARK, CALIFORNIA 90621

Tel: (714) 739-1669
Best Time to Call: **Early AM or Evenings**
Coordinator: **Jean Horn**

States/Regions Covered: **Anaheim, Bellflower, Costa Mesa, Cypress, Fullerton, Hermosa Beach, Santa Ana**

Rates (Single/Double):
  Modest: $25 $30
  Average: $30–$58 $36–$58
  Luxury: $58 $110

Credit Cards: No
Minimum Stay: 2 days

Jean offers comfortable accommodations in the areas of San Diego, Los Angeles, and Orange County (near Disneyland). Sightseeing, guided tours, and car rentals can be arranged. A directory of host homes is available for $2.

Seaview Reservations Bed & Breakfast ✪
P.O. BOX 1355, LAGUNA BEACH, CALIFORNIA 92652

Tel: (714) 494-8878
Best Time to Call: 9 AM–5 PM
Coordinator: Nancy Fine, Marcia Mordkin
States/Regions Covered: Laguna Beach, Newport Beach, Orange County, San Diego

Rates (Single/Double):
  Average: $35–$55 $45–$65
  Luxury: $55–$125 $70–$125
Credit Cards: MC, VISA

Nancy and Marcia have accommodations in private homes, small inns, and cottages. Homes are available on the oceanfront, near canyons, or walk-to-the-beach locations. Arts and crafts, music festivals, and the University of California at Irvine and San Diego are a few of the interesting "doings" in the area. This is a membership organization, with a $5 fee, paid only once, to join.

Anaheim Country Inn ✪
856 SOUTH WALNUT, ANAHEIM, CALIFORNIA 92802

Tel: (714) 778-0150
Host(s): Lois Ramont, Marilyn Watson
Location: 30 mi. S of Los Angeles
No. of Rooms: 8
No. of Private Baths: 1
Max. No. Sharing Bath: 6
Double/sb: $60–$75
Single/sb: $40
Suites: $100–$110

Open: All year
Breakfast: Full
Credit Cards: MC, VISA
Pets: No
Children: Welcome, over 12
Smoking: No
Social Drinking: Permitted
Airport/Station Pickup: Yes

This large, Princess Anne Victorian has beveled leaded glass windows, an elegant front stairway, and a pump organ. Guest rooms feature turn-of-the-century and country furnishings. Relax in the large living room, upstairs reading room, or one of three airy porches. Pause for light appetizers before dining out. Your hosts will gladly make your reservations. The Inn is located three blocks from the bus to Disneyland, Knott's Berry Farm, and the Convention Center. After touring, return to spacious grounds in a quiet, residential area.

The Blue Door ✪
13707 DURANGO DRIVE, DEL MAR, CALIFORNIA 92014

Tel: **(619) 755-3819**
Best Time to Call: **7 AM–10 PM**
Host(s): **Bob and Anna Belle Schock**
Location: **20 mi. N of San Diego**
No. of Rooms: **1 suite**
No. of Private Baths: **1**
Suites: **$40**
Open: **All year**

Reduced Rates: **After 2 nights**
Breakfast: **Full**
Pets: **No**
Children: **No**
Smoking: **No**
Social Drinking: **Permitted**
Airport/Station Pickup: **Yes**

Enjoy New England charm in a southern California setting overlooking exclusive Del Mar. A garden-level suite with wicker accessories and king-size bed is yours; it opens onto a private garden patio. Breakfast is served in the spacious country kitchen or in the dining room warmed by the fire on chilly days. Anna Belle prides herself on creative breakfast menus featuring homemade baked goods. She will gladly direct you to the nearby race track, beach, zoo, or University of California at San Diego.

Julian Gold Rush Hotel ✪
P.O. BOX 856, 2032 MAIN STREET, JULIAN, CALIFORNIA 92036

Tel: **(619) 765-0201**
Best Time to Call: **8 AM–9 PM**
Host(s): **Steve and Gig Ballinger**
Location: **60 mi. NE of San Diego**
No. of Rooms: **16**
No. of Private Baths: **4**
Max. No. Sharing Bath: **4**
Double/pb: **$50–$64**
Single/pb: **$50–$64**
Double/sb: **$38–$52**

Single/sb: **$21–$26**
Guest Cottage: **$65–$78; sleeps 2**
Open: **All year**
Reduced Rates: **20%, seniors; families**
Breakfast: **Full**
Pets: **No**
Children: **Welcome, weekdays**
Smoking: **Permitted**
Social Drinking: **Permitted**

This century-old landmark is listed in the National Register of Historic Places, and it is furnished with American antiques lovingly restored by your hosts. The lobby has a wood-burning stove, books and games, and an original, oak player piano. The historic town of Julian has been preserved to look much as it did 100 years ago and it has gold mine tours. Gig and Steve serve a man-sized breakfast, and tea and coffee are always available.

Stay-a-Nite ✪
1287-85 VIRGINIA WAY, LA JOLLA, CALIFORNIA 92037

Tel: **(619) 459-5888**
Host(s): **Noel and Paul Stuart**
Location: **12 miles north of San Diego**
No. of Rooms: **6**
No. of Private Baths: **2**
Max. No. Sharing Bath: **3**
Double/pb: **$52**
Single/pb: **$47**
Double/sb: **$42–$47**
Single/sb: **$37–$42**
Suites: **$50–$55**
Open: **All year**
Breakfast: **Continental**
Pets: **No**
Children: **Welcome, over 2**
Smoking: **No**
Social Drinking: **Permitted**
Foreign Languages: **Spanish, French, Italian**

Located in the heart of La Jolla village, it is a short walk to shops, restaurants, and the ocean. Guests are welcome to use the Jacuzzi, and the music and recreation room. Your hosts prepare a hearty buffet breakfast. They will be happy to help with tour information. Nearby sights include Sea World, San Diego Zoo, and the University of California at San Diego. Please check with Noel or Paul regarding minimum stay requirements.

Jean's Retreat ✪
2308 CALLE LAS PALMAS, SAN CLEMENTE, CALIFORNIA 92672

Tel: **(714) 492-1216 or 492-4121**
Best Time to Call: **Before 10 AM, after 6 PM**
Host(s): **Jean Spain**
Location: **60 mi. S of Los Angeles**
No. of Rooms: **2**
No. of Private Baths: **2**
Double/pb: **$45**
Single/pb: **$35**
Open: **All year**
Breakfast: **Continental**
Pets: **No**
Children: **Welcome, over 12**
Smoking: **No**
Social Drinking: **Permitted**

Jean's contemporary house, located in a quiet, exclusive area, is decorated in a comfortable blend of modern and antique pieces. The roses, exotic plantings, and vegetable garden attest to her green thumb. The house is two blocks from the beach, 10 minutes away from San Juan Capistrano, and 45 minutes from Disneyland. At home, there's a fireplace, spa, and large redwood deck for relaxing. Coffee, fruit, and snacks are always available.

Abigail
6310 RAYDEL COURT, SAN DIEGO, CALIFORNIA 92120

Tel: **(619) 583-4738**
Host(s): **Felix and Pearl Ammar**
Location: **200 feet from Freeway 8**
No. of Rooms: **1 suite**
No. of Private Baths: **1**
Suites: **$46**
Open: **All year**

Breakfast: **Full**
Pets: **No**
Children: **No**
Smoking: **No**
Social Drinking: **Permitted**
Foreign Languages: **French, German, Greek, Italian, Arabic**

Felix and Pearl live on the first floor, and they have created a haven for two on the second floor, offering privacy in the exclusive Del Cerro section. There is a separate entrance to the self-contained suite, which includes a kitchen where all the fixings for breakfast are provided; you can prepare what you wish, when you wish. San Diego Zoo, Balboa Park, Sea World, plus the Pacific Ocean and San Diego State University are all close by.

Britt House ✪
406 MAPLE STREET, SAN DIEGO, CALIFORNIA 92103

Tel: **(619) 234-2926**
Best Time to Call: **8 AM–10 PM**
Host(s): **Daun Martin**
Location: **1 mi. from Hwys. 5, 8, 163**
No. of Rooms: **9**
No. of Private Baths: **1**
Max. No. Sharing Bath: **5**
Double/pb: **$85**
Single/pb: **$85**

Double/sb: **$65–$95**
Single/sb: **$65–$95**
Open: **All year**
Breakfast: **Full**
Credit Cards: **MC, VISA**
Pets: **No**
Children: **Welcome, over 8**
Smoking: **Permitted**
Social Drinking: **Permitted**

Fresh flowers and original drawings are part of this historic Victorian house. A winding oak stairway bends past the two-story stained glass windows. A book-filled parlor and grand piano are available for your pleasure. It's close to Balboa Park, the Globe Theater, the San Diego Zoo, and The University of California, and you can walk to several fine restaurants. Breakfast features homemade delicacies and fresh-ground coffee. Daun serves afternoon tea, and there are cookies and fruit thoughtfully placed in each guest room.

The Cottage ✪
3829 ALBATROSS STREET, P.O. BOX 3292, SAN DIEGO, CALIFORNIA 92103

Tel: **(619) 299-1564**
Best Time to Call: **9 AM–6 PM**
Host(s): **Robert and Carol Emerick**
Location: **1 mi. from Rt. 5**
Guest Cottage: **$40–$55; sleeps 3**
Open: **All year**
Breakfast: **Continental**
Credit Cards: **MC, VISA**
Pets: **No**
Children: **Welcome**
Smoking: **No**
Social Drinking: **Permitted**

Located in the Hillcrest section, where undeveloped canyons and old houses dot the landscape, this private hideaway offers a cottage with a king-size bed in the bedroom, a single bed in the living room, full bath, and fully equipped kitchen. Decorated with turn-of-the-century furniture, the wood-burning stove and oak pump organ evoke memories of long ago. It's two miles to the zoo, less to Balboa Park, and it is within easy walking distance of restaurants, shops, and theater. The University of California and the University of San Diego are nearby.

Harbor Hill Guest House ✪
2330 ALBATROSS STREET, SAN DIEGO, CALIFORNIA 92101

Tel: **(619) 233-0638**
Host(s): **Dorothy A. Milbourn**
No. of Rooms: **6**
No. of Private Baths: **6**
Double/pb: **$50**
Single/pb: **$50**
Guest Cottage: **Available, sleeps 3**
Open: **All year**
Breakfast: **Continental**
Pets: **No**
Children: **Welcome**
Smoking: **Permitted**
Social Drinking: **Permitted**
Airport/Station Pickup: **Yes**

Each level in Dorothy's contemporary, three-story house has its own private entrance and a kitchen for your use. It is within walking distance of San Diego harbor, and only 40 minutes to the Wild Animal Park and all tourist attractions.

The Hide-A-Way ✪
4140 CAMPUS AVENUE, SAN DIEGO, CALIFORNIA 92103

Tel: **(619) 298-7260**
Best Time to Call: **Evenings**
Host(s): **Betty Soloff**
Location: **3 blocks from Rte. 163**
No. of Rooms: **1**
No. of Private Baths: **1**
Double/pb: **$35**
Single/pb: **$25**

Open: **Jan. 4–Nov. 15**
Breakfast: **Continental**
Pets: **No**
Children: **No**
Smoking: **No**
Social Drinking: **Permitted**
Airport/Station Pickup: **Yes**

Betty's 65-year-old, two-story pink stucco house has a porch for summer relaxing and a fireplace to gather 'round on cool evenings. Furnished with a cozy ambience, it has a lovely view of the city and bay. It's a mile to the zoo and four miles from the beach, with lots to see and do in-between. Breakfast features homemade banana nut bread or pear bread, and complimentary wine and cheese are offered in the evening.

Friends-We-Haven't-Met ✪
10071 STARBRIGHT CIRCLE, WESTMINSTER, CALIFORNIA 92683

Tel: **(714) 531-4269**
Best Time to Call: **7–11 AM**
Host(s): **Bob and Sandy Runkle**
Location: **3 mi. S of Anaheim**
No. of Rooms: **3**
Max. No. Sharing Bath: **6**
Double/sb: **$32**
Single/sb: **$26**

Open: **All year**
Reduced Rates: **10% weekly**
Breakfast: **Full**
Pets: **No**
Children: **Welcome**
Smoking: **Permitted**
Social Drinking: **Permitted**
Airport/Station Pickup: **Yes**

The Runkles' two-story house offers a private den for reading, playing cards, or listening to music. The delightful backyard patio with flowers and barbecue is yours to enjoy. For those interested in physical fitness, Bob and Sandy are members of a private, 17-acre sports club which you may utilize. You are welcome to help yourself to coffee, wine, and fresh fruit. Long Beach State and the U. of C. at Irvine are nearby.

SAN FRANCISCO AREA

American Family Inn ✪
P.O. BOX 349, SAN FRANCISCO, CALIFORNIA 94101

Tel: (415) 931-3083
Best Time to Call: 9 AM–5 PM
Coordinator: **Susan and Richard Kreibich**
States/Regions Covered: **Gold Country, Carmel, Monterey, Marin County, San Francisco, Wine Country**
	Rates (Single/Double):
	  Modest: $40 $50
	  Average: $45–$50 $55–$60
	  Luxury: $55–$75 $65–$85
	Credit Cards: **AMEX, MC, VISA**

The San Francisco locations are near all the famous sights, such as Fisherman's Wharf and Chinatown. Many are historic Victorian houses. Some homes offer hot tubs and sun decks; a few are on yachts and houseboats where the tariff ranges $100–$120.

Bed & Breakfast International—San Francisco ✪
151 ARDMORE ROAD, KENSINGTON, CALIFORNIA 94707

Tel: (415) 527-8836
Best Time to Call: 8 AM–5 PM
Coordinator: **Jean Brown**
States/Regions Covered:
  California—Berkeley, Palo Alto, San Francisco, Los Angeles, Lake Tahoe; **Nevada**—Las Vegas; **Hawaii**; **N.Y.C.**
	Rates (Single/Double):
	  Modest: $29 $36
	  Average: $37 $46
	  Luxury: $48–$72 $60–$90
	Credit Cards: **AMEX, DC, MC, VISA** (for Deposit only)

Jean was the first to bring the concept of a bed and breakfast reservation service to America. Her accommodations range from a townhouse apartment to a villa above an ocean beach with a private pool. Others are conveniently located near the seashore, Gold Country, museums, universities, ethnic areas, Marineworld, Disneyland, Hollywood, Tijuana, Mexico, and missions. A minimum stay of two nights is required.

Creekview
1840 SONOMA AVENUE, BERKELEY, CALIFORNIA 94707

Tel: **(415) 524-6523**
Best Time to Call: **8–10 AM; 6–10 PM**
Host(s): **Marvin and Donis Shapiro**
Location: **10 mi. E of San Francisco**
No. of Rooms: **1**
No. of Private Baths: **1**
Double/pb: **$32**
Single/pb: **$25**
Open: **All year**
Reduced Rates: **Weekly**
Breakfast: **Full**
Pets: **No**
Children: **Welcome**
Smoking: **No**
Social Drinking: **Permitted**
Airport/Station Pickup: **Yes**

This 1920s green-stucco bungalow is surrounded by trees and shrubs. The backyard deck overlooks a pretty creek with a bridge leading to a small sitting area. Marvin and Donis are cordial people. They'll direct you to the nearby jogging track, swimming pool, and to the multi-faceted interests provided by the University of California's Berkeley campus. For longer stays, you might consider the two-room apartment they rent for $100–$150 weekly, accommodating up to three guests.

Thirty-Nine Cypress
BOX 176, POINT REYES STATION, CALIFORNIA 94956

Tel: **(415) 663-1709**
Best Time to Call: **Before 8 AM; after 6 PM**
Host(s): **Julia Bartlett**
Location: **45 mi. N of San Francisco**
No. of Rooms: **3**
Max. No. Sharing Bath: **6**
Double/sb: **$47**
Single/sb: **$42**
Open: **All year**
Reduced Rates: **3-day stays**
Breakfast: **Full**
Pets: **No**
Children: **Sometimes**
Smoking: **No**
Social Drinking: **Permitted**

Ten miles from the Pacific, surrounded by hills, this handsome home is furnished with antiques, original art, and Oriental rugs. Point Reyes National Seashore is three miles away. Julia knows the area intimately and can always suggest a hike or day trip suited to the weather, energy level, and tastes of her guests. From January through April, one of the world's most beautiful spots for watching the migrating gray whale is only 25 miles away. Each guest room opens onto a private patio on a bluff overlooking grazing cattle and wild birds.

Albion House ⊘
135 GOUGH STREET, SAN FRANCISCO, CALIFORNIA 94102

Tel: **(415) 621-0896**
Best Time to Call: **8 AM–10 PM**
Host(s): **Richard Meyer**
No. of Rooms: **8**
No. of Private Baths: **8**
Double/pb: **$65–$75**
Single/pb: **$65**
Suites: **$85–$125**
Open: **All year**

Breakfast: **Full**
Credit Cards: **AMEX, MC, VISA**
Pets: **No**
Children: **Welcome**
Smoking: **Permitted**
Social Drinking: **Permitted**
Airport/Station Pickup: **Yes**
Foreign Languages: **French**

You will be enchanted by the elegance and charm of this urban gem which stylishly combines the romance of a European *pensione* with the luxury of a grand hotel. Every room is a designer's delight, combining English antique furnishings and California flair. It's a short walk to the Opera House, Symphony Hall, Museum of Modern Art, galleries, and fine restaurants. The spacious living room is a comforting place to return after a busy day. Richard will treat you to a glass of sherry before you retire.

Bed & Breakfast Near-The-Park ⊘
1387 SIXTH AVENUE, SAN FRANCISCO, CALIFORNIA 94122

Tel: **(415) 753-3574**
Host(s): **John and Alice Micklewright**
No. of Rooms: **3**
Max. No. Sharing Bath: **6**
Double/sb: **$42**
Single/sb: **$32**
Open: **All year**

Breakfast: **Continental**
Pets: **No**
Children: **Welcome**
Smoking: **Permitted**
Social Drinking: **Permitted**
Foreign Languages: **French**

Just two blocks from Golden Gate Park, this Edwardian-era house is within walking distance of the De Young Museum, Steinhart Aquarium, and Japanese Tea Gardens. John and Alice decorated the guest rooms with people-comfort in mind. One room has a large kitchen attached, most convenient for longer visits. The University of California Medical Center is three blocks away.

Casa Arguello ✪
225 ARGUELLO BOULEVARD, SAN FRANCISCO, CALIFORNIA 94118

Tel: **(415) 661-3842 or 752-9482**
Best Time to Call: **After 10 AM**
Host(s): **Emma Baires**
No. of Rooms: 5
No. of Private Baths: 2
Max. No. Sharing Bath: 6
Double/pb: **$45**
Single/pb: **$40**
Double/sb: **$35**

Single/sb: **$30**
Suites: **$70**
Open: **All year**
Breakfast: **Continental**
Pets: **No**
Children: **Welcome, over 7**
Smoking: **Permitted**
Social Drinking: **Permitted**
Foreign Languages: **Spanish**

This spacious duplex has an elegant living room, dining room, and cheerful bedrooms which overlook neighboring gardens. Tastefully decorated with modern and antique furnishings, it is convenient to Golden Gate Park, Golden Gate Bridge, Union Square, and fine shops and restaurants. Mrs. Baires allows her kitchen to be used for light snacks. The University of California Medical School is nearby.

Casita Blanca ✪
330 EDGEHILL WAY, SAN FRANCISCO, CALIFORNIA 94127

Tel: **(415) 564-9339**
Host(s): **Joan Bard**
No. of Rooms: **1 cottage**
No. of Private Baths: 1
Guest Cottage: **$60; sleeps 2**
Open: **All year**

Pets: **No**
Children: **No**
Smoking: **Permitted**
Social Drinking: **Permitted**
Foreign Languages: **Spanish**

Perched on a hill, nestled among trees, and overlooking the city and bay, this unique cottage is separated from the main house, affording you the luxury of privacy. Every detail has been attended to, down to condiments in the kitchen. Though limited to two people at a time, there is a three-day minimum stay. Joan will be happy to direct you to all the non-tourist spots that make this city so exciting. The University of California Medical Center is close by. Joan also offers B&B in Carmel Valley, Lake Tahoe, and Sonoma.

Le Petit Manoir ✪
468 NOE STREET, SAN FRANCISCO, CALIFORNIA 94114

Tel: **(415) 864-7232**	Open: **All year**
Best Time to Call: **Morning, Evening**	Breakfast: **Full**
Host(s): **Paul Bernard**	Pets: **No**
No. of Rooms: **3**	Children: **Welcome, over 12**
Max. No. Sharing Bath: **6**	Smoking: **Permitted**
Double/sb: **$55**	Social Drinking: **Permitted**
Single/sb: **$45**	Foreign Languages: **French**

Paul's experience with all phases of running a restaurant is evident in the superb breakfasts he prepares for guests and serves on elegant china and crystal, either in the formal dining room of this 1902 Edwardian house, or on the glass-enclosed deck by the hot tub. He may even surprise you with eggs Benedict, accompanied by homemade hollandaise sauce, while you are drinking freshly squeezed orange juice.

Glen Echo ✪
508 KILKARE ROAD, SONOL, CALIFORNIA 94586

Tel: **(415) 862-2046**	Reduced Rates: **10%, seniors**
Best Time to Call: **Morning**	Breakfast: **Continental**
Host(s): **Don and Jan Scheer**	Pets: **No**
Location: **45 mi. SE of San Francisco**	Children: **Welcome**
No. of Rooms: **2**	Smoking: **No**
Max. No. Sharing Bath: **4**	Social Drinking: **No**
Double/sb: **$25**	Airport/Station Pickup: **Yes**
Single/sb: **$20**	Foreign Languages: **French**
Open: **All year**	

This comfortable home is located in farm country, surrounded by woods, with a creek flowing in front—a fine place to relax. Jan is a vegetarian so whole grains and natural foods are breakfast ingredients. California almonds and fresh fruit are always available. Don is an engineer and enjoys sailing when he's not busy remodeling the house. It is a good home-base for side trips to San Francisco, Carmel, Yosemite, Lake Tahoe, and Wine Country. California State University-Hayward is nearby.

Gasthaus zum Bären
2113 BLACKSTONE DRIVE, WALNUT CREEK, CALIFORNIA 94598

Tel: (415) 934-8119
Host(s): **Lois D. Martin**
Location: **33 mi. E of San Francisco**
No. of Rooms: **3**
No. of Private Baths: **2**
Max. No. Sharing Bath: **2**
Double/pb: **$35**
Single/pb: **$30**
Double/sb: **$30**
Single/sb: **$25**
Open: **All year**

Reduced Rates: **10%, seniors, families**
Breakfast: **Continental**
Other Meals: **Available**
Pets: **No**
Children: **Welcome, must be swimmers**
Smoking: **No**
Social Drinking: **Permitted**
Foreign Languages: **German, Italian, Spanish**

This rambling ranch home is furnished with artifacts from around the world. A huge natural fireplace dominates the living and family rooms. In summer, the large swimming pool becomes the center of activity and a California-style breakfast is served in the garden. Guests are welcome to the Jacuzzi, grill, and bicycles. Your hostess will be happy to provide picnic suppers for performances at the nearby Concord Pavilion, an outdoor concert shell carved into Mount Diablo. Foreign-language tours of San Francisco, Sausalito, Muir Woods, and the Wine Country can be arranged on summer weekends. For nature lovers, Briones Regional Park and numerous wilderness areas are nearby.

SAN JOAQUIN VALLEY

Valley View Citrus Ranch ○
14801 AVENUE 428, OROSI, CALIFORNIA 93647

Tel: (209) 528-2275
Host(s): **Tom and Ruth Flippen**
Location: **40 mi. SE of Fresno**
No. of Rooms: **4**
No. of Private Baths: **3**
Max. No. Sharing Bath: **4 (washbasin in each bedroom)**
Double/pb: **$45**
Single/pb: **$42**

Double/sb: **$45**
Single/sb: **$42**
Open: **All year**
Breakfast: **Full**
Pets: **Sometimes**
Children: **Welcome**
Smoking: **Permitted**
Social Drinking: **Permitted**
Foreign Languages: **Spanish**

Located in the San Joaquin Valley (The Fruit Basket of the World), this modern ranch home is set in the foothills of the Sierra Nevadas. The 70-foot-long porch provides some beautiful views. Tom and Ruth will be happy to plan your itinerary, which might include a visit to Sequoia National Park, Kings Canyon, Crystal Caves, Grants Grove, or you can play tennis on their clay court. Breakfast specialties are Belgian waffles served in the delightful gazebo. Complimentary beverages are always available, as is fresh fruit in season.

SAN LUIS OBISPO AREA

Megan's Friends
1296 GALLEON WAY #2, SAN LUIS OBISPO, CALIFORNIA 93401

Tel: (805) 544-4406
Best Time to Call: 8–9 AM; 2–6 PM
Coordinator: **Megan Backer**
State/Regions Covered: **Baywood Park, Cambria, Los Osos, Pine Canyon, Shell Beach, Sunset Palisades, San Luis Obispo**

Rates (Single/Double):
  Average: $20–$30 $35–$40
  Luxury: $40 $50–$65
Credit Cards: **No**

Megan has exclusive listings that no other reservation agency has. Ranging from a contemporary showplace to a cozy, country cottage, you are certain to be accommodated in a B&B best suited to your interests and purse. A $10 annual membership covers you and your immediate family.

The Castles ✪
1826 CHORRO STREET, SAN LUIS OBISPO, CALIFORNIA 93401

Tel: (805) 543-2818 or 541-8165
Best Time to Call: **Mornings, or evenings**
Host(s): **Sharon Castle**
Location: 1 mi. from Hwy. 101
No. of Rooms: 2
No. of Private Baths: 2
Double/pb: $35
Single/pb: $35

Guest Cottage: **$45; sleeps 2**
Open: **June 11–Sept. 10**
Reduced Rates: **Weekly**
Breakfast: **Full**
Pets: **Sometimes**
Children: **Yes**
Smoking: **No**
Social Drinking: **Permitted**
Airport/Station Pickup: **Yes**

English-style flower gardens, separate entrances, handmade curtains, and antique decor make this a homey and private place to be. Picnic lunches and a decanter of wine are available. Guests are served a breakfast of home-baked breads, fruit and specialty foods on the garden patio or in their private quarters. Wineries, hot springs, the beach, Hearst Castle, and California Polytechnic University are nearby.

SANTA BARBARA AREA
Educators' Vacation Alternatives
317 PIEDMONT ROAD, SANTA BARBARA, CALIFORNIA 93105

Tel: **(805) 687-2947**
Coordinator: **LaVerne Long**
States/Regions Covered: **U.S., Canada, New Zealand**

Rates (Single/Double):
Modest: **$12–$17 $18**
Average: **$25 $30–$35**
Luxury: **$85 $125**
Credit Cards: **No**

EVA is an acronym for Educators' Vacation Alternatives, which caters exclusively to active or retired professional educators. There are hosts in the U.S. as well as home exchanges. The directory costs $5.50, plus $1 for U.S. postage; $2.50 overseas; you make reservations directly.

Rose Victorian Inn ✪
789 VALLEY ROAD, ARROYO GRANDE, CALIFORNIA 93420

Tel: **(805) 481-5566**
Host(s): **Ross and Diana Cox**
Location: **200 mi. N of Los Angeles**
No. of Rooms: **6**
No. of Private Baths: **1**
Max. No. Sharing Bath: **5**
Double/pb: **$105**
Single/pb: **$90**
Double/sb: **$85**
Single/sb: **$60**
Suites: **$155**

Open: **All year**
Reduced Rates: **Oct. 1–Apr. 30, Sun.–Wed.**
Breakfast: **Full**
Other Meals: **Dinner included**
Credit Cards: **AMEX, MC, VISA**
Pets: **No**
Children: **Welcome, over 16**
Smoking: **No**
Social Drinking: **Permitted**
Airport/Station Pickup: **Yes**

This majestic mansion (circa 1885) is painted four shades of rose and the gardens abound in rose bushes of every hue. An arbor leads to the gazebo which is surrounded by Koi ponds. Each room is decorated with authentic, ornate Victorian pieces. The parlor has an onyx fireplace, pump organ, and a collection of Chinese antiques. Breakfast is served in the family dining room and features such delicacies as eggs Benedict, stuffed croissants, cheese strata or eggs Florentine. It is close to the Oceano Sand Dunes, Hearst Castle, Solvang Danish Village, wineries, and the Pacific.

Bayview House ✪
1070 SANTA LUCIA AVENUE, BAYWOOD PARK, CALIFORNIA 93402

Tel: (805) 528-3098
Host(s): Jack and Frieda Murphy
Location: 15 mi. N of San Luis Obispo
No. of Rooms: 1 suite
Suite: $35–$45
Open: All year
Breakfast: Full

Pets: No
Children: Welcome
Smoking: Permitted
Social Drinking: Permitted
Airport/Station Pickup: Yes
Foreign Languages: Dutch, Indonesian

If you enjoy sunsets from a private deck, a bird sanctuary, lovely flowers, and peaceful tranquillity, you will surely enjoy your stay in this spacious suite with its fully equipped kitchen and dining room. Breakfast features home-baked bread and homemade sausages. It's just a short drive to Hearst Castle, Montana de Oro State Park and Cal. Poly.

D & B Schroeder Ranch ✪
1825 CRAVENS LANE, CARPINTERIA, CALIFORNIA 93013

Tel: (805) 684-1579
Host(s): Don and Beverly Schroeder
Location: 10 mi. E of Santa Barbara
No. of Private Baths: 1
Suites: $45
Open: All year

Breakfast: Continental
Pets: No
Children: Welcome
Smoking: No
Social Drinking: Permitted

This wood-and-glass contemporary beauty is on a ten-acre lemon and avocado ranch and boasts ocean and mountain views. You may pick fruit, play a hand of bridge, or enjoy the use of Bev and Don's spa or bicycles. All the attractions of Santa Barbara are close by. You are welcome to play tennis at the Polo and Racquet Club where the guest fee is $5 per person.

Blue Quail Inn ✪
1908 BATH STREET, SANTA BARBARA, CALIFORNIA 93101

Tel: (805) 687-2300
Best Time to Call: 8 AM–9 PM
Host(s): Jeanise Suding
Location: 100 mi. N of Los Angeles
No. of Rooms: 8
No. of Private Baths: 5
Max. No. Sharing Bath: 4
Double/pb: $58.50–$85
Double/sb: $45–$80
Suites: $54–$80
Guest Cottage: $67.50–$85; sleeps 2–3

Open: All year
Reduced Rates: Weekly; mid-week
Breakfast: Continental
Other Meals: Available
Credit Cards: MC, VISA
Pets: No
Children: Welcome, over 12
Smoking: No
Social Drinking: Permitted
Air/Station Pickup: Yes

The main house is a California-style bungalow and is adjacent to four quaint cottages. Each guest room is decorated with antiques and country charm. Jeanise is most cordial and offers complimentary spiced apple cider each evening. You're welcome to borrow her bikes to tour the beach, Santa Barbara Mission, and other historical landmarks. The University of California is close by.

The Glenborough Inn
1327 BATH STREET, SANTA BARBARA, CALIFORNIA 93101

Tel: (805) 966-0589
Host(s): Pat Hardy and JoAnn Bell
Location: ½ mi. from Rt. 101
No. of Rooms: 8
No. of Private Baths: 4
Max. No. Sharing Bath: 4
Double/pb: $70–$80
Single/pb: $65–$75
Double/sb: $55–$65
Single/sb: $50–$60
Suites: $100–$105

Open: All year
Reduced Rates: 10% off-season, mid-week
Breakfast: Full
Credit Cards: MC, VISA
Pets: No
Children: Welcome, over 12
Smoking: Permitted
Social Drinking: Permitted
Airport/Station Pickup: Yes

The main house of the Glenborough dates back to the turn of the century. All the guest rooms are quiet, romantic, and furnished with antiques. Fresh flowers, quilts, plants, and lace abound. A small Victorian cottage across the street has similar accommodations with private baths and entrances. Feel welcome to stroll the lush gardens and relax in the outdoor hot tub. Breakfast specialties include nutbreads, fresh fruit bowl, cheese blintzes, and specially blended coffee. Enjoy a glass of wine by the fire with your hosts. They will gladly direct you to beaches, shops, the harbor, and mission.

Long's Seaview Bed & Breakfast ◐
317 PIEDMONT ROAD, SANTA BARBARA, CALIFORNIA 93105

Tel: **(805) 687-2947**	Single/sb: **$35**
Best Time to Call: **Before 6 PM**	Open: **All year**
Host(s): **Bob and LaVerne Long**	Reduced Rates: **After 2nd night**
Location: **1½ mi. from Hwy. 101**	Breakfast: **Full**
No. of Rooms: **2**	Other Meals: **Available**
No. of Private Baths: **1**	Pets: **No**
Max. No. Sharing Bath: **4**	Children: **No**
Double/pb: **$48**	Smoking: **No**
Single/pb: **$35**	Social Drinking: **Permitted**
Double/sb: **$45**	Airport/Station Pickup: **Yes**

Overlooking Santa Barbara's prestigious north side, this ranch-style home is in a quiet, residential neighborhood. Breakfast is usually served on the patio where you can see the ocean, Channel Islands, and citrus orchard. Convenient to the beach, Solvang, and Santa Ynes Valley, the large, airy bedrooms are cheerfully furnished, with antiques and brass. You are welcome to use the spa.

Ocean View House ◐
P.O. BOX 20065, SANTA BARBARA, CALIFORNIA 93102

Tel: **(805) 966-6659**	Suites: **$60 for 4**
Best Time to Call: **Before 8 AM, or after 5 PM**	Open: **All year**
	Breakfast: **Continental**
Host(s): **Bill and Carolyn Canfield**	Pets: **Sometimes**
Location: **2 mi. from 101 Fwy.**	Children: **Welcome**
No. of Rooms: **2**	Smoking: **No**
No. of Private Baths: **1**	Social Drinking: **Permitted**
Double/pb: **$40**	Airport/Station Pickup: **Yes**

This California ranch house features a guest room furnished with a queen-size bed and antiques. The adjoining paneled den, with double-bed divan and color TV, is available together with the guest room as a suite. While you relax and sip wine on the patio, you can look out at the sailboats on the ocean. Children will be delighted with the playhouse. It's a short walk to the beach and local shops. Breakfast specialties are apple cake and beer bread served on Lenox china. The University of California at Santa Barbara is nearby.

Laurelwood Inn
232 NORTH 8TH STREET, SANTA PAULA, CALIFORNIA 93060

Tel: **(805) 525-3087**
Host(s): **Eva Paul**
Location: **15 mi. E of Ventura**
No. of Rooms: **2**
No. of Private Baths: **1**
Max. No. Sharing Bath: **3**
Double/pb: **$53.50**
Single/pb: **$43.50**
Double/sb: **$48.15**
Single/sb: **$38.15**

Open: **All year**
Reduced Rates: **15%, weekly**
Breakfast: **Continental**
Other Meals: **Available**
Pets: **No**
Children: **Welcome, over 13**
Smoking: **Permitted**
Social Drinking: **Permitted**
Airport/Station Pickup: **Yes**

This stately Victorian is on a quiet, tree-lined street, set in a picturesque valley of orchards and farms. Eva has decorated with lovely antiques, and lots of plants and flowers from her garden. She looks forward to spoiling you each morning with homemade breads, jams, and fresh-squeezed orange juice. It's only 15 minutes to the Pacific and the Oil Museum. The collection of old planes at the Santa Paula Airport makes for interesting sightseeing.

Solvang Castle Inn
1210 MISSION DRIVE, SOLVANG, CALIFORNIA 93463

Tel: **(805) 688-9338**
Host(s): **Gordon and Arline Heath**
Location: **45 mi. N of Santa Barbara**
No. of Rooms: **40**
No. of Private Baths: **18**
Max. No. Sharing Bath: **4**

Double/pb: **$45-$69**
Single/pb: **$42-$55**
Double/sb: **$32-$48**
Single/sb: **$30-$38**
Suites: **$55-$75**
Open: **All year**

Reduced Rates: **10% midweek, off-season**
Breakfast: **Continental**
Pets: **Sometimes**
Children: **Welcome**
Smoking: **Permitted**
Social Drinking: **Permitted**
Airport/Station Pickup: **Yes**

This romantic Inn is located in Solvang, a Danish village with gas lights, cobbled streets, and windmills. Cross the drawbridge and enter the main hall, with its curved stairway and floral ceilings. The turrets, spires and dormer windows are in keeping with older "royal" style. The guest rooms feature handmade headboards, lace and Danish curtains, and papered walls; some have canopied beds. Your hosts—third-generation innkeepers—serve fresh pastries in a homey breakfast room each morning. Relax in the spa before and after touring local wineries, horse farms, missions, and Lake Cachuma.

Country House Inn
91 MAIN STREET, P.O. BOX 179, TEMPLETON, CALIFORNIA 93465

Tel: **(805) 434-1598**
Host(s): **Barbara and Nick**
Location: **22 mi. N of San Luis Obispo**
No. of Rooms: **7**
Max. No. Sharing Bath: **6**
Double/sb: **$55**
Single/sb: **$35**
Open: **All year**
Reduced Rates: **10%, Dec.–Jan.**
Breakfast: **Continental**
Pets: **No**
Children: **No**
Smoking: **No**
Social Drinking: **Permitted**
Airport/Station Pickup: **Yes**

Step back in time to the warmth of a home built in 1886, a designated historic site. The spacious bedrooms are furnished with queen- and king-size beds and antiques. While you enjoy breakfast, watch the hummingbirds at the window. Walk in the rose-bordered gardens or play the player piano by the fireside. Hearst Castle is about 30 miles away, as are a dozen wineries with tasting rooms. Walk to dinner at one of the town's restaurants, and read about its history on the plaques of the old buildings.

COLORADO

Fort Collins • • Ault
Estes Park • • Greeley
• Longmont
Central City •
• Denver
Aspen •
Green • • Colorado Springs
Mtn Falls
Norwood • • Ouray
• Silverton
Dolores •
• Durango

Bed and Breakfast Colorado ✪
P.O. BOX 20596, DENVER, COLORADO 80220

Tel: **(303) 333-3340**	Rates (Single/Double):
Best Time to Call: **1–6 PM**	Average: $20 $40
Coordinator: **Rick Madden**	Luxury: $40 $60
States/Regions Covered: **Colorado**	Credit Cards: **MC, VISA**

Your home away from home could be a bedroom in an historic mansion overlooking a ski village, an apartment in the heart of Denver, or a small cottage all to yourself. Farm and ranch accommodations are available as well as homes in or near National Parks including Mesa Verde. Major colleges and universities are convenient to many B&Bs. Just mention your interests, hobbies, and other requirements, and Rick will do his best to comply. Send $3 for the descriptive directory.

Bed & Breakfast—Rocky Mountains ☯
P.O. BOX 804, COLORADO SPRINGS, COLORADO 80901

Tel: **(303) 630-3433**	Rates (Single/Double):
Coordinator: **Kate Peterson**	Modest: **$20** **$30**
States/Regions Covered: **Colorado,**	Average: **$30** **$40**
Montana, New Mexico, Wyoming	Luxury: **$95** **$109**
	Credit Cards: **No**

Kate's roster covers the whole gamut, from modest homes to elegant mansions, log cabins to working cattle ranches, ski chalets with beamed ceilings and hot tubs to homes near lakes and rivers. Send $2 with a self-addressed envelope (37-cent postage) for the descriptive directory.

The Copper Horse
P.O. BOX 4948, 328 WEST MAIN STREET, ASPEN, COLORADO 81612

Tel: **(303) 925-7525**	Open: **June 1–Apr. 14**
Host(s): **Tom Grady**	Breakfast: **Full**
No. of Rooms: **13**	Pets: **No**
Max. No. Sharing Bath: **7**	Children: **Welcome**
Double/sb: **$35–$46**	Smoking: **Permitted**
Single/sb: **$18–$23**	Social Drinking: **Permitted**

The Copper Horse used to be a large Victorian home dating back to the 1890s. Today it is a converted old-fashioned ski lodge where guests gather by the fire with wine and hot chocolate after a day on the slopes. Furnished in period pieces, a few rooms are large enough to sleep groups of 4–8. Breakfast specialties include pancakes, French toast, and eggs, and the coffee pot is always on. The house is within walking distance of the lifts, shops, and restaurants. The free Aspen Shuttle and buses to Snowmass and Buttermilk pass by the door.

The Adams House ☯
115 B. STREET, P.O. BOX 512, AULT, COLORADO 80610

Tel: **(303) 834-1587**	No. of Rooms: **1**
Host(s): **Sue and Jim Adams**	No. of Private Baths: **1**
Location: **11 mi. N of Greeley**	Double/pb: **$24**

Single/pb: **$16**
Open: **All year**
Breakfast: **Continental**
Pets: **No**

Children: **Welcome**
Smoking: **No**
Social Drinking: **No**

Sue and Jim offer a restful atmosphere in their 1907 frame house. Summer breakfasts, which feature homemade muffins and garden goodies, are served beneath the yellow umbrella on the patio. A waterfall and pool with rock garden will open your eyes if the coffee doesn't. A city park with tennis courts is just a block away. For cultural activities, the University of Northern Colorado is 12 miles away. The Cheyenne Frontier Days Rodeo is nearby.

Two Ten Casey ✪
BOX 154, 210 CASEY AVENUE, CENTRAL CITY, COLORADO 80427

Tel: **(303) 582-5906**
Best Time to Call: **6 AM–6 PM**
Host(s): **Esther Campbell**
Location: **35 mi. NW of Denver**
No. of Rooms: **1**
No. of Private Baths: **1**
Double/pb: **$30**

Single/pb: **$25**
Open: **Apr. 1–Oct. 31**
Breakfast: **Continental**
Pets: **No**
Children: **Welcome, over 5**
Smoking: **Permitted**
Social Drinking: **Permitted**

The bay windows of this comfortable clapboard cottage overlook Gregory Gulch, where gold was discovered in 1859. Esther, a retired nurse, will be happy to point out the historical sights. She is an experienced hiker and will lead you along the old trails. Area attractions include ski slopes, museums, shops, and restaurants.

Griffin's Hospitality House ✪
4222 NORTH CHESTNUT, COLORADO SPRINGS, COLORADO 80907

Tel: **(303) 599-3035**
Best Time to Call: **Mornings**
Host(s): **John and Diane Griffin**
Location: **5 mi. N of Colorado Springs**
No. of Rooms: **3**
No. of Private Baths: **1**
Max. No. Sharing Bath: **4**
Double/pb: **$35**
Single/pb: **$25**

Double/sb: **$30**
Open: **Closed July 21–Aug. 7**
Reduced Rates: **10%, families**
Breakfast: **Full**
Pets: **No**
Children: **Welcome (crib)**
Smoking: **Permitted**
Social Drinking: **Permitted**
Airport/Station Pickup: **Yes**

The welcome mat is always out at Diane and John's house. It's close to Pike's Peak, the Air Force Academy, and the Garden of the Gods. You can use the picnic table, TV, washing machine, and dryer. You will enjoy a fine view of Pike's Peak while eating the bountiful breakfast. In the evening, you are invited to relax in the living room with wine and good conversation. The University of Colorado is 4 miles away.

The Hearthstone Inn
506 NORTH CASCADE, COLORADO SPRINGS, COLORADO 80903

Tel: **(303) 473-4413**
Host(s): **Dorothy and Ruth Williams**
Location: **4 blocks E of I-25**
No. of Rooms: **25**
No. of Private Baths: **23**
Max. No. Sharing Bath: **2**
Double/pb: **$53–$85**
Single/pb: **$45–$80**
Double/sb: **$40**
Single/sb: **$35**
Suites: **$85**
Open: **All year**
Breakfast: **Full**
Credit Cards: **MC, VISA**
Pets: **No**
Children: **Welcome (crib)**
Smoking: **Permitted**
Social Drinking: **Permitted**

The inn is on a residential boulevard of splendid mansions, only three blocks from Colorado College and close to the city center and public transportation. Every bedroom is special in furnishings or its view. Breakfast may include cheese soufflé with Dijon sauce, hot pumpkin doughnuts and fresh peaches, or perhaps quiche or lemon bread with strawberries. The coffee pot is always on. Pike's Peak, Cave of the Winds, Will Rogers Shrine of the Sun, plus skiing and white-water rafting, are close by.

Four Seasons ✪
1300 MONROE 502, DENVER, COLORADO 80206

Tel: **(303) 393-8294**
Host(s): **Patricia Parks**
Location: **4 mi. from I-70**
No. of Rooms: **1**
No. of Private Baths: **1**
Double/pb: **$45**
Single/pb: **$40**
Open: **All year**
Breakfast: **Continental**
Pets: **Sometimes**
Children: **Welcome, over 12**
Smoking: **Permitted**
Social Drinking: **Permitted**
Airport/Station Pickup: **Yes**

The guest room is done in white wicker with a French provincial theme. Patricia is a walking tour guide for historic Denver and will show you Molly Brown's house and the governor's mansion. It's close to the park, zoo, Botanical Gardens, the mint, museums, and restaurants. In warm weather you'll enjoy having your breakfast on the balcony with a view of snowcapped mountains.

Simon Draw Guest House ○
13980 COUNTY ROAD 29, DOLORES, COLORADO 81323

Tel: **(303) 565-2153**
Host(s): **Richard and Evelyn Wagner**
Location: **4½ mi. from Hwy. 160**
Guest Cottage: **$30–$38; sleeps 2–4**
Open: **Apr.–Oct.**
Reduced Rates: **15%, weekly**

Breakfast: **Full**
Credit Cards: **MC, VISA**
Pets: **Yes**
Children: **Welcome (crib)**
Smoking: **Permitted**
Social Drinking: **Permitted**

This two-story cottage, complete with kitchen, living room, bedroom, and bath, is in the woods on the edge of a small canyon with a stream at the bottom. It contains a double bed and a twin-size couch in the living room. It is a charming home away from home while visiting Mesa Verde National Park.

Wanek's Lodge at Estes ○
P.O. BOX 898, 560 PONDEROSA DRIVE, ESTES PARK, COLORADO 80517

Tel: **(303) 586-5851**
Best Time to Call: **Evenings**
Host(s): **Jim and Pat Wanek**
Location: **71 mi. NW of Denver**
No. of Rooms: **6**
Max. No. Sharing Bath: **6**
Double/sb: **$34**
Single/sb: **$28**

Open: **All year**
Breakfast: **Continental**
Other Meals: **Available**
Pets: **No**
Children: **Welcome**
Smoking: **Permitted**
Social Drinking: **Permitted**

Pat and Jim invite you to share their modern mountain inn, with its wood beams, stone fireplace, old-fashioned hospitality, and gorgeous scenery. The emphasis is on excellent food, lovingly prepared. The Rocky Mountain National Park is minutes away, and boating on Lake Estes is fun. Former educators, the Waneks are people-oriented and warm.

Outlook Lodge ✪
P.O. BOX 5, GREEN MOUNTAIN FALLS, COLORADO 80819

Tel: (303) 684-2303
Best Time to Call: After 7 PM
Host(s): The Ahern Family
Location: 15 mi. W of Colorado Springs
No. of Rooms: 11
No. of Private Baths: 4
Max. No. Sharing Bath: 6
Double/pb: $39
Single/pb: $34

Double/sb: $32
Single/sb: $29
Open: May 27–Sept. 2
Breakfast: Continental
Credit Cards: MC, VISA
Pets: Yes
Children: Welcome (crib)
Smoking: Permitted
Social Drinking: Permitted
Foreign Languages: German, Spanish

This restored Victorian parsonage (1889) is set at the foot of Pike's Peak and is surrounded by pines on property fronted by a creek. The furnishings, stained glass, and rocking chair veranda all add to the feeling of "going to Grandma's." The gracious Aherns invite you to use the kitchen stove, refrigerator, barbecue, and picnic area. Located just a block away from a lake, pool, tennis court, stables, shops, and restaurants, it is also within easy driving of the Garden of the Gods, the Air Force Academy, Colorado College, Royal Gorge, and Cripple Creek.

The Knox Farm ✪
12384 OXFORD ROAD, LONGMONT, COLORADO 80501

Tel: (303) 776-3530
Best Time to Call: 6–9 AM or PM
Host(s): Barbara and Wally Knox
Location: 30 mi. NW of Denver
No. of Rooms: 2
Max. No. Sharing Bath: 6
Double/sb: $45
Single/sb: $35
Open: All year

Reduced Rates: Weekly
Breakfast: Continental
Other Meals: Available
Pets: Sometimes
Children: Welcome
Smoking: No
Social Drinking: Permitted
Airport/Station Pickup: Yes

The farm has a homespun atmosphere that will help urban dwellers to unwind. There is a 150-mile view of the Colorado Rockies, and you can see Long's Peak and Pike's Peak from the property. Barbara and Wally have a collection of fine art done by local artists, and antiques, many of them for sale. You can easily take one-day excursions to Estes Park, Big Thompson Canyon, and Colorado Springs.

The Nippersink ✪
106 SPENCER AVENUE, MANITOU SPRINGS, COLORADO 80829

Tel: **(303) 333-3340**
Host(s): **Larry and Memory Schorr**
Location: **On Hwy. 24**
No. of Rooms: **3**
Max. No. Sharing Bath: **5**
Double/sb: **$40**
Single/sb: **$35**
Open: **All year**
Breakfast: **Continental**
Pets: **No**
Children: **Welcome, over 12**
Smoking: **Permitted**
Social Drinking: **Permitted**

Located at the base of Pike's Peak, this 1885 Victorian house has been restored, and now offers restful and spacious accommodations with turn-of-the-century charm. You will enjoy the many attractions of Colorado Springs, the Air Force Academy, and the Broadmoor. There are many charming shops in the area. You're invited to observe your hosts' hobbies—Larry's photography; Memory's 14-room dollhouse and miniature collection. Complimentary evening sherry is served in the parlor.

Back Narrows Inn ✪
1550 GRAND AVENUE, BOX 156, NORWOOD, COLORADO 81423

Tel: **(303) 327-4417**
Best Time to Call: **11 AM–6 PM**
Host(s): **Joyce and Terre Bucknam**
Location: **125 mi. SE of Grand Junction**
No. of Rooms: **10**
No. of Private Baths: **3**
Max. No. Sharing Bath: **5**
Double/pb: **$27**
Single/pb: **$23**
Double/sb: **$18–$21**
Single/sb: **$16–$18**
Open: **All year**
Breakfast: **Continental**
Other Meals: **Available**
Credit Cards: **MC, VISA**
Pets: **Welcome**
Children: **Welcome**
Smoking: **Permitted**
Social Drinking: **Permitted**

At the edge of the San Juan Mountains, the inn, built in 1880, retains a flavor of the past, with its antique furnishings. The lobby invites relaxation, conversation, darts, and other games. It's 33 miles to historic Telluride town and ski area for winter fun. There's marvelous local cross-country skiing too. Summer diversions are fishing, hiking, gold-panning, and music and film festivals.

Baker's Manor Guest House ✪
317 SECOND STREET, OURAY, COLORADO 81427

Tel: (303) 325-4574	Open: June–Sept.
Best Time to Call: Evening	Reduced Rates: Families; long stays
Host(s): John and Nancy Nixon	Breakfast: Continental
Location: 37 mi. S of Montrose	Pets: No
No. of Rooms: 6	Children: Welcome (crib)
Max. No. Sharing Bath: 12	Smoking: Permitted
Double/sb: $20	Social Drinking: Permitted
Single/sb: $18	

This immaculate 100-year-old home was built in the mining days. Ouray is often called the Switzerland of America since it is 8,000 feet high in the San Juan Mountains. There is a natural hot springs municipal pool and Box Canyon Falls. Popular pastimes are jeeping, backpacking, fishing, and mountain climbing. Delightful restaurants and shops are close by.

The House of Yesteryear ✪
516 OAK STREET, P.O. BOX 440, OURAY, COLORADO 81427

Tel: (303) 325-4277	Single/sb: $26
Host(s): Raymond O'Brien	Open: June 6–Sept. 9
Location: 4 blocks from Hwy. 550	Reduced Rates: 10%, June; families
No. of Rooms: 8	Breakfast: Continental—$1.00
No. of Private Baths: 1	Pets: No
Max. No. Sharing Bath: 5	Children: Welcome (crib)
Double/pb: $35	Smoking: Permitted
Double/sb: $30	Social Drinking: Permitted

Perched on a hill overlooking spectacular scenery, this spotless home is filled with many museum-quality antiques. Each room is individual in decor, an eclectic mix of old and new. Mount Abrams and Bear Creek Falls are nearby. Take a daytime drive on the Million Dollar Highway—the views are breathtaking.

The Alma House ○
220 EAST 10TH STREET, SILVERTON, COLORADO 81433

Tel: **(303) 387-5336**
Host(s): **Don and Jolene Stott**
Location: **50 mi. N of Durango**
No. of Rooms: **10**
Max. No. Sharing Bath: **5**
Double/sb: **$30**
Single/sb: **$30**

Open: **June 20–Sept. 2**
Breakfast: **Continental**
Credit Cards: **MC, VISA**
Pets: **No**
Children: **Welcome**
Smoking: **No**
Social Drinking: **Permitted**

This 1898 stone-and-frame building has been lovingly restored and comfortably updated. Each spacious room has a deluxe queen-size bed, luxurious linens, antique dressers, and special touches. The plumbing in the bathrooms is up-to-date but the brass-and-walnut fixtures are faithful to a day gone by. Don and Jolene have a large video tape library for your evening entertainment. Ride the Durango–Silverton Narrow Gauge Railroad to the Mesa Verde National Park. Silverton retains the flavor of the old Western town it is. The Bent Elbow Saloon, just next door, is fun.

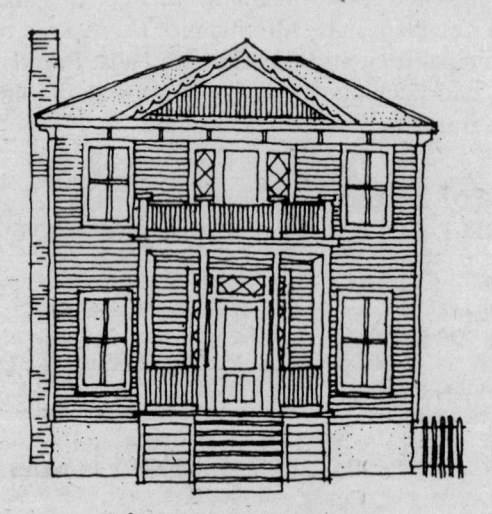

Baker's Manor Guest House

CONNECTICUT

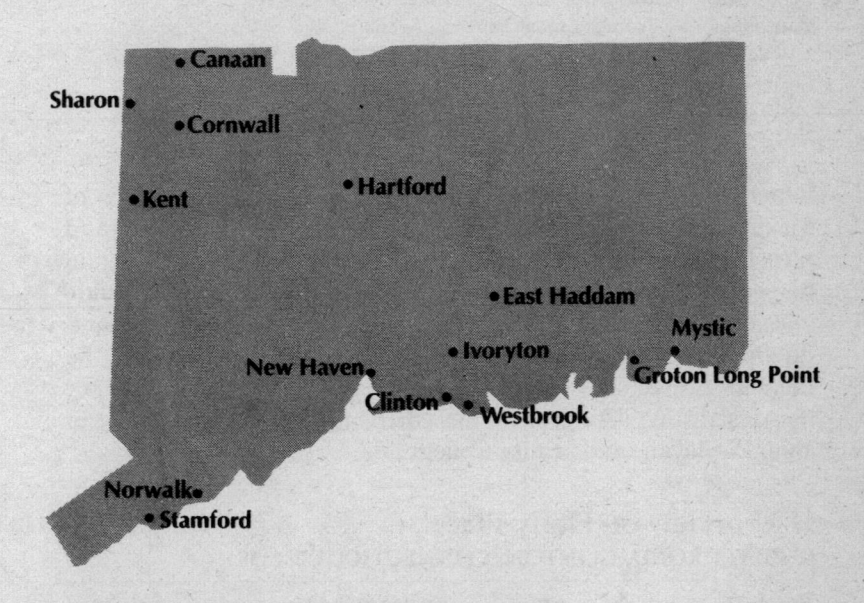

Covered Bridge Bed & Breakfast ✪
WEST CORNWALL, CONNECTICUT 06796

Tel: **(203) 672-6052**
Best Time to Call: **9 AM–7 PM**
Coordinator: **Rae Eastman**
Best Time to Call: **9 AM–7 PM**
States/Regions Covered:
   Connecticut—Canaan, Cornwall, Essex, Lakeville, Kent, Sharon; Massachusetts—Sheffield, Stockbridge, Williamstown

Rates (Single/Double):
   Modest: $30 $35
   Average: $40 $50
   Luxury: $50 $70
Credit Cards: **No**

If you enjoy historic homes, picture-postcard New England scenery, unsurpassed fall foliage, music festivals, theater, antiquing, auto racing, skiing, white-water rafting, or hiking, call Rae. Her host homes are located primarily in the northwest corner of Connecticut, and the Berkshires in western Massachusetts. Williams College and Bennington College are nearby.

Nutmeg Bed & Breakfast
56 FOX CHASE LANE, WEST HARTFORD, CONNECTICUT 06107

Tel: **(203) 236-6698**
Coordinator: **Maxine Kates**
States/Regions Covered: **Connecticut (statewide)**

Rates (Single/Double):
　Modest:　**$35–$40**
　Average:　**$45–$50**
　Luxury:　**$50–$70**
Credit Cards: **MC, VISA**
Minimum Stay: **2 days/holiday weekends**

Experience the Connecticut countryside under the auspices of Maxine, who has selected ideal B&Bs for your comfort and pleasure, spanning every conceivable ambience. You are certain to feel at home as soon as your host greets you. Maxine will guide you to the best the state offers, including cross-country and downhill skiing, brilliant fall foliage, the scenic coastline, the theaters, universities, and antique shops. Send two dollars for her descriptive listing of homes. B&Bs are within easy reach of Yale, Wesleyan, and Trinity College.

Harborview on Holly Place
63 PRATT ROAD, CLINTON, CONNECTICUT 06413

Tel: **(203) 481-0075 Days; (203) 669-5563 Evenings**
Host(s): **Gerald M. and Jill Ann Walthall**
Location: **20 mi. E of New Haven**
No. of Rooms: **3**
Max. No. Sharing Bath: **6**
Double/sb: **$75**
Single/sb: **$50**

Suites: **$60–$75**
Open: **All year**
Breakfast: **Continental**
Other Meals: **Available**
Pets: **Sometimes**
Children: **Welcome, over 12**
Smoking: **No**
Social Drinking: **Permitted**
Airport/Station Pickup: **Yes**

This Queen Anne Victorian dates back to 1896. It is a mansion with turrets and tower, porches and cozy fireplaces, plus parquet floors, French chandeliers and antiques. The house is next to Hammonasset State Park and a 10-minute walk from the water. It's an easy drive to Mystic, Essex, and New London. After a day of touring, all are invited to relax at the swimming pool. An antique car livery service is available (a Jaguar and a Rolls-Royce).

Bishopsgate Inn
GOODSPEED LANDING, EAST HADDAM, CONNECTICUT 06423

Tel: **(203) 873-1677**
Host(s): **Julie Bishop**
Location: **15 mi. from Rt. 95**
No. of Rooms: **6**
No. of Private Baths: **4**
Max. No. Sharing Bath: **4**
Double/pb: **$65**
Single/pb: **$40**
Double/sb: **$60**
Single/sb: **$40**
Suites: **$85**
Open: **All year**
Breakfast: **Continental**
Pets: **No**
Children: **Welcome, over 6**
Smoking: **Permitted**
Social Drinking: **Permitted**
Airport/Station Pickup: **Yes**

Bishopsgate was built on beautiful grounds in 1818. The guest rooms have brass plates on the doors that describe their personalities—The Rose Room, The Jenny Lind, named for its spool bed and fishnet canopy. Larger rooms have fireplaces; all contain antiques and heirlooms. Throughout the house there are bits of memorabilia from the famous Goodspeed Opera House, within walking distance. Fresh fruit and scones are served each morning at a harvest table in the fireplaced kitchen-dining room. Nearby attractions include fine shops, restaurants, river cruises, and historic tours.

Shore Inne ✪
54 EAST SHORE ROAD, GROTON LONG POINT, CONNECTICUT 06340

Tel: **(203) 536-1180**
Best Time to Call: **8 AM–8 PM**
Host(s): **Helen Ellison**
Location: **3½ mi. W of Mystic**
No. of Rooms: **7**
No. of Private Baths: **3**
Max. No. Sharing Bath: **2**
Double/pb: **$45**
Single/pb: **$43**
Double/sb: **$39**
Single/sb: **$37**
Open: **Apr.–Oct.**

Reduced Rates: **20%, April, May**
Breakfast: **Continental**
Credit Cards: **MC, VISA**
Pets: **No**

Children: **Welcome**
Smoking: **Permitted**
Social Drinking: **Permitted**

Capturing the charm of the Connecticut coast, the inn's gracious rooms command water views. It is within a few miles of Mystic Seaport, the Marine Life Aquarium, Fort Griswold, and the U.S. Submarine Base and Memorial. Connecticut College and the U.S. Coast Guard Academy are close by. Swimming, fishing, biking, and tennis are a few steps from the door, and harbor and day cruises are available. Helen encourages you to enjoy the TV, library, and sun-rooms.

Ivoryton Inn ✪
MAIN STREET, IVORYTON, CONNECTICUT 06442

Tel: **(203) 767-0422**
Best Time to Call: **9 AM–3 PM**
Host(s): **Jean and Doug Neumann**
Location: **30 mi. S of Hartford**
No. of Rooms: **28**
No. of Private Baths: **28**
Double/pb: **$52–$65**
Single/pb: **$47–$60**

Open: **All year**
Reduced Rates: **Available**
Breakfast: **Continental**
Credit Cards: **AMEX, MC, VISA**
Pets: **No**
Childen: **No**
Smoking: **Permitted**
Social Drinking: **Permitted**

The inn takes its name from the days back in 1800 when the ivory trade prospered here. It has a tap room with bar and fireplace, and a living room for relaxing. Many outstanding restaurants, the Ivoryton Playhouse, and historic Essex waterfront are all close by.

Comolli's Guest House ✪
36 BRUGGEMAN PLACE, MYSTIC, CONNECTICUT 06355

Tel: **(203) 536-8723**
Best Time to Call: **8–9 PM**
Host(s): **Dorothy M. Comolli**
Location: **Between Rtes. 1 & 27**
No. of Rooms: **2**
Max. No. Sharing Bath: **3**
Double/sb: **$50**
Single/sb: **$45**

Open: **All year**
Breakfast: **No**
Pets: **No**
Children: **No**
Smoking: **Permitted**
Social Drinking: **Permitted**
Airport/Station Pickup: **Yes**

Welcoming vacationers touring historic Mystic or the business person who desires a homey respite while traveling. Dorothy caters to discriminating, mature singles. Her immaculate home is on a quiet hill convenient to Olde Mistick Village. She will be delighted to provide tips on sightseeing, sporting activities, and nearby eating places where you'll get the best value for your money.

1833 House ✪
33 GREENMANVILLE AVENUE, MYSTIC, CONNECTICUT 06355

Tel: **(203) 572-0633**
Best Time to Call: **10 AM–Noon**
Host(s): **Joan Smith**
Location: **10 mi. E of New London**
No. of Rooms: **5**
No. of Private Baths: **2**
Max. No. Sharing Bath: **3**
Double/pb: **$44–$48**
Single/pb: **$36**
Double/sb: **$40**

Single/sb: **$22**
Suites: **$48–$60**
Open: **All year**
Reduced Rates: **Nov. 1–Apr.1**
Breakfast: **Continental**
Pets: **Welcome**
Children: **Welcome (crib)**
Smoking: **Permitted**
Social Drinking: **Permitted**
Airport/Station Pickup: **Yes**

This house is right at the entrance of the world-famous Seaport Museum of Mystic. From Joan's backyard and some of the bedrooms, you can glimpse the tall ships. At the 1833, you will find the atmosphere of old New England in everything. During your stay, you will want to visit the Seaport, the Aquarium, and Old Mistick Village. Joan will be happy to watch the family dog while you take in the sights.

The Pentway House ✪
ONE BROADWAY, MYSTIC, CONNECTICUT 06355

Tel: **(203) 536-1716**
Host(s): **Paula Norberg**
Location: **1 mi. from I-95**
No. of Rooms: **5**
No. of Private Baths: **2**
Max. No. Sharing Bath: **4**
Double/pb: **$50**
Single/pb: **$50**
Double/sb: **$45**

Single/sb: **$45**
Suites: **$85 (2-bedroom family unit)**
Open: **June–Sept.**
Breakfast: **No**
Pets: **Sometimes**
Children: **Welcome**
Smoking: **No**
Social Drinking: **Permitted**

Enjoy the nautical charm of Mystic and relax at this comfortable home located a few blocks from the seaport. Use the cable TV or cool off in the huge swimming pool, with a diving board and water slide, in the backyard. The bedrooms are newly furnished in dark pine. Paula's an experienced motel manager so expect all the necessary comforts teamed with special hospitality. The U.S. Coast Guard Academy and famous restaurants are nearby.

River Lodge & Boat Haven ○
25 SCHOOL STREET, WEST MYSTIC, CONNECTICUT 06388

Tel: **(203) 536-7296**
Host(s): **Arlene Baker**
Location: **10 mi. E of New London**
No. of Rooms: **6**
Max. No. Sharing Bath: **4**
Double/sb: **$55–$60**
Single/sb: **$45–$50**
Open: **All year**
Reduced Rates: **Off-season; weekly**
Breakfast: **Continental**
Credit Cards: **MC, VISA**
Pets: **No**
Children: **Welcome, over 3**
Smoking: **Permitted**
Social Drinking: **Permitted**

Arlene welcomes you to her small, restored 1889 hotel directly on the west bank of the Mystic River and less than a mile from downtown. Enjoy the homelike atmosphere in your comfortable, individually decorated room. Have your morning coffee in the yard or on the deck as you watch the tall ships go by. If you want to drop anchor in your own boat, you can dock right outside.

Captain Stannard House ○
138 SOUTH MAIN STREET, WESTBROOK, CONNECTICUT 06498

Tel: **(203) 399-7565**
Best Time to Call: **Evenings**
Host(s): **Al and Betty Barnett**
Location: **25 mi. E of New Haven**
No. of Rooms: **6**
No. of Private Baths: **6**
Double/pb: **$55**
Single/pb: **$50**
Open: **All year**
Breakfast: **Continental**
Credit Cards: **AMEX, MC, VISA**
Pets: **No**
Children: **Welcome, over 6**
Smoking: **Permitted**
Social Drinking: **Permitted**
Airport/Station Pickup: **Yes**

This Georgian Federal house with its fan window is the former home of a sea captain. Recapture the charm of yesteryear when you register in the country-store atmosphere. Play croquet or horseshoes, relax with a book, or browse through the on-premises antique shop. The village and the beach are close by. It is convenient to Mystic Seaport, Goodspeed Opera House, river cruises, fine restaurants, and charming shops. The U.S. Coast Guard Academy, Yale, and Wesleyan are nearby.

Shore Inne

DELAWARE

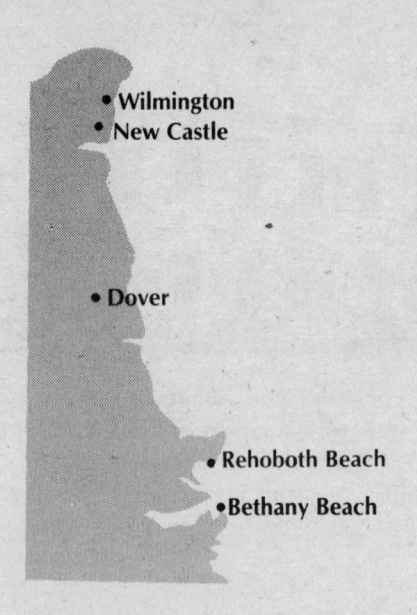

- Wilmington
- New Castle
- Dover
- Rehoboth Beach
- Bethany Beach

Bed & Breakfast of Delaware ✪
1804 BREEN LANE, WILMINGTON, DELAWARE 19810

Tel: (302) 475-2738
Best Time to Call: 3–6 PM
Coordinator: **Barbara Rogers**
States/Regions Covered:
  Delaware—Statewide;
  Maryland—Elkton;
  Pennsylvania—Chadds Ford

Rates (Single/Double):
  Modest: $18 $30
  Average: $25 $40
  Luxury: $30 $45
Credit Cards: No

Barbara's host homes are within easy reach of Philadelphia, the Pennsylvania Amish country, Annapolis, Chesapeake Bay, as well as the many historic and beautiful tourist regions within Delaware. They are convenient to historic and artistic communities, and all the accommodations have private baths. The University of Delaware, Widener University, Neumann College, and Delaware State College are conveniently located to many B&Bs in the area.

The Sand Box & Sea-Vista Villas ✪
BOX 62, BETHANY BEACH, DELAWARE 19930

Tel: **(302) 539-3354 or (202) 223-0322**	Single/pb: **$40**
Best Time to Call: **9 AM–5 PM**	Open: **May 15–Oct. 31**
Host(s): **Dale M. Duvall**	Breakfast: **Full**
Location: **½ mi. from Rte. 1**	Pets: **Sometimes**
No. of Rooms: **3**	Children: **Welcome at The Sand Box**
No. of Private Baths: **3**	Smoking: **Permitted**
Double/pb: **$45–$50**	Social Drinking: **Permitted**

Your cosmopolitan and most cordial host has two villas in a lovely wooded setting near Rehoboth Beach and Ocean City, Maryland. Guests will find the tennis court, swimming pool, terrace, and superb beach fine therapy after an urban winter. The Sandbox has two double bedrooms with baths, a deluxe kitchen, and a fireplace for chilly times. The Sea Vista features a double bedroom and bath. Dale offers Happy Hour on the house.

Biddles Bed and Breakfast ✪
101 WYOMING AVENUE, DOVER, DELAWARE 19901

Tel: **(302) 736-1570**	Single/sb: **$26**
Best Time to Call: **4–9 PM**	Open: **All year**
Host(s): **Millard and Hattye Mae Biddle**	Breakfast: **Continental**
	Pets: **No**
Location: **½ mi. from US 13**	Children: **No**
No. of Rooms: **3**	Smoking: **Permitted**
Max. No. Sharing Bath: **3**	Social Drinking: **Permitted**
Double/sb: **$30**	

At Biddles you will find old-fashioned hospitality in a contemporary setting. The guest rooms of this white frame house have been recently redecorated, with comfortable furnishings and special touches, such as fruit and mints. Breakfast features hot homemade muffins and biscuits. Your hosts will do all they can to make your stay in the capital city enjoyable. It's a short walk to the sights of the historic district. The beaches are 40 miles away. Dover Air Force Base is nearby.

William Penn Guest House ✪
206 DELAWARE STREET, NEW CASTLE, DELAWARE 19720

Tel: **(302) 328-7736**
Best Time to Call: **Early AM, or after 5 PM**
Host(s): **Mr. and Mrs. Richard Burwell**
Location: **1 mi. from Rte. 13**
No. of Rooms: **4**
Max. No. Sharing Bath: **4**
Double/sb: **$30**
Single/sb: **$30**
Open: **All year**
Breakfast: **No**
Pets: **No**
Children: **Welcome**
Smoking: **Permitted**
Social Drinking: **Permitted**
Foreign Languages: **Italian**

If you're a history buff, perhaps a stay in a 1682 house named for William Penn is what you've been seeking. Located in the heart of New Castle's historic district, the accommodations here are most comfortable. A lovely park for strolling and for the children to play in borders the Delaware shore, just two blocks away. The University of Delaware is 15 minutes from the house.

Beach House Bedroom ✪
BOX 138, REHOBOTH BEACH, DELAWARE 19971

Tel: **(302) 227-0937**
Best Time to Call: **8 AM, or after 5 PM**
Host(s): **Sally DeBelles**
Location: **125 mi. E of Washington, D.C.**
No. of Rooms: **2**
No. of Private Baths: **1**
Max. No. Sharing Bath: **4**
Double/pb: **$40**
Single/pb: **$40**
Double/sb: **$35**
Single/sb: **$35**
Open: **May–Sept.**
Reduced Rates: **10%, June, Sept.**
Breakfast: **Continental**
Pets: **No**
Children: **No**
Smoking: **Permitted**
Social Drinking: **Permitted**

This is a modern, tree-shaded beach cottage, with a screened-in porch made for relaxing. The beach is two blocks away, and tennis and sailing are nearby. The atmosphere is casual. It's just a bike ride away from great restaurants, shops, and the boardwalk. Minimum stay is two days; three days for holiday weekends.

DISTRICT OF COLUMBIA

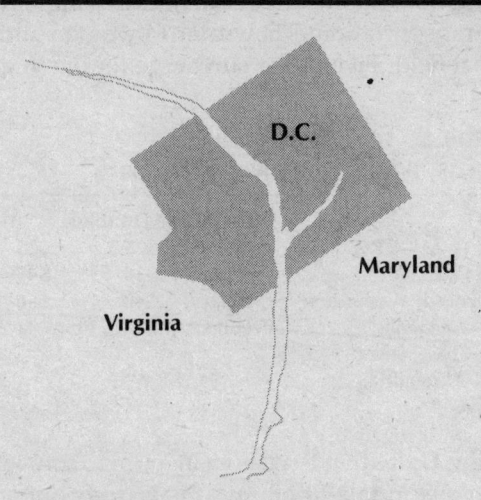

The Bed & Breakfast League, Ltd.
2855 29TH STREET, N.W., WASHINGTON, D.C. 20008

Tel: (202) 232-8718
Coordinator: **Diana Chapin MacLeish**
States/Regions Covered: **Washington, D.C.; U.S.A; England; France; New Zealand**

Rates (Single/Double):
  Average: $35–$45 $40–$80
Credit Cards: **AMEX, MC, VISA**

This is a full service B&B booking agency representing hosts in the United States and overseas. Airline tickets, car rentals, and foreign payments for booking abroad can be arranged for you.

Bed 'n' Breakfast Ltd. of Washington, D.C. ✪
P.O. BOX 12011, WASHINGTON, D.C. 20005

Tel: (202) 328-3510
Coordinators: **Mila Brooks, Jackie Reed**
States/Regions Covered: **Washington, D.C., Virginia and Maryland suburbs**

Rates (Single/Double):
  Modest: $30 $40
  Average: $35 $42–$45
  Luxury: $40–$50 $50–$65
Credit Cards: **No**

This service boasts a network of homes in the city's historic districts. Jackie and Mila have been on the Washington scene a long time, and they know that the best places need not cost the most. Several of their accommodations are located in gracious Georgetown and on Dupont Circle. All of the homes are convenient to public transportation. They cater to women and those in the international field. Five-dollar surcharge for one-night stay.

Sweet Dreams & Toast, Inc.
P.O. BOX 4835-0035, WASHINGTON, D.C. 20008

Tel: **(202) 483-9191**	Rates (Single/Double):
Best Time to Call: **11 AM–6 PM**	Modest: **$25** **$35**
Coordinator: **Ellie Chastain**	Average: **$30–$35** **$45**
States/Regions Covered: **Washington, D.C.; Maryland—Annapolis, Bethesda, Chevy Chase, Silver Spring; Virginia—Alexandria, Arlington, McLean**	Luxury: **$40** **$60**
	Credit Cards: **MC, VISA**

The capital of the United States is awe-inspiring. You will want to spend several days to take it all in. This is your opportunity to watch history in the making and to visit the glorious monuments erected to memorialize those who shaped America's history. Ellie's hosts will direct you to restaurants and special shops that are off the beaten tourist track, where you get the best values.

Adams Inn ✪
1744 LANIER PLACE NORTH WEST, WASHINGTON, D.C. 20009

Tel: **(202) 745-3600**	Open: **All year**
Host(s): **Gene and Nancy Thompson**	Reduced Rates: **Weekly, Nov. 1–Mar. 31**
No. of Rooms: **11**	
No. of Private Baths: **5**	Breakfast: **Continental**
Max. No. Sharing Bath: **6**	Credit Cards: **AMEX, MC, VISA**
Double/pb: **$40–$45**	Pets: **No**
Single/pb: **$35–$40**	Children: **Welcome (crib)**
Double/sb: **$30–$40**	Smoking: **No**
Single/sb: **$25–$35**	Social Drinking: **Permitted**
Guest Cottage: **$60–$75; sleeps 2–4**	

This turn-of-the-century town house is two blocks from the White House. It is located in a diverse, historic neighborhood, home to many diplomats and government workers. The rooms are furnished simply, and a library and parlor are available. Your hosts invite you to have a cup of coffee or tea anytime. They will gladly direct you to international restaurants, shops, and sightseeing of all kinds.

Kalorama Guest House ✪
1854 MINTWOOD PLACE, N.W., WASHINGTON, D.C. 20009

Tel: **(202) 667-6369**
Best Time to Call: **10 AM–4 PM**
Host(s): **Roberta Pieczenik, James Mench**
No. of Rooms: **22**
No. of Private Baths: **5**
Max. No. Sharing Bath: **3**
Double/pb: **$55–$65**
Single/pb: **$50–$60**
Double/sb: **$38–$48**
Single/sb: **$30–$40**
Suites: **$65 up**
Open: **All year**
Reduced Rates: **7th night free**
Breakfast: **Continental**
Credit Cards: **AMEX, MC, VISA, DC**
Pets: **No**
Children: **Welcome**
Smoking: **Permitted**
Social Drinking: **Permitted**

Located in the fashionable downtown embassy district, this Victorian town house maintains the ambience of its era. Guests enjoy breakfast in the dining room, and go to the upstairs parlor for sherry in the afternoon. The guest rooms are inviting and gracious, with brass headboards, plush comforters, Oriental carpets, and wing chairs. Jim is an actor; Roberta is a criminologist. Rely on their making your stay comfortable.

Meg's International Guest House ✪
1315 EUCLID STREET, N.W., WASHINGTON, D.C. 20009

Tel: **(202) 232-5837**
Best Time to Call: **1 PM–10 PM**
Host(s): **Sosena Yirga**
No. of Rooms: **5**
Max. No. Sharing Bath: **3**

Double/sb: **$35**
Single/sb: **$18**
Suites: **$60**
Open: **All year**
Reduced Rates: **Seniors; professors**

Breakfast: **Continental**
Pets: **No**
Children: **Welcome**
Smoking: **Permitted**

Social Drinking: **Permitted**
Airport/Station Pickup: **Yes**
Foreign Languages: **Amharic, French**

Located on one of the highest points in the city, there's a panoramic view of Washington's most notable monuments just down the street. The house is a four-story Victorian, built in 1894, with an enclosed front yard, porches, and fireplaces in two of the bedrooms. An apartment with cooking facilities on the first floor is especially nice for families. It is just 20 blocks from the White House, within walking distance of the city's international district with its scores of ethnic restaurants and shops.

The New Manse ✪
1415 Q STREET N.W., WASHINGTON, D.C. 20009

Tel: **(202) 232-9150**
Host(s): **Mila Brooks and Holly Van Fleet**
No. of Rooms: **3**
No. of Private Baths: **1**
Max. No. Sharing Bath: **3**
Double/sb: **$40**
Single/sb: **$33**

Suites: **$38–$45**
Open: **All year**
Breakfast: **Continental**
Pets: **Sometimes**
Children: **Welcome, over 8**
Smoking: **Permitted**
Social Drinking: **Permitted**
Foreign Languages: **Spanish**

Conveniently located, this is 12 blocks from the White House and five blocks from DuPont Circle, attractively furnished in an eclectic blend of Latin-American art and antiques. The bedrooms have television and telephones. Mila and Holly have both lived in South America and are now consultants to the State Department and the Agency for International Development. Wine and cheese is their way of saying, "We're so glad you're here."

The Reeds ✪
1310 Q STREET, N.W., WASHINGTON, D.C. 20009

Tel: **(202) 328-3510**
Best Time to Call: **9 AM–5 PM**
Host(s): **Charles and Jackie Reed**
No. of Rooms: **6**
Max. No. Sharing Bath: **4**

Double/sb: **$50–$55**
Single/sb: **$30–$40**
Open: **All year**
Breakfast: **Continental**
Pets: **Sometimes**

Children: **Welcome** Social Drinking: **Permitted**
Smoking: **Permitted** Foreign Languages: **French**

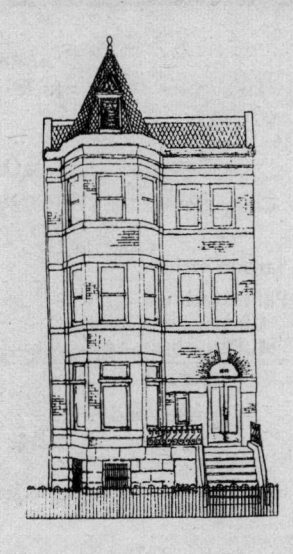

This 100-year-old Victorian mansion boasts landscaped gardens, a terrace, and a fountain. The interior features original wood paneling, elaborate oak staircases, nine fireplaces, ornate mantels as well as Art Nouveau antiques, and is centrally air-conditioned in summer. Adjoining the Logan Circle Historic District, is only 10 blocks from the White House. Charles is a senior partner with a prominent law firm; Jackie is an interior designer who was taught breakfast pastry-making by Nancy and Ronnie's chef!

FLORIDA

A & A Bed & Breakfast of Florida, Inc.
P.O. BOX 1316, WINTER PARK, FLORIDA 32790

Tel: (305) 628-3233
Best Time to Call: 9 AM–6 PM
Coordinator: **Brunhilde (Bruni) Fehner**
States/Regions Covered: **Orlando area**—Disney World, Epcot, Cape Kennedy, Sea World, Altamante Springs, Winter Park, Maitland, New Smyrna Beach

Rates (Single/Double):
Modest: $20 $30
Average: $25 $36–$50
Luxury: $40 $50–$65
Credit Cards: No
Minimum Stay: **2 nights**

You should allow several days to really savor all this area has to offer. Bruni's hosts will suggest hints on getting the most out of the major attractions, wonderful un-touristy restaurants, and tips on where to shop for unique gifts to take home. All of her homes have a certain "touch of class" to make you delighted with your visit. Rollins College is close by.

Bed & Breakfast Co. ◐
P.O. BOX 262, SOUTH MIAMI, FLORIDA 33243

Tel: (305) 661-3270
Coordinator: **Marcella Schaible**
States/Regions Covered: **Boca Raton, Key Biscayne, Ft. Lauderdale, Hollywood, Jupiter, Lakeland, Miami Beach, Palm Beach, The Keys**

Rates (Single/Double):
Modest: $20–$28 $28–$32
Average: $28–$40 $40–$45
Luxury: $38–$54 $54–$65
Credit Cards: **No**

Marcella's roster includes a restored Art Deco mansion on Biscayne Bay, a suite in Palm Beach a few steps from the ocean, a 59-foot Hatteras yacht, a studio room in chic Coconut Grove, and a secluded tree house on the ocean in the Keys. Accommodations to suit all budgets, with or without swimming pools, hot tubs, spas, but all with comfortable furniture and traditional hospitality. Many are convenient to the University of Miami, Barry College, and the University of South Florida. Discount tickets are provided to many attractions.

B&B Suncoast Accommodations
8690 GULF BOULEVARD, ST. PETERSBURG BEACH ISLAND, FLORIDA 33706

Tel: (813) 360-1753
Coordinator: **Ron and Danie Bernard**
State/Regions Covered: **Bonita Springs, Clearwater, Bellair, Ramrod Key, Sarasota, Tarpon**

Rates (Single/Double):
Modest: $25 $30
Average: $30 $35–$45
Luxury: $35 $46–$75

Florida, the land of sunshine, has always been a vacationer's dream. You can turn dreams into reality because Ron and Danie are specializing in accommodations on the west coast and in Orlando. The above rates quoted are the in-season (December–May) rates. Off-season rates are greatly reduced. There is a two-night minimum stay required except in the St. Petersburg Beach area.

Bed & Breakfast of the Florida Keys and East Coast ☉
5 MAN-O-WAR DRIVE, P.O. BOX 1373, MARATHON, FLORIDA 33050

Tel: (305) 743-4118	Rates (Single/Double):
Coordinator: **Joan E. Hopp**	Modest: $25 $30
States/Regions Covered: **Islamorada, Key Largo, Key West, Marathon, Delray, Palm and Vero Beach**	Average: $30 $40
	Luxury: $45 $90
	Credit Cards: **No**

Joan arranges placement in private homes, apartments, or condominiums with hospitable hosts who will share their knowledge of the best places to eat, where to find boat rentals, where to scuba dive or snorkel, and where the best seashells can be found. July 1–October 15 please call (201) 223-5979.

Florida & England Bed & Breakfast ☉
P.O. BOX 12, PALM HARBOR, FLORIDA 33563

Tel: (813) 784-5118	Rates (Single/Double):
Best Time to Call: **9 AM–6 PM**	Modest: $22 $28
Coordinator: **Carol J. Hart**	Average: $24 $35
State/Regions Covered: **Bradenton, Clearwater, Dunedin, Largo, Orlando, St. Petersburg, Sarasota, Tampa**	Luxury: $30 $50
	Credit Cards: **No**
	Minimum Stay: **2 days**

Carol's roster includes only gracious hosts who provide the best in hospitality and breakfast too! The homes are beautifully furnished and many have private swimming pools. The Gulf of Mexico, with its miles of beaches, golf courses, tennis, and water sports, is convenient to all the homes, as are the University of South Florida and the University of Tampa. Her directory is $3.

Quail's Nest ☉
260 BUTTERCUP CIRCLE, ALTAMONTE SPRINGS, FLORIDA 32714

Tel: (305) 788-6112	No. of Private Baths: **1**
Host(s): **Bubs Quail**	Double/pb: **$45**
Location: **4 mi. N of Orlando**	Single/pb: **$35**
No. of Rooms: **1**	Open: **All year**

Reduced Rates: **10% June 1–Nov. 30**
Breakfast: **Full**
Pets: **Sometimes**

Children: **No**
Smoking: **Permitted**
Social Drinking: **Permitted**

Guests rave about this Florida gem, located in an exclusive residential area, convenient to the elegant shops of Winter Park and the fun and excitement of Epcot and Disney World. Shrubbed gardens surround this contemporary home; the pool is set amid orange trees and tropical plants. Inside, sunny colors complement the lovely furnishings. A hearty breakfast is beautifully served in the cheery kitchen, often including home-baked goodies.

1735 House ✪
584 SOUTH FLETCHER, AMELIA ISLAND, FLORIDA 32034

Tel: **(904) 261-5878**
Best Time to Call: **9 AM–5 PM**
Host(s): **David and Susan Caples**
Location: **35 mi. NE of Jacksonville**
No. of Rooms: **5**
No. of Private Baths: **5**
Double/pb: **$55**
Single/pb: **$45**
Guest Cottage: **$85–$115; sleeps up to 6**

Open: **All year**
Reduced Rates: **5%, seniors; families**
Breakfast: **Continental**
Credit Cards: **AMEX, MC, VISA**
Pets: **No**
Children: **Welcome**
Smoking: **Permitted**
Social Drinking: **Permitted**
Airport/Station Pickup: **Yes**

This quaint country inn is situated on the beach of beautiful Amelia Island. The house is furnished with wicker and rattan, and the bedrooms have interesting antiques. David and Susan allow you to use the kitchen for light snacks, and supply bags so you can take home your seashell collection. There's surf-casting right on the beach, and deep-sea fishing or boat charters can be arranged. Don't miss the private tour of Greyfield Inn.

The Barnacle ✪
ROUTE 1, BOX 780 A, LONG BEACH ROAD, BIG PINE KEY, FLORIDA 33043

Tel: **(305) 872-3298**
Best Time to Call: **Before 9 PM**
Host(s): **Wood and Joan Cornell**
Location: **33 mi. E of Key West**

No. of Rooms: **4**
No. of Private Baths: **4**
Double/pb: **$40–$50**
Guest Cottage: **$60; sleeps 2**

Open: **All year**
Breakfast: **Full**
Pets: **No**
Children: **No**

Smoking: **Permitted**
Social Drinking: **Permitted**
Foreign Languages: **French**

GUESTHOUSE

The ultimate in privacy is the self-contained cottage—a tropical tree house with stained glass windows and private terrace. The main house guest room has an ocean view and overlooks the atrium, hot tub, and lush plants; two mini-apartments have private entrances and kitchenette. Every detail in and around their home reflects Wood and Joan's taste, attention to detail, and artistic flair. The structure was built to frame their outstanding collection of statuary, tapestries, and art. Their emphasis is on the sun and sea, with warm hospitality offered in abundance. You can scuba dive or fish right off "your own" beach. Bahia Honda State Park and Key West are close by.

Bed & Breakfast-on-the-Ocean ✪
P.O. BOX 378, BIG PINE KEY, FLORIDA 33043

Tel: (305) 872-2878
Best Time to Call: **10 AM–4 PM**
Host(s): **Jon and Kathleen Threlkeld**
Location: **1½ mi. from US 1**
No. of Rooms: **3**
No. of Private Baths: **2**
Maximum No. Sharing Bath: **4**
Double/pb: **$45**
Single/pb: **$40**

Double/sb: **$45**
Single/sb: **$40**
Open: **All year**
Breakfast: **Full**
Pets: **No**
Children: **No**
Smoking: **Permitted**
Social Drinking: **Permitted**

This spectacular, Spanish-style home facing the water was custom-designed to suit the natural beauty of the Keys. The large landscaped garden patio is where you'll enjoy Jon and Kathleen's bountiful breakfast. It is also the site of the hot tub/Jacuzzi for relaxing by day or under a moonlit sky. The large and airy guest rooms are comfortably cooled by Bahama fans. Key deer and birds abound. You'll enjoy swimming, fishing, snorkeling, bicycling, and jogging. A welcoming cocktail begins your pleasant stay.

Banyan House ✪
624 FONTANA LANE, BRADENTON, FLORIDA 33529

Tel: (813) 746-8633
Best Time to Call: **Before 8 AM, after 5 PM**
Host(s): **Sally DeBelles**
Location: **30 mi. S of St. Petersburg**
No. of Rooms: 1
No. of Private Baths: 1
Double/pb: $35
Single/pb: $35
Guest Cottage: **$55; sleeps 2**
Open: **Nov.–May**
Reduced Rates: **10–15% off-season; seniors; weekly**
Breakfast: **Continental**
Pets: **Sometimes**
Children: **No**
Smoking: **Permitted**
Social Drinking: **Permitted**

Sun yourself on the whitest sand, swim in the Gulf of Mexico, play tennis or golf, then return to Sally's home. The separate guest house shares a terrace with the main house; while the bedroom and private bath are in the main house. The guest house has light cooking facilities. The Ringling Museum, Sarasota, Busch Gardens, and Tampa are nearby.

Island Hotel
P.O. BOX 460, 2ND AND B STREETS, CEDAR KEY, FLORIDA 32625

Tel: **(904) 543-5111**
Best Time to Call: **9 AM–5 PM**
Host(s): **Marcia Rogers**
Location: **60 mi. W of Gainesville**
No. of Rooms: **10**
No. of Private Baths: **3**
Max. No. Sharing Bath: **4**
Double/pb: **$50**
Single/pb: **$50**
Double/sb: **$35–$40**
Single/sb: **$35–$40**
Open: **Feb. 1–Dec. 16**
Reduced Rates: **Weekly**
Breakfast: **$2.50 and up**
Other Meals: **Available**
Pets: **No**
Children: **Welcome**
Smoking: **Permitted**
Social Drinking: **Permitted**
Airport/Station Pickup: **Yes**

The exterior of this historic landmark (circa 1850) is covered with tabley, made from crushed oyster shell and limestone. The atmosphere, with ceiling fans, potbelly stove, and Chistopher, the resident parrot, will bring Casablanca to mind. French doors lead to the dining veranda, and classical music fills the air. Antiques, fresh flowers, oak rockers, and a hammock are there for you. The four-star gourmet dining room on the premises will impress you. Marcia will do everything she can to assure you a memorable stay in this sleepy fishing village.

Bed & Breakfast of Tampa Bay ✪
3234 TERN WAY, FEATHERSOUND, CLEARWATER, FLORIDA 33520

Tel: **(813) 576-5825**
Best Time to Call: **Before 10 AM, after 6 PM**
Host(s): **Vivian and David Grimm**
Location: **7 mi. W of Tampa**
No. of Rooms: **3**
No. of Private Baths: **1**
Max. No. Sharing Bath: **4**
Double/pb: **$30**
Single/pb: **$20**
Double/sb: **$25**
Single/sb: **$15**
Open: **All year**
Breakfast: **Full**
Pets: **Sometimes**
Children: **Welcome**
Smoking: **Permitted**
Social Drinking: **Permitted**
Airport/Station Pickup: **Yes**

The lovely gardens of this fine stucco home have an Oriental flair, and the interior is graced with fine Oriental and European art. Whenever Vivian and David travel, they bring home souvenirs to enhance their decor. Busch Gardens, St. Petersburg Fine Arts Museum, and Tarpon Springs are 15 miles away; Disney World, Circus World, and Sea World are 65 miles away. If you want to stay close to home, the Grimms will lend you their bikes. You're welcome to use the pool, play the piano, or use the kitchen for light snacks. It's close to the University of South Florida and the University of Tampa.

Lemon Bay B&B ✪
12 SOUTHWIND DRIVE, ENGLEWOOD, FLORIDA 33533

Tel: (813) 474-7571
Host(s): **Cy and Jean Rochon**
Location: **30 mi. N of Sarasota**
No. of Rooms: **1**
No. of Private Baths: **1**
Double/pb: **$35**
Single/pb: **$35**

Open: **Oct. 1–May 31**
Breakfast: **Full**
Pets: **Sometimes**
Children: **No**
Smoking: **Permitted**
Social Drinking: **Permitted**

Lemon Bay B&B is on a quiet cul-de-sac on the Intercoastal Waterway, across from the beach and the Gulf of Mexico. This white stucco home has large, comfortable rooms and a lovely view of the bay. Cy and Jean are retired schoolteachers who will make you feel at home. You can fish off their dock, relax with a book, or drive to the beach for fishing, fossil hunting, swimming, and shelling. Buttermilk corncakes and homemade jam are often featured at breakfast along with interesting conversation. This is unharried Florida, at its best.

Windsong Garden
5570-4 WOODROSE COURT, FORT MYERS, FLORIDA 33907

Tel: (813) 936-6378
Host(s): **Embe Burdick**
Location: **40 mi. N of Naples**
No. of Rooms: **1**
No. of Private Baths: **1**
Double/pb: **$35**
Single/pb: **$30**

Open: **All year**
Breakfast: **No**
Pets: **No**
Children: **No**
Smoking: **No**
Social Drinking: **Permitted**
Airport/Station Pickup: **Yes**

This modern cedar-shake-and-brick town house has a private courtyard and balcony for your enjoyment. The spacious combination bedroom-and-sitting room is most comfortable. Embe's varied interests include arts, crafts, and music. It's close to Sanibel and Captiva islands, fine shopping, good restaurants, and the University of Florida. You are welcome to use the barbecue and pool.

The Pines
1207 WEST DUVAL STREET, LAKE CITY, FLORIDA 32055

Tel: **(904) 752-2745**
Host(s): **George and Marian Hudson**
Location: **1 mi. from I-75**
No. of Rooms: **3**
Max. No. Sharing Bath: **4**
Double/sb: **$40**
Single/sb: **$20–$25**

Open: **All year**
Reduced Rates: **10% seniors; families**
Breakfast: **Continental**
Pets: **No**
Children: **Welcome, over 12**
Smoking: **No**
Social Drinking: **Permitted**

This brick Cape Cod home is set on five acres amid pine trees. The decor is a blend of contemporary and antique pieces. Guest accommodations consist of a set of twin beds, a single bed and a three-quarter spool bed. Lake City is known as the gateway to Florida. It's a good stopping off place if you're headed further south to points of interest such as Disney and Sea World.

Hopp-Inn Guest Home ✪
5 MAN-O-WAR DRIVE, MARATHON, FLORIDA 33050

Tel: **(305) 743-4118**
Host(s): **Joan and Joseph Hopp**
Location: **100 mi. W of Miami**
No. of Rooms: **3**
No. of Private Baths: **3**
Double/pb: **$38**
Single/pb: **$30**
Guest Cottage: **$50–$90; sleeps 2–6**
Open: **Oct. 15–June 30**

Reduced Rates: **10%, May, Oct., Nov.**
Breakfast: **Full**
Pets: **No**
Children: **Welcome (crib)**
Smoking: **Permitted**
Social Drinking: **Permitted**
Airport/Station Pickup: **Yes**
Foreign Languages: **German**

This oceanfront white stucco Florida Keys house is in a tropical setting. The temperature is 72° year-round, and there is scuba diving, snorkeling, and the best fishing nearby. In fact, if you catch the fish, Joan and Joseph will supply the gas grill. The house is attractively decorated; the atmosphere is casual and comfortable.

"The White House" ✪
8252 N.E. THIRD COURT, MIAMI, FLORIDA 33138

Tel: (305) 754-3191
Host(s): **Gene Leverett and Sandy O'Connor**
Location: **1 mi. E of I-95**
No. of Rooms: **1**
Max. No. Sharing Bath: **3**
Double/sb: **$50**

Single/sb: **$45**
Open: **All year**
Breakfast: **Full**
Pets: **No**
Children: **No**
Smoking: **Permitted**
Social Drinking: **Permitted**

This 1938 "salt-box" features a lovely garden, country kitchen, large back porch, gazebo with hot tub, sauna cabin, and deck. A tropical paradise, it's filled with wicker and turn-of-the-century furniture inside and a collection of specimen plants and flowers outside. Miami Beach is nearby, and fine ethnic restaurants are convenient to the house.

Feller House ✪
2473 LONGBOAT DRIVE, NAPLES, FLORIDA 33942

Tel: (813) 774-0182
Best Time to Call: **Evenings**
Host(s): **Wayne and Pat Feller**
Location: **35 mi. S of Ft. Myers**
No. of Rooms: **1**
No. of Private Baths: **1**
Double/pb: **$35**
Single/pb: **$28**

Open: **Oct. 1–June 1**
Breakfast: **Full**
Pets: **No**
Children: **Welcome, over 5**
Smoking: **Permitted**
Social Drinking: **Permitted**
Airport/Station Pickup: **Yes**
Foreign Languages: **German**

You are assured of a warm welcome in this attractive home on a canal in a quiet, residential neighborhood. Feel free to use the TV in the den, the pool, or the patio. Tennis courts are nearby and Gulf beaches are minutes away. Wayne and Pat, experienced travelers and home exchangers, will supply maps to take you to Everglades National Park, Corkscrew Bird Sanctuary, as well as directions to the fine shops and restaurants in town.

Avonelle's Bed & Breakfast ✪
4755 ANDERSON ROAD, ORLANDO, FLORIDA 32806

Tel: (305) 275-8733
Best Time to Call: 9–11 AM; 7–9 PM
Host(s): **Jan Ross**
Location: **4 mi. N of airport**
No. of Rooms: **2**
No. of Private Baths: **2**
Double/pb: **$35**
Single/pb: **$35**

Open: **All year**
Breakfast: **Continental**
Pets: **No**
Children: **Welcome**
Smoking: **No**
Social Drinking: **Permitted**
Airport/Station Pickup: **Yes**

Surrounded by giant oaks and citrus trees, Jan's home combines beauty with rustic charm. It is minutes away from Disney World, Epcot, and all central Florida attractions. Arrangements can be made to sail the Gulf of Mexico with Captain Ken Ross aboard his 35-foot trimaran. Rollins College is nearby.

Bed & Breakfast of Orlando ✪
8205 BANYAN BOULEVARD, ORLANDO, FLORIDA 32819

Tel: (305) 352-9157
Host(s): **Bobbie Jean Havlish**
Location: **2 mi. from I-4**
No. of Rooms: **3**
Max. No. Sharing Bath: **6**
Double/sb: **$45–$50**
Single/sb: **$40–$45**
Open: **All year**

Reduced Rates: **Apr. 15–Oct. 15**
Breakfast: **Full**
Pets: **No**
Children: **Welcome**
Smoking: **Permitted**
Social Drinking: **Permitted**
Airport/Station Pickup: **Yes**

Located in Sand Lake Hills, close to the country clubs of Bay Hills and Orange Tree, is Bobbie's lovely home. Weather permitting, she serves breakfast in the screened-in Florida room overlooking the orange groves. It is all very quiet and peaceful, yet minutes away from Epcot, Disney World, Sea World, the Orange County Convention Center, and the Factory Outlet Mall.

Dancing Palms
34 SURFSIDE DRIVE, ORMOND BEACH, FLORIDA 32074

Tel: (904) 441-8800
Host(s): **John and Barbara Pinney**
Location: **8 mi. N of Daytona Beach**

No. of Rooms: **2**
Max. No. Sharing Bath: **4**
Double/sb: **$45**

Single/sb: **$30**
Open: **All year**
Reduced Rates: **10%, seniors**
Breakfast: **Continental**
Pets: **Sometimes**

Children: **Welcome (crib)**
Smoking: **No**
Social Drinking: **Permitted**
Airport/Station Pickup: **Yes**

This charming ranch home is three short blocks from a quiet beach. Guests may choose an antique-filled bedroom with a brass bed, or a simpler, twin-bedded room. Breakfast is served overlooking the large pool; guests are welcome to a refreshing dip anytime. Your hosts offer wine and cheese in the afternoon. They suggest a riverboat cruise on the Halifax River just a short stroll from the house. Daytona Beach is close by; other area attractions include fishing, boardwalk amusements, summer theater, waterfront dining, and jai alai.

Sunrise Guest House ☉
117 SUNRISE DRIVE, PALM HARBOR, FLORIDA 33563

Tel: **(813) 934-7157**
Host(s): **Marjorie and Donald Havery**
Location: **6 mi. N of Clearwater**
No. of Rooms: **2**
No. of Private Baths: **2**
Double/pb: **$30**
Single/pb: **$25**

Open: **All year**
Breakfast: **Continental**
Pets: **No**
Children: **Welcome**
Smoking: **Permitted**
Social Drinking: **Permitted**

Surrounded by rustic pines and citrus trees, "Sunrise" is on the water leading to the Gulf of Mexico, a few blocks from the famous Tarpon Springs sponge docks. Located in a cul-de-sac, it is private and quiet. Use the piano, laundry facilities, and kitchen for light snacks. Coffee and tea are always on tap.

Sunshine Inn ☉
508 DECATUR AVENUE, PENSACOLA, FLORIDA 32507

Tel: **(904) 455-6781**
Best Time to Call: **After 2 PM**
Host(s): **The Jablonskis**
Location: **8 mi. from I-10**
No. of Rooms: **2**
Max. No. Sharing Bath: **4**
Double/sb: **$28**
Open: **All year**

Breakfast: **Full**
Pets: **No**
Children: **Welcome, over 10**
Smoking: **Permitted**
Social Drinking: **Permitted**
Airport/Station Pickup: **Yes**
Foreign Languages: **German**

Sun yourself on the whitest sand, swim in the Gulf of Mexico, and return to the Sunshine Inn for a dip in the pool. Or, walk a block to the bayou for fishing. Feel free to relax in the living room and seek touring advice from your knowledgeable hostess Renate. The University of West Florida is nearby.

Kenwood Inn ✪
38 MARINE STREET, ST. AUGUSTINE, FLORIDA 32084

Tel: **(904) 824-2116**	Single/sb: **$30**
Best Time to Call: **8 AM–8 PM**	Open: **All year**
Host(s): **Judy and Dick Smith**	Reduced Rates: **Seniors**
Location: **40 mi. S of Jacksonville**	Breakfast: **Continental**
No. of Rooms: **16**	Credit Cards: **MC, VISA**
No. of Private Baths: **14**	Pets: **No**
Max. No. Sharing Bath: **4**	Children: **Welcome, over 12**
Double/pb: **$35–$60**	Smoking: **Permitted**
Single/pb: **$35–$60**	Social Drinking: **Permitted**
Double/sb: **$30**	Airport/Station Pickup: **Yes**

If you are to discover a Victorian building in Florida, how appropriate that it should be in the historic section of St. Augustine, the oldest city in the U.S. This New England-style inn is a rarity in the South; this one has old-fashioned beds with color-coordinated touches right down to the sheets and linens. Breakfast may be taken in your room, in the courtyard surrounded by trees, or by the swimming pool. Tour trains, the waterfront shops, restaurants, and museums are within walking distance. Flagler College is three blocks away.

Victorian House Bed & Breakfast ✪
11 CADIZ STREET, ST. AUGUSTINE, FLORIDA 32084

Tel: **(904) 824-5214**	Suites: **$50**
Best Time to Call: **2–5 PM**	Separate Guest Cottage: **$65 for 4**
Host(s): **Daisy Morden**	Open: **All year**
No. of Rooms: **6**	Breakfast: **Continental**
No. of Private Baths: **4**	Credit Cards: **MC, VISA**
Max. No. Sharing Bath: **4**	Pets: **No**
Double/pb: **$45**	Children: **In cottage only**
Double/sb: **$30**	Smoking: **Permitted**
Single/sb: **$25**	Social Drinking: **Permitted**

From its location in the heart of the historic district, it's a short walk to fine restaurants, the waterfront, shops, museums, and the plaza. The rooms are charming with brass and canopy beds, handwoven coverlets, handmade quilts, stenciled walls and floors. One of the bedrooms is pictured on the back cover. The house is comfortably air-conditioned, but the warmth of your hosts is quite special.

Bayboro House
1719 BEACH DRIVE S.E., ST. PETERSBURG, FLORIDA 33701

Tel: **(813) 823-4955**
Best Time to Call: **After 4 PM; weekends**
Host(s): **Gordon and Antonia Powers**
Location: **½ mi. from I-275**
No. of Rooms: **3**
No. of Private Baths: **3**
Double/pb: **$35**
Single/pb: **$30**
Open: **All year**
Breakfast: **Continental**
Pets: **No**
Children: **Welcome, over 10**
Smoking: **No**
Social Drinking: **Permitted**

A unique three-story Queen Anne with airy, high-ceilinged rooms and a wraparound veranda in view of Tampa Bay, it is graced with antique furniture plus tropical plants and flowers. It is the ideal spot for sunning, beachcombing, and fishing. Relax in the hammock or visit unusual shops, fine restaurants, the Sunken Gardens, Salvador Dali museum, or the dog track. Complimentary champagne is served on the veranda when the moon is full; that's just one of the special touches offered by Antonia and Gordon. The University of South Florida is one mile away.

The Walters House ✪
1115 BOCA CIEGA ISLE, ST. PETERSBURG BEACH, FLORIDA 33706

Tel: **(813) 360-3372**
Host(s): **Karen and Dick Walters**
Location: **4 mi. from I-275**
No. of Rooms: **1**
No. of Private Baths: **1**
Double/pb: **$35**
Single/pb: **$30**
Open: **All year**
Breakfast: **Continental**
Pets: **No**
Children: **No**
Smoking: **Permitted**
Social Drinking: **Permitted**
Airport/Station Pickup: **Yes**
Foreign Languages: **French, German**

This spacious, immaculate, air-conditioned house has cathedral ceilings and lots of glass to enhance its tropical setting. Located on a private island, it is a half-mile from the Gulf of Mexico beaches, only 20 minutes to Busch Gardens in Tampa, and 90 minutes to Disney World, Epcot, and Sea World. Karen and Dick offer coffee or popcorn while you relax after a busy day. The University of South Florida and Eckerd College are nearby.

The Bay-View Home
1448 JOHN RINGLING PARKWAY, SARASOTA, FLORIDA 33577

Tel: **(813) 388-1772**
Host(s): **Mary Staup**
Location: **3 mi. from Rte. 41**
No. of Rooms: **1**
Max. No. Sharing Bath: **2**
Double/sb: **$40**
Single/sb: **$25**
Open: **All year**
Breakfast: **Continental**
Other Meals: **Available**
Pets: **No**
Children: **No**
Smoking: **Permitted**
Social Drinking: **Permitted**
Airport/Station Pickup: **Yes**
Foreign Languages: **Yugoslav**

This island home has a panoramic view of Sarasota Bay and the skyline. The rooms are furnished with contemporary pieces and feature king-sized beds. Your hostess will gladly prepare snacks and meals, and offers fresh pastries for breakfasts. Nearby attractions include sandy beaches, the Ringling Museum, and first-rate shops and restaurants.

Tallahassee Bed & Breakfast
3023 WINDY HILL LANE, TALLAHASSEE, FLORIDA 32308

Tel: **(904) 385-3768 or 421-5220**
Best Time to Call: **6 AM–11 PM**
Coordinator: **Martha Thomas**
States/Regions Covered: **Tallahassee**

Rates (Single/Double):
Modest: **$30**   **$40**
Luxury: **$50**   **$65**

Tallahassee is the capital of Florida, located in the beautiful Panhandle area near the Gulf of Mexico. The area has much to offer scenically, historically, and culturally. Martha's hosts look forward to having guests and will direct you to places that are tailored to your interests. Florida State University and Florida Agricultural and Mechanical University are close by.

GEORGIA

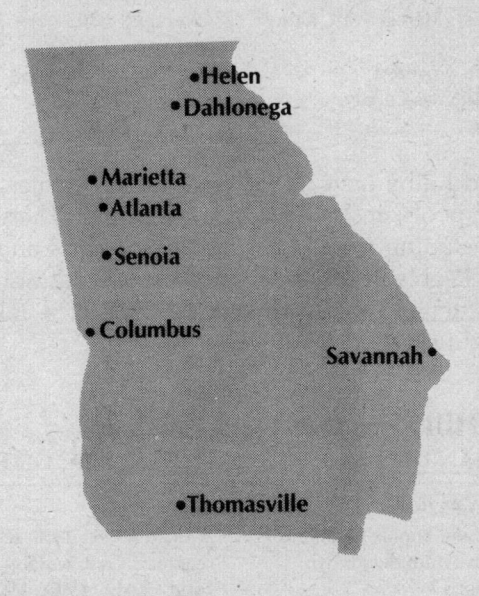

- Helen
- Dahlonega
- Marietta
- Atlanta
- Senoia
- Columbus
- Savannah
- Thomasville

Bed & Breakfast—Atlanta
1221 FAIRVIEW ROAD, N.E., ATLANTA, GEORGIA 30306

Tel: **(404) 378-6026**
Best Time to Call: **10 AM–Noon; 2–5 PM**
Coordinator(s): **Jane Carney, Madalyne Eplan, Paula Gris**
States/Regions Covered: **Atlanta, Decatur, Marietta, Stone Mountain**

Rates (Single/Double):
  Modest: **$24**   **$28**
  Average: **$28**   **$36**
  Luxury: **$36–$56**   **$40–$60**
Credit Cards: **No**

Visit one of America's most gracious cities, with the advantage of being a houseguest. Jane, Madalyne, and Paula consider transportation and language needs as well as other personal preferences in making your reservation. Locations are offered in the city's most desirable homes, and all offer a private bath. There is a $4 surcharge for a one-night stay. Georgia Tech., Emory University, and Georgia State University are close by.

Quail Country Bed & Breakfast, Ltd. ✪
1104 OLD MONTICELLO ROAD, THOMASVILLE, GEORGIA 31792

Tel: **(912) 226-7218 or 226-6882**
Coordinator(s): **Mercer Watt, Kathy Lanigan**
States/Regions Covered:
 Georgia—Thomas County, Thomasville

Rates (Single/Double):
 Average: **$30** **$40**
 Luxury: **$40** **$50**
Credit Cards: **MC, VISA**

Mercer and Kathy have a wide selection of homes, several with swimming pools, in lovely residential areas. There's lots to see and do, including touring historic restorations and plantations. Enjoy the Pebble Hill Plantation museum, historic Glen Arven Country Club, and the April Rose Festival. Five-dollar surcharge for one-night stay.

Beverly Hills Inn ✪
65 SHERIDAN DRIVE NORTH EAST, ATLANTA, GEORGIA 30305

Tel: **(404) 233-8520**
Host(s): **Lyle and Bonnie Kleinhans**
Location: **5 mi. from downtown**
No. of Rooms: **17**
No. of Private Baths: **17**
Double/pb: **$57**
Single/pb: **$48**
Suites: **$70**

Open: **All year**
Reduced Rates: **10%, seniors**
Breakfast: **Continental**
Credit Cards: **AMEX, MC, VISA**
Pets: **Sometimes**
Children: **Welcome**
Smoking: **Permitted**
Social Drinking: **Permitted**

This Inn was built as an apartment house in the late 1920s, when the Hollywood look was "in." Its period furnishings, private balconies, and old wood floors recall the architecture of that era. Guests may choose from 17 suites with kitchenettes. A library, parlor, and grand piano are available. Your hosts are happy to help plan visits to nearby shops, restaurants, museums, and historic homes.

House of Friends ☉
946 HIGHLAND VIEW N.E., ATLANTA, GEORGIA 30306

Tel: **(404) 874-0519**
Best Time to Call: **7–9 AM**
Host(s): **Hilary Jones**
Location: **1½ mi. from Peachtree St.**
No. of Rooms: **2**
No. of Private Baths: **1**
Double/pb: **$35**
Single/pb: **$20**
Double/sb: **$32**
Single/sb: **$18**
Open: **All year**
Reduced Rates: **Over 2 nights**
Breakfast: **Full**
Pets: **Sometimes**
Children: **Welcome, over 6**
Smoking: **No**
Social Drinking: **No**
Foreign Languages: **French**

You will enjoy the tranquillity of sitting on the porch, surrounded by lovely old trees, after seeing the many city sights. The house, of brick and redwood construction, contains some beautiful antiques and memorabilia Hilary has collected during her many travels abroad. A writer of children's books, she has a myriad of interests, especially people.

The DeLoffre House ☉
812 BROADWAY, COLUMBUS, GEORGIA 31901

Tel: **(404) 324-1144 or 1146**
Host(s): **Shirley and Paul Romo**
Location: **5 mi. from Rte. 185**
No. of Rooms: **6**
No. of Private Baths: **6**
Double/pb: **$50–$60**
Single/pb: **$43–$49**
Open: **All year**
Reduced Rates: **15%, weekly**
Breakfast: **Continental**
Credit Cards: **AMEX, MC, VISA**
Pets: **No**
Children: **Welcome, over 12**
Smoking: **Permitted**
Social Drinking: **Permitted**

This 1863 Italianate town house, located in the historic district, is elegantly furnished with Victorian and Empire antiques. Three of the bedrooms have original fireplaces. Each bedroom is supplied with a bowl of fruit, a decanter of sherry, good books, a private phone, and color TV, to make you comfortable. The opera, theater, museums, F.D.R.'s Little White House and Columbus College are all nearby.

Worley Homestead Inn ✪
410 WEST MAIN STREET, DAHLONEGA, GEORGIA 30533

Tel: (404) 864-7002	Guest Cottage: $65–$90; sleeps 4
Best Time to Call: 8 AM–10 PM	Open: All year
Host(s): Mick and Mitzi Francis	Reduced Rates: Nov. 1–Sept. 30
Location: 40 mi. N of Atlanta	Breakfast: Full
No. of Rooms: 9	Credit Cards: AMEX, MC, VISA
No. of Private Baths: 8	Pets: No
Max. No. Sharing Bath: 4	Children: Welcome
Double/pb: $45–$65	Smoking: Permitted
Single/pb: $40–$60	Social Drinking: Permitted

This country Victorian house is located three blocks from the historic town square. It is furnished with antiques, historic photographs, and documents, and gives you the feeling of going back in time. The staff dresses in period costumes and the 1800s-style Southern breakfast includes fruit, two meats, grits, gravy, and biscuits. The town is the site of the nation's first Gold Rush in 1832 and the Gold Museum and operating gold mines make for unusual sightseeing.

Hilltop Haus
P.O. BOX 154, CHATTAHOOCHEE STREET, HELEN, GEORGIA 30545

Tel: (404) 878-2388	Double/sb: $30
Host(s): Frankie Tysor and Barbara Nichols	Single/sb: $20
	Guest Cottage: $60; sleeps 4
Location: 60 mi. from I-85	Open: All year
No. of Rooms: 5	Breakfast: Full
No. of Private Baths: 2	Pets: No
Max. No. Sharing Bath: 4	Children: Welcome, over 12
Double/pb: $35	Smoking: Permitted
Single/pb: $25	Social Drinking: Permitted

This contemporary split-level overlooks Alpine Helen and the Chattahoochee River. It is near the foothills of the Smoky Mountains, six miles from the Appalachian Trail. Rich wood paneling and fireplaces create a homey atmosphere for the traveler. Guests may choose a private room or the efficiency cottage with separate entrance. Each morning a hearty breakfast includes homemade biscuits and preserves. Your hostess will direct you to many outdoor activities and sights.

GEORGIA • 143

Arden Hall Inn—1880
FOREST OF ARDEN, 1052 ARDEN DRIVE, S.W., MARIETTA,
GEORGIA 30060

Tel: **(404) 422-0780**
Best Time to Call: **9 AM–10 PM**
Host(s): **Dr. and Mrs. Wilkes Henry Davis, Jr.**
Location: **18 mi. NW of Atlanta**
No. of Rooms: **2**
No. of Private Baths: **2**
Double/pb: **$50**
Single/pb: **$45**

Open: **All year**
Reduced Rates: **$5 less for 2 nights**
Breakfast: **Full**
Pets: **No**
Children: **No**
Smoking: **No**
Social Drinking: **Permitted**
Foreign Languages: **French, German**

This gracious turn-of-the-century home is tastefully furnished with antiques, a grand piano, Oriental rugs, and cherished collected items from all over the world. Wilkes is an ophthalmologist and soloist with the Atlanta Symphony. Dotty is a master chef, professional photographer, and caterer. Don't miss the cruise on the Chattahoochee River and the Calloway Gardens. It's convenient to Kennesaw College and Southern Tech.

Savannah Historic Inns and Guest Houses
1900 LINCOLN STREET, SAVANNAH, GEORGIA 31401

Tel: **(912) 233-7666**
Coordinator: **Susan Earl**
State/Regions Covered: **Savannah**

Rates: **(Single/Double):**
Modest: **$30–$38**
Average: **$50–$65**
Luxury: **$70–$88**
Credit Cards: **AMEX, MC, VISA**

Savannah has 21 square miles known as the National Landmark Historic District, the largest such designated area in the country. Built as early as 1733, the homes have been restored to their original elegance, near museums, restaurants and the riverfront. You will be impressed with true Southern hospitality.

Bed & Breakfast Inn ○
117 GORDON STREET WEST AT CHATHAM SQUARE,
SAVANNAH, GEORGIA 31401

Tel: **(912) 238-0518**
Best Time to Call: **8 AM–5 PM**
Host(s): **Robert T. McAlister**
No. of Rooms: **10**

No. of Private Baths: **4**
Max. No. Sharing Bath: **4**
Double/pb: **$65**
Single/pb: **$55**

Double/sb: **$38**
Single/sb: **$30**
Open: **All year**
Breakfast: **Continental**
Credit Cards: **AMEX, MC, VISA**

Pets: **No**
Children: **Welcome (crib)**
Smoking: **Permitted**
Social Drinking: **Permitted**

Located in the heart of the historic district, this regal town house, built in 1853, has been beautifully restored. There are both upstairs bedrooms and four garden apartments, with private entrances, complete kitchens, sofa sleepers for extra guests, overlooking a lovely garden. Savannah is the epitome of elegance, and its floral displays, fountains, and varied architecture are delights. Don't forget to take a ride in an antique horse-drawn buggy over the cobblestone streets. Bob will advise you of the best restaurants in the area. Armstrong State College is nearby.

Four Seventeen—The Haslam-Fort House ✪
417 EAST CHARLTON STREET, SAVANNAH, GEORGIA 31401

Tel: **(912) 233-6380**
Best Time to Call: **After 6 PM**
Host(s): **Alan Fort**
Location: **12 mi. from I-95**
No. of Rooms: **1 suite**
No. of Private Baths: **1**
Suites: **$75 (for 2); $125 (for 4)**
Open: **All year**
Reduced Rates: **July 1 to Aug. 31, $68 for 2, $98 for 4**
Breakfast: **Continental**
Pets: **Welcome**
Children: **Welcome (crib)**
Smoking: **Permitted**
Social Drinking: **Permitted**
Foreign Languages: **German, Norwegian, Spanish**

Located in the famed historic district, the ground floor of this lovely town house has a private entrance with easy access for the handicapped, a delightful private garden, two bedrooms, a living room with fireplace, a private bath, and a country kitchen where all the fixings for a do-it-yourself breakfast are on hand. Alan will be happy to direct you to all the special attractions of the area.

The Stoddard-Cooper House ✪
19 W. PERRY STREET, SAVANNAH, GEORGIA 31401

Tel: **(912) 233-6809**
Host(s): **Barbara Hershey**
Location: **12 mi. from I-95**
No. of Rooms: **1 suite**
No. of Private Baths: **1**
Suites: **$75–$125 (for 2–4)**

Open: **All year**
Breakfast: **Continental**
Pets: **Sometimes**
Children: **Welcome (crib)**
Smoking: **Permitted**
Social Drinking: **Permitted**

Come stay in the secluded, garden-level suite of this carefully restored historic home (circa 1854), right on Chippewa Square in the heart of the historic district. There are two bedrooms, a wood-burning fireplace in the living room, and a modern kitchen with bountiful supplies for breakfast. The suite is beautifully appointed with antiques. The Savannah College of Art and Design is nearby.

The Culpepper House ✪
P.O. BOX 462, MORGAN AT BROAD, SENOIA, GEORGIA 30276

Tel: **(404) 599-8182**
Best Time to Call: **7 PM–10 PM**
Host(s): **Mary A. Brown**
Location: **37 mi. S of Atlanta**
No. of Rooms: **4**
No. of Private Baths: **1**
Max. No. Sharing Bath: **5**
Double/pb: **$45**
Double/sb: **$35**
Single/sb: **$30**

Suites: **$50**
Open: **All year**
Reduced Rates: **15%, weekly**
Breakfast: **Continental**
Credit Cards: **No**
Pets: **No**
Children: **Welcome, over 12**
Smoking: **Permitted**
Social Drinking: **Permitted**
Airport/Station Pickup: **Yes**

This Queen Anne Victorian was built in 1871. Gingerbread trim, stained glass, sliding doors, bay windows, and provincial furnishings recreate that turn-of-the-century feeling. Snacks and setups are offered. Your hostess will gladly direct you to surrounding antique and craft shops, state parks, and gardens.

HAWAII

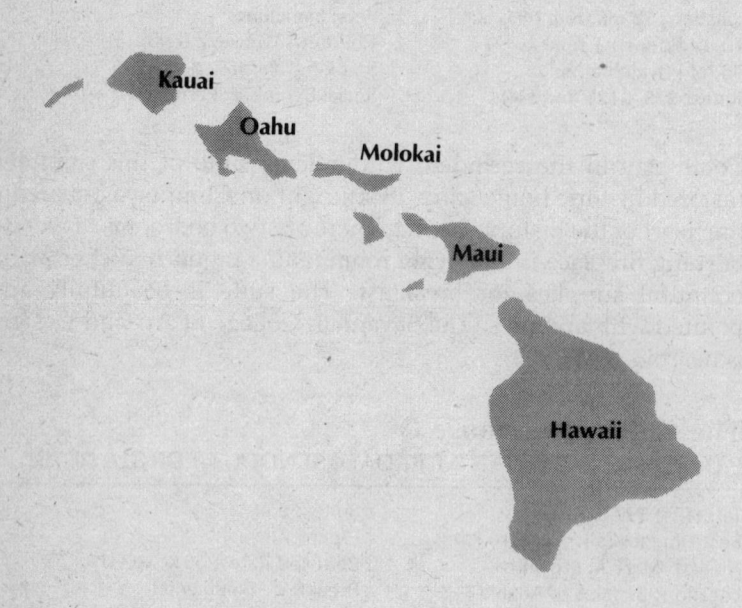

Bed & Breakfast—Hawaii ✪
P.O. BOX 449, KAPAA, HAWAII 96746

Tel: **(808) 822-7771**
Best Time to Call: **8:30 AM–4:30 PM**
Coordinators: **Evie Warner, Al Davis**
States/Regions Covered: **All of the Hawaiian Islands**

Rates (Single/Double):
  Modest: $15 $20–$25
  Average: $20 $30–$37.50
  Luxury: $50 $50–$70
Credit Cards: **No**

Hawaii is a group of diverse islands, offering traditional warmth and hospitality to the visitor through this membership organization. For a $5 membership fee, you will receive a descriptive directory of accommodations on all five islands. Some are separate units; others are in the main house. Most have private baths. Minimum stay is two nights. The University of Hawaii at Oahu is convenient to many B&Bs.

Pacific–Hawaii Bed & Breakfast ✪
19 KAI NANI PLACE, KAILUA, OAHU, HAWAII 96734

Tel: **(808) 262-6026 or 254-5115**
Coordinator: **Doris E. Epp**
States/Regions Covered: **All of the Hawaiian Islands**
	Rates (Single/Double):
	  Modest: **$18** **$20–$25**
	  Average: **$25** **$30–$40**
	  Luxury: **$30 and up $50–$100**
	Credit Cards: **No**
	Minimum Stay: **3 days**

Doris enjoys matching guests and hosts, and will find a home tailored to your taste on any of the major islands. For example, one of her oceanfront homes on a beautiful white sand beach, not yet discovered by tourists, is only $20, including a private bath. It's 20 minutes to Pearl Harbor and half an hour to Waikiki. Most of her B&Bs are on the island of Oahu (Honolulu).

Alohaland Guest House ✪
98-1003 OLIWA STREET, ALEA, HAWAII 96701

Tel: **(808) 487-0482** Best Time to Call: **6–9 PM** Host(s): **Mrs. Abaya** Location: **10 mi. from downtown Honolulu** No. of Rooms: **1** No. of Private Baths: **1** Double/pb: **$40**	Single/pb: **$32** Open: **Aug., Oct., Nov., Jan.** Breakfast: **Continental** Pets: **No** Children: **No** Smoking: **No** Social Drinking: **No** Airport/Station Pickup: **Yes**

Mrs. Abaya's home is in a residential area, convenient to all points of interest via public transportation. The inviting beaches of Hawaii, plus the sights and nightlife in Honolulu can be enjoyed to the fullest. A three-day minimum stay is requested.

Hale O'Makamaka ✪
2564 AINAOLA DRIVE, HILO, HAWAII 96720

Tel: **(808) 959-9789** Host(s): **Fabian and Nancy Toribio** Location: **6 mi. W of Hilo** No. of Rooms: **1** No. of Private Baths: **1** Double/pb: **$27**	Single/pb: **$16.50** Open: **All year** Reduced Rates: **15%, weekly** Breakfast: **Continental** Pets: **No** Children: **No**

Smoking: **No**　　　　　　　　Airport/Station Pickup: **yes**
Social Drinking: **Permitted**

Hale O'Makamaka means "house of friends." It is a modest cottage, elevation 1,200 feet, on the slopes of Mauna Loa. The house overlooks the bay city of Hilo, known for its beautiful gardens and orchidariums. Your hosts offer homemade bread as part of breakfast and are happy to advise on local dining. Nearby attractions include the volcano, Rainbow Falls, and the beaches.

For key to listings, see inside front or back cover.

○ This star means that rates are guaranteed through December 31, 1985 to any guest making a reservation as a result of reading about the B&B in BED & BREAKFAST U.S.A.—1985 edition.

Please enclose a self-addressed, stamped, business-sized envelope when contacting reservation services.

For more details on what you can expect in a B&B, see Chapter 1.

Always mention *Bed & Breakfast USA* when making reservations!

IDAHO

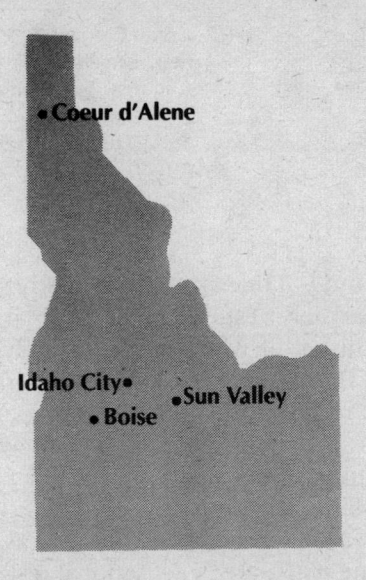

Sunnie's Guest House ✪
749 GOVERNMENT WAY, COEUR d'ALENE, IDAHO 83814

Tel: (208) 667-3078
Host(s): A. Sunnie Thomas
Location: 30 mi. E of Spokane, Wash.
No of Rooms: 2
Max. No. Sharing Bath: 4
Double/sb: $40
Single/sb: $30
Open: Apr. 1–Oct. 31

Reduced Rates: 10%, seniors
Breakfast: Full
Credit Cards: MC, VISA
Pets: No
Children: No
Smoking: Permitted
Social Drinking: Permitted
Airport/Station Pickup: Yes

Sunnie's two-story house has an early 1920s atmosphere. It is within walking distance of the downtown area and the city park with its own lake and public tennis courts. Lake Coeur d'Alene features boating and sailing. Sunnie, a retired rancher, homesteaded in Alaska, where she wrote for the local newspaper. She likes to spoil her guests with a real country breakfast which includes home-baked biscuits and gravy. North Idaho College is close by.

Ellsworth Inn ✪
P.O. BOX 1253, 715 THIRD AVENUE SOUTH, HAILEY, IDAHO 83333

Tel: **(208) 788-2298**
Host(s): **Sonja Tarnay**
Location: **11 mi. S of Sun Valley**
No. of Rooms: **8**
No. of Private Baths: **8**
Double/pb: **$55–$85**
Open: **All year**
Breakfast: **Full**
Credit Cards: **MC, VISA**
Pets: **Sometimes**
Children: **Sometimes**
Smoking: **Permitted**
Social Drinking: **Permitted**
Airport/Station Pickup: **Yes**
Foreign Language: **French, German, Norwegian**

Built in 1915, the inn is a fine example of "Early Craftsman" style architecture, remarkably restored to its original elegance. Sonja has tastefully furnished it with antiques, family heirlooms, and handsome quilts. It is close to Silver Creek, world famous for its fly fishing trout stream, and Sun Valley skiing. You can fill your days with hiking, soaring, ballooning, whitewater float trips, tennis, and swimming. Sonja can even arrange a llama pack-trip, if you're inclined to try the unusual. A delightful afternoon tea is served from 3–5 PM daily, except Sunday. Leave some room to enjoy dinner at one of the area's sensational restaurants.

Idaho City Hotel ✪
P.O. BOX 70, IDAHO CITY, IDAHO 83631

Tel: **(208) 392-4298**
Host(s): **Don Campbell**
Location: **37 mi. N of Boise**
No. of Rooms: **12**
No. of Private Baths: **12**
Double/pb: **$34**
Single/pb: **$30**
Suites: **$42 for 4**
Open: **All year**
Reduced Rates: **Weekly**
Breakfast: **Full**
Credit Cards: **MC, VISA**
Pets: **Welcome**
Children: **Welcome**
Smoking: **Permitted**
Social Drinking: **Permitted**
Foreign Languages: **German**

Don will be pleased to share with you the spectacular history of this old gold-mining town. The 1860s-style hotel is furnished with oak furniture and cast iron beds, but 20th century plumbing, fixtures and cable TV have been added for your comfort. Breakfast is a more-than-you-can-eat feast and always features three styles of Idaho (naturally!) potatoes as a delicious side dish. Your room rate includes free entry to the private Warm Springs resort, nearby, where you can use the swimming facilities.

For key to listings, see inside front or back cover.

○ This star means that rates are guaranteed through December 31, 1985 to any guest making a reservation as a result of reading about the B&B in *BED & BREAKFAST U.S.A.*—1985 edition.

Please enclose a self-addressed, stamped, business-sized envelope when contacting reservation services.

For more details on what you can expect in a B&B, see Chapter 1.

Always mention *Bed & Breakfast USA* when making reservations!

ILLINOIS

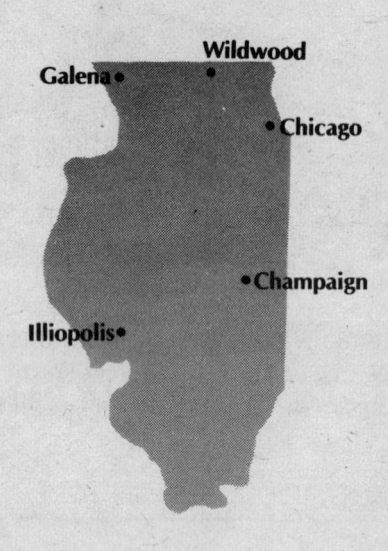

Morgan Residence ✪
311 WHEATON AVENUE, CHAMPAIGN, ILLINOIS 61820

Tel: **(217) 359-7698**
Host(s): **Beth and Bruce Morgan**
Location: **2 mi. from I-57, 74, 72**
No. of Rooms: **1**
No. of Private Baths: **1**
Double/pb: **$23**
Single/pb: **$18**
Open: **All year**

Reduced Rates: **Available**
Breakfast: **Continental**
Pets: **Sometimes**
Children: **Welcome (crib)**
Smoking: **Permitted**
Social Drinking: **Permitted**
Airport/Station Pickup: **Yes**
Foreign Languages: **French, Spanish**

This traditional, Midwestern-style home has a big yard and porch. The rooms are furnished with turn-of-the-century pieces and feature plants and newly restored woodwork. Guests are welcomed to a two-room suite in the finished attic. A breakfast of homemade breads, jams, and espresso is served in the sunny dining room. Your hosts will be glad to point out the sights of Abraham Lincoln country and the Amish community. The University of Illinois is nearby.

Belle Aire Mansion ✪
11410 RT. 20 WEST, GALENA, ILLINOIS 61036

Tel: **(815) 777-0893**
Best Time to Call: **Before noon; after 6 PM**
Hosts: **Evelyn and James Nemecek**
Location: **18 mi. E of Dubuque, Ia.**
No. of Rooms: **4**
No. of Private Baths: **2**
Max. No. Sharing Bath: **4**
Double/pb: **$40**

Double/sb: **$35**
Open: **All year**
Breakfast: **Full**
Pets: **Sometimes**
Children: **Welcome**
Smoking: **Permitted**
Social Drinking: **Permitted**
Airport/Station Pickup: **Yes**
Foreign Languages: **Bohemian, Czech**

Nestled in a parklike setting of towering pines, this Federal Period (circa 1834) gem is a visit into the past. It's furnished with elegant antiques, with some of the finest walnut high-backed beds and marble-topped dressers to be found anywhere. Beds are covered with hand-crocheted spreads; cushioned white wicker chairs add to your comfort, and there are wash basins in every bedroom. Sixteen manicured acres boast a barn and windmill. Hot air ballooning, antique shops, General Grant's home, and winter skiing are all nearby. Evelyn and James serve wine and fruit after your busy day.

Old Illiopolis Hotel ✪
608 MARY STREET, BOX 66, ILLIOPOLIS, ILLINOIS 62539

Tel: **(217) 486-6451**
Best Time to Call: **Evenings**
Host(s): **James and Kathleen Jensen-Browne**
Location: **19 mi. E of Springfield**
No. of Rooms: **6**
Max. No. Sharing Bath: **3**
Double/sb: **$20**

Single/sb: **$18**
Open: **All year**
Breakfast: **Continental**
Pets: **Sometimes**
Children: **Welcome**
Smoking: **No**
Social Drinking: **Permitted**

This 18-room clapboard dates back to 1854, when it served as a stopover for the Great Western Railway. Your hosts spent the better part of a year restoring the wainscoting and replacing porcelain fixtures. The ten small, quaint guest rooms are furnished in period pieces. The hotel remains the oldest standing structure in town, and it is said that Abe Lincoln often stopped there. Your hosts will gladly point the way to his home, in Springfield.

The Keplers ✪
33460 N. LAKE SHORE DRIVE, WILDWOOD, ILLINOIS 60030

Tel: **(312) 223-5680**
Host(s): **Theresa and Arthur Kepler**
Location: **40 mi. NW of Chicago**
No. of Rooms: **2**
Max. No. Sharing Bath: **4**
Double/sb: **$26**
Single/sb: **$20**

Open: **All year**
Breakfast: **Continental**
Pets: **No**
Children: **No**
Smoking: **Permitted**
Social Drinking: **Permitted**
Airport/Station Pickup: **Yes**

On Gages Lake, where you can swim, boat, and fish through the summer, the Keplers have a ranch-style home and private dock. Spend the afternoon in the rowboat or on the paddleboat, and then relax on the patio, complete with grill. Enjoy a quiet evening by the fire or drive to Lake Geneva, Great America, or Chicago. In winter, there is ice skating on the lake. A full breakfast is available for $2.50 each. The College of Lake County is nearby.

INDIANA

Duneland Beach Inn ✪
3311 POTTAWATTOMIE TRAIL, MICHIGAN CITY, INDIANA 46360

Tel: (219) 874-7729
Best Time to Call: 9 AM–6 PM
Host(s): **George and Kathleen Friederich**
Location: 56 mi. E of Chicago, Il.
No. of Rooms: **12**
No. of Private Baths: **1**
Max. No. Sharing Bath: **5**
Double/pb: **$49**
Double/sb: **$29**
Single/sb: **$24**

Open: **All year**
Reduced Rates: **15%, weekly**
Breakfast: **Full**
Other Meals: **Available**
Credit Cards: **MC, VISA**
Pets: **Sometimes**
Children: **Welcome, over 12**
Smoking: **Permitted**
Social Drinking: **Permitted**
Airport/Station Pickup: **Yes**

This country inn is nestled in a secluded residential area surrounded by lovely trees. A private white sand beach and clear Lake Michigan waters provide a unique setting for swimming, sunning, and boating. The rooms are clean and cozy with lovely antiques and special touches. Nearby recreational facilities, Notre Dame football weekends, Oktoberfest, and winter sports make this a fun place in all seasons.

Patchwork Quilt Bed and Breakfast
11748 Country Road #2, MIDDLEBURY, INDIANA 46540

Tel: **(219) 825-5645**	Open: **All year**
Best Time to Call: **10 AM–4 PM**	Reduced Rates: **Available**
Host(s): **Arletta Lovejoy**	Breakfast: **Continental**
Location: **18 mi. E of South Bend**	Other Meals: **Available**
No. of Rooms: 3	Pets: **No**
Max. No. Sharing Bath: 6	Children: **No**
Double/sb: **$45**	Smoking: **No**
Single/sb: **$35**	Social Drinking: **No**

The house on this 260-acre working farm is furnished with collectibles and antiques. Guests are greeted with cheese, fruit, and seasonal drinks. Homemade meals are prepared with farm-fresh ingredients. Breakfast and dinner are served in the oak dining room with adjoining open kitchen. Each guest room has its own patchwork quilt. Your hosts offer tours of the Amish farm country, including stops at orchards, weavers, mills, and craft shops.

Sunset House ✪
RURAL ROUTE 3, BOX 127, NASHVILLE, INDIANA 47448

Tel: **(812) 988-6118**	Open: **All Year**
Host(s): **Mary Margaret Baird**	Reduced Rates: **$5 less, Mon.–Thurs.; seniors**
Location: **2½ mi. N of Nashville**	
No. of Rooms: 3	Breakfast: **Continental**
No. of Private Baths: 3	Pets: **Sometimes**
Double/pb: **$45**	Children: **Welcome**
Single/pb: **$45**	Smoking: **Permitted**
Suites: **$55**	Social Drinking: **Permitted**

Mary's home is a magnificent contemporary house, with a deck and patio for relaxing. The guest rooms have separate entrances and all are furnished in fine cherry wood. The master suite has a handsome stone fireplace. Although there are many things to keep you busy, the Little Nashville Opry is a major attraction each Saturday, with Country-and-Western stars entertaining. Indiana University is nearby.

The Rockport Inn ☯
THIRD AT WALNUT, ROCKPORT, INDIANA 47635

Tel: **(812) 649-2664**	Reduced Rates: **30% weekly**
Best Time to Call: **8 AM–6 PM**	Breakfast: **$1.25–$3.25**
Host(s): **Emil and Carolyn Ahnell**	Other Meals: **Available**
Location: **40 mi. E of Evansville**	Pets: **Sometimes**
No. of Rooms: **6**	Children: **Welcome (crib)**
No. of Private Baths: **6**	Smoking: **Permitted**
Double/pb: **$25–$32**	Social Drinking: **Permitted**
Single/pb: **$19–$25**	Foreign Languages: **German, Swedish**
Open: **All year**	

Built in 1855, this white, frame, two-story residence has a porch and landscaped yard. It's furnished with antiques; plants and flowers add to its cozy atmosphere. Lincoln State Park, Santa Claus Land, and Kentucky Wesleyan College are nearby.

Green Meadow Ranch ☯
R.R. 2, BOX 592, SHIPSHEWANA, INDIANA 46565

Tel: **(219) 768-4221**	Reduced Rates: **Families**
Host(s): **Paul and Ruth Miller**	Breakfast: **Continental**
Location: **20 mi. E of South Bend**	Pets: **Welcome**
No. of Rooms: **4**	Children: **Welcome**
Max. No. Sharing Bath: **6**	Smoking: **Permitted**
Double/sb: **$30**	Social Drinking: **Permitted**
Single/sb: **$30**	Foreign Languages: **Pennsylvania German**
Open: **Mar. 1–Nov. 30**	

Shipshewana is a large Amish and Mennonite settlement. One of the largest flea markets in the country is held on summer Tuesdays and Wednesdays, and an antique auction every Wednesday, all year long. Ruth and Paul's brick colonial home, decorated with lovely country antiques, is on their 20-acre ranch. They raise horses, a miniature horse, fancy chickens, and ducks. They offer snacks, fruit, and soft drinks along with information about the Amish way of life. Ruth is expert in many crafts including her Amish-style dolls and quilts, which are for sale.

Camel Lot, Ltd. ✪
4512 WEST 131 STREET, WESTFIELD, INDIANA 46074

Tel: **(317) 873-4370**
Best Time to Call: **Evenings**
Host(s): **Moselle Schaffer**
Location: **10 mi. N of Indianapolis**
No. of Rooms: **1 Suite**
No. of Private Baths: **1**
Suites: **$40–$60**
Open: **All year**

Breakfast: **Full**
Air-Conditioning: **Yes**
Pets: **Sometimes**
Children: **Welcome, over 12**
Smoking: **Permitted**
Social Drinking: **Permitted**
Airport/Station Pickup: **Yes**

Be a guest in Moselle's three-room suite complete with a four-poster bed, private bath, and study, in a private wing of the house. On this exotic animal breeding farm, the camels, llamas, and zebras are kept out back. After breakfast on the terrace that overlooks Siberian tigers Deuchka and Ivan, you can roam the 50 acres of this unusual farm. It is twenty minutes from Indianapolis, two miles from the colonial village of Zionsville. Butler University is nearby.

IOWA

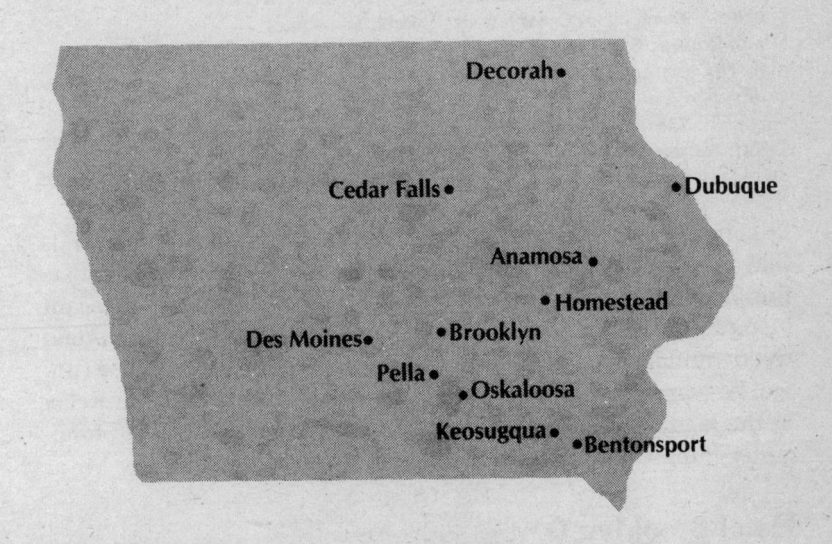

Bed & Breakfast in Iowa, Ltd. ✪
7104 FRANKLIN AVENUE, DES MOINES, IOWA 50322

Tel: (515) 277-9018
Best Time to Call: 9 AM–Noon;
  1 PM–5 PM
Coordinator: **Iona Ansorge**
States/Regions Covered: **Iowa
  (statewide)**

Rates (Single/Double):
  Modest: $18–$20 $25–$30
  Average: $25–$35 $35–$45
  Luxury: $38–$60 $50–$65
Credit Cards: MC, VISA

Iona has a vast variety of accommodations, ranging from working farms where you can participate in agricultural activities, National Registry homes, mansions overlooking the Mississippi River, and huge ranches overlooking the lakes, bluffs, and cliffs of northeast Iowa. The Iowa State Fair and over 200 statewide festivals will suit all interests, including cultural, historic, sports, and crafts. Please send $2 for a descriptive directory. The University of Iowa, Iowa State, and Drake University are close to several homes.

The Inn at Stone City ◐
RR 1, ANAMOSA, IOWA 52205

Tel: **(319) 462-4733**	Other Meals: **Available**
Host(s): **Mike and Lynette Richards**	Credit Cards: **MC, VISA**
Location: **20 mi. NE of Cedar Rapids**	Pets: **Sometimes**
No. of Rooms: **6**	Children: **Welcome**
Max. No. Sharing Bath: **12**	Smoking: **Permitted**
Double/sb: **$50**	Social Drinking: **Permitted**
Single/sb: **$35**	Airport/Station Pickup: **Yes**
Open: **All year**	Foreign Languages: **Spanish**
Breakfast: **Continental**	

This turn-of-the-century mansion nestles among the rolling hills that inspired Grant Wood's paintings. Many writers and artists find the Inn's oak furnishings and warm fireside a pleasant inspiration. In summer, canoe the Wapsipinicon and the Buffalo rivers (rentals are available). In winter, a mug of hot buttered rum will be waiting when you return from cross-country skiing. Relax in the Jacuzzi afterward. Your hosts suggest a visit to the Stonecutter Pub, Iowa's center for folk and acoustic music.

Hotel Brooklyn ◐
407 FRONT STREET, BROOKLYN, IOWA 52211

Tel: **(515) 522-9229**	Single/sb: **$16**
Host(s): **Kay Lawson**	Suites: **$38**
Location: **1½ mi. from I-80**	Open: **All year**
No. of Rooms: **9**	Reduced Rates: **Groups**
No. of Private Baths: **2**	Breakfast: **No**
Max. No. Sharing Bath: **5**	Pets: **No**
Double/pb: **$28**	Children: **Welcome**
Single/pb: **$20**	Smoking: **Permitted**
Double/sb: **$20**	Social Drinking: **Permitted**

The hotel, of solid brick with arched window hoods, bracketed eaves, and a three-story tower, was built in 1875. The imposing staircase, marble fireplace, fine woodwork, and hand-painted murals have secured it a spot in the National Register of Historic Places. Operated by the Lawson family for 40 years, the guest rooms are lovely and have been updated to include TV sets.

Fifth Avenue Guest House ✪
204 FIFTH AVENUE, DECORAH, IOWA 52101

Tel: **(319) 382-8110**
Best Time to Call: **Before 8 AM; after 4 PM**
Host(s): **Dan and Dave Kust**
Location: **65 mi. SE of Rochester, MN**
No. of Rooms: **4**
Max. No. Sharing Bath: **4**
Double/sb: **$20**
Single/sb: **$20**

Open: **June 1–Aug. 31**
Reduced Rates: **Groups; weekly**
Breakfast: **Continental**
Pets: **Sometimes**
Children: **Welcome**
Smoking: **Permitted**
Social Drinking: **Permitted**
Airport/Station Pickup: **Yes**

This comfortable home is conveniently located near the campus of Luther College and across the street from a small park. It's close to the Norwegian-American Museum and lovely shops. There's skiing in winter; summer fun can be found on the upper Iowa River, which flows parallel to Fifth Avenue and offers a view of the bluff-lined landscape. Breakfast is highlighted by fresh cinnamon rolls—enormous, light, and moist. Relax near the wood-burning stove and enjoy a complimentary glass of wine.

Montgomery Mansion ✪
812 MAPLE AVENUE, DECORAH, IOWA 52101

Tel: **(319) 382-5088**
Host(s): **Dave Kust**
Location: **65 mi. SE of Rochester, MN**
No. of Rooms: **4**
No. of Private Baths: **1**
Max. No. Sharing Bath: **6**
Double/pb: **$30**
Double/sb: **$25**
Open: **All year**
Breakfast: **Continental**
Pets: **No**
Children: **No**
Smoking: **No**
Social Drinking: **Permitted**

This appealing 10-room historic home is close to the heart of town. You are welcome to relax in the large living room, enjoy a good book, or visit with Dave and the other guests. There's a TV room for cable movies, a large front porch, and cross-country skiing and hiking for the ambitious. Luther College is 15 minutes away.

Die Heimat Country Inn ✪
AMANA COLONIES, MAIN STREET, HOMESTEAD, IOWA 52236

Tel: (319) 622-3937
Best Time to Call: **8 AM-10 PM**
Host(s): **Don and Sheila Janda**
Location: **18 mi. S of Cedar Rapids**
No. of Rooms: **19**
No. of Private Baths: **19**
Double/pb: **$26.50**
Single/pb: **$22.50**
Open: **All year**

Reduced Rates: **Dec.-Feb.**
Breakfast: **Continental**
Credit Cards: **MC, VISA**
Pets: **Sometimes**
Children: **Welcome**
Smoking: **Permitted**
Social Drinking: **Permitted**
Airport/Station Pickup: **Yes**

The Amana Colonies is a German enclave listed in the National Register of Historic Places. This 1853 inn has been restored and furnished with antiques and hand-crafted walnut and cherry furniture, plus modern TV, telephones, and air conditioning in all rooms. Museums, shops, and a winery are nearby. The woolen mill is a must; it uses wool from 12 breeds of sheep from around the world. Blankets, yard goods, and clothing are quite special—good buys! Don and Sheila offer snacks and will recommend fine restaurants in town.

Mason House Inn ✪
FRONT STREET, BENTONSPORT, KEOSAUQUA, IOWA 52565

Tel: (319) 592-3133
Host(s): **Herbert K. and Burretta Redhead**
Location: **22 mi. from Hwy. 34**
No. of Rooms: **8**
Max. No. Sharing Bath: **3**
Double/sb: **$30-$40**
Single/sb: **$25**

Open: **Apr. 1-Nov. 1**
Breakfast: **Full**
Other Meals: **Available**
Pets: **No**
Children: **No**
Smoking: **Permitted**
Social Drinking: **Permitted**

This Georgian brick inn has offered lodging since 1896. Many of the original furnishings have been preserved, accented with wood and glass pieces. There's coffee, tea, and fruit to snack on; special dishes are prepared for breakfast, and a variety of dinner choices are available. Your hosts, museum curators for 25 years, will be happy to advise on the historic homes, antique shops, and recreational activities in Bentonsport.

KANSAS

Colby
Modoc
Merriam
Tonganoxie
Prairie Village
Kansas City
Overland Park

Kansas City Bed & Breakfast ✪
P.O. BOX 14781, LENEXA, KANSAS 66215

Tel: **(913) 268-4214**
Best Time to Call: **5–9 PM or 9 AM–5 PM in summer**
Coordinator: **Diane C. Kuhn**
States/Regions Covered:
  Kansas—Lake Quivira, Leawood, Lenexa, Merriam, Overland Park, Modoc, Prairie Village, Shawnee; **Missouri**—Liberty, Parkville, Kansas City, Warrensburg

Rates (Single/Double):
  Modest: $25 $30
  Average: $30 $35
  Luxury: $48 $50
Credit Cards: **No**

As the song says, "Everything's up-to-date in Kansas City." You will enjoy visiting such places as Crown Center, Country Club Plaza, Arrowhead Stadium, Royals Stadium, Kemper Arena, and the Missouri Repertory Theatre. A directory fully describing all of the host homes is available. Please send a self-addressed envelope with 37¢ postage. Advise Diane of your selection and she will do the rest. Jewell College, Parkville College, the University of Missouri, and Central Missouri State are close by.

Bourquin's Bed and Breakfast on the Farm ⊙
ROUTE 3, COLBY, KANSAS 67701

Tel: **(913) 462-7447; 462-2998**	Double/sb: **$25**
Best Time to Call: **Evenings**	Single/sb: **$18**
Host(s): **Dan and Shirley Bourquin**	Open: **All year**
Location: **11 mi. NW of Colby**	Breakfast: **Full**
No. of Rooms: **3**	Pets: **Welcome**
No. of Private Baths: **1**	Children: **Welcome**
Max. No Sharing Bath: **4**	Smoking: **Permitted**
Double/pb: **$25**	Social Drinking: **Permitted**
Single/pb: **$18**	Airport/Station Pickup: **Yes**

This glass-and-cedar chalet is in the heart of the wheat belt. The house features passive solar heat, a patio, recreation area, and family room. Guest accommodations have a separate entrance. A tour of the wheat harvest and farming operation is a must. Children and adults will enjoy the Thomas County Museum's collections of Kuska dolls and "cut" glass. The farm offers plenty of space to jog, walk, or play in the shade of ponderosa pines and cedars.

Almeda's Inn ⊙
BOX 103, 220 SOUTH MAIN, TONGANOXIE, KANSAS 66086

Tel: **(913) 845-2295**	Open: **All year**
Host(s): **Almeda and Richard Tinberg**	Breakfast: **Continental**
Location: **20 mi. W of Kansas City**	Pets: **No**
No. of Rooms: **3**	Children: **Welcome, over 4**
Max. No. Sharing Bath: **6**	Smoking: **Permitted**
Double/sb: **$30**	Social Drinking: **Permitted**
Single/sb: **$25**	

Located in a picturesque small town, the inn dates back to World War I. You are welcome to sip a cup of coffee at the unique stone bar in the room once used as a bus stop in 1930. In fact, this room was the inspiration for *Bus Stop*. Almeda and Richard will be happy to direct you to the golf course, swimming facilities, the Starlight Theatre, or the University of Kansas at Lawrence.

For key to listings, see inside front or back cover.

✪ This star means that rates are guaranteed through December 31, 1985 to any guest making a reservation as a result of reading about the B&B in BED & BREAKFAST U.S.A.—1985 edition.

Please enclose a self-addressed, stamped, business-sized envelope when contacting reservation services.

For more details on what you can expect in a B&B, see Chapter 1.

Always mention *Bed & Breakfast USA* when making reservations!

KENTUCKY

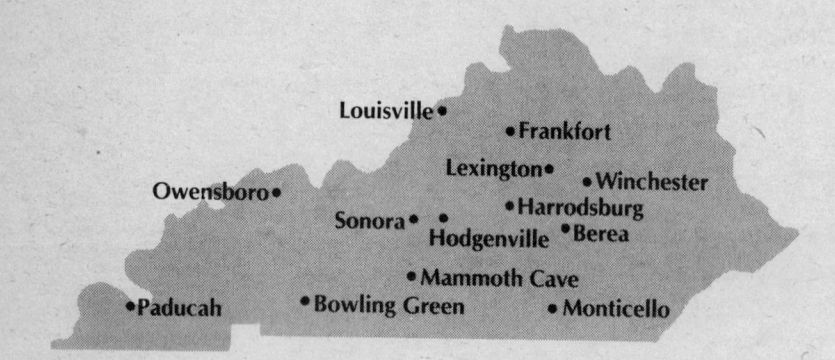

Kentucky Homes B&B ✪
1431 ST. JAMES COURT, LOUISVILLE, KENTUCKY 40208

Tel: (502) 635-7341 or 452-6629
Coordinator: **Jo DuBose Boone, Lillian B. Marshall**
States/Regions Covered:
   Kentucky—statewide; Indiana; Tennessee

Rates (Single/Double):
   Average: $29–$39 $34–$44
Credit Cards: **No**

Lillian and Jo cordially invite you to be a guest in friendly Kentucky at one of dozens of host homes. Fish in spectacular lakes, visit Mammoth Cave, drop in on Shakertown at Pleasant Hill, or reserve early and assure yourself of a spot at the next running of the Kentucky Derby (held the first Saturday in May). Stay in a gorgeous turn-of-the-century home in restored old Louisville, or a dairy farm that boards and trains racehorses, or many comfortable choices in-between. Efficiency apartments are also available for $36.

Bowling Green Bed & Breakfast ✪
659 EAST 14TH AVENUE, BOWLING GREEN, KENTUCKY 42101

Tel: **(502) 781-3861**
Best Time to Call: **Evenings**
Host(s): **Ronna Lee and Norman Hunter**
Location: **4 mi. from I-65**
No. of Rooms: **3**
No. of Private Baths: **1**
Max. No. Sharing Bath: **4**
Double/pb: **$30**
Single/pb: **$23**

Double/sb: **$30**
Single/sb: **$23**
Open: **All year**
Breakfast: **Continental**
Pets: **No**
Children: **Welcome, over 14**
Smoking: **No**
Social Drinking: **Permitted**
Airport/Station Pickup: **Yes**

This trim, gray-shingled, comfortably furnished, two-story home is situated on a wooded lot. You are welcome to watch TV, select a book from the library, crank out a tune on the old Victrola, or play ping-pong in the recreation room. It is an easy drive to state parks and Mammoth Cave. Ronna Lee and Norman teach at nearby Western Kentucky State College.

Ehrhardt's B&B ✪
285 SPRINGWELL DRIVE, PADUCAH, KENTUCKY 42001

Tel: **(502) 554-0644**
Best Time to Call: **7-10 AM; 4-6 PM**
Host(s): **Eileen and Phil Ehrhardt**
Location: **1 mi. from I-24**
No. of Rooms: **2**
Max. No. Sharing Bath: **4**
Double/sb: **$30**
Single/sb: **$25**

Open: **All year**
Reduced Rates: **10%, seniors**
Breakfast: **Full**
Pets: **Sometimes**
Children: **Welcome**
Smoking: **Permitted**
Social Drinking: **Permitted**
Airport/Station Pickup: **Yes**

This brick colonial ranch home is just a mile off I-24, which is famous for its beautiful scenery. Your hosts hope to make you feel at home in antique-filled bedrooms and a fireplaced den. Homemade biscuits, jellies, country ham and gravy are breakfast specialties. Enjoy swimming and boating at nearby Lake Barkley, Ky Lake, and Land between the Lakes. Fine dining and Paducah's historic riverfront are nearby.

LOUISIANA

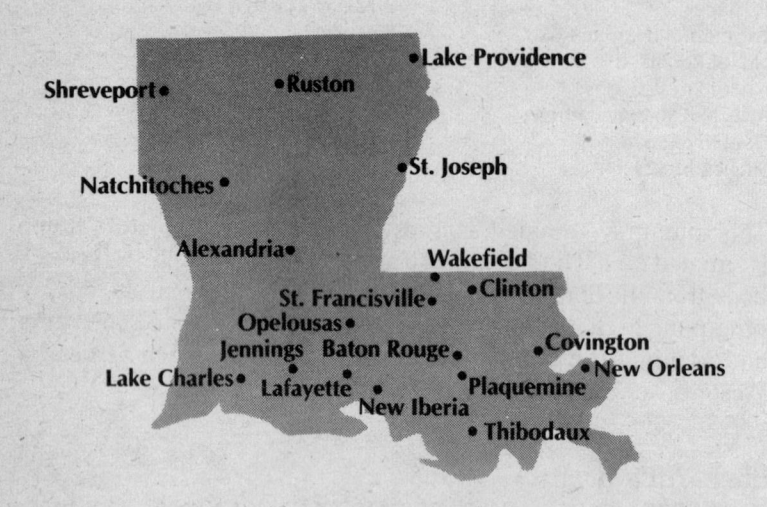

Louisiana Hospitality Services, Inc.
P.O. BOX 80717, BATON ROUGE, LOUISIANA 70898

Tel: **(504) 769-0366**
Best Time to Call: **9 AM–9 PM**
Coordinator: **Melissa D. Folks**
State/Regions Covered: **Clinton, Jackson, Ruston, Shreveport, La.; Natchez, Vicksburg, Miss.**

Rates (Single/Double):
Modest: **$25–$40**
Average: **$40–$70**
Luxury: **$60–$100**
Credit Cards: **No**

The above represents only a partial listing of areas covered by Melissa's reservation service. All the homes on her roster must meet specific qualifications: they must be historic properties, with at least 25% of the lodging facility being of pre-1930 construction. The hosts must be 100% dedicated to cordial hospitality. Antebellum homes, National Register Historic Districts, and plantations are typical accommodations.

Southern Comfort Bed & Breakfast
2856 HUNDRED OAKS, BATON ROUGE, LOUISIANA 70808

Tel: (504) 346-1928 or 926-9784
Best Time to Call: 8 AM–8 PM
Coordinators: Susan Morris and Helen Heath
State/Regions Covered: Louisiana—Baton Rouge, Clinton, Jennings, Lafayette; Mississippi—Columbus, Picayune; New Mexico

Rates (Single/Double):
  Modest: $20–$35 $30–$40
  Average: $35–$50 $40–$60
  Luxury: $55–$95 $65–$125
Credit Cards: MC, VISA

Susan and Helen offer you the best of the Old and the New South with hosts in urban and rural areas. The above is only a sample list. Special attractions are Civil War and other historic sites; fabulous New Orleans; Acadian (Cajun) country; sports, deep-sea fishing, and racetracks in Louisiana and New Mexico. Their descriptive directory is $1.

Plantation Bell Guest House ✪
204 WEST 24th AVENUE, COVINGTON, LOUISIANA 70433

Tel: (504) 892-1952
Best Time to Call: Before 8 AM
Host(s): Lila Rapier
Location: 35 mi. N of New Orleans
No. of Rooms: 3
No. of Private Baths: 3
Double/pb: $30–$35
Single/pb: $25–$30

Open: All year
Reduced Rates: Weekly
Breakfast: Full
Air-Conditioning: Yes
Pets: Sometimes
Children: Welcome
Smoking: Permitted
Social Drinking: Permitted

This late Victorian house has an old-fashioned porch with rocking chairs overlooking a quiet street. Inside, the ceilings are 13 feet high, and the old-time fans add to the nostalgic motif. The guest rooms are decorated with cheerful wallpapers and are very comfortable. Local possibilities include canoeing, cycling, and shopping in Covington.

Mintmere Plantation
1400 EAST MAIN STREET, NEW IBERIA, LOUISIANA 70560

Tel: **(318) 364-6210**
Best Time to Call: **10 AM–5 PM**
Host(s): **Virginia Jones**
Location: **150 mi. NW of New Orleans**
No. of Rooms: **5 suites**
No. of Private Baths: **4**
Suites: **$100 (for 2); $150 (for 4)**

Open: **All year**
Breakfast: **Full**
Pets: **No**
Children: **Welcome, over 12**
Smoking: **Permitted**
Social Drinking: **Permitted**
Foreign Languages: **French**

This magnificent Greek Revival raised cottage was built in 1857. It is furnished with Louisiana antiques and overlooks historic Bayou Teche. The house is on the National Register of Historic Places. Don't miss Konrico, the oldest operating rice mill and country store in the country. The University of Southwestern Louisiana is close by.

Bed & Breakfast, Inc. ✪
1236 DECATUR STREET, NEW ORLEANS, LOUISIANA 70116

Tel: **(504) 525-4640**
Coordinator: **Hazell Boyce**
States/Regions Covered: **New Orleans**

Rates (Single/Double):
    Modest: **$25–$35**   **$25–$35**
    Average: **$30–$55**   **$40–$65**
    Luxury: **$60 and up $70 and up**
Credit Cards: **No**

New Orleans is called the "City That Care Forgot." You are certain to be carefree, visiting the French Quarter, taking Mississippi riverboat rides, going to the Superdome, taking plantation tours, and enjoying the Mardi Gras, as well as dining in fine restaurants or attending jazz concerts. Hazell's hosts will help you get the most out of your stay. Sample listings on request.

New Orleans Bed & Breakfast ✪
P.O. BOX 8163, NEW ORLEANS, LOUISIANA 70182

Tel: (504) 949-6705 (toll-free outside Louisiana: 1-800-541-9852)
Best Time to Call: 8 AM–7 PM
Coordinator: Sarah-Margaret Brown
States/Regions Covered:
   Louisiana—Baton Rouge, Covington, Cottonport, Lafayette, Lake Charles, New Iberia, New Orleans, Shreveport, Vinton;
   Mississippi—Biloxi, Ocean Springs, Waveland

Rates (Single/Double):
   Modest: $25 $25–$35
   Average: $35–$50 $40–$65
   Luxury: $60 $65–$150
Credit Cards: MC, VISA (for deposits only)

Sarah-Margaret offers a range from the youth-hostel type for the backpacker crowd, to modest accommodations in all areas of the city, to deluxe B&Bs in lovely and historic locations. If the past intrigues you, treat yourself to an overnight stay in a great Louisiana or Mississippi plantation home, or revel in the warm sun and sand of the Gulf Coast in Waveland, Mississippi.

The Cornstalk Fence Guest House ✪
915 ROYAL STREET, NEW ORLEANS, LOUISIANA 70116

Tel: (504) 523-1515
Best Time to Call: 1–3 PM
Host(s): Debi and David Spencer
No. of Rooms: 14
No. of Private Baths: 14
Double/pb: $65–$85
Single/pb: $60–$80
Open: All year

Reduced Rates: Corporate; military
Breakfast: Continental
Credit Cards: AMEX, MC, VISA
Pets: No
Children: Welcome (crib)
Smoking: Permitted
Social Drinking: Permitted
Foreign Languages: French, German

This exquisite Georgian mansion (circa 1780) is surrounded by a fabulous cast-iron fence fashioned like Iowa corn growing in a field. Stained glass windows, fireplaces, Oriental rugs, and antiques embellish the interior. The balcony overlooks Royal Street in the famed French Quarter, and you will be close to world-class restaurants, galleries, museums, shops, and jazz spots. You may enjoy breakfast along with the morning paper, in the comfort of your room, or the balcony porch, or patio. Debi and David offer a complimentary glass of liquor to help you unwind after a busy day.

Lafitte Guest House
1003 BOURBON STREET, NEW ORLEANS, LOUISIANA 70117

Tel: **(504) 581-2678**
Host(s): **Steve Guyton**
No. of Rooms: **14**
No. of Private Baths: **14**
Double/pb: **$75–$105**
Single/pb: **$65–$95**
Open: **All year**

Reduced Rates: **10% June 1–Aug. 31**
Breakfast: **Continental**
Credit Cards: **AMEX, MC, VISA**
Pets: **No**
Children: **Welcome**
Smoking: **Permitted**
Social Drinking: **Permitted**

This three-story French manor house was built in 1849 and is located in the heart of the world famous French Quarter. Furnished with Victorian antiques, it is a comfortable place to return to after dining in the area's marvelous restaurants or shopping in fine shops.

The Estorge House
427 NORTH MARKET STREET, OPELOUSAS, LOUISIANA 70570

Tel: **(318) 948-4592**
Best Time to Call: **9 AM–6 PM**
Host(s): **Margaret Eagle**
Location: **100 mi. NW of New Orleans**
No. of Rooms: **2 suites**
No. of Private Baths: **2**

Suites: **$100**
Open: **All year**
Breakfast: **Full**
Pets: **No**
Children: **Welcome, over 12**
Smoking: **Permitted**
Social Drinking: **Permitted**

This house, built in 1827, in the neo-classic style, is furnished with beautiful period pieces. Opelousas is an historic town which served as the capital of Louisiana during the Civil War. Many historic sites and fine antebellum homes can be seen in the area. Margaret is a tour guide and is very adept at many handcrafts. Her thorough knowledge of her home town will make your visit special. The University of Southwestern Louisiana is nearby.

Twin Gables
711 NORTH VIENNA STREET, RUSTON, LOUISIANA 71270

Tel: **(318) 244-4452**
Host(s): **Carol Hudson and Beulah Laster**
Location: **²/₁₀ mi. from I-20**

No. of Rooms: **5**
No. of Private Baths: **5**
Double/pb: **$45–$50**
Single/pb: **$40–$45**

Open: **All year**
Breakfast: **Continental**
Credit Cards: **MC, VISA**
Pets: **No**

Children: **Welcome, over 12**
Smoking: **Permitted**
Social Drinking: **Permitted**
Airport/Station Pickup: **Yes**

Built in 1882, this refurbished Victorian mansion will please discriminating visitors. Antiques, good paintings, and lots of plants are used in the decor. Teapots and cakes are available for afternoon tea, and the kitchen may be used for snacks. Carol and Beulah will allow you the use of the washer-dryer to freshen your travel wardrobe. D'Arbonne Lake, Claiborne Lake, and the Sandy Hill Golf Club are close by, as is Louisiana Tech. University.

Cottage Plantation ○
ROUTE 5, BOX 425, ST. FRANCISVILLE, LOUISIANA 70775

Tel: **(504) 635-3674**
Best Time to Call: **4–6 PM**
Host(s): **Mr. & Mrs. J. E. Brown**
Location: **30 mi. N of Baton Rouge**
No. of Rooms: **5**
No. of Private Baths: **5**
Double/pb: **$60**

Single/pb: **$40**
Open: **All year**
Breakfast: **Full**
Pets: **No**
Children: **Welcome**
Smoking: **Permitted**
Social Drinking: **Permitted**

This sprawling antebellum home is a working plantation listed in the National Register of Historic Places. Andrew Jackson once slept here, and today you can see much of the same furnishings he did. A full Southern-style breakfast is offered. Guests are welcome to tour the 15 original buildings built over a century ago. Nearby attractions include Audubon Memorial Park and the historic sites of St. Francisville.

MAINE

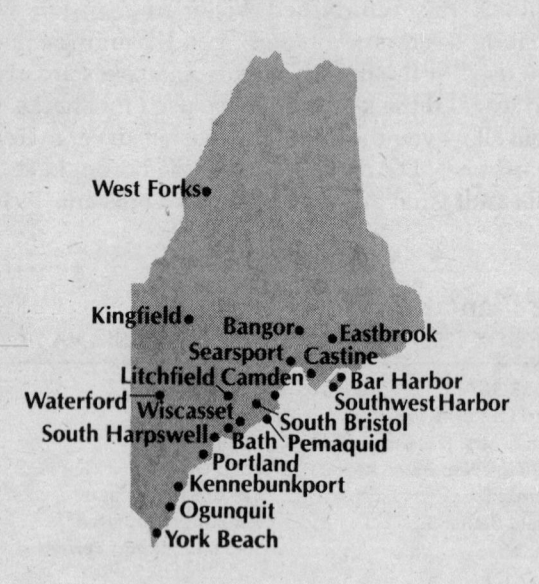

Bed & Breakfast Down East, Ltd. ○
BOX 547, MACOMBER MILL ROAD, EASTBROOK, MAINE 04634

Tel: (207)565-3517
Coordinator: **Sally B. Godfrey**
States/Regions Covered: **Maine (statewide)**

Rates (Single/Double):
Modest: $25 $35
Average: $30 $40–$45
Luxury: $35 $55
Credit Cards: **MC, VISA**

There are delightful accommodations waiting for you, from Kittery Point at the New Hampshire border to "way down East" in Eastport, near F.D.R.'s Campobello Island in New Brunswick, Canada. You are certain to enjoy Bar Harbor, Acadia National Park, the rugged coastline, and inland forest and streams. All of Sally's hosts will make you feel welcome.

INLAND MAINE

The Country Cupboard Guesthouse
ROUTE 27, NORTH MAIN STREET, RD1 BOX 1270, KINGFIELD, MAINE 04947

Tel: **(207) 265-2193**
Best Time to Call: **Before 10 PM**
Host(s): **Sharon and Bud Jordan**
Location: **45 mi. W of Waterville**
No. of Rooms: **7**
Max. No. Sharing Bath: **6**
Double/sb: **$42–$52**
Open: **All year**

Reduced Rates: **Weekly**
Breakfast: **Full**
Other Meals: **Available**
Credit Cards: **MC, VISA**
Pets: **No**
Children: **Welcome**
Smoking: **Permitted**
Social Drinking: **Permitted**

This cozy clapboard farmhouse is only 18 miles from Sugarloaf Mountain. All the bedrooms are carpeted and comfortably furnished with color-coordinated linens. Sharon and Bud will be pleased to suggest fun things to do in all seasons. There's great fishing, hiking, and marvelous skiing. The fall foliage is fabulous.

Crab Apple Acres Inn ✪
ROUTE 201, WEST FORKS, MAINE 04985

Tel: **(207) 663-2218**
Host(s): **Chuck and Sharyn Peabody**
Location: **140 mi. S of Quebec City, Canada**
No. of Rooms: **7**
Max. No. Sharing Bath: **7**
Double/sb: **$30**
Single/sb: **$15**

Open: **All year**
Breakfast: **Full—$4**
Other Meals: **Available**
Credit Cards: **MC**
Pets: **No**
Children: **Welcome**
Smoking: **Permitted**
Social Drinking: **Permitted**

This fine old farmhouse, built in 1835, overlooks the Kennebec River; its hosts welcome you with congenial, country hospitality. The house has polished, wide-board pine floors, a wood cookstove, and colorful quilts on the beds. Your hosts are licensed professional white-water outfitters, and Chuck guides raft trips on the Kennebec and Dead rivers. The coffee pot is always on.

ALONG THE COAST

Birch Haven Bed & Breakfast ✪
RFD#1, BOX 190L, BAR HARBOR, MAINE 04609

Tel: **(207) 288-3571**
Host(s): **Virginia and Dale Kohr**
Location: **10 mi. S of Ellsworth**
No. of Rooms: **2**
Max. No. Sharing Bath: **4**
Double/sb: **$45–$55**
Reduced Rates: **Oct. 15–May 15**
Open: **All year**

Breakfast: **Full**
Other Meals: **Available**
Credit Cards: **AMEX, VISA**
Pets: **No**
Children: **Welcome, over 6**
Smoking: **Permitted**
Social Drinking: **Permitted**

This secluded woodland hideaway is set back on five acres near Acadia National Park. The area is ideal for cross-country skiing, bird watching, and a multitude of recreational activities in all seasons. Virginia and Dale pride themselves on over 40 ways to prepare eggs for breakfast; their menu is a gourmet's delight.

Grane's Fairhaven Inn ✪
NORTH BATH ROAD, BATH, MAINE 04530

Tel: **(207) 443-4391**
Best Time to Call: **9–11 AM, Evenings**
Host(s): **Jane Wyllie, Gretchen Williams**
Location: **3 mi. N of Bath**
No. of Rooms: **9**
No. of Private Baths: **1**
Max. No. Sharing Bath: **5**
Double/pb: **$40–$50**

Double/sb: **$30–$40**
Single/sb: **$22–$33**
Open: **All year**
Reduced Rates: **Weekly; 4-night stays**
Breakfast: **$2–$4**
Pets: **Yes**
Children: **Welcome**
Smoking: **Permitted**
Social Drinking: **Permitted**

The Fairhaven is a rambling colonial inn on 27 acres, overlooking the Kennebec River. The original family quarters date back to 1790. Now the 20-room inn includes a library, a "bring your own" tavern, and is furnished with lots of antiques, wood, and glass. Breakfast specials include orange French toast and homemade sausage. Golf, tennis, the beach, and ski slopes are nearby. Bowdoin, Bates, and Beal colleges are nearby.

Goodspeed's Guest House
60 MOUNTAIN STREET, ROUTE 52, CAMDEN, MAINE 04843

Tel: **(207) 236-8077**
Best Time to Call: **8 AM–8 PM**
Host(s): **Don and Linda Goodspeed**
Location: **¼ mi. from Rt 1**
No. of Rooms: **8**
Max. No. Sharing Bath: **6**
Double/sb: **$45**
Single/sb: **$35**

Suites: **$65**
Open: **All year**
Breakfast: **Continental**
Pets: **No**
Children: **Welcome, over 12**
Smoking: **Permitted**
Social Drinking: **Permitted**

This grey clapboard house features antique clocks, wicker furniture, plants, and stained glass windows. Guest rooms are furnished in oak, maple, and pine, with iron or brass beds. Breakfast includes homemade pastries and fresh-ground coffee. Your hosts welcome you to lemonade, iced tea in season, and will gladly provide setups for BYOB guests. It's just six blocks to the outdoor theater. The lakes and ski slopes are within a few miles of the house.

Hawthorn Inn
9 HIGH STREET, CAMDEN, MAINE 04843

Tel: **(207) 236-8842**
Best Time to Call: **7–8:30 AM**
Host(s): **Douglas and Jocelyn Morrison**
Location: **150 mi. N of Boston**
No. of Rooms: **7**
No. of Private Baths: **2**
Max. No. Sharing Bath: **3**
Double/pb: **$55–$65**
Double/sb: **$40–$55**
Open: **All year**

Reduced Rates: **$10 less daily, Nov. 1–June 25**
Breakfast: **Continental**
Credit Cards: **MC, VISA**
Pets: **No**
Children: **Welcome**
Smoking: **Permitted**
Social Drinking: **Permitted**
Airport/Station Pickup: **Yes**

The airy rooms of this Victorian inn are an elegant mixture of the old and the new. Guests are welcome to wine or coffee while relaxing on the deck or getting warm by the fire. Breakfast is served in a sunny dining room. All rooms overlook either Mt. Battle or Camden Harbor. A score of winter sports can be enjoyed in the area, and shops and restaurants are a short walk away.

Maine Stay Bed and Breakfast ○
22 HIGH STREET, CAMDEN, MAINE 04843

Tel: (207) 236-9636
Best Time to Call: **Evenings**
Host(s): **Sally and Bob Tierney, Pat and Bruce Hunt**
Location: **97 mi. NE of Portland**
No. of Rooms: **7**
Max. No. Sharing Bath: **4**
Double/sb: **$45–$50**
Single/sb: **$35–$40**

Open: **All year**
Reduced Rates: **10% seniors, 10% weekly**
Breakfast: **Continental**
Pets: **No**
Children: **Welcome, over 10**
Smoking: **Permitted**
Social Drinking: **Permitted**
Foreign Languages: **French**

This is one of Camden's treasured colonials, built in 1813. Choose from seven large bedrooms decorated with period pieces. Relax with a cup of coffee or catch up on a book in one of the spacious parlors. Breakfast is served on an attractive deck in warm weather. It's only a five-minute walk to the shops and restaurants of Camden Harbor. Windjammer cruises, a Shakespeare theater, skiing, and Camden Hills State Park are just a few of the local attractions.

Wooden Goose Inn
RTE. 1, BOX 195, CAPE NEDDICK, MAINE 03902

Tel: (207) 363-5673
Host(s): **Jerry D. Rippetoe, Anthony V. Sienicki**
Location: **70 mi. N of Boston**
No. of Rooms: **5**
No. of Private Baths: **1**
Max. No. Sharing Bath: **4**
Double/pb: **$55**
Double/sb: **$50–$55**

Single/sb: **$30**
Suites: **$85–$105**
Open: **Feb. 1–Dec. 31**
Breakfast: **Full**
Pets: **No**
Children: **Welcome, over 12**
Smoking: **Permitted**
Social Drinking: **Permitted**

This 19th-century farmhouse was built by a sea captain. It is decorated with porcelain, crystal, and Oriental rugs. Guests are served afternoon tea with croissants and paté, and the coffee pot is always on. Breakfast might feature either eggs Benedict or Florentine, and sausage. Portsmouth and Ogunquit are nearby.

The Captain Lord Mansion ✪
PLEASANT STREET, BOX 527, KENNEBUNKPORT, MAINE 04046

Tel: **(207) 967-3141**
Best Time to Call: **8 AM–11 PM**
Host(s): **Bev Davis, Rick Litchfield**
Location: **35 mi. S of Portland**
No. of Rooms: **16**
No. of Private Baths: **16**
Double/pb: **$69–$99**
Single/pb: **$69–$99**

Open: **All year**
Breakfast: **Continental**
Pets: **No**
Children: **Welcome, over 12**
Smoking: **No**
Social Drinking: **Permitted**
Airport/Station Pickup: **Yes**

Bev and Rick have lovingly restored their home to its 1812 elegance. It is listed in the National Historic Register. The guest rooms are filled with antiques, thick carpets, plus handmade quilts and pillows. Eleven rooms have working fireplaces. Breakfast is served in the country kitchen. The beach, galleries, and restaurants are close by.

The Green Heron Inn
DRAWER 151, OCEAN AVENUE, KENNEBUNKPORT, MAINE 04046

Tel: **(207) 967-3315**
Best Time to Call: **Evenings**
Host(s): **Virginia and Wallace Reid**
Location: **4½ mi. from U.S. 1**
No. of Rooms: **10**
No. of Private Baths: **10**
Double/pb: **$30–$40**
Single/pb: **$20.50–$30.50**
Suites: **$42–$60**

Guest Cottage: **$42–$60; sleeps 4**
Open: **June 3–Oct. 14**
Reduced Rates: **15%, weekly; families**
Breakfast: **Full**
Pets: **Welcome**
Children: **Welcome (crib)**
Smoking: **Permitted**
Social Drinking: **Permitted**
Airport/Station Pickup: **Yes**

This immaculate inn (circa 1908) with its inviting porch and striped awnings, furnished simply and comfortably, is located between the river and the ocean in this colonial resort village. The full Yankee breakfast is a rib-buster! This is a saltwater fisherman's heaven, with boating, golf, swimming, and tennis all nearby, close to shops and galleries. Virginia and Wallace will be happy to suggest the best place for lobster. Reserve early because this is a super value in this resort town.

Old Fort Inn ⚬
P.O. BOX 759H, OLD FORT AVENUE, KENNEBUNKPORT, MAINE 04046

Tel: **(207) 967-5353**
Host(s): **Sheila and David Aldrich**
Location: **Near Exit 3, Maine Turnpike**
No. of Rooms: **12**
No. of Private Baths: **12**
Double/pb: **$63–$85**
Suites: **$105**
Open: **May to Oct.**
Reduced Rates: **20%, May 1 to June 13**
Breakfast: **Continental**
Credit Cards: **AMEX, MC, VISA**
Pets: **No**
Children: **Welcome, over 7**
Smoking: **Permitted**
Social Drinking: **Permitted**

Built in 1880, the inn has yesterday's charm and today's conveniences. The guest rooms are in a brick-and-stone carriage house, and are beautifully decorated with early pine and oak furniture. Each has a fully equipped kitchen unit, TV, and maid service. There's a large pool, tennis court, and shuffleboard on premises, and it is an easy walk to the ocean.

Old Tavern Inn ⚬
POST ROAD, P.O. BOX 445, LITCHFIELD, MAINE 04350

Tel: **(207) 268-4965**
Host(s): **Virginia Albert**
Location: **12 mi. SW of Augusta**
No. of Rooms: **6**
Max. No. Sharing Bath: **4**
Double/sb: **$30**
Single/sb: **$27**
Open: **All year**
Breakfast: **Full**
Pets: **Sometimes**
Children: **Welcome**
Smoking: **Permitted**
Social Drinking: **Permitted**

Virginia's home was built as a tavern in 1808, and the hitching posts that flank it go back to the time when stagecoach horses were tethered there. Furnished with traditional pieces, comfortable antiques, and plants, it is warm and cozy. There's a heated in-ground pool and a pond for fishing; it's an easy walk to Tacoma Lake for boating and fishing. Bates College is nearby.

Bed 'n' Breakfast at Penury Hall ✪
BOX 68, MAIN STREET, SOUTHWEST HARBOR, MT. DESERT ISLAND, MAINE 04679

Tel: **(207) 244-7102**
Host(s): **Gretchen and Toby Strong**
Location: **15 mi. W of Bar Harbor**
No. of Rooms: **3**
Max. No. Sharing Bath: **5**
Double/sb: **$40**
Single/sb: **$32**
Open: **All year**

Reduced Rates: **November 1 to April 1**
Breakfast: **Full**
Pets: **No**
Children: **Welcome, over 16**
Smoking: **Permitted**
Social Drinking: **Permitted**
Airport/Station Pickup: **Yes**

This grey frame house has a red door and a crisp, welcoming air. Built in 1830, it is comfortably furnished with traditional pieces, antiques, and original art. Gretchen and Toby are cosmopolitan and cordial. Their motto is: "Each guest is an honorary member of the family," and you'll soon feel at home. Knowledgeable about the area's highlights, they'll direct you to special shops and restaurants and all the best things to see and do.

The Harbor Lights ✪
P.O. BOX 593, SOUTHWEST HARBOR, MT. DESERT ISLAND, MAINE 04679

Tel: **(207) 244-3835**
Host(s): **Hilda Leighton**
Location: **15 mi. W of Bar Harbor**
No. of Rooms: **9**
No. of Private Baths: **7**
Max. No. Sharing Bath: **4**
Double/pb: **$20–$30**
Single/pb: **$20–$30**
Double/sb: **$18–$25**

Single/sb: **$18–$25**
Open: **All year**
Breakfast: **No**
Credit Cards: **MC, VISA**
Pets: **Sometimes**
Children: **Welcome (crib)**
Smoking: **Permitted**
Social Drinking: **Permitted**
Airport/Station Pickup: **Yes**

This area is a fabulous combination of mountains, ocean, caves, forests, quaint villages, and stately homes. Acadia National Park is here, and it rivals Yellowstone in popularity. This is a spacious, comfortable home with wide porch and a living room with fireplace and TV. It is close to many fine restaurants. Don't miss the lobster pier for the best buy in a delicious meal.

Hearthside Inn
7 HIGH STREET, BAR HARBOR, MT. DESERT ISLAND, MAINE 04609

Tel: **(207) 288-4533**
Host(s): **Lois Gregg**
No. of Rooms: **9**
No. of Private Baths: **7**
Max. No. Sharing Bath: **4**
Double/pb: **$54–$62**
Single/pb: **$48–$56**
Double/sb: **$44–$48**
Single/sb: **$40–$44**

Open: **June 21 to September 2**
Reduced Rates: **No**
Breakfast: **Continental**
Credit Cards: **MC, VISA**
Pets: **No**
Children: **Welcome, over 10**
Smoking: **Permitted**
Social Drinking: **Permitted**

On a quiet street, just a short walk to town, is this gracious home, furnished in the manner of a country cottage. You are invited to share the special ambience of a living room with a cozy fireplace and brimming with books, or the music room with its grand piano and game table. Some rooms have a balcony or a fireplace. Complimentary coffee and iced tea are offered.

Hartwell House ✪
116 SHORE ROAD, OGUNQUIT, MAINE 03907

Tel: **(207) 646-7210**
Best Time to Call: **Mornings**
Host(s): **Jennifer Delmont**
Location: **75 mi. N of Boston**
No. of Rooms: **9**
No. of Private Baths: **9**
Double/pb: **$95**
Single/pb: **$95**

Open: **All year**
Breakfast: **Full**
Credit Cards: **MC, VISA**
Pets: **No**
Children: **Welcome, over 14**
Smoking: **Permitted**
Social Drinking: **Permitted**
Foreign Languages: **French**

Jennifer offers the serenity of Maine country life, although it's only minutes from the bustle of this thriving summer resort. Each guest room is tastefully furnished with early American and English antiques. Most have private balconies overlooking the lawn with its sculptured flower gardens. Flowers in every room add to the charm. The University of Maine is nearby.

High Tor ✪
FRAZIER PASTURE ROAD, OGUNQUIT, MAINE 03907

Tel: **(207) 646-8232**
Best Time to Call: **5–8 PM**
Host(s): **Julie O'Brien, Cleda Farris Wiley**
Location: **75 mi. N of Boston**
No. of Rooms: **2**
No. of Private Baths: **2**

Double/pb: **$60**
Open: **May 1–Oct. 30**
Breakfast: **Continental**
Pets: **No**
Children: **Welcome, over 10**
Smoking: **Permitted**
Social Drinking: **Permitted**

This gracious home, with a panoramic view of the Atlantic, overlooks Marginal Way, a coastal footpath, and is midway between town and Perkins Cove. In this exclusive residential area, the quiet is broken only by the sound of the surf. The wood interior, beamed ceiling, fieldstone fireplace, and lovely antiques add to the easy atmosphere. Guest rooms, looking over the sea, have queen-size beds and down comforters, plus a guest refrigerator. Coffee is provided in each room. You'll enjoy the theater, museums, and auctions as well as seaside activities. Minimum stay is two nights.

Little River Inn ✪
ROUTE 130, PEMAQUID, MAINE 04558

Tel: (207) 677-3678
Best Time to Call: **Evenings**
Host(s): **Jeffrey and Judith Burke**
Location: **9½ mi. S of Damariscotta**
No. of Rooms: **7**
No. of Private Baths: **2**
Max. No. Sharing Bath: **4**
Double/pb: **$40**
Single/pb: **$35**
Double/sb: **$35–$45**

Single/sb: **$30–$40**
Open: **All year**
Reduced Rates: **Off-season; weekly**
Breakfast: **Full**
Credit Cards: **MC, VISA**
Pets: **Sometimes**
Children: **Welcome**
Smoking: **Permitted**
Social Drinking: **Permitted**
Foreign Languages: **Spanish**

This handsome home is located in a historic area on the bank of the river and above the waterfalls. Jeffrey has painstakingly refurbished each room to reflect its original charm. Judy's breakfast quiche is the best, and her talent for setting a lovely table will be obvious. It's close to the beach, Fort William Henry, and archeological digs.

The Inn at Parkspring ✪
135 SPRING STREET, PORTLAND, MAINE 04101

Tel: (207) 774-1059
Host(s): **Wendy Wickstrom**
Location: **2 mi. from I-295**
No. of Rooms: **7**
No. of Private Baths: **5**
Max. No. Sharing Bath: **4**
Double/pb: **$85**
Double/sb: **$75**

Open: **All year**
Reduced Rates: **Winter**
Breakfast: **Continental**
Credit Cards: **MC, VISA**
Pets: **Sometimes**
Children: **Welcome, over 12**
Smoking: **Permitted**
Social Drinking: **Permitted**

Built in 1835, the Inn reflects the 19th-century architecture Portland is famous for. First floor rooms feature period decor, with floor to ceiling windows. Third floor accommodations reflect today's style, with skylights overlooking the city. The second floor blends the old and the contemporary. Guests are welcomed with fresh flowers and imported chocolates. In the afternoon, enjoy a glass of brandy or a cup of tea with your hosts. They also offer setups, and early or late breakfast.

The Tide's Inn ✪
BOX 589 ROUTE 129, SOUTH BRISTOL, MAINE 04568

Tel: **(207) 644-8130**
Host(s): **Richard and Barbara Hawkins**
Location: **12 mi. S of Damariscotta**
No. of Rooms: **4**
No. of Private Baths: **2**
Max. No. Sharing Bath: **4**
Double/pb: **$40**
Single/pb: **$30**
Double/sb: **$35**
Single/sb: **$25**
Open: **All year**
Reduced Rates: **Weekly**
Breakfast: **Full**
Pets: **Welcome**
Children: **Welcome (crib)**
Smoking: **Permitted**
Social Drinking: **Permitted**

Tide's Inn is built on a hillside overlooking Bradstreet Cove, offering a large living room with cathedral ceiling, piano, and many books. Guest rooms are comfortably furnished with antiques and all have water views. A gourmet breakfast featuring soufflés, eggs Benedict and homemade breads is served on a large deck in season. Use the grill and picnic tables. Your hosts will be happy to pack a picnic lunch. The small fishing village of South Bristol is nearby. Other area attractions include golf, tennis, cross-country skiing, and a trip to the lighthouse at Pemaquid Point is a must.

The Maine Stay ✪
RD2, BOX 355, SOUTH HARPSWELL, MAINE 04079

Tel: **(207) 729-1373**
Best Time to Call: **4–8 PM**
Host(s): **Paul and Barbara Hansen**
Location: **6 mi. S of Brunswick**
No. of Rooms: **2**
Max. No. Sharing Bath: **4**
Double/sb: **$35**
Single/sb: **$20**
Open: **June 1–Oct. 31**
Reduced Rates: **After 3 nights**
Breakfast: **Full**
Pets: **Sometimes**
Children: **Welcome**
Smoking: **Permitted**
Social Drinking: **Permitted**

Paul and Barbara have a sprawling 19th-century home on two acres dotted with berry bushes and old apple trees, and just a short walk to the ocean. Inside, the curved staircase leads up to the guest rooms, art studios, and darkroom. There are cultural events at Bowdoin College in Brunswick close by, and the symphony in Portland. Advance reservations are requested.

The Artemus Ward House ⊙
WATERFORD, MAINE 04088

Tel: (207) 583-4106
Best Time to Call: 7–10 AM, 3–7 PM
Host(s): Lynn Baker
Location: 50 mi. NW of Portland
No. of Rooms: 4
No. of Private Baths: 2
Max. No. Sharing Bath: 4
Double/pb: $40
Single/pb: $35
Double/sb: $35

Single/sb: $32
Open: May 15–Jan. 15
Reduced Rates: 10%, weekly
Breakfast: Full
Other Meals: Available
Pets: No
Children: Welcome
Smoking: Permitted
Social Drinking: Permitted

This white clapboard farmhouse is set on five acres. Guests will enjoy the lakefront beach and equestrian center. Inside, the decor is antique, and there is a special tearoom done in a blue and white motif. Nearby sights include the picturesque village and the White Mountains, offering sports in all seasons.

Roberts House Bed & Breakfast ⊙
MAIN STREET AND PLEASANT STREET, P.O. BOX 413,
WISCASSET, MAINE 04578

Tel: (207) 882-5055
Best Time to Call: Before 10 AM, after 7 PM
Host(s): Alice and Ed Roberts
Location: 40 mi. NE of Portland
No. of Rooms: 3
Max. No. Sharing Bath: 3
Double/sb: $36–$40

Single/sb: $30
Open: All year
Breakfast: Full
Pets: No
Children: Welcome, over 5
Smoking: Permitted
Social Drinking: Permitted
Foreign Languages: French, German

Beautifully furnished in a blend of contemporary comfort and lovely antiques, this 18th-century home is a fine base for day trips. Alice and Ed request a two-night minimum stay, so that you can truly take advantage of seeing Bath, Brunswick, Boothbay Harbor, and Pemaquid. Don't miss the spectacular Portland Museum of Modern Art. Wiscasset may be Maine's prettiest village and abounds in classic homes, lovely gardens, antique shops, and fine restaurants. There's fine boating and fishing in the Sheepscott River.

The Jo-Mar B&B on-the-Ocean ✪
41 FREEMAN STREET, BOX 838, YORK BEACH, MAINE 03910

Tel: (207) 363-4826
Host(s): **Mary Della Puietra, Joan Curtis**
Location: **5 mi. from I-95**
No. of Rooms: **6**
Max. No. Sharing Bath: **5**
Double/sb: **$42**
Single/sb: **$30**
Guest Cottage: **$265 weekly**

Open: **May 15–Oct. 15**
Reduced Rates: **15% to June 26, after Sept. 2**
Breakfast: **Continental**
Pets: **No**
Children: **Welcome**
Smoking: **Permitted**
Social Drinking: **Permitted**
Foreign Languages: **Italian**

This comfortable home is located on a bluff overlooking Short Sands Beach. Most guest rooms have ocean views and are furnished with antique pieces. The backyard has a barbecue and picnic table, and you can view the mighty Atlantic from a comfortable lawn chair. Store your snacks in the refrigerator and visit in the cozy living room. The amusement park, galleries, and craft shops are just minutes away. It is convenient to Ogunquit's great restaurants and renowned summer theater. Mary and Joan enjoy having visitors.

MARYLAND

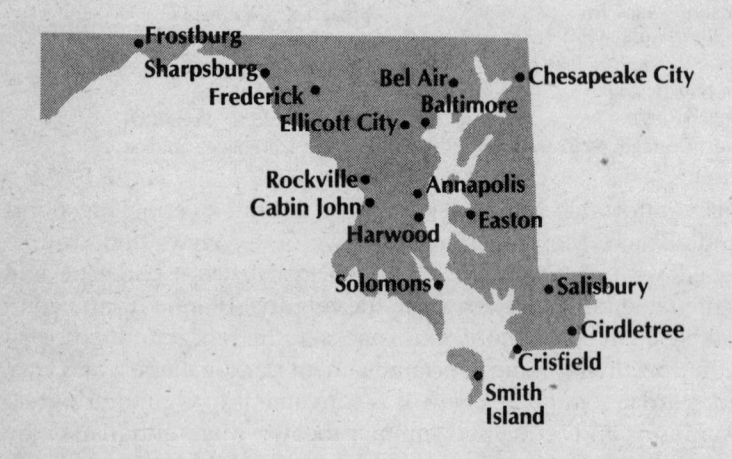

The Maryland Registry ✪
C/O SHARP-ADAMS, INC., 33 WEST STREET, ANNAPOLIS, MARYLAND 21401

Tel: (301) 269-6232 or 261-2233
Best Time to Call: 9 AM–5 PM
Coordinator(s): B. J. Adams and Cecily Sharp-Whitehill
States/Regions Covered:
Maryland—Annapolis, Baltimore, Eastern Shore, South and West Counties; D.C. suburbs

Rates (Single/Double):
  Average: $30–40 $38–$50
  Luxury: $40 and up $50 and up
Credit Cards: AMEX, MC, VISA

Maryland lies between the Atlantic Ocean and the Allegheny Mountains. Chesapeake Bay offers marvelous fishing and boating, and Washington, D.C., is convenient to many of the B&Bs. Don't miss the U.S. Naval Academy at Annapolis. Many of the B&Bs are located close to Goucher College, Johns Hopkins University, and the University of Maryland.

The Unicorn House ✪
327 EAST 29TH STREET, BALTIMORE, MARYLAND 21218

Tel: **(301) 889-4066**
Best Time to Call: **After 6 PM**
Host(s): **Thomas Migliaccio**
No. of Rooms: **2**
No. of Private Baths: **1**
Max. No. Sharing Bath: **4**
Double/pb: **$50**
Single/pb: **$35**

Double/sb: **$50**
Single/sb: **$35**
Open: **All year**
Breakfast: **Full**
Pets: **No**
Children: **Welcome**
Smoking: **Permitted**
Social Drinking: **Permitted**

Built in 1927, this brick-and-stone row house is located in the Waverly–Charles Village district, near Johns Hopkins University. Furnished in Art Deco, it has a relax-and-put-your-feet-up ambience. Tom is interested in fashion, theater, writing, and yoga. He'll welcome you with coffee and pastry, and give you a complimentary copy of *Baltimore* magazine.

Heritage Hill
304 VALE ROAD, BEL AIR, MARYLAND 21014

Tel: **(301) 879-7595**
Best Time to Call: **9 AM–5 PM**
Host(s): **June and Frank Wanek**
Location: **15 mi. N of Baltimore**
No. of Rooms: **2 suites**
No. of Private Baths: **2**
Suites: **$30–$35**
Open: **All year**

Reduced Rates: **Extended stays**
Breakfast: **Full**
Pets: **No**
Children: **Welcome**
Smoking: **No**
Social Drinking: **Permitted**
Airport/Station Pickup: **Yes**

This 200-year-old handsome white colonial house is located in a historic area. Each suite consists of a living room with a sleep-sofa, a bedroom with twin beds, fully equipped kitchen, and bath. Both have private entrances and lovely views of the surrounding countryside and nearby horse farms. They are attractively furnished with antique wardrobes, poster beds, and restored Mission pieces. June and Frank stock the kitchen with everything you'll need for breakfast.

The Winslow Home ✪
8217 CARAWAY STREET, CABIN JOHN, MARYLAND 20818

Tel: **(301) 229-4654**
Best Time to Call: **After 5 PM**
Host(s): **Jane Winslow**
Location: 7 mi. W of D.C.
No. of Rooms: **2**
Max. No. Sharing Bath: **4**
Double/sb: **$35**
Single/sb: **$25**

Open: **All year**
Reduced Rates: **Seniors; families**
Breakfast: **Full**
Pets: **Welcome**
Children: **Welcome**
Smoking: **No**
Social Drinking: **No**
Airport/Station Pickup: **Yes**

You may enjoy the best of two worlds while staying at Jane's. This comfortable home is located in a lovely residential section of Bethesda, just 20 minutes from downtown Washington, D.C. Imagine touring the capital with some extra pocket money saved on high hotel costs. You are welcome to use the kitchen, laundry facilities, and piano. Georgetown, George Washington, and American universities are close by.

Hynson Tourist Home
804 DOVER ROAD, EASTON, MARYLAND 21601

Tel: **(301) 822-2777**
Host(s): **Nellie Hynson**
Location: **35 mi. N of Annapolis**
No. of Rooms: **6**
Max. No. Sharing Bath: **5**
Double/sb: **$30**
Single/sb: **$15–$17**

Open: **All year**
Reduced Rates: **Dec.–Feb., $15–$25**
Breakfast: **No**
Pets: **No**
Children: **Welcome**
Smoking: **Permitted**
Social Drinking: **No**

With the great attractions and conveniences this area affords, many visitors make it a base from which to visit Washington, D.C., and tour the surrounding region. Located on the eastern shore of Maryland, its recreational activities are plentiful. The oldest Quaker meeting house in the U.S. is in town; William Penn worshipped here. St. Michaels, the historic waterfront town, featuring fine seafood and an interesting museum, is nearby.

Hayland Farm ✪
5000 SHEPPARD LANE, ELLICOTT CITY, MARYLAND 21043

Tel: (301) 531-5593 or (301) 596-9119
Host(s): **Louis and Dorothy Mobley**
Location: **Bet. Baltimore & D.C.**
No. of Rooms: **2**
Max. No. Sharing Bath: **4**
Double/sb: **$35**
Single/sb: **$25**

Open: **All year**
Breakfast: **Full**
Pets: **No**
Children: **Welcome (crib)**
Smoking: **No**
Social Drinking: **Permitted**

When you breathe the country-fresh air, it may surprise you that Baltimore and Washington, D.C., are only a short drive away. At Hayland Farm you will find gracious living in a large manor house furnished in a handsome yet comfortable style. Louis and Dorothy are retired and have traveled extensively. They enjoy sharing conversation with their guests. In warm weather, the 20' by 50' swimming pool is a joy.

The Stockmans ✪
P.O. BOX 125, TAYLOR LANDING ROAD, GIRDLETREE, MARYLAND 21829

Tel: (301) 632-3299
Best Time to Call: **After 6 PM**
Host(s): **John and Joan Stockman**
Location: **6 mi. S of Snow Hill**
No. of Rooms: **2**
Max. No. Sharing Bath: **4**
Double/sb: **$28**
Single/sb: **$26**

Open: **Mar.–Dec.**
Reduced Rates: **Nov.–Apr.**
Breakfast: **Continental**
Pets: **Sometimes**
Children: **Welcome, over 4**
Smoking: **No**
Social Drinking: **Permitted**

This large Victorian country house is comfortably furnished with a blend of antiques and charm. Fishing, crabbing, and swimming are nearby, as well as interesting historic sites. The coffee pot is usually full and you are welcome to enjoy a cup while relaxing on the front porch.

Oakwood ✪
4566 SOLOMONS ISLAND ROAD, HARWOOD, MARYLAND 20776

Tel: (301) 261-5338
Host(s): **Dennis and Joan Brezina**
Location: **25 mi. SE of D.C.**
No. of Rooms: **2**
Max. No. Sharing Bath: **4**
Double/sb: **$45**
Single/sb: **$40**

Open: **Mar. 1–Dec. 14**
Reduced Rates: **Weekly; families**
Breakfast: **Full**
Pets: **No**
Children: **Welcome, over 12**
Smoking: **Permitted**
Social Drinking: **Permitted**

This elegant antebellum manor house, featured on Maryland House Tours, has six fireplaces, 11-foot ceilings, and handmade rugs. Guests are welcome to relax on the veranda or stroll in the terraced gardens. Your hosts serve an English-style breakfast in the open-hearthed kitchen. They are happy to advise on day trips to Washington, D.C., or nearby Chesapeake Bay and Annapolis.

Swift's B&B ✪
13819 LOREE LANE, ROCKVILLE, MARYLAND 20853

Tel: (301) 460-4648
Best Time to Call: **7 AM–9 AM**
Host(s): **Marietta and Jerry Swift**
Location: **13 mi. N of D.C.**
No. of Rooms: **5**
No. of Private Baths: **1**
Max. No. Sharing Bath: **2**
Double/pb: **$39**
Single/pb: **$29**
Double/sb: **$39**

Single/sb: **$29**
Open: **All year**
Breakfast: **Full**
Pets: **No**
Children: **Welcome (crib)**
Smoking: **Permitted**
Social Drinking: **Permitted**
Airport/Station Pickup: **Yes**
Foreign Languages: **French, German, Hungarian**

Jerry and Marietta offer Old World hospitality just miles from the White House. Having worked and traveled extensively in Europe, they know the importance of neighborliness, especially to foreign visitors. You will be welcomed with flowers in true Continental tradition. Maps, guidance, and personal tours are available in English, or in your own language. Beautiful linen and china add graciousness to hearty breakfasts that feature homemade breads from European recipes. Montgomery College is nearby.

Inn at Antietam ✪
220 EAST MAIN STREET, P.O. BOX 119, SHARPSBURG, MARYLAND 21782

Tel: (301) 432-6601
Best Time to Call: **Mornings; Evenings**
Host(s): **Betty and Cal Fairbourn**
Location: **15 mi. SW of Hagerstown**
No. of Rooms: **4**
No. of Private Baths: **1**
Max. No. Sharing Bath: **4**
Double/pb: **$55–$60**
Single/pb: **$55**
Double/sb: **$35**

Suites: **$65 for 3**
Open: **All year**
Reduced Rates: **Weekly**
Breakfast: **Continental**
Other Meals: **Available**
Credit Cards: **AMEX**
Pets: **No**
Children: **Welcome, over 6**
Smoking: **Permitted**
Social Drinking: **Permitted**

This classic Victorian, located next to the historic Antietam Battlefield, was built in 1908. The wraparound porch with its rockers and swing is a great place to relax. The house is decorated in a pleasant mix of styles with Victorian accents. Coffee and cookies are always available. It is close to the C & O Canal, Harpers Ferry, and less than an hour from Gettysburg. Shepard College in Shepardstown, West Virginia, is four miles away.

Frances Kitching's ✪
SMITH ISLAND, EWELL, MARYLAND 21824

Tel: (301) 425-3321
Best Time to Call: **3–6:30 PM**
Host(s): **Frances Kitching**
Location: **Rte. 413 S to waterfront**
No. of Rooms: **5**
Max. No. Sharing Bath: **5**
Double/sb: **$70**
Single/sb: **$35**

Open: **Apr. 1–Sept. 30**
Breakfast: **Full**
Other Meals: **Dinner included**
Pets: **No**
Children: **Welcome**
Smoking: **Permitted**
Social Drinking: **Permitted**

You can reach this comfortable house only by *The Island Bell II* boat from Crisfield at 12:30 PM or 5 PM ($5 round trip). Frances is the author of a cookbook, so picture the delicious breakfasts, seafood dinners, and homemade desserts she serves, family-style. The major summer industry of this island is crabbing, so both hard-shell and soft-shell crabs are often featured at mealtime.

MASSACHUSETTS

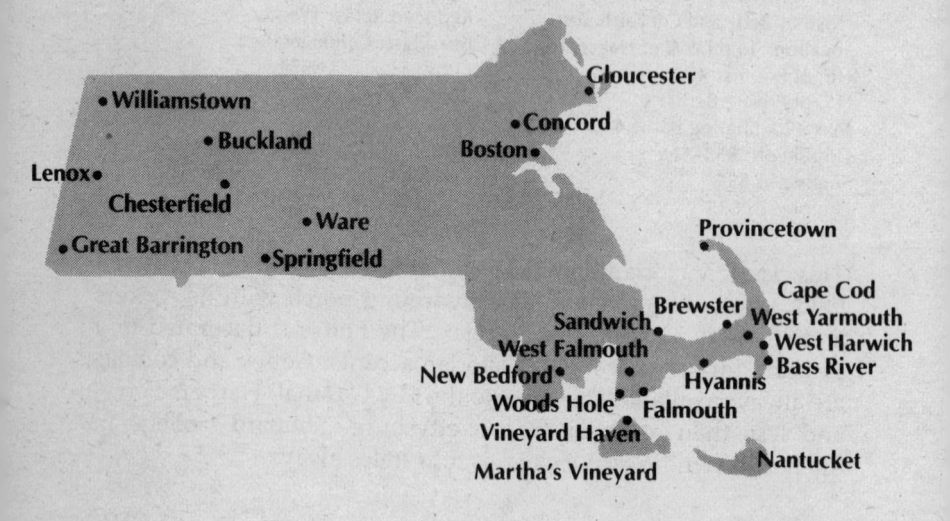

Map of Massachusetts showing: Williamstown, Buckland, Lenox, Chesterfield, Great Barrington, Ware, Springfield, Gloucester, Concord, Boston, Provincetown, Brewster, Cape Cod, Sandwich, West Yarmouth, West Falmouth, West Harwich, New Bedford, Bass River, Hyannis, Woods Hole, Falmouth, Vineyard Haven, Martha's Vineyard, Nantucket

Bed & Breakfast Associates—Bay Colony
P.O. BOX 166, BABSON PARK, BOSTON, MASSACHUSETTS 02157

Tel: **(617) 449-5302**
Best Time to Call: **10–12 AM; 1:30–5 PM**
Coodinators: **Arline Kardasis, Phyllis Levenson, Marilyn Mitchell**
States/Regions Covered: **Eastern Massachusetts**

Rates (Single/Double):
Modest: **$30**   **$35**
Average: **$35–$45**   **$40–$50**
Luxury: **$50–$55**   **$55–$65**
Credit Cards: **MC, VISA**
Minimum Stay: **2 days**

A wide variety of host homes is available in the city, in the country, and at the shore. They range from pre-Revolutionary horse farms to contemporary condominiums. Many are convenient to the major colleges and universities. Send $2 for the descriptive directory, or contact Arline, Phyllis, and Marilyn.

Pineapple Hospitality, Inc.
384 RODNEY FRENCH BOULEVARD, NEW BEDFORD, MASSACHUSETTS 02744

Tel: (617) 990-1696
Coordinator: **Joan A. Brownhill**
States/Regions Covered: **All six New England states**

Rates (Single/Double):
Modest: $27–$29 $33–$34
Average: $30–$32 $35–$49
Luxury: $45–$52 $50–$85
Credit Cards: **No**

The pineapple has been the symbol of rare hospitality since early colonial days, and the host homes on Joan's roster personify this spirit. They are located in cities and in the countryside, at beach resorts and lakeside communities, in historic districts and near hundreds of schools and colleges; you are bound to find just the spot to call home. Send $3.32 for a descriptive directory so that you may make your reservations directly.

BOSTON AREA

Greater Boston Hospitality ✪
P.O. BOX 1142, BROOKLINE, MASSACHUSETTS 02146

Tel: (617) 734-0807
Coordinator: **Lauren A. Simonelli**
States/Regions Covered: **Boston, Brookline, Cambridge, Newton, Needham, Wellesley**

Rates (Single/Double):
Modest: $25 $30
Average: $30 $35
Luxury: $35 $50
Credit Cards: **No**

Lauren's homes are convenient to many of the 75 colleges and universities in the greater Boston area. What a boon it is for people applying to school, and to parents visiting undergrads, to have a home-away-from-home nearby.

Host Homes of Boston
P.O. BOX 117, NEWTON, MASSACHUSETTS 02168

Tel: (617) 244-1308
Coordinator: **Marcia Whittington**
State/Regions Covered: **Belmont, Boston, Brookline, Cambridge, Chestnut Hill, Newton**

Rates (Single/Double):
Average: $32–$35 $45–$55
Credit Cards: **MC, VISA**

Marcia has culled a variety of select private homes in excellent areas convenient to good public transportation. Most hosts prepare a full breakfast although only continental breakfast is required. It's their special way of saying welcome to their city of colleges, universities, museums, and cultural life.

New England Bed & Breakfast ✪
1045 CENTRE STREET, NEWTON, MASSACHUSETTS 02159

Tel: **(617) 244-2112 or 498-9810**
Coordinator(s): **John and Maggie Gardiner**
States/Regions Covered:
Massachusetts—Boston, Brookline, Cambridge; Maine; New Hampshire; Vermont

Rates (Single/Double):
 Average: **$21–$32 $39–$52**
Credit Cards: **No**

While John and Maggie have many homes in several New England states, they feature moderate-priced host homes in the greater Boston area convenient to public transportation. There is a stunning carriage house in posh Brookline. At another, a retired State Department official delights in picking guests up at the airport and giving tours of Harvard Square as part of her hospitality.

Williams Guest House ✪
136 BASS AVENUE, GLOUCESTER, MASSACHUSETTS 01930

Tel: **(617) 283-4931**
Best Time to Call: **8 AM–5 PM**
Host(s): **Betty Williams**
Location: **30 mi. N of Boston**
No. of Rooms: **7**
No. of Private Baths: **5**
Max. No. Sharing Bath: **4**
Double/pb: **$40–$45**
Single/pb: **$40–$45**
Double/sb: **$32**

Single/sb: **$32**
Guest Cottage: **$350 (week) sleeps 4**
Open: **May 1–Oct. 31**
Reduced Rates: **Off-season**
Breakfast: **Continental**
Pets: **No**
Children: **Welcome in cottage**
Smoking: **Permitted**
Social Drinking: **Permitted**

Located five miles from Rockport and one and a half miles from Rocky Neck, Gloucester is a quaint fishing village on the North Shore. Betty's colonial-revival house borders the finest beach, Good Harbor. The guest rooms are furnished with comfort in mind, and her homemade breakfast muffins are delicious. Betty will be happy to suggest many interesting things to do, such as boat tours, sport fishing, whale-watching trips, sightseeing cruises around Cape Ann, the Hammond Castle Museum, and the shops and galleries of the artist colony.

CAPE COD/MARTHA'S VINEYARD

Bed & Breakfast—Cape Cod ✪
BOX 341, W. HYANNISPORT, MASSACHUSETTS 02672

Tel: (617) 775-2772	Rates (Single/Double):
Best Time to Call: 9:30 AM–4 PM	Modest: $28 $32
Coordinator(s): Elaine Borowick, Kay Traywick	Average: $28 $42
	Luxury: $40 $60
States/Regions Covered: Cape Cod	Credit Cards: MC, VISA

It is just a little over an hour's drive from sophisticated Boston to the relaxed, quaint charm of the Cape. Year-'round, you can choose from Elaine and Kay's roster of homes. The house you stay in may be a vine-covered cottage, a Victorian estate, a sea captain's home, or an oceanfront house. Your hosts will direct you to the restaurants and shops off the tourist trail.

House Guests—Cape Cod ✪
BOX 8-AR, DENNIS, MASSACHUSETTS 02638

Tel: (617) 398-0787	Rates (Single/Double):
Coordinator: Ellie C. Greenberg	Average: $28–$36 $40–$60
States/Regions Covered: Cape Cod, Martha's Vineyard, Nantucket	Credit Cards: No
	Minimum Stay: 2 days: June–Aug.

Ellie's accommodations range from a simple single bedroom with shared bath to historic homes furnished with antiques. Some are on the ocean; others are in wooded country areas. There are even a few self-contained guest cottages on private estates. The area is beautiful in all seasons. Her descriptive directory is $2.

Old Cape House ✪
108 OLD MAIN STREET, BASS RIVER, MASSACHUSETTS 02664

Tel: **(617) 398-1068**
Host(s): **George and Linda Arthur**
Location: **5 mi. E of Hyannis**
No. of Rooms: **6**
No. of Private Baths: **2**
Max. No. Sharing Bath: **3**
Double/pb: **$45–$60**
Double/sb: **$35**
Single/sb: **$28**
Guest Cottage: **$60 for 2**
Open: **May–Oct.**
Reduced Rates: **Weekly, 10% off-season**
Breakfast: **Continental**
Pets: **No**
Children: **Welcome, over 10**
Smoking: **No**
Social Drinking: **Permitted**
Foreign Languages: **French, Italian**

This fine home was built in 1815 and is convenient to fine beaches, restaurants, and scenic attractions of Cape Cod. You will enjoy home-baked items at breakfast, plus the use of a spacious porch and garden. All the rooms are charmingly decorated in New England style. It's a great place to stay in the fall for visits to antique shops and craft fairs. Linda is from London, and George also lived in Europe for many years, so they know how to bring the bed-and-breakfast tradition here.

Old Sea Pines Inn ✪
2553 MAIN STREET, BREWSTER, MASSACHUSETTS 02631

Tel: **(617) 896-6114**
Host(s): **Michele and Steve Rowan**
Location: **16 mi. E of Hyannis**
No. of Rooms: **13**
No. of Private Baths: **8**
Max. No. Sharing Bath: **3**
Double/pb: **$36–$45**
Double/sb: **$29**
Open: **May 1–Oct. 31**
Breakfast: **Continental**
Credit Cards: **MC, VISA**
Pets: **No**
Children: **Welcome, over 10**
Smoking: **Permitted**
Social Drinking: **Permitted**
Airport/Station Pickup: **Yes**
Foreign Languages: **German, Italian**

Originally a women's finishing school, this sprawling inn has kept many of its turn-of-the-century features, such as brass and iron beds, plus antique and wicker furniture. Your hosts invite you to share wine and cheese next to the fire. A breakfast of homemade specialties is served on the porch or in the sunny dining room. Located on over three acres, the inn is close to beaches, bike paths, shops, and restaurants.

Old Sea Pines Inn

Mostly Hall Bed & Breakfast Inn ✪
27 MAIN STREET, FALMOUTH, MASSACHUSETTS 02540

Tel: **(617) 548-3786**
Host(s): **Jim and Ginny Austin**
Location: **67 mi. S of Boston**
No. of Rooms: **6**
No. of Private Baths: **5**
Max. No. Sharing Bath: **2**
Double/pb: **$50–$65**
Single/pb: **$45–55**
Double/sb: **$40–$45**
Single/sb: **$30–$35**
Open: **All year**
Reduced Rates: **Winter, spring, fall**
Breakfast: **Full**
Pets: **No**
Children: **Welcome, over 16**
Smoking: **Permitted**
Social Drinking: **Permitted**
Airport/Station Pickup: **Yes**

Located in the historic district on the village green, and convenient to the Martha's Vineyard and Nantucket ferries, this 1849 house is a faithful copy of a Mississippi River mansion. It's on a beautiful lawn with a charming gazebo, and is decorated with poster beds in classic country style, accented with antiques. The bountiful breakfast often features popovers with creamed eggs or stuffed French toast. Jim and Ginny serve complimentary lemonade in summer, and tea or sherry in winter. Mostly Hall is pictured on the front cover.

Somerset House ✪
378 COMMERCIAL STREET, PROVINCETOWN, MASSACHUSETTS 02657

Tel: **(617) 487-0383**
Best Time to Call: **10 AM–10 PM**
Host(s): **Jon Gerrity**
Location: **124 mi. E of Boston**
No. of Rooms: **13**
No. of Private Baths: **10**
Max. No. Sharing Bath: **6**
Double/pb: **$44–$60**

Single/pb: **$38–$55**
Double/sb: **$36–$40**
Single/sb: **$30–$34**
Guest Cottage: **$425 weekly for 2**
Open: **Apr. 1–Nov. 30**
Reduced Rates: **25%, off-season**
Breakfast: **No**

Credit Cards: **MC, VISA**
Pets: **No**
Children: **Welcome**
Smoking: **Permitted**
Social Drinking: **Permitted**
Foreign Languages: **German**

This historic inn dates back to 1850. The guest rooms are large, high-ceilinged, and comfortably decorated with Victorian and contemporary pieces. The inn is located in the center of town, and your host will be glad to advise on nearby restaurants. It's 100 feet to the beach. Other possibilities include tennis, whale-watching trips, sailing, biking, and the Provincetown Playhouse.

The Summer House
P.O. BOX 341, 158 OLD MAIN STREET, SANDWICH, MASSACHUSETTS 02563

Tel: **(617) 888-4991**
Host(s): **Pamela Hunt**
Location: **2 mi. from Rt. 6**
No. of Rooms: **4**
Max. No. Sharing Bath: **4**
Double/sb: **$40**
Open: **May 1–Nov. 30**

Breakfast: **Continental**
Credit Cards: **MC, VISA**
Pets: **Sometimes**
Children: **Welcome**
Smoking: **Permitted**
Social Drinking: **Permitted**
Airport/Station Pickup: **Yes**

The Summer House is a Greek Revival dating back to 1835. Antique furniture, fireplaces, original woodwork, and hardwood floors bring back the original aura of this newly restored home. A sunny breakfast room filled with books and the adjoining parlor provide for comfortable relaxation. Your hostess invites you to enjoy the surrounding lawns and gardens. Pamela is happy to direct guests to the famous Sandwich glass shops and the beach, a half mile away.

Captain Dexter House
BOX 2457, 100 MAIN STREET, VINEYARD HAVEN, MASSACHUSETTS 02568

Tel: **(617) 693-6564**
Host(s): **Lara and Beyer Parker**
Location: **7 mi. by Woods Hole ferry**
No. of Rooms: **7**
No. of Private Baths: **5**
Max. No. Sharing Bath: **4**
Double/pb: **$60–$75**
Single/pb: **$60–$75**
Double/sb: **$55–$58**
Single/sb: **$55–$58**
Open: **All year**
Reduced Rates: **Off-season**
Breakfast: **Continental**
Pets: **No**
Children: **Welcome, over 7**
Smoking: **Permitted**
Social Drinking: **Permitted**

This gracious Inn was once the home of a 19th-century sea captain. It has been elegantly refurbished with period antiques. The bedrooms feature fresh flowers and fine linens; several have canopied beds and fireplaces. Your hosts offer homemade breads, freshly squeezed juices, and preserves each morning. Choose a book and relax by the living room fire. The Inn is just a short walk from the beach, ferry, historic homes, shops, and restaurants.

Haven Guest House ✪
278 MAIN STREET, P.O. BOX 1022, VINEYARD HAVEN, MARTHA'S VINEYARD, MASSACHUSETTS 02568

Tel: **(617) 693-3333**	Open: **All year**
Best Time to Call: **9 AM–10 PM**	Reduced Rates: **Off-season**
Host(s): **Karl and Lynn Buder**	Breakfast: **Full**
Location: **70 mi. S of Boston**	Credit Cards: **AMEX, MC, VISA**
No. of Rooms: **10**	Pets: **No**
No. of Private Baths: **10**	Children: **Welcome, over 12**
Double/pb: **$80–$90**	Smoking: **Permitted**
Single/pb: **$80–$90**	Social Drinking: **Permitted**

This rambling, two-chimney home was built in 1918. It is situated in a quiet, residential neighborhood and completely surrounded by woodlands, despite its proximity to the ocean. Karl and Lynn will direct you to all the special attractions.

The Elms
495 WEST FALMOUTH HIGHWAY, WEST FALMOUTH, MASSACHUSETTS 02574

Tel: **(617) 540-7232**	Single/sb: **$35**
Host(s): **Elizabeth and Joseph Mazzucchelli**	Guest Cottages: **$275 (weekly) for 2**
	Open: **All year**
Location: **½ mi. from Rte. 28A**	Reduced Rates: **10% Oct. 12– Sept. 2**
No. of Rooms: **9**	
No. of Private Baths: **6**	Breakfast: **Full**
Max. No. Sharing Bath: **4**	Pets: **No**
Double/pb: **$52**	Children: **Welcome, over 12**
Single/pb: **$42**	Smoking: **Permitted**
Double/sb: **$45**	Social Drinking: **Permitted**

The Elms is a refurbished Victorian home built in the 1800s, filled with antiques and plants, and boasting cool breezes from Buzzards Bay. Enjoy a stroll to Chapoquoit Beach, only half a mile away. Golf, tennis, antique shops, the historic district and Woods Hole Oceanographic Institute are nearby. Your hosts invite you for afternoon sherry, served with snacks, in the parlor. They serve homemade Irish bread, muffins, quiche, or eggs Benedict each morning.

Sjöholm Inn Bed & Breakfast ○
17 CHASE ROAD, WEST FALMOUTH, MASSACHUSETTS 02574

Tel: **(617) 540-5706**
Best Time to Call: **7 AM–8 PM**
Host(s): **Karen and Alan Cassidy**
Location: **½ mi. from Rte. 28A**
No. of Rooms: **17**
No. of Private Baths: **4**
Max. No. Sharing Bath: **4**
Double/pb: **$54**
Single/pb: **$36**
Double/sb: **$37–$47**
Single/sb: **$24–$29**

Guest Cottage: **$380; sleeps 4**
Open: **All year**
Reduced Rates: **Off-season**
Breakfast: **Full**
Credit Cards: **AMEX, MC, VISA**
Pets: **No**
Children: **Welcome, over 10**
Smoking: **Permitted**
Social Drinking: **Permitted**
Foreign Languages: **French**

This white, rambling Cape Cod homestead (circa 1870) is furnished with a comfortable blend of styles and lots of plants. Located in a quiet, country setting, it is close to all the activities the Cape is known for. Karen and Alan assure that each guest is given individual attention. They offer sailing day trips on their 38' sailing yacht.

Lion's Head Inn ○
P.O. BOX 444, 186 BELMONT ROAD, WEST HARWICH, MASSACHUSETTS 02671

Tel: **(617) 432-7766**
Host(s): **Laurie and Djordje Soc**
Location: **4 mi. from Mid Cape Hwy.**
No. of Rooms: **4**
No. of Private Baths: **2**
Max. No. Sharing Bath: **4**
Double/pb: **$48–$50**
Single/pb: **$43–$45**
Double/sb: **$38–$40**
Single/sb: **$33–$35**
Guest Cottage: **$300–$350; sleeps 3 to 5**

Open: **All year**
Reduced Rates: **Off-season**
Breakfast: **Full**
Pets: **No**
Children: **Welcome**
Smoking: **Permitted**
Social Drinking: **Permitted**
Airport/Station Pickup: **Yes**
Foreign Languages: **French, Italian**

The original pine floors, root cellar, and captain's stairs are part of this inn's traditional flavor. Laurie and Djordje will be happy to point out the best things to see and do on the Cape; after a busy day, a complimentary glass of wine will await you. After dinner at one of the fine restaurants close by, you are welcome to visit or play chess or backgammon in the living room.

The Manor House
57 MAINE AVENUE, WEST YARMOUTH, MASSACHUSETTS 02673

Tel: **(617) 771-9211**
Best Time to Call: **Summer 9 AM–9 PM**
Host(s): **Sherry Braun**
Location: **1 mi. E of Hyannis**
No. of Rooms: **6**
No. of Private Baths: **6**
Double/pb: **$38–$42**
Single/pb: **$38–$42**
Open: **May 15–Oct. 14**
Reduced Rates: **Off-season**
Breakfast: **Continental**
Pets: **No**
Children: **Welcome**
Smoking: **Permitted**
Social Drinking: **Permitted**

This large, white Dutch colonial is two blocks from the beach and overlooks Lewis Bay. It is decorated with lovely antiques, handmade quilts, plants, and dried flower arrangements. It is close to golf, tennis, antique shops, fine restaurants, and the ferry dock. Sherry is a science teacher interested in crafts.

The Marlborough ✪
320 WOODS HOLE ROAD, WOODS HOLE, MASSACHUSETTS 02543

Tel: **(617) 548-6218**
Host(s): **Patricia Morris**
Location: **2½ mi. from Rte. 28**
No. of Rooms: **7**
No. of Private Baths: **3**
Max. No. Sharing Bath: **6**
Double/pb: **$65**
Double/sb: **$55**
Open: **All year**
Reduced Rates: **Sept. 2–Oct. 14**
Breakfast: **Full**
Pets: **Sometimes**
Children: **Welcome**
Smoking: **Permitted**
Social Drinking: **Permitted**
Foreign Languages: **French**

This faithful reproduction of a Full Cape house is decorated with collectibles, antiques, designer quilts, and handcrafted spreads. It is situated on a shaded half-acre that includes a paddle tennis court, swimming pool, a hammock, croquet, and picnicking facilities. A private beach is nearby with a three-mile bike path running past it. It's a mile from the Martha's Vineyard and Nantucket ferries. Patricia serves a pre-dinner treat of cheese and sherry, and her gourmet breakfast is a celebration. The Oceanographic and Marine Biological laboratories are in town.

NANTUCKET

Carlisle House O
26 NORTH WATER STREET, NANTUCKET, MASSACHUSETTS 02554

Tel: (617) 228-0720
Best Time to Call: **Mornings**
Host(s): **Peter Conway**
Location: **30 mi. S of Cape Cod**
No. of Rooms: 15
No. of Private Baths: 5
Max. No. Sharing Bath: 6
Double/pb: $75–$85
Single/pb: $75–$85
Double/sb: $53–$60

Single/sb: **$30**
Open: **All year**
Reduced Rates: **15%–20%, Oct.–May**
Breakfast: **Continental**
Pets: **No**
Children: **Welcome, over 10**
Smoking: **Permitted**
Social Drinking: **Permitted**

This 1765 home is graced with a veranda, fireplace, canopied or brass beds, wicker furniture, and plants. It offers travelers a warm, comfortable place to spend vacation days. Weather permitting, breakfast is served on the sun porch. Peter will be happy to tell you of restaurants and local happenings. He'll also lend you inner tubes to enjoy at the beach.

The Carriage House O
5 RAY'S COURT, NANTUCKET, MASSACHUSETTS 02554

Tel: (617) 228-0326
Best Time to Call: **8 AM–10 PM**
Host(s): **Jeanne and Bill McHugh**
No. of Rooms: 7
No. of Private Baths: 7

Double/pb: **$50–$90**
Single/pb: **$40–$70**
Open: **All year**
Breakfast: **Continental**
Pets: **No**

Children: **Welcome, over 5** Social Drinking: **Permitted**
Smoking: **Permitted**

Located in the center of town, this landmark was built in 1865. It is a charming example of early Victorian architecture, restored and transformed into an inviting home. Guests enjoy the quiet serenity of a country lane. The home-baked muffins are delicious at breakfast. Suggestions by Jeanne and Bill will help you explore the island to its fullest.

Cliff Lodge
9 CLIFF ROAD, NANTUCKET, MASSACHUSETTS 02554

Tel: **(617) 228-0893**
Best Time to Call: **Evenings**
Host(s): **Kay and Andy Lynch**
Location: **30 mi. from Hyannis**
No. of Rooms: **12**
No. of Private Baths: **6**
Max. No. Sharing Bath: **8**
Double/pb: **$55–$60**
Single/pb: **$35**
Double/sb: **$35–$43**

Single/sb: **$20–$25**
Suites: **$400 per week (for 4)**
Open: **Apr. 15–Nov. 1**
Reduced Rates: **Off-season**
Breakfast: **No**
Pets: **No**
Children: **Welcome**
Smoking: **Permitted**
Social Drinking: **Permitted**

Located in a superb spot away from the traffic and noise stands this gracious old captain's home built in 1771. The attractively furnished bedrooms are immaculate. Kay and Andy will enjoy having you visit in their antiques-filled living room or relax on the lush lawn. It's convenient to the beaches, tennis courts, and great restaurants.

CENTRAL/WESTERN MASSACHUSETTS

Berkshire Bed & Breakfast ✪
141 NEWTON ROAD, SPRINGFIELD, MASSACHUSETTS 01118

Tel: **(413) 783-5111**
Coordinator(s): **Mary and Tim Allen**
States/Regions Covered:
  Massachusetts—Lenox, Pittsfield, Sheffield, Williamstown, Great Barrington; New York—Canaan, Lebanon Springs, Berlin

Rates (Single/Double):
  Modest: **$20–$35**   **$25–$35**
  Average: **$25–$35**   **$40–$55**
  Luxury: **$60–$85**   **$60–$100**
Credit Cards: **MC, VISA**

Most of Tim and Mary's host homes are off the beaten track, offering the visitor pastoral, historical, and cultural attractions. Many are close to Albany, New York, the area near the Tanglewood Music Festival, Williams College, or Jiminy Peak for skiing. The homes vary from a 1750 colonial farmhouse to a large manor house with pool and tennis court. A two-day minimum stay is required on summer weekends.

Pioneer Valley Bed & Breakfast ✪
141 NEWTON ROAD, SPRINGFIELD, MASSACHUSETTS 01118

Tel: (413) 783-5111
Coordinator(s): **Mary and Tim Allen**
States/Regions Covered: **Amherst, Northampton, Springfield, Longmeadow**

Rates (Single/Double):
Modest: $20–$30 $25–$35
Average: $25–$35 $30–$40
Luxury: $35–$55 $45–$55
Credit Cards: **MC, VISA**

Many of the host homes are located close to Smith College, Mt. Holyoke, the University of Massachusetts, and Amherst. Accommodations vary from a farmhouse offering fresh goats' milk, to a restored 1800 colonial, to an historic mansion. The Basketball Hall of Fame, the Eastern States Exposition, and the fall foliage are highlights of the area.

Sturbridge Bed & Breakfast ✪
141 NEWTON ROAD, SPRINGFIELD, MASSACHUSETTS 01118

Tel: (413) 783-5111
Coordinator(s): **Mary and Tim Allen**
States/Regions Covered:
  Belchertown, Brimfield, Charlton, Sturbridge, Worcester

Rates (Single/Double):
Modest: $25–$35 $25–$35
Average: $35–$45 $35–$45
Luxury: $45–$55 $45–$55
Credit Cards: **MC, VISA**

Colonial Old Sturbridge Village is New England's answer to Williamsburg, Virginia. On weekends, local craftsmen will teach their crafts to interested visitors. The Brimfield Flea Market is a mecca for antiques collectors. Host homes vary from a traditional house near the village green to a chalet nestled in the forest. Many are convenient to Clark University and Holy Cross.

Amacord
CHARLEMONT ROAD AND UPPER STREET, BUCKLAND, MASSACHUSETTS 01338

Tel: (413) 625-2975 (6–10 PM); 625-2697 (9 AM–5 PM)
Host(s): Janet Turley
Location: 13 mi. W of Greenfield
No. of Rooms: 2
No. of Private Baths: 1
Max. No. Sharing Bath: 4
Double/pb: $40–$45
Single/pb: $30–$33
Double/sb: $36–$41
Single/sb: $28–$30
Suite: $65 for 4
Open: All year
Breakfast: Full
Other Meals: Available
Pets: No
Children: No
Smoking: Permitted
Social Drinking: Permitted

This white, center-hall colonial (circa 1797) has a lovely screened-in porch for summer enjoyment and four fireplaces for cozy winter pleasure. Prestigious Deerfield Academy, Old Deerfield, Sturbridge Village, and the historic sights of Pioneer Valley are all close by. The University of Massachusetts, Smith, Amherst, and Williams are convenient to Janet's home.

The Turning Point Inn
R.D. 2, BOX 140, ROUTE 23 AND LAKE BUEL ROAD, GREAT BARRINGTON, MASSACHUSETTS 01230

Tel: (413) 528-4777
Best Time to Call: Early AM
Host(s): Irving and Shirley Yost
Location: 10 mi. from Mass. Pike
No. of Rooms: 7
No. of Private Baths: 1
Max. No. Sharing Bath: 4
Double/pb: $70
Double/sb: $55
Single/sb: $40
Open: All year
Reduced Rates: 10% Mon.–Thurs.
Breakfast: Full
Pets: No
Children: Welcome (crib)
Smoking: No
Social Drinking: Permitted

Irv and Shirley offer old-style comfort in an atmosphere of informality and warmth. Situated in the Berkshire Mountains, the house is 15 minutes from the music of Tanglewood and within walking distance of Butternut Ski Basin. The inn is 200 years old and has been lovingly restored and refurbished with antiques and fine reproductions. A naturally delicious homemade breakfast of eggs, whole grain pancakes, cereals, and fresh fruits is served. A two-day minimum stay is required on summer weekends. Simon's Rock of Bard College is nearby.

The Wildwood Inn ✪
121 CHURCH STREET, WARE, MASSACHUSETTS 01082

Tel: **(413) 967-7798**
Best Time to Call: **5–8 PM**
Host(s): **Margaret, Geoffrey, Heather, and Lori Lobenstine**
Location: **70 mi. W of Boston**
No. of Rooms: **5**
Max. No. Sharing Bath: **3**
Double/sb: **$35–$55**
Single/sb: **$35–$55**
Open: **All year (Nov.–Apr., weekends only)**
Reduced Rates: **10%, weekly**
Breakfast: **Continental**
Pets: **No**
Children: **Welcome, over 6**
Smoking: **Permitted**
Social Drinking: **Permitted**

Everything about this old-fashioned Victorian home with its rambling two acres is designed to help you unwind. There's a swing on the porch, a hammock under the firs, a blazing fire in the winter, a Norman Rockwell-esque brook-fed swimming hole in the summer. Your hosts have furnished their guest rooms with heirloom quilts, family treasures, and rockers, all of which work to spell welcome. Homemade bread and Margaret's own peach butter are included with continental breakfast, while "country yummies" are offered for one dollar extra. Sturbridge Village, Old Deerfield, and Amherst offer recreational activities that are all close by. You can stroll to the tennis court or borrow the canoe.

MICHIGAN

Windermere Inn ✪
747 CRYSTAL DRIVE, BEULAH, MICHIGAN 49617

Tel: **(616) 882-7264**
Best Time to Call: **1–6 PM**
Host(s): **Loralee and Bill Ludwig**
Location: **200 mi. N of Detroit**
No. of Rooms: **4**
No. of Private Baths: **4**
Double/pb: **$55**
Single/pb: **$55**

Open: **All year**
Reduced Rates: **10%, Nov.–Mar.**
Breakfast: **Continental**
Credit Cards: **MC, VISA**
Pets: **No**
Children: **No**
Smoking: **Permitted**
Social Drinking: **Permitted**

Set among century-old pine trees, this many-gabled white farmhouse is delightfully decorated with antiques. Loralee and Bill put fruit and flowers in each room daily, and coffee and snacks are always available. There's a fine view of Crystal Lake, and you're close to Sleeping Bear National Lakeshore and Interlochen Arts Academy. Recreational activities are plentiful in all seasons.

Bannicks B&B ✪
4608 MICHIGAN ROAD, DIMONDALE, MICHIGAN 48821

Tel: **(517) 646-0224**
Host(s): **Pat and Jim Bannick**
Location: **5 mi. SW of Lansing**
No. of Rooms: **2**
No. of Private Baths: **1**
Max. No. Sharing Bath: **3**
Double/pb: **$30**
Single/pb: **$15**
Double/sb: **$30**
Single/sb: **$15**
Open: **All year**
Breakfast: **Full**
Pets: **No**
Children: **Welcome**
Smoking: **No**
Social Drinking: **No**

This large ranch-style home features a stained glass entry, nautical-style basement, and a Mona Lisa bathroom. Guest accommodations consist of comfortable bedrooms and a den-TV room. Your hosts invite you to share a cup of coffee anytime. They will be happy to advise on the sights of Michigan's capital city, just five minutes away. For a break from touring, an above-ground swimming pool is available in season. Michigan State University is eight miles away.

Rosemont Inn ✪
83 LAKESHORE DRIVE, P.O. BOX 541, DOUGLAS, MICHIGAN 49406

Tel: **(616) 857-2637**
Best Time to Call: **8 AM–8 PM**
Host(s): **Ric and Cathy Gillette**
Location: **10 mi. S of Holland**
No. of Rooms: **14**
No. of Private Baths: **14**
Double/pb: **$65–$70**
Open: **All year**
Reduced Rates: **Weekly; Off-season**
Breakfast: **Continental**
Credit Cards: **MC, VISA**
Pets: **No**
Children: **Welcome**
Smoking: **Permitted**
Social Drinking: **Permitted**

The Rosemont is a Victorian inn with gingerbread trim. It began receiving guests in 1886 and still maintains a tradition of country living and hospitality. The house is furnished in country prints and antiques reproductions, with fireplaces in ten of the guest rooms. On a large porch, enjoy the cool breezes from Lake Michigan, whose beaches are directly across the street. Or swim in the Inn's heated pool. Your hosts will gladly supply information on boat trips, golf, and the sights of Saugatuck.

Wellman Accommodations ✪
P.O. BOX 58, 205 MAIN STREET, HORTON, MICHIGAN 49246

Tel: **(517) 563-2231**
Best Time to Call: **Evenings**
Host(s): **Karen D. Gauntlett**
Location: **10 mi. SW of Jackson**
No. of Rooms: **1 suite**
No. of Private Baths: **1**
Suites: **$38.50–$55 (2–4)**
Open: **All year**
Breakfast: **$5.50 (each)**
Other Meals: **Available**
Pets: **No**
Children: **Welcome, over 12**
Smoking: **Permitted**
Social Drinking: **Permitted**
Airport/Station Pickup: **Yes**

Karen's B&B is a designer apartment that was previously a turn-of-the-century general store. A large, carpeted living room/sleeping area where the dry goods and groceries used to be kept contains a double bed, color TV, leather card table, and phone. Settle down by the fire and enjoy the original art, or sun yourself in the garden or patio. The adjacent mill pond is great for swimming and fishing, and cross-country skiing is everywhere in winter. Karen is well-traveled, a former professional cook. Her gourmet four-course dinner is served with complimentary wines. Detroit is one and a half hours away and Chicago is four hours distant.

Seven Oaks Farm ✪
7891 HOLLISTER ROAD, LAINGSBURG, MICHIGAN 48848

Tel: **(517) 651-5598**
Host(s): **Terry and Mary Brock**
Location: **15 mi. NE of East Lansing**
No. of Rooms: **2**
Max. No. Sharing Bath: **4**
Double/sb: **$40**
Single/sb: **$20**
Open: **All year**
Breakfast: **Full**
Other Meals: **Available**
Pets: **Welcome**
Children: **Welcome (crib)**
Smoking: **Permitted**
Social Drinking: **Permitted**
Airport/Station Pickup: **Yes**

Seven Oaks is a large, comfortable home on a quiet country road. There are 100 acres to roam, a fishing pond, and ample opportunity for bird watching, snowmobiling and cross-country skiing. The house dates back 100 years, with spacious, double-bedded rooms now newly remodeled. Guests are invited to browse in the library or relax on the screened-in porch. Breakfast features griddle cakes or eggs and sausage. Nearby are country auctions, bowling, movies, golf, and museums as well as Michigan State University.

The Pebble House
15197 LAKESHORE ROAD, LAKESIDE, MICHIGAN 49116

Tel: **(616) 469-1416**
Host(s): **Jean and Ed Lawrence**
Location: **80 mi. E of Chicago**
No. of Rooms: **9**
No. of Private Baths: **7**
Max. No. Sharing Bath: **5**
Double/pb: **$65–$75**
Single/pb: **$60–$70**
Double/sb: **$45–$55**
Single/sb: **$40–$50**
Suites: **$65–$75**
Open: **Mar.–Dec.**
Reduced Rates: **10%, weekdays**
Breakfast: **Continental**
Pets: **No**
Children: **Welcome**
Smoking: **Permitted**
Social Drinking: **Permitted**
Airport/Station Pickup: **Yes**

Located in a quiet village only 90 minutes from Chicago's Loop, this restored 1900 stone-and-block house, coach house, and cottage comprise the inn. You are surrounded by farmland, orchards and vineyards, while dunes and white sand beaches skirt the Lake Michigan shore. Comfortably furnished, each room is color coordinated. Rest on the rocking chairs lining the porch, or by the fireplace in the book-lined living room. It's like "going back to grandma's." The Scandinavian buffet breakfast is a delight.

Governor's Inn ✪
7277 SIMONS STREET, P.O. BOX 471, LEXINGTON, MICHIGAN 48450

Tel: **(313) 359-5770**
Host(s): **Jane and Bob MacDonald**
Location: **20 mi. N of Port Huron**
No. of Rooms: **3**
No. of Private Baths: **3**
Double/pb: **$30**
Single/pb: **$30**
Open: **May 1–Sept. 30**
Breakfast: **Continental**
Pets: **No**
Children: **Welcome, over 12**
Smoking: **Permitted**
Social Drinking: **Permitted**

A handsome residence built in 1859, it is located near the shore of Lake Huron. It has been refurbished to its original "summer home" style. Wicker furniture, rag rugs, iron beds, and green plants accent the light, airy decor. You can stroll to the nearby beach, browse through interesting shops, fish from the breakwater, or play golf or tennis. Jane and Bob, both educators, look forward to sharing their quaint village surroundings with you.

Blue Lake Lodge ✪
9765 BLUE LAKE LODGE LANE, P.O. BOX 1, MECOSTA, MICHIGAN 49332

Tel: **(616) 972-8391 or (517) 482-0066**
Host(s): **Frank and Elaine Huisgen and Ray and Florence Gibbs**
Location: **65 mi. NE of Grand Rapids**
No. of Rooms: **6**
Max. No. Sharing Bath: **6**
Double/sb: **$30**
Single/sb: **$30**
Open: **Apr. 1–Nov. 30**
Reduced Rates: **Seniors; weekly rates**
Breakfast: **Continental**
Credit Cards: **MC, VISA**
Pets: **Sometimes**
Children: **Welcome**
Smoking: **Permitted**
Social Drinking: **Permitted**
Airport/Station Pickup: **Yes**

This is a large, informal home built in 1913 and located on the shore of a beautiful lake. All lakeside activities, such as swimming, boating, and fishing, are available. It's close to restaurants, but cooking grills, guest refrigerator, and picnic tables will help you cut down on dining costs.

MICHIGAN • 215

Raymond House Inn
111 SOUTH RIDGE STREET, PORT SANILAC, MICHIGAN 48469

Tel: **(313) 622-8800**
Best Time to Call: **9 AM–9 PM**
Host(s): **Shirley Denison**
Location: **30 mi. N of Port Huron**
No. of Rooms: **6**
No. of Private Baths: **4**
Max. No. Sharing Bath: **4**
Double/pb: **$45**
Single/pb: **$45**
Double/sb: **$35**
Single/sb: **$35**
Open: **May–Sept.**
Breakfast: **Continental**
Pets: **No**
Children: **Welcome, over 12**
Smoking: **Permitted**
Social Drinking: **Permitted**

Shirley will put you right at ease in her antique-filled inn with the conveniences of today and the ambience of 1895. Each bedroom is furnished with period furniture, brightly colored spreads, and lace curtains. There's an old-fashioned parlor, and a dining room where you are served breakfast. Sport fishermen and sailboat enthusiasts will enjoy this area; cultural activities, quilting bees, and the annual summer festival are longtime traditions here. There is an art gallery and an antique shop in the inn.

Colonial House Inn
90 NORTH STATE STREET, ST. IGNACE, MICHIGAN 49781

Tel: **(906) 643-6900**
Host(s): **Ailene and Joel Wittstein**
Location: **40 mi. NE of Petoskey**
No. of Rooms: **5**
Max. No. Sharing Bath: **6**
Doube/sb: **$27–$44**
Single/sb: **$23–$40**
Open: **All year**
Reduced Rates: **Nov. 1–Apr. 30**
Breakfast: **Continental**
Credit Cards: **MC, VISA**
Pets: **No**
Children: **Welcome**
Smoking: No
Social Drinking: **Permitted**
Airport/Station Pickup: **Yes**

Only minutes away from Mackinac Bridge, the longest suspension bridge in the world, Joel and Ailene's house is for those who appreciate history, the warmth of rich woods, the grace of antique furnishings, and breakfast served on century-old china. They are former teachers, interested in poetry, music, crafts, and weaving. Their handsome home is listed in the National Historic Register.

Wickwood Inn ⊙
510 BUTLER STREET, SAUGATUCK, MICHIGAN 49453

Tel: (616) 857-1097
Best Time to Call: 9–5 PM weekdays
Host(s): **Sue and Stub Louis**
Location: **20 mi. S of Holland**
No. of Rooms: **10**
No. of Private Baths: **10**
Double/pb: **$75**
Single/pb: **$75**
Suites: **$85–$110**

Open: **All year**
Reduced Rates: **Off-season, weekdays**
Breakfast: **Continental**
Credit Cards: **AMEX, MC, VISA**
Pets: **No**
Children: **No**
Smoking: **Permitted**
Social Drinking: **Permitted**
Airport/Station Pickup: **Yes**

The bedrooms of this stately Federal-style inn have pleasant British accents, with Laura Ashley fabrics and wallpapers; in each bath there are fine soaps and shampoos from London. The rooms are named for the four seasons. All have fine antiques of pine, walnut, and cherry. Relax in the sunken garden room, screened gazebo, and library-bar, which is designed like an English gentlemen's club. Guests will find hospitable touches throughout their stay, such as fresh flowers, afternoon teas, and homemade cakes at breakfast. The beaches at Lake Michigan, golf, tennis, and historic homes are all close by.

The Victorian Villa Guesthouse ⊙
601 NORTH BROADWAY STREET, UNION CITY, MICHIGAN 49094

Tel: (517) 741-7383
Best Time to Call: **7:30 AM–10 PM**
Host(s): **Ron and Sue Gibson**
Location: **20 mi. S of Battle Creek**
No. of Rooms: **8**
No. of Private Baths: **3**
Max. No. Sharing Bath: **4**
Double/pb: **$65**
Single/pb: **$60**
Double/sb: **$45–$50**

Single/sb: **$40–$45**
Suites: **$65**
Open: **Feb. 1–Dec. 31**
Breakfast: **Continental**
Credit Cards: **MC, VISA**
Pets: **No**
Children: **Welcome**
Smoking: **No**
Social Drinking: **Permitted**

The Victorian Villa is a 19th-century estate house furnished with antiques. Guests may choose from five private chambers, all elegantly appointed. Chilled champagne, wine, cheese, and a private "tea-for-two" can be arranged. Fancy chocolates, a specialty of the house, are placed on the pillows at night. Your hosts will help make your visit as sparkling as you like, directing you to summer theater, museums, antique shops, and restaurants.

Villa Hammer
3133 BENSTEIN, WALLED LAKE, MICHIGAN 48088

Tel: (313) 624-1071
Host(s): **Reinhold and Veronica Hammer**
Location: **35 mi. NW of Detroit**
No. of Rooms: **2**
No. of Private Baths: **1**
Max. No. Sharing Bath: **3**
Double/pb: **$35**
Single/pb: **$25**
Double/sb: **$30**
Single/sb: **$20**
Open: **All year**
Reduced Rates: **20%, families**
Breakfast: **Full**
Pets: **No**
Children: **Welcome, over 10**
Smoking: **No**
Social Drinking: **Permitted**
Foreign Languages: **German**

This spacious Tudor home is set on three acres in a quiet area. The Huron River runs the length of the property and can be seen through many windows in the house. The rooms are comfortably decorated and boast many plants. Breakfast menus include German specialties and old standbys like waffles and bacon. The river provides fine fishing and canoeing, as do the other nearby lakes. Your hosts will gladly direct you to Alpine Ski area, Greenfield Village, and local dining.

MINNESOTA

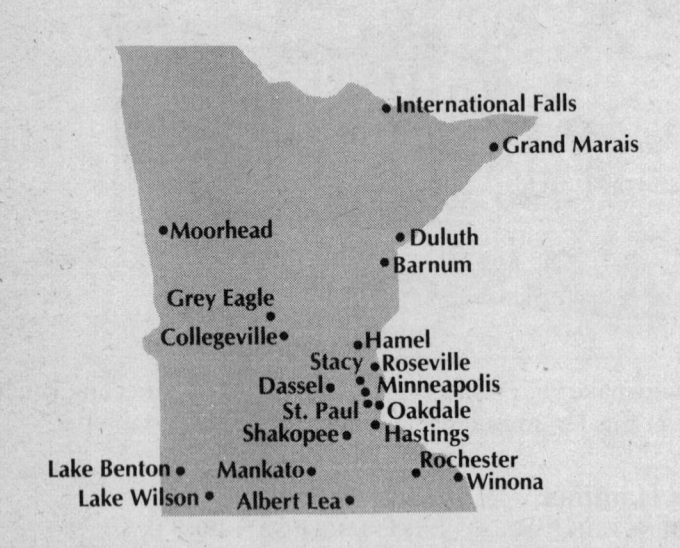

Bed & Breakfast Registry—North America
P.O. BOX 80174, ST. PAUL, MINNESOTA 55108

Tel: **(612) 646-4238**	Rates (Single/Double):
Best Time to Call: **9 AM–9 PM**	Modest: $16–$25 $20–$35
Coordinator: **Mary Winget**	Average: $20–$35 $30–$45
States/Regions Covered: **Statewide** and national	Luxury: $40 and up $45 and up
	Credit Cards: **MC, VISA**

The Twin City attractions of the Guthrie Theater, Walker Art Center, Art Institute, Omni Theater, Science Center, and the live Prairie Home Companion radio show draw people from all over the country. There are delightful urban accommodations on Mary's roster, as well as more rural B&Bs for quiet serenity. A directory describing hosts in 39 states is available for $5.95.

Gabrielson's B&B ✪
RURAL ROUTE 1, DASSEL, MINNESOTA 55325

Tel: **(612) 275-3609**
Best Time to Call: **Late afternoon**
Host(s): **Elaine and Don Gabrielson**
Location: **60 mi. W of Minneapolis**
No. of Rooms: **1**
No. of Private Baths: **1**
Double/pb: **$25**
Single/pb: **$18**

Open: **All year**
Breakfast: **Continental**
Pets: **Sometimes**
Children: **Welcome, over 9**
Smoking: **Permitted**
Social Drinking: **Permitted**
Airport/Station Pickup: **Yes**

Perched on a hilltop, this 1910 white clapboard farmhouse, decorated in early American style, overlooks a private lake. You are welcome to use the paddleboat for getting to the little island, where you can picnic. Or, try your hand at archery, trap shooting, or pond fishing. Elaine and Don are busy raising corn and beans but they'll happily arrange a farm tour of Meeker County. Wine, cheese, and rolls are stocked in the guest refrigerator. The University of Minnesota is nearby.

Thorwood Bed & Breakfast ✪
FOURTH AND PINE, HASTINGS, MINNESOTA 55033

Tel: **(612) 437-3297**
Host(s): **Dick and Pam Thorsen**
Location: **19 mi. SE of St. Paul**
No. of Rooms: **3**
No. of Private Baths: **1**
Max. No. Sharing Bath: **4**
Double/pb: **$45**
Single/pb: **$39**
Double/sb: **$35**
Single/sb: **$29**
Open: **All year**
Reduced Rates: **Available**
Credit Cards: **AMEX, VISA**
Breakfast: **Continental**
Pets: **Welcome**
Children: **Welcome**
Smoking: **Permitted**
Social Drinking: **Permitted**
Foreign Languages: **Norwegian**
Airport/Station Pickup: **Yes**

Enjoy comfort and warm hospitality in this elegant 1880 French Second Empire home, which boasts such details as frescoed ceilings and marble fireplaces. The town is located on the Mississippi and the town's bluff views are beautiful. Dick and Pam serve a generous breakfast, put wine and goodies in your room, and if you are a midnight snacker, they won't send you to bed hungry. The area abounds in history, fine restaurants, specialty shops, and nature trails.

Evelo's Bed & Breakfast ✪
2301 BYRANT AVENUE SOUTH, MINNEAPOLIS, MINNESOTA 55405

Tel: **(612) 374-9656**	Open: **All year**
Best Time to Call: **After 4 PM**	Reduced Rates: **Weekly**
Host(s): **David and Sheryl Evelo**	Breakfast: **Full**
No. of Rooms: 3	Pets: **No**
Max. No. Sharing Baths: 6	Children: **Welcome**
Double/sb: $30–$40	Smoking: **No**
Single/sb: $20	Social Drinking: **Permitted**

Located in the historic Lowry Hill East neighborhood, this century-old Victorian has one of the best-preserved interiors in the area and is furnished with fine period pieces. David and Sheryl are both schoolteachers. Breakfast often features quiche or egg casseroles. The house is within walking distance of the Guthrie Theater and the Walker Art Center.

Oakdale Tanners Lake ✪
886 GLENBROOK AVENUE NORTH, OAKDALE, MINNESOTA 55119

Tel: **(612) 739-0193**	Single/sb: $25
Host(s): **Ray and Audrey Furchner**	Open: **All year**
Location: **10 mi. E of St. Paul**	Breakfast: **Continental**
No. of Rooms: 2	Pets: **No**
No. of Private Baths: 1	Children: **No**
Max. No. Sharing Bath: 2	Smoking: **Permitted**
Double/pb: $35	Social Drinking: **Permitted**

You can take in the excitement of nearby Minneapolis and St. Paul and return "home" to Ray and Audrey's contemporary split-level home to relax. Thoughtful touches such as a phone and TV are part of your accommodations. Their hobby is constructing and furnishing doll houses. You are welcome to use the pool table and the backyard; the coffee pot is always on.

Canterbury Inn Bed & Breakfast
723 SECOND STREET S.W., ROCHESTER, MINNESOTA 55902

Tel: (507) 289-5553
Host(s): **Mary Martin and Jeffrey Van Sant**
Location: **90 mi. S of Minneapolis**
No. of Rooms: **4**
No. of Private Baths: **4**
Double/pb: **$60**
Single/pb: **$50**
Open: **Feb. 16–Jan. 14**

Reduced Rates: **10%, weekly**
Breakfast: **Full**
Credit Cards: **AMEX, MC, VISA**
Pets: **No**
Children: **Sometimes**
Smoking: **Permitted**
Social Drinking: **Permitted**
Airport/Station Pickup: **Yes**
Foreign Languages: **Italian**

This is a huge Victorian structure, just three blocks from the Mayo Clinic, with polished hardwood floors, stained glass windows, and a cozy fireplace complete with carved mantel. Lace curtains and eclectic furnishings give it an air in keeping with its age. Enjoy games, music, and conversation in the parlor. Breakfast is served in the formal dining room and may include such delicious fare as eggs Benedict and German apple pancakes. Afternoon tea at 4:30 generally lingers into the evening.

Kings Oakdale Park Guest House ○
6933 232 AVENUE N.E., STACY, MINNESOTA 55079

Tel: (612) 462-5598
Host(s): **Donna and Charles Solem**
Location: **38 mi. N of St. Paul**
No. of Rooms: **3**
No. of Private Baths: **2**
Double/pb: **$28**
Single/pb: **$25**
Double/sb: **$20**
Single/sb: **$18**

Suites: **$28**
Open: **All year**
Breakfast: **Continental**
Pets: **Sometimes**
Children: **No**
Smoking: **Permitted**
Social Drinking: **Permitted**
Foreign Languages: **French**

This comfortable home is situated on four landscaped acres on the banks of Typo Creek. The picnic tables, volleyball net, and horseshoe game are sure signs of a hospitable country place. It is a serene retreat for people on business trips to the Twin Cities.

The Wisconsin border and the scenic St. Croix River, where boat trips are offered, are minutes from the house. Charles and Donna will direct you to the most reasonable restaurants in town. For late snacks, refrigerators in the bedrooms are provided.

For key to listings, see inside front or back cover.

✪ This star means that rates are guaranteed through December 31, 1985 to any guest making a reservation as a result of reading about the B&B in BED & BREAKFAST U.S.A.—1985 edition.

Please enclose a self-addressed, stamped, business-sized envelope when contacting reservation services.

For more details on what you can expect in a B&B, see Chapter 1.

Always mention *Bed & Breakfast USA* when making reservations!

MISSISSIPPI

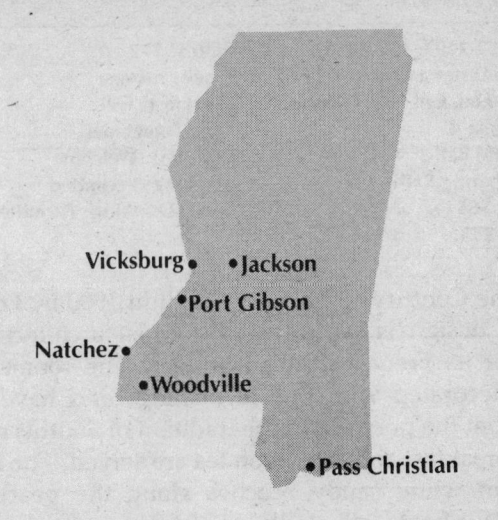

Vicksburg • • Jackson
• Port Gibson
Natchez •
• Woodville

• Pass Christian

Monmouth Plantation
P.O. BOX 1736, 36 MELROSE AVENUE, NATCHEZ, MISSISSIPPI 39120

Tel: (601) 442-5852
Best Time to Call: 9 AM–5 PM
Host(s): **Harvey and Sarah Cotten**
Location: **40 mi. from I-55**
No. of Rooms: **11**
No. of Private Baths: **11**
Double/pb: **$75–$95**
Single/pb: **$70–$90**

Open: **All year**
Breakfast: **Full**
Credit Cards: **AMEX, MC, VISA**
Pets: **No**
Children: **Welcome, over 12**
Smoking: **No**
Social Drinking: **Permitted**

Monmouth is a Greek Revival mansion built in 1818. The rooms are totally of their time, with lavish period furnishings. Guests will also appreciate the central air-conditioning, television, and modern conveniences. Your hosts offer complimentary afternoon wine and snacks, and a Southern breakfast each morning. They will advise on tours of the local antebellum homes, beginning with their own. The old slave quarter is now a museum, housing rare and interesting relics of the Civil War. After a day of sightseeing, relax beside the pond or stroll the spacious grounds.

Turn of the Century Cottage ○
MENGE AVENUE, ROUTE 4, BOX 214, PASS CHRISTIAN, MISSISSIPPI 39571

Tel: (601) 452-2402; 452-2868
Host(s): Jan Lester and Marla Elmer
Location: 60 mi. E of New Orleans
No. of Rooms: 4
No. of Private Baths: 1
Max. No. Sharing Bath: 4
Double/pb: $65
Double/sb: $55

Suites: $72
Open: All year
Breakfast: Full
Pets: Sometimes
Children: Welcome
Smoking: Permitted
Social Drinking: Permitted

Turn of the Century Cottage was built in 1900 by Louis Dubuisson. The design is typical of the Coast architecture and the designs of its French Acadian builder. The rooms are professionally decorated with fine furnishings and have private entrances from the porches. In the tradition of Southern hospitality, a hearty breakfast and afternoon tea are served. The house is two miles from white sandy beaches along the peaceful Gulf of Mexico. Your hosts will gladly provide information on the better restaurants, antebellum homes, and boat excursions to Ship Island.

Oak Square ○
1207 CHURCH STREET, PORT GIBSON, MISSISSIPPI 39150

Tel: (601) 437-4350 or 437-5771
Best Time to Call: Morning; evening
Host(s): Mr. and Mrs. William D. Lum
Location: 60 mi. SW of Jackson on Hwy. 61
No. of rooms: 7
No. of Private Baths: 7
Double/pb: $55–$65
Single/pb: $50–$60

Guest Cottage: Available
Open: All year
Breakfast: Full
Credit Cards: AMEX, MC, VISA
Pets: No
Children: Welcome
Smoking: Permitted
Social Drinking: Permitted

Port Gibson is the town that Union General Ulysses S. Grant said was "too beautiful to burn." Oak Square is the largest and most palatial antebellum mansion (circa 1850) in Port Gibson, and is listed in the National Historic Register. The guest rooms are all furnished with family heirlooms, and most have canopied beds.

Guests will enjoy the courtyard, gazebo, and beautiful grounds. A chairlift for upstairs rooms is available. You will enjoy the delightful Southern breakfast and tour of the house. Your hosts offer complimentary wine, tea, or coffee, and will enlighten you on the many historic attractions in the area.

Square Ten Inn ✪
242 DEPOT STREET, P.O. BOX 371, WOODVILLE, MISSISSIPPI 39669

Tel: **(601) 888-3993**	Open: **All year**
Host(s): **Elizabeth M. Treppendahl**	Reduced Rates: **25%, 5 day stay**
Location: **35 mi. S of Natchez**	Breakfast: **Continental**
No. of Rooms: **3**	Pets: **No**
No. of Private Baths: **3**	Children: **Welcome, over 6**
Double/pb: **$34**	Smoking: **Permitted**
Suites: **$39.50**	Social Drinking: **Permitted**

This one-story town house was built in 1830 and is located close to Courthouse Square, a National Historic District. Elizabeth has artistically furnished it with lovely antiques and brass beds. You are welcome to relax in the comfortable living room or secluded courtyard. Complimentary wine, coffee, or tea is served.

MISSOURI

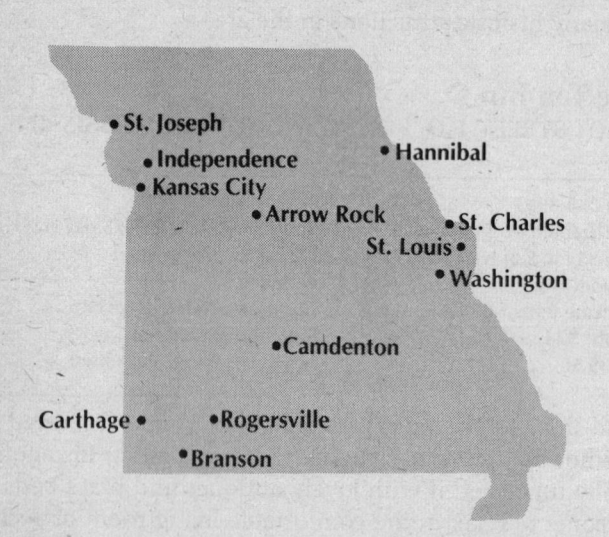

B&B St. Louis—River Country of Missouri & Illinois, Inc. ✪
1 GRANDVIEW HEIGHTS, ST. LOUIS, MISSOURI 63131

Tel: (314) 965-4328	Rates (Single/Double):
Best Time to Call: 8 AM–4 PM	Modest: $20–$25 $25–$30
Coordinator: Mike Warner	Average: $30 $35
States/Regions Covered:	Luxury: $45 $45–$75
Missouri-Statewide; Southern Illinois	Credit Cards: MC, VISA

Whether you'd enjoy roughing it in a rustic cabin in Clark National Forest, or having breakfast in bed in an historic lakeside inn, or even bringing your horse along for "bed and bale" at a cattle ranch, Miss Mike Warner has the extraordinary or the traditional B&B just tailored to your taste. Delightful spots such as St. Genevieve, Kansas City, or accommodations convenient to the University of Missouri and Stephens College in Columbia. Send $3 for her descriptive directory.

Ozark Mountain Country B&B Service
BOX 295, BRANSON, MISSOURI 65616

Tel: **(417) 334-5077 or 334-4720**
Coordinator: **Linda Johnson, Kay Cameron**
States/Regions Covered:
  Missouri—Branson, Cape Fair, Forsyth, Galena, Hollister;
  Arkansas—Eureka Springs, Pindall

Rates (Single/Double):
  Average: **$20–$33 $25–$38**
Credit Cards: **No**

Linda and Kay will send you a complimentary copy of their descriptive listing of homes, so you can select the host of your choice; they'll take care of making your reservation.

Borgman's Bed & Breakfast ✪
ARROW ROCK, MISSOURI 65320

Tel: **(816) 837-3350**
Best Time to Call: **7–9 AM**
Host(s): **Helen and Kathy Borgman**
Location: **100 mi. E of Kansas City**
No. of Rooms: **4**
Max. No. Sharing Bath: **4**
Double/sb: **$30–$40**
Single/sb: **$30**

Open: **All year**
Reduced Rates: **10%, three nights**
Breakfast: **Continental**
Other Meals: **Dinner (winter only)**
Pets: **Sometimes**
Children: **Welcome**
Smoking: **No**
Social Drinking: **Permitted**

This 1860 home is spacious and comfortable, and it is furnished with cherished family pieces. Helen is a seamstress, artisan, and baker. Wait till you taste her fresh breads! Daughter Kathy is a town tour guide, so you will get first-hand information on this National Historic Landmark town. A fine repertory theater, the Lyceum, is open in summer. Craft shops, antique stalls, and the old country store are fun places to browse in. Good restaurants are within walking distance.

Lakeside Guest House ✪
R.R. 2, BOX 41, NORMAC, CAMDENTON, MISSOURI 65020

Tel: **(314) 346-3767**	Single/pb: **$30**
Best Time to Call: **Evenings**	Open: **May 1–Oct. 31**
Host(s): **Virginia Dyck**	Breakfast: **Continental**
Location: **170 mi. S of Kansas City**	Pets: **No**
No. of Rooms: **2**	Children: **No**
No. of Private Baths: **2**	Smoking: **No**
Double/pb: **$35**	Social Drinking: **Permitted**

Virginia's lovely home is a bi-level, modified A-frame just 50 feet from the Lake of the Ozarks, with cathedral ceilings and many glass doors opening onto the patio and deck. You will be lulled to sleep by the sound of lapping water. HaHa Tonka Mansion and Trails, Bridal Cave, country music shows, antique shops and many fine restaurants are all close by.

Morgan's Woodhaven ✪
RR 70, BOX 833, CAMDENTON, MISSOURI 65020

Tel: **(314) 346-3944**	Open: **May 1–Oct. 31**
Host(s): **Gladys Morgan**	Breakfast: **Continental**
Location: **¼ mi. from Hwy. 54**	Pets: **Sometimes**
No. of Rooms: **1**	Children: **No**
No. of Private Baths: **1**	Smoking: **No**
Double/pb: **$30**	Social Drinking: **Permitted**
Single/pb: **$20**	

This ranch-style home, well-furnished, is located two miles from all the recreational activities to be found on and around the Lake of the Ozarks. The guest room has a sliding glass door which provides a private entrance and opens onto the deck which overlooks the woods. Gladys wants you to feel at home; use her kitchen should you tire of the excellent restaurants in the area.

Hill House ✪
1157 SOUTH MAIN STREET, CARTHAGE, MISSOURI 64836

Tel: **(417) 358-6145**	No. of Rooms: **2**
Best Time to Call: **Evenings**	No. of Private Baths: **2**
Host(s): **Dean and Ella Mae Scoville**	Double/pb: **$40**
Location: **60 mi. SW of Springfield**	Single/pb: **$25**

Open: **All year**
Breakfast: **Full**
Pets: **No**
Children: **Welcome**

Smoking: **No**
Social Drinking: **No**
Airport/Station Pickup: **Yes**

A stay at this brick Victorian mansion, located in the Historic District, includes the grand tour of all the rooms. The house has stained glass, sliding-pocket doors, 10 fireplaces, and rare period furnishings. Your hosts will prepare dietetic foods to order, and the coffee pot is always on. Breakfast includes homemade muffins and jams. Carthage Square, a mining museum, Harry Truman's birthplace, and Missouri Southern State College are nearby.

The Victorian Guest House ✪
3 STILLWELL PLACE, HANNIBAL, MISSOURI 63401

Tel: **(314) 221-3093**
Best Time to Call: **After 5 PM**
Host(s): **Katherine and Beth McKinney**
Location: **117 mi. N of St. Louis**
No. of Rooms: **3**
No. of Private Baths: **1**
Max. No. Sharing Bath: **5**
Double/pb: **$35**
Single/pb: **$30**

Double/sb: **$30**
Single/sb: **$25**
Open: **All year**
Reduced Rates: **10%, seniors**
Breakfast: **Continental**
Pets: **Sometimes**
Children: **Welcome, over 6**
Smoking: **No**
Social Drinking: **Permitted**

Located in a residential area, this gracious Victorian brick home is attractively furnished and is eight blocks from the historic Mark Twain area. Katherine's connection with Hannibal Tourist Information will enable her to give you added assistance with touring ideas. A full breakfast is served September through May. It is convenient to Hannibal La Grange College.

Truman Country Bed & Breakfast ✪
P.O. BOX 14, INDEPENDENCE, MISSOURI 64050

Tel: **(816) 254-6657**
Best Time to Call: **8 AM–6 PM**
Coordinator: **Barbara Earley**
State/Regions Covered:
  Independence

Rates (Single/Double):
  Modest: **$20–$25**
  Average: **$25–$35**
  Luxury: **$37.50–$40–$45**
Credit Cards: **No**

Barbara's hosts are proud of their historic home town and will do all they can to make your visit rich and rewarding. Do stay long enough to visit the Truman Library and Museum, President Truman's Home, Fort Osage, Honey Farm, and Liberty Jail. Park College and the University of Missouri-Kansas City are close by.

Anchor Hill Lodge ○
ANCHOR HILL RANCH, ROUTE 1, ROGERSVILLE, MISSOURI 65742

Tel: **(417) 753-2930**	Open: **All year**
Best Time to Call: **After 7 PM**	Breakfast: **Continental**
Host(s): **Dr. and Mrs. T. E. Atkinson**	Pets: **No**
Location: **20 mi. SE of Springfield**	Children: **Welcome (crib)**
No. of Rooms: **2**	Smoking: **Permitted**
No. of Private Baths: **2**	Social Drinking: **Permitted**
Double/pb: **$35**	Airport/Station Pickup: **Yes**
Single/pb: **$25**	

If your horse hasn't taken a vacation in a while, he's most welcome to accompany you to this rural ranch in the foothills of the Ozark Mountains. For $5 he will have a box stall and all he can eat, while you enjoy the comfort of an old-fashioned country home. Your hosts breed and ride Arabian horses and there are miles of trails for you to enjoy. In addition, there's lots to do and see, including an exotic animal farm, theater, museums, water sports, hiking, and craft fairs. Enjoy the relaxing hot tub on-premises, as well as the beautiful views.

McNally House Bed & Breakfast ○
1105 SOUTH 15TH STREET, ST. JOSEPH, MISSOURI 64503

Tel: **(816) 232-0623**	Open: **All year**
Best Time to Call: **Evenings, weekends**	Reduced Rates: **10%, seniors**
Host(s): **Reva Allen, Charles St. Clair**	Breakfast: **Continental**
Location: **50 mi. N of Kansas City**	Pets: **No**
No. of Rooms: **2**	Children: **Welcome**
Max. No. Sharing Bath: **3**	Smoking: **No**
Double/sb: **$25**	Social Drinking: **Permitted**
Single/sb: **$20**	

There are lots of plants, leaded stained glass windows, wicker furniture, and a grand piano set in the bay window of this 75-

year-old clapboard house. It boasts two porches and a variety of gardens. In this historic area you can visit the Pony Express Stables, Patee House, and the Jesse James Home. Reva is a professor of social work at Missouri Western State College nearby, and Charles is a community development specialist. They both enjoy travel and travelers.

Bed & Breakfast St. Louis ✪
16 GREEN ACRES, ST. LOUIS, MISSOURI 63137

Tel: **(314) 868-2335**	Rates (Single/Double):
Coordinator: **Evelyn Ressler**	Modest: **$25** **$30-$32**
States/Regions Covered: **St. Louis and suburbs**	Average: **$30-$35** **$35-$40**
	Luxury: **$35-45** **$45-$50**
	Credit Cards: **No**

"Show me. I'm from Missouri" works in reverse for visitors, because Missourians will want to show *you* what makes their area so special. You can't miss the Gateway Arch, and shouldn't miss a tour of the Anheuser-Busch Brewery, the Museum of Transport, Six Flags Amusement Park, Busch Stadium, and the symphony, theater, and historic sites. Send for Evelyn's descriptive directory and select your host home. St. Louis University, Washington University, and The University of Missouri are nearby.

The Schwegmann House B&B Inn ✪
438 WEST FRONT STREET, WASHINGTON, MISSOURI 63090

Tel: **(314) 239-5025**	Double/sb: **$35**
Best Time to Call: **Friday evenings**	Single/sb: **$35**
Host(s): **George Bocklage, Barbara Lee, Cathy French**	Months of Operation: **All year**
	Breakfast: **Continental**
Location: **50 mi. W of St. Louis**	Credit Cards: **MC, VISA**
No. of Rooms: **9**	Pets: **No**
No. of Private Baths: **7**	Children: **Welcome, over 7**
Max. No. Sharing Bath: **4**	Smoking: **Permitted**
Double/pb: **$50**	Social Drinking: **Permitted**
Single/pb: **$50**	Foreign Languages: **French**

A three-story 1861 Georgian brick house included in the National Historic Register, it is located on the Missouri River. It is tastefully furnished with antiques; handmade quilts complement the decor of each guest room. It is close to Daniel Boone's home, Meramec

232 • MISSOURI

Caverns, Missouri's Rhineland wineries, unique shops, and fine restaurants. Relax in the graceful parlor by the fireside or stroll the gardens that overlook the river. George, Barbara, and Cathy serve a bountiful breakfast including fresh-ground coffee, imported cheeses, croissants, homemade bread, and grape juice from Missouri's vineyards.

Voss Inn, Montana

MONTANA

Western Bed & Breakfast Hosts O
P.O. BOX 322, KALISPELL, MONTANA 59901

Tel: (406) 257-4476	Rates (Single/Double):
Best Time to Call: 9 AM–5 PM	Modest: $18-$22 $22-$28
Coordinator: **Sylva Jones**	Average: $25-$30 $30-$45
States/Regions Covered: **Montana** (statewide)	Luxury: $35-40 $45-$50

Sylva brings you the opportunity of experiencing the vast and beautiful region between Canada, in the north, and Yellowstone National Park in the south. This area includes Glacier National Park, the National Bison Range, and Bob Marshall Wilderness. The whole region is popular for hiking, hunting, fishing, skiing, and gorgeous mountain scenery. The University of Montana is near several B&Bs.

Voss Inn ✪
319 SOUTH WILLSON, BOZEMAN, MONTANA 59715

Tel: **(406) 587-0982**
Host(s): **Ken and Ruthmary Tonn**
Location: **3 mi. from I-90**
No. of Rooms: **6**
No. of Private Baths: **6**
Double/pb: **$45-$55**
Single/pb: **$45-$55**
Open: **All year**

Reduced Rates: **Available**
Breakfast: **Full**
Credit Cards: **MC, VISA**
Pets: **No**
Children: **Sometimes**
Smoking: **Permitted**
Social Drinking: **Permitted**

This handsome 100-year-old brick mansion flanked by Victorian gingerbread porches is set like a gem on a tree-lined street in historic Bozeman. The bedrooms are elegantly wallpapered and furnished with brass and iron beds, ornate lighting, Oriental throw rugs over polished hardwood floors . . . a perfect spot for a first or second honeymoon. The parlor has a fireplace, candle-topped mantel, good selection of books, as well as a chess set for your pleasure. It's north of Yellowstone, on the way to Glacier, with trout fishing, mountain lakes, and skiing within easy reach. Don't miss the Museum of the Rockies on the Montana State University campus 10 blocks away.

Duck Inn ✪
1305 COLUMBIA AVENUE, WHITEFISH, MONTANA 59937

Tel: **(406) 862-DUCK**
Host(s): **Ken and Phyllis Adler**
Location: **25 mi. from Glacier Nat'l. Park**
No. of Rooms: **10**
No. of Private Baths: **10**
Double/pb: **$48**
Open: **All year**

Reduced Rates: **Off-season, families**
Breakfast: **Continental**
Credit Cards: **MC, VISA**
Pets: **No**
Children: **Welcome**
Smoking: **Permitted**
Social Drinking: **Permitted**
Airport/Station Pickup: **Yes**

The Duck Inn is on the Whitefish River, six blocks from downtown. Each guest room features a brass or white iron bed, cozy fireplace, deep soak tub, and a balcony. A large living room with a view of Big Mountain and the river is a relaxing spot. Your hosts offer a different kind of fresh-baked bread each morning, and can provide information on Glacier National Park, wilderness areas, and spots to swim, sail, and fish. A Jacuzzi is available after a heavy day of touring.

NEBRASKA

Map showing: North Platte, Lexington, Grand Island, Lincoln, Omaha

Bed & Breakfast of Nebraska ✪
1464 28TH AVENUE, COLUMBUS, NEBRASKA 68601

Tel: **(402) 564-7591**
Best Time to Call: **After 5 PM**
Coordinator: **Marlene Van Lent**
States/Regions Covered: **Statewide**

Rates (Single/Double):
  Average: $25 $35
  Luxury: $36 $55
Credit Cards: **No**

Marlene has delightful homes in cities, towns, villages, and on farms and ranches. Many are located close to I-80, making it convenient for cross-country travelers. Visit the vacation area of Chadron, the wagon trails of Scotts Bluff, the Bill Cody Museum in North Platte, the Indian culture of Fort Robinson, the De Soto Bend Wildlife Refuge, and the world renowned Boys Town in Omaha. Many areas feature fine fishing and hunting, and the Missouri River has many tourist attractions. You are assured of warm welcomes wherever you stop. Creighton University and the University of Nebraska are convenient to several B&Bs.

Rogers House ✪
2145 B STREET, LINCOLN, NEBRASKA 68502

Tel: **(402) 476-6961**
Host(s): **Nora Houtsma**
No. of Rooms: **5**
No. of Private Baths: **5**
Double/pb: **$45–$55**
Single/pb: **$40–$50**
Suites: **$90–$110**
Open: **All year**
Breakfast: **Full**
Credit Cards: **MC, VISA**
Pets: **No**
Children: **Welcome**
Smoking: **Permitted**
Social Drinking: **Permitted**

This Jacobean Revival style brick mansion was built in 1914 and is a local historic landmark. There are three sunporches, attractively furnished with wicker and plants, and the air-conditioned house is decorated with lovely antiques. Nora can arrange walking tours in the historic district and will direct you to the diverse cultural attractions available at the nearby University of Nebraska. Don't miss a visit to the Children's Zoo and the beautiful Sunken Gardens. Breakfast is hearty and delicious and often features a quiche or souffle.

For key to listings, see inside front or back cover.

✪ This star means that rates are guaranteed through December 31, 1985 to any guest making a reservation as a result of reading about the B&B in *BED & BREAKFAST U.S.A.*—1985 edition.

Please enclose a self-addressed, stamped, business-sized envelope when contacting reservation services.

For more details on what you can expect in a B&B, see Chapter 1.

Always mention *Bed & Breakfast USA* when making reservations!

NEVADA

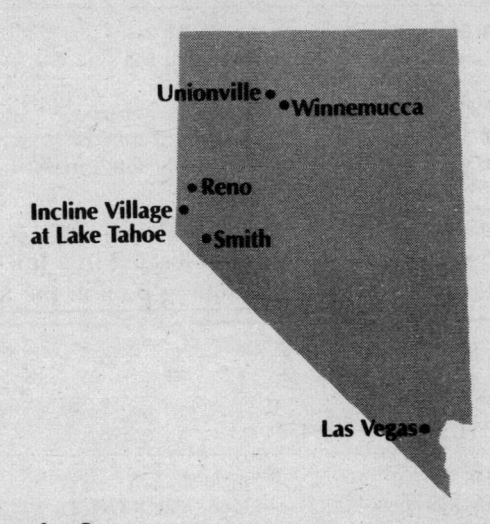

Haus Bavaria ⊙
P.O. BOX 3308, 593 NORTH DYER CIRCLE, INCLINE VILLAGE, LAKE TAHOE, NEVADA 89450

Tel: (702) 831-6122
Best Time to Call: 9 AM–8 PM
Host(s): **Wolfgang and Anna Zimmermann**
Location: 35 mi. SW of Reno
No. of Rooms: 5
No. of Private Baths: 5
Double/pb: $50
Single/pb: $40

Open: **All year**
Reduced Rates: **10%, weekly**
Breakfast: **Full**
Pets: **No**
Children: **Welcome, over 10**
Smoking: **Permitted**
Social Drinking: **Permitted**
Foreign Languages: **German**

This immaculate residence is framed by the mountains and convenient to the lake. It's hard to believe you're not in the Swiss Alps! Each guest room opens onto a balcony. Continental hosts Wolfgang and Anna set a breakfast table with bountiful platters of cold cuts, imported cheeses, sliced fruits, boiled eggs, cake, rolls, and endless cups of delicious coffee or tea. It's close to the gambling casinos and shows, all water sports and, in winter, the challenging slopes of Mount Rose and Heavenly Valley.

Las Vegas B&B
CONTACT: BED AND BREAKFAST INTERNATIONAL, 151 ARDMORE ROAD, KENSINGTON, CALIFORNIA 94707

Tel: **(415) 527-8836**
Host(s): **Jean Brown**
No. of Rooms: **2**
No. of Private Baths: **1**
Double/pb: **$46**
Suite: **$82 for 4**

Open: **All year**
Breakfast: **Full**
Pets: **No**
Children: **Welcome**
Smoking: **Permitted**
Social Drinking: **Permitted**

The hosts are writers and interested in genealogy, geology, and traveling. Their single-story home is located in a fine neighborhood. Guests may enjoy the swimming pool in the landscaped garden.

Windybrush Ranch
BOX 85, SMITH, NEVADA 89430

Tel: **(702) 465-2481**
Best Time to Call: **Mornings**
Host(s): **Frank and Margaret Parsons**
Location: **75 mi. SE of Reno**
No. of Rooms: **2**
No. of Private Baths: **1**
Max. No. Sharing Bath: **4**
Double/pb: **$46**
Single/pb: **$23**
Double/sb: **$46**

Single/sb: **$23**
Open: **May 1–Oct. 31**
Breakfast: **Full**
Other Meals: **Lunch & Dinner**
Pets: **Welcome**
Children: **Welcome (crib)**
Smoking: **Permitted**
Social Drinking: **Permitted**
Airport/Station Pickup: **Yes**

The rooms of this clapboard farmhouse have mountain views and country furnishings. This is a children's paradise, with acres to explore, animals to pet, games and swings. Your hosts will provide transportation to nearby fishing, swimming, and river rafting. They will also give local tours or will watch the kids while the adults take in Lake Tahoe. Three hearty meals are included in the tariff. Snacks and picnics are never a problem. In the evening, enjoy a sing-a-long, slideshow, or the gentle breeze from a front porch rocker.

Old Pioneer Garden
79 UNIONVILLE, NEVADA 89418

Tel: (702) 538-7585
Best Time to Call: **Early AM**
Host(s): **Lew and Mitzi Jones**
Location: **20 mi. from I-80**
No. of Rooms: **5**
No. of Private Baths: **2**
Max. No. Sharing Bath: **3**
Double/pb: **$25**
Double/sb: **$25**

Open: **All year**
Breakfast: **Full**
Other Meals: **Available**
Pets: **Welcome**
Children: **Welcome**
Smoking: **Permitted**
Social Drinking: **Permitted**
Airport/Station Pickup: **Yes**
Foreign Languages: **German**

Located in the middle of peaceful nowhere, with endless Humboldt Mountain and valley vistas, is this historic clapboard farmhouse. The mining community that surrounds it was established in 1860, and many things have not changed. It is quiet, unique, and restful. The old-fashioned casinos with their contemporary games of chance are in sharp contrast to Mitzi and Lew's home.

Shone House ✪
602 BRIDGE STREET, WINNEMUCCA, NEVADA 89445

Tel: (702) 623-3285
Best Time to Call: **Afternoon**
Host(s): **Mrs. Crutcher**
Location: **170 mi. E of Reno**
No. of Rooms: **15**
Max. No. Sharing Bath: **6**
Double/sb: **$17**

Single/sb: **$15**
Open: **All year**
Breakfast: **Full**
Pets: **Sometimes**
Children: **Welcome**
Smoking: **Permitted**
Social Drinking: **Permitted**

Only two minutes from I-80, and less than that to the gambling casinos, Winnemucca is a ranching and mining center. The frontier-style house dating back to 1900 has Victorian furnishings. Seven rooms of boutique treasures and antiques from around the world are for sale. Mrs. Crutcher serves refreshments in the garden.

NEW HAMPSHIRE

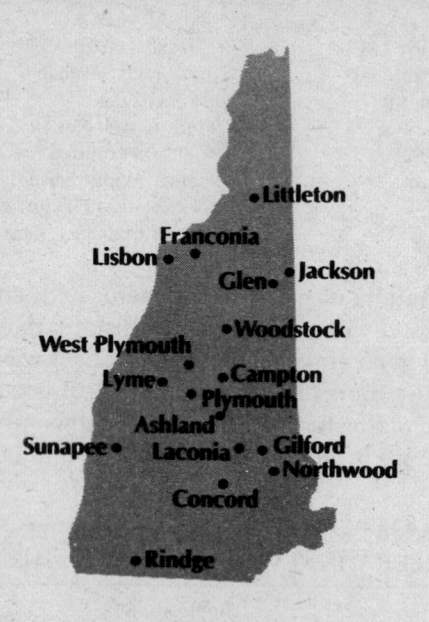

New Hampshire Bed & Breakfast
RFD 3, BOX 53, LACONIA, NEW HAMPSHIRE 03246

Tel: (603) 279-8348
Best Time to Call: 1–6 PM
Coordinator: Martha W. Dorais
States/Regions Covered: Statewide

Rates (Single/Double):
Modest: $20 $30
Average: $25 $35–$40
Luxury: $35 $50
Credit Cards: No

New Hampshire is a haven for the sports-minded, having facilities for every type of recreation. Shoppers will find it a bargain haven since there's no sales tax on merchandise. Martha's roster ranges from an 18th-century Cape house where the hostess makes her own cheese, to a mountainside home overlooking Lake Winnipesaukee with its own pool and tennis court, to a contemporary home convenient to the Manchester factory outlets. Send $1 for her descriptive directory, make your selection, and she will make the reservation for you.

Cheney House ○
P.O. BOX 683, 40 HIGHLAND STREET, ASHLAND, NEW HAMPSHIRE 03217

Tel: **(603) 968-7968**
Best Time to Call: **Afternoons, Evenings**
Host(s): **Michael and Daryl Mooney**
Location: **1 mi. from I-93**
No. of Rooms: **3**
Max. No. Sharing Bath: **6**
Double/sb: **$34–$40**
Single/sb: **$28–$32**
Open: **May 27–Oct. 14**
Breakfast: **Full**
Pets: **No**
Children: **Welcome**
Smoking: **Permitted**
Social Drinking: **Permitted**

Michael and Daryl cordially invite you to their Victorian home on a residential street where pastureland and old village homes meet. This is a great base for seeing New Hampshire. It's one mile to the beach on Squam Lake, six miles to Plymouth State College, and in 20 minutes you're at the White Mountain parks, Waterville Valley, and Lake Winnipesaukee. Relax on a porch overlooking stone walls and flower gardens, help feed the chickens, or take in the New Hampshire Symphony.

The Campton Inn ○
RT. 175 NORTH, BOX 282, CAMPTON, NEW HAMPSHIRE 03223

Tel: **(603) 726-4449**
Best Time to Call: **Mornings, evenings**
Host(s): **Bill and Arlene Roberts**
Location: **45 mi. N of Concord**
No. of Rooms: **10**
No. of Private Baths: **1**
Max. No. Sharing Bath: **4**
Double/pb: **$48**
Single/pb: **$30**
Double/sb: **$42**
Single/sb: **$25**
Open: **All year**
Reduced Rates: **Available**
Breakfast: **Full**
Other Meals: **Available**
Credit Cards: **MC, VISA**
Pets: **Sometimes**
Children: **Welcome (crib)**
Smoking: **Permitted**
Social Drinking: **Permitted**
Airport/Station Pickup: **Yes**

This 1835 country home is a friendly place to stay while visiting the lakes, Waterville Valley, and White Mountain region. Awake to the aroma of fresh-brewed coffee and sizzling bacon. After a busy day enjoying the slopes, Polar Caves, Old Man of the Mountains, The Flume, Franconia Notch, and the delightful shops, come back and relax by the fireplace. Bill and Arlene are known for their hearty country meals.

Mountain-Fare Inn ✪
BOX 553, CAMPTON, NEW HAMPSHIRE 03223

Tel: **(603) 726-4283**
Best Time to Call: **After 5 PM**
Host(s): **Susan and Dick Preston**
Location: **40 mi. N of Concord**
No. of Rooms: **10**
No. of Private Baths: **5**
Maxi. No. Sharing Bath: **4**
Double/pb: **$44**
Single/pb: **$25**
Double/sb: **$38**
Single/sb: **$22**
Open: **All year**
Reduced Rates: **Mid-week, Off-season**
Breakfast: **Full**
Other Meals: **Sometimes**
Pets: **Sometimes**
Children: **Welcome**
Smoking: **No**
Social Drinking: **Permitted**

Built in the 1800s, this white clapboard farmhouse is located in the foothills of the White Mountains, just minutes away from Franconia Notch and the Waterville Valley Resort. Susan and Dick are professional skiers and into physical fitness. Their enthusiasm is contagious! Generous seasonal snacks are offered. During the ski season, you are invited to have a family-style dinner for $7.50 per person. Plymouth State College is nearby.

Sugar Hill Inn
ROUTE 117, FRANCONIA, NEW HAMPSHIRE 03580

Tel: **(603) 823-5621**
Host(s): **Carolyn and Richard Bromberg**
Location: **7 mi. S of Littleton**
No. of Rooms: **16**
No. of Private Baths: **16**
Double/pb: **$50–70**
Guest Cottage: **$50–$70; sleeps 2–3**
Open: **All year**
Reduced Rates: **Off-season; families**
Breakfast: **Full**
Other Meals: **Available**
Credit Cards: **AMEX, MC, VISA**
Pets: **No**
Children: **Welcome (crib)**
Smoking: **No**
Social Drinking: **Permitted**

The Sugar Hill was built in 1826 as a farmhouse. About 100 years later the first guests were welcomed to this fine lodging overlooking Franconia Notch. Wide-board floors, stenciled walls, and antiques accent the rooms. The dining room features old brass tools and a player piano. It is the B&B for Swiss eggs and walnut pancakes. Plan the day from a comfortable wicker rocker on the porch. Local attractions include the Appalachian Trail, Cannon Mountain, and the Flume.

Cartway House
OLD LAKE SHORE ROAD, GILFORD, NEW HAMPSHIRE 03246

Tel: **(603) 528-1172**
Host(s): **The Shortway family**
Location: **33 mi. N of Concord**
No. of Rooms: **10**
Max. No. Sharing Bath: **7**
Double/sb: **$38.50**
Single/sb: **$24.60**
Suites: **$69.55**
Open: **All year**

Breakfast: **Full**
Other Meals: **Available**
Credit Cards: **MC, VISA**
Pets: **No**
Children: **Welcome**
Smoking: **Permitted**
Social Drinking: **Permitted**
Airport/Station Pickup: **Yes**
Foreign Languages: **French, Italian**

This clapboard colonial, built in 1771, is set on a hill overlooking fields and mountains. Recent renovations include a French country kitchen where special desserts are served Saturday nights. Some of the guest rooms have bunk beds, suitable for groups of skiers and hikers. The more private rooms have double beds, and there is a suite with separate entrance. Breakfast specialties include eggs Benedict and French toast. Afternoon tea is served to wind down your busy day. Ski areas, a private beach, and Lake Winnipesaukee are just a few of the area attractions.

Bridgehouse Bed and Breakfast
RFD 2 BOX 7B, LISBON, NEW HAMPSHIRE 03585

Tel: **(603) 838-6370**
Host(s): **Helene Hymoff & Mark Guerin**
Location: **10 mi. from I-91**
No. of Rooms: **4**
Max. No. Sharing Bath: **4**
Double/sb: **$28–$40**
Single/sb: **$25**

Open: **All year**
Reduced Rates: **Groups**
Breakfast: **Continental**
Pets: **Sometimes**
Children: **Welcome, over 12**
Smoking: **Permitted**
Social Drinking: **Permitted**
Foreign Languages: **French, Spanish**

This restored 19th-century farmhouse is located on a scenic road in the White Mountains. The guest rooms are furnished with country antiques. A comfortable lounge with an upright piano is available for your pleasure. Your hosts will gladly help plan activities over morning coffee and croissants. Skiing, hiking, golf, fishing, and Franconia Notch State Park are minutes away.

The Beal House Inn
247 WEST MAIN STREET, LITTLETON, NEW HAMPSHIRE 03561

Tel: **(603) 444-2661**
Best Time to Call: **10 AM–4 PM**
Host(s): **Doug and Brenda Clickenger**
Location: **85 mi. N of Concord**
No. of Rooms: **15**
No. of Private Baths: **10**
Max. No. Sharing Bath: **9**
Double/pb: **$40–$60**
Single/pb: **$33**
Double/sb: **$32**
Single/sb: **$27**
Suites: **$55–$75**
Open: **All year**
Reduced Rates: **Groups**
Breakfast: **Available**
Credit Cards: **AMEX, DC, MC, VISA**
Pets: **No**
Children: **Welcome (crib)**
Smoking: **Permitted**
Social Drinking: **Permitted**
Foreign Languages: **Spanish**
Airport/Station Pickup: **Yes**

Doug and Brenda have an antique shop and have furnished their Federal-style home with choice pieces. The decor is constantly changing since so many guests buy these pieces and take them away. Breakfast costs $4.50 and features hot popovers served by the fireside. The inn is conveniently accessible to six great ski areas, Franconia Notch, and the famed Old Man of the Mountain.

1895 House ✪
74 PLEASANT STREET, LITTLETON, NEW HAMPSHIRE 03561

Tel: **(603) 444-5200**
Host(s): **Susanne Watkins**
Location: **180 mi. N of Boston**
No. of Rooms: **6**
No. of Private Baths: **1**
Max. No. Sharing Bath: **6**
Double/pb: **$65**
Single/pb: **$65**
Double/sb: **$55**
Single/sb: **$55**
Open: **July 15–Oct. 31**
Reduced Rates: **Summer; families**
Breakfast: **Full**
Credit Cards: **MC, VISA**
Pets: **Sometimes**
Children: **Welcome**
Smoking: **Permitted**
Social Drinking: **Permitted**

A Queen Anne three-story Victorian house, its interior is an excellent example of artistry, craftsmanship, and Susanne's exquisite taste. It is centrally located, so you can explore the delights of the White Mountains in all seasons. Summer is for water sports, the fall foliage is fabulous, spring is for antiquing, and winter is for skiing down Cannon Mountain. Breakfast often features zucchini muffins, cinnamon butter, raspberry jam, and freshly ground amaretto coffee. The dining room of 1895 House is pictured on the back cover.

The Scottish Lion Inn
ROUTE 16, NORTH CONWAY, NEW HAMPSHIRE 03860

Tel: (603) 356-6381
Host(s): John and Phyllis Morris
Location: 1 mi. N of North Conway
No. of Rooms: 8
Max. No. Sharing Bath: 4
Double/sb: $45
Open: All year
Breakfast: Full

Other Meals: Available
Credit Cards: AMEX, DC, MC, VISA
Pets: No
Children: Welcome
Smoking: Permitted
Social Drinking: Permitted
Foreign Languages: French

This white clapboard inn offers a taste of Scotland in the White Mountains. Guest accommodations are comfortably furnished, with touches from the Highlands. Scottish paintings hang in the pub, where 40 brands of Scotch are served. In the dining room, mushroom pie and veal are house specialties. Breakfast includes hot scones and freshly baked coffee cake. The presidential Mountain Range, Appalachian Trail, and the Scenic Railway are nearby.

The Resort at Lake Shore Farm ✪
JENNESS POND ROAD, NORTHWOOD, NEW HAMPSHIRE 03261

Tel: (603) 942-5921
Host(s): Ellis and Eloise Ring
Location: 20 mi. E of Concord
No. of Rooms: 28
No. of Private Baths: 20
Max. No. Sharing Bath: 4
Double/pb: $90
Single/pb: $45
Double/sb: $80
Single/sb: $40

Open: All year
Reduced Rates: Weekly
Breakfast: Full
Other Meals: Includes lunch & dinner
Pets: Sometimes
Children: Welcome (crib)
Smoking: Permitted
Social Drinking: Permitted
Airport/Station Pickup: Yes

This fine old farmhouse, built in 1848, is surrounded by 150 acres. Guests have been coming since 1926, and each year additions have been made to provide every comfort. Beach, lake, tennis, and fishing are some of the summer recreations on the premises. Winter features snow sports. Your hosts Ellis and Eloise serve large meals and look forward to your hearty appetite.

Woodstock Inn
BOX 118, NORTH WOODSTOCK, NEW HAMPSHIRE 03262

Tel: **(603) 745-3951**
Host(s): **Scott and Eileen Rice**
Location: **2 mi. from Rt. 93**
No. of Rooms: **6**
Max. No. Sharing Bath: **4**
Double/sb: **$32–$55**
Open: **All year**
Reduced Rates: **Available**
Breakfast: **Full**
Pets: **No**
Children: **Welcome**
Smoking: **Permitted**
Social Drinking: **Permitted**

Warm and comfortable, snuggled in the heart of the scenic White Mountains, this 100-year-old Victorian home has been fully restored to its original beauty. It is close to Loon and Cannon Mountains for skiing. A complimentary shuttle bus will transport guests to the slopes. Breakfast specialties include eggs Benedict, Red Flannel Hash, and a variety of omelettes. Do visit Fantasy Farm, Clark's Trading Post, the gondola sky ride, and the Arts and Crafts Barn.

Tokfarm Inn ✪
BOX 229, WOOD AVENUE, RINDGE, NEW HAMPSHIRE 03461

Tel: **(603) 899-6646**
Beat Time to Call: **Early AM, evenings**
Host(s): **Mrs. W. B. Nottingham**
Location: **45 mi. NW of Boston**
No. of Rooms: **5**
Max. No. Sharing Bath: **4**
Double/sb: **$27–$30**
Single/sb: **$15**
Open: **Apr. 16 to Nov. 14**
Breakfast: **Continental**
Pets: **No**
Children: **No**
Smoking: **No**
Social Drinking: **Permitted**
Airport/Station Pickup: **Yes**
Foreign Languages: **Dutch, French, German**

This 100-year-old farmhouse has a spectacular view of three states from its 1,400-foot hilltop. Mt. Monadnock, the second most climbed peak in the world (Mt. Fuji is first), is practically in its backyard! Mrs. Nottingham raises Christmas trees, is a world traveler, and loves to ski. She'll recommend things to keep you busy in all seasons. Don't miss the lovely Cathedral of the Pines. Franklin Pierce College is nearby.

Times Ten Inn ✪
ROUTE 103B, BOX 572, SUNAPEE, NEW HAMPSHIRE 03782

Tel: **(603) 763-5120**
Host(s): **Audrey and Dick Kelly**
Location: **90 mi. NW of Boston**
No. of Rooms: **3**
Max. No. Sharing Bath: **4**
Double/sb: **$30–$35**
Single/sb: **$25**
Open: **All year**

Reduced Rates: **Families**
Breakfast: **Full**
Pets: **Sometimes**
Children: **Welcome**
Smoking: **Permitted**
Social Drinking: **Permitted**
Airport/Station Pickup: **Yes**

An 1820 New England farmhouse, with floor-to-ceiling living room windows overlooking a wildlife preserve. It's 25 miles to Dartmouth College, recreational Lake Sunapee, and skiing. Audrey and Dick offer a huge breakfast of Swedish pancakes, real maple syrup, homemade preserves, bacon, or sausage. Complimentary wine and good conversation are always on tap.

Crab Apple Inn
ROUTE 25, WEST PLYMOUTH, NEW HAMPSHIRE 03264

Tel: **(603) 536-4476**
Host(s): **Janene Davis**
Location: **4 mi. from Rte. 93**
No. of Rooms: **4**
No. of Private Baths: **2**
Max. No. Sharing Bath: **4**
Double/pb: **$53.50**
Single/pb: **$45**
Double/sb: **$48.50**
Single/sb: **$40**

Suites: **$52.50**
Open: **All year**
Reduced Rates: **10%, Mon.–Thurs.**
Breakfast: **Full**
Pets: **No**
Children: **Welcome, over 10**
Credit Cards: **MC, VISA**
Smoking: **Permitted**
Social Drinking: **Permitted**
Airport/Station Pickup: **Yes**

Of Federal design, the inn is an 1835 brick building situated beside a small brook at the foot of Tenney Mountain. The bedrooms on the second floor have fireplaces; those on the third floor have a panoramic view of the mountains. All are tastefully furnished. There are several fine restaurants nearby, and the inn is within a 10-minute drive of Plymouth State College. Gift studios, handcraft and antique shops in the area provide treasures for both the discerning and casual buyer.

Times Ten Inn

NEW JERSEY

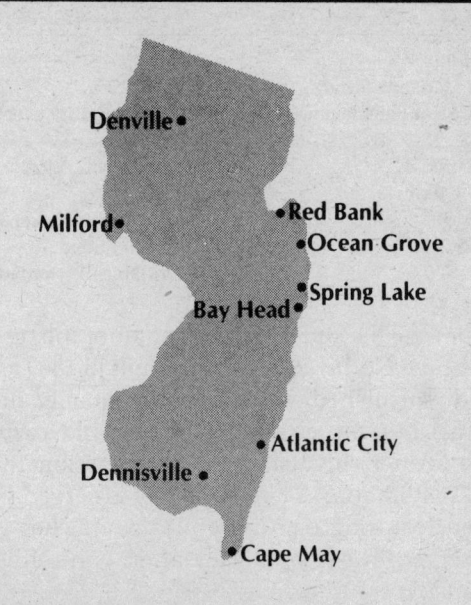

Conover's Bay Head Inn ✪
646 MAIN AVENUE, BAY HEAD, NEW JERSEY 08742

Tel: **(201) 892-4664**
Best Time to Call: **Mornings**
Host(s): **Carl and Beverly Conover**
Location: **50 mi. S of Newark**
No. of Rooms: **12**
No. of Private Baths: **6**
Max. No. Sharing Bath: **4**
Double/pb: **$70–$90**
Single/pb: **$60–$85**

Double/sb: **$45–$50**
Single/sb: **$40–$45**
Open: **Feb. 15–Dec. 15**
Reduced Rates: **Feb. 15–Apr. 7**
Breakfast: **Continental**
Pets: **No**
Children: **Welcome, over 13**
Smoking: **Permitted**
Social Drinking: **Permitted**

This is the 16th season Carl and Beverly have been receiving guests in their lovely home, but the Bay Head Inn has been treating travelers to a homespun atmosphere since 1916. Tastefully furnished with antiques, original artwork, old-fashioned photographs, and other special touches, this is a delightful summer and winter retreat. Located a block from the beach, it is also convenient to fine restaurants and shops. A full breakfast is served off-season. Monmouth College is nearby.

The Abbey
COLUMBIA AVENUE AND GURNEY STREET, CAPE MAY, NEW JERSEY 08204

Tel: **(609) 884-4506**
Host(s): **Jay and Marianne Schatz**
Location: **95 mi. SE of Philadelphia**
No. of Rooms: **7**
No. of Private Baths: **4**
Max. No. Sharing Bath: **6**
Double/pb: **$50–$85**
Single/pb: **$40–$75**
Double/sb: **$65–$70**
Single/sb: **$55–$60**
Open: **Apr.–Nov.**
Reduced Rates: **10%, weekly**
Breakfast: **Full**
Credit Cards: **MC, VISA**
Pets: **No**
Children: **Welcome, over 12**
Smoking: **Permitted**
Social Drinking: **Permitted**

One block from the beach and in the center of the historic district sits this handsome Gothic Revival villa built in 1869 and authentically restored. Furnished with museum quality antiques, the decor is formal but the attitude is warm and casual. Jay and Marianne are former chemists who have passionate interests in antiques and restoration. A full breakfast is served in the spring and fall, often featuring egg casseroles or quiches. Continental breakfast is served in summer. Late-afternoon refreshments are always available.

Albert G. Stevens Inn ✪
127 MYRTLE AVENUE, CAPE MAY, NEW JERSEY 08204

Tel: **(609) 884-4717**
Best Time to Call: **After 5 PM**
Host(s): **Dean Krumrine, Dick Flynn**
Location: **40 mi. S of Atlantic City**
No. of Rooms: **6**
No. of Private Baths: **6**
Double/pb: **$50–$55**
Suites: **$70**
Open: **Apr.–Oct.**
Breakfast: **Full**
Pets: **No**
Children: **No**
Smoking: **Permitted**
Social Drinking: **Permitted**

This 80-year-old Victorian is located next door to historic Wilbrahan Mansion and three blocks from the beach. The antique decor includes mother-of-pearl inlay in the parlor suite, an oak mantel, and other treasures throughout. The wraparound veranda is a wonderful place for sipping your second cup of coffee or for relaxing later in the day. Breakfast often features ham and cheese quiche or waffles with whipped cream.

Barnard-Good House ✪
238 PERRY STREET, CAPE MAY, NEW JERSEY 08204

Tel: **(609) 884-5381**
Best Time to Call: **8 AM–9 PM**
Host(s): **Nan and Tom Hawkins**
No. of Rooms: **6**
No. of Private Baths: **3**
Max. No. Sharing Bath: **2**
Double/pb: **$68**
Single/pb: **$63**
Double/sb: **$58**
Single/sb: **$53**
Suites: **$78**
Open: **Apr. 1–Nov. 1**
Reduced Rates: **10%, weekly**
Breakfast: **Full**
Pets: **No**
Children: **No**
Smoking: **Permitted**
Social Drinking: **Permitted**
Airport/Station Pickup: **Yes**

Nan and Tom cordially invite you to their Second Empire Victorian cottage (circa 1869), just two blocks from the "swimming" beach. They love antiques and are continually adding to their collection. They use them generously to create the warm and comfortable atmosphere. Nan's breakfast includes homemade exotic juices, delicious home-baked breads, and unusual preserves. In spring and fall, added gourmet entrées and side dishes make for an epicurean feast. Iced tea and snacks are served evenings.

The Brass Bed Inn ✪
719 COLUMBIA AVENUE, CAPE MAY, NEW JERSEY 08204

Tel: **(609) 884-8075**
Best Time to Call: **1–3 PM**
Host(s): **John and Donna Dunwoody**
No. of Rooms: **8**
No. of Private Baths: **2**
Max. No. Sharing Bath: **4**
Double/pb: **$65–$70**
Single/pb: **$65**
Double/sb: **$57–$62**
Single/sb: **$45–$50**
Open: **All year**
Reduced Rates: **Sept. 16–May 15**
Breakfast: **Full**
Pets: **No**
Children: **Welcome, over 12**
Smoking: **Permitted**
Social Drinking: **Permitted**
Airport/Station Pickup: **Yes**

This Gothic Revival home was built in 1872. The original furnishings have all been restored, and you are welcome to visit in the handsome parlor and dining room. It is two blocks to the ocean, shops, and restaurants on the mall. John and Donna suggest that you bring your bikes to truly enjoy this historic town; there's a lock-up area to keep them safe.

The Gingerbread House ☉
28 GURNEY STREET, CAPE MAY, NEW JERSEY 08204

Tel: **(609) 884-0211**
Best Time to Call: **7–10 PM**
Host(s): **Joan and Fred Echevarria**
No. of Rooms: **6**
No. of Private Baths: **3**
Max. No. Sharing Bath: **5**
Double/pb: **$65–$75**
Single/pb: **$65–$75**
Double/sb: **$52**
Single/sb: **$45**
Suites: **$75**
Open: **All year**
Reduced Rates: **Oct. 1–May 31**
Breakfast: **Continental**
Pets: **No**
Children: **Welcome, over 7**
Smoking: **Permitted**
Social Drinking: **Permitted**

Listed in the National Register of Historic Places, this charming seaside cottage features cozy guest rooms. The house is cheerfully decorated with plants, lots of fresh flowers, period furniture, and photographs by Fred Echevarria. Located a block from the beach and two blocks from the mall, the house has a comfortable living room and breezy porch that are the gathering places for friendly conversation.

The Mainstay Inn ☉
635 COLUMBIA AVENUE, CAPE MAY, NEW JERSEY 08204

Tel: **(609) 884-8690**
Best Time to Call: **10 AM–4 PM**
Host(s): **Tom and Sue Carroll**
No. of Rooms: **12**
No. of Private Baths: **8**
Max. No. Sharing Bath: **4**
Double/pb: **$54–$85**
Single/pb: **$44–$75**
Double/sb: **$44–$73**
Single/sb: **$34–$63**
Suites: **$58–$85**
Open: **Apr. 1–Oct. 31**
Reduced Rates: **Off-season; weekdays**
Breakfast: **Full**
Pets: **No**
Children: **Welcome, over 12**
Smoking: **No**
Social Drinking: **Permitted**

Located in the heart of the historic district, this 110-year-old mansion was originally built as a private gambling club. Except for a few 20th-century concessions, it still looks much as it did when the gamblers were there, with 14-foot ceilings, elaborate chandeliers, and outstanding Victorian antiques. Tom and Sue serve breakfast either in the formal dining room or on the veranda; afternoon tea and homemade snacks are a ritual. Breakfast often features ham and apple pie, or corn quiche with baked ham. Continental breakfast is served in summer. Rock on the wide veranda; enjoy croquet in the garden; or retreat to the cupola.

The Open Hearth Guest House O
705 COLUMBIA AVENUE, CAPE MAY, NEW JERSEY 08204

Tel: (609) 884-4933
Host(s): Harold and Eileen Kirsch
No. of Rooms: 5
Max. No. Sharing Bath: 3
Double/sb: $30–$50
Open: May–Oct.

Breakfast: No
Pets: No
Children: Welcome
Smoking: Permitted
Social Drinking: Permitted

Located in the historic district, this comfortable home is close to everything. Eileen and Harold invite you to share their living room and its most unusual fireplace. You can read, watch TV, or just visit. The lovely porch is a relaxing spot too. They have thoughtfully provided an outside shower/dressing room for your après-beach convenience. There are also two efficiency apartments with private baths available.

The Queen Victoria
102 OCEAN STREET, CAPE MAY, NEW JERSEY 08204

Tel: (609) 884-8702
Best Time to Call: 10 AM–10 PM
Host(s): Joan and Dane Wells
No. of Rooms: 12
No. of Private Baths: 4
Max. No. Sharing Bath: 7
Double/pb: $84
Single/pb: $79
Double/sb: $48–$58
Single/sb: $43–$53
Suites: $135 (for 4)

Open: All year
Reduced Rates: 20% off-season
Breakfast: Full
Credit Cards: MC, VISA
Pets: No
Children: No
Smoking: Permitted
Social Drinking: Permitted
Airport/Station Pickup: Yes
Foreign Languages: French

This 100-year-old seaside inn is a celebration of Victorian elegance. Curl up beside the evening fire and perhaps a friendly cat will curl up next to you. Retire amid colorful quilts, antique furnishings, and fresh flowers. Walk to the beach or ride through the charming village on bicycles provided by Joan and Dane. Breakfast and complimentary afternoon tea are served in the dining room. Minimum stays are required on weekends.

The Seventh Sister Guest House
10 JACKSON STREET, CAPE MAY, NEW JERSEY 08204

Tel: **(609) 884-2280**
Best Time to Call: **9 AM–10 PM**
Host(s): **Bob and Jo-Anne Myers**
No. of Rooms: **6**
Max. No. Sharing Bath: **4**
Double/sb: **$49**
Single/sb: **$49**
Open: **All year**
Reduced Rates: **Off-season; weekly**
Breakfast: **Available**
Pets: **No**
Children: **Welcome, over 7**
Smoking: **Permitted**
Social Drinking: **Permitted**
Foreign Languages: **Spanish, German**

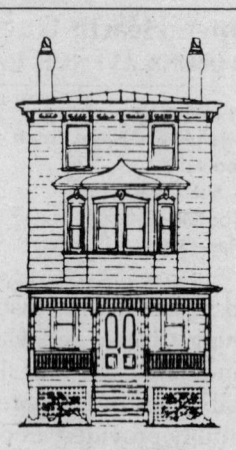

This seaside cottage was built in 1888 and is beautifully restored. It is registered in the Library of Congress as a historic American building. The guest rooms have ocean views and are appropriately furnished. Bob and Jo-Anne invite you to visit in the living room, spacious yard, or on the breeze-cooled sun porch. They have an unusual wicker collection. The beach is 100 feet away.

The Henry Ludlum Inn ✪
124 S. DELSEA DRIVE, DENNISVILLE, NEW JERSEY 08214

Tel: **(609) 861-5847**
Host(s): **Ann and Marty Thurlow**
Location: **25 mi. SW of Atlantic City**
No. of Rooms: **3**
Max. No. Sharing Bath: **4**
Double/pb: **$60**
Double/sb: **$50**
Open: **All year**
Breakfast: **Full**
Pets: **No**
Children: **Welcome, over 12**
Smoking: **Permitted**
Social Drinking: **Permitted**
Airport/Station Pickup: **Yes**

Built in 1803, Ann and Marty's home is furnished with antiques, handmade quilts, plants, and other nice touches to complete the decor. It's located on a 55-acre lake, 20 minutes from the Stone Harbor beaches. During cold months, breakfast is served in the Keeping Room; in warm months, on the porch overlooking the lake. All the bedrooms have working fireplaces for cozy comfort. Afternoon tea and wine are served.

Lakeside Bed & Breakfast ✪
11 SUNSET TRAIL, DENVILLE, NEW JERSEY 07834

Tel: **(201) 625-5129**	Open: **All year**
Host(s): **Annette and Al Bergins**	Breakfast: **Full**
Location: **35 mi. W of NYC**	Pets: **Welcome**
No. of Rooms: **1**	Children: **Welcome**
No. of Private Baths: **1**	Smoking: **Permitted**
Double/pb: **$35**	Social Drinking: **Permitted**
Single/pb: **$25**	Airport/Station Pickup: **Yes**

Just off Route 80, midway between Manhattan and the Pocono Mountains, is this modern, two-story home with private guest quarters on the ground level. There's a stunning view of the bay leading to Indian Lake. Al and Annette, both teachers, will provide you with a rowboat and beach passes, as well as wine and cheese afterward. Relax on the deck overlooking the bay, or explore the unspoiled towns and points of interest off the tourist trail. Good restaurants of every variety and price range abound.

Chestnut Hill on-the-Delaware ✪
63 CHURCH STREET, MILFORD, NEW JERSEY 08848

Tel: **(201) 995-9761**	Suites: **$75**
Host(s): **Linda and Rob Castagna**	Open: **All year**
Location: **15 mi. from Rte. 78**	Reduced Rates: **Weekly**
No. of Rooms: **5**	Breakfast: **Full**
No. of Private Baths: **2**	Pets: **No**
Max. No. Sharing Bath: **4**	Children: **Welcome**
Double/sb: **$70**	Smoking: **No**
Single/sb: **$55**	Social Drinking: **Permitted**

The veranda of this 1860 Neo-Italianate Victorian overlooks the peaceful Delaware River. Linda, Rob, and teenage son Michael have refurbished and restored their home with charm, grace, and beauty. The historic countryside is great for antique hunting, water sports, art shows, and restaurants. It's only minutes to New Hope and Bucks County delights, and to dozens of factory outlets.

Cordova ○
26 WEBB AVENUE, OCEAN GROVE, NEW JERSEY 07756

Tel: **(201) 774-3084**
  Winter: **212-751-9577**
Host(s): **The Chernik Family**
Location: **30 miles from Newark**
No. of Rooms: **20**
No. of Private Baths: **3**
Max. No. Sharing Bath: **8**
Double/pb: **$45–$47**
Double/sb: **$21–$37**
Single/sb: **$18–$23**
Guest Cottage: **$330 (week) sleeps 4**

Open: **May 27–Sept. 2**
Reduced Rates: **Stay 7 days, pay for 5;**
  10%, seniors; 10%, groups; 10%,
  families
Breakfast: **Continental**
Pets: **No**
Children: **Welcome (crib)**
Smoking: **Permitted**
Social Drinking: **Permitted**
Foreign Languages: **French, Russian**

This century-old Victorian is located in a lovely beach community. It has a friendly family atmosphere with Old World charm. There's a white sandy beach, a wooden boardwalk, and no honky tonk. Many rooms have oak chests, rockers, and washbasins. If you stay a week, the Cherniks invite you to their family barbecue.

Cape Associates ○
340 46TH PLACE, SEA ISLE CITY, NEW JERSEY 08243

Tel: **(609) 263-8700 or 263-4461**
Host(s): **Wish Zurawski, Eileen Rodan**
Location: **2 mi. from Rte. 9**
No. of Rooms: **4**
No. of Private Baths: **1**
Max. No. Sharing Bath: **5**
Double/pb: **$45–$60**
Single/pb: **$35–$45**
Double/sb: **$35–$50**
Single/sb: **$20–$35**

Open: **All year**
Reduced Rates: **$15 off Oct. 1–**
  May 15; seniors 10%
Breakfast: **Continental**
Pets: **Sometimes**
Children: **Welcome**
Smoking: **Permitted**
Social Drinking: **Permitted**
Airport/Station Pickup: **Yes**

It's four blocks to the beach from this 1962 brick-and-wood colonial house on the bay. It's casual and comfortable with lots of books, records, and artwork, and close to historic Cape May and

Atlantic City. Eileen and Wish will arrange to escort you to the casinos. Use the kitchen for light snacks, and the laundry facilities. Cooled by the bay breezes, the deck is a lovely place to relax.

Normanday Inn ✪
21 TUTTLE AVENUE, SPRING LAKE, NEW JERSEY 07762

Tel: **(201) 449-7172**
Best Time to Call: **10 AM–10 PM**
Host(s): **Michael and Susan Ingino**
Location: **80 mi. from NYC and Philadelphia**
No. of Rooms: **18**
No. of Private Baths: **18**
Double/pb: **$55–$85**

Single/pb: **$45–$75**
Open: **All year**
Reduced Rates: **Weekly; Off-season**
Breakfast: **Full**
Pets: **No**
Children: **Welcome**
Smoking: **Permitted**
Social Drinking: **Permitted**

This Victorian inn dates back to 1888. White wicker tables and chairs adorn the wraparound porch where guests can enjoy a complimentary glass of wine. Antique clocks, walnut and oak period pieces, and old-fashioned beds carry the 19th-century style into the many rooms. A breakfast of blueberry pancakes, homemade Irish oatmeal, or soda bread is served in the sunny dining room. The beach is down the street, and shops, restaurants, golf, tennis, and riding are nearby.

NEW MEXICO

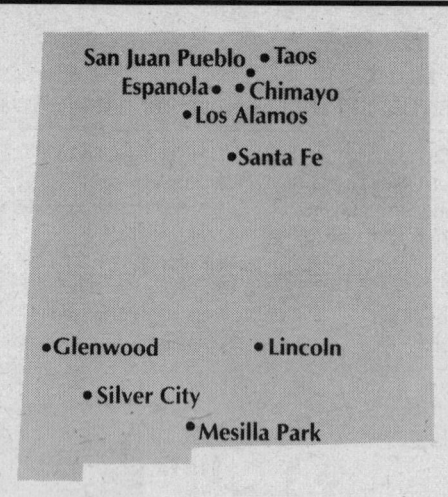

Casa Escondida ✪
P.O. BOX 142, CHIMAYO, NEW MEXICO 87522

Tel: (505) 351-4805	Open: All year
Best Time to Call: 7 AM–7 PM	Reduced Rates: 10%, 2 nights
Host(s): Jaramillo Family	Breakfast: Continental
Location: 25 mi. N of Santa Fe	Other Meals: Available
No. of Rooms: 2	Pets: No
No. of Private Baths: 2	Children: No
Double/pb: $55	Smoking: No
Single/pb: $45	Social Drinking: Permitted
Suites: $140 for 6	Foreign Languages: Spanish

Open the gate and drive down a winding dirt road to a quiet, secluded adobe home set on 17 acres in an old mountain village. The house has hand-plastered walls, pine *vigas* (beams), a Kiva corner fireplace, earth-and-brick floors with polished fir in the kitchen, and Mexican tiled baths. Eclectic furnishings include antiques and locally handcrafted rugs, pottery, and quilts. Minutes away is Santuario de Chimayo, renowned for its Spanish-Colonial art and miraculous, curative earth. The Jaramillo family are descendants of the first Spanish settlers who arrived here around 1730. They can direct you to the Santa Fe Opera, Indian villages and ruins, and other areas of historic interest.

La Puebla House ✪
ROUTE 1, BOX 172 A, ESPANOLA, NEW MEXICO 87532

Tel: (505) 753-3981
Best Time to Call: **After 6 PM**
Host(s): **Elvira Bain**
Location: **4 mi. E of Espanola**
No. of Rooms: **4**
Max. No. Sharing Bath: **6**
Double/sb: **$29**
Single/sb: **$23**
Open: **All year**
Reduced Rates: **Off-season, weekly**
Breakfast: **Continental**
Credit Cards: **MC, VISA**
Pets: **Sometimes**
Children: **Welcome**
Smoking: **No**
Social Drinking: **Permitted**

The house is situated between the famous landscapes of Santa Cruz and Chimayo. Elvira will be happy to direct you to the sights of nearby Santa Fe. Occasionally, Elvira, a gourmet cook, will invite you to be seated at her table for a reasonable price. If you prefer to cook and clean up on your own, the kitchen is available. She offers snacks to go along with your self-supplied cocktails.

The Wortley Hotel ✪
BOX 96, LINCOLN, NEW MEXICO 88338

Tel: (505) 653-4381
Best Time to Call: **7 AM–2 PM**
Host(s): **Jerre Pace**
No. of Rooms: **8**
No. of Private Baths: **8**
Double/pb: **$55**
Single/pb: **$45**
Open: **All year**
Reduced Rates: **Weekly**
Breakfast: **Full**
Other Meals: **Available**
Credit Cards: **MC, VISA**
Pets: **Sometimes**
Children: **Welcome**
Smoking: **Permitted**
Social Drinking: **Permitted**

Back in 1878, the Wortley provided meals and lodging for the workers at the general store. The store is now a museum and the Wortley continues to provide fine country lodging. The guest rooms feature ceiling fans, brass beds, and fireplaces. Enjoy fine dining in a quiet dining room where blueberry pancakes, homemade breads and a variety of dinner specialties are served. Nestled at the foothills of the Capitan Mountains, the hotel is near skiing, hiking, and horseracing. Be sure to take a guided tour of Lincoln's historic buildings during your stay.

Los Alamos Bed & Breakfast ✪
BOX 1212, LOS ALAMOS, NEW MEXICO 87544

Tel: **(505) 662-6041**	Open: **All year**
Best Time to Call: **Evenings**	Reduced Rates: **10%, seniors; families**
Host(s): **Mary and Roland Pettitt**	Breakfast: **Full**
Location: **32 mi. N of Santa Fe**	Other Meals: **Dinner ($5.00)**
No. of Rooms: **2**	Pets: **No**
No. of Private Baths: **1**	Children: **Welcome (crib)**
Max. No. Sharing Bath: **2**	Smoking: **No**
Double/pb: **$35**	Social Drinking: **Permitted**
Single/pb: **$30**	Foreign Languages: **Spanish**
Single/sb: **$10–$15**	

This comfortable ranch-style home has a charming, fully equipped apartment with a separate entry adjoining the patio and garden. At an elevation of 7,500 feet, this town is truly a breath of fresh air. It is close to the Los Alamos National Laboratory (where Roland is a geologist) and within minutes of ski slopes, hiking trails, and Indian pueblos. Mary likes exchanging travel talk.

Orange Street Bed & Breakfast ✪
3496 ORANGE STREET, LOS ALAMOS, NEW MEXICO 87544

Tel: **(505) 662-2651**	Open: **All year**
Best Time to Call: **Early AM**	Breakfast: **Full**
Host(s): **Phil and Hester Sargent**	Pets: **No**
Location: **32 mi. N of Santa Fe**	Children: **No**
No. of Rooms: **3**	Smoking: **No**
Max. No. Sharing Bath: **5**	Social Drinking: **Permitted**
Double/sb: **$28–$35**	Airport/Station Pickup: **Yes**
Single/sb: **$22–$25**	

At an elevation of 7,300 feet in the Jemez Mountains, the fresh air is exhilarating. Hester is a tennis coach, and Phil plays well too. They also ski, hike, and bike, and they will suggest how you can enjoy these pursuits during your stay. The Indian pueblos and old mining towns are just two of the not-to-be-missed sights. A bowl of fruit and homemade goodies are placed in your room daily. The University of New Mexico is nearby.

The Elms ✪
1110 CARVER RD, P.O. BOX 1176, MESILLA PARK, NEW MEXICO 88047

Tel: (505) 524-1513
Best Time to Call: **After 5 PM**
Host(s): **Margaret B. Dalton**
Location: **2 mi. from I-10, I-25**
No. of Rooms: **3**
No. of Private Baths: **1**
Max. No. Sharing Bath: **2**
Double/pb: **$40**

Single/sb: **$30**
Open: **All year**
Breakfast: **Continental**
Pets: **No**
Children: **Welcome**
Smoking: **No**
Social Drinking: **Permitted**

This large redwood-and-stucco house is set on five acres and shaded by 100-year-old elm trees. Guest rooms are furnished with solid oak antiques and Oriental rugs. Your hosts offer farm-fresh eggs, homemade breads, and preserves for breakfast. They will gladly direct you to historic sights, White Sands Missile Range, and NASA.

Chinguague Compound
P.O. BOX 1118, SAN JUAN PUEBLO, NEW MEXICO 87566

Tel: (505) 852-2194
Host(s): **Phil and Joan Blood**
Location: **34 mi. N of Santa Fe**
No. of Rooms: **3**
No. of Private Baths: **3**
Double/pb: **$39–$70**
Single/pb: **$25**
Guest Cottages: **$125; sleeps 4**

Open: **Apr. 15–Sept. 30**
Breakfast: **Full**
Other Meals: **Available**
Pets: **Sometimes**
Children: **Welcome**
Smoking: **Permitted**
Social Drinking: **Permitted**
Airport/Station Pickup: **Yes**

This quiet, secluded compound is located on the banks of the Rio Grande River, with a view of the Sangre de Christo and Jemez Mountains. Two adobe cottages surrounded by cottonwoods are also available. Both have *kiva* fireplaces and fully equipped kitchens. The larger one sleeps six and features a porch and terrace. Three can share the smaller cottage. Your hosts serve organically grown fruits, vegetables, and home-baked breads. They are happy to point out the sights of Santa Fe, old mountain villages, and ancient Indian lands.

Bear Mountain Guest Ranch
P.O. BOX 1163, SILVER CITY, NEW MEXICO 88062

Tel: (505) 538-2538
Best Time to Call: 7–9 AM; 6–9 PM
Host(s): **Myra B. McCormick**
Location: **160 mi. NW of El Paso**
No. of Rooms: **10**
No. of Private Baths: **10**
Double/pb: **$58**
Single/pb: **$39**
Guest Cottage: **$56; sleeps 4**
Open: **All year**
Reduced Rates: **10%, seniors; military**
Breakfast: **Full**
Other Meals: **Lunch and dinner (included)**
Pets: **Welcome**
Children: **Welcome**
Smoking: **Permitted**
Social Drinking: **Permitted**
Airport/Station Pickup: **Yes**
Foreign Languages: **French, Spanish, Tagalog**

At an elevation of 6,250 feet, on 160 acres, the ranch adjoins the Gila National Forest. Home-baked breads, natural foods, and family-style meals are featured. The rate quoted for the guest cottage is without meals. If you prefer Myra's cooking to your own, add $12 per person. Myra leads groups of guests into the area's four life zones in search of southwestern birds, tropical-looking wild plants, archeological sites, and scenery. You will enjoy investigating the Gila Cliff Dwellings, Glenwood Catwalk, hot springs, the Gila Wilderness, and the Gila River Bird Habitat. Western New Mexico University is nearby.

American Artists Gallery-House ✪
FRONTIER ROAD, P.O. BOX 584, TAOS, NEW MEXICO 87571

Tel: (505) 758-0311
Best Time to Call: **Mornings**
Host(s): **Benjamin and Myra Carp**
Location: **¼ mi. from Rt. 68**
No. of Rooms: **1**
No. of Private Baths: **1**
Double/pb: **$34**
Single/pb: **$34**
Open: **All year**
Reduced Rates: **10%, seniors**
Breakfast: **Full**
Pets: **No**
Children: **Welcome**
Smoking: **No**
Social Drinking: **Permitted**
Airport/Station Pickup: **Yes**

This charming adobe-style home is filled with regional works of art. A large, comfortable bedroom with a splendid view of Taos Mountain awaits you. Your hosts, gallery owners, will gladly advise on local craft shops and boutiques. Their home is close to Rio Grande Gorge State Park, 900-year-old Taos Pueblo, and places to go fishing and rafting. Varied cuisine of the Southwest is featured at breakfast.

Mountain Light Bed & Breakfast ✪
P.O. BOX 241, TAOS, NEW MEXICO 87571

Tel: **(505) 776-8474**
Best Time to Call: **Early AM or evenings**
Host(s): **Gail Russell**
Location: **12 mi. N of Taos**
No. of Rooms: **3**
No. of Private Baths: **1**
Max. No. Sharing Bath: **4**
Double/pb: **$42**
Single/pb: **$25**

Double/sb: **$37**
Single/sb: **$20**
Open: **All year**
Reduced Rates: **$3 less 2nd night**
Breakfast: **Continental**
Pets: **Sometimes**
Children: **Welcome**
Smoking: **Permitted**
Social Drinking: **Permitted**
Airport/Station Pickup: **Yes**

This large, traditional adobe home is perched on the edge of a mesa and commands a spectacular view. Gail is a professional photographer and the house is her home, studio, and gallery. Her photographs have appeared in many national magazines. There are cozy fireplaces and a wood-burning stove. It is close to the D. H. Lawrence Ranch, the Millicent Rogers Museum, Ski Valley, and the Rio Grande. This is "where the buffalo roam" and good trout fishing is nearby. The coffee pot is always on.

For key to listings, see inside front or back cover.

✪ This star means that rates are guaranteed through December 31, 1985 to any guest making a reservation as a result of reading about the B&B in *BED & BREAKFAST U.S.A.*—1985 edition.

Please enclose a self-addressed, stamped, business-sized envelope when contacting reservation services.

For more details on what you can expect in a B&B, see Chapter 1.

Always mention *Bed & Breakfast USA* when making reservations!

NEW YORK

THE CATSKILLS

The Lanigan Farmhouse ✪
BOX 399, RD1, STAMFORD, NEW YORK 12167

Tel: **(607) 652-7455/6263**	Open: **All year**
Host(s): **June and Richard Lanigan**	Breakfast: **Full**
Location: 23 mi. E of Oneonta	Pets: **Welcome**
No. of Rooms: 3	Children: **Welcome**
Max. No. Sharing Bath: 6	Smoking: **Permitted**
Double/sb: $40	Social Drinking: **Permitted**
Single/sb: $30	

The Lanigan Farmhouse offers the charm of rural life, and is convenient to cultural activities. Guests are welcome to wine and cheese, and are served a breakfast of homemade breads and jams, ham, and omelettes. The well-stocked library is a good place for relaxing. Deer Run ski area, golf courses, hiking, tennis, swimming, and antique shops are all nearby.

The Eggery Inn ✪
COUNTY ROAD 16, TANNERSVILLE, NEW YORK 12485

Tel: **(518) 589-5363**	Open: **May 16–Mar. 31**
Best Time to Call: **10 AM–8 PM**	Reduced Rates: **Families**
Host(s): **Julie and Abe Abramczyk**	Breakfast: **Full**
Location: **125 mi. N of New York City**	Other Meals: **Available**
No. of Rooms: **12**	Credit Cards: **MC, VISA**
No. of Private Baths: **10**	Pets: **Sometimes**
Max. No. Sharing Bath: **4**	Children: **Welcome**
Double/pb: **$48**	Smoking: **Permitted**
Single/pb: **$38**	Social Drinking: **Permitted**
Double/sb: **$42**	Foreign Languages: **Yiddish**
Single/sb: **$35**	

The inn, with its wraparound porch, is nestled amid the majestic ridges of the Catskills at an elevation of 2,200 feet. The sitting room is enhanced by a beautiful oak balustrade leading to cozy guest rooms furnished with antiques, rockers, and warm comforters. The player piano, Mission Oak furnishings, and abundance of plants lend a homey atmosphere. It is convenient to the Catskill Game Preservation, Hunter, Cortina, and Windham Mountains for skiing, hiking and seasonal recreational activities. On weekends and holiday periods the above rates change, since dinner is included.

CENTRAL NEW YORK/LEATHERSTOCKING AREA

Bed & Breakfast of Central New York
1846 BELLEVUE AVENUE, SYRACUSE, NEW YORK 13204

Tel: **(315) 472-5050**	**Marcellus, Oswego, Syracuse,**
Coordinator(s): **Mary Lou Karrat,**	**Skaneateles, Thousand Islands, Utica**
Linda Rackard	Rates (Single/Double):
States/Regions Covered: **Cazenovia,**	Average: **$28** **$36**
Dewitt, Fayetteville, Ithaca,	Credit Cards: **MC, VISA**

Mary Lou and Linda have a network of host homes convenient to Syracuse University, Lemoyne College, and Cornell University, as well as the recreational area of the Finger Lakes. Beautiful country in all seasons, there are many historic sites to see and cultural activities to enjoy.

Bed & Breakfast—Leatherstocking ✪
BOX 389, BROCKWAY ROAD, FRANKFORT, NEW YORK 13340

Tel: **(315) 733-0040**
Best Time to Call: **5 PM–7 PM**
Coordinator: **Floranne McCraith**
States/Regions Covered: **Central NY**

Rates (Single/Double):
Modest: **$20**   **$30**
Average: **$35**   **$45**
Credit Cards: **No**

Leatherstocking Country is a seven-county region of New York which extends from the Catskills, across the Mohawk Valley to the Central Adirondacks. It's a region to be visited in all seasons for all reasons, and its residents warmly welcome visitors. Recreational sports and activities, outlet shopping, antiques hunting, and fine dining are waiting for you and your B&B host will tell you where to find the best of everything.

B&B Adagio ✪
FOUR CIRCLE DRIVE, BINGHAMTON, NEW YORK 13905

Tel: **(607) 724-5803**
Best Time to Call: **10 AM–Noon**
Host(s): **Jean Adagio**
Location: **2 mi. from Rte. 17**
No. of Rooms: **2**
Max. No. Sharing Bath: **3**
Double/sb: **$35**

Single/sb: **$25**
Open: **All year**
Breakfast: **Continental**
Pets: **No**
Children: **Welcome**
Smoking: **Permitted**
Social Drinking: **Permitted**

Located in a quiet, residential area, Jean's home has a lovely screened porch for restful relaxation. It's only minutes to the tennis courts at Broome Community College, and SUNY-Binghamton is nearby. Jean loves to quilt and her bedrooms show samples of her fine handiwork.

Erie Bridge Inn
FLORENCE HILL ROAD, CAMDEN, NEW YORK 13316

Tel: **(315) 245-1555**
Host(s): **The Maleys**
Location: **20 mi. W of Rome**
No. of Rooms: **7**
No. of Private Baths: **4**
Max. No. Sharing Bath: **6**
Double/pb: **$42**

Single/pb: **$39**
Double/sb: **$39**
Single/sb: **$39**
Open: **May 1–Nov. 15**
Reduced Rates: **10%, seniors**
Breakfast: **Full**
Credit Cards: **MC, VISA**

Pets: **No**
Children: **Welcome**
Smoking: **Permitted**

Social Drinking: **Permitted**
Airport/Station Pickup: **Yes**

This is a casual, comfortable home that has a swimming pool and a hot tub for your seasonal enjoyment. It is close to Rome Canal Village, Fort Stanwich, and the Charles Town Outlet Mall. Homemade breads, jams, and omelettes are breakfast specialties.

The Inn at Brook Willow Farm ✪
R.D. 2, BOX 514, MIDDLEFIELD CENTER ROAD, COOPERSTOWN, NEW YORK 13326

Tel: **(607) 547-9700**
Best Time to Call: **After 6 PM**
Host(s): **Joan and Jack Grimes**
Location: **28 mi. N of Oneonta**
No. of Rooms: **5**
No. of Private Baths: **3**
Max. No. Sharing Bath: **4**
Double/pb: **$38**
Single/pb: **$38**

Double/sb: **$38**
Single/sb: **$38**
Open: **All year**
Breakfast: **Full**
Pets: **No**
Children: **Welcome (crib)**
Smoking: **Permitted**
Social Drinking: **Permitted**

Located on 14 acres of meadow and woods, nestled among the pines and willows, this charming Victorian cottage with its restored barn is furnished with lovely antiques, wicker, and plants. Enjoy homemade blueberry muffins at breakfast, and wine, fresh fruit, and fresh flowers in your room. The world-famous Baseball Hall of Fame is here, as well as countless historic and cultural sites to visit. Recreational activities abound on unspoiled Lake Otsego.

Litco Farms Bed and Breakfast ✪
P.O. BOX 148, FLY CREEK, NEW YORK 13337

Tel: **(607) 547-2501**
Host(s): **Margaret and Jim Wolff**
Location: **2 mi. NW of Cooperstown**
No. of Rooms: **3**
No. of Private Baths: **1**
Max. No. Sharing Bath: **5**
Double/pb: **$35–$40**
Single/pb: **$25–$30**
Double/sb: **$35–$40**
Single/sb: **$25–$30**

Suites: **$70–$75**
Open: **All year**
Reduced Rates: **Families; Off-season**
Breakfast: **Full**
Pets: **No**
Children: **Welcome**
Smoking: **Permitted**
Social Drinking: **Permitted**
Airport/Station Pickup: **Yes**

Seventy acres of unspoiled meadows and woodlands are yours to explore at Litco Farms. The day begins with fresh-baked breads, fresh eggs, milk, and local bacon, served in the dining room-library. Borrow a canoe to fish on Canadarago Lake, which is stocked with freshwater salmon. There are other places to paddle, including Glimmerglass, the lake made famous by James Fenimore Cooper. After spending a day at the Baseball Hall of Fame, guests may relax and unwind around the large in-ground pool. Your hosts recommend a visit to the Cider Mill and the quaint craft and antique shops.

Libby's Lodgings ✪
32 EVELYN STREET, JOHNSON CITY, NEW YORK 13790

Tel: **(607) 729-6839**
Host(s): **Elizabeth Pert Ashcraft**
Location: **1 mi. from Binghamton**
No. of Rooms: **2**
Max. No. Sharing Bath: **4**
Double/sb: **$30**
Single/sb: **$20**

Open: **All year**
Breakfast: **Continental**
Pets: **Sometimes**
Children: **No**
Smoking: **Permitted**
Social Drinking: **Permitted**
Airport/Station Pickup: **Yes**

This comfortable house is located in a quiet neighborhood, with a shaded back porch for relaxing. In the scenic southern tier of the state, it is convenient to malls, restaurants, state parks, historical sites, and Harper College. Libby has decorated with Junktique (little inexpensive treasures). Her hand-hooked rugs and carpentry add a special touch. She is ever ready with conversation and a limitless coffee pot.

FINGER LAKES AREA

Wheeler Bed and Breakfast
RD2, BOX 455, BATH, NEW YORK 14810

Tel: **(607) 776-6756**
Host(s): **Irene Verity**
Location: **30 mi. N of Corning**
No. of Rooms: **3**
Max. No. Sharing Bath: **4**
Double/sb: **$55**
Single/sb: **$55**
Suites: **$75**

Open: **All year**
Reduced Rates: **10%, seniors**
Breakfast: **Full**
Pets: **Sometimes**
Children: **No**
Smoking: **Permitted**
Social Drinking: **Permitted**
Airport/Station Pickup: **Yes**

This stately Greek Revival home is nestled in the heart of the Finger Lakes region. There are 365 acres to stroll and three porches to relax on. The rooms are furnished with gracious antiques, crafts, and plants. Choose from double, twin or king-sized beds. In warm weather, breakfast is served outdoors or on the screened-in porch. House specialties are omelettes and home-made jams. Enjoy a glass of local wine with your hosts. They will gladly direct you to Watkins Glen, Corning Glass, and several nearby state parks.

Bristol Bed & Breakfast ✪
4861 ROUTE 64, BRISTOL VALLEY ROAD, CANANDAIGUA, NEW YORK 14424

Tel: **(716) 229-2003**
Host(s): **Patricia M. Rodger**
Location: **7 mi. from Rtes. 5 and 20**
No. of Rooms: **4**
No. of Private Baths: **1**
Max. No. Sharing Bath: **4**
Double/pb: **$45**
Single/pb: **$22**
Double/sb: **$45**
Single/sb: **$22**

Open: **All year**
Reduced Rates: **15%, seniors; weekly**
Breakfast: **Full**
Credit Cards: **MC, VISA**
Pets: **Sometimes**
Children: **Welcome**
Smoking: **Permitted**
Social Drinking: **Permitted**
Airport/Station Pickup: **Yes**
Foreign Languages: **French, German**

This gracious Federal-style home was built in 1790. The rooms are decorated with paintings and crafts of local artists, and the bedrooms have the original fireplaces. In winter, Bristol Valley is a skiers' wonderland. In other seasons, you can use the lighted tennis court, the hot tub, skate, or borrow Pat's bikes for a tour of the beautiful surroundings. Charming shops, restaurants, and cultural activities are nearby.

The Country House ✪
37 MILL STREET, CANASERAGA, NEW YORK 14822

Tel: **(607) 545-6439**
Best Time to Call: **11–1 PM, 5–7 PM**
Host(s): **Robert and Renée Coombs**
Location: **50 mi. S of Rochester**
No. of Rooms: **6**
Max. No. Sharing Bath: **4**
Double/sb: **$25**
Single/sb: **$15**

Open: **All year**
Breakfast: **Continental**
Pets: **Welcome**
Children: **Welcome (crib)**
Smoking: **Permitted**
Social Drinking: **Permitted**
Airport/Station Pickup: **Yes**

This 100-year-old Victorian home stands on a quiet street in a charming rural village. Guest rooms are comfortably furnished with antiques. Home-baked pastries and fresh fruit are served each morning in the breakfast room or dining room. Your hosts will happily direct you to the many valleys, forests, and streams nearby for hunting, fishing, hiking, and scenic solitude. Swain Ski Center slopes, Corning Glassworks, and Letchworth State Park are minutes away.

Laurel Hill Guest House ☉
2670 POWDERHOUSE ROAD, CORNING, NEW YORK 14830

Tel: **(607) 936-3215**
Best Time to Call: **Evenings**
Host(s): **Dick and Marge Woodbury**
Location: **1.7 mi. from Rte. 17**
No. of Rooms: **2**
Max. No. Sharing Bath: **4**
Double/sb: **$39**
Single/sb: **$29**

Open: **All year**
Breakfast: **Continental**
Pets: **Sometimes**
Children: **Welcome**
Smoking: **Permitted**
Social Drinking: **Permitted**
Airport/Station Pickup: **Yes**

This traditional Cape Cod house is nestled on a wooded hillside. The solar greenhouse is perfect for bird watching while breakfasting on homemade muffins, breads, and granola. Spacious guest rooms are furnished with brass beds; both the music room with grand piano, and the breezy screened porch are inviting. Nearby attractions include the Corning Glass Center, Finger Lakes wineries, and Watkins Glen.

Rosewood Inn ☉
134 EAST FIRST STREET, CORNING, NEW YORK 14830

Tel: **(607) 962-3253**
Best Time to Call: **Before noon**
Host(s): **Winnie and Dick Peer**
Location: **1 block off Rte. 17**
No. of Rooms: **6**
No. of Private Baths: **4**
Max. No. Sharing Bath: **4**
Double/pb: **$44**
Single/pb: **$37**
Double/sb: **$34**

Single/sb: **$29**
Suites: **$50**
Open: **All year**
Reduced Rates: **Weekly; families**
Breakfast: **Continental**
Pets: **Sometimes**
Children: **Welcome (crib)**
Smoking: **Permitted**
Social Drinking: **Permitted**
Airport/Station Pickup: **Yes**

This two-story stucco English Tudor is decorated with both antiques and originality. Each guest room is named for a famous person and the accessories echo the personality of that individual's era. It's within walking distance of the Corning Glass Museum and the Rockwell Museum of Western Art. Winnie teaches school, and Dick is the editor of the daily newspaper. They look forward to your arrival and greet you with refreshments.

Victoria House ✪
222 PINE STREET, CORNING, NEW YORK 14830

Tel: **(607) 962-3413**	Open: **All year**
Best Time to Call: **After 4 PM**	Reduced Rates: **Families; weekly**
Host(s): **Billie Jean and Ron Housel**	Breakfast: **Continental**
Location: **¼ mi. S of Rte. 17**	Pets: **No**
No. of Rooms: **4**	Children: **Welcome**
Max. No. Sharing Bath: **4**	Smoking: **Permitted**
Double/sb: **$35**	Social Drinking: **Permitted**
Single/sb: **$25**	

This turn-of-the-century home has been restored to its former charm, and is located in a quiet residential area within walking distance of the Corning Glass Center, Rockwell Museum, and the unique shops and restaurants of Market Street. The rooms are furnished with antiques. You are invited to relax in the spacious reception rooms and on the portico in summer.

"Millstones" Guest House
742 GARDEN ROAD, ELMIRA, NEW YORK 14905

Tel: **(607) 732-6812**	Open: **Mar. 1–Nov. 30**
Host(s): **Mr. and Mrs. John Lowman**	Breakfast: **Full**
Location: **1½ mi. from Rte. 17**	Pets: **No**
No. of Rooms: **2**	Children: **Welcome, over 12**
Max. No. Sharing Bath: **4**	Smoking: **No**
Double/sb: **$35**	Social Drinking: **Permitted**

"Millstones" offers the atmosphere of an English Cotswold cottage with its old beams, leaded glass windows, large stone fireplaces, and comfortable antiques. The bedrooms are tucked under the eaves, away from the owners' quarters and are carefully furnished with such special touches as hooked rugs and pretty quilts. There's a terrace under the trees where you may relax and where breakfast is served on pleasant days. Jack's steaming hot oatmeal is an old-fashioned treat and lunch is packed on request. Visit the National Soaring Museum, Watkins Glen, the Corning Glass Museum, the wineries, and the Finger Lakes. All of these attractions are less than an hour away; Elmira College is in town.

The Cobblestones ✪
RD 2, GENEVA, NEW YORK 14456

Tel: **(315) 789-1896**
Best Time to Call: **7–9:30 PM**
Host(s): **The Lawrence Graceys**
Location: **3½ mi. W of Geneva**
No. of Rooms: **4**
Max. No. Sharing Bath: **6**
Double/sb: **$10 and up**

Single/sb: **$10**
Open: **All year**
Breakfast: **No**
Pets: **Welcome**
Children: **Welcome**
Smoking: **Permitted**
Social Drinking: **Permitted**

This example of Greek Revival cobblestone architecture was built in 1848. The fluted columns crowned by Ionic capitals at the entrance add to its beauty. There are precious antiques and Oriental rugs, which reflect the fine taste of your gracious hosts. Located in the heart of the Finger Lakes area, tours are available at nearby wineries. Hobart and William Smith Colleges are right in town.

Elmshade Guest House ✪
402 SOUTH ALBANY STREET, ITHACA, NEW YORK 14850

Tel: **(607) 273-1707**
Best Time to Call: **2–3 PM**
Host(s): **Ethel D. Pierce**
Location: **3 blocks from Rte. 13**
No. of Rooms: **9**
Max. No. Sharing Bath: **4**
Double/sb: **$36–$40**

Single/sb: **$18–$20**
Open: **All year**
Breakfast: **No**
Pets: **No**
Children: **Welcome, over 6**
Smoking: **Permitted**
Social Drinking: **Permitted**

Located in a lovely residential area, the house is convenient to shopping and excellent, inexpensive restaurants. The guest rooms are large, bright, comfortable, and immaculate. Ethel limits guest occupancy to nine at a time so that she can give personal attention to everyone. Cornell University and Ithaca College are nearby.

Rose Inn
813 AUBURN ROAD, ROUTE 34, BOX 6576, ITHACA, NEW YORK 14851

Tel: **(607) 533-4202**	Reduced Rates: **$10 less Dec. 1– Mar. 31**
Host(s): **Sherry and Charles Rosemann**	Breakfast: **Continental**
Location: **50 mi. SW of Syracuse**	Other Meals: **Available**
No. of Rooms: **5**	Pets: **No**
No. of Private Baths: **4**	Children: **Welcome, over 12**
Max. No. Sharing Bath: **2**	Smoking: **No**
Double/pb: **$55–$85**	Social Drinking: **Permitted**
Double/sb: **$55–$85**	Airport/Station Pickup: **Yes**
Guest Cottage: **$160; sleeps 4**	Foreign Languages: **German, Spanish**
Open: **All year**	

The showpiece of this 19th-century mansion is a circular staircase of solid Honduras mahogany, stretching three stories to the cupola on the roof. Guest rooms and sitting parlors are furnished in elegant period pieces. Special touches such as fresh apples, local wine, huge bath sheets, soft robes, and baskets filled with toiletries are thoughtfully provided. Fresh croissants and homemade jams are served in the fireplaced country kitchen. On request, a honeymoon breakfast cart can be wheeled into your bedroom. Local attractions of the Finger Lakes region include Watkins Glen, Greek Peak Ski Area, and the wine district.

Varna Inn ✪
933 DRYDEN ROAD, ITHACA, NEW YORK 14850

Tel: **(607) 273-0595**	Breakfast: **Continental**
Host(s): **Ann and Chuck Johns**	Credit Cards: **AMEX, MC, VISA**
Location: **2 mi. E of Ithaca**	Pets: **No**
No. of Rooms: **7**	Children: **Welcome**
No. of Private Baths: **7**	Smoking: **Permitted**
Double/pb: **$45**	Social Drinking: **Permitted**
Open: **All year**	Airport/Station Pickup: **Yes**

The comfortably furnished guest rooms of this colonial inn have individual TVs and coffeemakers. Guests are welcomed with ice-cold splits of champagne; you might like to take yours outside to enjoy beside the pool. Continental breakfast is brought to your private quarters in a wicker basket. At night, the beds are turned down and mints are placed on the pillows. Your hosts can direct you to nearby waterfalls, Cayuga Lake, and local wineries. Cornell University and Ithaca College are minutes away.

Ivy Chimney
143 DIDAMA STREET, SYRACUSE, NEW YORK 13224

Tel: (315) 446-4199
Best Time to Call: **10:30 AM–9 PM**
Host(s): **Elaine Samuels**
Location: **3 mi. from I-90**
No. of Rooms: **2**
Max. No. Sharing Bath: **2**
Double/sb: **$35**
Single/sb: **$20**

Open: **All year**
Breakfast: **Continental**
Pets: **Sometimes**
Children: **No**
Smoking: **No**
Social Drinking: **Permitted**
Airport/Station Pickup: **Yes**

This cozy white colonial (circa 1920) with its wide porch is located on a quiet residential street. The bedrooms are cheerful and furnished with some antiques and collectibles. It is close to the Civic Center, Syracuse University, Lemoyne College and recreational sports facilities. Elaine's interests are fine arts, theater, and music.

HUDSON VALLEY/ALBANY/KINGSTON AREA

Bed & Breakfast, U.S.A., Ltd. ✪
P.O. BOX 606, CROTON-ON-HUDSON, NEW YORK 10520

Tel: (914) 271-6228
Best Time to Call: **8–8:30 AM**
Coordinator: **Barbara Notarius**
States/Regions Covered: **Hudson Valley, Westchester county, upstate New York, NYC**

Rates (Single/Double):
  Modest: **$25**   **$30**
  Average: **$30**   **$30–40**
  Luxury: **$35**   **$50–$75**
Credit Cards: **MC, VISA**

Barbara's extensive network of host homes are convenient to colleges, corporate headquarters, historic sites, recreational activities, and cultural events. Some have easy access to New York City, and others are rustic country places; the ambience ranges from a simple cabin to an elegant mansion, with many choices in between. The $25 annual membership fee includes unlimited reservations and the informative newsletter. If you choose not to be a member, there is a $15 processing fee for each booking. Sarah Lawrence, Manhattanville, Russell Sage, Vassar, West Point, and Skidmore are but a few of the major colleges nearby.

Bed and Breakfast Barn ✪
R.D. 1, CAMBRIDGE, NEW YORK, 12816

Tel: **(518) 677-8868**	Open: **All year**
Host(s): **Veronica and Walter Piekarz**	Breakfast: **Continental**
Location: **30 mi. E of Saratoga**	Other Meals: **Available**
No. of Rooms: **2**	Pets: **No**
Max. No. Sharing Bath: **4**	Children: **No**
Double/sb: **$30**	Smoking: **Permitted**
Single/sb: **$20**	Social Drinking: **Permitted**

The post-and-beam structure of this Yankee barn contemporary can be spotted throughout its interior. Guests will enjoy the gourmet meals served by their hosts who are interested in music and a back-to-basics way of life. Bromley Mountain, Saratoga Performing Arts Center, Manchester, Vermont, and Bennington College in Vermont are close by.

Olde Post Inn
43 MAIN STREET, COLD SPRING, NEW YORK 10516

Tel: **(914) 265-2510**	Open: **All year**
Best Time to Call: **Wed.–Sun.**	Reduced Rates: **Mon.–Thur.**
Host(s): **Carole Zeller, George Argila**	Breakfast: **Continental**
Location: **50 mi. N of NYC**	Credit Cards: **MC, VISA**
No. of Rooms: **4**	Pets: **No**
Max. No. Sharing Bath: **8**	Children: **Welcome, over 5**
Double/sb: **$50**	Smoking: **Permitted**
Single/sb: **$50**	Social Drinking: **Permitted**

Built in 1820 as a post office and customhouse, the inn is listed in the National Historic Register. The wide-plank floors, exposed beam ceilings, and original moldings have been retained. It is comfortably decorated in country style. George is a musician who graduated from Juilliard, and Carole enjoys hostessing and crafts.

One Market Street
COLD SPRING ON HUDSON, NEW YORK 10516

Tel: (914) 265-3912
Host(s): **Philip and Esther Baumgarten**
Location: **50 mi. N of NYC**
No. of Rooms: **1 suite**
No. of Private Baths: **1**
Suites: **$55**
Open: **All year**

Reduced Rates: **Weekly**
Breakfast: **Continental**
Credit Cards: **VISA**
Pets: **No**
Children: **Welcome, over 10**
Smoking: **Permitted**
Social Drinking: **Permitted**

This beautiful Federal-style building dates back to the 1800s and looks out on the Hudson, surrounding mountains, and the foliage of the valley. The suite's kitchenette is stocked with rolls, juice, tea, and coffee for a make-it-at-your-leisure breakfast. Don't miss nearby West Point, Vassar College, and the Vanderbilt Mansion. Philip and Esther will direct you to the fine restaurants and antique shops in their historic town.

Barbara's Bed & Breakfast ✪
49 VAN WYCK STREET, CROTON-ON-HUDSON, NEW YORK 10520

Tel: (914) 271-6228
Best Time to Call: **7–8:30 AM**
Host(s): **Barbara and George Klein**
Location: **30 mi. N of NYC**
No. of Rooms: **2**
No. of Private Baths: **1**
Max. No. Sharing Bath: **4**
Double/pb: **$50**
Single/pb: **$35**
Double/sb: **$40**
Single/sb: **$30**

Open: **All year**
Reduced Rates: **Weekly; families**
Breakfast: **Full**
Credit Cards: **MC, VISA**
Pets: **No**
Children: **Welcome**
Smoking: **No**
Social Drinking: **Permitted**
Foreign Languages: **Russian, French**
Airport/Station Pickup: **Yes**

A handsome 95-year-old Victorian mansion, it is eclectically furnished with antiques, Oriental rugs, and unusual decorator touches. Lush landscaping punctuates the pool area and the lovely view from the rear garden is of the Hudson River and the Palisades. It is close to the Sleepy Hollow restoration, Pace College, Cold Spring, and West Point. Barbara is interested in art and history; George is a computer consultant interested in woodworking. Breakfast often includes such delicacies as raspberry pancakes, baked eggs, and homemade challah.

Golden Eagle Inn
GARRISON'S LANDING, GARRISON, NEW YORK 10524

Tel: **(914) 424-3067**
Host(s): **George and Stephanie Templeton**
Location: **50 mi. N of NYC**
No. of Rooms: **5**
No. of Private Baths: **4**
Max. No. Sharing Bath: **4**
Double/pb: **$70**
Single/pb: **$70**
Double/sb: **$60**
Single/sb: **$60**
Suites: **$85**
Open: **April 1–Jan. 15**
Reduced Rates: **$10 less Mon.–Thurs.**
Breakfast: **Continental**
Other Meals: **Lunch on weekends, May–Oct.**
Credit Cards: **AMEX, MC, VISA**
Pets: **Sometimes**
Children: **No**
Smoking: **Permitted**
Social Drinking: **Permitted**

Built in the highlands on the banks of the Hudson River, this gracious brick mansion (circa 1848) is listed in the National Register of Historic Places. It's close to West Point and Boscobel, as well as to Hyde Park and the Sleepy Hollow restorations. All the rooms are decorated with antiques and original artwork. The Templetons will direct you to some of the best restaurants in the area. The U.S. Military Academy at West Point is nearby.

House on the Hill ◎
P.O. BOX 86, OLD ROUTE 213, HIGH FALLS, NEW YORK 12440

Tel: **(914) 687-9627**
Best Time to Call: **Before 8 PM**
Host(s): **Shelley and Sharon Glassman**
Location: **10 mi. S of Kingston**
No. of Rooms: **4**
No. of Private Baths: **2**
Max. No. Sharing Bath: **4**
Double/pb: **$55**
Single/pb: **$50**
Double/sb: **$50–$60**
Single/sb: **$45**
Suites: **$65**
Open: **All year**
Reduced Rates: **Families**
Breakfast: **Full**
Pets: **No**
Children: **Welcome**
Smoking: **Permitted**
Social Drinking: **Permitted**
Airport/Station Pickup: **Yes**

A bowl of fruit, a bouquet of flowers, and handmade quilts give the suites in this spacious colonial a special charm. Breakfast is served by the fireside in the living room, or on the glass porch facing the pond. There are woods to explore, lawns for the children to play on, and ice-skating on the pond in winter. Tennis, golf, and fine skiing are all nearby. Lake Mohonk and historic Kingston are minutes away. Complimentary wine and cheese are served, and Shelley and Sharon will direct you to the two four-star restaurants within walking distance of their home. SUNY-New Paltz is nearby.

Elaine's Guest House ✪
P.O. BOX 27, JOHNSON, NEW YORK 10933

Tel: **(914) 355-8811**	Double/sb: **$30**
Host(s): **Elaine Scott**	Single/sb: **$15**
Location: **10 mi. from I-84**	Open: **All year**
No. of Rooms: **2**	Breakfast: **Full**
No. of Private Baths: **1**	Pets: **No**
Max. No. Sharing Bath: **2**	Children: **Welcome**
Double/pb: **$30**	Smoking: **No**
Single/pb: **$15**	Social Drinking: **Permitted**

Located ten minutes from Middletown, between Westown and Slate Hill, Elaine's home features hospitality and comfort. It is furnished with choice items from her on-premises antique and collectibles shop. She will be pleased to direct you to the area's points of special interest and will suggest good places to dine, suited to your budget.

Brookside Manor ✪
MAIN STREET, LEBANON SPRINGS, NEW YORK 12114

Tel: **(518) 794-9620**	Reduced Rates: **10%, off-season, midweek**
Host(s): **Leslie and Arnold Gallo**	Breakfast: **Full**
Location: **8 mi. W of Pittsfield, MA**	Pets: **Sometimes**
No. of Rooms: **5**	Children: **Welcome**
Max. No. Sharing Bath: **4**	Smoking: **Permitted**
Double/sb: **$65–$90**	Social Drinking: **Permitted**
Single/sb: **$55–$75**	
Open: **All year**	

This 1860 Victorian Georgian mansion is situated on 60 acres in a historic area. It has been newly renovated to emphasize its original beauty. It is convenient to skiing at Jiminy Peak and Brodie Mountain and close to the Tanglewood Music Festival, Shaker Village, and many antique shops and restaurants. There is a pool on-premises and tennis is nearby.

Locust Tree House ✪
P.O. BOX 31, OLD CHATHAM, NEW YORK 12136

Tel: **(518) 794-8651**	Reduced Rates: **10% seniors**
Host(s): **Dot and Russ Petterson**	Breakfast: **Full**
Location: **23 mi. SE of Albany**	Pets: **No**
No. of Rooms: **4**	Children: **Welcome (crib)**
Max. No. Sharing Bath: **4**	Smoking: **No**
Double/sb: **$35**	Social Drinking: **Permitted**
Suites: **$60 (Private bath)**	Airport/Station Pickup: **Yes**
Open: **Apr. 1–Dec. 15**	

The name of this historic 18th-century home is derived from the 200-year-old locust trees on the front lawn. It was once the stagecoach stop for the first night on the ride from Albany to Boston. It is comfortably furnished with antiques that enhance many of the original architectural features. The Old Chatham Shaker Museum is nearby; Tanglewood and Albany are less than an hour away.

Maggie Towne's B&B
PHILLIPS ROAD, PITTSTOWN, NEW YORK (mailing: Box 82, RD 2, Valley Falls, New York 12185)

Tel: **(518) 663-8369; 686-7331**	Reduced Rates: **10% seniors; families**
Host(s): **Maggie Towne**	Breakfast: **Full**
Location: **14 mi. E of Troy**	Other Meals: **Available**
No. of Rooms: **3**	Pets: **Sometimes**
Max. No. Sharing Bath: **4**	Children: **Welcome (crib)**
Double/sb: **$35**	Smoking: **No**
Single/sb: **$15**	Social Drinking: **Permitted**
Open: **All year**	

This lovely old colonial is located amid beautiful lawns and trees. Enjoy a cup of tea or glass of wine before the huge fireplace in the family room. Use the music room or curl up with a book on the screened-in porch. Mornings, your hostess serves home-baked goodies. She will gladly prepare a lunch for you to take on tour or enjoy at the house. It's 20 miles to historic Bennington, Vermont, and 30 to Saratoga.

Tibbitt's House Inn ✪
100 COLUMBIA TURNPIKE, CLINTON HEIGHTS, RENSSELAER, NEW YORK 12144

Tel: (518) 472-1348
Host(s): Claire and Herb Rufleth
Location: 2 mi. E of Albany
No. of Rooms: 5
Max. No. Sharing Bath: 4
Double/sb: $22
Single/sb: $20

Open: All year
Reduced Rates: $35 less, weekly
Breakfast: $2–$4
Pets: No
Children: No
Smoking: Permitted
Social Drinking: No

This cozy, cheerful clapboard farmhouse is 127 years old and is surrounded by trees and flowers. You will enjoy relaxing on the porch and breathing the fresh air. If you are more ambitious, try out the bike/hike path along the Hudson River. Claire and Herb look forward to your visit and will direct you to the area sights. It's just across the river from Albany, and near Fort Crailo, which was built by the Dutch in 1642 and is the oldest fort preserved in the country. (It is also where "Yankee Doodle" was composed.) Rensselaer Polytechnic Institute, Union College, Russell Sage College, and SUNY-Albany are nearby campuses.

Corner House ✪
110 EAST MARKET STREET, RHINEBECK, NEW YORK 12572

Tel: (914) 876-4758
Best Time to Call: 7–10 AM; 5–7 PM
Host(s): Mary Decker
Location: 90 mi. N of NYC
No. of Rooms: 2
Max. No. Sharing Bath: 4
Double/sb: $30–35
Single/sb: $20–25

Open: All year
Breakfast: Full
Pets: No
Children: Welcome
Smoking: Permitted
Social Drinking: Permitted
Foreign Languages: Spanish

Through all its 180 years, the Corner House has had just two owners. The furnishings range from country Chippendale to all vintages of Victorian. Each morning a hearty breakfast including homemade muffins is served. The sights of Hudson county, its wineries, universities, farms, and ski slopes are all within easy reach. The mansions of the Vanderbilts and Roosevelts are just two of the stops you might make on a historic tour of the area. Bard College is nearby.

Two Brooks Bed & Breakfast ○
ROUTE 42, SHANDAKEN, NEW YORK 12480

Tel: **(914) 688-7101**	Reduced Rates: **Mon.–Thurs.; weekly**
Host(s): **Doris and Jerry Bartlett**	Breakfast: **Full**
Location: **30 mi. from I-87**	Pets: **Sometimes**
No. of Rooms: **4**	Children: **Welcome**
Max. No. Sharing Bath: **4**	Smoking: **Permitted**
Double/sb: **$35–$40**	Social Drinking: **Permitted**
Single/sb: **$29–$35**	Airport/Station Pickup: **Yes**
Open: **All year**	

This 19th-century home is off the road, across two bridges, at the confluence of two brooks teeming with trout. Guest rooms have views of the woods and streams, and there are wood stoves, a piano, books, and cable TV for cozy comfort. In summer, have breakfast on the shaded front porch. There's a solar greenhouse where you can sunbathe in February or November. Fill your days antiquing, visiting Woodstock arts and crafts shops, hiking Catskill area trails, skiing at Belleayre, Hunter or Windham, fishing on Esopus Creek, or just help weed the garden!

Spencertown Guests ○
BOX 122, SPENCERTOWN, NEW YORK 12165

Tel: **(518) 392-3583 or 392-2358**	Open: **April–Nov.**
Host(s): **Mary and Isabel Zander**	Reduced Rates: **20% weekly**
Location: **On Route 203**	Breakfast: **Continental**
No. of Rooms: **4**	Pets: **Sometimes**
Max. No. Sharing Bath: **4**	Children: **Welcome, over 12**
Double/sb: **$25**	Smoking: **Permitted**
Single/sb: **$18**	Social Drinking: **Permitted**

This 18th-century saltbox is surrounded by a white picket fence. It is located in the center of Spencertown, said to be one of the 10 best small towns in America. The living room has a stone fireplace, and the bedrooms are low-ceilinged and have wide-plank floors. The rolling hills of Columbia county are a riot of color in autumn. You will enjoy the county fair, holiday parades, church or firehouse suppers, band concerts, and bazaars. Recreational activities are available in all seasons.

Best One Yet ✪
17 OLD ENGLISH WAY, WAPPINGERS FALLS, NEW YORK 12590

Tel: **(914) 297-1002; 297-1817**
Best Time to Call: **9–Noon; 5–9 PM**
Host(s): **Peggy and Don Ryan**
Location: **4 mi. S of Poughkeepsie**
No. of Rooms: **1 suite**
No. of Private Baths: **1**
Suites: **$35–$50 (1–4)**
Open: **All year**
Breakfast: **Continental**
Other Meals: **Available**
Pets: **No**
Children: **Welcome**
Smoking: **Permitted**
Social Drinking: **Permitted**
Airport/Station Pickup: **Yes**
Foreign Languages: **Portuguese**

This two-story colonial is on a quiet residential street where guests are welcomed with refreshments. The private suite consists of a living and dining rooms and newly remodeled bathroom and full kitchen facilities. Your hosts will gladly stock the refrigerator and the freezer. The barbecue is in use all year 'round. If you prefer not to cook, there are many fine restaurants nearby. The family swimming pool is the center of activity in warm weather. Nearby attractions include hiking, skiing, and touring the Roosevelt and Vanderbilt mansions. Vassar College is nearby.

Tranquality Guest Home ✪
P. O. BOX 347, WEST STREET EXTENSION, WARWICK, NEW YORK 10990

Tel: **(914) 986-4364**
Best Time to Call: **Evenings**
Host(s): **Virginia Beckert, Frances Scalza**
Location: **60 mi. NW of NYC**
No. of Rooms: **2**
No. of Private Baths: **1**
Max. No. Sharing Bath: **2**
Double/pb: **$40**
Single/pb: **$20**
Double/sb: **$36**
Single/sb: **$18**
Open: **All year**
Reduced Rates: **10%, weekly, seniors**
Breakfast: **Continental**
Other Meals: **Available**
Pets: **No**
Children: **No**
Smoking: **No**
Social Drinking: **Permitted**

This century-old farmhouse with its comfortable full porch features the best of the old and the new. You can enjoy the cable TV, extensive library, and music room. Take a stroll on the spacious lawns or into Warwick for international restaurants and fine antique shops. It is close to tennis, golf, and the Appalachian Trail. Virginia and Frances offer complimentary wine and cheese along with bright conversation.

Willow Brook Farm ✪
P. O. BOX 375, WARWICK TURNPIKE, WARWICK, NEW YORK 10990

Tel: **(201) 853-7728**	Reduced Rates: **10%, seniors**
Host(s): **Frances Jacobsen**	Breakfast: **Full**
Location: **2 mi. from Rte. 94**	Other Meals: **Available**
No. of Rooms: **25**	Pets: **No**
Max. No. Sharing Bath: **6**	Children: **Welcome**
Double/sb: **$40**	Smoking: **Permitted**
Single/sb: **$20**	Social Drinking: **Permitted**
Open: **All year**	

Situated in a lovely setting, the Willow Brook offers recreational activities in all seasons. The fishing pond is big enough for summer rowboating and is well lit in winter for nighttime skating. Located on the New York/New Jersey state line, it's minutes to the Appalachian Trail, Vernon Valley Action Park, and Great Gorge. It is also an easy drive to Sterling Forest, Mt. Peter, Waywayanda State Park, and Hidden Valley. Frances is a cordial hostess and will make you feel at home.

LAKE GEORGE AREA

Hayes's B&B Guest House ✪
P.O. BOX 537, 7161 LAKESHORE DRIVE, BOLTON LANDING, NEW YORK 12814

Tel: **(518) 644-5941**	Suites: **$50**
Best Time to Call: **9 AM–9 PM**	Open: **June 1–Apr. 30**
Host(s): **Dick Hayes, Mrs. Martha Hayes**	Reduced Rates: **No**
	Breakfast: **Continental**
Location: **250 mi. N of NYC**	Air-Conditioning: **Unnecessary**
No. of Rooms: **3**	Pets: **No**
No. of Private Baths: **3**	Children: **Welcome, over 12**
Double/pb: **$45**	Smoking: **Permitted**
Single/pb: **$35**	Social Drinking: **Permitted**

Close to the shores of Lake George, this elegantly appointed 1920s Cape Cod estate is located across from the town beach, picnic area, and public docks. A five-minute walk to town brings you to tennis courts, shops, and fine restaurants. The Hayes family will arrange boat tours and a picnic lunch for a nominal fee in summer and fall. Cable TV and HBO are available. It's only 40 minutes to Saratoga and its famous racetrack. There's a private trout stream on the property, so pack your fishing gear.

East Lake George House ✪
MAILING ADDRESS: 492 GLEN STREET, GLENS FALLS, NEW YORK 12801

Tel: **(518) 656-9452 (summer); 792-9296 (winter)**
Best Time to Call: **Evenings**
Host(s): **Joyce and Harold Kirkpatrick**
Location: **10 mi. N of Glens Falls**
No. of Rooms: **7**
No. of Private Baths: **4**
Max. No. Sharing Bath: **4**
Double/pb: **$65**
Single/pb: **$65**
Double/sb: **$65**
Single/sb: **$65**
Suites: **$100 for 4**
Open: **July and Aug.**
Breakfast: **Full**
Credit Cards: **MC, VISA**
Pets: **No**
Children: **Welcome (crib)**
Smoking: **Permitted**
Social Drinking: **Permitted**
Foreign Languages: **French**

The view across the water to the mountains on the eastern shore is well worth the trip to this 19th-century country inn. Relax on the screened-in porch overlooking the lawn, and swim in the clear waters of Lake George. Joyce and Harold invite you to use the sailboat and canoes. Lake George Village, the opera festival, Glens Falls, and the Saratoga Performing Arts Center are nearby.

Willow Glen Hill ✪
RD 1, BOX 40, GRANVILLE, NEW YORK 12832

Tel: **(518) 642-2079**
Best Time to Call: **Before 9 AM; after 7 PM**
Host(s): **Jim and Jo Keats**
Location: **25 mi. NE of Glens Falls**
No. of Rooms: **3**
Max. No. Sharing Bath: **5**
Double/sb: **$20**
Single/sb: **$12**
Open: **All year**
Breakfast: **Continental**
Pets: **Sometimes**
Children: **Welcome (crib)**
Smoking: **Permitted**
Social Drinking: **Permitted**
Airport/Station Pickup: **Yes**

This lovely farmhouse is set on top of a hill with a magnificent view of the Green Mountains. It is just 1,500 feet from the Vermont border. In summer, enjoy Lake St. Catherine, Lake George, and Lake Champlain. Drive down Route 30 to the Dorset Playhouse and the Southern Vermont Art Center. Skiers may choose from Pico, Stratton, Killington and Bromley, all within an hour's drive. Jim and Jo offer coffee, tea, and cold drinks as a pleasant extra. Green Mountain College is nearby.

Corner Birches Guest House ✪
86 MONTCALM STREET, LAKE GEORGE, NEW YORK 12845

Tel: **(518) 668-2837**
Host(s): **Ray and Janice Dunklee**
Location: **60 mi. N of Albany**
No. of Rooms: **4**
Max. No. Sharing Bath: **8**
Double/sb: **$21.50–$30.50**
Single/sb: **$21.50–$30.50**

Open: **All year**
Reduced Rates: **$2 less Off-season**
Breakfast: **Continental**
Pets: **Welcome**
Children: **Welcome**
Smoking: **Permitted**
Social Drinking: **Permitted**

This green-shuttered white house has a comfortable front porch for relaxed rocking. It is located in the village, three blocks from the shore of Lake George. The attractively furnished bedrooms are all cross-ventilated to capture the fresh mountain air. For skiers, Gore and West Mountains are close by. You are invited to visit in the living room with Ray and Janice, who welcome everyone from children to senior citizens.

LAKE PLACID/ADIRONDACKS AREA

North Country B&B Reservation Service ✪
THE BARN, BOX 286, LAKE PLACID, NEW YORK 12946

Tel: **(518) 523-3739**
Best Time to Call: **10 AM–10 PM**
Coordinator: **Lyn Witte**
States/Regions Covered:
  **Chestertown, Cranberry Lake,
  Keene, Lake George, Lake Placid,
  Old Forge, Port Henry, Saranac**

**Lake, Severance, Westport,
Wilmington**
Rates (Single/Double):
  Modest: **$15** **$25**
  Average: **$20** **$40**
  Luxury: **$30** **$90**
Credit cards: **No**

Lyn has dozens of hosts waiting to show you Adirondack mountain hospitality. Your choice may be convenient to Champlain Valley, Revolutionary War forts, John Brown's farm, or Camp Sagamore. Lake Placid, The Olympic Village, and Lake George offer an endless choice of sports in all seasons. St. Lawrence University, Clarkson, SUNY-Potsdam, and Plattsburgh are nearby.

Bark Eater Inn ✪
ALSTEAD MILL ROAD, KEENE, NEW YORK 12942

Tel: (518) 576-2221
Best Time to Call: Mornings
Host(s): Joe and Pete Wilson, Harley McDevitt
Location: 135 mi. N of Albany
No. of Rooms: 7
Max. No. Sharing Bath: 6
Double/sb: $60
Single/sb: $30
Guest Cottage: $394; sleeps 15

Open: All year
Reduced Rates: 10%, for 5 days
Breakfast: Full
Other Meals: Available
Pets: Sometimes
Children: Welcome
Smoking: Permitted
Social Drinking: Permitted
Airport/Station Pickup: Yes

This 150-year-old farmhouse has two fireplaces, a beautiful view of the Adirondack Mountains, and is furnished with antiques. It is close to Whiteface Mountain, Ausable Chasm, and seasonal recreational sports. The cottage has two baths, a kitchen, and is perfect for a group of friends vacationing together.

Sports Palace ✪
3 HIGHLAND PLACE, LAKE PLACID, NEW YORK 12946

Tel: (518) 523-2377
Host(s): Cathy and Teddy Blazer
No. of Rooms: 8
No. of Private Baths: 3
Max. No. Sharing Bath: 4
Double/pb: $28
Single/pb: $24
Double/sb: $28
Single/sb: $14
Suites: $52

Open: All year
Reduced Rates: Families
Breakfast: Full
Pets: Sometimes
Children: Welcome
Smoking: Permitted
Social Drinking: Permitted
Airport/Station Pickup: Yes
Foreign Languages: French

The Sports Palace is in the center of the Olympic Village, in walking distance from Mirror Lake. Your host directs the Alpine Ski Racing Program at White Face Mountain, eight miles away. Guest rooms have one or two sets of bunk beds, perfect for groups. The decor is country style. Before a day of activity, a hearty breakfast is served, including pancakes and eggs. Excellent facilities to care for sports gear are provided.

Stagecoach Inn ✪
OLD MILITARY ROAD, LAKE PLACID, NEW YORK 12946

Tel: **(518) 523-9474**	Double/sb: **$30**
Best Time to Call: **6 PM**	Single/sb: **$25**
Host(s): **Peter and Sherry Moreau**	Suites: **$50**
Location: **285 mi. N of NYC**	Open: **All year**
No. of Rooms: **6**	Breakfast: **Continental**
No. of Private Baths: **4**	Pets: **Sometimes**
Max. No. Sharing Bath: **2**	Children: **Welcome, over 3**
Double/pb: **$35**	Smoking: **Permitted**
Single/pb: **$30**	Social Drinking: **Permitted**

The wainscoted, high-ceilinged common room, and five fireplaces will make you feel that you've arrived as the inn's original guests did—by stagecoach. Several thousand lakes and ponds for fishing and canoeing are in nearby Adirondack State Park. Local possibilities include golf, tennis, and the village of Lake Placid.

"Adirondack Hotel" on-the-Lake ✪
ONE LAKE STREET, LONG LAKE, NEW YORK 12847

Tel: **(518) 624-4700**	Single/sb: **$20**
Host(s): **Robert and Marijane Lucci**	Open: **May 24–Dec. 1**
Location: **55 mi. S of Lake Placid**	Breakfast: **Continental**
No. of Rooms: **30**	Other Meals: **Available**
No. of Private Baths: **12**	Pets: **No**
Max. No. Sharing Bath: **6**	Children: **Welcome, over 3**
Double/pb: **$30**	Smoking: **Permitted**
Single/pb: **$20**	Social Drinking: **Permitted**
Double/sb: **$25**	

It's called a hotel, but to Marijane and Robert, it's home; making you feel at home is their prime ambition. The atmosphere is back-to-basics involvement with their guests. There's lots to do, including free tennis, swimming at the protected beach across the way, hiking, and trout fishing in the pond. If you're ambitious, you can canoe all the way to Saranac Lake or the Hudson River. Or just enjoy the scenery. Clarkson University is nearby.

LONG ISLAND

A Reasonable Alternative ✪
117 SPRING STREET, PORT JEFFERSON, NEW YORK 11777

Tel: **(516) 928-4034**
Best Time to Call: **9 AM–1 PM**
Coordinator: **Kathleen B. Dexter**
States/Regions Covered: **Long Island**

Rates (Single/Double):
  Modest: **$20** **$28**
  Average: **$28** **$36**
  Luxury: **$40** **$48–$80**
Credit Cards: **MC, VISA**

Bounded by Long Island Sound and the Atlantic Ocean, from the New York City border to Montauk 100 miles to the east, the cream of host homes has been culled by Kathleen for you. There's much to see and do, including museums, historic homes, theater, horse racing, and the famous beaches, including Jones Beach, Fire Island, Shelter Island, and the exclusive Hamptons. (The Hamptons require a two-day minimum stay in July and August.) Adelphi College, Hofstra University, C. W. Post, Stony Brook, and St. Joseph's are a few of the nearby schools.

Hampton-on-the-Water ✪
33 RAMPASTURE ROAD, HAMPTON BAYS, NEW YORK 11946

Tel: **(516) 728-3560**
Best Time to Call: **8–9 AM, 8–9 PM**
Host(s): **Ute Lambur**
Location: **90 mi. E of NYC**
No. of Rooms: **2**
No. of Private Baths: **2**
Double/pb: **$35–$70**
Single/pb: **$30–$65**
Open: **May–Dec.**

Reduced Rates: **30% Off-season**
Breakfast: **Full**
Other Meals: **Available**
Pets: **No**
Children: **No**
Smoking: **Permitted**
Social Drinking: **Permitted**
Foreign Languages: **French, German, Spanish**

A spanking-white ranch-style home right on the water of Shinnecock Bay awaits your visit. There's a terrace and large garden for relaxing when you aren't clamming, fishing, or swimming. Ute permits you to use her windsurfer, small motorboat, or bicycles when the mood strikes you. It's only seven miles from the shops of Southampton. Minimum stay is three days in July and August; two days the rest of the time. Ute also has a fabulous spot in Acapulco, Mexico, available from January 15 until April 15.

Duvall Bed and Breakfast ☉
237 CATHEDRAL AVENUE, HEMPSTEAD, NEW YORK 11550

Tel: **(516) 292-9219**
Best Time to Call: **4–9 PM**
Host(s): **Wendy and Richard Duvall**
Location: **20 mi. E of NYC**
No. of Rooms: **2**
No. of Private Baths: **2**
Double/pb: **$45–$55**
Single/pb: **$35**
Open: **All year**
Reduced Rates: **10%, weekly**
Breakfast: **Full**
Other Meals: **Available**
Pets: **Sometimes**
Children: **Welcome (crib)**
Smoking: **No**
Social Drinking: **Permitted**
Airport/Station Pickup: **Yes**
Foreign Languages: **Spanish, German**

Guests feel right at home in this Dutch colonial with four-poster beds and antiques reproductions. Refreshments are served on arrival and breakfast ranges from pancakes to muffins and homemade breads. Jones Beach, Fire Island, Westbury Gardens, and Bethpage Village are nearby. Guests are welcome to use the patio, garden, barbecue, and bicycles. Adelphi, Hofstra, and C. W. Post Colleges are close by.

Seafield House ☉
2 SEAFIELD LANE, WESTHAMPTON BEACH, NEW YORK 11978

Tel: **(516) 288-1559**
Best Time to Call: **After 4 PM**
Host(s): **Elsie Collins**
Location: **90 mi. E of NYC**
No. of Rooms: **2**
No. of Private Baths: **2**
Double/pb: **$45**
Suites: **$60**
Open: **Sept.–May**
Breakfast: **Full**
Pets: **No**
Children: **No**
Smoking: **No**
Social Drinking: **Permitted**
Airport/Station Pickup: **Yes**

This 100-year-old home in posh Westhampton is five blocks from the beach but boasts its own pool. Victorian lounges, a caned rocker, piano, hurricane lamps, Shaker benches, Chinese porcelain all combine to create the casual, country inn atmosphere. When the sea air chills Westhampton Beach, the parlor fire keeps the house toasty warm. The aromas of freshly brewing coffee and Mrs. Collins' breads and rolls baking in the oven are likely to wake you in time for breakfast. You'll leave this hideaway relaxed, carrying one of Mrs. Collins' homemade goodies.

NEW YORK CITY AREA

The B&B Group (New Yorkers at Home)
301 EAST 60TH STREET, NEW YORK, NEW YORK 10022

Tel: **(212) 838-7015**
Best Time to Call: **9 AM–4 PM**
Coordinator: **Farla Zammit**
States/Regions Covered: **New York City, the Hampton Beaches**

Rates (Single/Double):
  Modest: **$35–$40**   **$50**
  Average: **$45**   **$55**
  Luxury: **$50–$55**   **$65–$95**
Credit Cards: **No**
Minimum Stay: **2 days**

Accommodations appropriate to your purpose and purse are available, from the chic East Side to the arty West Side, to Greenwich Village, SoHo, Chelsea, and the Wall Street area. They range from luxury high-rise apartments to historic brownstone mansions, and are hosted by a variety of people, including artists, actors, doctors, engineers, and writers. All are enthusiastic about the Big Apple and eager to share it with you.

Urban Ventures
P.O. BOX 426, NEW YORK, NEW YORK 10024

Tel: **(212) 594-5650**
Best Time to Call: **9 AM–5 PM**
Coordinators: **Mary McAulay and Fran Tesser**
State/Regions Covered: **Manhattan, Brooklyn, Queens**

Rates (Single/Double):
  Modest: **$23–$32**   **$32–$44**
  Average: **$34–$52**   **$44–$54**
  Luxury: **$54–$60**   **$54–$85**
Credit Cards: **AMEX, MC, VISA**
Minimum Stay: **2 days**

The biggest bargains since the Indians sold Manhattan for $24 are offered by this registry. Mary and Fran have bedrooms and complete apartments located throughout the best areas of New York City, including landmarked historic districts. They will be happy to help with theater tickets, restaurant information, current museum exhibits, as well as special tours.

The Tilted Barn ○
41 DEERFIELD AVENUE, EASTCHESTER, NEW YORK 10707

Tel: **(914) 779-5061**
Host(s): **Sud and Lydia Sudler**

Location: **10 mi. N of NYC**
No. of Rooms: **3**

Max. No. Sharing Bath: **6**
Double/sb: **$40**
Single/sb: **$30**
Open: **All year**
Reduced Rates: **Available**
Breakfast: **Full**
Other Meals: **Available**
Pets: **No**
Children: **Welcome, school-age**
Smoking: **Permitted**
Social Drinking: **Permitted**
Airport/Station Pickup: **Yes**

Only two miles from the Hutchinson River Parkway, this updated Victorian house was originally built in 1895. It is attractively furnished with family heirlooms. Weather permitting, you can enjoy breakfast on the screened-in porch. Lydia will share her kitchen for light snacks, and offers you use of the barbecue, washer, and dryer to help you cut down on expenses. Sud is an antique car buff. It's just minutes away from Sarah Lawrence College, horseback riding, and tennis, and you are welcome guests at the swim club.

I-Love-New York Bed & Breakfast ✪
190-11 HILLSIDE AVENUE, HOLLISWOOD, NEW YORK 11423

Tel: **(212) 776-6434**
Host(s): **Helena and Fred Sommer**
Location: **15 mi. E of Manhattan**
No. of Rooms: **2**
No. of Private Baths: **1**
Max. No. Sharing Bath: **2**
Double/pb: **$30**
Single/pb: **$25**
Double/sb: **$25**
Open: **All year**
Breakfast: **Full**
Other Meals: **Available**
Pets: **No**
Children: **Welcome**
Smoking: **Permitted**
Social Drinking: **Permitted**
Airport/Station Pickup: **Yes**
Foreign Languages: **Lithuanian, Polish**

This gracious, white, center-hall colonial is located in Queens, a borough of New York City. This is a lovely residential section, convenient to excellent buses or subways to whisk you to the Big Apple in a half hour. LaGuardia and Kennedy airports are 10 minutes away. It's also close to Shea Stadium, famous racetracks, and several beaches. Helena and Fred have traveled widely and have many interesting collectibles accenting their comfortable furnishings. St. John's University is two miles away.

A Bit o' the Apple—New York City ✪
Contact: TRAILS END, RD 2 BOX 355A, GREENTOWN, PENNSYLVANIA 18426

Tel: (212) 321-2930 or (717) 857-0856	Open: **All year**
Best Time to Call: **Weekends**	Breakfast: **Continental**
Location: **Manhattan**	Pets: **No**
No. of Rooms: **1 Suite**	Children: **No**
No. of Private Baths: **1**	Smoking: **Permitted**
Suites: **$55 for 2; $70 for 3**	Social Drinking: **Permitted**

This pied-à-terre in a luxury high-rise building on the Battery is within walking distance of the World Trade Center, the Wall Street Stock Exchanges, Trinity Church, the Statue of Liberty ferry, and the South Street Seaport. The accommodations consist of a one-bedroom, self-contained apartment with twin beds, a hide-a-bed sofa in the living room, fully-equipped kitchen, and commodious bath. It is tastefully furnished in a traditional style with fine furniture, antiques, and lots of plants. Your hosts, native New Yorkers, have the adjacent apartment and will happily suggest special restaurants and shops off the tourist trail that will make your visit affordable and memorable.

Sixteen Firs ✪
352 ST. PAULS AVENUE, STATEN ISLAND, NEW YORK 10304

Tel: (212) 727-9188	Breakfast: **Continental**
Host(s): **Drs. Karl and Shirley Leone**	Pets: **No**
Location: **5 mi. W of Manhattan**	Children: **Welcome**
No. of Rooms: **3**	Smoking: **Permitted**
Max. No. Sharing Bath: **4**	Social Drinking: **Permitted**
Double/sb: **$35–$40**	Airport/Station/Ferry Pickup: **Yes**
Open: **All year**	

This gracious Victorian is located in a residential borough. It's a 25-minute ferry ride across fabulous New York Harbor to the Wall Street area of Manhattan. Karl and Shirley are native New Yorkers and will help you plan a low-cost visit to the Big Apple. There's a guest refrigerator and coffee is always available. A two-night minimum stay is required. Wagner College and St. John's University are nearby.

Beehive Bed & Breakfast ✪
82 VERMONT TERRACE, TUCKAHOE, NEW YORK 10707

Tel: **(914) 779-6411**
Best Time to Call: **After 5 PM**
Host(s): **Gloria and Norman Bantz**
Location: **10 mi. N of NYC**
No. of Rooms: **5**
No. of Private Baths: **1**
Max. No. Sharing Bath: **6**
Double/pb: **$44**
Single/pb: **$40**
Double/sb: **$40**

Single/sb: **$32**
Open: **All year**
Reduced Rates: **Weekly; families**
Breakfast: **Full**
Other Meals: **Available**
Pets: **No**
Children: **Welcome (crib)**
Smoking: **No**
Social Drinking: **Permitted**
Airport/Station Pickup: **Yes**

This large, brick Federal-style home is located in a lovely residential section of Westchester County, yet it's less than 30 minutes away from Manhattan. The rooms are immaculate. You may use the kitchen for light snacks and the laundry facilities; complimentary wine, cheese, and beverages are always offered. Gloria and Norman are hobby beekeepers so you know the homemade honey bread is the real thing. They'll lend you bikes so you can work off the effects of the hearty breakfast, by following the 25 miles of cycling and jogging paths along the Bronx River, which passes in front of the door. Fordham University and Sarah Lawrence College are nearby.

NIAGARA/BUFFALO/ROCHESTER AREA

Bed & Breakfast—Rochester ✪
P.O. BOX 444, FAIRPORT, N.Y. 14450

Tel: **(716) 223-8510 or 223-8877**
Coordinator: **Betty Kinsman**
States/Regions Covered: **Bluff Point, Fairport, Penfield, Wyohing**

Rates (Single/Double):
 Modest: **$30–$40 $35–$50**
 Luxury: **$45 $50**
Credit Cards: **No**

Picture yourself in a ranch-style home where your nutrition-conscious hostess is whipping up apple-oatmeal muffins for your breakfast; or in a beautiful ranch home on Lake Ontario; or in a tri-level cottage where your hosts are a college professor and artist. All will be happy to advise you on the sights and "doings" in their areas. Don't miss the International Museum of Photography at George Eastman House, founder of the Kodak firm. The University of Rochester, Colgate and SUNY-Brockport are three local campuses.

The Eastwood House ✪
45 SOUTH MAIN STREET, CASTILE, NEW YORK 14427

Tel: **(716) 493-2335**
Best Time to Call: **After 6 PM**
Host(s): **Joan Ballinger**
Location: **63 mi. SE of Buffalo**
No. of Rooms: **2**
Max. No. Sharing Bath: **4**
Double/sb: **$21**

Single/sb: **$18**
Open: **All year**
Breakfast: **Continental**
Pets: **Sometimes**
Children: **Welcome, over 5**
Smoking: **No**
Social Drinking: **Permitted**

This comfortable house is a few minutes' drive from Letchworth State Park. Your hostess offers coffee, fresh fruit, and juice on arrival. Hot biscuits, freshly whipped cream, and jam are featured at breakfast each morning. Local sights include the Historical Society and the Indian Museum.

Back of the Beyond ✪
7233 LOWER EAST HILL ROAD, COLDEN, NEW YORK 14033

Tel: **(716) 652-0427**
Best Time to Call: **Early AM**
Host(s): **Bill and Shash Georgi**
Location: **30 mi. S of Buffalo**
No. of Rooms: **3**
Max. No. Sharing Bath: **6**
Double/sb: **$40**

Single/sb: **$35**
Open: **All year**
Breakfast: **Full**
Pets: **Sometimes**
Children: **Welcome**
Smoking: **No**
Social Drinking: **Permitted**

Bill and Shash have a small country estate near a ski area and an hour from Niagara Falls. They maintain a greenhouse, and grow their vegetables organically. Breakfast reflects all this "healthiness" with delicious herbal omelettes, organic juice, plus other surprise goodies. The guest quarters are in a separate three-bedroom chalet, fully equipped even to the fireplace. There is a $25 rate for children over 12.

Highland Springs ✪
ALLEN ROAD, EAST CONCORD, NEW YORK 14055

Tel: **(716) 592-4323**
Best Time to Call: **5 PM–9 PM**
Host(s): **Lew and Judy Markle**
Location: **40 mi. S of Buffalo**
No. of Rooms: **3**
No. of Private Baths: **2**
Max. No. Sharing Bath: **4**
Double/pb: **$40**
Single/pb: **$35**

Double/sb: **$40**
Single/sb: **$35**
Open: **All year**
Breakfast: **Continental**
Pets: **No**
Children: **Welcome (crib)**
Smoking: **No**
Social Drinking: **Permitted**

This 70-acre country estate offers a comfortable, homey ambience. Alpine and Nordic skiing are close by, and summer pleasures may be enjoyed in the on-premises pond where you can swim and fish. Judy loves to bake with natural ingredients; her vegetarian breakfast is delicious and bountiful.

Bebaks Guest House ✪
S 5047 MOUNT VERNON BOULEVARD, HAMBURG, NEW YORK 14075

Tel: **(716) 627-9094**
Host(s): **Joe and Sally Bebak**
Location: **12 mi. S of Buffalo**
No. of Rooms: **3**
Max. No. Sharing Bath: **5**
Double/sb: **$30**
Single/sb: **$20**
Guest Cottage: **$50; sleeps 4–6**
Open: **All year**

Reduced Rates: **Seniors, families**
Breakfast: **Continental**
Other Meals: **Available**
Pets: **Sometimes**
Children: **Welcome (crib)**
Smoking: **Permitted**
Social Drinking: **Permitted**
Airport/Station Pickup: **Yes**

Tastefully furnished guest rooms await you in this modest colonial. Your hosts enjoy raising plants and have filled the house with greenery. They serve either a continental or full breakfast, depending on your needs. They can direct guests to local dining or will occasionally prepare other meals. Nearby attractions include Niagara Falls, Rich Stadium, and the beaches.

Crafts' Place B&B ○
10283 RIDGE ROAD AT JEDDO, MEDINA, NEW YORK 14103

Tel: (716) 735-7343
Best Time to Call: 4 PM–7 PM
Host(s): Peg and Bob Crafts
Location: On Rte. 104
No. of Rooms: 4
Max. No. Sharing Bath: 4
Double/sb: $25
Single/sb: $20

Open: April 15–Nov. 15
Reduced Rates: Seniors, families
Breakfast: Full
Pets: Sometimes
Children: Welcome
Smoking: Permitted
Social Drinking: Permitted
Foreign Languages: Spanish

Located in the historic Lake Ontario–Lake Erie area, this comfortable century-old home with its handsome stone porch is convenient to everything. Local museums, wineries, arts and crafts shows, boating, swimming, and fishing will keep you busy. Buffalo, Rochester, and Niagara Falls are nearby. Bob and Peg, longtime residents of the area, will be happy to help with your plans.

The Franklin House
1331 WEST DANBY ROAD, NEWFIELD, NEW YORK 14867

Tel: (607) 272-5858
Host(s): Lynne Tucker
Location: 3 mi. S of Ithaca
No. of Rooms: 5
No. of Private Baths: 2
Max. No. Sharing Bath: 5
Double/pb: $75
Double/sb: $50
Single/sb: $20
Suites: $75

Open: All year
Reduced Rates: Families
Breakfast: Continental
Other Meals: Available
Credit Cards: AMEX, MC, VISA
Pets: Sometimes
Children: Welcome
Smoking: Permitted
Social Drinking: Permitted
Airport/Station Pickup: Yes

This restored clapboard farmhouse offers country-style lodging amid acres of rolling hills. Browse through the well-stocked library and relax in a magnificent living room. The stone room is the place for TV, bridge, or chess. It opens onto a patio with large in-ground pool and adjacent tennis courts. Local wine, homemade popcorn, spiced apple cake, granola parfaits, and pies are specialties of the house. Your hosts will gladly point out places to ski, sled, ice skate, and hike.

Strawberry Castle Bed & Breakfast ✪
1883 PENFIELD ROAD, PENFIELD, NEW YORK 14526

Tel: **(716) 385-3266**
Best Time to Call: **Evenings**
Host(s): **Charles and Cynthia Whited**
Location: **8 mi. E of Rochester**
No. of Rooms: **2 suites**
Max. No. Sharing Bath: **4**
Double/sb: **$55**
Single/sb: **$45**
Open: **All year**
Reduced Rates: **15%, weekly**
Breakfast: **Continental**
Credit Cards: **MC, VISA**
Pets: **No**
Children: **Welcome, over 12**
Smoking: **Permitted**
Social Drinking: **Permitted**
Airport/Station Pickup: **Yes**

An outstanding example of the Italian villa style of architecture, the Whiteds' home (circa 1878) features columned porches, heavy plaster moldings, high sculptured ceilings, and a white marble fireplace, and is appropriately furnished with antiques and brass beds. Wander the lawns and gardens, sun on the patio, or take a dip in the pool. Charles and Cynthia will direct you to fine restaurants, golf courses, and all the nearby Rochester attractions. Complimentary wine and fruit are graciously served.

THOUSAND ISLANDS AREA

Pink House Inn ✪
9125 SOUTH MAIN STREET, P.O. BOX 85, SANDY CREEK, NEW YORK 13145

Tel: **(315) 387-3276**
Host(s): **Evelyn Sadowski**
Location: **46 mi. N of Syracuse**
No. of Rooms: **5**
Max. No. Sharing Bath: **3**
Double/sb: **$35**
Single/sb: **$25**
Open: **All year**
Breakfast: **Continental**
Pets: **Sometimes**
Children: **Welcome**
Smoking: **Permitted**
Social Drinking: **Permitted**
Airport/Station Pickup: **Yes**

Evelyn owns an antique shop, and many fine pieces accent her comfortable home. This clapboard house, built in 1872, has an inviting screened-in porch. If you are heading for Canada, this is a fine place to rest up, since the house is located on Route 11. It is only five miles to Lake Ontario. Your hostess truly enjoys people.

Le Muguet ✪
2553 CHURCH STREET, THREE MILE BAY, NEW YORK 13693

Tel: **(315) 649-5896**
Best Time to Call: **7–10 PM**
Host(s): **Elisabeth Dibrell**
Location: **18 mi. W of Watertown**
No. of Rooms: **2**
Max. No. Sharing Bath: **3**
Double/sb: **$25**
Single/sb: **$20**
Suite: **$35**
Open: **June–Oct.**
Breakfast: **Continental**
Pets: **Sometimes**
Children: **Welcome, over 6**
Smoking: **No**
Social Drinking: **No**
Airport/Station Pickup: **Yes**
Foreign Languages: **French**

This 100-year-old farmhouse is cozily furnished with antiques, plants, and lots of decorator touches. Elisabeth specialized in fine arts and has a good eye for innovative decor. There are many things to do in this lovely area of the scenic Thousand Islands.

House on the Hill

NORTH CAROLINA

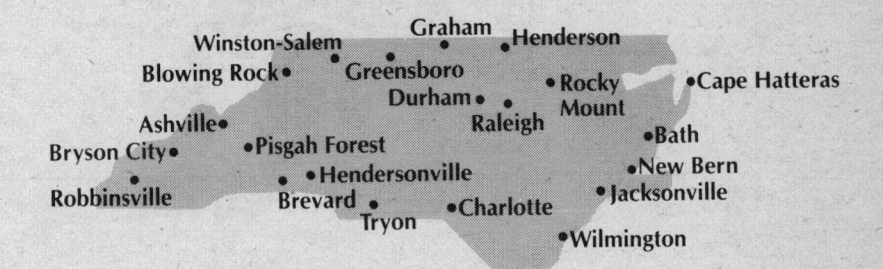

Flint Street Inn ✪
116 FLINT STREET, ASHEVILLE, NORTH CAROLINA 28801

Tel: (704) 253-6723
Host(s): **Rick and Lynne Vogel**
Location: ¼ mi. from Rte. 240
No. of Rooms: **4**
No. of Private Baths: **2**
Max. No. Sharing Bath: **4**
Double/pb: **$50**
Single/pb: **$45**
Double/sb: **$45**
Single/sb: **$40**

Guest Cottage: **$100; sleeps 4–6**
Open: **All year**
Reduced Rates: **Weekly**
Breakfast: **Full**
Credit Cards: **AMEX**
Pets: **No**
Children: **Welcome, over 12**
Smoking: **Permitted**
Social Drinking: **Permitted**
Airport/Station Pickup: **Yes**

This turn-of-the-century home is listed in the National Register of Historic Places. Stained glass, pine floors, and a claw-footed bathtub are part of the Victorian decor. Guests are served wine, coffee, and soft drinks; at breakfast, homemade biscuits with honey and jam are featured. The Art Deco buildings and craft shops of downtown Asheville are minutes away. The Blue Ridge Parkway and the University of North Carolina are close by.

The Ray House ☉
83 HILLSIDE STREET, ASHEVILLE, NORTH CAROLINA 28801

Tel: **(704) 252-0106**
Best Time to Call: **10 AM–9 PM**
Host(s): **Will and Alice Curtis**
Location: **5 mi. from I-40**
No. of Rooms: **3**
Max. No. Sharing Bath: **5**
Double/sb: **$37**
Single/sb: **$26**
Suites: **$42**

Open: **All year**
Reduced Rates: **Weekly**
Breakfast: **Continental**
Pets: **Sometimes**
Children: **Welcome**
Smoking: **Permitted**
Social Drinking: **Permitted**
Airport/Station Pickup: **Yes**
Foreign Languages: **French**

This restored 1891 home sits on an acre of towering trees which provide leafy privacy in a parklike setting. Interior features include windows of unusual design, beamed ceilings, and handsome woodwork. A breakfast of homemade breads, sweet cakes, and jellies is served in the formal dining room or on the shaded wraparound porch.

Balsam Lodge
BOX 279, RIVER ROAD, BALSAM, NORTH CAROLINA 28707

Tel: (704) 456-6528
Best Time to Call: **9 AM–10 PM**
Host(s): **Marie and Gordon Pike**
Location: **35 mi. W of Asheville**
No. of Rooms: **8**
No. of Private Baths: **4**
Max. No. Sharing Bath: **7**
Double/pb: **$35**
Single/pb: **$30**

Double/sb: **$25**
Single/sb: **$20**
Open: **June 1–Oct. 31**
Reduced Rates: **10%, weekly**
Breakfast: **Continental**
Pets: **Sometimes**
Children: **Welcome**
Smoking: **Permitted**
Social Drinking: **Permitted**

Local crafts, fresh flowers, and period pieces fill the rooms of this turn-of-the-century home. The depot, which once served the town of Balsam, is now divided into private accommodations for guests. At the main house, enjoy an evening on a porch rocker; in the morning, your hosts offer homemade muffins and cakes. They are glad to advise on trips to nearby Great Smoky National Park, Blue Ridge Parkway, and the Cherokee Indian Reservation. Western Carolina University is nearby.

Bath Guest House ✪
SOUTH MAIN STREET, BATH, NORTH CAROLINA 27808

Tel: (919) 923-6811
Best Time to Call: **9 AM–9 PM**
Host(s): **Paul and Irene Komarow**
No. of Rooms: **5**
No. of Private Baths: **1**
Max. No. Sharing Bath: **4**
Double/pb: **$45**
Single/pb: **$40**
Double/sb: **$40**

Single/sb: **$35**
Open: **All year**
Breakfast: **Full**
Other Meals: **Available**
Credit Cards: **MC**
Pets: **Sometimes**
Children: **Welcome**
Smoking: **Permitted**
Social Drinking: **Permitted**

This is a fine, historic inn, on the beautiful Pamlico River. You can absorb the abundant history of the town, join the sailing enthusiasts, enjoy hunting and fishing, or just relax on the back porch rocking chairs and watch the sun set over the river. Everything is within walking distance, but bicycles are available for your use. There's no charge for the use of small boats or for docking your own. Special duck hunting packages are available in season, including experienced guide service and meals. Paul and Irene's Southern breakfasts are special.

Ragged Garden Inn and Restaurant
BOX 1927 SUNSET DRIVE, BLOWING ROCK, NORTH CAROLINA 28605

Tel: **(704) 295-9703**
Best Time to Call: **Mornings**
Host(s): **Joe and Joyce Villani**
Location: **35 mi. N of Hickory**
No. of Rooms: **4**
No. of Private Baths: **4**
Double/pb: **$60**
Single/pb: **$55**
Suites: **$85**
Open: **Apr. 15–Jan. 1**
Reduced Rates: **Apr.–May; Nov.–Dec.**
Breakfast: **Continental**
Other Meals: **Dinner available**
Credit Cards: **AMEX, MC, VISA**
Pets: **No**
Children: **Welcome, over 12**
Smoking: **Permitted**
Social Drinking: **Permitted**
Foreign Languages: **Italian**

You will discover a touch of the past in this grand turn-of-the-century chestnut-bark home set on an acre surrounded by majestic trees and lovely flower gardens. Joe and Joyce have restored and refurbished it with taste and comfort. In addition to the guest rooms, they have an on-premises gourmet dining room, featuring continental cuisine. It's close to interesting sightseeing as well as fine seasonal recreational activities. Appalachian State University is nearby.

The Inn at Brevard ◯
410 EAST MAIN STREET, BREVARD, NORTH CAROLINA 28712

Tel: **(704) 884-2105**
Host(s): **Bertrend and Eileen Bourget**
Location: **25 mi. W of Hendersonville**
No. of Rooms: **12**
No. of Private Baths: **10**
Max. No. Sharing Bath: **4**
Double/pb: **$45**
Single/pb: **$38**
Double/sb: **$45**
Single/sb: **$38**
Open: **All year**
Reduced Rates: **$10 less, Nov. 16–Apr. 15**
Breakfast: **Full**
Pets: **No**
Children: **Welcome**
Smoking: **Permitted**
Social Drinking: **No**

This white-columned inn is listed in the National Register of Historic Places and has retained the original brass hardware, carved fireplace mantels, and antique furnishings to recall old-time Southern charm. The bedrooms are comfortable and the clear air and mountain breezes will refresh you. Explore the many splendors of this Land of Waterfalls, and return to spend a peaceful evening with other guests on the porch or sitting room.

Folkestone Lodge
ROUTE 1, BOX 310, BRYSON CITY, NORTH CAROLINA 28713

Tel: (704) 488-2730
Host(s): Irene and Bob Kranich
Location: 60 mi. W of Asheville
No. of Rooms: 5
No. of Private Baths: 5
Double/pb: $48
Single/pb: $34
Open: May–Nov.

Breakfast: Full
Credit Cards: MC, VISA
Pets: No
Children: Welcome
Smoking: No
Social Drinking: Permitted
Foreign Languages: Spanish

The lodge is a quaint mountain retreat; small, secluded, and old-fashioned, it is located 10 minutes from Great Smoky Mountain National Park. The park offers hiking, trout fishing, camping, and tubing. The Cherokee Indian Reservation is also close by. Bob and Irene have tastefully furnished the guest rooms; antiques, fresh flowers, high headboards, hand-crocheted bedspreads, and Oriental rugs add to the charm. A grand country breakfast awaits you each morning.

Hampton Manor
3327 CARMEL ROAD, CHARLOTTE, NORTH CAROLINA 28226

Tel: (704) 542-6299
Host(s): Rebecca Triggs
Location: 3 mi. from Hwy. 51
No. of Rooms: 5
No. of Private Baths: 5
Double/pb: $150
Single/pb: $150
Suites: $300

Open: All year
Breakfast: Full
Credit Cards: AMEX, DC, MC, VISA
Pets: No
Children: Welcome (crib)
Smoking: Permitted
Social Drinking: Permitted
Airport/Station Pickup: Yes

This English manor has de luxe accommodations in the style of the 1840s. Private bedroom suites, two splendidly furnished sitting rooms, an Empire-style dining room, and an informal pub await you. All are superbly appointed, with antiques. A skilled staff will attend to your needs and chauffeured limousines are available. An English breakfast of thick bacon, eggs any style, heavy cream and croissants is served in your private quarters. Your hosts invite you to stroll the gardens and relax at the swimming pool.

The Library Suite ☯
326 WEST EIGHTH STREET, CHARLOTTE, NORTH CAROLINA 28202

Tel: (704) 334-8477
Host(s): **Robert Carpenter, Calvin Hefner**
Location: 1 mi. from I-77
No. of Rooms: 2
No. of Private Baths: 1
Suites: $65–$80

Open: **All year**
Reduced Rates: **10% corporate**
Breakfast: **Continental**
Pets: **No**
Children: **Welcome**
Smoking: **Permitted**
Social Drinking: **Permitted**

The Library Suite is a Victorian-style retreat in the luxurious Overcarsh House. The private entrance into the suite leads to a wraparound gallery overlooking Fourth Ward Park. The adjoining sleeping quarters feature a draped French bed. Your hosts have stocked the floor-to-ceiling bookcases with plenty of books and periodicals. They also provide wine and a wet bar, fresh flowers, cable TV, and coffeemaker. Overcarsh House is listed in the National Register of Historic Places, close to the uptown area, performing arts center, shopping, and restaurants.

The Lords Proprietors' Inn
300 NORTH BROAD STREET, EDENTON, NORTH CAROLINA 27932

Tel: (919) 482-3641
Host(s): **Arch and Jane Edwards**
Location: 75 mi. SW of Norfolk, Va.
No. of Rooms: 12
No. of Private Baths: 12
Double/pb: $50
Single/pb: $41

Open: **All year**
Breakfast: **Continental**
Pets: **No**
Children: **Welcome (crib)**
Smoking: **Permitted**
Social Drinking: **Permitted**
Airport/Station Pickup: **Yes**

Originally built in 1783 and remodeled in 1906, the inn consists of two adjacent Victorian houses, one a large brick dwelling and the other a smaller frame house. Both have stained glass windows and comfortable porches. The elegant bedrooms are furnished by local antique dealers and craftsmen. You can enjoy the decor and perhaps buy what you like! Located on Albemarle Sound, it is near Nags Head, Hope Plantation, and Somerset House.

Mulberry Hill Guest House ✺
ROUTE 2, EDENTON, NORTH CAROLINA 27932

Tel: **(919) 482-4175 or 828-1339**	Double/sb: **$50**
Best Time to Call: **Before 8 AM; after 6 PM**	Open: **All year**
	Reduced Rates: **Dec. 1–Feb. 28**
Host(s): **Janie Wood**	Breakfast: **Continental**
Location: **5½ mi. from Hwy. 17**	Pets: **Sometimes**
No. of Rooms: **4**	Children: **Welcome, over 6**
No. of Private Baths: **2**	Smoking: **Permitted**
Max. No. Sharing Bath: **4**	Social Drinking: **Permitted**
Double/pb: **$50**	

Situated on over a thousand acres, this handsome Georgian-style plantation house (circa 1780) overlooks Albemarle Sound. There is excellent sailing, fishing, and boating on hand, plus a sandy beach for swimming. It is convenient to the country club for tennis, golf, and pool. You are welcome to use the kitchen for light snacks and the outdoor grill for a barbeque.

The Franklin Terrace ✺
67 HARRISON AVENUE, FRANKLIN, NORTH CAROLINA 28734

Tel: **(704) 524-7907**	Guest Cottage: **Available**
Best Time to Call: **After 2 PM**	Open: **May–Oct.**
Host(s): **Mike and Pat Giampola**	Breakfast: **Continental**
Location: **135 mi. N of Atlanta**	Credit Cards: **MC, VISA**
No. of Rooms: **7**	Pets: **No**
No. of Private Baths: **7**	Children: **Welcome**
Double/pb: **$38–$42**	Smoking: **Permitted**
Single/pb: **$34–$38**	Social Drinking: **Permitted**

Located close to the Cowee Valley ruby mines and the Standing Indian campground, this 95-year-old home, wrapped on three sides by comfortable porches, is listed in the National Register of Historic Places. Pat and Mike are in the antiques business so you can picture the special furnishings with which they have decorated their home. On the premises is an elegant old-fashioned ice cream parlor that will coddle your sweet tooth.

Mountain High ✪
BIG RIDGE ROAD, GLENVILLE, NORTH CAROLINA 28736

Tel: **(704) 743-3094**	Open: **June–Nov.**
Host(s): **Margaret and George Carter**	Reduced Rates: **Weekly**
Location: **2 mi. from Rte. 107**	Breakfast: **Full**
No. of Rooms: **3**	Pets: **No**
No. of Private Baths: **1**	Children: **No**
Max. No. Sharing Bath: **4**	Smoking: **No**
Double/sb: **$30**	Social Drinking: **Permitted**
Single/sb: **$15**	

It is located 4,200 feet high in the Smoky Mountains, only a short distance from the Carolina Highlands. Margaret and George offer warm hospitality to their guests. You are invited to take a horseback ride on the premises or join your hosts in a fox hunt (the hounds are trained not to kill the fox—just to chase him). You are welcome to use the kitchen for light snacks, and may freshen your wardrobe in the washer and dryer. Western Carolina University-Cullowhee is nearby.

Leftwich House ✪
215 EAST HARDEN STREET, GRAHAM, NORTH CAROLINA 27253

Tel: **(919) 226-5978**	Open: **All year**
Host(s): **Carolyn Morrow**	Breakfast: **Full**
Location: **2 mi. from Burlington**	Pets: **No**
No. of Rooms: **1**	Children: **Welcome, over 6**
No. of Private Baths: **1**	Smoking: **No**
Double/pb: **$35**	Social Drinking: **No**
Single/pb: **$25**	Airport/Station Pickup: **Yes**

Leftwich House has the high ceilings and crystal chandeliers typical of the 1920s. The rooms are filled with handicrafts, needlework, and antiques. The guest room has a queen-size bed of cherry wood, floral wallpaper, and an old rocker. Enjoy cookies and tea on arrival and a complimentary evening snack. Morning coffee, homemade breads, and omelettes are served on the porch in season. Your hostess will gladly point the way to Burlington, with its 200 outlet stores. Historic Alamanace Battleground is 10 miles away.

Greenwood ✪
P.O. BOX 6948, GREENSBORO, NORTH CAROLINA 27405

Tel: **(919) 656-7908**
Best Time to Call: **Mornings**
Host(s): **Lee and Jo Anne Green**
Location: **1 mi. from US 29**
No. of Rooms: **5**
No. of Private Baths: **1**
Max. No. Sharing Bath: **4**
Double/pb: **$45**
Single/pb: **$30**
Double/sb: **$35**
Single/sb: **$25**

Suites: **$80**
Open: **All year**
Reduced Rates: **Weekly; monthly; seniors**
Breakfast: **Continental**
Credit Cards: **MC, VISA, AMEX**
Pets: **Sometimes**
Children: **Welcome**
Smoking: **Permitted**
Social Drinking: **Permitted**

In the center of this 15-acre property are a pool and patio. Inside the house, the decor includes wood carvings and art from all over the world. Guests are welcome to relax by the fireside and enjoy wine or soft drinks. Breakfast features fresh fruit, cereals, breads, and jam. Golf, tennis, boating, and hiking are nearby, in Bryan Park. UNC-Greensboro is nearby.

Havenshire Inn
ROUTE 4, BOX 455, HENDERSONVILLE, NORTH CAROLINA 28739

Tel: **(704) 692-4097**
Host(s): **Cindy Findley, Kay Coppock**
Location: **20 mi. from Asheville**
No. of Rooms: **6**
No. of Private Baths: **2**

Max. No. Sharing Bath: **4**
Double/pb: **$60**
Single/pb: **$45**
Double/sb: **$60**
Single/sb: **$45**

Open: **Apr. 15–Oct. 31**
Reduced Rates: **After 2 nights**
Breakfast: **Continental**
Credit Cards: **MC, VISA**
Pets: **No**

Children: **Welcome, over 10**
Smoking: **Permitted**
Social Drinking: **Permitted**
Airport/Station Pickup: **Yes**
Foreign Languages: **Spanish**

Located on the French Broad River, this restored English home was built in 1880. The house is surrounded by 40 acres of magnificent landscaping and boasts a pond. The Carl Sandburg Home, Biltmore House, Pisgah National Forest, and the Blue Ridge Mountain Parkway are all within a 20-minute drive. Cindy and Kay will direct you to the best restaurants to suit your palate and purse.

Ye Olde Cherokee Inn
MILE POST 8, BEACH ROAD, KILL DEVIL HILLS, NORTH CAROLINA 27948

Tel: **(919) 441-6127**
Host(s): **Robert and Phyllis Combs**
Location: **80 mi. S of Norfolk, Virginia**
No. of Rooms: **7**
No. of Private Baths: **7**
Double/pb: **$35–$65**
Single/pb: **$35–$65**
Open: **Mar. 1–Dec. 31**

Reduced Rates: **March, Nov.**
Breakfast: **Continental**
Credit Cards: **AMEX, MC, VISA**
Pets: **No**
Children: **Welcome, over 12**
Smoking: **Permitted**
Social Drinking: **Permitted**

Situated 600 feet from the Atlantic Ocean, on the Outer Banks of North Carolina, this pink beach cottage has big porches for relaxing, with an interior that is cozy and restful. It's close to the Wright Brothers Monument, Jockey Ridge Sand Dunes, and Roanoke Island. Robert and Phyllis are genealogy buffs.

Kings Arms Inn ○
212 POLLACK STREET, P.O. BOX 1085, NEW BERN, NORTH CAROLINA 28560

Tel: **(919) 638-4409**
Host(s): **The Thomas, Paramore and Peterson families**
No. of Rooms: **8**
No. of Private Baths: **8**
Double/pb: **$58**
Single/pb: **$52**

Open: **All year**
Breakfast: **Continental**
Credit Cards: **AMEX, MC, VISA**
Pets: **Sometimes**
Children: **Welcome (crib)**
Smoking: **Permitted**
Social Drinking: **Permitted**

The Kings Arms is named for an old town tavern, said to have hosted members of the First Continental Congress. The Inn boasts its own historic significance, as many of its rooms date back to the early 1800s. Today its rooms are available to those seeking superior accommodations in the historic district. The bedrooms have fireplaces, antiques, brass, canopied or poster beds, plus color TV. Homemade biscuits and assorted sweets are brought to guests each morning. Your hosts will gladly direct you to the waterfront, Tryon Palace, and fine restaurants.

Beach House
BOX 443, OCRACOKE, NORTH CAROLINA 27960

Tel: **(919) 928-6471**
Best Time to Call: **4–10 PM**
Host(s): **Carol Beach**
Location: **On State Highway 12**
No. of Rooms: **2**
Max. No. Sharing Bath: **6**
Double/sb: **$40**

Open: **Apr. 1–Sept. 30**
Breakfast: **Full**
Pets: **No**
Children: **Welcome**
Smoking: **Permitted**
Social Drinking: **Permitted**
Airport/Station Pickup: **Yes**

This beach cottage has an old-fashioned front porch with gingerbread details. It offers a fine view of the harbor. Inside, the furnishings are comfortable, some dating back to the 1930s. Your hosts prepare homemade breads, preserves, and eggs for breakfast. They will be happy to advise on the sights of the Cape Hatteras National Seashore. Ocracoke is an island reached by ferry or private plane.

Mountain Key Lodge ✪
15 SEVENSPRINGS ROAD, PISGAH FOREST, NORTH CAROLINA 28768

Tel: **(704) 884-7400; (803) 232-7400**
Host(s): **Daniel Stewart and Debbie Harbinson**
Location: **35 mi. SW of Asheville**
No. of Rooms: **5**
No. of Private Baths: **3**
Max. No. Sharing Bath: **5**
Double/pb: **$56**
Single/pb: **$28**
Double/sb: **$56**

Single/sb: **$28**
Suites: **$112**
Open: **Apr. 1–Oct. 31**
Breakfast: **Full**
Credit Cards: **MC, VISA**
Pets: **No**
Children: **Welcome, over 6**
Smoking: **No**
Social Drinking: **Permitted**
Airport/Station Pickup: **Yes**

Mountain Key Lodge is a white frame country farmhouse overlooking Pisgah National Forest. The house was built in the late 19th century of walnut and chestnut from a nearby mountain. Inside, the house looks as it might have in the 1800s, with period pieces in the bedrooms and parlors. Your hosts provide soft drinks and afternoon snacks. Brevard Music Center, Biltmore House, and hiking are some area attractions.

Wilson's Guest House ✪
P.O. BOX 47, CIRCLE STREET, ROBBINSVILLE, NORTH CAROLINA 28771

Tel: **(704) 479-8679**
Host(s): **Mellie and Thomas Wilson**
Location: **2 blocks from Hwy. 129**
No. of Rooms: **6**
No. of Private Baths: **2**
Max. No. Sharing Bath: **5**
Double/pb: **$20**
Single/pb: **$16**
Double/sb: **$18**

Single/sb: **$16**
Open: **Apr. 1–Sept. 30**
Reduced Rates: **10%, seniors**
Breakfast: **Continental**
Pets: **Sometimes**
Children: **Welcome**
Smoking: **Permitted**
Social Drinking: **No**

Flowers and shrubs surround this comfortable porched home. Your cordial hosts, Mellie and Thomas, look forward to welcoming you to the heart of Graham County. There's much to see and do nearby, including the 3,800-acre Joyce Kilmer Memorial Forest and the Great Smoky Mountains. Several lakes offer backpacking, boating, fishing, or just a shady rest for reading and relaxing. It's only 60 miles to Knoxville.

Mill Farm Inn ✪
P.O. BOX 1251, TRYON, NORTH CAROLINA 28782

Tel: **(704) 859-6992**
Best Time to Call: **Mornings**
Host(s): **Chip and Penny Kessler**
Location: **45 mi. SE of Asheville**
No. of Rooms: **8**
No. of Private Baths: **8**
Double/pb: **$48**
Single/pb: **$40**

Suites: **$80–90**
Open: **Mar. 1–Nov. 30**
Breakfast: **Continental**
Pets: **No**
Children: **Welcome**
Smoking: **Permitted**
Social Drinking: **Permitted**
Foreign Languages: **French**

The Pacolet River flows past the edge of this three-and-one-half-acre property in the foothills of the Blue Ridge Mountains. Sitting porches and the living room with fireplace are fine spots to relax. A hearty breakfast of fresh fruit, cereal, specialty breads, and preserves is served daily. Your hosts offer kitchen privileges and will advise you on nearby dining.

Anderson Guest House ✪
520 ORANGE STREET, WILMINGTON, NORTH CAROLINA 28401

Tel: **(919) 343-8128**
Best Time to Call: **8 AM–5 PM**
Host(s): **Landon and Connie Anderson**
No. of Rooms: **2**
No. of Private Baths: **2**
Double/pb: **$55**
Single/pb: **$50**

Open: **All year**
Breakfast: **Full**
Pets: **Sometimes**
Children: **Welcome**
Smoking: **Permitted**
Social Drinking: **Permitted**
Airport/Station Pickup: **Yes**

This 19th-century town house has a private guest house overlooking a garden. The bedrooms have ceiling fans, fireplaces, and air-conditioning. Enjoy cool drinks upon arrival and a liqueur before bed. Breakfast specialties are eggs Mornay, blueberry cobbler, and crepes. Your hostess can point out the sights of this historic town and direct you to the beaches.

Mill Farm Inn

NORTH DAKOTA

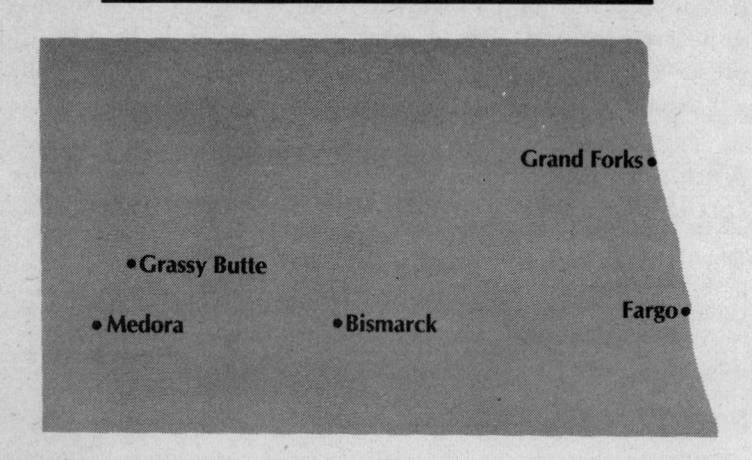

Long X Trail Ranch ⊙
GRASSY BUTTE, NORTH DAKOTA 58634

Tel: (701) 842-2128
Host(s): **Merv and Doreen Wike**
Location: **60 mi. SE of Williston on Hwy. 85**
No. of Rooms: **6**
No. of Private Baths: **6**
Double/pb: **$32**
Single/pb: **$29**

Open: **All year**
Reduced Rates: **Weekly; families**
Breakfast: **Full**
Other Meals: **Available**
Pets: **Sometimes**
Children: **Welcome**
Smoking: **Permitted**
Social Drinking: **Permitted**

Soothe your jangled nerves and treat yourself to a respite in the wide open spaces. The only jangle here is that of spurs as you and your new friends embark upon a trail ride or pack trip into the surrounding Badlands country. Merv and Doreen's dude ranch is a typical western environment, clean, quiet, and most hospitable, without frills or pretense. Their ranch, on the Little Missouri River, adjoins the northern part of the Theodore Roosevelt National Park where, on summer evenings, you're sure to enjoy the outdoor drama and music performances. Your hosts will be happy to arrange a stagecoach ride or direct you to historic restorations and museums nearby. Please note that meals are served only from Memorial Day through Labor Day.

The Rough Riders
MEDORA, NORTH DAKOTA 58645

Tel: **(701) 623-4422**	Breakfast: **Continental**
Host(s): **John Conway**	Other Meals: **Available**
Location: **135 mi. W of Bismarck**	Credit Cards: **AMEX**
No. of Rooms: **9**	Pets: **No**
No. of Baths: **9**	Children: **Welcome**
Double/pb: **$43**	Smoking: **Permitted**
Single/pb: **$37**	Social Drinking: **Permitted**
Open: **May 24–Sept. 2**	Airport/Station Pickup: **Yes**

Located at the center of town, the hotel is constructed inside and out of rough lumber. The facade bears the many branding marks of cattle barons, including that of Theodore Roosevelt. The "cow-town" atmosphere has been retained, down to the wooden sidewalk. The center staircase leads to the guest quarters, which are furnished with antiques. Don't miss the Outdoor Memorial Musical, an extravaganza complete with horses, stagecoaches, and a rousing tribute to Teddy Roosevelt. The Museum of Wildlife, the Doll House Museum, and the spectacular beauty of the Badlands will make your visit memorable.

For key to listings, see inside front or back cover.

✪ This star means that rates are guaranteed through December 31, 1985 to any guest making a reservation as a result of reading about the B&B in *BED & BREAKFAST U.S.A.*—1985 edition.

Please enclose a self-addressed, stamped, business-sized envelope when contacting reservation services.

For more details on what you can expect in a B&B, see Chapter 1.

Always mention *Bed & Breakfast USA* when making reservations!

OHIO

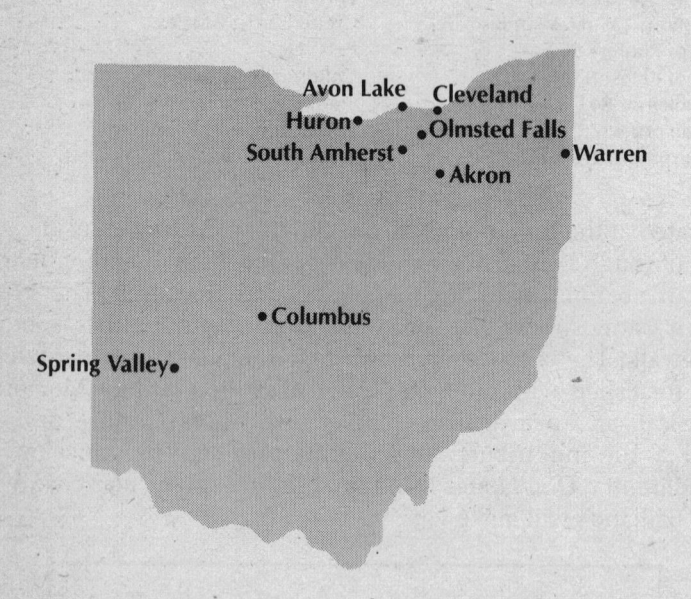

Portage House ✪
601 COPLEY ROAD, STATE ROUTE 162, AKRON, OHIO 44320

Tel: **(216) 535-9236**
Best Time to Call: **Before 11 PM**
Host(s): **Jeanne and Harry Pinnick**
Location: **2 mi. from I-77**
No. of Rooms: **5**
No. of Private Baths: **1½**
Max. No. Sharing Bath: **7**
Double/pb: **$24**
Single/pb: **$18**
Double/sb: **$24**
Single/sb: **$18**
Open: **All year**
Reduced Rates: **$3 off 2nd night**
Breakfast: **Full**
Other Meals: **Available**
Pets: **Yes**
Children: **Welcome (crib)**
Smoking: **Permitted**
Social Drinking: **Permitted**
Foreign Languages: **French, Spanish**

Steeped in history, nestled in a parklike setting, this gracious Tudor home dates back to 1917. There is a stone wall down the street that was the western boundary of the United States in 1785.

Harry is a physics professor at the university, and Jean is a gracious hostess. The coffee pot is always on, refreshments are available, and if bread is being baked, you'll be given some with butter. It's close to Akron University.

Williams House ✪
249 VINEWOOD, AVON LAKE, OHIO 44012

Tel: **(216) 933-5089**	Open: **Closed Christmas, Easter weeks**
Best Time to Call: **4–9 PM**	Reduced Rates: **10%, seniors**
Host(s): **Edred and Margaret Williams**	Breakfast: **Full**
Location: **20 mi. W of Cleveland**	Pets: **No**
No. of Rooms: **1**	Children: **No**
No. of Private Baths: **1**	Smoking: **No**
Double/pb: **$40**	Social Drinking: **Permitted**
Single/pb: **$25**	Airport/Station Pickup: **Yes**

Located a mile from the Lake Erie public beach, Edred and Margaret live in a quiet, residential neighborhood. The house is comfortably decorated in a harmonious blend of styles. They serve beverages and snacks upon your arrival, and will help you plan a pleasant visit. Breakfast is a dandy, from juice to cereal to eggs to bacon to coffee or tea.

Private Lodgings
P.O. BOX 18590, CLEVELAND, OHIO 44118

Tel: (216) 321-3213	Rate: (Single/Double):
Best Time to Call: 9 AM–5 PM	Modest: $20 $30
Coordinator: Jane McCarroll	Average: $25 $35
States/Regions Covered: Cleveland	Luxury: $35 $65
	Credit Cards: No

This is a city with world-renowned cultural and biomedical resources, as well as major corporations and recreational areas. Special attention is given to the needs of relocating and visiting professionals, out-patients, and relatives of hospital in-patients, as well as vacationers. Every effort is made to accommodate persons with physical handicaps. Discounted rates are provided for extended stays. Case Western Reserve, John Carroll, and Cleveland State Universities are convenient to the B&Bs.

The Sarah Frisch House ✪
1564 SOUTH TAYLOR ROAD, CLEVELAND, OHIO 44118

Tel: (216) 321-5694	Single/sb: $10
Best Time to Call: 5–8 PM	Open: All year
Host(s): Sarah Frisch	Reduced Rates: Weekly
Location: 4 mi. from I-90	Breakfast: $1.50
No. of Rooms: 2	Other Meals: Available
No. of Private Baths: 1	Pets: Sometimes
Max. No. Sharing Bath: 2	Children: Welcome
Double/pb: $20	Smoking: No
Single/pb: $15	Social Drinking: Permitted
Double/sb: $15	Airport/Station Pickup: Yes

Sarah's brick-and-shingle, comfortably furnished bungalow has a large yard and pretty garden. Sarah will make you feel at home. It is convenient to good shopping, fine restaurants, sports facilities, and all the cultural activities that Cleveland is famous for.

The Tudor House
P.O. BOX 18590, CLEVELAND, OHIO 44118

Tel: (216) 321-3213	No. of Rooms: 2
Host(s): Jane McCarroll	No. of Private Baths: 2
Location: 5 mi. from Rt. 271	Double/pb: $40–$50

Single/pb: $35–$45
Suite: $60
Open: **All year**
Breakfast: **Full**

Pets: **No**
Children: **Welcome**
Smoking: **Permitted**
Social Drinking: **Permitted**

This lovely 1920s Tudor-style house is listed in the National Register of Historic Places. Situated on an acre of landscaped grounds, it is within minutes of Cleveland's major business district as well as the cultural, academic, and biomedical establishments. Fine restaurants and shops are within easy walking distance. The house is attractively furnished with period furniture and antiques. Your hosts are a professional couple who have traveled widely and enjoy sharing their home and conversation with their guests. Case Western Reserve and John Carroll Universities are nearby.

Columbus Bed & Breakfast
763 S. THIRD STREET, GERMAN VILLAGE, COLUMBUS, OHIO 43206

Tel: **(614) 443-3680 or 444-8888**
Coordinator(s): **Fred Holdridge, Howard Burns**
States/Regions Covered: **Columbus**

Rates (Single/Double):
   Average: **$26**   **$36**
   Luxury: **$30**   **$40**
Credit Cards: **No**

Historic German Village is a registered National Historic Area. It's close to downtown Columbus but a century away in character. Small brick houses, brick sidewalks and streets, and wrought-iron fences combine to create an Old World atmosphere. Charming shops and restaurants are within easy walking distance.

The Beach House
213 KIWANIS AVENUE, CHASKA BEACH, HURON, OHIO 44839

Tel: **(419) 433-5839**
Best Time to Call: **Early AM**
Host(s): **Donna Lendrum**
Location: **60 mi. W of Cleveland**
No. of Rooms: **3**
Max. No. Sharing Bath: **6**
Double/sb: **$50**

Single/sb: **$50**
Open: **May–Sept.**
Breakfast: **Continental**
Pets: **No**
Children: **Welcome, over 12**
Smoking: **Permitted**
Social Drinking: **Permitted**

Located on the shore of Lake Erie, this spacious home is tastefully furnished with antiques. The guest rooms are in a separate wing of the house with a private entrance. You will enjoy the private sandy beach, the local fishing pier, the summer theater, or a side trip to Milan with its antiques shops and museums. Depending on the weather, Donna serves breakfast on the porch overlooking the lake or around the cozy kitchen table. A guest refrigerator and picnic table are available.

Hamilton B. Maxon House
6651 COLUMBIA ROAD, OLMSTED FALLS, OHIO 44138

Tel: **(216) 235-5204**
Best Time to Call: **Evenings**
Host(s): **Otto and Judith Ramlow**
Location: **20 mi. SW of Cleveland**
No. of Rooms: **2**
Max. No. Sharing Bath: **4**
Double/sb: **$36**
Single/sb: **$32**

Open: **All year**
Reduced Rates: **10%, seniors**
Breakfast: **Continental**
Pets: **Sometimes**
Children: **Welcome, over 15**
Smoking: **Permitted**
Social Drinking: **Permitted**
Airport/Station Pickup: **Yes**

This Victorian farmhouse is set on two acres next to Sunset Memorial Park. The house was built in 1872 and has been lovingly remodeled. The kitchen, furnished with a loveseat and chairs, is decorated with many antiques. One can see the 19th-century theme throughout the house in dark-toned wallpaper, handmade wreaths, family pieces, and some lucky auction finds. Share a glass of wine with your hosts while they point out interesting places to visit and dine. Baldwin Wallace College is 5 miles away.

Birch Way Villa ⚬
111 WHITE BIRCH WAY, SOUTH AMHERST, OHIO 44001

Tel: **(216) 986-2090**
Host(s): **Marjorie and Isaac Simon**
No. of Rooms: **3**
No. of Private Baths: **2**
Max. No. Sharing Bath: **3**
Double/pb: **$35**
Double/sb: **$35**
Open: **Dec. 31–Feb. 28; Apr. 1–Nov. 15**

Reduced Rates: **Seniors; families**
Breakfast: **Full**
Other Meals: **Available**
Pets: **No**
Children: **Welcome (crib)**
Smoking: **Permitted**
Social Drinking: **Permitted**
Airport/Station Pickup: **Yes**

Marjorie and Isaac's up-to-date home is part of a 30-acre wooded estate with a 10-acre spring-fed lake. The house is comfortably furnished and air-conditioned in summer. The living room has a fireplace and piano for your enjoyment. There are outdoor games, a tennis court, and basketball to keep you in shape. It's only 30 miles to Cleveland; Oberlin College is close by.

3B's Bed 'n' Breakfast ⚬
103 RACE STREET, SPRING VALLEY, OHIO 45370

Tel: **(513) 862-4241 or 878-9944**
Best Time to Call: **After 5 PM**
Host(s): **Pat and Herb Boettcher**
Location: **16 mi. SE of Dayton**
No. of Rooms: **3**
Max. No. Sharing Bath: **4**
Double/sb: **$29**
Single/sb: **$24**
Open: **All year**

Reduced Rates: **25% weekly**
Breakfast: **Full**
Other Meals: **Available**
Pets: **Sometimes**
Children: **Welcome, over 4**
Smoking: **Permitted**
Social Drinking: **Permitted**
Airport/Station Pickup: **Yes**

This restored 19th-century farmhouse is a great place to unwind. The rooms are spacious and airy, and abound with family heirlooms and homemade crafts. The quilts on the beds are handmade. Nearby attractions include historic Lebanon, Kings Island,

Dayton's Air Force Museum, and Sugarcreek Ski Hills at Bellbrook. Pat and Herb are retired from the Air Force and look forward to visiting with you. Wright State University is nearby.

Shirlee's Chambers ✪
535 ADELAIDE NORTH EAST, WARREN, OHIO 44483

Tel: (216) 372-1118
Host(s): **Shirlee and Wayne Chambers**
Location: **7 mi. from I-80**
No. of Rooms: **3**
Max. No. Sharing Bath: **3**
Double/sb: **$30**
Single/sb: **$22**
Open: **All year**

Reduced Rates: **10%, seniors**
Breakfast: **Full**
Pets: **No**
Children: **No**
Smoking: **Permitted**
Social Drinking: **Permitted**
Airport/Station Pickup: **Yes**

Shirlee welcomes you to her colonial home with wine, cheese, or tea and cookies. Her guest rooms are comfortably furnished. Start the day with a French mushroom omelette, the specialty of the house. Your hosts can direct you to the many nearby antique shops. Local attractions include summer theater and fine dining.

Hattle House ✪
502 NORTH KING STREET, XENIA, OHIO 45385

Tel: (513) 372-2315
Host(s): **Mary and Bill Hattle**
No. of Rooms: **3**
No. of Private Baths: **3**
Double/pb: **$35**
Single/pb: **$30**

Open: **All year**
Breakfast: **Continental**
Pets: **No**
Children: **Welcome (crib)**
Smoking: **Permitted**
Social Drinking: **Permitted**

This 100-year-old Victorian home is furnished with fine period antiques. Bedroom accommodations are large and comfortable. Xenia is the home of the epic outdoor drama "Blue Jacket," shown June through September. Other attractions include Dayton Air Force Museum, Kings Island, Cincinnati Riverfront Stadium and Zoo, and numerous state parks. A treat for history buffs is a visit to Lebanon or Waynesville, the antiques capitals of the Midwest.

OKLAHOMA

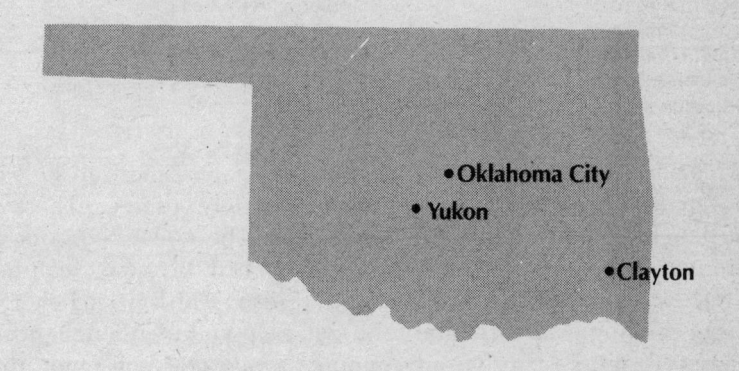

Clayton Country Inn ✪
ROUTE 1, BOX 8, HIGHWAY 271, CLAYTON, OKLAHOMA 74536

Tel: (918) 569-4165 or 627-1956
Host(s): **Jean Houze and Betty Lundgren**
Location: **140 mi. SE of Tulsa**
No. of Rooms: **9**
No. of Private Baths: **9**
Double/pb: **$26**
Single/pb: **$22**
Guest Cottage: **$28–$40; sleeps 2–4**

Open: **All year**
Breakfast: **$3**
Other Meals: **Available**
Credit Cards: **MC, VISA**
Pets: **No**
Children: **Welcome**
Smoking: **Permitted**
Social Drinking: **Permitted**

Perched on a hill amid 135 acres and surrounded by the Kiamichi Mountains is this 40 year old, two-story, stone and wood inn. It's furnished in a simple, traditional style with a beamed ceiling and fireplace. The restaurant on-premises is noted for "down home cooking." Bass fishing at Lake Sardis is two miles away, and an 18,000 acre game preserve is just across the highway. Feel free to bring your horse and enjoy trail rides under the vast western skies.

Tulp House
1210 KOUBA DRIVE, YUKON, OKLAHOMA 73099

Tel: **(405) 354-3280**
Host(s): **Margaret and John Tulp**
Location: **12 mi. W of Oklahoma City**
No. of Rooms: **1**
No. of Private Baths: **1**
Double/pb: **$30**
Single/pb: **$20**
Open: **All year**

Breakfast: **Continental**
Pets: **No**
Children: **No**
Smoking: **Permitted**
Social Drinking: **Permitted**
Airport/Station Pickup: **Yes**
Foreign Languages: **French, Spanish**

This two-story Dutch colonial furnished in early American style is located on a residential street lined with stately old trees. There is a delightful patio and garden out back. The guest bedroom is immaculate and has a comfortable double bed. Breakfast features fresh-ground coffee and homemade bread; use the kitchen for light cooking. Margaret and John will help you plan a delightful stay. Oklahoma City is only minutes away; you will enjoy the Western flavor of the area. Don't miss the Cowboy Hall of Fame, Indian City (site of the Artifacts of the Five Civilized Tribes), and a tour of the Oklahoma State Capitol, with operating oil well and the Pioneer Museum.

For key to listings, see inside front or back cover.

✪ This star means that rates are guaranteed through December 31, 1985 to any guest making a reservation as a result of reading about the *B&B in BED & BREAKFAST U.S.A.*—1985 edition.

Please enclose a self-addressed, stamped, business-sized envelope when contacting reservation services.

For more details on what you can expect in a B&B, see Chapter 1.

Always mention *Bed & Breakfast USA* when making reservations!

OREGON

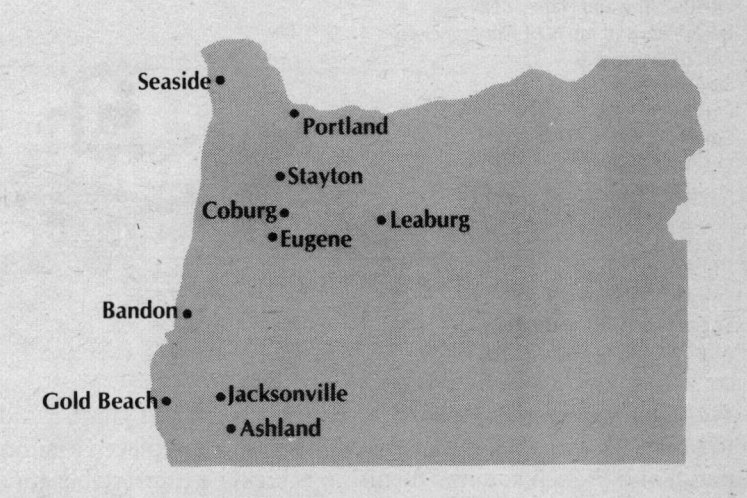

Northwest Bed and Breakfast
7707 SW LOCUST STREET, PORTLAND, OREGON 97223

Tel: (503) 246-8366
Best Time to Call: **8:30 AM–6 PM**
Coordinator: **Laine Friedman and Gloria Shaich**
States/Regions Covered: **Washington, Oregon, California, Idaho, Montana, Nevada, Illinois, Wyoming;** **Canada—Alberta, British Columbia; United Kingdom**
Rates (Single/Double):
　Average: $18–$30　$24–$45
　Luxury: $35–$55　$50–$65
Credit Cards: **No**

Laine and Gloria have a network of hundreds of host homes throughout the Pacific Northwest and Canada. They charge an annual membership fee of $15 (individual) or $20 (two or more in the same family). Upon joining, you will receive a directory of all the lodgings, which range from city to suburban to rural to coast, mountains, and desert. A variety of package tours, complete with car rental if required, can be arranged with stops at suitable B&Bs along the way.

Chanticleer ✪
120 GRESHAM STREET, ASHLAND, OREGON 97520

Tel: **(503) 482-1919**
Best Time to Call: **9 AM–5 PM**
Host(s): **Jim and Nancy Beaver**
Location: **350 mi. N of San Francisco**
No. of Rooms: **6**
No. of Private Baths: **6**
Double/pb: **$64–$69**
Single/pb: **$59–$64**
Open: **All year**
Reduced Rates: **25% Nov.–Feb.**
Breakfast: **Full**
Pets: **No**
Children: **Welcome**
Smoking: **Permitted**
Social Drinking: **Permitted**
Airport/Station Pickup: **Yes**

The Chanticleer overlooks Bear Creek Valley and the Cascade foothills. A large living room with a stone fireplace, a sunny patio, and French country furnishings create a comfortable atmosphere. Guests are welcome to juices, coffee, and sherry. Some of the specialty breakfast items include, Italian roast coffee, blintzes, and cheese-baked eggs. Shops, restaurants, and the site of the Shakespeare Festival are a short walk away. Mount Ashland ski area and the Rogue River are a 30-minute drive from the house. Southern Oregon State College is nearby.

The Coach House Inn ✪
70 COOLIDGE STREET, ASHLAND, OREGON 97520

Tel: **(503) 482-2257**
Best Time to Call: **Evenings**
Host(s): **Pamela and Jack Evans**
No. of Rooms: **3**
Max. No. Sharing Bath: **6**
Double/sb: **$43**
Single/sb: **$38**
Open: **Feb. 20–Oct. 31**
Breakfast: **Continental**
Pets: **No**
Children: **Welcome, over 12**
Smoking: **No**
Social Drinking: **Permitted**
Airport/Station Pickup: **Yes**
Foreign Languages: **German**

The guest rooms at this Victorian inn are decorated with antiques and offer mountain views. Enjoy soaking in the claw-foot bathtub, or a game of croquet on the spacious lawn. Breakfast features fresh fruit cobblers and homemade jams. Guests are welcome to join daily picnic tours of the local creamery and vineyards. The Shakespeare Theatre, historic homes, and antique shops are all nearby.

Neil Creek House O
341 MOWETZA DRIVE, ASHLAND, OREGON 97520

Tel: **(503) 482-1334**
Best Time to Call: **After 10 AM**
Host(s): **Edith and Thomas Heumann**
No. of Rooms: **2**
No. of Private Baths: **2**
Double/pb: **$65**
Single/pb: **$60**
Open: **All year**
Reduced Rates: **10%, weekly; $10 less Nov.–Feb.**

Breakfast: **Full**
Pets: **No**
Children: **No**
Smoking: **Permitted**
Social Drinking: **Permitted**
Airport/Station Pickup: **Yes**
Foreign Languages: **French, German**

This country house is set on five wooded acres with a duck pond for boating. Guests are welcome to relax by the swimming pool or on the deck. Wine, sherry, tea, and coffee are served. Breakfast treats may include homemade jams and syrups, ranch eggs, sausage, bacon, or Ebelskivers. The guest rooms overlook the creek or mountains, and are furnished with antiques and 19th-century art. Skiing, sailing, river rafting, and Shakespeare performances are nearby.

Royal Carter House O
514 SISKIYOU BOULEVARD, ASHLAND, OREGON 97520

Tel: **(503) 482-5623**
Best Time to Call: **Mornings**
Host(s): **Alyce and Roy Levy**
No. of Rooms: **4**
No. of Private Baths: **4**
Double/pb: **$45–$55**
Suites: **$60**

Open: **All year**
Breakfast: **Full**
Pets: **No**
Children: **Welcome, over 7**
Smoking: **No**
Social Drinking: **Permitted**
Airport/Station Pickup: **Yes**

This beautiful 1909 home is listed in the National Historic Register. Located four blocks from Ashland's famous Shakespeare Theatre, it is surrounded by lovely old trees in a parklike setting. It is suitably modernized but retains the original room structure. Alyce has added decorator touches of vintage hats and old periodicals to the antique furnishings. The Levys have traveled extensively abroad and will share stories of their experiences with you. Southern Oregon State College is four blocks away.

Shutes Lazy "S" Farm B&B ✪
200 MOWETZA DRIVE, ASHLAND, OREGON 97520

Tel: (503) 482-5498	Single/pb: $45
Best Time to Call: **Before 9 AM; after 7 PM**	Open: **All year**
	Breakfast: **Full**
Host(s): **Denny and Rodna Shutes**	Pets: **No**
No. of Rooms: 1	Children: **No**
No. of Private Baths: 1	Smoking: **No**
Double/pb: $47.50	Social Drinking: **Permitted**

Denny and Rodna have a ranch-style home with a long porch—perfect for taking in the fabulous mountain views. You may observe or participate in feeding the kids and lambs. Breakfast is prepared from the organically grown food that they raise on their five-acre farm. Rodna is a retired college drama instructor; Denny is a retired college instructor of ecology and geography. Complimentary beverages are served on arrival and after an evening at the famed Shakespeare Theatre. A two-day minimum stay is requested.

Spindrift Bed & Breakfast ✪
2990 BEACH LOOP ROAD, BANDON, OREGON 97411

Tel: (503) 347-2275	Single/sb: $35
Best Time to Call: **8 AM–1 PM**	Open: **All year**
Host(s): **Don and Robbie Smith**	Reduced Rates: **10%, Nov. 1–Mar. 1**
Location: **1 mi. from Rte. 101**	Breakfast: **Full**
No. of Rooms: 2	Credit Cards: **MC, VISA**
No. of Private Baths: 1	Pets: **Sometimes**
Max. No. Sharing Bath: 3	Children: **Welcome**
Double/pb: $45	Smoking: **Permitted**
Single/pb: $40	Social Drinking: **Permitted**
Double/sb: $40	Airport/Station Pickup: **Yes**

Enjoy the breathtaking beauty of the Oregon Coast from this lovely home, perched on a bluff just 40 feet above a long, sandy beach and framed by massive offshore rock formations. Uninterrupted vistas are yours from floor-to-ceiling windows, or from the deck with its direct beach access. Relax in the sunken living room with its vaulted beamed ceiling and inviting fireplace. Breakfast is a real feast, and afternoon refreshments are offered by Don and Robbie.

Wheeler's Bed & Breakfast O
BOX 8201, COBURG, OREGON 97401

Tel: **(503) 344-1366**
Host(s): **Joe and Isabel Wheeler**
Location: **7 mi. N of Eugene**
No. of Rooms: **3**
Max. No. Sharing Bath: **5**
Double/sb: **$30**
Single/sb: **$25**
Open: **Mar. 1–Dec. 31**

Breakfast: **Continental**
Other Meals: **Available**
Pets: **Sometimes**
Children: **No**
Smoking: **Permitted**
Social Drinking: **Permitted**
Airport/Station Pickup: **Yes**
Foreign Languages: **Spanish**

Joe and Isabel welcome you to their historic town which offers a unique atmosphere of antique shops and century-old homes. Whether you stroll the few blocks to the world renowned Coburg Inn (circa 1857) which boasts its own ghost, or bicycle down the country lanes, your stay will be rewarding. The guest quarters are separate from the rest of the house, offering complete privacy. Visit in the living room, use the washer-dryer, and make yourselves "at home."

Copper Windmill Ranch O
33263 DILLARD ROAD, EUGENE, OREGON 97405

Tel: **(503) 686-2194**
Host(s): **Bill and Lyn Neel**
Location: **6 mi. S of Eugene**
No. of Rooms: **1**
No. of Private Baths: **1**
Double/pb: **$48**
Single/pb: **$35**
Open: **All year**
Breakfast: **Full**

Other Meals: **Available**
Credit Cards: **MC, VISA**
Pets: **No**
Children: **Welcome, over 3**
Smoking: **Permitted**
Social Drinking: **Permitted**
Airport/Station Pickup: **Yes**
Foreign Languages: **Spanish**

You will enjoy your visit on this 80-acre ranch if Bill and Lyn have their say. The house is a replica of the original homestead, including hand-hewn timber beams and an antique cast-iron kitchen stove for cozy breakfasts. There's a small pond with a rowboat for your pleasure. Trips on the McKenzie River can be arranged. Most of the food served is raised on the ranch, and you can collect your own eggs for breakfast. Your horse may come along too. Stall and pasturing cost $8. The University of Oregon is nearby.

Griswold Bed & Breakfast ○
522 W. BROADWAY, EUGENE, OREGON 97401

Tel: (503) 683-6294
Coordinator: **Phyllis Griswold**
States/Regions Covered: **Eugene, Coburg, Elmira, Leaburg**

Rates (Single/Double):
   Average: **$20–$60**   **$30–$80**
Credit Cards: **No**

Nestled in Willamette Valley between the mountains and the ocean, Eugene is the Jogging Capital of the U.S. The miles of bicycle and pedestrian trails lead to the University of Oregon or to fabulous shopping. The Performing Arts Center is a main attraction.

The Cottage ○
95629 JERRYS FLAT ROAD, GOLD BEACH, OREGON 97444

Tel: (503) 247-2335, 6745
Best Time to Call: **Early morning, early evening**
Host(s): **Forrest and Lucille Pendergast**
Location: **3 mi. from Rt. 101**
No. of Rooms: **2**
Double/pb: **$35**
Single/pb: **$30**

Guest Cottage: **$40–$45**
Open: **All year**
Breakfast: **Full**
Pets: **Sometimes**
Children: **Welcome**
Smoking: **No**
Social Drinking: **Permitted**
Foreign Languages: **French**

This homey cottage is situated on the south bank of the Rogue River, near the beach and all the river recreations. Furnished with memorabilia collected from the hosts' travels to Europe and China, each room has a beautiful river view. The guest room in the house has its own entrance; the cottage is very private. You are welcome to use the barbecue and picnic table; complimentary wine and coffee are available.

Livingston Mansion ✪
4132 LIVINGSTON ROAD, BOX 1476, JACKSONVILLE, OREGON 97530

Tel: **(503) 899-7107**
Best Time to Call: **Early AM**
Host(s): **Wally and Sherry Lossing**
No. of Rooms: **6**
No. of Private Baths: **4**
Max. No. Sharing Bath: **4**
Double/pb: **$65–$75**
Single/pb: **$65–$75**
Double/sb: **$45**
Single/sb: **$45**
Suite: **$75**

Open: **All year**
Reduced Rates: **10% Off-season, mid-week**
Breakfast: **Full**
Credit Cards: **MC, VISA**
Pets: **No**
Children: **Welcome**
Smoking: **Permitted**
Social Drinking: **Permitted**
Airport/Station Pickup: **Yes**

This stately inn dates to the turn of the century. The porch, pool, patio, and the window seats inside are fine spots to relax. Wine, snacks, and sherry are complimentary. Breakfast cookies and eggs prepared in a variety of ways are served each morning. Nearby, you can enjoy skiing, white-water rafting, and performances of Shakespeare. Southern Oregon State College is close by.

Marjon Bed and Breakfast Inn ✪
44975 LEABURG DAM ROAD, LEABURG, OREGON 97489

Tel: **(503) 896-3145**
Host(s): **Margie Haas**
Location: **24 mi. E of Eugene**
No. of Rooms: **2**
No. of Private Baths: **2**
Double/pb: **$60**

Suites: **$80**
Open: **All year**
Reduced Rates: **10% Sun.–Thurs.; weekly**
Breakfast: **Full**
Pets: **No**

Children: **No**
Smoking: **Permitted**

Social Drinking: **Permitted**
Airport/Station Pickup: **Yes**

This cedar chalet is surrounded by rivers, lush woods, and towering mountains. One guest room overlooks a secluded Japanese garden and features a sunken bath. The other has a fish bowl shower and a view of a 100-year-old apple tree. Relax in the living room with its wraparound seating and massive stone fireplace. One of the walls is made entirely of glass with sliding doors that lead to a terrace. A multi-course breakfast is served there on balmy days. Waterfalls, trout fishing, white-water rafting, and skiing are all nearby.

Corbett House B & B ✪
7533 SOUTH WEST CORBETT AVENUE, PORTLAND, OREGON 97219

Tel: (503) 245-2580
Host(s): **Sylvia Malagamba**
Location: **3½ mi. S of Portland**
No. of Rooms: **3**
Max. No. Sharing Bath: **3**
Double/sb: **$35-$45**
Single/sb: **$30-$40**
Open: **All year**

Reduced Rates: **20%, 5 days**
Breakfast: **Continental**
Credit Cards: **AMEX, MC, VISA**
Pets: **No**
Children: **Welcome, over 10**
Smoking: **No**
Social Drinking: **Permitted**

Corbett House is located in a gracious neighborhood, five minutes from downtown. The inn has views of Mount St. Helens, the Willamette River, and Mount Hood. Sixty-year-old hardwood floors, artwork, antiques, and contemporary pieces create a look of casual elegance. Queen, twin, or full-sized beds are available. Your hosts provide robes and hair dryers for your convenience. They will gladly pack you a picnic lunch to take to nearby Riverfront Park. Interesting restaurants and shops are minutes from the inn.

The Riverside Inn Bed & Breakfast ✪
430 SOUTH HOLLADAY, SEASIDE, OREGON 97138

Tel: (503) 738-8254
Best Time to Call: **After 3 PM**

Host(s): **Catherine and Kay Matthias**
Location: **79 mi. W of Portland**

No. of Rooms: 7
No. of Private Baths: 7
Single/pb: **$23**
Suites: **$29–$43**
Open: **All year**
Reduced Rates: **Off-season**

Breakfast: **Continental**
Credit Cards: **MC, VISA**
Pets: **No**
Children: **Welcome (crib)**
Smoking: **Permitted**
Social Drinking: **Permitted**

Situated on the Necanicum River on the northern Oregon coast, the inn is an easy walk to the beach and shops. Furnished with a country flavor, each suite has its own entrance, and television. It is fresh and clean, reminiscent of grandmother's summer cottage. Breakfast is graciously served in the library lounge.

Horncroft ○
42156 KINGSTON LYONS DRIVE, STAYTON, OREGON 97383

Tel: **(503) 769-6287**
Best Time to Call: **Before 9 AM, after 6 PM**
Host(s): **Dorothea and Kenneth Horn**
Location: **17 mi. E of Salem**
No. of Rooms: 3
No. of Private Baths: 1
Max. No. Sharing Bath: 4
Double/pb: **$30**
Single/pb: **$20**

Double/sb: **$25**
Single/sb: **$15**
Open: **All year**
Breakfast: **Full**
Pets: **No**
Children: **Welcome (crib)**
Smoking: **No**
Social Drinking: **Permitted**
Foreign Languages: **German**

This lovely home is situated in the foothills of the Cascade Mountains on the edge of Willamette Valley. In summer, swim in the heated pool or hike on one of the scenic nature paths. The area is dotted with farms, and the valley is abundant in fruits, berries, and vegetables. Willamette and Oregon State universities are nearby. The Mount Jefferson Wilderness hiking area is an hour away.

PENNSYLVANIA

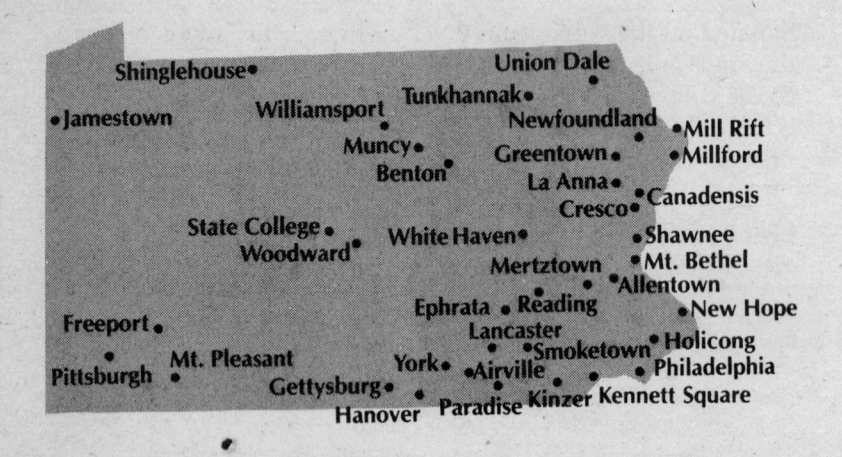

ALLENTOWN AREA

Longswamp Bed and Breakfast
RD 2 BOX 26, MERTZTOWN, PENNSYLVANIA 19539

Tel: (215) 682-6197
Host(s): Elsa Dimick and Dr. Dean Dimick
Location: 12 mi. SW of Allentown
No. of Rooms: 5
No. of Private Baths: 1
Max. No. Sharing Bath: 4
Double/pb: $55
Single/pb: $45
Double/sb: $55
Single/sb: $45
Open: All year
Reduced Rates: 15%, weekly
Breakfast: Full
Pets: No
Children: Welcome, over 8
Smoking: Permitted
Social Drinking: Permitted
Airport/Station Pickup: Yes
Foreign Languages: French

This guest house was originally built around 1750 and served as the first post office in town. The main house, completed in 1863, was a stop on the underground railroad. Today, Longswamp is a comfortable place with high ceilings, antiques, large fireplaces, plants, and bookcases full of reading pleasure. Breakfast specialties include home-dried fruits, *pain perdu*, quiche, and homemade breads. Your hostess offers wine, cheese, and coffee anytime. She will gladly direct you to antiques shops, auction houses, Reading, and the Amish country.

BUCKS COUNTY

Barley Sheaf Farm ☻
ROUTE 202, BOX 66, HOLICONG, PENNSYLVANIA 18928

Tel: (215) 794-5104
Host(s): **Ann and Don Mills**
Location: **40 mi. N of Philadelphia**
No. of Rooms: **10**
No. of Private Baths: **7**
Max. No. Sharing Bath: **6**
Double/pb: **$65**
Single/pb: **$65**
Double/sb: **$55**
Single/sb: **$45–$55**
Suites: **$80**
Open: **Mar. 7–Dec. 16**
Breakfast: **Full**
Pets: **No**
Children: **Welcome, over 8**
Smoking: **Permitted**
Social Drinking: **Permitted**
Airport/Station Pickup: **Yes**

Between New Hope and Doylestown, just around the bend from the antiques stalls and shops of Peddlers' Village, this charming 30-acre farm awaits you. The old stone (circa 1740) house is a National Historic Site. The bank barn, swimming pool, pond, and old trees round out a peaceful setting, the serenity of which may be broken by the sound of sheep in the meadow or the honking of Canada geese. Ann and Don will make you feel welcome.

Pineapple Hill ☻
RD 3, BOX 34C, RIVER ROAD, NEW HOPE, PENNSYLVANIA 18938

Tel: (215) 862-9608
Host(s): **Suzie and Randy Leslie**
Location: **40 mi. N of Philadelphia**
No. of Rooms: **4**
Max. No. Sharing Bath: **4**
Double/sb: **$55**
Single/sb: **$55**
Open: **All year**
Reduced Rates: **$45 Mon.–Thurs.**
Breakfast: **Continental**
Credit Cards: **AMEX**
Pets: **Sometimes**
Children: **Welcome (crib)**
Smoking: **No**
Social Drinking: **Permitted**

The 18-inch walls, fireplace, and traditional woodwork attest to the 18th-century origin of this charming farmhouse. Suzie and Randy have furnished it with family heirlooms and spool and brass beds. An elegant afternoon tea is served in the parlor in winter or at poolside in summer. When you return from the dozens of activities the area offers, relax in front of the fire, read, play backgammon, and visit.

The Wedgwood Bed & Breakfast Inn ✪
111 WEST BRIDGE STREET, NEW HOPE, PENNSYLVANIA 18938

Tel: **(215) 862-2570**
Best Time to Call: **After 10 AM**
Host(s): **Nadine Silnutzer, Carl Glassman**
No. of Rooms: **7**
No. of Private Baths: **3**
Maximum No. Sharing Bath: **4**
Double/pb: **$85**
Single/pb: **$79**
Double/sb: **$65–$75**
Single/sb: **$55–$65**

Suites: **$120**
Open: **All year**
Reduced Rates: **10%, midweek, off-season**
Breakfast: **Continental**
Pets: **Sometimes**
Children: **Welcome**
Smoking: **No**
Social Drinking: **Permitted**
Foreign Languages: **Dutch, Spanish**

Listed in the Historic Register, this gracious 1870 Victorian features a veranda for leisurely relaxing. It is surrounded by manicured lawns. Nadine and Carl take pride in their home, which features guest rooms beautifully furnished with antiques and original artwork and cooled by brass-fitted ceiling fans. You can use their kitchen for light snacks or curl up in the parlor with a book. A complimentary decanter of Amaretto, chocolate mints, plus discounts in many of the local shops are some of the little extras that will make your stay special.

Whitehall Farm
R.D. 2, BOX 250, NEW HOPE, PENNSYLVANIA 18938

Tel: **(215) 598-7945**
Best Time to Call: **8–9 AM**
Host(s): **Joyce Brickman**
No. of Rooms: **9**
No. of Private Baths: **6**
Max. No. Sharing Bath: **2**

Double/pb: **$80–$85**
Double/sb: **$65–$75**
Open: **All year**
Reduced Rates: **Off-season, mid-week**
Breakfast: **Full**
Credit Cards: **MC, VISA**

Pets: **Sometimes**
Children: **Welcome, over 14**
Smoking: **Permitted**

Social Drinking: **Permitted**
Airport/Station Pickup: **Yes**

This is an elegant, plastered stone manor house (circa 1794) set amid towering trees in lush horse country. Four bedrooms have fireplaces. Joyce invites you to use the tennis court and pool, and there's horseback riding too if you wish. You're only minutes from Peddlers' Village and the famed Bucks County Playhouse. Afternoon tea is served daily. The furnishings are both eclectic and comfortable.

CENTRAL PENNSYLVANIA

Rest & Repast Bed & Breakfast Service ✪
P.O. BOX 126, PINE GROVE MILLS, PENNSYLVANIA 16868

Tel: **(814) 238-1484**
Coordinators: **Linda Feltman, Brent Peters**
States/Regions Covered: **State College, Bellefonte, Aaronsburg, Houserville, Julian, Lemont, Potters Mills, Tyrone**
Rates (Single/Double):
Average: **$20–$27 $28–$37**
Credit Cards: **No**

You will enjoy touring historic mansions, Penns Cave, Woodward Cave, and several Civil War museums in this lovely area. A two-day minimum stay is required for the second week in July, the time of the annual Central Pennsylvania Festival of the Arts, and for the Penn State University Homecoming Football game in autumn. Rates are increased ten dollars per night during football weekends only, to a maximum of $47.00 per night double. (No single rates on football weekends.) Pennsylvania State University and Bucknell University are close by.

GETTYSBURG AREA

The Homestead ✪
785 BALTIMORE STREET, GETTYSBURG, PENNSYLVANIA 17325

Tel: **(717) 334-2037**
Host(s): **Ruth S. Wisler**
No. of Rooms: **2**
Maximum No. of Guests Sharing Bath: **4**
Double/sb: **$18**
Single/sb: **$13**

Open: **May–Oct.**
Breakfast: **No**
Pets: **No**
Children: **Welcome, over 4**
Smoking: **No**
Social Drinking: **No**

The Homestead is a gracious home standing on the historic battlefield, near the National Cemetery. It was originally an orphanage for children made homeless during the Civil War. It is comfortably furnished with family antiques and boasts several Civil War relics. Ruth is a retired English teacher who grows African violets. She likes helping her guests get the most out of their visit to the area. Store your perishable snacks in her refrigerator. Gettysburg has four-score and more things to see. Historic Gettysburg College is close to "Homestead."

Twin Elms ✪
228 BUFORD AVENUE, GETTYSBURG, PENNSYLVANIA 17325

Tel: (717) 334-4520
Best Time to Call: 9 AM-5 PM
Host(s): **Estella Williams**
No. of Rooms: 3
Max. No. Sharing Bath: 6
Double/sb: $15
Single/sb: $15

Open: **All year**
Reduced Rates: **10%, families**
Breakfast: **No**
Pets: **No**
Children: **Welcome, over 4**
Smoking: **Permitted**
Social Drinking: **No**

Estella's comfortable brick home is surrounded by the historic Gettysburg Battlefield. It is within walking distance of museums, the National Cemetery, swimming, golfing; the Eisenhower farm is close by, as well as diverse eating places. Your hostess is a former teacher and history buff who enjoys having guests.

Beck Mill Farm ✪
R.D. 1, BOX 452, BECK MILL ROAD, HANOVER, PENNSYLVANIA 17331

Tel: (717) 637-8992
Best Time to Call: **Evenings**
Host(s): **Alan and Teena Smith**
Location: **18 mi. SW of York**
No. of Rooms: 2
Max. No. Sharing Bath: 4
Double/sb: $32
Single/sb: $25

Open: **All year**
Reduced Rates: **10%, Nov. 1–Mar. 31**
Breakfast: **Full**
Other Meals: **Available**
Pets: **Sometimes**
Children: **Welcome**
Smoking: **No**
Social Drinking: **Permitted**

Outside this 60-year-old farmhouse are fruit trees, a swimming pool, and a barn. The interior features chestnut woodwork, early American furnishings, and a player piano in the living room.

Guests may have breakfast in their private quarters or the country kitchen. Attractions such as the Hanover and Lana Lobell Standardbred horse farms and Gettysburg National Military Park are nearby. Boating and sailing are minutes away.

PENNSYLVANIA DUTCH AREA
Spring House ✪
MUDDY CREEK FORKS, AIRVILLE, PENNSYLVANIA 17302

Tel: **(717) 927-6906**
Best Time to Call: **Early AM**
Host(s): **Ray Constance Hearne**
Location: **18 mi. S of York**
No. of Rooms: **4**
Max. No. Sharing Bath: **6**
Double/sb: **$50**
Single/sb: **$42**

Open: **Mar.–Dec.**
Reduced Rates: **10%, 5 days**
Breakfast: **Full**
Pets: **No**
Children: **Welcome**
Smoking: **No**
Social Drinking: **Permitted**
Foreign Languages: **Spanish**

This unique 200-year-old stone house, situated in a charming, 18th-century valley village, is decorated with whitewashed and stenciled walls, and furnished with a pleasant mixture of antiques, paintings, and handmade pottery. The antique beds have handmade quilts and featherbeds. Ray is never too busy to direct you to the river for water sports, show you where to hike, or explain where the award-winning wine is made. She gets raves for her fabulous breakfasts, and has won blue ribbons for her pies and bread.

Greystone Motor Lodge
2658 OLD PHILADELPHIA PIKE, P.O. BOX 270, BIRD-IN-HAND, PENNSYLVANIA 17505

Tel: (717) 393-4233	Open: All year
Best Time to Call: Weekdays AM	Reduced Rates: Sept. 4–June 15
Host(s): Jim and Phyllis Reed	Breakfast: No
No. of Rooms: 12	Credit Cards: AMEX, MC, VISA
No. of Private Baths: 12	Pets: No
Double/pb: $36	Children: Welcome (crib)
Single/pb: $36	Smoking: Permitted
Suites: $48	Social Drinking: Permitted

Situated on two acres of lush lawn and trees, the lodge was built in 1883. Back then, this French Victorian mansion and carriage house did not boast of air-conditioning, TV, and suites with kitchens, as it does today. Though a great deal of renovation has taken place, the antique features and charm of the mansion are intact. Good restaurants are nearby.

Smithton–Henry Miller 1763 House ✪
904 WEST MAIN STREET, EPHRATA, PENNSYLVANIA 17522

Tel: (717) 733-6094	Single/sb: $35–$45
Best Time to Call: 10 AM-9 PM	Suites: $125 for 2
Host(s): Dorothy Graybill	Open: All year
Location: 12 mi. NW of Lancaster	Breakfast: Full
No. of Rooms: 5	Credit Cards: MC, VISA
No. of Private Baths: 3	Pets: Welcome
Max. No. Sharing Bath: 4	Children: Welcome
Double/pb: $45–$75	Smoking: Permitted
Single/pb: $35–$65	Social Drinking: Permitted
Double/sb: $45–$55	

Picture yourself returning "home" after seeing the Pennsylvania Dutch sights and trudging wearily to your bedroom. Waiting for you are candle sconces, canopy beds, Amish quilts, down pillows and, on cool nights, a cozy fire. There's even a flannel nightshirt to snuggle in, and a trundle bed for the children. And, after a restful sleep, come down to a breakfast of hot waffles with whipped cream served with seasonal fruit.

Groff Tourist Farm Home ✪
R.D. 1, BOX 36, BRACKBILL ROAD, KINZER, PENNSYLVANIA 17535

Tel: (717) 442-8223	Double/sb: $18
Best Time to Call: 7–8 AM, 5–7 PM	Single/sb: $16
Host(s): **Harold and Mary Ellen Groff**	Open: **All year**
Location: **15 mi. E of Lancaster**	Breakfast: **No**
No. of Rooms: 5	Pets: **Sometimes**
No. of Private Baths: 1	Children: **Welcome**
Max. No. Sharing Bath: 6	Smoking: **No**
Double/pb: $28	Social Drinking: **No**
Single/pb: $25	

This old-fashioned stone farmhouse, recently redecorated, has a porch on which to relax; each comfortable bedroom is cross-ventilated, so you can enjoy the crisp country air. In her spare time, hostess Mary enjoys visiting with her guests, while stitching the gorgeous quilts her grandmother taught her to make. Nearby restaurants serve good food.

Sycamore Haven Farm Guest House ✪
35 SOUTH KINZER ROAD, KINZER, PENNSYLVANIA 17535

Tel: (717) 442-4901	Guest Cottage: **$24 for 4**
Best Time to Call: **9 AM–9 PM**	Open: **Dec.–Oct.**
Host(s): **Charles and Janet Groff**	Breakfast: **Continental, 75¢**
No. of Rooms: 3	Pets: **Sometimes**
Max. No. Sharing Bath: 8	Children: **Welcome**
Double/sb: $15	Smoking: **No**
Single/sb: $15	Social Drinking: **No**

This spacious home is a dairy farm where 40 cows are milked each day. You are welcome to watch the process. The children will be kept busy enjoying the swing, kittens, sheep, and games. You may use the Groff kitchen to fix light snacks and the guest refrigerator for storing them.

Groff Farm—"Abend-Ruhe" ✪
2324 LEAMAN ROAD, LANCASTER, PENNSYLVANIA 17602

Tel: **(717) 687-0221**
Best Time to Call: **Mornings**
Host(s): **Herb and Debbie Groff**
Location: **4 mi. E of Lancaster**
No. of Rooms: **4**
No. of Private Baths: **2**
Max. No. Sharing Bath: **4**
Double/pb: **$22**
Single/pb: **$22**
Double/sb: **$17**
Single/sb: **$17**
Open: **All year**
Breakfast: **Continental**
Pets: **Sometimes**
Children: **Welcome**
Smoking: **No**
Social Drinking: **Permitted**

This roomy 110-year-old brick farmhouse has an inviting wrap-around porch and lovely shade trees. It is comfortably furnished with simple country charm. Herb is a woodsmith with a shop located on the farm, and Debbie is a fulltime hostess interested in handicrafts. Her homemade breads and jams are delicious. Don't miss the famous Strasburg Railroad and Train Museum, just five minutes away. Franklin and Marshall College is nearby.

Meadowview Guest House ✪
2169 NEW HOLLAND PIKE, LANCASTER, PENNSYLVANIA 17601

Tel: **(717) 299-4017**
Host(s): **Edward and Sheila Christie**
No. of Rooms: **4**
No. of Private Baths: **2**
Max. No. Sharing Bath: **5**
Double/pb: **$22**
Single/pb: **$21**
Double/sb: **$17**
Single/sb: **$16**
Open: **April–Nov.**
Reduced Rates: **$3 off after 2 days**
Breakfast: **No**
Pets: **No**
Children: **Welcome (crib)**
Smoking: **No**
Social Drinking: **Permitted**

Situated in the heart of Pennsylvania Dutch country, the house has a pleasant blend of modern and traditional furnishings. Your hosts offer a fully equipped guest kitchen where you can store and prepare your own breakfast. Ed and Sheila supply coffee and tea. The area is known for great farmers' markets, antique shops, craft shops, country auctions, and wonderful restaurants.

Witmer's Tavern–Historic 1725 Inn ✪
2014 OLD PHILADELPHIA PIKE, LANCASTER, PENNSYLVANIA 17602

Tel: **(717) 299-5305**
Host(s): **Brant E. Hartung**
Location: **½ mi. from Rte. 30**
No. of Rooms: **5**
Max. No. Sharing Bath: **6**
Double/sb: **$45**
Suites: **$65**

Open: **All year**
Breakfast: **Continental**
Pets: **No**
Children: **Welcome**
Smoking: **Permitted**
Social Drinking: **Permitted**

Lafayette and Washington undoubtedly stopped by for grog in this pre-Revolutionary inn, now a National Historic Landmark. Decorated with authentic antiques, there are working fireplaces in each bedroom. ($10 charge for firewood.) Modern conveniences such as air conditioning and electric heat will keep you comfortable in all seasons. Brandt will happily share interesting information on local attractions and historic sites.

Maple Lane Guest House ✪
505 PARADISE LANE, PARADISE, PENNSYLVANIA 17562

Tel: **(717) 687-7479**
Host(s): **Marion and Edwin Rohrer**
Location: **60 mi. W of Philadelphia**
No. of Rooms: **4**
No. of Private Baths: **1**
Max. No. Sharing Bath: **4**
Double/pb: **$24**
Single/pb: **$20**
Double/sb: **$20**

Single/sb: **$18**
Open: **All year**
Reduced Rates: **No**
Breakfast: **Coffee or tea**
Pets: **Sometimes**
Children: **Welcome**
Smoking: **No**
Social Drinking: **Permitted**

From the hill nearby you can see for 40 miles. Stroll the 200 acres of this working farm, with its stream and woodland. Your hosts welcome you to rooms decorated with homemade quilts, needlework, and antiques. The sights of the Amish country, such as the farmers' market, antique shops, flea markets, and restaurants, are within easy reach.

Neffdale Farm ✪
604 STRASBURG ROAD, PARADISE, PENNSYLVANIA 17562

Tel: **(717) 687-7837**
Host(s): **Roy and Ellen Neff**
Location: **13 mi. SE of Lancaster**
No. of Rooms: **3**
No. of Private Baths: **1**
Max. No. Sharing Bath: **8**
Double/pb: **$22**
Single/pb: **$20**
Double/sb: **$20**
Single/sb: **$18**
Open: **Mar.–Nov.**
Breakfast: **No**
Pets: **Sometimes**
Children: **Welcome**
Smoking: **No**
Social Drinking: **No**

This 200-year-old farmhouse has large, comfortable rooms overlooking 115 acres of beautiful croplands, woods, meadows, and shady lawns. You are invited to watch the huge farm machinery in action, feed the calves, gather eggs, and visit the pigs and ducks. Roy is a busy dairy farmer and Ellen enjoys quilting and making sure that her guests have an enjoyable visit. Restaurants are close by.

Rayba Acres Farm ✪
183 BLACK HORSE ROAD, PARADISE, PENNSYLVANIA 17562

Tel: **(717) 687-6729**
Host(s): **J. Ray and Reba Ranck**
No. of Rooms: **6**
No. of Private Baths: **2**
Max. No. Sharing Bath: **6**
Double/pb: **$26**
Single/pb: **$26**
Double/sb: **$20**
Single/sb: **$20**
Open: **All year**
Reduced Rates: **10%, 5 days**
Breakfast: **No**
Pets: **No**
Children: **Welcome**
Smoking: **No**
Social Drinking: **No**

Five generations of the Ranck family have worked this dairy farm. The kids will enjoy visiting the animals, especially at milking time. You are welcome to help milk a cow, if you wish! The farmhouse is comfortably furnished, and your hosts will cordially help arrange your tour. Local possibilities include the antiques shops, restaurants, and the Pennsylvania Dutch shops and farmland.

El Shaddai ☉
229 MADISON AVENUE, HYDE VILLA, READING, PENNSYLVANIA 19605

Tel: (215) 929-1341 or 373-6639	Reduced Rates: **Families**
Host(s): **Dale and Joan Gaul**	Breakfast: **Full**
No. of Rooms: **3**	Pets: **No**
No. of Private Baths: **3**	Children: **No**
Double/pb: **$32**	Smoking: **No**
Single/pb: **$22**	Social Drinking: **No**
Open: **All year**	Airport/Station Pickup: **Yes**

El Shaddai is a stone farmhouse over 100 years old. Guests will enjoy relaxing in the sitting room with cooking hearth and spacious outdoor side porch. Each morning a hearty breakfast featuring homemade jam is prepared by your hostess. Nearby places of interest include the factory outlet in Reading, the historical sites of Berks County, and the Pennsylvania Dutch country. Albright College and Kutztown University are nearby.

Smoketown Village Tourist Home ☉
2495 OLD PHILADELPHIA PIKE, ROUTE 340, SMOKETOWN, PENNSYLVANIA 17576

Tel: (717) 393-5975	Single/sb: **$14**
Host(s): **Paul and Margaret Reitz**	Open: **All year**
Location: **5 mi. E of Lancaster**	Breakfast: **No**
No. of Rooms: **5**	Pets: **No**
No. of Private Baths: **1**	Children: **Welcome (crib)**
Max. No. Sharing Bath: **5**	Smoking: **Permitted**
Double/pb: **$15**	Social Drinking: **Permitted**
Double/sb: **$15**	

A stately brick colonial with white shutters, surrounded by lush lawns, this lovely home is graced with a comfortable porch where you may relax after touring the local sights. You are welcome to store your breakfast makings in the guest refrigerator, use the kitchen to prepare it, and enjoy it on the picnic table while breathing in the clean, country air.

Fairhaven ✪
RD 12, BOX 445, KELLER ROAD, YORK, PENNSYLVANIA 17406

Tel: (717) 252-3726
Best Time to Call: 8AM, 5–7 PM
Host(s): **Adelaide and George Price**
Location: **8 mi. from I-83**
No. of Rooms: **3**
Max. No. Sharing Bath: **6**
Double/sb: **$30**
Single/sb: **$20**

Open: **All year**
Reduced Rates: **Seniors; families**
Breakfast: **Full**
Pets: **Sometimes**
Children: **Welcome (crib)**
Smoking: **No**
Social Drinking: **No**

Relax in an old German farmhouse furnished with treasures handed down for generations. A bountiful breakfast, featuring homemade goodies and eggs fresh from the henhouse, is prepared on an antique stove. Take a dip in the pool or visit where history was made in Gettysburg or York. Visit Lancaster for museums and local attractions, Hershey's Chocolate World, and numerous outlet shops. Penn State and York College are close by.

Memory Lane Bed & Breakfast ✪
1950 MEMORY LANE, YORK, PENNSYLVANIA 17402

Tel: (717) 755-7409
Best Time to Call: **After 4:30 PM**
Host(s): **Patricia Wilson**
Location: **2 mi. from Rte. 83**
No. of Rooms: **2**
Max. No. Sharing Bath: **4**
Double/sb: **$35**
Single/sb: **$30**

Open: **All year**
Breakfast: **Full**
Pets: **Sometimes**
Children: **Welcome**
Smoking: **No**
Social Drinking: **Permitted**
Foreign Languages: **Spanish**

Come to the nation's first capital and enjoy this grey stone English country house surrounded by lovely trees. The newly decorated upstairs bedrooms offer ample space and comfort. Breakfast is always hearty and is served in a nook that overlooks a vista of birds, trees, and pasture. If you wish to cut down on expenses, feel free to use the guest refrigerator, gas barbecue, and picnic table. Patricia has extensive collections of Will Rogers memorabilia and first editions of contemporary writers. York College is nearby.

PHILADELPHIA AREA

Bed & Breakfast—Center City ✪
1908 SPRUCE STREET, PHILADELPHIA, PENNSYLVANIA 19103

Tel: (215) 735-1137 or 923-5459	Rates (Single/Double):
Best Time to Call: 8 AM–5 PM weekdays	Modest: $25 $35
	Average: $35 $40–$45
Coordinators: Nancy Frenze, Stella Pomerantz	Luxury: $50 $50–$65
	Credit Cards: No
States/Regions Covered: Philadelphia	

Lodgings range from Dickensian-type houses in lamplit cobblestone courtyards, to restored town houses, to elegant high-rise apartments with spectacular views of the city, and the entire spectrum between. There are unique and charming homes in the best sections of the city including Society Hill, Rittenhouse Square, Antique Row, University City, and Fitler Square. All are within easy reach of theaters, museums, fine restaurants, elegant shops, galleries, and all the major schools, colleges, and universities.

Bed & Breakfast of Chester County ✪
P.O. BOX 825, KENNETT SQUARE, PENNSYLVANIA 19348

Tel: (215) 444-1367	Rates (Single/Double):
Coordinator: Doris Passante	Modest: $18–$20 $25–$30
States/Regions Covered: Chester County, Chadds Ford, suburban Philadelphia	Average: $21–$30 $31–$40
	Luxury: $31–$40 $41–$50
	Credit Cards: No

Doris has a wide selection of homes located in the beautiful and historic Brandywine Valley, which is known for the River Museum, Longwood Gardens, Winterthur, Brandywine Battlefield, and Valley Forge. The area is convenient to the Pennsylvania Dutch Country. Send for her brochure which fully describes each B&B. The University of Delaware, Lincoln University, and West Chester University are close by.

Bed & Breakfast of Philadelphia ✪
P.O. BOX 680, DEVON, PENNSYLVANIA 19333

Tel: (215) 688-1633	Rates (Single/Double):
Best Time to Call: **9 AM–9 PM**	Modest: $25 $35
Coordinators: **Sandra Fullerton,**	Average: $30 $55
Joanne Goins, Carol Yarrow	Luxury: $55 $125
State/Regions Covered: **Philadelphia and suburbs; New Jersey—Riverton, Moorestown; Delaware—Wilmington**	Credit Cards: **MC, VISA**

Philadelphia is the "City of Brotherly Love" and you'll be made to feel like family in the B&Bs. Selections include luxury town houses in the heart of Society Hill, refurbished Victorians, suburban manor homes, country guest cottages, apartments near the museums, and places that are convenient to all the universities. Send $5 for a descriptive directory.

Meadow Spring Farm
201 EAST STREET ROAD, KENNETT SQUARE, PENNSYLVANIA 19348

Tel: (215) 444-3903	Open: **All year**
Host(s): **Anne and John Hicks**	Reduced Rates: **10%, families**
Location: **20 mi. E of Philadelphia**	Breakfast: **Full**
No. of Rooms: **4**	Other Meals: **Available**
No. of Private Baths: **1**	Pets: **Welcome**
Max. No. Sharing Bath: **4**	Children: **Welcome (crib)**
Double/pb: **$45**	Smoking: **Permitted**
Single/pb: **$35**	Social Drinking: **Permitted**
Double/sb: **$40**	Airport/Station Pickup: **Yes**
Single/sb: **$30**	

This large stone house dates back to the 1830s. A hot tub and screened-in porch are two of the recent additions. The rooms are decorated with family antiques and Victorian whimsy. Your hostess welcomes you with tea, wine, and goodies. In season she serves corn fritters, fresh eggs, and homemade breads on the porch. Local attractions include Longwood Gardens, Brandywine River Museum, and downtown Philadelphia.

Mrs. K's ○
404 RIDGE AVENUE, KENNETT SQUARE, PENNSYLVANIA 19348

Tel: **(215) 444-5559 or (302) 478-3000**	Single/sb: **$20**
Best Time to Call: **Before 8 AM, or after 6 PM**	Open: **All year**
	Breakfast: **Full**
Host(s): **Charlotte Kanofsky**	Pets: **No**
Location: **30 mi. S of Philadelphia**	Children: **Welcome, over 3**
No. of Rooms: **2**	Smoking: **No**
Max. No. Sharing Bath: **4**	Social Drinking: **Permitted**
Double/sb: **$30–$35**	

Arriving guests are greeted with cheese, crackers, and appropriate beverages. Charlotte has made her guest-house business a labor of love. Her lovely home is on a quiet residential street but close to many attractions. This is Andrew Wyeth's territory (Chadds Ford). Longwood Gardens, Brandywine Battlefield, and Brandywine River Museum are all worthwhile stops to make. It's less than a half hour from Wilmington, Delaware, home of Winterthur, the Hagley and the Natural History museums. You are welcome to use the kitchen for snacks, and the laundry facilities. West Chester University and the University of Delaware are close by.

POCONO MOUNTAINS

Bed & Breakfast Pocono Northeast
P.O. BOX 115, BEAR CREEK, PENNSYLVANIA 18602

Tel: **(717) 472-3145**	**Honesdale, Milford, Mountainhome,**
Best Time to Call: **9 AM–Noon; 7–10 PM**	**Paupack, Sayre, Tobyhanna, Wilkes-Barre**
Coordinator: **Ann Magagna**	Rates (Single/Double):
States/Regions Covered:	Average: **$12–30 $24–$50**
Albrightsville, Bushkill, Hawley,	Credit Cards: **No**

The above is merely a partial listing of the area covered by this registry. A variety of accommodations has been chosen by Ann for visitors coming to the northeastern corner of the state. Whatever your recreational bent, you are certain to find it, in all seasons, in this land of fresh air and mountain beauty, from skiing to water and land sports, antiquing, country fairs, theater, historic sites, fine restaurants, and handicraft shops. Business travelers, vacationers, and visitors to the renowned Geisinger and Robert Packer medical centers will all be made to feel perfectly at home.

Dreamy Acres ⊙
P.O. BOX 7, SEESE HILL ROAD AND RTE. 447, CANADENSIS, PENNSYLVANIA 18325

Tel: **(717) 595-7115**
Best Time to Call: **8 AM–11 PM**
Host(s): **Esther and Bill Pickett**
Location: **16 mi. N of Stroudsburg**
No. of Rooms: **6**
No. of Private Baths: **4**
Max. No. Sharing Bath: **4**
Double/pb: **$32–$38**
Single/pb: **$32–$38**
Double/sb: **$28**
Single/sb: **$28**
Guest Cottage: **$38 for 2**
Open: **All year**
Breakfast: **Continental—May–Oct.**
Pets: **No**
Children: **Welcome, over 4**
Smoking: **Permitted**
Social Drinking: **Permitted**

Situated in the heart of the Pocono Mountains, this comfortably furnished 100-year-old lodge is on over three acres, with a stream and a pond. Year-'round recreation includes fishing, tennis, state parks, golf, horseback riding, skiing, and skating. There are many fine restaurants, boutiques, and churches in the area. Esther and Bill have been entertaining guests for over 23 years; their motto is: "You are a stranger here but once."

Nearbrook ⊙
ROUTE 447, CANADENSIS, PENNSYLVANIA 18325

Tel: **(717) 595-3152**
Best Time to Call: **6–11 PM**
Location: **15 mi. N of Stroudsburg**
Host(s): **Barbie and Dick Robinson**
No. of Rooms: **3**
Max. No. Sharing Bath: **6**
Double/sb: **$25–$30**
Single/sb: **$15**
Open: **All year**
Reduced Rates: **Weekly**
Breakfast: **Full**
Pets: **Sometimes**
Children: **Welcome**
Smoking: **No**
Social Drinking: **Permitted**

Enjoy the Poconos while making Barbie and Dick's charming home your base. Meander through rock gardens and down a woodland path to a clear mountain stream. Nearby are well-marked hiking trails and vacation activities in all seasons. Each bedroom has its own sink and there are seven fine restaurants within a four-mile radius.

La Anna Guest House ✪
R.D. 2, BOX 1051, CRESCO, PENNSYLVANIA 18326

Tel: (717) 676-4225
Best Time to Call: **After 6 PM**
Host(s): **Kay and Julie Swingle**
Location: **9 mi. from I-84**
No. of Rooms: **4**
Max. No. Sharing Bath: **4**
Double/sb: **$24**
Single/sb: **$15**

Open: **All year**
Reduced Rates: **Families**
Breakfast: **Continental**
Pets: **Welcome**
Children: **Welcome (crib)**
Smoking: **Permitted**
Social Drinking: **Permitted**

This Victorian home has large rooms furnished with antiques; it is nestled on 25 acres of lush, wooded land, and has its own pond. Kay will happily direct you to fine dining spots that are kind to your wallet. Enjoy scenic walks, waterfalls, mountain vistas, Tobyhanna and Promised Land state parks; there's cross-country skiing right on the property. Lake Wallenpaupack is only 15 minutes away.

The Mountain House ✪
P.O. BOX 253, MOUNTAIN ROAD, DELAWARE WATER GAP, PENNSYLVANIA 18327

Tel: (717) 424-2254
Host(s): **Frank and Yolanda Brown**
Location: **½ mi. from I-80**
No. of Rooms: **32**
No. of Private Baths: **8**
Max. No. Sharing Bath: **8**
Double/pb: **$40**
Single/pb: **$30**
Double/sb: **$35**
Single/sb: **$25**

Open: **All year**
Breakfast: **Continental**
Other Meals: **Available**
Credit Cards: **AMEX, DC, MC, VISA**
Pets: **Sometimes**
Children: **Welcome (crib)**
Smoking: **Permitted**
Social Drinking: **Permitted**
Airport/Station Pickup: **Yes**
Foreign Languages: **German**

This 1870 yellow clapboard inn has a huge screened-in veranda and is filled with rare antiques and lots of wicker. The parlor has a piano and rocking chairs, and the dining room has a fine display of exquisite "cut" glass. All the attractions of the Poconos are nearby. Delaware River sports are a block away and the house is on the Appalachian Trail. Frank and Yolanda welcome you to use the pool, shuffleboard court, washing machine, and dryer. East Stroudsburg University is nearby.

Four County View B&B ✪
BOX 211, GREENTOWN, PENNSYLVANIA 18426

Tel: (717) 676-3417
Best Time to Call: **6–9 PM**
Host(s): **Philip Stuhlmuller**
No. of Rooms: **2**
No. of Private Baths: **1**
Max. No. Sharing Bath: **4**
Double/pb: **$40**

Double/sb: **$35**
Open: **All year**
Breakfast: **Continental**
Pets: **Sometimes**
Children: **Welcome**
Smoking: **No**
Social Drinking: **Permitted**

The moment you arrive at Phil's door you will be taken with the peaceful ambience of this country retreat and your cosmopolitan host's warm welcome. Phil can direct you to all the recreational activities that abound on Lake Wallenpaupack, only five miles away, and can suggest excellent nearby restaurants.

Trails End ✪
R.D. 2 BOX 355A, GREENTOWN, PENNSYLVANIA 18426

Tel: (717) 857-0856; (212) 321-2930
Best Time to Call: **Weekends; evenings**
Host(s): **Betty and Bob Rundback**
No. of Rooms: **2**
No. of Private Baths: **1**
Max. No. Sharing Bath: **2**
Double/pb: **$40**
Single/pb: **$35**
Double/sb: **$35**
Single/sb: **$30**
Open: **All year**
Breakfast: **Full**
Pets: **No**
Children: **Welcome, over 12**
Smoking: **Permitted**
Social Drinking: **Permitted**

Drive down a steep, wooded lane to this bi-level country home perched on a knoll. It boasts an unobstructed view of 17-mile Lake Wallenpaupack framed by the dramatic landscape of the mountains. The lake is the center of activity in all seasons. Summer offers swimming, picnicking, fishing, boating, and relaxing on the large deck or nearby island. Tennis, golf, and horse stables are nearby. Winter offers snowmobiling, downhill and cross-country skiing, and ice-fishing. After a day in the country air, you are invited to have a pre-dinner cocktail and complimentary cheese and crackers. When conditions permit, Betty and Bob will take you sailing or waterskiing.

The Vines
107 EAST ANN STREET, MILFORD, PENNSYLVANIA 18337

Tel: (717) 296-6775
Host(s): **Joan and Don Voce**
Location: **1 mi. from I-84**
No. of Rooms: **4**
Max. No. Sharing Bath: **3**
Double/sb: **$40–$50**
Single/sb: **$20–$40**
Open: **All year**
Reduced Rates: **Weekly**
Breakfast: **Full**
Credit Cards: **MC, VISA**
Pets: **No**
Children: **Welcome**
Smoking: **No**
Social Drinking: **Permitted**

The Vines is a Queen Anne Victorian, built in 1864, and has been completely restored. There are parks, flea markets, canoeing, antiquing, historical sites, skiing, fishing, and many charming restaurants within a short distance. Coffee and tea are available upon request; Saturday nights often have the added attraction of wine and cheese. It is a mile from Grey Towers, Apple Valley with its quaint little shops, and the Milford Theatre.

Bonny Bank
P.O. BOX 481, MILL RIFT, PENNSYLVANIA 18340

Tel: (717) 491-2250
Best Time to Call: 6–10 PM
Host(s): **Doug and Linda Hay**
Location: 5 mi. from I-84
No. of Rooms: 1
No. of Private Baths: 1
Double/sb: $35
Single/sb: $25

Open: **May 1–Oct. 31**
Reduced Rates: **15% weekly; seniors**
Breakfast: **Continental**
Credit Cards: **MC, VISA**
Pets: **No**
Children: **Welcome, over 10**
Smoking: **No**
Social Drinking: **Permitted**

Stay in a picture-book small town on a dead-end road. The sound of the rapids will lull you to sleep in this charming bungalow perched on the banks of the Delaware River. Doug and Linda invite you to use their private swimming area and will lend you inner-tubes for float trips. Nearby attractions include the Zane Grey house, Minisink Battlefield, Grey Towers Historical Site, the Victorian village of Milford, and all the sports and variety of restaurants the Poconos are known for.

Elvern Country Lodge
P.O. BOX 177, STONE CHURCH-FIVE POINTS ROAD, MOUNT BETHEL, PENNSYLVANIA 18343

Tel: (215) 588-1922
Host(s): **Dos and Herb Deen**
Location: 16 mi. N of Easton
No. of Rooms: 4
No. of Private Baths: 3
Max. No. Sharing Bath: 4
Double/pb: $40
Single/pb: $30
Double/sb: $30
Single/sb: $20

Open: **All year**
Reduced Rates: **Seniors, families**
Breakfast: **Full**
Other Meals: **Available**
Pets: **Sometimes**
Children: **Welcome (crib)**
Smoking: **Permitted**
Social Drinking: **Permitted**
Airport/Station Pickup: **Yes**

This is a working farm in the foothills of the Pocono Mountains. The house dates back to the Victorian period and includes a sundeck and patio. Guest quarters have cool summer breezes, individual thermostats, and wall-to-wall carpeting. Your hosts raise their own beef, vegetables, and fruit. They prepare a breakfast of country bacon, fresh eggs, and homemade jams. Fishing, boating, and swimming can be enjoyed in the two-acre lake on the farm. The Delaware Water Gap Recreation Area, Appalachian Trail, and summer theater are nearby.

White Cloud ✪
R.D. 1, BOX 215, NEWFOUNDLAND, PENNSYLVANIA 18445

Tel: (717) 676-3162
Host(s): **George Wilkinson, Judy Jordan**
Location: **25 mi. SE of Scranton**
No. of Rooms: **20**
No. of Baths: **8**
Max. No. Sharing Bath: **3**
Double/pb: **$40**
Single/pb: **$34**
Double/sb: **$32.50**
Single/sb: **$25**

Open: **All year**
Reduced Rates: **Available**
Breakfast: **Full**
Other Meals: **Available**
Credit Cards: **AMEX, MC, VISA, DC**
Pets: **Sometimes**
Children: **Welcome (crib)**
Smoking: **No**
Social Drinking: **Permitted**
Airport/Station Pickup: **Yes**

This is a quiet country place where the emphasis is on natural, wholesome living, away from the clatter of modern life. There's a pool and tennis court for your summer pleasure, and the surrounding area offers a spectrum of activities, including skiing in winter and all sports on 17-mile Lake Wallenpaupack. Accommodations are simple but comfortable. The dining room serves ample meals. Fruits and vegetables are organically grown in season, and the homemade breads and herb teas are outstanding. No meat is served. The library features books on metaphysical and philosophical subjects.

Eagle Rock Lodge ✪
BOX 265, RIVER ROAD, SHAWNEE, PENNSYLVANIA 18356

Tel: (717) 421-2139
Host(s): **The Cox Family**
Location: **75 mi. W of NYC**

No. of Rooms: **7**
Max. No. Sharing Bath: **6**
Double/sb: **$45**

Single/sb: **$30**
Open: **All year**
Reduced Rates: **Weekdays; groups**
Breakfast: **Full**

Pets: **Sometimes**
Children: **Welcome**
Smoking: **Permitted**
Social Drinking: **Permitted**

Eagle Rock is a 19th-century inn with an 80-foot porch overlooking the river, at the entrance to the Delaware Water Gap National Recreation Area. It is steps away from white-water canoeing, hiking, fishing, skiing, swimming, and horseback riding. The Shawnee Playhouse, open air concerts, art shows, and antique shops are nearby. Doris, Randy, and George provide a rib-buster of a breakfast! They have an antique shop on-premises that you'll want to browse in. The University of East Stroudsburg is close.

The Redwood House ✪
BOX 9B EAST SIDE BORO, WHITE HAVEN, PENNSYLVANIA 18661

Tel: **(717) 443-7186; (215) 446-4066**
Host(s): **Mr. and Mrs. John Moore**
Location: **10 mi. E of Hazelton**
No. of Rooms: **4**
No. of Private Baths: **2**
Max. No. Sharing Bath: **3**
Double/pb: **$35**
Single/pb: **$20**
Double/sb: **$30**

Single/sb: **$15**
Suites: **$60**
Open: **All year**
Reduced Rates: **5%, seniors**
Breakfast: **Continental**
Pets: **Sometimes**
Children: **Welcome, well behaved**
Smoking: **Permitted**
Social Drinking: **Permitted**

This frame chalet is minutes from the slopes at Big Boulder and Jack Frost. In summer enjoy sunning and swimming at Hickory Run State Park. Nearby Lehigh River offers fishing and rafting. Your hosts recommend a visit to Eckley, where the movie *The Molly Maguires* was filmed—a true example of what life was like in a 19th-century mining community. After a day of touring, come and relax on the large, comfortable porch.

SCRANTON/NORTH CENTRAL PENNSYLVANIA

Endless Mountains Reservation Service
BOX 294B, UNION DALE, PENNSYLVANIA 18470

Tel: **(717) 679-2425**
Best Time to Call: **Evenings after 6 PM**
Coordinator: **Jeanne R. Spillane**
States/Regions Covered: **Bradford, Susquehanna, Tioga, Wayne Counties in Pa.; Broome, Sullivan Counties in N.Y.**

Rates (Single/Double):
Modest: **$15** $24
Average: **$20** $30
Luxury: **$35** $50
Credit Cards: **No**

Accommodations on Jeanne's roster were carefully selected to bring you the best. There are gracious mansions with elegant suites, a rustic cabin close to nature, estates with hot tubs and private stables, as well as simple farmhouses with country charm. The areas represented have a multitude of recreational activities in all seasons.

The Bodine House ✪
307 SOUTH MAIN STREET, MUNCY, PENNSYLVANIA 17756

Tel: **(717) 546-8949**
Best Time to Call: **Evenings**
Host(s): **David and Marie Louise Smith**
Location: **15 mi. S of Williamsport**
No. of Rooms: **4**
No. of Private Baths: **2**
Max. No. Sharing Bath: **4**
Double/pb: **$30**
Double/sb: **$25**

Single/sb: **$20**
Open: **All year**
Breakfast: **Full**
Other Meals: **Available**
Pets: **No**
Children: **Welcome, over 6**
Smoking: **Permitted**
Social Drinking: **Permitted**

This restored town house dates back to 1805. A baby grand piano, four fireplaces, and a candlelit living room add to its old-fashioned appeal. A full country breakfast and wine and cheese are on the house; a light supper is served by arrangement. Local attractions include the Susquehanna River, the Endless Mountains, and the fall foliage.

Anderson Acres ✪
R.D. 1, STEVENS LAKE, TUNKHANNOCK, PENNSYLVANIA 18657

Tel: **(717) 836-5228**
Best Time to Call: **After 4 PM**
Host(s): **John and Doris Anderson**
Location: **26 mi. W of Scranton**
No. of Rooms: **2**
No. of Private Baths: **1**
Maximum No. Sharing Bath: **4**
Double/pb: **$25**
Single/pb: **$20**

Double/sb: **$25**
Single/sb: **$20**
Open: **All year**
Breakfast: **Continental**
Pets: **Welcome**
Children: **Welcome**
Smoking: **Permitted**
Social Drinking: **Permitted**

This 45-acre hobby farm is located in the Endless Mountains. The farm animals are kept in the barn area and the children will surely want to visit them. In town, five minutes away, there is a theater, roller skating rink, and golf course. The house has a lovely view of Steven's Lake. It's a 40-minute ride to Elk Mt. skiing.

Powder Mill Farms ✪
BOX 294B, UNION DALE, PENNSYLVANIA 18470

Tel: **(717) 679-2425**
Best Time to Call: **After 6 PM**
Host(s): **Jeanne and Paul Spillane**
Location: **35 mi. N of Scranton**
No. of Rooms: **3**
Max. No. Sharing Bath: **3**
Double/pb: **$40**
Double/sb: **$36**
Single/sb: **$30**

Guest Cottage: **$50–$70**
  for 6
Open: **All year**
Reduced Rates: **10%, families**
Breakfast: **Full**
Pets: **Sometimes**
Children: **Welcome**
Smoking: **Permitted**
Social Drinking: **Permitted**

Jeanne and Paul offer warm hospitality and country comfort in a picturesque 1826 home nestled in the Endless Mountains, filled with "cut" glass and fine antiques. It's only three miles to Elk Mountain for great skiing. This colonial grey home is surrounded by 42 wooded acres, a fishing pond, a bubbling trout stream, and lovely country trails. You are welcome to use the guest refrigerator, barbecue, and hot tub.

WESTERN PENNSYLVANIA

Pittsburgh Bed & Breakfast ✪
P.O. BOX 25353, PITTSBURGH, PENNSYLVANIA 15221

Tel: **(412) 241-5746**
Best Time to Call: **Mornings, evenings**
Coordinator: **Karen Krull**
States/Regions Covered: **Pittsburgh and western Pennsylvania**

Rates (Single/Double):
Modest: **$20**   **$28**
Average: **$25**   **$38**
Luxury: **$40**   **$50**
Credit Cards: **No**

Karen has many comfortable accommodations in the historic Northside, Southside, Shadyside, Squirrel Hill, and Mount Washington areas. Many homes are convenient to Carnegie-Mellon University, Duquesne, and the University of Pittsburgh. This is a great place to stop off en route to Cleveland (80 miles), Chicago (400 miles), and West Virginia (60 miles).

Hobby Horse Farm ✪
174 SRADER GROVE ROAD, FREEPORT, PENNSYLVANIA 16229

Tel: **(412) 295-3123**
Best Time to Call: **Mornings; evenings**
Host(s): **The Magra Family**
Location: **60 mi. NE of Pittsburgh**
No. of Rooms: **1 suite**
No. of Private Baths: **1**
Double/pb: **$35**
Single/pb: **$25**

Suites: **$25–$35**
Open: **All year**
Breakfast: **Full**
Pets: **Sometimes**
Children: **Welcome**
Smoking: **No**
Social Drinking: **Permitted**
Airport/Station Pickup: **Yes**

This restored brick farmhouse is perched on one of the highest hills in Armstrong County. Each room boasts a fireplace, antiques, and country crafts. A trencherman breakfast of locally produced bacon, omelettes, or French toast is served each morning. Your hosts offer afternoon tea and hot cider in season. If you like, they will take you on a walking tour of historic Freeport. Other local attractions include Todd Sanctuary, Freeport Park, the Allegheny River, and the Baker Trail. The front-porch rockers are a fine place for viewing the change of seasons.

Das Tannen-Lied (The Singing Pines) ✪
1195 EAST LAKE ROAD, JAMESTOWN, PENNSYLVANIA 16134

Tel: **(412) 932-5029**
Best Time to Call: **8 AM–9 PM**
Host(s): **Marian Duecker**
Location: **85 mi. N of Pittsburgh**
No. of Rooms: **2**
Max. No. Sharing Bath: **4**
Double/sb: **$30**

Single/sb: **$25**
Open: **Apr. 2–Oct. 31**
Breakfast: **Full**
Pets: **No**
Children: **Welcome, over 10**
Smoking: **Permitted**
Social Drinking: **Permitted**

This Victorian home, built in 1872, is set on the shore of Pymatuning Lake, which offers many recreational activities. Or, you may simply sit on the big front porch and watch the boats go by. Marian is a retired home economics teacher and dietitian, and on advance notice she will prepare picnic baskets, lunch, or dinner at reasonable prices. You are welcome to play the piano, browse in her library, and enjoy a cool beverage whenever you wish. Thiel College is close by.

RHODE ISLAND

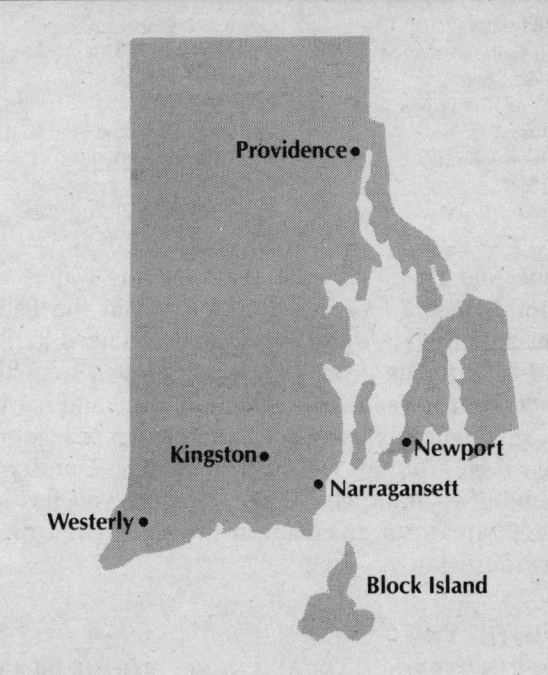

Old Town Inn ✪
P.O. BOX 351, BLOCK ISLAND, RHODE ISLAND 02807

Tel: **(401) 466-5958**
Host(s): **Ralph, Monica and David Gunter**
Location: **40 mi. SW of Providence**
No. of Rooms: **12**
No. of Private Baths: **8**
Max. No. Sharing Bath: **7**
Double/pb: **$58–$70**
Double/sb: **$45**

Single/sb: **$30**
Open: **May 27–Sept. 30**
Breakfast: **Full**
Pets: **No**
Children: **Welcome over 5**
Smoking: **Permitted**
Social Drinking: **Permitted**
Airport/Station Pickup: **Yes**

This modernized 150-year-old farmhouse, with its spacious grounds and special play area for the children, is just a mile from the beach. If you've never tasted Maine blueberries, wait 'til you've tried Monica's blueberry muffins. Afternoon tea is served, along with warm hospitality.

House of Snee ✪
191 OCEAN ROAD, NARRAGANSETT, RHODE ISLAND 02882

Tel: **(401) 783-9494**
Best Time to Call: **After 6 PM**
Host(s): **Mildred Snee**
Location: **15 mi. SW of Newport**
No. of Rooms: **2**
Max. No. Sharing Bath: **4**
Double/sb: **$35**
Single/sb: **$25**
Open: **All year**
Reduced Rates: **10%, seniors**
Breakfast: **Full**
Pets: **No**
Children: **Welcome over 4**
Smoking: **Permitted**
Social Drinking: **Permitted**
Airport/Station Pickup: **Yes**

This century-old Dutch colonial overlooks the waters of Rhode Island Sound. It's just across the street from the fishing pier where you can buy tackle and everything you need to hook a big one. It's a mile to the beach and just minutes from the Block Island Ferry. Mildred's kitchen is her kingdom and her breakfast often features delicious specialties such as crepes, johnnycake, and Scotch ham. You are welcome to use the laundry facilities and just about anything else that will make you feel at home. Winery tours are a fun diversion in the area. The University of Rhode Island is nearby.

The Richards ✪
104 ROBINSON STREET, NARRAGANSETT, RHODE ISLAND 02882

Tel: **(401) 789-7746**
Best Time to Call: **8–9 AM; 9–11 PM**
Host(s): **Steven and Nancy Richards**
Location: **35 mi. S of Providence**
No. of Rooms: **3**
No. of Private Baths: **1**
Max. No. Sharing Bath: **5**
Double/pb: **$45**
Double/sb: **$40**
Single/sb: **$35**
Open: **All year**
Reduced Rates: **Oct. 1–May 20**
Breakfast: **Full**
Pets: **No**
Children: **Welcome (crib)**
Smoking: **No**
Social Drinking: **Permitted**

Wicker, antiques, and chintz lend a country air to this half-century-old Cape on a beautifully landscaped acre. A quiet deck and patio surrounded by flowers make this the spot to relax after a day at the beach. The Manunuck Theatre-By-The-Sea, summer concerts, great restaurants, and shopping are nearby. Leave your alarm clock home, because the delightful aromas of such breakfast delights as johnnycakes, cheese blintzes, blueberry muffins, and fresh-ground gourmet coffee or herb tea will get you up.

Brinley Victorian ✪
23 BRINLEY STREET, NEWPORT, RHODE ISLAND 02840

Tel: **(401) 849-7645**
Best Time to Call: **9 AM–9 PM**
Host(s): **Amy Weintraub, Edwina Sebest**
Location: **70 mi. S of Boston**
No. of Rooms: **17**
No. of Private Baths: **8**
Maximum No. Sharing Bath: **6**
Double/pb: **$50–$70**
Single/pb: **$45–$60**
Double/sb: **$45–$65**
Single/sb: **$40–$55**
Suites: **$75**
Open: **All year**
Breakfast: **Continental**
Pets: **No**
Children: **Welcome, over 12**
Smoking: **Permitted**
Social Drinking: **Permitted**

Located in the prestigious Kay Street and Bellevue Avenue area, this lovely home offers the charm of the Victorian era, plus contemporary comfort and a convenient central location. It's an easy walk to the mansions, harbor, quaint shops, restaurants, and historic sites. Amy and Edwina prepare a delightful breakfast; appropriate beverages are available all day. Salve Regina College is nearby.

Ellery Park House ✪
44 FAREWELL STREET, NEWPORT, RHODE ISLAND 02840

Tel: **(401) 847-6320**
Best Time to Call: **After 5 PM**
Host(s): **Margo and Michael Waite**
Location: **25 mi. from I-95**
No. of Rooms: **2**
Max. No. Sharing Bath: **4**
Double/sb: **$45**
Single/sb: **$45**
Open: **All year**
Breakfast: **Continental**
Pets: **No**
Children: **No**
Smoking: **Permitted**
Social Drinking: **Permitted**
Airport/Station Pickup: **Yes**

Enjoy European hospitality in a turn-of-the-century home, just four blocks from the waterfront. Guest rooms are small and cozy, featuring fluffy towels and lots of reading material. Fresh juice, homemade jam, muffins, and freshly ground coffee are served mornings. You may like a peek at the kitchen with its restaurant stove and array of copper cookware. Your hosts will gladly direct you to the beach, waterfront restaurants, and historic homes.

Queen Anne Inn
16 CLARKE STREET, NEWPORT, RHODE ISLAND 02840

Tel: **(401) 846-5676**
Host(s): **Peg McCabe**
Location: **1½ mi. S of Boston**
No. of Rooms: **12**
Max. No. Sharing Bath: **3**
Double/sb: **$35–$55**
Single/sb: **$25**

Open: **Apr. 1–Nov. 15**
Breakfast: **Continental**
Pets: **No**
Children: **Welcome**
Smoking: **Permitted**
Social Drinking: **Permitted**

The Queen Anne is a rose-colored Victorian in the heart of the historic district. The guest rooms are decorated with gay, end-of-century-style wallpapers and furnishings. Enjoy breakfast in the garden before touring the city. It's just two blocks to the waterfront shops and restaurants. Your hostess will be happy to point the way to the beaches and Mauve Decade mansions.

Woody Hill Guest House ✪
RR1 BOX 676E, WOODY HILL ROAD, WESTERLY, RHODE ISLAND 02891

Tel: **(401) 322-0452**
Best Time to Call: **After 5 PM, during school year**
Host(s): **Ellen L. Madison**
Location: **¾ mi. from Rt 1**
No. of Rooms: **2**
Max. No. Sharing Bath: **6**
Double/sb: **$42**

Single/sb: **$36**
Open: **All year**
Reduced Rates: **Off-season**
Breakfast: **Full**
Pets: **No**
Children: **Welcome**
Smoking: **No**
Social Drinking: **Permitted**

This colonial reproduction is set on a hilltop among informal gardens and fields. Antiques, wide-board floors, and handmade quilts create an early American atmosphere. Your hostess serves homemade jams, muffins, and fresh raspberries in the morning. She can direct you to Mystic Seaport, Block Island, and historic areas. Newport's famous beaches, where "The 400" played, are just two miles away.

SOUTH CAROLINA

Twelve Oaks Inn ✪
ROUTE 2, BOX 293, HIGHWAY 280, BEAUFORT, SOUTH CAROLINA 29902

Tel: **(803) 524-1530**
Best Time to Call: **Mornings**
Host(s): **Garland and Gloria Bishop**
Location: **45 mi. N of Savannah**
No. of Rooms: **5**
No. of Private Baths: **1**
Max. No. Sharing Bath: **4**
Double/pb: **$45**
Double/sb: **$39–$45**
Single/sb: **$35**

Suites: **$70–90**
Open: **All year**
Reduced Rates: **10% Weekly; Seniors**
Breakfast: **Full**
Pets: **No**
Children: **Welcome, over 12**
Smoking: **Permitted**
Social Drinking: **Permitted**
Foreign Languages: **Spanish**

This plantation-style home is surrounded by magnificent trees and Spanish moss. The rooms have hardwood floors, high ceilings, and fine furnishings. Guests are welcome to relax by the fire, or on one of two large porches or sundeck perhaps. The large pond stocked with bass will entice you. Your hosts serve a Southern-style breakfast, including fresh fruits in season. They will gladly direct you to historic downtown Beaufort, Parris Island, Hunting Island State Park, area beaches, or the University of South Carolina-Beaufort campus nearby.

The Carriage House O
1413 LYTTLETON STREET, CAMDEN, SOUTH CAROLINA 29020

Tel: **(803) 432-2430**
Best Time to Call: **After 10 AM**
Host(s): **Dr. and Mrs. Robert Watkins**
Location: **30 mi. N of Columbia**
No. of Rooms: **2**
No. of Private Baths: **1½**
Double/pb: **$45**
Single/pb: **$45**

Open: **All year**
Breakfast: **Full**
Pets: **No**
Children: **Welcome (crib)**
Smoking: **Permitted**
Social Drinking: **Permitted**
Airport/Station Pickup: **Yes**

The Carriage House is an antebellum cottage with window boxes and a picket fence. Located in the center of historic Camden, it is within walking distance of tennis, parks, and shops. The guest rooms have twin or double beds and are decorated with colorful fabrics and lovely antiques. Visitors are welcomed to their quarters with complimentary sherry, fruit, and cheese. Your hosts serve a Southern-style breakfast featuring grits, eggs, and fresh-squeezed juices.

The Inn O
1308-10 BROAD STREET, CAMDEN, SOUTH CAROLINA 29020

Tel: **(803) 425-1806**
Best Time to Call: **10 AM–5 PM**
Host(s): **John, Katherine, and Ted de Loach**
Location: **32 mi. NE of Columbia**
No. of Rooms: **12**
No. of Private Baths: **12**
Double/pb: **$55–$75**
Single/pb: **$35–$65**
Suites: **$65**
Open: **All year**

Reduced Rates: **June 1–Sept. 1; weekly**
Breakfast: **Continental**
Other Meals: **Available**
Credit Cards: **AMEX, MC, VISA**
Pets: **Sometimes**
Children: **Welcome**
Smoking: **Permitted**
Social Drinking: **Permitted**
Airport/Station Pickup: **Yes**
Foreign Languages: **French**

The two historic houses which comprise The Inn were built in 1825 and 1890. Their remodeling was done with care to retain their gracious ambience and to include all modern comforts. Camden is the oldest inland town in the state and is filled with homes of historic and architectural significance. The Carolina Cup and Colonial Cup steeplechase races are held here in the spring and fall, respectively. The Veranda Restaurant, widely acclaimed for its fine cuisine and unique atmosphere, is managed separately but is located on the premises.

Charleston East Bed & Breakfast
1031 TALL PINE ROAD, MOUNT PLEASANT, SOUTH CAROLINA 29464

Tel: **(803) 884-8208**
Coordinator: **Bobbie Auld**
State/Regions Covered: **East Cooper, Sullivan's Island, Isle of Palms**

Rates (Single/Double):
Average $10–$20 $20–30

Bobbie has lovely homes in the geographic area known as East Cooper, three miles from downtown historic Charleston. Several are furnished in antiques; others are contemporary. One is in the small fishing village north of Charleston, where the host offers cruises in the evening on his houseboat. The non-commercial beaches of Sullivan's Island and the Isle of Palms are close by.

Historic Charleston Bed & Breakfast
43 LEGARE STREET, CHARLESTON, SOUTH CAROLINA 29401

Tel: **(803) 722-6606**
Best Time to Call: **1–6 PM**
Coordinator: **Charlotte Fairey**
State/Regions Covered: **Charleston**

Rates (Single/Double):
Modest: $30 $45
Average $50 $65
Luxury: $75 $100
Credit Cards: **No**

This port city is one of the most historic in the U.S. Through the auspices of Charlotte, you will enjoy your stay in a private home, carriage house, or mansion in a neighborhood of enchanting walled gardens, cobblestoned streets and moss-draped oak trees. Each home is unique, yet each has a warm and friendly atmosphere provided by a host who sincerely enjoys making guests welcome. All are historic properties dating from 1720 to 1890, yet all are up to date with air-conditioning, phones, and television. Reduced rates are available for weekly stays but there is a $5 surcharge for one night visits.

Holland's Guest House ✪
15 NEW STREET, CHARLESTON, SOUTH CAROLINA 29401

Tel: **(803) 723-0090**	Open: **All year**
Best Time to Call: **After 6 PM**	Reduced Rates: **Weekly, $300**
Host(s): **Betty and Wallace Holland**	Breakfast: **Full**
Location: **1½ mi. from I-26**	Pets: **No**
No. of Rooms: **1**	Children: **No**
No. of Private Baths: **1**	Smoking: **Permitted**
Guest Cottage: **$55; sleeps 2**	Social Drinking: **Permitted**

Betty and Wallace live in the historic district, a short distance from the downtown area. Attached to their 100-year-old house is a newly renovated guest cottage. It has a small kitchen stocked with breakfast foods and snacks, and an enclosed porch with an eating area. The bedroom, private bath, phone, and TV are perfect for travelers seeking home-style living and a little privacy. Complimentary wine and cheese are part of the Southern hospitality. The Citadel and College of Charleston are close by.

Two Meeting Street Inn ✪
2 MEETING STREET, CHARLESTON, SOUTH CAROLINA 29401

Tel: **(803) 723-7322**	Single/sb: **$40**
Host(s): **David Spell**	Open: **All year**
No. of Rooms: **7**	Reduced Rates: **10%, weekly**
No. of Private Baths: **5**	Breakfast: **Continental**
Max. No. Sharing Bath: **3**	Pets: **No**
Double/pb: **$75–$85**	Children: **Welcome**
Single/pb: **$60–$70**	Smoking: **Permitted**
Double/sb: **$50**	Social Drinking: **Permitted**

This Queen Anne Victorian mansion was originally built as a wedding gift for a wealthy banker's daughter. Today, the inn specializes in honeymooners and appreciative visitors. Tiffany glass windows, carved oak paneling, beautifully arched piazzas, antiques, and Oriental rugs set the elegant tone. Afternoon and evening sherry are gladly provided. Your hosts can point out the local sights and lend you bicycles for touring.

Two Meeting Street Inn

Coosaw Plantation ✪
DALE, SOUTH CAROLINA 29914

Tel: **(803) 846-8225**
Best Time to Call: **After 6 PM**
Host(s): **Peggy Sanford**
Location: **50 mi. S of Charleston**
Guest Cottage: **$35 (for 2);
$40 (for 4)**
Open: **Mar. 1–Dec. 31**

Breakfast: **Continental**
Pets: **Welcome**
Children: **Welcome**
Smoking: **Permitted**
Social Drinking: **Permitted**
Foreign Languages: **Spanish, French**

This sprawling plantation offers a relaxed setting on the Coosaw River. Each guest cottage has a living room with fireplace, a full kitchen, and a bath. Your hosts will prepare a breakfast of muffins or casseroles, or will leave the fixings in your cottage. Boating, fishing, or a visit to Beaufort and Savannah are just a few of the local possibilities. Or, stay "home" and use the pool and tennis court on-premises.

Shaw House
8 CYPRESS COURT, GEORGETOWN, SOUTH CAROLINA 29440

Tel: **(803) 546-9663**
Host(s): **Mary Shaw**
Location: **1 block off Hwy. 17**
No. of Rooms: **2**
No. of Private Baths: **2**
Double/pb: **$40**
Single/pb: **$40**

Open: **All year**
Breakfast: **Full**
Pets: **No**
Children: **Welcome**
Smoking: **Permitted**
Social Drinking: **Permitted**
Airport/Station Pickup: **Yes**

Shaw House is a two-story colonial with a beautiful view of the Willowbank Marsh. Your hostess is knowledgeable about antiques and has filled the rooms with nostalgia. The rocking chairs and cool breeze will tempt you to the porch. Each morning a pot of coffee and Southern-style casserole await you. Fresh fruit and homemade snacks are available all day. The house is within walking distance of the historic district and is near Myrtle Beach, Pawleys Island, golf, tennis, and restaurants.

Serendipity, An Inn
407 71ST AVENUE NORTH, MYRTLE BEACH, SOUTH CAROLINA 29577

Tel: **(803) 449-5268**
Host(s): **Cos and Ellen Ficarra**
Location: **½ block from I-17**
No. of Rooms: 15
No. of Private Baths: 15
Double/pb: **$50–$58**
Single/pb: **$45**
Suites: **$70**
Open: **Mar. 16–Oct. 14**

Reduced Rates: **Off-season**
Breakfast: **Continental**
Credit Cards: **MC, VISA**
Pets: **No**
Children: **Welcome (crib)**
Smoking: **No**
Social Drinking: **Permitted**
Airport/Station Pickup: **Yes**
Foreign Languages: **Spanish, Italian**

The Serendipity is a Spanish Mission-style inn, 300 yards from the ocean. The spacious rooms are furnished in different period styles using oak, pine, mahogany, or wicker. Relax in a heated pool or spend a quiet moment by the patio fountain. The cheery garden room is the spot for breakfast and friendly conversation. Free bikes, shuffleboard, ping pong, and bumper pool are available. Miles of open beach, golf courses, restaurants, and shopping are all nearby. The University of South Carolina is a short drive from the Inn.

A Country Place ◊
ROUTE 1, BOX 585, SALEM, SOUTH CAROLINA 27676

Tel: **(803) 944-0477**
Best Time to Call: **8–10 AM; 7–10 PM**
Host(s): **Polly Medlicott, Manfred Mueller**
Location: **30 mi. from I-85**
No. of Rooms: 4

Max. No. Sharing Bath: 3
Double/sb: **$30**
Single/sb: **$20**
Guest Cottage: **$350 weekly; sleeps 6–8**
Open: **Feb.–Nov.**

Reduced Rates: **Weekly**
Breakfast: **Full**
Pets: **Sometimes**
Children: **Welcome (crib)**

Smoking: **Permitted**
Social Drinking: **Permitted**
Foreign Languages: **German**

If you have ever wanted your own place in the country, this will come close. There are 100 acres of meadows, woods, and streams, a fish pond, and a cedar-shingled farmhouse with a long porch for relaxing. Polly and Manfred live next door and have stocked "your home" with fresh breakfast ingredients as well as such conveniences as a dishwasher, washer, and dryer. It's 10 minutes to state parks, lakes, Whitewater Falls, and the Chattooga River, and close to the mountains of Georgia and North Carolina. Don't miss local activities like country music concerts, and antiquing.

Prospect Hill Plantation
BOX 173, YONGES ISLAND, CHARLESTON COUNTY, SOUTH CAROLINA 29494

Tel: **(803) 889-3807**
Host(s): **Suzy Merck**
Location: **30 mi. S of Charleston**
No. of Rooms: **4**
No. of Private Baths: **3**
Max. No. Sharing Bath: **3**
Double/pb: **$65**
Single/sb: **$38**
Suites: **$55**

Open: **Oct. 1–July 1**
Breakfast: **Continental**
Other Meals: **Available**
Pets: **Sometimes**
Children: **Welcome**
Smoking: **Permitted**
Social Drinking: **Permitted**
Airport/Station Pickup: **Yes**
Foreign Languages: **French**

This lovely residence (circa 1845), in the National Register of Historic Places, is at the end of a 900-foot-long oak-lined avenue. The family antiques, baby grand piano, fine linens, and lovely appointments speak of a rich past and comfortable present. It is close to South Edisto River for boating and fishing. Breakfast features home-grown corn for grits and bread, fresh eggs, and homemade jams.

SOUTH DAKOTA

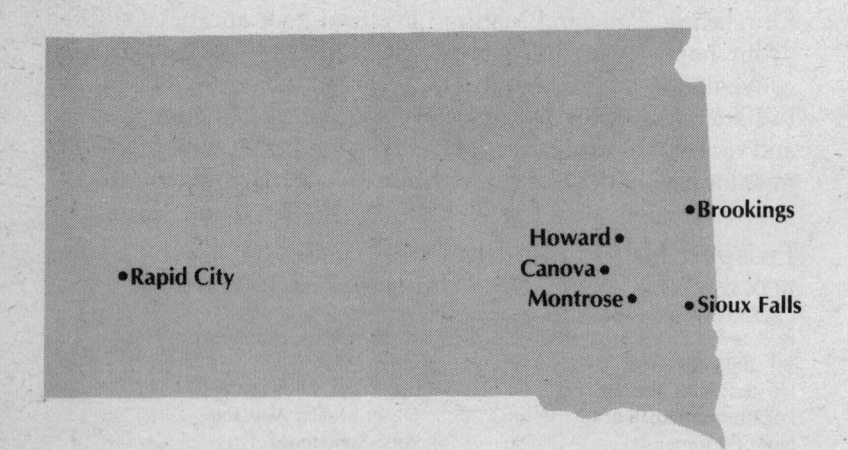

Bed and Breakfast of South Dakota
P.O. BOX 80137, SIOUX FALLS, SOUTH DAKOTA 57116

Tel: (605) 528-6571 or 339-0759
Coordinators: **Kathy Hales and Karen Olson**
State/Regions Covered: **Academy, Armour, Buffalo, Deadwood, Rapid City, Salem, Sioux Falls**

Rates (Single/Double):
  Average: $20 $27.50
Credit Cards: **No**

From the majestic Black Hills across rolling prairie to the city and to awesome Mt. Rushmore, you will be treated to Midwestern hospitality at its best. Whether traveling through the state, skiing, hunting, or on business, you will enjoy staying in a private home of one of Kathy and Karen's hosts.

Skoglund Farm ✪
CANOVA, SOUTH DAKOTA 57321

Tel: **(605) 247-3445**	Reduced Rates: **Under 18**
Best Time to Call: **Early AM, evenings**	Breakfast: **Full**
Host(s): **Alden and Delores Skoglund**	Other Meals: **Dinner included**
Location: **12 miles from I-90**	Pets: **Welcome**
No. of Rooms: **5**	Children: **Welcome (crib)**
Max. No. Sharing Bath: **3**	Smoking: **Permitted**
Double/sb: **$50**	Social Drinking: **Permitted**
Single/sb: **$25**	Airport/Station Pickup: **Yes**
Open: **All year**	

This is a working farm where the emphasis is on the simple, good life. It is a welcome escape from urban living. You may, if you wish, help with the farm chores, or just watch everyone else work; the family raises cattle, fowl, and peacocks. You may ride the horses over the wide, open spaces. You are welcome to use the laundry facilities or play the piano. The coffee pot is always on.

Lakeside Farm
RR2, BOX 52, WEBSTER, SOUTH DAKOTA 57274

Tel: **(605) 486-4430**	Open: **All year**
Host(s): **Joy and Glenn Hagen**	Breakfast: **Full**
Location: **60 mi. E of Aberdeen on Hwy. 12**	Pets: **No**
No. of Rooms: **2**	Children: **Welcome**
Double/sb: **$25**	Smoking: **No**
Single/sb: **$20**	Social Drinking: **No**

This hundred year old, 750 acre farmstead where Joy and Glen raise oats, corn, and a herd of 50 Holstein dairy cows, is located in the Lake Region where recreational activities abound. You are certain to be comfortable in their farmhouse, built in 1970 and furnished in a simple, informal style. You will awaken to the delicious aroma of Joy's heavenly cinnamon rolls or bread and enjoy breakfast served on the enclosed porch in view of the pretty garden. Nearby attractions include Fort Sisseton and the June festival that recounts Sam Browne's historic ride. You will also enjoy the Blue Dog fish hatchery, and the Game Reserve. Don't leave 'til you've watched the cows being milked and had a dish of home-churned ice cream!

TENNESSEE

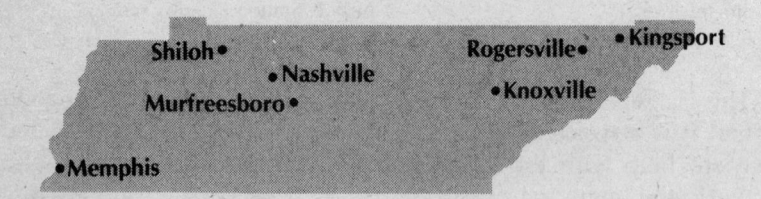

Host Homes of Tennessee (a B&B Group) ✪
P.O. BOX 110227, NASHVILLE, TENNESSEE 37222

Tel: **(615) 331-5244**
Coordinator: **Fredda Odom**
States/Regions Covered: **Statewide**

Rates (Single/Double):
Average: $26–$30 $32–$35
Luxury: $32–$35 $45–$50
Credit Cards: **MC, VISA**

From the Great Smoky Mountains to the Mississippi, here is a diversity of attractions that includes fabulous scenery, Nashville's Grand Ole Opry and Opryland, universities, Civil War sites, horse farms, and much more. Fredda will arrange sightseeing tours, car rentals, tickets to events, and everything she can to assure you a pleasant stay.

Shallowford Farm ✪
ROUTE 6, BOX 142, KINGSPORT, TENNESSEE 37660

Tel: **(615) 245-0798**
Best Time to Call: **Evenings**
Host(s): **Jane and Bill Walley**
Location: **15 mi. from I-81**
No. of Rooms: **2**
Max. No. Sharing Bath: **4**
Double/sb: **$30**
Single/sb: **$25**
Open: **All year**
Breakfast: **Full**
Pets: **Sometimes**
Children: **Welcome**
Smoking: **No**
Social Drinking: **Permitted**

This Dutch colonial farmhouse overlooks a river and the Tennessee hills. You will enjoy relaxing on the porch or using the swimming pool. Take a walk in the herb garden, or watch the cattle and poultry. A breakfast featuring fresh eggs, jams, jellies, and fruit is served by the fireside in winter or on the screened porch in summer. The Bays Mountain Nature Center and historic Netherland Inn are nearby.

Three Chimneys of Knoxville
1302 WHITE AVENUE, KNOXVILLE, TENNESSEE 37916

Tel: **(615) 521-4970**
Host(s): **Alfred and Margo Akerman**
Location: **½ mi. from I-40/I-75**
No. of Rooms: **4**
No. of Private Baths: **2**
Max. No. Sharing Bath: **2**
Double/pb: **$50**
Single/pb: **$45**
Double/sb: **$40–$45**
Single/sb: **$35–$40**
Open: **All year**
Breakfast: **Full**
Pets: **No**
Children: **Welcome**
Smoking: **Permitted**
Social Drinking: **Permitted**
Foreign Languages: **French, German**

This Queen Anne Victorian mansion is located in a historic neighborhood on the University of Tennessee campus. The large guest rooms are carpeted and furnished in antiques. Breakfast is served on a glassed-in porch; a magnolia blooms nearby beginning in May. Breakfast may include grits, biscuits, wheat pancakes, and Southern cured bacon; the coffee pot starts perking at dawn for early risers.

Bed & Breakfast in Memphis ✪
P.O. BOX 41621, MEMPHIS, TENNESSEE 38174

Tel: (901) 726-5920
Best Time to Call: 8 AM–6 PM, Weekdays
Coordinator: Helen Denton
States/Regions Covered:
  Tennessee—Bolivar, Eads, Fisherville, Germantown, Memphis;
  Arkansas—Hughes;
  Mississippi—Holly Springs
Rates (Single/Double):
  Modest: $26 $32
  Average: $34 $40
  Luxury: $45 $80
Credit Cards: MC, VISA

A sampler of Memphis sights includes the mighty Mississippi River, Mud Island, historic Beale Street, Victorian Village, Memphis Brooks Art Gallery, and Overton Park and Zoo. Helen will send you a descriptive listing of all the accommodations offered by her hosts. The $2.50 directory charge will be credited to your reservation. The University of Tennessee Medical College, Rhodes College, and Memphis State University are convenient to many of the homes.

Clardy's Guest House ✪
435 EAST MAIN STREET, MURFREESBORO, TENNESSEE 37130

Tel: (615) 893-6030
Best Time to Call: Before 11 PM
Host(s): Frank and Barbara Clardy
Location: 2 mi. from I-24
No. of Rooms: 8
No. of Private Baths: 6
Max. No. Sharing Bath: 4
Double/pb: $20
Single/pb: $15
Double/sb: $15
Single/sb: $12.50
Open: All year
Breakfast: No
Pets: Yes
Children: Welcome (crib)
Smoking: Permitted
Social Drinking: Permitted

This Romanesque-style Victorian dates back to 1898. The 20 rooms are filled with antiques; with 40 antique dealers in town, you can guess what Murfreesboro is best known for. The world championship horse show at Shelbyville is 30 minutes away. Your hosts will be glad to advise on local tours and can direct you to the home of Grand Ole Opry, one hour away in Nashville, and fine eating places. Middle Tennessee State University is close by.

Miss Anne's Bed & Breakfast
3033 WINDEMERE CIRCLE, NASHVILLE, TENNESSEE 37214

Tel: **(615) 885-1899**	Single/sb: **$21**
Best Time to Call: **After 4 PM**	Open: **All year**
Host(s): **Anne Cowell**	Reduced Rates: **10%, seniors,**
Location: **2 mi. from I-40**	**off-season**
No. of Rooms: **4**	Breakfast: **Full**
No. of Private Baths: **1**	Pets: **No**
Max. No. Sharing Bath: **4**	Children: **Welcome**
Double/pb: **$27**	Smoking: **Permitted**
Single/pb: **$24**	Social Drinking: **Permitted**
Double/sb: **$24**	Airport/Station Pickup: **Yes**

Visiting Anne is easy and pleasant in her comfortable home furnished with a cozy blend of antiques and lots of wood and glass. Her collection of doll dishes is quite special. Breakfast features such delectables as French toast, German pancakes, and homemade raspberry preserves. Opryland, the Hermitage, and the Parthenon are all nearby, as is Vanderbilt University.

Hale Springs Inn ✪
ROGERSVILLE, TENNESSEE 37857

Tel: **(615) 272-5171**	Open: **All year**
Host(s): **Lola Moore, Captain and Mrs.**	Breakfast: **$1.50**
Carl Netherland Brown	Other Meals: **Available**
Location: **60 mi. NE of Knoxville**	Credit Cards: **MC, VISA**
No. of Rooms: **10**	Pets: **Sometimes**
No. of Private Baths: **10**	Children: **Welcome**
Double/pb: **$35**	Smoking: **Permitted**
Single/pb: **$30**	Social Drinking: **Permitted**
Suites: **$55**	Foreign Languages: **Spanish**

This three-story Federal inn dates from 1824. George Washington did not sleep here, but Andrew Jackson did. Large, high-ceilinged rooms with fireplaces, antiques, and four-poster beds continue the hosting tradition. Guests will enjoy touring the rest of the historic district. Davy Crockett's home, Lake Cherokee, and the Smoky Mountains are nearby. Rogersville is one of Tennessee's oldest towns.

TEXAS

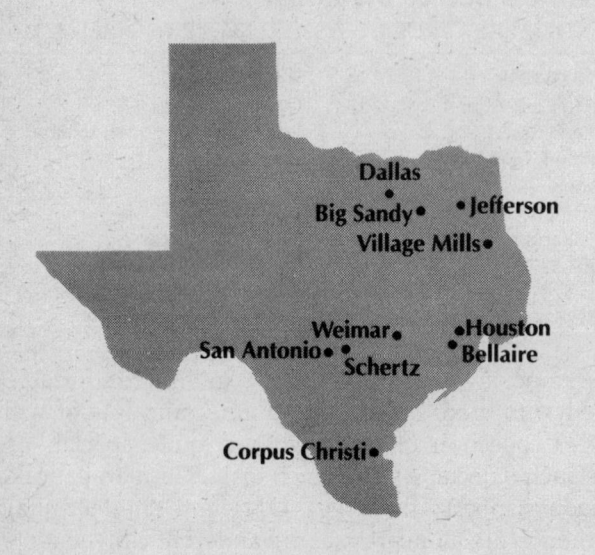

Bed & Breakfast Texas Style ✪
4224 W. RED BIRD LANE, DALLAS, TEXAS 75237

Tel: **(214) 298-8586**
Best Time to Call: **9 AM–6 PM**
Coordinator: **Ruth Wilson**
States/Regions Covered: **Austin, Dallas, Denison, Fort Worth, El Paso, Galveston, Garland, Houston, San Antonio, Waco**

Rates (Single/Double):
Modest: $20 $30
Average: $29 $40
Luxury: $35 $60
Credit Cards: No

The above cities are only a small sample of the locations of hosts waiting to give you plenty of warm hospitality. Ruth's register includes comfortable accommodations in condos, restored Victorians, lakeside cottages, and ranches. To make your choice, please send $2 for her descriptive directory. Texas University, Southern Methodist University, Baylor University, Rice University, and Texas Christian University are convenient to many B&Bs.

Annie's Bed and Breakfast ✪
106 NORTH TYLER, BIG SANDY, TEXAS 75755

Tel: (214) 636-4307
Host(s): **Christopher and Jolinda Klotz**
Location: **10 mi. from I-20**
No. of Rooms: **13**
No. of Private Baths: **8**
Max. No. Sharing Bath: **4**
Double/pb: **$58–$100**
Single/pb: **$48–$90**
Double/sb: **$45–$48**
Single/sb: **$35–$38**
Suites: **$100**

Open: **All year**
Reduced Rates: **Available**
Breakfast: **Full**
Other Meals: **Available**
Credit Cards: **MC, VISA**
Pets: **No**
Children: **Welcome (crib)**
Smoking: **No**
Social Drinking: **Permitted**
Airport/Station Pickup: **Yes**

This restored Victorian is in the heart of the stately pines region of northeast Texas. The house is surrounded by a white picket fence, and features decorative porches and balconies. Each guest room is furnished with antiques, imported rugs, handmade quilts, and fresh flowers. Breakfast specialties include pecan rolls, blueberry muffins, Belgian waffles, and strawberry soup. Your hosts will gladly point the way to local craft shops, restaurants, and the Tyler Rose Gardens.

Sand Dollar Hospitality B&B
3605 MENDENHALL, CORPUS CHRISTI, TEXAS 78415

Tel: (512) 853-1222
Best Time to Call: **8 AM–7 PM**
Coordinator: **Pat Hirsbrunner**
States/Regions Covered: **Corpus Christi**

Rates (Single/Double):
  Modest: **$20**   **$25**
  Average: **$25**   **$30**
  Luxury: **$35**   **$40**
Credit Cards: **No**

Enjoy Southern hospitality in this sparkling city-by-the-sea, touted as the Texas Riviera. It combines urban life with an abundance of outdoor pleasures. There's the Padre Island National Seashore. Go crabbing in Bird Island. Visit King Ranch, with its real cowboys, or the art colony of Rockport. Shopping in Mexico is only 2½ hours away by car. Take in an evening at the symphony or participate in genuine country-and-western dancing. Great Mexican food, barbecue, fresh fish, and shrimp are regional specialties. Corpus Christi State University is nearby.

The Bed & Breakfast Society of Houston ✪
4432 HOLT, BELLAIRE, TEXAS 77401

Tel: **(713) 666-6372**	Rates (Single/Double):
Best Time to Call: **9 AM–5 PM**	Modest: **$25** **$35**
Coordinator: **Debbie Herman Siegel**	Average: **$25** **$35**
States/Regions Covered: **Houston and suburbs**	Luxury: **$60** **$100**
	Credit Cards: **No**

Whether you're traveling for business or pleasure, Debbie's hosts offer the kind of friendliness and individualized care that will make your stay pleasant. The area is known for the Astrodome, Galveston Bay, NASA, and the Texas Medical Center. There are wonderful restaurants, shops, museums, and historic sights, and Baylor, Rice, and the University of Houston are nearby.

The Hostess House B&B ✪
10601 WILLOWGROVE, HOUSTON, TEXAS 77035

Tel: **(713) 721-5202**	Single/sb: **$30**
Host(s): **Arthur and Naomi McCall**	Open: **All year**
Location: **3 mi. from I-10**	Reduced Rates: **Seniors; families**
No. of Rooms: **6**	Breakfast: **Continental**
No. of Private Baths: **2**	Other Meals: **Available**
Max. No. Sharing Bath: **3**	Pets: **No**
Double/pb: **$50**	Children: **Welcome, over 12**
Single/pb: **$40**	Smoking: **Permitted**
Double/sb: **$40**	Social Drinking: **Permitted**

This contemporary two-story home is in a quiet, residential area, less than 15 minutes from the Medical Center or the Astrodome, and within walking distance of a large shopping center with movies and restaurants. Furnished with a comfortable mix of antiques, collectibles, and family mementoes, it will feel like "home." Naomi is a registered nurse and a hostess who enjoys cooking Southern-style. Rice University is nearby.

Bed & Breakfast Hosts of San Antonio
166 ROCKHILL, SAN ANTONIO, TEXAS 78209

Tel: **(512) 824-8036**	Rates (Single/Double):
Best Time to Call: **9 AM–5 PM**	Modest: **$29** **$42.50**
Coordinator: **Lavern Campbell**	Average: **$40.50** **$53.50**
States/Regions Covered: **San Antonio**	Luxury: **$51.50** **$59**
	Credit Cards: **MC, VISA**

You'll find hospitable hosts waiting to welcome you and to suggest how best to enjoy this beautiful and historic city. Don't miss the Paseo del Rio (a bustling river walk), the Alamo, the Arneson River Theatre showplace, El Mercado (which is a restored Mexican and Farmers Market), the Southwest Craft Center, wonderful restaurants, marvelous shops, and delightful, friendly folks. The University of Texas, Trinity University, and St. Mary's University are nearby.

Cardinal Cliff ✪
3806 HIGHCLIFF, SAN ANTONIO, TEXAS 78218

Tel: **(512) 655-2939**	Open: **All year**
Host(s): **Roger and Alice Sackett**	Breakfast: **Full**
No. of Rooms: **3**	Pets: **Sometimes**
Max. No. Sharing Bath: **4**	Children: **Welcome (crib)**
Double/sb: **$25**	Smoking: **Permitted**
Single/sb: **$18**	Social Drinking: **Permitted**

This is a suburban ranch-style home, overlooking a wooded river valley, and furnished in Victorian style. It is located close to the Lyndon B. Johnson ranch and major San Antonio attractions. Roger, a retired army officer, and Alice, a retired librarian, enjoy having guests and welcome you with coffee or iced tea. Trinity University is nearby.

Seventh Haven ✪
140 PATRICK HENRY, SCHERTZ, TEXAS 78154

Tel: **(512) 658-6474**	No. of Rooms: **2**
Host(s): **Walter and Janie Sargeant**	Max. No. Sharing Bath: **4**
Location: **3 mi. from Randolph A. F. Base**	Double/sb: **$25**
	Single/sb: **$18**

Open: **All year**
Reduced Rates: **15% weekly; 10% seniors**
Breakfast: **Full**

Pets: **No**
Children: **Sometimes**
Smoking: **No**
Social Drinking: **Permitted**

Walter and Janie have a clean, comfortable home in a small development in a rural area. It is in a pleasant, quiet neighborhood in the Greenfield Village section. You can be in San Antonio in less than a half hour, and the LBJ Ranch is two hours away. Texas Lutheran College and Trinity University are close by.

Big Thicket Guest House ✪
BOX 91, VILLAGE MILLS, TEXAS 77663

Tel: **(409) 834-2875**
Best Time to Call: **Evenings**
Host(s): **Paul and Mary Betzner**
Location: **30 miles from I-10**
No. of Rooms: **2**
Max. No. Sharing Bath: **4**
Double/sb: **$40**
Single/sb: **$35**

Open: **All year**
Reduced Rates: **15% seniors, families**
Breakfast: **Full**
Other Meals: **Available**
Pets: **Sometimes**
Children: **Welcome**
Smoking: **No**
Social Drinking: **Permitted**

This comfortable country home is furnished with antiques, some of which are for sale. Guests are welcome to enjoy a complimentary glass of wine. Breakfast specialties include homemade biscuits or waffles. Your hosts are happy to point the way to nearby tennis, golf, swimming, biking, and touring the Big Thicket National Forest. An Indian reservation and quite a few historic sights are within a half-hour's ride.

Weimar Country Inn ✪
P.O. BOX 782, WEIMAR, TEXAS 78962

Tel: **(409) 725-8888**
Host(s): **Kelly Koenig**
Location: **82 mi. W of Houston**
No. of Rooms: **9**
No. of Private Baths: **7**
Max. No. Sharing Bath: **4**
Double/pb: **$38–$65**
Double/sb: **$30**
Suites: **$125**

Open: **All year**
Breakfast: **Continental**
Meals: **Available**
Credit Cards: **AMEX, MC, VISA**
Pets: **No**
Children: **Welcome, over 8**
Smoking: **Permitted**
Social Drinking: **Permitted**

The Weimar is constructed in the wood clapboard style of the late 19th century. The rooms are furnished with antiques, lovely quilts, and harmonized wallpaper. Your hosts welcome you to cocktails and fine dining on the premises. Breakfast features homemade jams and strudel. Nearby, enjoy a tour of the historic district, golfing, and antiquing.

For key to listings, see inside front or back cover.

◐ This star means that rates are guaranteed through December 31, 1985 to any guest making a reservation as a result of reading about the *B&B in BED & BREAKFAST U.S.A.*—1985 edition.

Please enclose a self-addressed, stamped, business-sized envelope when contacting reservation services.

For more details on what you can expect in a B&B, see Chapter 1.

Always mention *Bed & Breakfast USA* when making reservations!

UTAH

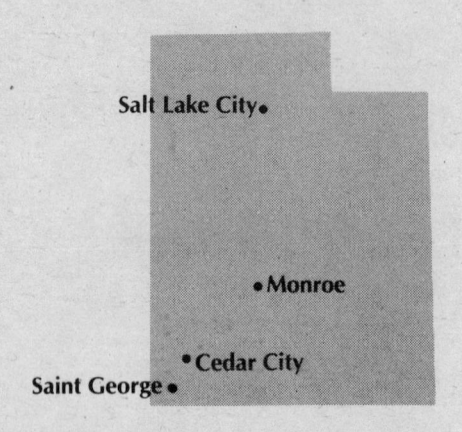

Bed 'n' Breakfast Association of Utah
P.O. BOX 16465, SALT LAKE CITY, UTAH 84116

Tel: **(801) 532-7076**
Best Time to Call: **9 AM–5 PM**
Coordinators: **Barbara Baker, Nadine Smith**
States/Regions Covered: **Statewide**

Rates (Single/Double):
　Modest:　$20–$30　　$30–$40
　Average:　$30–$50　　$40–$60
　Luxury:　$50–$70　　$60–$100
Credit Cards: **No**
Minimum Stay: **2 nights**

Utah has something for everyone, and Barbara and Nadine have a roster of hosts who delight in making you feel at home. A full breakfast is included with most of the accommodations. Location and season are taken into consideration in the rate, and discounts are offered to senior citizens, families, and for extended stays. Send $1 and a SASE for a directory. Brigham Young University, University of Utah, Southern Utah State College (site of the Utah Shakespeare Festival in summer) are near many B&Bs.

Meadeau View Lodge ✪
P.O. BOX 356, HIGHWAY 14, DUCK CREEK VILLAGE, CEDAR CITY, UTAH 84720

Tel: (801) 682-2495
Best Time to Call: 7 AM–10 PM
Host(s): Harry and Gaby Moyer
Location: 30 mi. E of Cedar City
No. of Rooms: 9
No. of Private Baths: 9
Double/pb: $38–$49
Single/pb: $25
Suites: $49
Open: All year

Reduced Rates: 10% weekly
Breakfast: Full
Other Meals: Available
Pets: No
Children: Welcome (crib)
Smoking: Permitted
Social Drinking: Permitted
Airport/Station Pickup: Yes
Foreign Languages: German

The lodge is nestled in a pine and aspen forest, 8,400 feet above sea level. In the back meadow, there's trout fishing in Duck Pond; Aspen Mirror Lake is down the road. Harry and Gaby will direct you to nearby Zion National Park and Bryce Canyon, about an hour's drive away. Coffee and cookies are always available, but if you want something stronger, bring your own; this is Utah!

Peterson's Bed and Breakfast ✪
95 NORTH 300 WEST, MONROE, UTAH 84754

Tel: (801) 527-4830
Best Time to Call: After 6 PM
Host(s): Mary Ann & Howard Peterson
Location: 10 mi. SW of Richfield
No. of Rooms: 2 (Suite)

No. of Private Baths: 1
Double/pb: $30
Single/pb: $20
Suite: $55
Open: All year
Reduced Rates: 5%, seniors

Breakfast: **Full**
Other Meals: **Available**
Pets: **Sometimes**

Children: **Welcome**
Smoking: **No**
Social Drinking: **No**

This modern farmhouse, casual and comfortable, is surrounded by 10,000-foot mountains in the heart of hunting and fishing country. The Petersons have traveled extensively, and Mary Ann has written a marvelous cookbook called *Country Cooking*. If you're interested in your ancestral roots, you can use the genealogical files in Richfield for tracing your beginnings; there is no charge for this information service. Monroe Hot Springs is nearby. It's a few hours' drive to Provo, Salt Lake City, or St. George.

Larkin Inn ✪
4750 400 EAST, ST. GEORGE, UTAH 84770

Tel: **(801) 673-2303**
Best Time to Call: **8 AM**
Host(s): **Montrue Larkin**
Location: **On Rte. 475**
No. of Rooms: **3**
No. of Private Baths: **1**
Max. No. Sharing Bath: **3**
Double/pb: **$35**
Single/pb: **$25**
Double/sb: **$25**

Single/sb: **$15**
Suites: **$37**
Open: **All year**
Breakfast: **Continental**
Pets: **Sometimes**
Children: **Welcome**
Smoking: **No**
Social Drinking: **No**
Airport/Station Pickup: **Yes**

Montrue teaches a class in furniture restoration and refinishing, so it is not surprising that this comfortable B&B has some beautiful antiques. Zion National Park is 50 miles away. There are many interesting things to see and do right in St. George. Breakfast features homemade breads and jams but no coffee is served.

Seven Wives Inn ✪
217 NORTH 100 WEST, ST. GEORGE, UTAH 84770

Tel: **(801) 628-3737**
Best Time to Call: **After 9 AM**
Host(s): **Jay and Donna Curtis**
Location: **120 mi. NE of Las Vegas**
No. of Rooms: **8**
No. of Private Baths: **6**
Max. No. Sharing Bath: **5**

Double/pb: **$30–$50**
Single/pb: **$30-$50**
Double/sb: **$25–$35**
Single/sb: **$20–$35**
Open: **All year**
Breakfast: **Full**
Credit Cards: **MC, VISA**

Pets: **Sometimes**
Children: **Welcome, over 12**
Smoking: **No**

Social Drinking: **Permitted**
Airport/Station Pickup: **Yes**

This delightful inn is featured on the walking tour of St. George; it is just across from the Brigham Young home and two blocks from the historic Washington County Court House. Jay and Donna offer traditional Western hospitality. Their home is decorated with antiques collected in America and Europe. Each bedroom is named after one of the seven wives of Donna's polygamous great-grandfather. A gourmet breakfast is served in the elegant dining room that will give you a hint of the past. St. George is located near Zion and Bryce National Parks, boasts four golf courses, and is noted for its mild winters. Dixie College is nearby.

Eller Bed and Breakfast ✪
164 SOUTH 900 EAST, SALT LAKE CITY, UTAH 84102

Tel: **(801) 533-8184**
Host(s): **Margaret and LaVon Eller**
Location: **1 mi. from I-80**
No. of Rooms: **5**
Max. No. Sharing Bath: **6**
Double/sb: **$35**
Single/sb: **$25**

Open: **All year**
Breakfast: **Full**
Pets: **No**
Children: **Welcome**
Smoking: **No**
Social Drinking: **Permitted**
Airport/Station Pickup: **Yes**

This clean, comfortable, 80-year-old home is listed in the Utah Historical Register. If you're not traveling by car, you should know that restaurants, shops, the University of Utah, and the downtown attractions of Salt Lake are within walking distance. Margaret and LaVon are natural hosts. Wait until you smell breakfast being prepared. It often includes homemade cinnamon rolls or ableskeivers, fresh from the old Majestic stove.

VERMONT

[Map of Vermont showing locations: Montgomery, North Hero, West Charlston, St. Albans, Colchester, East Burke, Burlington, Stowe, Waterbury Center, Montpelier, Barre, Waitsfield, Lisbon, Franconia, Middlebury, Warren, Brookfield, Fairlee, Rochester, Bethel, West Hartford, White River Junction, Brownsville, South Wallingford, Ludlow, Proctorsville, Dorset, Perkinsville, Manchester, Bondville, West Dover, Bennington, Brattleboro, Woodford, Wilmington]

American Bed & Breakfast—New England ✪
P.O. BOX 983, ST. ALBANS, VERMONT 05478

States/Regions Covered: New Hampshire, Maine, Massachusetts, Vermont	Rates (Single/Double):	
	Modest: $18	$25
	Average: $25	$35
	Credit Cards: No	

This group of B&B hosts asks the prospective visitor to select the home of his choice from a descriptive directory and to make reservations directly with the host. The directory costs $3 and lists accommodations at farms, country villages, or ski chalets in New England and northern New York State. Many B&Bs are close to the University of Vermont, Trinity College, Dartmouth College, Bennington College, Smith College, Mt. Holyoke, Amherst, and the University of Massachusetts.

Woodruff House ☉
13 EAST STREET, BARRE, VERMONT 05641

Tel: **(802) 476-7745**
Best Time to Call: **Evenings**
Host(s): **Robert and Terry Somaini**
Location: **60 mi. S of Montreal**
No. of Rooms: **2**
Max. No. Sharing Bath: **4**
Double/sb: **$35**
Single/sb: **$28**

Open: **All year**
Breakfast: **Full**
Pets: **No**
Children: **Welcome**
Smoking: **No**
Social Drinking: **Permitted**
Airport/Station Pickup: **Yes**

Woodruff House is located in a quiet park in the heart of town. The house is painted Victorian style, using three colors: blue with white trim and cranberry shutters. Guest rooms are furnished in antiques and decorated with flair. Guests are welcome to relax in the two living rooms and use the TV and piano. Breakfast specialties include homemade breads and eggs prepared with Vermont cheddar. Your host will point the way to the state capital, five ski areas, museums, and some of the greatest fall foliage in the state.

Greenhurst Inn ☉
RIVER STREET, BETHEL, VERMONT 05032

Tel: **(802) 234-9474**
Host(s): **Lyle and Barbara Wolf**
Location: **30 mi. E of Rutland**
No. of Rooms: **12**
No. of Private Baths: **4**
Max. No. Sharing Bath: **5**
Double/pb: **$50–$60**
Single/pb: **$45–$55**
Double/sb: **$40–$45**

Single/sb: **$35–$40**
Open: **All year**
Breakfast: **Continental**
Credit Cards: **MC, VISA, AMEX**
Pets: **Welcome**
Children: **Welcome (crib)**
Smoking: **Permitted**
Social Drinking: **Permitted**

Located 100 yards from the White River, this elegant Queen Anne mansion is listed in the National Register of Historic Places. Built in 1891, the heavy brass hinges, embossed floral brass doorknobs, and etched windows at the entry have withstood the test of time. The cut crystal collection is magnificent, and the stereoscope and old Victrola add to the old-fashioned atmosphere. It's close to many points of historic interest, and seasonal recreational activities are abundant. There's tennis and croquet on the premises, and afternoon tea and snacks are served. Vermont Law School is close by.

Poplar Manor ✪
RD 2, BETHEL, VERMONT 05032

Tel: (802) 234-5426	Reduced Rates: 10%, weekly
Host(s): Carmen and Bob Jaynes	Breakfast: Continental
Location: 16 mi. N of Woodstock	Pets: Sometimes
No. of Rooms: 5	Children: Welcome
Max. No. Sharing Bath: 4	Smoking: Permitted
Double/sb: $26	Social Drinking: Permitted
Single/sb: $18	Airport/Station Pickup: Yes
Suites: $26	Foreign Languages: Spanish
Open: All year	

This 19th-century colonial is surrounded by green meadows and cornfields. The rooms are large and bright, with exposed beam ceilings, collectibles, and plants. Your hosts offer wine and mulled cider, served "spiked," if you wish. The fields back up to the White River and a swimming hole. Other area attractions include skiing, the Federal Fish Hatchery, and the shops of Woodstock. Vermont Law School is nearby.

The Barn Lodge
WINHALL HOLLOW ROAD, BONDVILLE, VERMONT 05340

Tel: (802) 297-1877	Open: June 1–Oct. 31
Host(s): Barbara and Paul Dittmer, Gertrude Rebecchi	Reduced Rates: 10%, AARP
	Breakfast: Full
Location: 12 mi. W of Manchester	Credit Cards: MC, VISA
No. of Rooms: 9	Pets: No
No. of Private Baths: 5	Children: Welcome
Max. No. Sharing Bath: 5	Smoking: Permitted
Double/pb: $50–$56	Social Drinking: Permitted
Double/sb: $50–$56	

This rustic lodge, on a quiet country road in the Green Mountains, was built in 1968, entirely of native rough-sawn pine. Inside, the fireplaced living room, playroom, knick-knacks and plants create a homey atmosphere. The guest rooms have wall-to-wall carpeting and twin beds. Your hosts invite you to swim in the outdoor pool or enjoy a game of golf at the local country club. Other nearby activities include theater, hiking, hunting, fishing, and crafts shows.

Green Trails Country Inn ✪
POND VILLAGE, BROOKFIELD, VERMONT 05036

Tel: (802) 276-3412
Host(s): **Betty and Jack Russell**
Location: **6 mi. from I-89**
No. of Rooms: **15**
No. of Private Baths: **9**
Max. No. Sharing Bath: **4**
Double/pb: **$55**
Single/pb: **$39.50**
Double/sb: **$49**
Single/sb: **$36.50**
Suites: **$52–$65**

Open: **All year**
Reduced Rates: **10%, weekly; seniors; families**
Breakfast: **Full**
Other Meals: **Available**
Pets: **Sometimes**
Children: **Welcome (crib)**
Smoking: **Permitted**
Social Drinking: **Permitted**
Airport/Station Pickup: **Yes**

The inn consists of two buildings. One is an 1840 farmhouse; the other was built in the late 1700s and has pumpkin pine floorboards. They are located across from the famous Floating Bridge. Furnished in antiques and "early nostalgia," the rooms have handmade quilts and fresh flowers. The historic village is a perfect base for seasonal excursions to the Shelburne Museum or Woodstock. Cross-country skiers can start at the doorstep, while downhill enthusiasts can try Sugarbush and Killington. Jack and Betty serve afternoon tea.

The Inn at Mt. Ascutney ✪
BROWNSVILLE, VERMONT 05037

Tel: (802) 484-7725
Best Time to Call: **Early evening**
Host(s): **Margaret and Eric Rothchild**
Location: **8 mi. from I-91**
No. of Rooms: **9**
No. of Private Baths: **5**
Max. No. Sharing Bath: **4**
Double/pb: **$58–$65**
Single/pb: **$50–$65**
Double/sb: **$38–$45**
Single/sb: **$32**

Open: **Dec. 1–Mar. 31; May 1–Oct. 31**
Breakfast: **Continental**
Other Meals: **Available**
Credit Cards: **MC, VISA**
Pets: **Sometimes**
Children: **Welcome (crib)**
Smoking: **Permitted**
Social Drinking: **Permitted**
Airport/Station Pickup: **Yes**

The inn is directly across the valley from the ski area where magnificent views are always in season. It was converted from an old farmhouse, parts of which date back to the American Revolution. The Rothchilds have achieved a comfortable balance between the old and the new. Their dining room and cocktail lounge feature an open hearth and kitchen with the original low wood beams from the old carriage house. After a day of skiing, tennis, fishing, hiking, or antiquing, you may dine on Margaret's continental-style country cooking, Monday through Thursday.

Stone Hearth Inn
ROUTE 11, CHESTER, VERMONT 05143

Tel: **(802) 875-2525**
Host(s): **Sharon and Andy Papineau**
Location: **10 mi. from I-91**
No. of Rooms: **8**
No. of Private Baths: **3**
Max. No. Sharing Bath: **6**
Double/pb: **$56–$64**
Single/pb: **$40–$44**
Double/sb: **$44–$56**
Single/sb: **$30–$40**
Open: **All year**
Reduced Rates: **Off-season**
Breakfast: **Full**
Pets: **No**
Children: **Welcome (crib)**
Smoking: **Permitted**
Social Drinking: **Permitted**

This white 19th-century colonial is set on five acres of fields and wooded land. The rooms have been lovingly restored and feature wide-board pine floors and open beams, floral wallpapers, antiques, quilts, and a player piano. A fireplaced game room is available in the remodeled attached barn. After a busy day, relax in the pub and enjoy a light snack. Horseback riding, downhill and cross-country skiing, and swimming in the river across the road are but a handful of the local pleasures. Your hosts offer fresh-baked breads, Belgian waffles, and French toast for breakfast.

The Little Lodge at Dorset ✪
ROUTE 30, BOX 673, DORSET, VERMONT 05251

Tel: (802) 867-4040
Host(s): **Allan and Nancy Norris**
Location: **6 mi. N of Manchester**
No. of Rooms: **5**
No. of Private Baths: **3**
Max. No. Sharing Bath: **4**
Double/pb: **$54–$60**
Single/pb: **$44–$50**
Double/sb: **$44–$49**

Single/sb: **$34–$39**
Open: **May–Oct., Dec.–Apr.**
Reduced Rates: **10%, weekly**
Breakfast: **Continental**
Credit Cards: **AMEX**
Pets: **Sometimes**
Children: **Welcome (crib)**
Smoking: **Permitted**
Social Drinking: **Permitted**

Situated in one of the prettiest little towns in Vermont, this delightful 1890 colonial house is perched on a hillside overlooking its own trout pond that's used for skating in winter or canoeing in summer. The original paneling and wide floorboards set off the splendid antiques. After skiing at nearby Stratton or Bromley, toast your feet by the fireplace while sipping hot chocolate. If you prefer, bring your own liquor, and Nancy and Allan will provide Vermont cheese and crackers.

Maplewood Colonial House
BOX 1019, ROUTE 30, DORSET, VERMONT 05251

Tel: (802) 867-4470
Best Time to Call: **After 5 PM**
Host(s): **Marge and Leon Edgerton**

Location: **7 mi. from Rt. 7**
No. of Rooms: **5**
Max. No. Sharing Bath: **4**

Double/sb: **$45**
Single/sb: **$30**
Open: **All year**
Reduced Rates: **Weekly; family**
Breakfast: **Full**

Pets: **Sometimes**
Children: **Welcome (crib)**
Smoking: **No**
Social Drinking: **Permitted**

This large, 20-room white colonial with green shutters is in a lovely setting. The five corner bedrooms are airy, comfortably furnished with antiques; the dining table is pre–Civil War vintage. You are welcome to wander the acreage, canoe on the pond, bicycle, or browse in Marge and Leon's library. In winter, skiing at Bromley or Stratton is convenient. The fall foliage is fabulous.

Blue Wax Farm
PINKHAM ROAD, EAST BURKE, VERMONT 05832

Tel: **(802) 626-5542**
Host(s): **Kenneth and Ingrid Parr**
Location: **45 mi. N of White River Junction**
No. of Rooms: **4**
No. of Private Baths: **2**
Max. No. Sharing Bath: **3**
Double/pb: **$26**
Single/pb: **$13**
Double/sb: **$24**

Single/sb: **$12**
Open: **All year**
Breakfast: **Continental**
Credit Cards: **MC, VISA**
Pets: **No**
Children: **Welcome**
Smoking: **Permitted**
Social Drinking: **Permitted**
Foreign Languages: **Finnish, Spanish**

If you want to ski Vermont without bedding down at resorts with bars and discos, reserve a room here. Kenneth and Ingrid have a quiet retreat adjoining the Burke Mountain ski resort. There is cross-country skiing on the property, in addition to the downhill trails on Burke. Both casual and serious hikers will find this an ideal spot. The cordiality of your hosts and the view of the countryside, especially the fall foliage, are well worth the trip in all seasons. Lyndon State College is nearby.

Burke Green Lodging ✪
RURAL ROUTE 1, EAST BURKE, VERMONT 05832

Tel: **(802) 467-3472**
Best Time to Call: **10 AM–9 PM**
Host(s): **Harland and Beverly Lewin**
Location: **15 mi. N of St. Johnsbury**

No. of Rooms: **3**
No. of Private Baths: **2**
Max. No. Sharing Bath: **5**
Double/pb: **$30**

Single/pb: **$22**
Double/sb: **$28**
Single/sb: **$20**
Open: **All year**
Reduced Rates: **Weekly**

Breakfast: **Full**
Pets: **Sometimes**
Children: **Welcome (crib)**
Smoking: **Permitted**
Social Drinking: **Permitted**

You will enjoy the quiet, 25-acre country setting and spacious 1840 farmhouse, remodeled with modern conveniences but retaining the original wooden beams and old-fashioned fixtures. The view of Burke Mountain is spectacular. Sit in the family room and enjoy the warmth of the cozy fireplace. It is 10 minutes from skiing and snow sports; summertime fun includes swimming, fishing, and hiking. The kitchen is always open for cookies and beverages, and you are welcome to use the laundry facilities, guest refrigerator, and picnic table. Lyndon State College is nearby.

Jericho House
249 JERICHO ROAD, ESSEX JUNCTION, VERMONT 05452

Tel: **(802) 899-2147**
Host(s): **Stacy and Matt Glavin**
Location: **12 mi. E of Burlington**
No. of Rooms: **3**
Max. No. Sharing Bath: **3**
Double/sb: **$30**
Single/sb: **$25**

Open: **All year**
Breakfast: **Continental**
Pets: **No**
Children: **Welcome (crib)**
Smoking: **Permitted**
Social Drinking: **Permitted**
Airport/Station Pickup: **Yes**

This 175-year-old brick farmhouse is registered with the Vermont Historical Society. Stacy and Matt carefully selected antiques to combine country elegance with an informal touch. It's 45 minutes from the ski slopes of Stowe; summer fun includes the fishing hole within walking distance. The coffee pot is always on, and cookies and wine are offered in the evening. The University of Vermont is at Burlington.

The Combes Family Inn
RFD 1, BOX 275, LUDLOW, VERMONT 05149

Tel: **(802) 228-8799**
Host(s): **Ruth and Bill Combes**
Location: **2 mi. from Rt. 100**

No. of Rooms: **10**
No. of Private Baths: **6**
Max. No. Sharing Bath: **8**

Double/pb: **$69**
Single/pb: **$53**
Double/sb: **$69**
Single/sb: **$53**
Suites: **$85–$117**
Open: **May 15–Apr. 15**
Reduced Rates: **Summer**
Breakfast: **Full**
Other Meals: **Available**
Credit Cards: **AMEX, MC, VISA**
Pets: **Welcome**
Children: **Welcome (crib)**
Smoking: **Permitted**
Social Drinking: **Permitted**
Airport/Station Pickup: **Yes**
Foreign Languages: **French**

This century-old farmhouse is set on 50 country acres. The meadows and woods offer wonderful exploring and cross-country skiing. Enjoy Vermont-style cooking in a handsome dining room with exposed beams and large bay window overlooking Okemo Mountain. BYOB to the fireplaced lounge, paneled in barnboard and furnished with end-of-century oak. The children will enjoy the family goats that share the farm. There is fine downhill skiing; many lakes, hiking areas, and picnic spots beckon. Your hosts will gladly pack a box lunch.

Brook 'n' Hearth O
STATE ROAD 11/30, BOX 508, MANCHESTER CENTER, VERMONT 05255

Tel: **(802) 362-3604**
Best Time to Call: **After 2 PM**
Host(s): **Larry and Terry Greene**
Location: **1 mi. E of U.S. 7**
No. of Rooms: **4**
No. of Private Baths: **3**
Max. No. Sharing Bath: **4**
Double/pb: **$28–$38**
Single/pb: **$16–$24**
Suites: **$44–$55**
Open: **May 17–Oct. 31; Nov. 22–Apr. 27**
Reduced Rates: **10%, 5 days; off-season; families**
Breakfast: **Full**
Credit Cards: **AMEX**
Pets: **No**
Children: **Welcome (crib)**
Smoking: **Permitted**
Social Drinking: **Permitted**

True to its name, a brook runs through the property and a fire warms the living room of this country home. Terry and Larry offer setups and happy-hour snacks for your self-supplied cocktails. You're within five miles of the ski slopes at Bromley and Stratton; it is also convenient to art centers, summer theater, restaurants, and a score of sports that include hiking on the Long Trail.

Brookside Meadows
RD 3, MIDDLEBURY, VERMONT 05753

Tel: (802) 388-6429
Host(s): **The Cole Family**
No. of Rooms: **2**
No. of Private Baths: **2**
Double/pb: **$40**
Single/pb: **$25**

Open: **All year**
Breakfast: **Full**
Pets: **No**
Children: **Welcome**
Smoking: **Permitted**
Social Drinking: **Permitted**

This attractive farmhouse was built in 1979, based on a 19th-century design. The house is on a country road, on 20 acres of meadowland. The property borders on a brook. It is also home to geese, goats, two dogs, and a cat; the children are welcome to play with the animals. Comfortable twin-bedded rooms are available. Relax on cedar lawn chairs and enjoy a view of the Green Mountains. Area attractions include alpine and cross-country skiing, hiking, spring syrup operations, the beach on Lake Dunmore, Middlebury College, and the University of Vermont Horse Farm.

Fallbrook House ✪
HILL WEST ROAD, MONTGOMERY, VERMONT 05470

Tel: (802) 326-4614 or 863-3241
Host(s): **Herb and Lucille Rubin**
Location: **25 mi. from I-89**
No. of Rooms: **2**
No. of Private Baths: **2**
Double/pb: **$40–$58**
Open: **June 15–Oct. 15; Dec. 1– Mar. 31**

Reduced Rates: **After 4 nights**
Breakfast: **Full**
Pets: **Sometimes**
Children: **Welcome**
Smoking: **Permitted**
Social Drinking: **Permitted**
Airport/Station Pickup: **Yes**

Built a few years ago by a master craftsman, this beautifully appointed house has pine walls and beamed ceilings, massive fireplaces, stained glass windows, and sliding doors opening onto three separate decks. Surrounded by the mountains, the sound of the falls from the hillside brook breaks the silence. There's a heated swimming pool on the grounds, and tennis and fishing are nearby. Skiing at Jay Peak with its aerial tramway is 10 miles away. After enjoying the Rubin's 6-course breakfast, you may want to take the 60-mile drive to Montreal, Canada.

Charlie's Northland Lodge ✪
BOX 88, NORTH HERO, VERMONT 05474

Tel: **(802) 372-8822**
Best Time to Call: **Before 8 PM**
Host(s): **Charles and Dorice Clark**
Location: **60 mi. S of Montreal, Canada**
No. of Rooms: **4**
Max. No. Sharing Bath: **6**
Double/sb: **$36**
Single/sb: **$30**

Guest Cottage: **$230–$325 (4–6)**
Open: **All year**
Reduced Rates: **Sept. 2–Dec. 25**
Breakfast: **Continental**
Pets: **No**
Children: **Welcome, over 5**
Smoking: **Permitted**
Social Drinking: **Permitted**

The lodge is a 200-year-old restored colonial located on Lake Champlain, where bass and walleye abound. A sport and tackle shop is on the premises. Fall and winter fishing should appeal to all anglers. Cross-country ski buffs will love the 10 miles of groomed trails. In summer, tennis, hiking, or relaxing in the reading room are pleasant activities.

Peregrine's Rest ✪
UPPER FALLS ROAD, PERKINSVILLE, VERMONT 05151

Tel: **(802) 263-5784**
Host(s): **Anneke Mayer**
Location: **10 mi. from I-91**
No. of Rooms: **4**
No. of Private Baths: **2**
Max. No. Sharing Bath: **4**
Double/sb: **$30**
Single/sb: **$20**

Open: **All year**
Breakfast: **Continental**
Pets: **Welcome**
Children: **Welcome**
Smoking: **No**
Social Drinking: **Permitted**
Airport/Station Pickup: **Yes**
Foreign Languages: **French**

This white clapboard farmhouse is on a back road lined with ancient sugar maples. The house dates back to the 1830s and its charisma is enhanced by lots of plants and sunny rooms. Wood stoves, wide pine floors, floral rugs, stenciled walls, and chintz curtains create a relaxed and friendly atmosphere. Your hostess invites you to cool off in the swimming hole after touring. There are many nearby places to ski, hike, explore, and sample restaurants and antiques dealers.

Pittsfield Inn ✪
ROUTE 100, BOX 526, PITTSFIELD, VERMONT 05762

Tel: **(802) 746-8943**
Best Time to Call: **After 4 PM**
Host(s): **Tom and Sue Yennerell**
Location: **20 mi. N of Rutland**
No. of Rooms: **8**
No. of Private Baths: **2**
Max. No. Sharing Bath: **4**
Double/pb: **$60**
Single/pb: **$50**
Double/sb: **$50**
Single/sb: **$40**
Open: **All year**
Breakfast: **Full**
Other Meals: **Available**
Credit Cards: **MC, VISA**
Pets: **No**
Children: **Welcome**
Smoking: **Permitted**
Social Drinking: **Permitted**

The inn is located at the end of the village green, where it has stood since 1835. Guests are invited to the parlor, porch, or tavern, where fine food is served. The rooms are filled with antiques, and you may find your treasures at the many craft shops in town. If you choose, professional guides will escort you over the Green Mountains. Skiing at Pico and Killington is 10 miles away.

Okemo Lantern Lodge
P.O. BOX 247, PROCTORSVILLE, VERMONT 05153

Tel: **(802) 226-7770**
Best Time to Call: **Mornings**
Host(s): **Charles and Joan Racicot**
Location: **25 mi. S of Rutland**
No. of Rooms: **7**
No. of Private Baths: **1**
Max. No. Sharing Bath: **4**
Double/pb: **$48**
Single/pb: **$38**
Double/sb: **$48**
Single/sb: **$38**
Open: **All year**
Breakfast: **Full**
Other Meals: **Dinner available**
Credit Cards: **AMEX, MC, VISA**
Pets: **No**
Children: **Welcome, over 6**
Smoking: **Permitted**
Social Drinking: **Permitted**
Airport/Station Pickup: **Yes**

A 19th-century Victorian lodge nestled in the village, in the heart of ski country, awaits your visit. It is decorated with canopy beds, antiques, and original stained glass windows. Charles and Joan charge $50 to $60 per person during ski season, which includes dinner and breakfast. There are countless activities in all seasons, including the gondola at Killington and the spectacular fall foliage.

The Peeping Cow Inn ○
ROUTE 106, READING, VERMONT 05062

Tel: **(802) 484-5036**	Double/sb: **$35**
Best Time to Call: **7–10 AM; 5:30–7 PM**	Open: **All year**
	Reduced Rates: **After 3 nights**
Host(s): **Nancy and Frank Lynch**	Breakfast: **Continental**
Location: **6 mi. from I-95**	Pets: **No**
No. of Rooms: **2**	Children: **Welcome, over 10**
No. of Private Baths: **1**	Smoking: **Permitted**
Max. No. Sharing Bath: **4**	Social Drinking: **Permitted**
Double/pb: **$35**	Airport/Station Pickup: **Yes**
Single/pb: **$30**	Foreign Languages: **French**

The "peeping bovines" are 50 Swiss Jerseys in the meadows surrounding Nancy and Frank's circa-1800 white farmhouse. Outdoor mountain recreation abounds in all seasons. Mt. Ascutney is five minutes away, convenient to many downhill ski areas, and cross-country skiing starts outside the door. Fishing, horseback riding, tennis, golf, bicycling, swimming, fun summer festivals, hot air ballooning, steamboat rides on Lake Sunapee are just a few things to do. Dartmouth College is a short drive.

Harvey Farm Country Inn ○
ROCHESTER, VERMONT 05767

Tel: **(802) 767-4273**	Reduced Rates: **Families**
Host(s): **Don and Maggie Harvey**	Breakfast: **Full**
Location: **35 mi. N of Rutland**	Other Meals: **Dinner included**
No. of Rooms: **8**	Pets: **No**
Max. No. Sharing Bath: **4**	Children: **Welcome, over 4**
Double/sb: **$60**	Smoking: **Permitted**
Single/sb: **$38**	Social Drinking: **Permitted**
Open: **All year**	

You can find serenity in this inn that combines modern country living with the beauty of mountains, open meadows, woods, and farmland. After a hearty breakfast, children are invited to help feed the small animals and ride the pony. Everyone is welcome to swim in the pool or go fishing. Picnic lunches are available and delectable dinners are served in the antique-filled dining room. Your last cup of coffee can be enjoyed on the porch or in front of the TV. In winter, the ski slopes of Sugarbush, Middlebury Snowbowl, and Killington are close by.

Hillcrest Guest House ○
RD 1, MCKINLEY AVENUE, RUTLAND, VERMONT 05701

Tel: **(802) 775-1670**	Open: **All year**
Host(s): **Bob and Peg Dombro**	Breakfast: **Continental**
Location: **3/10 mi. from Rte. 7**	Pets: **No**
No. of Rooms: **3**	Children: **Welcome**
Max. No. Sharing Bath: **5**	Smoking: **No**
Double/sb: **$30**	Social Drinking: **Permitted**
Single/sb: **$20**	Airport/Station Pickup: **Yes**

This 150-year-old farmhouse, with a comfortable screened porch for warm weather relaxing, is furnished with country antiques. Pico and Killington ski areas are 7 and 16 miles away. Summer brings the opportunity to explore charming villages, covered bridges, and antiques and craft centers. Country auctions, marble quarries, trout streams, and Sunday evening band concerts are pleasant pastimes. Bob and Peg always offer something in the way of between-meal refreshments.

Munro-Hawkins House
HISTORIC ROUTE 7A, SHAFTSBURY, VERMONT 05262

Tel: **(802) 447-2286**	Open: **All year**
Host(s): **Ruth Ann Myers**	Reduced Rates: **Weekly**
Location: **4 mi. N of Bennington**	Breakfast: **Full**
No. of Rooms: **5**	Other Meals: **Available**
No. of Private Baths: **2**	Pets: **Sometimes**
Max. No. Sharing Bath: **3**	Children: **Welcome (crib)**
Double/sb: **$40**	Smoking: **Permitted**
Single/sb: **$35**	Social Drinking: **Permitted**
Suites: **$60**	Airport/Station Pickup: **Yes**

The Munro-Hawkins House is a classic Georgian-style home, familiar in New England. It is a symmetrical white clapboard with high ceilings, marble fireplaces, and handcarved moldings. Have a country breakfast in the dining room or in your room. The guest rooms are furnished with antiques, pewter pieces, and each has a cozy fireplace. Your hosts will direct you to the pleasures of the Green Mountains—state parks, cool lakes, skiing, sugaring operations, restaurants, and more. Bennington College is nearby.

Watercourse Way
ROUTE 132, SOUTH STAFFORD, VERMONT 05070

Tel: (802) 765-4314
Host(s): Lincoln Alden
Location: 10 mi. from I-91
No. of Rooms: 3
Max. No. Sharing Bath: 5
Double/sb: $35
Single/sb: $25

Open: **All year**
Reduced Rates: **Available**
Breakfast: **Continental**
Pets: **Sometimes**
Children: **Welcome**
Smoking: **Permitted**
Social Drinking: **No**

Watercourse Way is a large white farmhouse dating back to 1850. It is set on the Ompompanoosuc River, among evergreen and herb gardens. The river is a charming place to wade, fish, or kayak. A country store, horse farm, and restaurant are close by. Your host will gladly direct you to the historical meeting house at Stafford Green, Lake Fairlee, Hanover, and Woodstock. Dartmouth College is nearby.

Ski Inn ○
ROUTE 108, STOWE, VERMONT 05672

Tel: (802) 253-4050
Best Time to Call: **9–11 AM; Evenings**
Host(s): **Larry and Harriet Heyer**
Location: **47 mi. NE of Burlington**
No. of Rooms: **10**
No. of Private Baths: **4**
Max. No. Sharing Bath: **5**
Double/pb: **$27–$70**
Single/pb: **$21–$55**
Double/sb: **$20–$47**

Single/sb: **$18–$45**
Open: **All year**
Reduced Rates: **10% Jan.; families**
Breakfast: **Continental**
Other Meals: **Included in winter**
Pets: **Sometimes**
Children: **Welcome**
Smoking: **Permitted**
Social Drinking: **Permitted**

In appearance, this is a traditional New England inn, but everything is modern inside. Set back from the highway among evergreens on a gentle sloping hillside, this is a quiet place to relax and sleep soundly. In winter, it's a skier's delight, close to downhill and cross-country trails. A full breakfast and delicious dinner are included in winter rates of $55–$70. In summer, the rates drop to $21–$27 per room, including a continental breakfast. Larry and Harriet offer warm hospitality in all seasons.

Timberhölm Inn ✪
COTTAGE CLUB ROAD, RR 1 BOX 810, STOWE, VERMONT 05672

Tel: **(802) 253-7603**
Host(s): **Johanna and Lee Darrow**
Location: **2.5 mi. N of Stowe**
No. of Rooms: **10**
No. of Private Baths: **4**
Max. No. Sharing Bath: **6**
Double/sb: **$29**
Single/sb: **$20**
Suites: **$70 (for 4); $60 (for 3)**

Open: **All year**
Reduced Rates: **Off-season**
Breakfast: **Full—$3.50**
Credit Cards: **MC, VISA**
Pets: **Sometimes**
Children: **Welcome**
Smoking: **Permitted**
Social Drinking: **Permitted**

Set on a wooded hillside overlooking the lush valley and mountains, Johanna and Lee's home is close to famous ski areas, summer attractions, and special events. The large living room with its huge stone fireplace and picture windows is filled with antiques and books. The game room has another fireplace, piano, and guest refrigerator. During the ski season, enjoy a complimentary bowl of homemade soup by the hearth, guaranteed to warm body and soul.

Knoll Farm Country Inn ☉
BRAGG HILL ROAD, R.F.D. BOX 179, WAITSFIELD, VERMONT 05673

Tel: **(802) 496-3939**	Open: **Dec. 1–Apr. 1; May 1–Nov. 1**
Best Time to Call: **8–9 AM**	Reduced Rates: **Families; 5 nights**
Host(s): **Ann Day Heinzerling and Ethel and Harvey Horner**	Breakfast: **Full**
	Other Meals: **Dinner included**
Location: **22 mi. S of Montpelier on Rte. 100**	Pets: **No**
	Children: **Welcome, over 5**
No. of Rooms: **4**	Smoking: **Permitted**
Max. No. Sharing Bath: **3**	Social Drinking: **Permitted**
Double/sb: **$76**	Airport/Station Pickup: **Yes**
Single/sb: **$44**	

From the porch of this informal, converted farmhouse, one can see the Mad River Glen and Sugarbush ski areas four miles away. You can hike or cross-country ski, swim and boat on the pond, or help care for the farm animals. Horseback riding is especially popular. The hosts raise their own meat and eggs so you've never had a fresher breakfast of bacon, sausage, and eggs; even the vegetables are grown organically. Meals are served family-style. Dinner is a candlelit feast with wine and classical music. Picture yourself on a cold winter night sipping mulled cider and nibbling on Vermont cheese by the wood stove, chatting with your hosts. Vermont College is nearby.

Schneider Haus ☉
ROUTE 100, BOX 1595, WATERBURY, VERMONT 05676

Tel: **(802) 244-7726**	Open: **June 1–Apr. 15**
Best Time to Call: **8–11 AM, 4–9 PM**	Reduced Rates: **Ski weeks**
Host(s): **George and Irene Ballschneider**	Breakfast: **Full**
	Other Meals: **Available**
Location: **13 mi. W of Montpelier**	Pets: **No**
No. of Rooms: **10**	Children: **Welcome, over 3**
Max. No. Sharing Bath: **6**	Smoking: **Permitted**
Double/sb: **$29–$46**	Social Drinking: **Permitted**
Single/sb: **$25–$28**	

This Austrian chalet is nestled in the Green Mountains. A lounge with fireplace and floor-to-ceiling windows, plus quilts, hot tub, and sauna create a warm and comforting atmosphere. Breakfast specialties include French toast and homemade muffins. Enjoy nearby fishing, hiking, fall foliage, and winter excitement on the slopes of Sugarbush and Sugarbush North. Snacks and coffee are always on tap.

Hunt's Hideaway ○
RFD MORGAN ROAD, WEST CHARLESTON, VERMONT 05872

Tel: **(802) 895-4432 or 334-8322**	Single/sb: **$18**
Best Time to Call: **7 AM–11 PM**	Open: **Dec. 11–Oct. 9**
Host(s): **Pat and Paul Hunt**	Breakfast: **Full**
Location: **6 mi. from I-91**	Pets: **Sometimes**
No. of Rooms: **3**	Children: **Welcome**
Max. No. Sharing Bath: **4**	Smoking: **Permitted**
Double/sb: **$25**	Social Drinking: **Permitted**

This modern, split-level home is located on 100 acres of woods and fields, with a brook, pond, and large swimming pool. Pancakes with Vermont maple syrup are featured at breakfast. Ski Jay Peak and Burke, or fish and boat on Lake Seymour, two miles away. Visiting antique shops or taking a trip to nearby Canada are other local possibilities.

Snow Den ○
P.O. BOX 615, ROUTE 100, WEST DOVER, VERMONT 05356

Tel: **(802) 464-9355 or 464-5537**	Breakfast: **Full**
Host(s): **Jean and Milt Cummings**	Other Meals: **Available**
No. of Rooms: **8**	Credit Cards: **MC, VISA**
No. of Private Baths: **8**	Pets: **No**
Double/pb: **$46–$70**	Children: **Welcome, over 8**
Single/pb: **$46–$70**	Smoking: **Permitted**
Open: **All year**	Social Drinking: **Permitted**
Reduced Rates: **April 15–Dec. 1**	

Located in the heart of the Mount Snow, Haystack, and Corinthia ski areas, this delightful home's guest rooms are tastefully furnished with antiques; four bedrooms have fireplaces. In spring, summer, and fall, there's swimming, golf, and tennis to keep you busy. Jean and Milt will be happy to steer you to the diverse attractions the area offers.

Waldwinkel Inn ⊙
P.O. BOX 364, ROUTE 100, WEST DOVER, VERMONT 05356

Tel: **(802) 464-5281**
Best Time to Call: **Evenings**
Host(s): **Linda and Mickey Kersten**
No. of Rooms: **11**
No. of Private Baths: **10**
Max. No. Sharing Bath: **5**
Double/pb: **$50**
Single/pb: **$50**
Double/sb: **$45**
Single/sb: **$45**
Open: **All year**
Reduced Rates: **10%, 4-day stays**
Breakfast: **Full**
Pets: **No**
Children: **Welcome (crib)**
Smoking: **Permitted**
Social Drinking: **Permitted**

A snowball's throw from Mount Snow, this alpine-style lodge is made cozy by the warmth and geniality of Linda and Mickey. In addition to the area's famed sports and skiing facilities, they provide pool and ping-pong tables, games, and friendship around the fireplaces. An outdoor swimming pool is a summer attraction. Some rooms have balconies overlooking the valley.

The Weathervane
DORR FITCH ROAD, BOX 57, WEST DOVER, VERMONT 05356

Tel: **(802) 464-5426**
Host(s): **The Chabots**
Location: **1 mi. from Rte. 100**
No. of Rooms: **10**
No. of Private Baths: **4**
Max. No. Sharing Bath: **5**
Double/pb: **$55**
Single/pb: **$28**
Double/sb: **$44**
Single/sb: **$24**
Suites: **$60**
Open: **All year**
Reduced Rates: **Ski-weeks; off-season**
Breakfast: **Full**
Other Meals: **Dinner**
Pets: **No**
Children: **Welcome (crib)**
Smoking: **Permitted**
Social Drinking: **Permitted**

Only four miles from Haystack, Mount Snow, and Corinthia, this Tyrolean-style ski lodge is decorated with authentic antiques and colonial charm. The lounge and recreation room have fireplaces and a bring-your-own bar. Winter rates are $35–$50 per person, including breakfast, dinner, cross-country ski equipment, sleds, and snowshoes, so that you may explore the lovely marked trails. Summer brings lakeshore swimming, boating, fishing, tennis, riding, museums, and the Marlboro Music Festival.

The Colonial House
ROUTE 100, BOX 138, WESTON, VERMONT 05161

Tel: (802) 824-6286	Single/sb: $27
Best Time to Call: 8 AM–10 PM	Open: All year
Host(s): Betty and John Nunnikhoven	Reduced Rates: 10%, 4 days, seniors
Location: 35 mi. SE of Rutland	Breakfast: Full
No. of Rooms: 15	Other Meals: Available
No. of Private Baths: 9	Credit Cards: AMEX, MC, VISA
Max. No. Sharing Bath: 6	Pets: Sometimes
Double/pb: $44–$60	Children: Welcome (crib)
Single/pb: $38	Smoking: Permitted
Double/sb: $38–$42	Social Drinking: Permitted

Built in 1790, this cozy farmhouse offers you a country-living experience. Enjoy leisurely farm breakfasts, with snacks in the afternoon. There's a guest living room with a player piano, fireplace, and warm hospitality. Cross-country skiing starts at the doorstep and seasonal activities are all nearby.

Holly Tree ◐
RD1, BOX 315A, LAKE RAPONDA, WILMINGTON, VERMONT 05363

Tel: (802) 464-5251	Suites: $45 (for 4)
Best Time to Call: Evenings	Open: All year
Host(s): Norma Naudain	Breakfast: Continental
Location: 20 mi. W of Brattleboro	Pets: Sometimes
No. of Rooms: 2	Children: Welcome
Max. No. Sharing Bath: 4	Smoking: Permitted
Double/sb: $35	Social Drinking: Permitted
Single/sb: $20	

Norma operated a bed and breakfast in England, so you will find New England hospitality spiced with a genuine European accent. Wilmington provides a beautiful setting for swimming, fishing, hiking, cycling, skiing, skating, snowmobiling, and hunting. It is close to Mount Snow, the Marlboro Music Festival, and historic Bennington. Whenever you wish, the coffee pot is ready.

Nutmeg Inn ✪
ROUTE 9W, P.O. BOX 818, WILMINGTON, VERMONT 05363

Tel: (802) 464-3351
Best Time to Call: **9:30 AM–9:30 PM**
Host(s): **Joan and Rich Combes**
Location: **1 mi. W of Wilmington**
No. of Rooms: **9**
No. of Private Baths: **4**
Max. No. Sharing Bath: **6**
Double/pb: **$48–$63**
Single/pb: **$40–$50**
Double/sb: **$45–$55**
Single/sb: **$35–$45**

Open: **Dec. 27–Apr. 15; June 1– Oct. 31**
Reduced Rates: **Ski weeks**
Breakfast: **Full**
Other meals: **Dinner (in winter)**
Credit Cards: **AMEX**
Pets: **No**
Children: **Welcome, over 9**
Smoking: **Permitted**
Social Drinking: **Permitted**

Joan and Rich are proud of their home which was built in the 1700s; it still shows the original posts and beams. In winter, the focus is on skiing at Mount Snow, Corinthia, and Haystack. In summer, the mountain lakes beckon. The autumn colors are spectacular. Guests always enjoy the informal atmosphere of the living room with fireplace, piano, books, and bring-your-own-cocktail bar.

Knoll Farm Country Inn

VIRGINIA

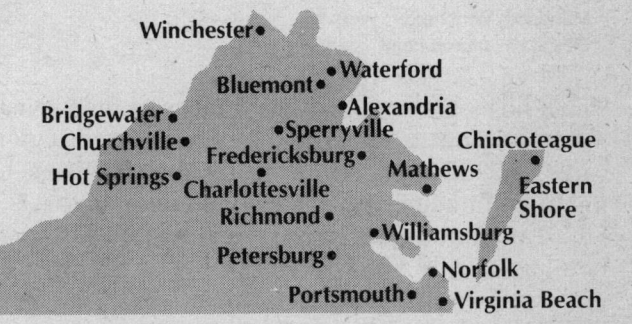

Princely/Bed & Breakfast, Ltd.
819 PRINCE STREET, ALEXANDRIA, VIRGINIA 22314

Tel: (703) 683-2159
Coordinator: **E. J. Mansmann**
States/Regions Covered: **Alexandria**

Rates (Single/Double):
    Luxury: $50–$65 $50–$65
Credit Cards: **No**
Minimum Stay: **2 nights**

Alexandria is eight miles from Washington, D.C., and nine miles from Mount Vernon. Mr. Mansmann, a former State Department official, has an exclusive roster of de luxe accommodations ready for you; they include an 18th-century Federal-style mansion in historic Old Town Alexandria, as well as other historic houses (circa 1751 to 1838) filled with museum-quality antiques. You will be made to feel like visiting royalty, whichever place you choose.

Blue Ridge Bed & Breakfast
ROUTE 1, BOX 517, BLUEMONT, VIRGINIA 22012

Tel: (703) 955-3955
Best Time to Call: 8 AM–10 PM
Coordinator: Sara Genthner
States/Regions Covered:
  Virginia—Berryville, Bluemont, Boyce, Lorettsville, Purcellville, Front Royal, Waterford, Lincoln, Millwood, Winchester; West Virginia—Summit Point

Rates (Single/Double):
  Modest: $18
  Average: $20 $30
  Luxury: $35 $45–$70
Credit Cards: No

Sara's hosts are within 25 to 75 miles of the capital, perfect for those wishing to visit rural areas near Washington, D.C. The variety includes houses in the Historic Register, mountain retreats, and traditional private homes in small towns. This beautiful area is known for its part in American history, horses, and farming.

Jean's Bed & Breakfast ✪
117 SOUTH MAIN STREET, BRIDGEWATER, VIRGINIA 22812

Tel: (703) 828-3982
Host(s): Jean and Hub Allen
Location: 4 mi. from I-81
No. of Rooms: 4
No. of Private Baths: 2
Max. No. Sharing Bath: 4
Double/pb: $30
Single/pb: $25
Double/sb: $25
Single/sb: $20
Guest Cottage: $50

Open: All year
Reduced Rates: Seniors; families
Breakfast: Full
Pets: Sometimes
Children: Welcome
Smoking: Permitted
Social Drinking: Permitted
Airport/Station Pickup: Yes
Foreign Languages: French, Spanish, Swedish

This charming frame guest house is in the area of the Shenandoah Valley, the beautiful Skyline Drive, and Natural Bridge. Jean and Hub have a flair for decorating, evident in their artistic mix of antique and contemporary pieces. They constantly add to their antiques collection, and many of their things are for sale. Warm hospitality, interesting conversation, wine, snacks, and a good game of bridge are their hallmark.

Sandy Hill Farm Bed and Breakfast
ROUTE 1, BOX 55, SANDY HILL FARM, CAPRON, VIRGINIA 23829

Tel: (804) 658-4281
Best Time to Call: 7–8:30 AM;
  7–11:30 PM
Host(s): **Anne and Roger Kitchen**
Location: **11 mi. from I-95**
No. of Rooms: **2**
Max. No. Sharing Bath: **4**
Double/sb: **$25**
Single/sb: **$20**

Open: **All year**
Reduced Rates: **Families; 5 nights**
Breakfast: **Continental**
Other Meals: **Available**
Pets: **Welcome**
Children: **Welcome (crib)**
Smoking: **Permitted**
Social Drinking: **Permitted**

Experience the pleasures of an unspoiled rural setting at this ranch-style farmhouse. There are animals to visit, quiet places to stroll and a lighted tennis court on the grounds. This is an ideal hub from which to tour southeastern and central Virginia—day trips to Williamsburg, Norfolk, Richmond. Your hosts serve fresh fruits and homemade breads each morning. They will gladly prepare other meals, or can direct you to good restaurants.

Guesthouses Reservation Service
P.O. BOX 5737, CHARLOTTESVILLE, VIRGINIA 22905

Tel: (804) 979-8327
Best Time to Call: **1–6 PM**
Coordinator: **Sally Reger**
States/Regions Covered:
  Charlottesville, Luray

Rates (Single/Double):
  Average: **n/a**   **$40–$48**
  Luxury: **n/a**   **$56–$64**
  Estate cottages: **$72 up**
Credit Cards: **MC, VISA**

Charlottesville is a gracious town. The hosts in Sara's hospitality file offer you a genuine taste of Southern hospitality. All places are close to Thomas Jefferson's Monticello and James Madison's Ash Lawn, as well as the University of Virginia. Unusual local activities include ballooning, steeplechasing, and wine festivals. Please note that the office is closed from Christmas through New Year's day. Reduced rates are available for additional nights, and most hosts offer a full breakfast.

The English Inn Guest House ⊙
316 14TH STREET NORTHWEST, CHARLOTTESVILLE, VIRGINIA 22903

Tel: (804) 295-7707
Best Time to Call: 8 AM–9 PM
Host(s): The Klee Family
Location: 3 mi. from I-64
No. of Rooms: 8
No. of Private Baths: 2
Max. No. Sharing Bath: 4
Double/pb: $40
Single/pb: $40
Double/sb: $35
Single/sb: $27

Suites: $70
Open: All year
Reduced Rates: 10%, Nov. 15–Mar. 20
Breakfast: Continental
Pets: Welcome
Children: Welcome
Smoking: No
Social Drinking: Permitted
Foreign Languages: Greek

This brick colonial is located in the historic district; it is close to shops, restaurants, and two blocks from the University of Virginia. For relaxing, there are a porch and a garden, and a sitting room with fireplace. Continental breakfast includes homemade breads. Area attractions include the home of Thomas Jefferson, plus Ash Lawn, Castle Hill, and Swannanoa mansions.

Miss Molly's Inn ⊙
113 NORTH MAIN STREET, CHINCOTEAGUE, VIRGINIA 23336

Tel: (804) 336-6686
Host(s): Dr. and Mrs. James Stam
Location: 50 mi. S of Salisbury
No. of Rooms: 7
No. of Private Baths: 1
Max. No. Sharing Bath: 2
Double/pb: $65
Double/sb: $55
Single/sb: $45

Open: Apr.–Dec.
Reduced Rates: Off-season
Breakfast: Full
Other Meals: Available
Pets: No
Children: Welcome, over 12
Smoking: Permitted
Social Drinking: Permitted

The 22 rooms of this seaside Victorian have been lovingly restored to their 19th-century charm. Relax in an ambience of lace curtains, stained glass windows, and period pieces. While writing her book *Misty*, Marguerite Henry stayed here. The ponies made famous by that story roam wild at the nearby National Wildlife Refuge. You too may find "Miss Molly's" cool breezes, five porches, and afternoon teas worth writing about. Chincoteague has beaches, gourmet restaurants, and the NASA museum. Your hosts will gladly direct you to these sights, beginning with the Bay, which is 150 feet from the front door.

Buckhorn Inn O
STAR ROUTE BOX 139, ROUTE 250, CHURCHVILLE, VIRGINIA 24421

Tel: **(703) 885-2900**
Host(s): **Roger and Eileen Lee**
Location: **12 mi. W of Staunton**
No. of Rooms: **6**
No. of Private Baths: **1**
Max. No. Sharing Bath: **5**
Double/pb: **$38**
Single/pb: **$28**
Double/sb: **$28**
Single/sb: **$18**

Open: **All year**
Reduced Rates: **Groups; families**
Breakfast: **Continental**
Credit Cards: **MC, VISA**
Pets: **Sometimes**
Children: **Welcome (crib)**
Smoking: **Permitted**
Social Drinking: **Permitted**
Airport/Station Pickup: **Yes**

This vintage inn (circa 1811) has lovely open porches, and the guest rooms are decorated with fine colonial reproductions. Located in the heart of the Shenandoah Valley, adjoining George Washington National State Forest, it is close to the Natural Bridge as well as to an antiques mall that houses over 100 dealers. Coffee, tea, and lemonade are always available, and you are welcome to use the washer and dryer. The inn also hosts a four-star restaurant, famous for all-you-can-eat country buffets. Mary Baldwin College is nearby.

The McGrath House ✪
225 PRINCESS ANNE STREET, FREDERICKSBURG, VIRGINIA 22401

Tel: (703) 371-4363
Best Time to Call: **Mornings**
Host(s): **Sylvia McGrath**
Location: **50 mi. S of Washington, D.C.**
No. of Rooms: **3**
Max. No. Sharing Bath: **6**
Double/sb: **$30**

Single/sb: **$25**
Open: **All year**
Reduced Rates: **Weekly**
Breakfast: **Continental**
Pets: **Sometimes**
Children: **Welcome**
Smoking: **No**
Social Drinking: **Permitted**

This carefully restored house, featured on walking tours, dates back to the early 19th century and is located in the oldest part of Fredericksburg on a quiet, tree-lined street. You'll enjoy breakfast in the country kitchen that overlooks a small colonial herb garden. In the evening, you are welcome to a drink and snacks with Sylvia before retiring. Don't miss seeing the President James Monroe Law Offices, Rising Sun Tavern, and the Battlefield. Mary Washington College is nearby.

Riverfront House ✪
ROUTE 14 EAST PO BOX 310, MATHEWS, VIRGINIA 23109

Tel: (804) 725-5655
Host(s): **Annette Goldreyer**
Location: **30 mi. from U.S. 17**
No. of Rooms: **6**
No. of Private Baths: **1**
Max. No. Sharing Bath: **4**
Double/pb: **$50**
Single/pb: **$50**
Double/sb: **$35–$60**

Single/sb: **$35–$60**
Open: **Apr.–Nov.**
Reduced Rates: **Sun.–Thurs.**
Breakfast: **Continental**
Pets: **Sometimes**
Children: **Welcome, over 3**
Smoking: **Permitted**
Social Drinking: **Permitted**

This clapboard farmhouse is set on seven acres near the mouth of the East River. The 19th-century design features a gracious front hall and mahogany mantelpieces. The bedrooms blend contemporary with antique furnishings. A buffet of fruit, cheese, and muffins is offered each morning. Breakfast can be enjoyed inside or on the wraparound porch. Sun bathe right on the dock, or drop a crab line and try your luck. Your hosts invite you to share a glass of wine in the parlor. The beach on Chesapeake Bay is only five miles away.

Bed & Breakfast of Tidewater Virginia O
P.O. BOX 3343, NORFOLK, VIRGINIA 23514

Tel: (804) 627-1983 or 627-9409
Best Time to Call: 8–10 AM; 5–7 PM
Coordinator: Ashby Willcox and
  Susan Hubbard
States/Regions Covered: Chesapeake,
  Chincoteague, Eastern Shore of

Virginia, Hampton, Norfolk,
Portsmouth, Virginia Beach
Rates (Single/Double):
- Modest: $25 $30
- Average: $30 $35–$40
- Luxury: $40 $55
Credit Cards: No

The world's largest naval base is in Norfolk, as are the famed Chrysler Museum and MacArthur Memorial. It is also a cultural hub in which top-rated opera, symphony, and stage productions abound. There are miles of scenic beaches to explore on Chesapeake Bay and the Atlantic Ocean. Old Dominion University, Eastern Virginia Medical School, and Virginia Wesleyan College are conveniently located.

Cameron Residence O
1605 BILL STREET, NORFOLK, VIRGINIA 23518

Tel: (804) 587-0673
Host(s): Jessie Cameron
No. of Rooms: 1
No. of Private Baths: 1
Double/pb: $20
Single/pb: $15
Open: All year

Breakfast: Continental
Pets: Sometimes
Children: No
Smoking: Permitted
Social Drinking: Permitted
Airport/Station Pickup: Yes

This comfortable ranch home is close to Busch Gardens, Colonial Williamsburg, and Virginia Beach. Your hostess offers guests the use of the washing machine and dryer, private living room, and backyard patio. Swimming and fishing are nearby.

Bensonhouse of Richmond O
P. O. BOX 15131, RICHMOND, VIRGINIA 23227

Tel: (804) 648-7560 or 321-6277
Best Time to Call: 10 AM–5 PM
Coordinator: Lyn Benson
States/Regions Covered: Petersburg,
  Richmond

Rates (Single/Double):
  Modest: $22–$26 $30–$34
  Average: $28–$38 $36–$46
  Luxury: $40–$72 $48–$84
Credit Cards: MC, VISA ($50
  minimum charge)

With a history dating back to 1607, Richmond offers a blend of the historic and contemporary. Houses on Lyn's list are of architectural or historic interest, offering charm in the relaxed comfort of a home. The hosts delight in guiding you to the best sights, and advising you on how to get the most out of your visit.

Griffin House
9601 NORTHRIDGE COURT, RICHMOND, VIRGINIA 23235

Tel: **(804) 272-2741**	Open: **All year**
Host(s): **Phyllis and Roger Griffin**	Breakfast: **Full**
Location: **11 mi. from I-95**	Pets: **No**
No. of Rooms: **1**	Children: **No**
No. of Private Baths: **1**	Smoking: **No**
Double/pb: **$35**	Social Drinking: **Permitted**
Single/pb: **$30**	

Only nine miles from historic Richmond, this lovely private house is on a quiet suburban street. Phyllis and Roger, having traveled extensively, know exactly how to make visitors feel welcome. They will be happy to suggest side trips to nearby Williamsburg, Petersburg, Yorktown, and Gloucester. Take advantage of the new Performing Arts Center, where you can see memorable music and dance performances. You can decide what to see first while enjoying the delightful British breakfast.

The Conyers House ✪
SLATE MILLS ROAD, SPERRYVILLE, VIRGINIA 22740

Tel: **(703) 987-8025**	Guest Cottage: **$85–$100; sleeps 2**
Host(s): **Norman and Sandra Cartwright-Brown**	Open: **All year**
	Breakfast: **Full**
Location: **78 mi. SW of D.C.**	Other Meals: **Available**
No. of Rooms: **8**	Pets: **Sometimes**
No. of Private Baths: **4**	Children: **Welcome, over 16**
Max. No. Sharing Bath: **4**	Smoking: **Permitted**
Double/pb: **$85–$150**	Social Drinking: **Permitted**
Single/pb: **$75–$140**	Airport/Station Pickup: **Yes**
Double/sb: **$80–$85**	Foreign Languages: **French, German, Italian**
Single/sb: **$70–$75**	

Built in 1770, what was once a country store and post office has been lovingly restored and enlarged to accommodate 20th-century conveniences. It is now eclectically and elegantly furnished with antiques, family pieces, and Oriental rugs. Sandra, an avid, sophisticated horsewoman, encourages everyone to enjoy a trail ride; tennis and swimming are nearby. She's a gracious hostess, as is her capable housekeeper, Debbie Racer Keys. Norman, English by birth, is a cosmopolitan raconteur. Afternoon tea is served daily.

Angie's Guest Cottage ✪
302 24TH STREET, VIRGINIA BEACH, VIRGINIA 23451

Tel: **(804) 428-4690**
Best Time to Call: **10 AM–10 PM**
Host(s): **Barbara, Garnette and Bob Yates**
Location: **20 mi. E of Norfolk**
No. of Rooms: **6**
No. of Private Baths: **1**
Max. No. Sharing Bath: **4**
Double/pb: **$48**
Single/ pb: **$44**
Double/sb: **$36–$44**
Single/sb: **$32–$40**
Guest Cottage: **$300–$345; sleeps 2 to 5**
Open: **All year**
Reduced Rates: **30%–50% off-season**
Breakfast: **Continental**
Credit Cards: **MC, VISA**
Children: **Welcome (crib)**
Smoking: **Permitted**
Social Drinking: **Permitted**

Just a block from the beach, shops, restaurants, and across the street from the Greyhound bus station is this bright and comfortable beach house. Former guests describe it as: "cozy, cute, and clean." Barbara recalls having guests from 14 different nations from all over the world at the same time. Deep-sea fishing, nature trails, and harbor tours are but a few things to keep you busy. Freshly baked croissants in various flavors are a breakfast delight.

The Graters' Residence
209 GREAT MEADOWS COURT, VIRGINIA BEACH, VIRGINIA 23452

Tel: (804) 486-4982	Reduced Rates: **Off-season**
Host(s): **Robert and Roberta Grater**	Breakfast: **Continental**
Location: **15 mi. W of Virginia Beach**	Pets: **No**
No. of Rooms: **2**	Children: **No**
Max. No. Sharing Bath: **3**	Smoking: **No**
Double/sb: **$25**	Social Drinking: **No**
Single/sb: **$18**	Airport/Station Pickup: **Yes**
Open: **All year**	Foreign Languages: **French**

Guests are greeted at the Grater home with homemade Scottish shortbread and tea. Your hostess, a native of Scotland, has decorated the rooms with country furnishings and floral wallpapers. Relax in the fireplaced den or on the attractive wooden deck. Each morning, homemade breads and fresh fruits are offered on fine English china. It's 15 minutes to the beach, and just a short walk to the lake and tennis courts.

The Pink House O
WATERFORD, VIRGINIA 22190

Tel: (703) 882-3453	Breakfast: **Full**
Host(s): **Charles and Marie Anderson**	Other Meals: **Available**
Location: **38 mi. W of D.C.**	Pets: **Sometimes**
No. of Rooms: **2 three-room suites**	Children: **Welcome, over 12**
No. of Private Baths: **2**	Smoking: **Permitted**
Suites: **$70**	Social Drinking: **Permitted**
Open: **All year**	Airport/Station Pickup: **Yes**
Reduced Rates: **Families**	

Pink House is in the center of Waterford, one of the few villages entirely designated as a national landmark. Through the years, the house has been a Civil War officers' billet and an apothecary shop. Today, two three-room suites overlook a formal garden, with private entrance, terrace, color TV, and whirlpool among the luxurious features. A breakfast of homemade breads, grits, and sausage is served each morning. Gourmet dinners served with fine wines and cocktails are also available. Nearby sights include plantations, museums, and the equestrian center at Morvan Park.

The Travel Tree
P. O. BOX 838, WILLIAMSBURG, VIRGINIA 23187

Tel: (804) 565-2236 or 229-6477
Best Time to Call: 5–9 PM only
Coordinator(s): **Joann Proper and Sheila Zubkoff**
States/Regions Covered:
Williamsburg, Jamestown, Yorktown

Rates (Single/Double):
Modest: **$20–$24**   **$25–$30**
Average: **$28–$32**   **$35–$40**
Luxury: **$40–$60**   **$50–$75**
Credit Cards: **No**

You will thoroughly enjoy colonial Williamsburg, historic Jamestown and Yorktown, Busch Gardens, and Carter's Grove Plantation. Your bedroom might be furnished with canopy beds and antiques, or tucked under the eaves in a wooded setting, or a two-room cottage in a sylvan setting, complete with brass bed and kitchenette.

Brass Lantern Lodge ✪
1782 JAMESTOWN ROAD, WILLIAMSBURG, VIRGINIA 23185

Tel: **(804) 229-4320 or 229-9089**
Host(s): **Marge and Bill Fisher**
No. of Rooms: **16**
No. of Private Baths: **14**
Max. No. Sharing Bath: **6**
Double/pb: **$35–$40**
Double/sb: **$35–$40**
Suites: **$50–$80**

Guest Cottage: **$125; sleeps 6**
Open: **All year**
Breakfast: **Continental**
Pets: **No**
Children: **Welcome (crib)**
Smoking: **Permitted**
Social Drinking: **Permitted**

Minutes away from the historic restoration, the Fishers have transformed a motor lodge into a homey B&B. The rooms are decorated with antiques and stenciled walls. Outside, swings and a play area are provided for the younger set. Coffee, cold drinks, and tea are always offered when you return from touring.

Carter's Guest House
903 LAFAYETTE STREET, WILLIAMSBURG, VIRGINIA 23185

Tel: **(804) 229-1117**
Best Time to Call: **8 AM–10 PM**
Host(s): **Mrs. H. J. Carter**
No. of Rooms: **2**
Max. No. Sharing Bath: **4**
Double/sb: **$18–$20**
Single/sb: **$18**

Open: **All year**
Breakfast: **No**
Pets: **No**
Children: **Welcome**
Smoking: **Permitted**
Social Drinking: **No**

This brick Cape Cod home is located in town, three-quarters of a mile from the restored area, and five miles from the popular Williamsburg Pottery. Mrs. Carter enjoys meeting people and her hobby of beautiful needlework is evident in the decor. She will direct you to restaurants to suit your palate and purse.

The Cedars ☉
616 JAMESTOWN ROAD, WILLIAMSBURG, VIRGINIA 23185

Tel: **(804) 229-3591**
Host(s): **Rose deB. Harris**
No. of Rooms: **6**
No. of Private Baths: **6**
Max. No. Sharing Bath: **n/a**
Double/pb: **$35–$40**
Single/pb: **$32–$35**
Guest Cottage: **$80–85; sleeps 6**
Open: **All year**
Breakfast: **No**
Pets: **Sometimes**
Children: **Welcome**
Smoking: **Permitted**
Social Drinking: **Permitted**

A guest house of distinction, attractively furnished in the Williamsburg tradition, this stately home is within walking distance of the restored area and is located opposite Phi Beta Kappa Hall of the College of William and Mary, where many cultural activities are presented.

The Chateau ☉
330 INDIAN SPRINGS ROAD, WILLIAMSBURG, VIRGINIA 23185

Tel: **(804) 253-2323**
Host(s): **Evelyn Charbeneau**
No. of Rooms: **3 Suites**
No. of Private Baths: **3**
Suite: **$40–$45**
Open: **All year**
Breakfast: **No**
Pets: **Sometimes**
Children: **Welcome**
Smoking: **No**
Social Drinking: **No**

The Chateau offers three separate guest units located a short walk from Williamsburg's restored district. All have private entrances and overlook a shady ravine. The house was designed by a local architect and is comfortably furnished. Shops, restaurants, and Merchant's Square are a short walk from the house. Other local sights include Busch Gardens, and William and Mary College.

Country Cottage Guest House ⊙
701 MONUMENTAL AVENUE, WILLIAMSBURG, VIRGINIA 23185

Tel: **(804) 229-6914**
Host(s): **Heidi and Rick Dunlap**
No. of Rooms: **3**
No. of Private Baths: **2**
Max. No. Sharing Bath: **6**
Double/pb: **$35**
Single/pb: **$30**
Double/sb: **$30**
Single/sb: **$25**

Open: **All year**
Reduced Rates: **4-night stays**
Breakfast: **Continental**
Pets: **No**
Children: **Welcome**
Smoking: **Permitted**
Social Drinking: **Permitted**
Airport/Station Pickup: **Yes**

This brick Cape Cod is within walking distance of the restored area. The rooms have a colonial decor, with poster beds, stenciled walls, and folk art. Guests are welcomed with a generous fruit basket, and a cup of coffee is always available. Your hosts offer fresh muffins or sweet rolls in the morning. They will advise on nearby tourist attractions and restaurants. William and Mary College is nearby.

Mi Casa ⊙
208 THOMAS NELSON LANE, WILLIAMSBURG, VIRGINIA 23185

Tel: **(804) 253-1104**
Best Time to Call: **Mornings; evenings**
Host(s): **Hope Jimenez**
Location: **50 mi. from Norfolk**
No. of Rooms: **1**
No. of Private Baths: **1**
Double/pb: **$40**

Open: **All year**
Breakfast: **No**
Pets: **Sometimes**
Children: **Welcome**
Smoking: **Permitted**
Social Drinking: **Permitted**
Foreign Languages: **Spanish**

Mi Casa is located five minutes from Colonial Williamsburg. A comfortable guest room has a private entrance, cable TV, refrigerator, individually controlled air conditioning, and an oversized bath among its amenities. The house is in the vicinity of fine dining of every variety. Other local attractions are a wax museum, candle factory, and famous pottery stores. Your hosts urge you to arrive early, drop off your bags, and begin touring. William and Mary College is nearby.

Thompson Guest House ☉
1007 LAFAYETTE STREET, WILLIAMSBURG, VIRGINIA 23185

Tel: **(804) 229-3455**
Host(s): **Alma Thompson**
No. of Rooms: **3**
No. of Private Baths: **1**
Max. No. Sharing Bath: **4**
Double/pb: **$25**
Single/pb: **$25**
Double/sb: **$18**

Single/sb: **$18**
Open: **All year**
Breakfast: **No**
Pets: **No**
Children: **Welcome**
Smoking: **Permitted**
Social Drinking: **No**

This charming house is located close to the historic district, where you can get the look and feel of another century. Alma is a most gracious hostess and will take the time to direct you to the not-to-be-missed sights, fine restaurants, and interesting shops.

Wood's Guest Home ☉
1208 STEWART DRIVE, WILLIAMSBURG, VIRGINIA 23185

Tel: **(804) 229-3376**
Host(s): **Lonnie and Betty Wood**
No. of Rooms: **3**
Max. No. Sharing Bath: **5**
Double/sb: **$26**
Single/sb: **$26**

Open: **All year**
Breakfast: **Continental**
Pets: **Sometimes**
Children: **Welcome**
Smoking: **Permitted**
Social Drinking: **Permitted**

This comfortable, rambling house is filled with handmade crafts, antiques, and modern pieces. Relax on the screened-in porch or in the living room with a fresh cup of coffee and a cookie. Colonial Williamsburg, Busch Gardens, Jamestown, Yorktown, and Carter's Grove Plantation are just a few of the local sights.

WASHINGTON

Pacific Bed & Breakfast ✪
701 N.W. 60TH STREET, SEATTLE, WASHINGTON 98107

Tel: **(206) 784-0539**
Best Time to Call: **8 AM–6 PM**
TELEX: **329473 ATT PBB 580**
Coordinator: **Irmgard Castleberry**
States/Regions Covered: **Anacortes, Ashford, Bellevue, Gig Harbor, Mercer Island, Seattle, Spokane, Tacoma, Vashon Island**

Rates (Single/Double):
  Modest: **$20**   **$25**
  Average: **$30**   **$35**
  Luxury: **$40**   **$49**
Credit Cards: **MC, VISA**

The above is but a partial list of the host homes available through Irmgard. There are Victorians, contemporaries, island cottages, waterfront houses, and private suites with full kitchens available. Most are close to downtown areas, near bus lines, in fine residential neighborhoods, or within walking distance of a beach. Many extras are included, such as pickup service, free use of laundry facilities, guided tours and more. The University of Washington and the University of Puget Sound are nearby.

Traveller's Bed & Breakfast—Seattle
BOX 492 MERCER ISLAND, WASHINGTON 98040

Tel: **(206) 232-2345**
Coordinator: **Jean Knight**
States/Regions Covered: **Bainbridge, Portland, Port Angeles, Port Townsend, Seattle, Tacoma, Vashon Island, Whidbey Island, Spokane, Olympia, Victoria, B.C.**

Rates (Single/Double):
Modest: **$25** **$35**
Average: **$35** **$45**
Luxury: **$65** **$65**
Credit Cards: **MC, VISA**

Jean has a roster of beautiful homes, deluxe accommodations, rooms with views of Puget Sound, and more. Rental cars and local tours can be arranged. Don't miss the Space Needle, Mount St. Helens, Mount Rainier. A ferry ride will take you to the surrounding islands and the most gorgeous scenery anywhere. Send $5 for her annotated listing of homes. Let Jean know your choice; she'll do the rest. Many B&Bs are near the University of Washington.

The Channel House ✪
2902 OAKES AVENUE, ANACORTES, WASHINGTON 98221

Tel: **(206) 293-9382**
Best Time to Call: **8 AM–10 PM**
Host(s): **Sam and Kathy Salzinger**
Location: **65 mi. N of Seattle**
No. of Rooms: **4**
Max. No. Sharing Bath: **4**
Double/sb: **$45**
Single/sb: **$38**
Open: **All year**

Reduced Rates: **10%, Sept. 15– June 15**
Breakfast: **Continental**
Pets: **No**
Children: **Welcome, over 10**
Smoking: **No**
Social Drinking: **Permitted**
Airport/Station Pickup: **Yes**

Built in 1902 by an Italian count, this three-story Victorian house has stained glass windows, rare antiques, gracious ambience, and is in mint condition. The guest rooms have beautiful views of Puget Sound and the San Juan islands. It's an ideal getaway for relaxing in the "cleanest corner of the country." Kathy serves gourmet breakfasts in front of the fireplace, and Sam's 23-foot sloop is ideal for sailing. The communal hot tub is a treat after salmon fishing, tennis, or golf. And it's only minutes from the ferry for visiting Victoria, British Columbia.

Phoenix House ✪
10472 N.E. SOUTH BEACH DRIVE, BAINBRIDGE ISLAND, WASHINGTON 98110

Tel: (206) 842-7170
Best Time to Call: **Before 9 AM; after 5 PM**
Host(s): **Diane and George Moser**
Location: **6 mi. from Hwy. 305**
Guest Cottage: **$36–$42; sleeps 2–3**
Open: **All year**

Reduced Rates: **Weekly**
Breakfast: **Continental**
Pets: **Sometimes**
Children: **Welcome**
Smoking: **Permitted**
Social Drinking: **Permitted**

This is a charmingly decorated private cottage adjoining Diane and George's beachfront home. Furnished with antiques, the large bed-sitting room has a double bed, color TV, and comfortable sitting area. There's a brass claw-foot tub, stained glass windows, and country wallpaper. Tea and coffee are always on tap. It's only minutes from Winslow for restaurants and shopping.

Palmer's Chart House ✪
P.O. BOX 51, ORCAS ISLAND, DEER HARBOR, WASHINGTON 98243

Tel: (206) 376-4231
Host(s): **Majean and Don Palmer**
Location: **50 mi. N of Seattle**
No. of Rooms: **2**
No. of Private Baths: **2**
Double/pb: **$60**
Single/pb: **$45**
Open: **All year**

Breakfast: **Full**
Other Meals: **Dinner (included)**
Pets: **No**
Children: **No**
Smoking: **No**
Social Drinking: **Permitted**
Airport/Station Pickup: **Yes**
Foreign Languages: **Spanish**

It's just an hour's ride on the Washington State ferry from Anacortes to Orcas Island. This is an adult, private paradise—quiet and informal. Seasoned travelers, Majean and Don know how to make your stay special. The guest rooms are carpeted, spacious, spic-and-span. Each has a private deck from which you may survey the harbor scene. Local seafood often provides the basis for Majean's special dinners, included in the rate. *Amante*, the 33-foot sloop, is available for sailing when Don, the skipper, is free.

The Harrison House ○
210 SUNSET AVENUE, EDMONDS, WASHINGTON 98020

Tel: **(206) 776-4748**
Best Time to Call: **Mornings**
Host(s): **Jody and Harve Harrison**
Location: **15 mi. N of Seattle**
No. of Rooms: **1**
No. of Private Baths: **1**
Double/pb: **$35**

Single/pb: **$25**
Open: **All year**
Breakfast: **Continental—$2**
Pets: **No**
Children: **No**
Smoking: **Permitted**
Social Drinking: **Permitted**

This new, informal, waterfront home has a sweeping view of Puget Sound and the Olympic Mountains. It is a block north of the ferry dock and three blocks from the center of this historic town. Many fine restaurants are within walking distance. Your spacious room has a private deck. The University of Washington is nearby.

Heather House ○
1011 "B" AVENUE, EDMONDS, WASHINGTON 98020

Tel: **(206) 778-7233**
Best Time to Call: **5–6:30 PM**
Host(s): **Harry and Joy Whitcutt**
Location: **15 mi. N of Seattle**
No. of Rooms: **1**
No. of Private Baths: **1**
Double/pb: **$35**
Single/pb: **$25**

Open: **All year**
Breakfast: **Continental—$3**
Pets: **No**
Children: **No**
Smoking: **Permitted**
Social Drinking: **Permitted**
Foreign Languages: **French, German**

This contemporary home has a spectacular view of Puget Sound and the Olympic Mountains. The guest room has a comfortable king-size bed and opens onto a private deck. Joy and Harry are world travelers and enjoy their guests. The homemade jams, jellies, and marmalades are delicious. A full English breakfast is $4. You can work off breakfast by walking a mile to the shops, beaches, and fishing pier.

Santopolo House ✪
1111 NINTH AVENUE NORTH, EDMONDS, WASHINGTON 98020

Tel: (206) 778-7093
Host(s): **Mike and Gayle**
Location: **20 mi. N of Seattle**
No. of Rooms: **1**
No. of Private Baths: **1**
Double/pb: **$35**
Single/pb: **$25**

Open: **All year**
Breakfast: **Full**
Pets: **Sometimes**
Children: **Sometimes**
Smoking: **Permitted**
Social Drinking: **Permitted**
Airport/Station Pickup: **Yes**

It is only 25 minutes to Seattle from Mike and Gayle's 101-year-old house. Furnished with antiques, lovely stained glass, and lots of wood, its views are of the mountains and Puget Sound. It's within walking distance of downtown as well as the beach. The University of Washington is nearby.

Lockhart's Retreat ✪
841 SEVENTH LANE, FOX ISLAND, WASHINGTON 98333

Tel: (206) 549-2179
Best Time to Call: **8:30 AM**
Host(s): **Tom and Janet Lockhart**
Location: **15 mi. W of Tacoma**
No. of Rooms: **2**
Max. No. Sharing Bath: **4**
Double/sb: **$40–$45**
Single/sb: **$30**
Open: **All year**

Reduced Rates: **15% weekly; 10% seniors**
Breakfast: **Full**
Credit Cards: **MC, VISA**
Pets: **Sometimes**
Children: **Sometimes**
Smoking: **Permitted**
Social Drinking: **Permitted**
Airport/Station Pickup: **Yes**

Five wooded acres in the center of Fox Island provide a "green curtain" atmosphere of peace and tranquillity. The farmhouse kitchen always has available a cookie and a cup of coffee. Tom and Janet are proud of their large, contemporary farmhouse. Do visit the Historical Museum and enjoy the nearby fishing village with its charming shops.

San Juan Inn
P.O. BOX 776, 50 SPRING STREET, FRIDAY HARBOR,
WASHINGTON 98250

Tel: **(206) 378-2070**	Reduced Rates: **10%, Oct. 15–May 15**
Host(s): **Joan and Norm Schwinge**	Breakfast: **Continental**
Location: **80 mi. N of Seattle**	Credit Cards: **MC, VISA**
No. of Rooms: **10**	Pets: **Sometimes**
Max. No. Sharing Bath: **6**	Children: **Welcome, over 5**
Double/sb: **$38**	Smoking: **Permitted**
Single/sb: **$29**	Social Drinking: **Permitted**
Open: **All year**	Airport/Station Pickup: **Yes**

Built in 1873, the San Juan is 100 feet from the ferry dock and steps away from restaurants and shops. Each guest room has quaint wallpaper, antique furnishings, and overlooks the harbor or the gardens. Norm and Joan provide bike rentals and will direct you to boating, fishing, national parks, a whaling museum, and the marine laboratory. In crisp weather, a crackling fire in the old nickel-plated parlor stove makes it a cozy spot to relax.

Hillside Gardens Bed and Breakfast ✪
6915 SILVER SPRINGS DRIVE N.W., GIG HARBOR,
WASHINGTON 98335

Tel: **(206) 851-5007**	Open: **All year**
Best Time to Call: **After 5 PM**	Reduced Rates: **10%, weekly**
Host(s): **Carol and Dick Unrue**	Breakfast: **Full**
Location: **10 mi. from Tacoma**	Pets: **No**
No. of Rooms: **1**	Children: **No**
No. of Private Baths: **1**	Smoking: **No**
Double/pb: **$35**	Social Drinking: **Permitted**
Single/pb: **$30**	Airport/Station Pickup: **Yes**

This comfortable home, set on a hillside, is surrounded by trees and flowers. Guests are welcome to relax by the fireside or in the garden or sun rooms. Arriving guests are greeted with coffee or tea and crackers and cheese. Fresh fruit muffins, blueberry pancakes, and eggs are served for breakfast. Gig Harbor and Point Defiance Park are nearby. Fishing, local theater, and golf are in the vicinity.

The Olde Glencove Hotel ✪
9418 GLENCOVE ROAD, GIG HARBOR, WASHINGTON 98335

Tel: (206) 884-2835
Host(s): **Larry and Luciann Nadeau**
Location: **20 mi. from Tacoma**
No. of Rooms: **2**
No. of Private Baths: **2**
Max. No. Sharing Bath: **2**
Double/pb: **$45–$50**
Single/pb: **$40**
Double/sb: **$35–$40**

Single/sb: **$30–$35**
Open: **All year**
Reduced Rates: **15%, weekly**
Breakfast: **Full**
Pets: **No**
Children: **Welcome, over 8**
Smoking: **Permitted**
Social Drinking: **Permitted**

This 1896 residence, listed in the National Historic Register, is located in a quiet cove on Puget Sound. Larry and Luciann have been restoring it to its original appearance, and they have decorated it with antiques and handcrafted stained glass. There's biking, boating, badminton, and croquet. Larry is known locally for his horseshoe game and backgammon expertise. The breakfast is special; champagne and *hors d'oeuvres* are offered for your pre-dinner enjoyment.

Flying L Guest Ranch
ROUTE 2, BOX 28, GLENWOOD, WASHINGTON 98619

Tel: (509) 364-3488
Host(s): **Ilse Lloyd**
Location: **35 mi. from I-84**
No. of Rooms: **7**
No. of Private Baths: **7**
Double/pb: **$33–$37**
Single/pb: **$22.50**
Open: **May–Oct.**

Reduced Rates: **Weekly; families**
Breakfast: **Full**
Pets: **No**
Children: **Welcome**
Smoking: **Permitted**
Social Drinking: **Permitted**
Airport/Station Pickup: **Yes**

The Flying L is in a quiet, picturesque farming and logging valley at the foot of Mount Adams. About half of the 280 acres are densely wooded, and the rest are covered with lush meadows. A two-story guest house and light housekeeping cabins are available. Ranch-style breakfasts are served in the rustic dining room of the main house. Lounge on the porch or swim in a shallow meadow lake. Hiking trails, canyons, a wildlife refuge, and white-river rafting are all nearby.

Brown's Farm ✪
11150 HIGHWAY 209, LEAVENWORTH, WASHINGTON 98826

Tel: **(509) 548-7863**
Best Time to Call: **Evenings**
Host(s): **Steve and Wendi Brown**
Location: **115 mi. from Seattle**
No. of Rooms: **2**
Max. No. Sharing Bath: **5**
Double/sb: **$45–$50**
Single/sb: **$45–$50**
Open: **All year**
Breakfast: **Full**
Pets: **No**
Children: **Welcome (crib)**
Smoking: **No**
Social Drinking: **Permitted**

It's like visiting Bavaria, because Leavenworth overlooks the snowcapped Icicle Ridge, the Wenatchee River, and is filled with European-style shops. The farm boasts a wooded setting for the delightful home built by Steve, Wendi and their children, furnished with antiques, handmade stained glass, lovely quilts, and a collection of family treasures. Breakfast is a feast. Children love the farm because there are eggs to gather, and rabbits to hug. Children in the crib stay for free. You are requested to bring sleeping bags for older children.

Edel Haus Bed 'n' Breakfast
320 9TH STREET, LEAVENWORTH, WASHINGTON 98826

Tel: **(509) 548-4412**
Best Time to Call: **10 AM–10 PM**
Host(s): **Betsy and Mark Montgomery**
Location: **2 blocks from Rte. 2**
No. of Rooms: **5**
No. of Private Baths: **2**
Maximum No. of Guests Sharing Bath: **6**
Double/pb: **$55**
Double/sb: **$49.50**
Single/sb: **$44.75**
Guest Cottage: **$60 (for 2)**
Open: **All year**
Reduced Rates: **10% Sun.–Thurs.**
Breakfast: **Full**
Other Meals: **Available (off-season)**
Air-Conditioning: **Yes**
Pets: **No**
Children: **Welcome**
Smoking: **No**
Social Drinking: **Permitted**
Airport/Station Pickup: **Yes**

Located in the Bavarian village in the central Cascades, this white stucco two-story home was built in 1930. The rooms are light and airy, furnished with antiques. The view is of the riverfront park. In winter, the accent is on skiing, as well as high camp adventure in the Scottish Lake area. In all seasons, relax in the hot tub.

Lake Pateros B&B ✪
206 WEST WARREN, BOX 595, PATEROS, WASHINGTON 98846

Tel: **(509) 923-2626**
Host(s): **Bob and Charlene Knoop**
Location: **19 mi. N of Chelan**
No. of Rooms: **2**
Max. No. Sharing Bath: **4**
Double/sb: **$35**
Single/sb: **$30**
Open: **All year**

Reduced Rates: **20% Off-season; seniors**
Breakfast: **Full**
Pets: **Sometimes**
Children: **Welcome**
Smoking: **No**
Social Drinking: **Permitted**

This white Dutch colonial has a red roof, red shutters, and is furnished with oak, wicker, and plants. The beds have handmade quilts and fluffy down pillows. It is located in the north central part of the state, the heart of Apple Country. Columbia River provides fabulous year-round fishing and water sports. Bob and Charlene invite you to use the kitchen for light snacks, as well as the washing machine and dryer.

Lizzie's ✪
731 PIERCE, PORT TOWNSEND, WASHINGTON 98368

Tel: (206) 385-4168
Best Time to Call: 9:30 AM–8 PM
Host(s): Thelma Scudi, Gabrielle and Charlie Ross
Location: 50 mi. NW of Seattle
No. of Rooms: 7
No. of Private Baths: 2½
Max. No. Sharing Bath: 5
Double/pb: $59–$79
Single/pb: $53–$73
Double/sb: $47–$66
Single/sb: $41–$61
Open: All year
Breakfast: Continental
Credit Cards: MC, VISA
Pets: No
Children: Welcome, over 12
Smoking: Permitted
Social Drinking: Permitted

History has been beautifully preserved here. Relax amid fireplaces, leather sofas, and Parisian wallpaper; try your hand on the rosewood piano. Sandy beaches, charter and surf fishing, galleries, book and antique shops, hiking, and bicycling are close by. The famous Olympic Peninsula warrants closer inspection. There are breathtaking views of the Olympic and Cascade mountains, as well as Puget Sound. The coffee pot is always on. Lizzie's is a state-licensed, fire-safe facility.

Palace Hotel ✪
1004 WATER STREET, PORT TOWNSEND, WASHINGTON 98368

Tel: (206) 385-0773
Host(s): Liz and Bill Svensson
No. of Rooms: 11
No. of Private Baths: 8
Max. No. Sharing Bath: 6
Double/pb: $35–$58
Single/pb: $30–$53
Double/sb: $30
Single/sb: $25
Suites: $48 (for 2)
Open: All year
Reduced Rates: 10% Oct.–Apr.; midweek
Breakfast: No
Credit Cards: MC, VISA
Pets: No
Children: Welcome (crib)
Smoking: Permitted
Social Drinking: Permitted
Foreign Languages: Danish

This three-story Victorian hotel, located on the downtown waterfront, is listed in the National Historic Register. The comfortable rooms are spacious, with 14-foot ceilings, and are furnished with antiques. Three rooms feature a water view. Liz is an artist, Bill's an architect. Although no breakfast is offered, the individual guest rooms are equipped with electric pots for making tea or coffee. Each suite has a fully equipped kitchen. Fine restaurants are nearby.

Chambered Nautilus Bed and Breakfast Inn
5005 22ND AVENUE NORTH EAST, SEATTLE, WASHINGTON 98105

Tel: **(206) 522-2536**
Host(s): **Kate McDill and Deborah Sweet**
Location: **4 mi. NE of downtown**
No. of Rooms: **6**
Max. No. Sharing Bath: **4**
Double/sb: **$35–$65**
Open: **All year**
Reduced Rates: **Over 3 nights**

Breakfast: **Continental**
Credit Cards: **MC, VISA**
Pets: **No**
Children: **Welcome**
Smoking: **Permitted**
Social Drinking: **Permitted**
Foreign Languages: **American sign language**

This 1915 Georgian mansion faces the Cascade Mountains and Lake Washington. Guests are welcomed with a glass of wine. One bedroom is romantic, with lots of oak; another is sunny, with inlaid mahogany pieces; several have balconies. Take homemade pastries to your room each morning, or enjoy breakfast in the fireplaced dining room. Your hosts will be happy to direct you to local theaters, restaurants, and sports activities. The University of Washington is nearby.

The College Inn Guest House
4000 UNIVERSITY WAY N.E., SEATTLE, WASHINGTON 98105

Tel: **(206) 633-4441**
Best Time to Call: **7 AM–11 PM**
Host(s): **Gladys Louise Fred**
No. of Rooms: **27**
Max. No. Sharing Bath: **5**
Double/sb: **$37–$44**
Single/sb: **$30–$32**
Open: **All year**

Breakfast: **Continental**
Credit Cards: **AMEX, MC, VISA, DC, CB**
Pets: **No**
Children: **Welcome**
Smoking: **Permitted**
Social Drinking: **Permitted**

Built in 1909, the inn is now in the National Register of Historic Places. Recently refurbished, this English Tudor building is an old-fashioned respite within a cosmopolitan city. It is next door to the University of Washington, within walking distance of shops, theaters, parks, restaurants, and museums. Each guest room has a sink in it. Coffee and tea are always available.

Inge's Place
6809 LAKE GROVE S.W., TACOMA, WASHINGTON 98499

Tel: (206) 584-4514
Host(s): **Ingeborg Deatherage**
Location: **3 mi. from I-5**
No. of Rooms: **3**
No. of Private Baths: **1**
Max. No. Sharing Bath: **4**
Double/pb: **$40**
Single/pb: **$30**
Double/sb: **$40**
Single/sb: **$30**
Suites: **$60**

Open: **All year**
Reduced Rates: **After 3 nights**
Breakfast: **Full**
Credit Cards: **MC, VISA**
Pets: **No**
Children: **Welcome**
Smoking: **Permitted**
Social Drinking: **Permitted**
Airport/Station Pickup: **Yes**
Foreign Languages: **German**

This spic-and-span home is in a lovely Tacoma suburb called Lakewood. Feel welcome to use the hot tub, large backyard, and patio. There are many restaurants and shopping centers within walking distance, and several nearby lakes where fishing is excellent. Tacoma is the gateway to Mount Rainier. Inge is a world traveler, teacher, and enthusiast about B&Bs.

Keenan House ✪
2610 NORTH WARNER, TACOMA, WASHINGTON 98407

Tel: (206) 752-0702
Host(s): **Lenore Keenan**
Location: **2½ mi. from I-5**
No. of Rooms: **5**
Max. No. Sharing Bath: **4**
Double/sb: **$30**
Single/sb: **$25**

Open: **All year**
Breakfast: **Full**
Pets: **No**
Children: **Welcome**
Smoking: **Permitted**
Social Drinking: **Permitted**

This spacious Victorian house is located in the historic district near Puget Sound. It is furnished in antiques and period pieces. Afternoon tea is served, and ice is available for cocktails; fruit and croissants are served with breakfast. Local possibilities include Puget Sound, Vashon Island, the state park, zoo, and ferry. It's only five blocks to the University of Puget Sound.

The Swallow's Nest ○
ROUTE 3, BOX 221, VASHON, WASHINGTON 98070

Tel: (206) 463-2646
Best Time to Call: **Mornings**
Host(s): **Kathryn Brown Keller**
Location: **15 minutes from Seattle by ferry**
No. of Rooms: **2 cottages**
No. of Private Baths: **2**
Guest Cottage: **$40; sleeps 2**

Open: **All year**
Reduced Rates: **$200 weekly**
Breakfast: **Continental—$2.50**
Credit Cards: **MC, VISA**
Pets: **No**
Children: **Welcome**
Smoking: **No**
Social Drinking: **Permitted**

The "nest" actually consists of two lovely cottages overlooking Puget Sound and Mount Rainier. Fresh flowers and a basket of fruit help welcome guests. There are 20 acres of forest, fruit trees, and open fields to explore. Your breakfast is brought on a tray to the cottage.

Guest House Bed & Breakfast ○
835 EAST CHRISTENSON ROAD, GREENBANK, WHIDBEY ISLAND, WASHINGTON 98253

Tel: (206) 678-3115
Best Time to Call: **Before 10 PM**
Host(s): **Don and Mary Jane Creger**
Location: **49 mi. NW of Seattle**
No. of Rooms: **6**
Max. No. Sharing Bath: **4**
Double/sb: **$35–$43**
Single/sb: **$35–$43**
Guest Cottage: **$55–$90**

Open: **All year**
Reduced Rates: **Available**
Breakfast: **$2.50**
Credit Cards: **MC, VISA**
Pets: **Sometimes**
Children: **Welcome, over 14**
Smoking: **No**
Social Drinking: **Permitted**

It is a delightful 15-minute ferry ride from Mukilteo to this lovely island. A variety of accommodations is offered, including two charming country guest rooms in the 1920 farmhouse, with shared bath; three self-contained private guest cottages cozily furnished with antiques, stained glass, fireplaces, and mini-kitchens; and the luxurious log lodge that sleeps up to five. Continental breakfast is included with farmhouse accommodations. A full breakfast setup in the cottages is $2.50 per person per day. Vancouver and Victoria, B.C., are in easy reach.

Sally's Bed and Breakfast Manor
215 6TH STREET, P.O. BOX 459, WHIDBEY ISLAND, LANGLEY, WASHINGTON 98260

Tel: **(206) 221-8709**
Host(s): **Sally De Felice**
Location: **40 mi. N of Seattle**
No. of Rooms: **2**
No. of Private Baths: **2**
Double/pb: **$65**
Single/pb: **$60**

Open: **Feb.–Dec.**
Breakfast: **Full**
Pets: **Sometimes**
Children: **Welcome, over 16**
Smoking: **No**
Social Drinking: **Permitted**
Airport/Station Pickup: **Yes**

This 55-year-old farmhouse is set on three acres overlooking Puget Sound. The decor is country-style, with coordinating wallpapers, fabrics, and traditional furnishings, in guest rooms overlooking the mountains and the sea. Enjoy a lazy morning in the sun room, or linger over coffee in the dining area. Your hosts offer hot cider by the fire and occasionally serve light *hors d'oeuvres*. It's a short walk to the beach, village shops, galleries, theaters, and restaurants.

For key to listings, see inside front or back cover.

✪ This star means that rates are guaranteed through December 31, 1985 to any guest making a reservation as a result of reading about the B&B in *BED & BREAKFAST U.S.A.*—1985 edition.

Please enclose a self-addressed, stamped, business-sized envelope when contacting reservation services.

For more details on what you can expect in a B&B, see Chapter 1.

Always mention *Bed & Breakfast USA* when making reservations!

WEST VIRGINIA

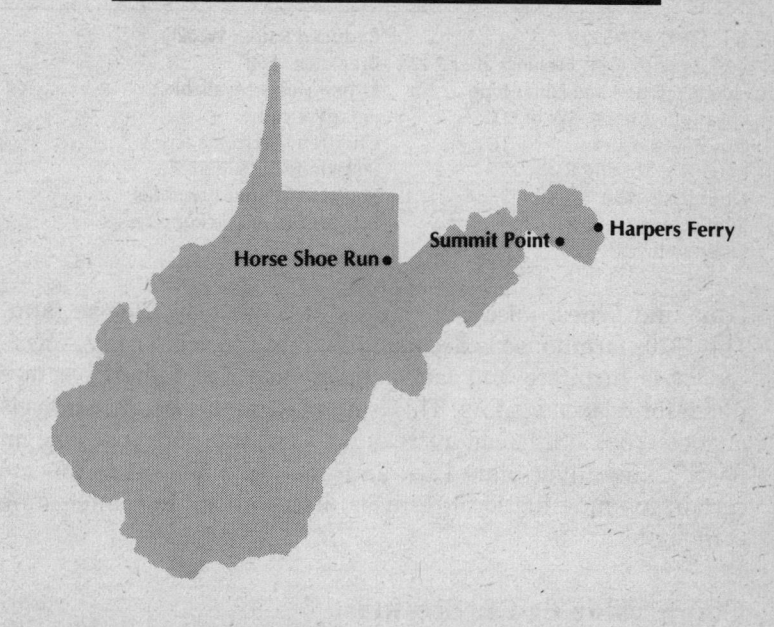

Mountain Village Inn ✪
ROUTE 219, HORSE SHOE RUN, WEST VIRGINIA 26769

Tel: (304) 735-6344
Host(s): **Bill and Sheila Reeves**
Location: **200 mi. W of D.C.**
No. of Rooms: **3**
Max. No. Sharing Bath: **6**
Double/sb: **$80**
Single/sb: **$40**
Open: **Nov. 1–Apr. 30**

Breakfast: **Full**
Other Meals: **Dinner included**
Credit Cards: **MC, VISA**
Pets: **No**
Children: **Welcome**
Smoking: **Permitted**
Social Drinking: **Permitted**
Foreign Languages: **Spanish**

Atop the Allegheny Mountains, at an elevation of 2,500 feet, is this natural wood home trimmed with antique shutters. There's a porch on which to relax, overlooking the lake. Bill and Sheila love to cook, and pride themselves on such goodies as buckwheat cakes and sausage, hot tortillas, and marvelous biscuits. Wine, coffee, and snacks are always on hand. This is a very rural area, framed by mountains, close to several recreational areas.

Valley View Farm ✪
RT. 1, BOX 467, MATHIAS, WEST VIRGINIA 26812

Tel: (304) 897-5229
Best Time to Call: **Evenings after 7 PM**
Host(s): **Ernest and Edna Shipe**
Location: **130 mi. SW of D.C.**
No. of Rooms: **4**
Max. No. Sharing Bath: **7**
Double/sb: **$30**
Single/sb: **$15**
Open: **All year**

Reduced Rates: **Weekly**
Breakfast: **Full**
Other Meals: **Available**
Pets: **Welcome**
Children: **Welcome (crib)**
Smoking: **Permitted**
Social Drinking: **Permitted**
Airport/Station Pickup: **Yes**

Edna and Ernest raise cattle and sheep on their 250-acre farm. The 1920s farmhouse is decorated with comfortable Early American style furniture and family mementoes, and there's a nice porch for relaxed visiting. This is no place to diet because Edna is a good cook. Seasonal recreational activities are available in nearby Lost River State Park and on Rock Cliff Lake. You are certain to enjoy the local festivals, house tours, and interesting craft shops.

Countryside Bed & Breakfast
BOX 57, SUMMIT POINT, WEST VIRGINIA 25446

Tel: (304) 725-2614
Host(s): **Lisa and Daniel Hileman**
Location: **8 mi. from Rtes. 7, 50**
No. of Rooms: **2**
No. of Private Baths: **2**
Double/pb: **$35**
Single/pb: **$30**

Open: **All year**
Breakfast: **Continental**
Children: **Welcome**
Smoking: **Permitted**
Social Drinking: **Permitted**
Foreign Languages: **Spanish**

In the Shenandoah Valley of the Eastern Panhandle, only 20 minutes from Harpers Ferry, this country home with white shutters, large yard, and patio is on a quiet street in a charming old village. It is furnished with country oak furniture, antique quilts, and original art. Lisa and Daniel offer hospitable touches of fruit and candy, placed in each guest room. Afternoon tea is served; snacks and beverages are always available.

WISCONSIN

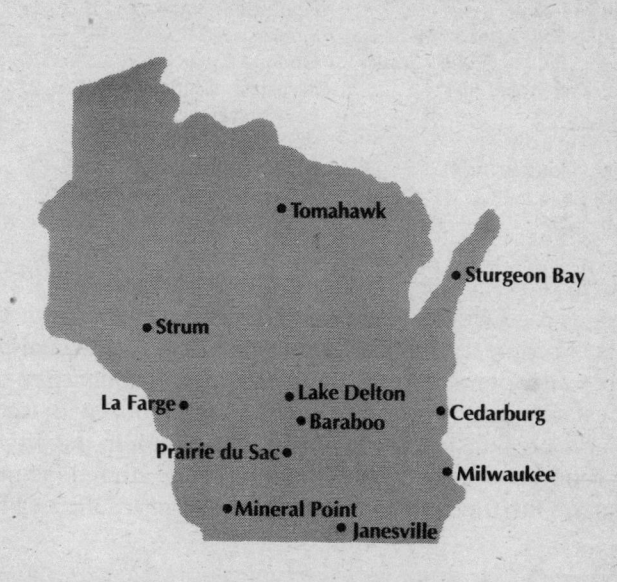

The House of Seven Gables ✪
215 6TH STREET, BARABOO, WISCONSIN 53913

Tel: **(608) 356-8387**
Best Time to Call: **8 AM–10 PM**
Host(s): **Ralph and Pamela W. Krainik**
Location: **13 mi. from I-90**
No. of Rooms: **2 suites**
No. of Private Baths: **2**
Suite: **$50**

Open: **All year**
Breakfast: **Continental**
Credit Cards: **MC**
Pets: **No**
Children: **Welcome**
Smoking: **No**
Social Drinking: **Permitted**

Seven Gables is a restored 1860 Gothic Revival home. It is in the National Register of Historic Places as one of the best examples of this architecture. The 17 rooms are furnished entirely in the Civil War period. Pamela and Ralph will be happy to direct you to the activities, restaurants, and shops that make their area special. The University of Wisconsin is close by.

Sessler's Guest House ✪
210 SOUTH JACKSON STREET, JANESVILLE, WISCONSIN 53545

Tel: **(608) 754-7250**
Best Time to Call: **After 3 PM**
Host(s): **Mr. and Mrs. Robert Sessler**
Location: **2 mi. from I-90**
No. of Rooms: **3**
No. of Private Baths: **1**
Max. No. Sharing Bath: **4**
Double/pb: **$36**
Single/pb: **$25**
Double/sb: **$36**
Single/sb: **$25**
Open: **All year**
Breakfast: **Continental**
Pets: **Sometimes**
Children: **Welcome**
Smoking: **Permitted**
Social Drinking: **Permitted**
Airport/Station Pickup: **Yes**

This turn-of-the-century home is finely appointed, with brass fixtures, leaded beveled glass windows, and Italian fireplace mantels. The guest rooms are in soft colors with colonial-period English wallpaper, fancy pillows, dust ruffles, and cozy quilts. The guest sitting room has books and a refrigerator with ice. Your hosts serve breakfast on the screened-in porch or in the fireplaced dining room, overlooking the grounds. Local attractions include the beach, Old Town restorations, hiking trails, golf, and museums.

Rainbow Retreat ✪
ROUTE 2, BOX 121, LA FARGE, WISCONSIN 54639

Tel: **(608) 625-4492**
Best Time to Call: **Mornings; evenings**
Host(s): **Joe Swanson and Rosanne Boyett**
Location: **40 mi. SE of LaCrosse**
Guest Cottage: **$45–$60; 1–4**
Open: **All year**
Reduced Rates: **10%, weekly**
Breakfast: **Continental**
Pets: **No**
Children: **Welcome (crib)**
Smoking: **Permitted**
Social Drinking: **Permitted**
Airport/Station Pickup: **Yes**

This private cottage is on a working farm located in the heart of a thriving Amish community. It is surrounded by an orchard, garden, and a lovely tree-shaded yard. There's a path beside the stream that winds through woods and fields. The cottage is light and airy, with comfortable wicker furniture. Rosanne and Joe stock your kitchen with homemade breads, jams, cheese, farm-fresh eggs, coffee, tea, and even goat's milk if you wish. Recreational activities abound in the area: art studios, craft shops, and Amish woodworking shops are fun to visit.

O.J.'s Victorian Village Guest House ✪
P.O. BOX 98, LAKE DELTON, WISCONSIN 53940

Tel: (608) 254-6568	Open: All year
Best Time to Call: 5 PM	Reduced Rates: 10% Nov. 1–May 31
Host(s): O. J. and Lois Thompto	Breakfast: Continental
Location: 50 mi. W of Madison	Pets: Sometimes
No. of Rooms: 4	Children: Sometimes
No. of Private Baths: 4	Smoking: No
Double/pb: $30–$35	Social Drinking: Permitted
Single/pb: $25	Airport/Station Pickup: Yes
Guest Cottage: $55 for 4	

Located midway between Milwaukee and the Twin Cities, this brand-new house was built especially for B&B. It is situated on a major waterway; there's access to an enchanting creek and lake for fishing, swimming, and boating. It's five miles from the International Crane Foundation where you can watch cranes from Africa, Asia, and America. O. J. and Lois look forward to greeting you, and will arrange for discounts in many restaurants and shops. The University of Wisconsin at Baraboo is nearby.

Bed & Breakfast of Milwaukee, Inc. ✪
3107 N. DOWNER AVENUE, MILWAUKEE, WISCONSIN 53211

Tel: (414) 342-5030	Rates (Single/Double):
Coordinator: Claudette McShane	Modest: $20–$30 $25–$35
State/Regions Covered: Cedarburg, Milwaukee	Average: $30–$40 $35–$45
	Luxury: $45–$55 $50–$60
	Credit Cards: No

A city of great ethnic diversity, Milwaukee is the site of many festivals and cultural celebrations. There is no shortage of fine restaurants; your host will be happy to make suitable recommendations to suit your taste and purse. There is a fine zoo, museums, and renowned cultural attractions. Major league sports and miles of Lake Michigan offer diversion and fun. The University of Wisconsin and Marquette University are convenient to many of Claudette's accommodations.

The Duke House ☉
618 MAIDEN STREET, MINERAL POINT, WISCONSIN 53565

Tel: (608) 987-2821
Host(s): **Tom and Darlene Duke**
Location: **48 mi. SW of Madison**
No. of Rooms: **3**
Max. No. Sharing Bath: **6**
Double/sb: **$35**
Single/sb: **$25**
Open: **All year**
Breakfast: **Continental**
Pets: **No**
Children: **No**
Smoking: **Permitted**
Social Drinking: **Permitted**

This colonial corner house is furnished with antique beds and hardwood floors. Tea and pastries or wine and cheese are served in the afternoon. Breakfast features homemade breads and coffee cakes. Local possibilities include House-on-the-Rock, Frank Lloyd Wright architecture, Governor Dodge State Park, the Wisconsin River, and the Pendarvis Historical Site.

Farmhand Cottage ☉
ROUTE 1, BOX 216, PRAIRIE DU SAC, WISCONSIN 53578

Tel: (608) 643-4258
Best Time to Call: **Early evening**
Host(s): **Robert and Joan Weiss**
Location: **1 mi. W of Hwy. 12**
No. of Rooms: **1 cottage**
No. of Private Baths: **1**
Guest Cottage: **$25–$35; 1–4**
Open: **All year**
Breakfast: **Full**
Pets: **No**
Children: **Welcome**
Smoking: **Permitted**
Social Drinking: **Permitted**
Foreign Languages: **German**

Joan and Bob have a working beef-hog farm located halfway between the Dells and the House-on-the-Rock in Dodgeville. The self-contained guest cottage is 90 years old and furnished with antiques. The fixings for a do-it-yourself breakfast are supplied and include freshly laid eggs, homemade bread, and jam from homegrown strawberries.

The Lake House ✪
515 ELM STREET, RR2, BOX 217, STRUM, WISCONSIN 54770

Tel: **(715) 695-3519**
Best Time to Call: **Evenings**
Host(s): **Florence Gullicksrud**
Location: **20 mi. S of Eau Claire**
No. of Rooms: **2**
No. of Private Baths: **1**
Max. No. Sharing Bath: **4**
Double/pb: **$20**
Single/pb: **$15**
Double/sb: **$20**

Single/sb: **$15**
Suites: **$35**
Open: **May 30–Sept. 2**
Breakfast: **Continental**
Pets: **Sometimes**
Children: **Welcome, over 4**
Smoking: **Permitted**
Social Drinking: **Permitted**
Airport/Station Pickup: **Yes**

This lovely lakeside home is surrounded by parks and hills. There are miles of hiking trails through scenic farm country, as well as a nine-hole golf course and free tennis. Or, you can just stay "home" and use the canoe, rowboat, and picnic table. Florence is a retired nurse, is interested in art, and devotes herself to making her guests feel at home. The two-bedroom suite is best suited to a couple with children or friends traveling together. It's a half-hour to the University of Wisconsin, theater, and concerts.

White Lace Inn—A Victorian Guest House ✪
16 NORTH FIFTH AVENUE, STURGEON BAY, WISCONSIN 54235

Tel: **(414) 743-1105**
Host(s): **Dennis and Bonnie Statz**
Location: **175 mi. N of Milwaukee**
No. of Rooms: **11**
No. of Private Baths: **11**
Double/pb: **$52–$74**
Single/pb: **$45–$67**
Open: **Jan.–Mar.; May–Oct.**

Reduced Rates: **Jan.–Mar.**
Breakfast: **Continental**
Credit Cards: **AMEX, MC, VISA**
Pets: **No**
Children: **Welcome, over 6**
Smoking: **Permitted**
Social Drinking: **Permitted**
Airport/Station Pickup: **Yes**

This elegant Victorian guest house is beautifully furnished with quality antiques, down pillows, cozy comforters, brass canopy beds, lace curtains, and fine rugs. Located in a residential area close to the bay, it is near shops and historic sites. Winter features great cross-country skiing, snow sports, and hot chocolate in front of the fireplace. Summer offers boating, tennis, and swimming, with iced tea served on the front porch.

WYOMING

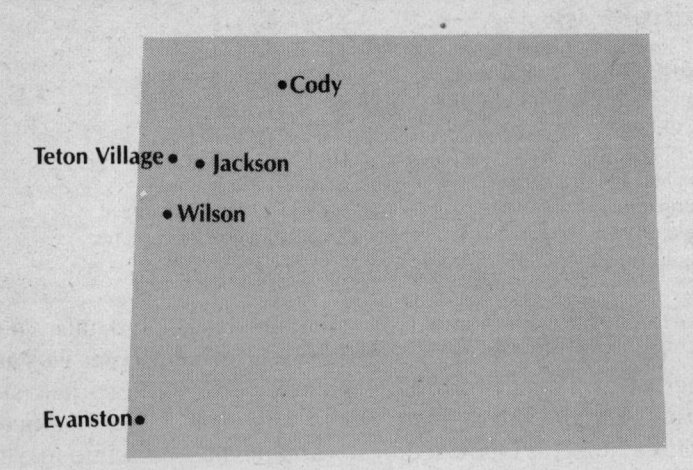

The Lockhart Inn ✪
109 WEST YELLOWSTONE AVENUE, CODY, WYOMING 82414

Tel: (307) 587-6074
Host(s): Verene and Lloyd Londerville
No. of Rooms: 6
No. of Baths: 6
Double/pb: $40
Single/pb: $35
Months of operation: All year
Reduced Rates: 15% less Nov.–May

Breakfast: Full
Credit Cards: MC, VISA
Pets: Sometimes
Children: Welcome over 3
Smoking: Permitted
Social Drinking: Permitted
Airport/Station Pickup: Yes

Once the home of Cody's famous turn-of-the-century novelist, Caroline Lockhart, Verene and Lloyd and their daughters Vicki and Lisa have updated this historic frontier home while retaining the flavor of the old West. Located 50 miles from the eastern entrance to Yellowstone National Park, there's plenty to do in addition to relaxing on the front porch. The Trail Town Museum, Buffalo Bill Historical Center, and the Cody Nightly Rodeo are just some of the attractions. Hunting is a popular sport, and the inn offers special rates that include all meals to hunters. The breakfast is an all-you-can-eat feast, and coffee or tea are always available.

Pine Gables Bed and Breakfast Inn ✪
1049 CENTER STREET, EVANSTON, WYOMING 82930

Tel: (307) 789-2069
Best Time to Call: 7 AM–10 PM
Host(s): Jessie and Arthur Monroe
Location: 85 mi. E of Salt Lake City
No. of Rooms: 6
No. of Private Baths: 2
Max. No. Sharing Bath: 4
Double/pb: $28.50
Single/pb: $26.50
Double/sb: $28.50
Single/sb: $26.50

Suites: $32.50
Open: All year
Reduced Rates: 15%, Nov.–Apr.; 20%, seniors
Breakfast: Continental
Credit Cards: CB, DC, MC, VISA
Pets: Sometimes
Children: Welcome
Smoking: Permitted
Social Drinking: Permitted
Airport/Station Pickup: Yes

This antiques-filled inn is a site on the tour of Evanston's historic district. Each bedroom is furnished with collectibles and decorated using different woods—oak, cherry, mahogany, and walnut. Your hosts operate an antique shop on-premises. They prepare a breakfast of homemade breads and pastries. Hiking, fishing, skiing, and hunting are nearby.

Captain Bob Morris
BOX 261, TETON VILLAGE, JACKSON HOLE, WYOMING 83025

Tel: (307) 733-4413
Best Time to Call: 6–10 AM
Host(s): Captain Bob Morris
Location: 12 mi. NW of Jackson
No. of Rooms: 2
No. of Private Baths: 1
Max. No. Sharing Bath: 3
Double/pb: $30
Single/pb: $25
Double/sb: $25

Single/sb: $20
Open: Dec. 1–Apr. 15; May 30–Oct. 15
Reduced Rates: Non-smokers
Breakfast: Continental
Pets: Yes
Children: Welcome
Smoking: Permitted
Social Drinking: Permitted

It's just 400 yards from the longest tram in the U.S. Bob's 5,000-square-foot passive solar house is your home-away-from-home. Skiing is the keynote here but the other wonderful things to do include visiting Yellowstone or Grand Teton (nearby) national parks, experiencing Snake River in a raft, or riding Western-style.

Heck-of-a-Hill Homestead ✪
P.O. BOX 105, WILSON, WYOMING 83014

Tel: **(307) 733-8023**
Host(s): **Bill and Mimi Schultes**
Location: **7 mi. W of Jackson**
No. of Rooms: **2**
No. of Baths: **2**
Double/pb: **$60**
Single/pb: **$48**
Open: **All year**

Breakfast: **Full**
Other Meals: **Available**
Pets: **Welcome**
Children: **Welcome**
Smoking: **Permitted**
Social Drinking: **Permitted**
Airport/Station Pickup: **Yes**

Bill and Mimi's spacious home, adjacent to Teton National Forest, personifies western charm and hospitality. You may spot a moose, elk, or deer roaming their three-acre property and the barn houses farm animals, including champion French Lop rabbits. You and the children are welcome to gather eggs or try your hand at milking the goat. There's a rustic cabin on the grounds that is perfect for older children wishing a camp-out-in-the-woods experience in summer. Great ski areas are less than an hour away for winter fun. The Schultes' delicious food is home-grown, home-baked or homemade.

For key to listings, see inside front or back cover.

✪ This star means that rates are guaranteed through December 31, 1985 to any guest making a reservation as a result of reading about the B&B in *BED & BREAKFAST U.S.A.*—1985 edition.

Please enclose a self-addressed, stamped, business-sized envelope when contacting reservation services.

For more details on what you can expect in a B&B, see Chapter 1.

Always mention *Bed & Breakfast USA* when making reservations!

5

CANADA

Note: *All prices listed in this section are quoted in Canadian dollars.*

ALBERTA

Alberta Bed & Breakfast O
4327 86TH STREET, EDMONTON, ALBERTA, CANADA T6K 1A9

Tel: **(403) 462-8885**
Best Time to Call: **Before 9 AM**
Coordinator: **June Brown**
States/Regions Covered: **Calgary, Edmonton, Canmore, Cochrane, Redwood Meadows, Westerose**

Rates (Single/Double):
  Modest: **$15**   **$20**
  Average: **$20–$25**   **$30–$35**
Credit Cards: **No**

Try a bit of Canadian western hospitality by choosing from June's variety of lovely homes in the majestic Rocky Mountains. Make a circle tour of Calgary, Banff, Lake Louise, the Columbia Icefields, Jasper, and Edmonton and stay in B&Bs all the way. Send one dollar for a descriptive list of the cordial hosts on her roster, make your selections, and June will do the rest.

BRITISH COLUMBIA

Grouse Mountain Bed and Breakfast ⚬
900 CLEMENTS AVENUE, NORTH VANCOUVER, BRITISH COLUMBIA, CANADA V7R2K7

Tel: **(604) 986-9630**
Best Time to Call: **Early Morning; Evening**
Host(s): **Lyne and John Armstrong**
Location: **1 mi. N of Vancouver**
No. of Rooms: **2**
No. of Private Baths: **1**
Max. No. Sharing Bath: **2**
Double/pb: **$30**
Single/pb: **$20**

Double/sb: **$28**
Single/sb: **$18**
Open: **All year**
Reduced Rates: **10% weekly**
Breakfast: **Full**
Pets: **Welcome**
Children: **Welcome (crib)**
Smoking: **No**
Social Drinking: **Permitted**
Airport/Station Pickup: **Yes**

Your hosts welcome you to a comfortable, modern home in the foothills of Grouse Mountain. Enjoy views of Vancouver Island from two sun decks overlooking the secluded grounds, with close proximity to Stanley Park, the beaches, and downtown. Large rooms await you, one with cedar-paneled bath, the other with flagstone fireplace. Both have ample sitting room. Breakfast features something different each day, such as French toast or omelettes with homemade jam. Skiing is only five minutes away. (Rates are quoted here in U.S. Funds.)

NOVA SCOTIA

Bread & Roses ✪
82 VICTORIA STREET, P.O. BOX 177, ANNAPOLIS ROYAL, NOVA SCOTIA B0S 1A0

Tel: **(902) 532-5727**
Host(s): **Ronald C. Phillips**
No. of Rooms: 7
No. of Private Baths: 7
Double/pb: **$40–$44**
Single/pb: **$36**
Open: **All year**
Breakfast: **$2.50–$3.50**

Credit Cards: **MC, VISA**
Pets: **Sometimes**
Children: **Welcome**
Smoking: **No**
Social Drinking: **Permitted**
Airport/Station Pickup: **Yes**
Foreign Languages: **French**

This restored home was built in 1882 during Nova Scotia's golden age. Enjoy the craftsmanship and use of rare woods in the grand staircase and throughout the house. Etched glass, sunny bay windows, and tiled fireplaces highlight the living and dining rooms. Your comfort is assured in spacious guest rooms with period furnishings. Use the library in the living room, or watch TV in the den. There are many recreational activities as well as historical sites to keep you busy.

Bute Arran
P.O. BOX 75, BADDECK, NOVA SCOTIA, CANADA B0E 1B0

Tel: **(902) 295-2786**
Best Time to Call: **After 6 PM**
Host(s): **Donald and Margot MacAulay**
Location: **2 mi. from Hwy. 105**
No. of Rooms: **4**
No. of Private Baths: **1**
Max. No. Sharing Bath: **5**
Double/pb: **$32**
Single/pb: **$30**

Double/sb: **$27**
Single/sb: **$22**
Open: **June 15–Oct. 15**
Breakfast: **Full**
Credit Cards: **AMEX, MC, VISA**
Pets: **Sometimes**
Children: **Welcome (crib)**
Smoking: **Permitted**
Social Drinking: **Permitted**

This rambling Cape Cod cottage is on the shore of Bras d'Or Lake, convenient to the famed Cabot Trail, a scenic 185-mile drive around northern Cape Breton. It is one mile east of the Alexander Graham Bell Museum. It is furnished in a comfortable blend of antique and modern pieces, with lots of books and games for guests of all ages. Breakfast features hearty oatcakes and scones. The MacAulays serve tea in the evening.

Confederation Farm ✪
RR3, PARRSBORO, DILIGENT RIVER, NOVA SCOTIA, CANADA B0M 1S0

Tel: **(902) 254-3057**
Best Time to Call: **Evenings**
Host(s): **Bob and Julia Salter**
Location: **45 mi. S of Amherst**
No. of Rooms: **4**
No. of Baths: **2**
Max. No. Sharing Bath: **4**
Double/sb: **$25**
Single/sb: **$19**

Open: **May 1–Nov. 15**
Reduced Rates: **No**
Breakfast: **Full**
Other Meals: **Available**
Pets: **Sometimes**
Children: **Welcome (crib)**
Smoking: **Permitted**
Social Drinking: **Permitted**
Airport/Station Pickup: **Yes**

This peaceful berry and fruit farm overlooks Cape Split on the Bay of Fundy. The farmhouse is homey, comfortable, and immaculate. Julia sets a table fit for royalty, featuring the seafood specialties that the area is famous for. Prices are modest and portions are hefty. Be sure to ask to see Bob's Horse and Buggy Days museum containing a collection of family memorabilia from way back when. The highest tides in the world may be viewed here, and it is a rock buff's paradise. The Salters have three housekeeping cottages as well as a picnic park on their property.

ONTARIO

Bed & Breakfast—Kingston ✪
10 WESTVIEW ROAD, KINGSTON, ONTARIO, CANADA K7M 2C3

Tel: (613) 542-0214
Coordinator: **Ruth MacLachlan**
Best Time to Call: **Mornings**
States/Regions Covered:
  Ontario—Bath, Gananoque,

Kingston, Perth, Westport
Rates (Single/Double):
  Average: $25 $35
Credit Cards: **No**

Situated at the eastern end of Lake Ontario, at the head of the St. Lawrence River, Kingston has much to offer besides gorgeous scenery. There's Old Fort Henry, boat cruises through the Thousand Islands, historic sites, museums, and sports activities of every sort; the Rideau Nature Trail starts here and heads northeast toward Ottawa. Send $1 for the detailed directory.

Ottawa Area Bed & Breakfast
P.O. BOX 4848, STATION E, OTTAWA, ONTARIO, CANADA K1S 5J1

Tel: (613) 563-0161
Coordinators: **Suzan Bissett, Al Martin**
States/Regions Covered:
  Ontario—Kanata, Nepean, Gloucester, Ottawa; Quebec—Hull

Rates (Single/Double):
  Modest: $18 $25
  Average: $22 $30
Credit Cards: **No**

If you are seeking an interesting but inexpensive holiday, then Canada's capital, Ottawa, is the place for you. The city is packed with free activities including museums, the House of Parliament, art galleries, and historic sites. You can skate on the Rideau Canal or bike on miles of parkways and trails. There is a $25 membership fee to join the organization.

Ambassador B&B ✪
266 ONTARIO STREET, STRATFORD, ONTARIO, CANADA N5A 3H5

Tel: (519) 271-5385
Coordinator: **Grace Brunk**
States/Regions Covered: **Stratford**

Rates (Single/Double):
  Modest: $22 $28
  Average: $25 $30
  Luxury: $45 $55
Credit Cards: **No**

Stratford's Shakespeare Theatre is world renowned, and the beautiful parks, art galleries, excellent restaurants, and the Mennonite country will keep you busy and happy. Grace's hosts look forward to sharing their knowledge of their home town with you.

The Maples ✪
220 CHURCH STREET, STRATFORD, ONTARIO, CANADA N5A 2R6

Tel: **(519) 273-0810**
Host(s): **Lina and Ed Morley**
Location: **18 mi. from Hwy. 401**
No. of Rooms: **5**
Max. No. Sharing Bath: **5**
Double/sb: **$30–$35**
Single/sb: **$25**
Open: **All year**

Breakfast: **Continental**
Pets: **No**
Children: **Welcome, over 10**
Smoking: **Permitted**
Social Drinking: **Permitted**
Airport/Station Pickup: **Yes**
Foreign Languages: **German, Polish**

This 90-year-old red brick house is surrounded by a lovely garden, large maple trees, and a veranda. It is tastefully furnished with a warm blend of the old and the new. Your hosts are particularly hospitable. It is convenient to the Shakespeare Theatre, Kitchener Farmer's Market, and the African Lion Safari.

Toronto Bed & Breakfast ✪
P.O. BOX 74, STATION M, TORONTO, ONTARIO, M6S 4T2

Tel: **(416) 233-3887 or 233-4041**
Best Time to Call: **Evenings; weekends**
Coordinator: **Randy Lee**
States/Regions Covered: **Toronto**

Rates (Single/Double):
Modest: $30 $40
Average: $35 $45
Luxury: $40 $50
Credit Cards: **No**
Minimum Stay: **2 nights**

Toronto, located on Lake Ontario, is a sophisticated city, but the hosts in Randy's network of homes are warm, friendly, and helpful. Accommodations vary from a bedroom in a British colonial to a terraced penthouse suite in a luxury condo; full breakfast is included. All homes are convenient to public transportation, so that you can easily visit the CN Tower, the Ontario Science Centre, Fort York, and the exciting Harbourfront with its craft galleries and ethnic restaurants. Send $3 for the descriptive directory and make your reservations directly with the host of your choice.

Oppenheim's ✪
153 HURON STREET, TORONTO, CANADA M5T 2B6

Tel: **(416) 598-4562 or 598-4063**
Best Time to Call: **Before 8 AM**
Host(s): **Susan Oppenheim**
Location: **Downtown Toronto**
No. of Rooms: **4**
Max. No. Sharing Bath: **3**
Double/sb: **$40–$46**
Single/sb: **$30–$36**

Open: **All year**
Breakfast: **Full**
Pets: **No**
Children: **No**
Smoking: **No**
Social Drinking: **Permitted**
Foreign Languages: **French, German**

Susan is a singer-lyricist, and you are welcome to accompany her on one of the four pianos in this restored Victorian house that is furnished with memorabilia, warmth, and humor. She shops at the international Kensington Market, so breakfast often features seasonal specials like banana buttermilk pancakes, glazed maple syrup pears, or dilled Havarti omelets. It is served in her huge kitchen whimsically decorated to resemble a turn-of-the-century country store. It's located three blocks from the Art Gallery of Ontario, the Royal Museum, Parliament, and the University of Toronto. A three-day minimum stay is preferred.

Glenbellart House ✪
285 MARY STREET, P.O. BOX 445, WIARTON, ONTARIO, CANADA N0H 2T0

Tel: **(519) 534-2422**
Best Time to Call: **Evenings**
Host(s): **Sally and John Wright**
Location: **120 mi. NW of Toronto**

No. of Rooms: **3**
Max. No. Sharing Bath: **8**
Double/sb: **$35**
Single/sb: **$30**

Open: **All year**
Breakfast: **Full**
Pets: **No**
Children: **Welcome, over 10**

Smoking: **Permitted**
Social Drinking: **Permitted**
Airport/Station Pickup: **Yes**
Foreign Languages: **French, German**

Built in 1886, this magnificent Victorian mansion on the Bruce Peninsula has hand-carved rosewood fireplaces, stained glass windows, oak floors, a library, spacious bedrooms, and a full veranda overlooking flowers and lawns, with a view of Colpoy Bay. It's close to sandy beaches, clear water swimming, sailing, and fishing for salmon and trout. John will happily describe outings and activities for all seasons, while Sally prepares a hearty breakfast.

PRINCE EDWARD ISLAND

Sea Breeze Bed & Breakfast ✪
KENSINGTON RR #1, PRINCE EDWARD ISLAND, CANADA C0B 1M0

Tel: **(902) 836-5275**
Best Time to Call: **Mornings**
Host(s): **Fran and Leslie Harding**
Location: **40 mi. N of Charlottetown**
No. of Rooms: **3**
Max. No. Sharing Bath: **6**
Double/sb: **$27**
Single/sb: **$13.50**

Open: **All year**
Reduced Rates: **10%, Sept.–June**
Breakfast: **Full**
Other Meals: **Available**
Pets: **Sometimes**
Children: **Welcome (crib)**
Smoking: **Permitted**
Social Drinking: **Permitted**

This modern home overlooks the harbor of a quiet island community. For those who like to fish, deep-sea or tuna excursions can be arranged. The beaches, shops, and Cabot Provincial Park are nearby.

Woodington's Country Inn ✪
RR 2, KENSINGTON, PRINCE EDWARD ISLAND, C0B 1M0 CANADA

Tel: **(902) 836-5518**
Best Time to Call: **Noon**
Host(s): **Marion and Claude "Woody" Woodington**
No. of Rooms: **5**
Max. No. Sharing Bath: **5**
Double/sb: **$28**
Single/sb: **$14**

Open: **All year**
Reduced Rates: **10%, after Aug. 25**
Breakfast: **Full**
Other Meals: **Available**
Pets: **Welcome**
Children: **Welcome**
Smoking: **Permitted**
Social Drinking: **Permitted**

Relax on the spacious lawns surrounding this immaculate Victorian farmhouse or stroll to the private beach. You'll feel at home immediately. Marion is a fabulous cook and her table reflects all that is fresh and wholesome. Woody hand-carves the most realistic duck decoys you've ever seen. Marion's spare time is spent making gorgeous quilts. A wood carving or quilt would make a memorable souvenir to take home.

Smallman's Bed and Breakfast
KNUTSFORD, O'LEARY, RR1, PRINCE EDWARD ISLAND, CANADA C0B IV0

Tel: **(902) 859-3469**
Host(s): **Arnold and Eileen Smallman**
Location: **7½ mi. from Rte. 2**
No. of Rooms: **4**
Max. No. Sharing Bath: **6**
Double/sb: **$20**
Single/sb: **$10**
Suites: **$25**

Open: **All year**
Reduced Rates: **Nov.–Apr.**
Breakfast: **Full**
Pets: **Sometimes**
Children: **Welcome**
Smoking: **Permitted**
Social Drinking: **No**
Airport/Station Pickup: **Yes**

This comfortable, split-level home is just 10 minutes from the beach. The kids will enjoy the backyard sandbox as well as a private track where the family racehorses train. Your hostess is a dedicated baker, always ready with coffee and a homemade snack. Breakfast specialties include homemade biscuits and cereals. Many local restaurants serve fresh lobster, clams, and oysters in season. Your hosts can direct you to the better buys in town, as well as the Gulf of St. Lawrence, golf courses, mills, and museums.

Dyment Bed & Breakfast
RR 3, WILMOT VALLEY, SUMMERSIDE, PRINCE EDWARD ISLAND, CANADA C1N 4J9

Tel: **(902) 436-9893**
Best Time to Call: **Before noon; after 6 PM**
Host(s): **Earle and Wanda Dyment**
Location: **32 mi. W of Charlottetown**
No. of Rooms: **3**
Max. No. Sharing Bath: **6**
Double/sb: **$23**

Single/sb: **$20**
Open: **May 20–Oct. 31**
Breakfast: **Full**
Pets: **Sometimes**
Children: **Welcome (crib)**
Smoking: **Permitted**
Social Drinking: **Permitted**

This spanking-clean house is set in a picturesque farming area overlooking the Wilmost River. Wanda delights in having people stay, and allows you to use her kitchen for light snacks. There is much to do and see, including swimming, golf, deep-sea fishing, and going to the racetrack.

For key to listings, see inside front or back cover.

❂ This star means that rates are guaranteed through December 31, 1985 to any guest making a reservation as a result of reading about the *B&B* in *BED & BREAKFAST U.S.A.*—1985 edition.

Please enclose a self-addressed, stamped, business-sized envelope when contacting reservation services.

For more details on what you can expect in a B&B, see Chapter 1.

Always mention *Bed & Breakfast USA* when making reservations!

QUEBEC

Montreal Bed & Breakfast
5020 ST. KEVIN, SUITE B, MONTREAL, QUEBEC, CANADA H3W 1P4

Tel: **(514) 735-7493 or 738-3859**
Best Time to Call: **Mornings**
Coordinator: **Marian Kahn**
States/Regions Covered: **Montreal, Ste. Adele (Laurentian Mountains), Sutton**

Rates (Single/Double):
Modest: **$28**   **$40**
Average: **$30–$35**   **$45–$50**
Luxury: **$40**   **$55–$60**
Credit Cards: **No**

Marian has a list of lovely homes in Montreal and surrounding countryside. Many hosts are French Canadian and the full breakfasts included in the rate often reflect a gourmet's touch. Visit Old Montreal and The Harbor for a glimpse of history, the Museum of Fine Arts, Place Des Arts for a touch of culture. McGill University, Mount Royal Park, St. Helen's Island, and the Laurentian Mountains are all worth a visit too. There are marvelous restaurants, wonderful shops, and the people are warm and friendly.

Montrealers at Home
331 CLARKE, SUITE 29, WESTMOUNT, MONTREAL, CANADA H3Z 2E7

Tel: **(514) 932-9690**
Coordinator: **Robert Finkelstein**
State/Regions Covered: **Montreal, Westmount, Outremont**

Rates (Single/Double):
Average: **$25–$30**   **$35**
Credit Cards: **No**

Bob has nearly 100 enthusiastic hosts ready to introduce you to good shopping, diverse restaurants, and places of special interest with an experienced eye on good value. After a day of hectic activity that might include a *caleche* ride through the cobbled streets of the Old Quarter, or a visit to the futuristic high-fashion urban area, and samples of excellent cuisine from all over the world, your hosts look forward to having you return to relax in their homes.

1550 Pine Avenue West
1550 PINE AVENUE WEST, MONTREAL, CANADA H3G 1B4

Tel: (514) 933-1866
Host(s): **Leo and Nicole Perron**
No. of Rooms: **6**
No. of Private Baths: **3**
Max. No. Sharing Bath: **2**
Double/pb: **$45**
Single/pb: **$35**
Double/sb: **$40**
Single/sb: **$30**

Open: **All year**
Reduced Rates: **10%, families**
Breakfast: **Full**
Pets: **No**
Children: **Welcome**
Smoking: **Permitted**
Social Drinking: **Permitted**
Airport/Station Pickup: **Yes**
Foreign Languages: **French**

The stained glass windows, fireplaces, and antiques of this Victorian mansion recall the elegance of the 1900s. A private apartment that sleeps six is also available. Your hosts will serve a homemade dinner, or can recommend international restaurants. Ride through the cobblestone streets, or on the modern Metro; linger at a cafe before visiting the wonderfully preserved buildings, famous galleries, and shops this city has to offer. Evenings, your hosts invite you to relax with mixed drinks, wine, and cheese.

6

PUERTO RICO AND THE VIRGIN ISLANDS

Buena Vista Guest House ✪
2218 GENERAL DEL VALLE, OCEAN PARK, SAN JUAN, PUERTO RICO 00913

Tel: **(809) 726-2796**
Best Time to Call: **8 AM–10 PM**
Hosts: **Raymond and Norma Mondin**
Location: **Suburb of San Juan**
No. of Rooms: **11**
No. of Private Baths: **7**
Max. No. Sharing Bath: **4**
Double/pb: **$35**
Single/pb: **$29**
Double/sb: **$32**
Single/sb: **$26**

Open: **All year**
Reduced Rates: **10%, Apr. 15–Dec. 15**
Breakfast: **Full**
Other Meals: **Available**
Pets: **No**
Children: **Welcome**
Smoking: **Permitted**
Social Drinking: **Permitted**
Airport/Station Pickup: **Yes**
Foreign Languages: **French, Spanish**

You won't miss an ounce of sunshine on the terrace, patio, or porch of this comfortable tropical home. You're welcome to strum the guitar, play the piano, use the kitchen for light snacks, and generally make yourself at home. It's a half block from the beach and all water sports are available. In the evenings you can visit the hotel casinos and clubs for glamorous excitement.

The Cottage—Hart House ✪
P.O. BOX 7158, ST. THOMAS, U.S. VIRGIN ISLANDS 00801

Tel: **(809) 775-6651**
Host(s): **Dr. and Mrs. F. Donnell Hart**
Location: **6 mi. E of Charlotte Amalie**
No. of Rooms: **2**
No. of Private Baths: **2**
Double/pb: **$55**
Guest Cottage: **$375 week; sleeps 2**

Open: **All year**
Breakfast: **Continental**
Pets: **No**
Children: **Welcome, over 15**
Smoking: **Permitted**
Social Drinking: **Permitted**

On the quiet, residential east end of this informal island, Hart House is a short distance from the powdery white Caribbean beach, where sailboats dot the turquoise cove waters. Taxis and a restaurant are available down the hill. The private swimming pool is three steps from your front door, and shopping, water sports, golf, and tennis are nearby. The trade winds are cooling, even on the warmest days, but air-conditioning is available for a surcharge. A lovely guest room in the main house is used when the cottage is not available. A two-day minimum is required. Donn and Bobbe pride themselves on their Sunday brunch and delicious rum punch. Reserve as early as possible for February through April and holidays.

Appendix:
STATE TOURIST OFFICES

Listed here are the addresses and telephone numbers for the tourist offices of every U.S. state. When you write or call one of these offices, be sure to request a map of the state and a calendar of events. If you will be visiting a particular city or region, or if you have any special interests, be sure to specify them as well.

Alabama Bureau of Publicity
and Information
532 South Perry Street
Montgomery, Alabama 36104
(205) 832-5510 or (800) 252-2262
(out of state) or (800) 392-8096
(within Alabama)

Alaska Division of Tourism
Pouch E-445
Juneau, Alaska 99801
(907) 465-2010

Arizona Office of Tourism
3507 North Central Avenue, Suite 506
Phoenix, Arizona 85012
(602) 255-3618

Arkansas Department of Parks
and Tourism
1 Capitol Mall
Little Rock, Arkansas 72201
(501) 371-7777 or (800) 643-8383
(out of state) or (800) 482-8999
(within Arkansas)

California Office of Tourism
1121 L Street First Floor
Sacramento, California 95814
(916) 322-1396

Colorado Office of Tourism
5500 South Syracuse Circle
Suite 267
Englewood, Colorado 80111
(303) 779-1067

Connecticut Department of Economic
Development-Vacations
210 Washington Street
Hartford, Connecticut 06106
(203) 566-3948 or (800) 243-1685
(out of state) or (800) 842-7492
(within Connecticut)

Delaware State Travel Service
99 Kings Highway, P.O. Box 1401
Dover, Delaware 19903
(302) 736-4254 or (800) 441-8846
(out of state) or (800) 282-8667
(in Delaware)

Washington, D.C. Convention
and Visitors' Assoc.
Suite 250
1575 I Street, N.W.
Washington, D.C. 20005
(202) 789-7000

Florida Division of Tourism
126 Van Buren Street
Tallahassee, Florida 32301
(904) 487-1462

Georgia Tour
Box 1776
Atlanta, Georgia 30301
(404) 656-3590

Hawaii Visitors Bureau
2270 Kalakaua Avenue, Suite 801
Honolulu, Hawaii 96815
(808) 923-1811
      or
New York Office
441 Lexington Avenue, Room 1407
New York, N.Y. 10017
(212) 986-9203

Idaho Division of Tourism
Capitol Building, Room 108
Boise, Idaho 83720
(208) 334-2470 or (800) 635-7820

Illinois Office of Tourism
310 South Michigan Avenue
Suite 108
Chicago, Illinois
(312) 793-2094 or (800) 252-8987
 (within Illinois) or (800) 637-8560
 (neighboring states)

Indiana Tourism Development
1 North Capitol, Suite 700
Indianapolis, Indiana 46204-2243
(317) 232-8860 or (800) 662-4464
 (within Indiana) or (800) 858-8073
 in Illinois, Iowa, Kentucky,
 Michigan, Missouri, Ohio,
 Tennessee, Wisconsin

Iowa Development Commission
Tourist Development Division
600 East Court
Suite A
Des Moines, Iowa 50309-2882
(515) 281-3679

Kansas Department of Economic
 Development-Travel
503 Kansas Avenue
Sixth Floor
Topeka, Kansas 66603
(913) 296-2009

Kentucky Travel
Frankfort, Kentucky 40601
(502) 564-4930 or (800) 372-2961
 (within Kentucky) or (800) 626-8000
 (in most states east of the Rockies)

Louisiana Office of Tourism
Inquiry Department
P.O. Box 44291
Baton Rouge, Louisiana 70804
(504) 925-3860 or (800) 231-4730 (out
 of state)

Maine Publicity Bureau
97 Winthrop St.
Hallowell, Maine 04347
(207) 289-2423

Maryland Office of Tourist
 Development
45 Calvert Street
Annapolis, Maryland 21401
(301) 269-3517

Massachusetts Division of Tourism
Department of Commerce and
 Development
100 Cambridge Street—13th Floor
Boston, Massachusetts 02202
(617) 727-3201 or (800) 343-9072
 (out of state)

Michigan Travel Bureau
Department of Commerce
P.O. Box 30226
Lansing, Michigan 48909
(517) 373-1195 or (800) 248-5700
 (outside Michigan) or
 (800) 292-2520 (in Michigan)

Minnesota Tourist Information Center
240 Bremer Building
419 North Robert St.
St. Paul, Minnesota 55101
(612) 296-5029 or (800) 328-1461 (out
 of state) or (800) 652-9747 (in
 Minnesota)

Mississippi Division of Tourism
P.O. Box 22825
Jackson, Mississippi 39205
(601) 359-3414 or (800) 647-2290
 (out of state) or (800) 962-2346
 (within Mississippi)

Missouri Division of Tourism
P.O. Box 1055
Jefferson City, Missouri 65102
(314) 751-4133

Montana Promotion Division
1424 9th Avenue
Helena, Montana 59620
(406) 444-2654 or (800) 548-3390

Nebraska Division of Travel and
 Tourism
P.O. Box 94666
Lincoln, Nebraska 68509
(402) 471-3796 or (800) 228-4307

Nevada Commission of Tourism
Capitol Complex
600 East Williams Street
Carson City, Nevada 89710
(702) 885-4322

New Hampshire Office of Vacation
   Information
P.O. Box 856
Concord, New Hampshire 03301
(603) 271-2343 or (800) 258-3608 (in
   the Northeast outside of New
   Hampshire)

New Jersey Division of Travel
   and Tourism
C.N. 826
Trenton, New Jersey 08625
(609) 292-2470

New Mexico Travel Division
Bataan Memorial Building, Room 751
Santa Fe, New Mexico 87503
(505) 827-6230 or (800) 545-2040

New York State Division of Tourism
1 Commerce Plaza
Albany, New York 12245
(518) 474-4116 or (800) 225-5697 (in
   the Northeast except Maine)

North Carolina Travel and Tourism
   Division
Raleigh, North Carolina 27611
(919) 733-4171 or (800) 438-4404 (out
   of state) or (800) 334-1051 (within
   North Carolina)

North Dakota Tourism Promotion
State Capitol Grounds
Bismarck, North Dakota 58505
(701) 224-2525 or (800) 472-2100
   (within North Dakota) or (800)
   437-2077 (out of state)

Ohio Office of Tourism
P.O. Box 1001
Columbus, Ohio 43216
(614) 466-8844 or (800) 282-5393
   (within Ohio)

Oklahoma Division of Tourism
215 N.E. 28th Street
Oklahoma City, Oklahoma 73105
(405) 521-2409 or (800) 652-6552 (in
   neighboring states)

Oregon Travel Information Office
595 Cottage Street, N.E.
Salem, Oregon 97310
(503) 373-1200 or (800) 547-7842
   (out of state) or (800) 233-3306
   (within Oregon)

Pennsylvania Bureau of Travel
   Development
Department of Commerce
416 Forum Building
Harrisburg, Pennsylvania 17120
(717) 787-5453 or (800) 847-4872

Rhode Island Department of
   Economic Development
Tourism Division
7 Jackson Walkway
Providence, Rhode Island 02903
(401) 277-2601 or (800) 556-2484 (out
   of state from Maine to Virginia)

South Carolina Division of Tourism
P.O. Box 71
Columbia, South Carolina 29202
(803) 758-8735

South Dakota Division of Tourism
Box 1000
Pierre, South Dakota 57501
(605) 773-3301 or (800) 843-1930

Tennessee Tourist Development
P.O. Box 23170
Nashville, Tennessee 37202
(615) 741-2158

Texas Tourist Development
P.O. Box 5064
Austin, Texas 78763
(512) 465-7401

Utah Travel Council
Council Hall
Capitol Hill
Salt Lake City, Utah 84114
(801) 533-5681

Vermont Travel Division
134 State Street
Montpelier, Vermont 05602
(802) 828-3236

Virginia State Travel Service
202 North 9th Street
Suite 500
Richmond, Virginia 23219
(804) 786-4484

Washington State Department
of Commerce and Economic
Development
Travel Information
101 General Administration Building
Olympia, Washington 98504
(206) 753-5600 or (800) 541-9274 (out
of state) or (800) 562-4570 (within
Washington)

West Virginia Travel
Capitol Complex
Charleston, West Virginia 25305
(304) 348-2286 or (800) 624-9110

Wisconsin Division of Tourism
P.O. Box 7606
Madison, Wisconsin 53707
(608) 266-2161 or (800) 372-2737
(within Wisconsin and neighboring
states)

Wyoming Travel Commission
Frank Norris, Jr. Travel Center
Cheyenne, Wyoming 82002
(307) 777-7777

BED AND BREAKFAST RESERVATION REQUEST FORM

Dear _____
     Host's Name

I read about your home in *Bed & Breakfast USA 1985,* and would be interested in making reservations to stay with you.

My name: _____

Address: _____
     street

_____
    city   state   zip

Telephone: _____
     area code

Business address/telephone: _____

_____

Number of adult guests: _____

Number and ages of children: _____

Desired date and time of arrival: _____

Desired length of stay: _____

Mode of transportation: _____
(car, bus, train, plane)

Additional information/special requests: _____

_____

_____

_____

_____

_____

I look forward to hearing from you soon.

                                                  Sincerely,

APPLICATION FOR MEMBERSHIP
(Please type or print)

Name of Bed & Breakfast: _____

Address: _____

City: _____ State: _____ Zip: _____ Phone: ( ) _____

Best Time to Call: _____

Host(s): _____

Located: No. of miles _____ Compass Direction _____ of

    Major City _____

    No. of miles _____ from Major Route _____

Accommodations: Total number of guest bedrooms: _____
        Total number of private baths: _____
        Maximum number of guests who must share one bathroom: _____

Room Rates:
$_____ Double—private bath $_____ Double—shared bath
$_____ Single—private bath $_____ Single—shared bath
$_____ Children 12 or under $_____ Suites
Separate Guest Cottage $_____ Sleeps _____

Are you open year-round? ☐ Yes   ☐ No
If "No," specify when you are open: _____

Do you discount rates at any time? ☐ No   ☐ Yes If "Yes," specify (i.e., 10% less during March, April, November; 15% less than daily rate if guests stay a week; $10 less per night Sunday through Thursday). _____

Do you offer a discount to senior citizens? ☐ No   ☐ Yes: ____ %
Do you offer a discount for families? ☐ No   ☐ Yes: ____ %

Breakfast: Type of breakfast included in rate:
    ☐ Full ☐ Continental
    Breakfast is not included: ☐ cost: $ _____
Are any other meals provided? ☐ No   ☐ Yes
 Lunch ☐ cost: $_____   Dinner ☐ cost: $_____
 Meals are included in rate quoted with room ☐ Yes   ☐ No

Do you accept Credit Cards? ☐ No ☐ Yes:
☐ AMEX ☐ DINERS ☐ MASTERCARD ☐ VISA

Will you GUARANTEE your rates from January through December, 1986? (   )Yes (   ) No

Note: This Guarantee applies only to those guests making reservations having read about you in *Bed & Breakfast USA, 1986*.

Do you have household pets? ☐ Dog ☐ Cat ☐ Bird
Can you accommodate a guest's pet?
  ☐ Yes ☐ No ☐ Sometimes
Are children welcome? ☐ No ☐ Yes If "Yes," any age restriction? _____

Do you permit smoking in your house? ☐ Yes ☐ No
Do you object to social drinking? ☐ Yes ☐ No

Guests can be met at ☐ Airport ____ ☐ Train ____ ☐ Bus ____

Can you speak a foreign language fluently? ☐ No ☐ Yes

Describe: _____

GENERAL AREA OF YOUR B&B (i.e., Boston Historic District; 20 minutes from Chicago Loop):

GENERAL DESCRIPTION OF YOUR B&B (i.e., brick colonial with white shutters; Victorian mansion with stained glass windows):

AMBIENCE OF YOUR B&B (i.e., furnished with rare antiques; lots of wood and glass):

THE QUALITIES THAT MAKE YOUR B&B SPECIAL ARE:

THINGS OF HISTORIC, SCENIC, CULTURAL, OR GENERAL INTEREST NEARBY (i.e., 1 mile from the San Diego Zoo; walking distance to the Lincoln Memorial):

YOUR OCCUPATION and SPECIAL INTERESTS (i.e., a retired teacher of Latin interested in woodworking; full-time hostess interested in quilting):

If you do welcome children, are there any special provisions for them (i.e., crib, playpen, highchair, play area, baby-sitter)?

Breakfast is prepared by ☐ Host ☐ Guest
Breakfast specialties of the house are (i.e., homemade breads and jams; blueberry pancakes):

Do you offer snacks (i.e., complimentary wine and cheese; pretzels and chips but BYOB)?

Can guests use your kitchen for light snacks? ☐ Yes ☐ No
Do you offer the following amenities: ☐ Guest Refrigerator ☐ Air-conditioning ☐ TV ☐ Piano ☐ Washing Machine ☐ Dryer ☐ Sauna ☐ Pool ☐ Tennis Court Other _____

What major college or university is within 10 miles?
_____

Do you offer a discount for other B&B hosts in our Association? ☐ No ☐ Yes: ____ %

Please supply the name, address, and phone number of three personal references from people not related to you (please use a separate sheet).

Please enclose a copy of your brochure, if possible, along with a photo of your B&B. If you have a black and white line drawing, send it along too. If you have a special breakfast recipe that you'd like to share, send it along too. (Of course, credit will be given to your B&B.) Nobody can describe your B&B better than you. If you'd like to try your hand, please do so. We will of course reserve the right to edit. As a member of the Tourist House Association of America, your B&B will be described in the next edition of our book, *BED & BREAKFAST USA*, published by E. P. Dutton, Inc. and distributed to bookstores and libraries throughout the U.S. The book is also used as a reference for B&Bs in our country by major offices of tourism throughout the world.

Note: If the publisher or authors receive negative reports from your guests regarding a deficiency in our standards of CLEANLINESS, COMFORT, and CORDIALITY, we reserve the right to cancel your Membership.

This Membership Application has been prepared by:

_____
(Signature)
Please enclose your $15 Membership Dues.   Date: _____

Return to:
Tourist House Association of America
Box 355A, R.D. 2
Greentown, Pennsylvania 18426

APPLICATION FOR MEMBERSHIP FOR A BED & BREAKFAST RESERVATION SERVICE

NAME OF BED & BREAKFAST SERVICE:_____

ADDRESS: _____

CITY: _____ STATE: _____ ZIP: _____ PHONE:(   ) _____

BEST TIME TO CALL: _____

COORDINATOR: _____

Names of State(s), Cities, and Towns where you have Hosts (in alphabetical order, please, and limit to 10):

Number of Hosts on your roster: _____

THINGS OF HISTORIC, SCENIC, CULTURAL, OR GENERAL INTEREST IN THE AREA(S) YOU SERVE:

Range of Rates:
  Modest: Single $_____   Double $_____
  Average: Single $_____   Double $_____
  Luxury: Single $_____   Double $_____

Will you GUARANTEE your rates through December, 1986? ( ) Yes ( ) No

Do you accept Credit Cards? ☐ No ☐ Yes:
☐ AMEX ☐ DINERS ☐ MASTERCARD ☐ VISA

Is the guest required to pay a fee to use your service?
☐ No ☐ Yes—The fee is $_____

Do you publish a Directory of your B&B listings?
☐ No ☐ Yes—The fee is $_____

Are any of your B&Bs within 10 miles of a University? Which?___
_____

Briefly describe a sample Host Home in each of the above categories: e.g., A cozy farmhouse where the host weaves rugs; a restored 1800 Victorian where the host is a retired general; a contemporary mansion with a sauna and swimming pool.

Please supply the name, address, and phone number of three personal references from people not related to you (please use a separate sheet of paper). Please enclose a copy of your brochure. This Membership Application has been prepared by:

_____
(Signature)

Please enclose your $15 Membership Dues.   Date: _____

If you have a special breakfast recipe that you'd like to share, send it along. (Of course, credit will be given to your B&B agency.) As a member of the Tourist House Association of America, your B&B agency will be described in the next edition of our book, *BED & BREAKFAST USA*, published by E. P. Dutton, Inc. Return to: Tourist House Association, R.D. 2, Box 355A, Greentown, PA 18426.

WE WANT TO HEAR FROM YOU!

Name: _____

Address: _____
        street

_____
city   state   zip

Please contact the following B&Bs; I think that they would be great additions to the next edition of *Bed & Breakfast USA*.

Name of B&B: _____

Address: _____
        street

_____
city   state   zip

Comments:

Name of B&B: _____

Address: _____
        street

_____
city   state   zip

Comments:

_____

The following is our report on our visit to the home of:

Name of B&B: _____ Date of visit: _____

Address: _____ I was pleased. ☐

_____ I was disappointed. ☐

Comments:

Just tear out this page and mail it to us. It won't ruin your book!

Return to:
Tourist House Association of America
Box 355A, R.D. 2
Greentown, Pennsylvania 18426

INFORMATION ORDER FORM

We are constantly expanding our roster to include new members in the Tourist House Association of America. Their facilities will be fully described in the next edition of *Bed & Breakfast USA*. In the meantime, we will be happy to send you a list including the name, address, telephone number, minimum rates, etc.

For those of you who would like to order additional copies of the book or perhaps send one to a friend as a gift, we will be happy to fill mail orders. If it is a gift, let us know and we'll enclose a special gift card from you.

ORDER FORM

To:
Tourist House
Association
R.D. 2, Box 355A
Greentown, PA
18426

From: _____
      (Print your name)
Address: _____

_____
City   State   Zip

Date: _____

Please send:
- ☐ List of new B&Bs ($2.00)
- ☐ ____ copies of *Bed & Breakfast, USA* @ $7.95 each plus $1 for 4th class mail; $3 for 1st class mail.

Send to: _____

Address: _____

_____
City   State   Zip

☐ Enclose a gift card from:

Please make check or money order payable to Tourist House Association.